New York City

"All you've got to do is decide to go
and the hardest part is over.

So go!"

TONY WHEELER, CO

THIS EDITION WRITTEN AND RESEARCHED BY

Regis St Louis,
Cristian Bonetto, Zora O'Neill

Contents

Plan Your Trip 4

Explore New York City 58

Understand New York City 351

Survival Guide 383

New York City Maps 407

(left) Escape the city's madness in **Central Park (p230)**.

(above) Wander through **Washington Square Park (p135)**.

(right) Spot squirrels in Lower Manhattan's **Battery Park (p74)**.

Harlem & Upper Manhattan
p246

Upper West Side & Central Park
p228

Upper East Side
p211

West Village, Chelsea & the Meatpacking District
p130

Midtown
p175

Union Square, Flatiron District & Gramercy
p161

Queens
p302

SoHo & Chinatown
p83

East Village & Lower East Side
p105

Lower Manhattan & the Financial District
p62

Brooklyn
p263

Welcome to New York City

One of the world's most captivating places, New York City has it all: celebrated concert halls, a renowned dining and drinking scene, and fascinating neighborhoods filled with people from every corner of the globe.

Nexus of the Arts

The Met, MoMA and the Guggenheim are just the beginning of a dizzying list of art-world icons. You'll find museums devoted to everything from fin de siècle Vienna to immigrant life in the Lower East Side, and sprawling galleries filled with Japanese sculpture, postmodern American painting, Himalayan textiles and New York City lore. For a glimpse of current and future greats, delve into the cutting-edge galleries of Chelsea and the Lower East Side, with their myriad exhibition spaces and festive opening-night parties (usually Thursday night if you want to join in).

Urban Wanderers

With its compact size and streets packed with eye-candy of all sorts – architectural treasures, Old World cafes, atmospheric booksellers and curio shops – NYC is an urban wanderer's delight. Crossing continents is as easy as walking over a few avenues in this jumbled city of 200-plus nationalities. You can lose yourself in the crowds of Chinatown amid brightly painted Buddhist temples, steaming noodle shops and fragrant fishmongers, then stroll up to Nolita for enticing boutiques and coffee-tasting among the craft-minded scenesters. Every neighborhood offers a dramatically different version of New York City – from the 100-year-old Jewish delis of the Upper West Side to the meandering cobblestone lanes of Greenwich Village. And the best way to experience this city is to walk its streets.

The Night Is Young

When the sun sinks slowly beyond the Hudson and luminous skyscrapers light up the night, New York transforms into one grand stage. Well-known actors take to the legendary theaters of Broadway as world-class soloists, dancers and musicians perform at venues large and small across town. Whether high culture or low, New York embraces it all: in-your-face rock shows at Williamsburg dives, lavish opera productions at the Lincoln Center, and everything in between. This is a city of experimental theater, improv comedy, indie cinema, ballet, poetry readings, burlesque, world music, jazz and so much more. If you can dream it up, it's probably happening in NYC.

MATT MUNRO / LONELY PLANET ©

Why I Love New York City

By Regis St Louis, Writer

While there are many reasons to fall for New York, I've always loved the energy here. There's so much creativity in the air, with wildly imaginative works filling the city's galleries and concert halls – not to mention its restaurants, with ever more inventive mash-ups of global cuisines. Despite living for many years in New York, I never tire of exploring the metropolis. You can cross continents with the mere swipe of a MetroCard, visiting colorful neighborhoods that contain an astonishing variety of cultures and ethnicities (particularly in Queens). The people, the food, the art: NYC has many virtues, which is why so many of us can't imagine living anywhere else. **For more about our writers, see p452**

Top: The High Line (p132)

New York City's Top 16

Statue of Liberty & Ellis Island (p64)

1 Since its unveiling in 1886, Lady Liberty has welcomed millions of immigrants, sailing into New York Harbor in the hope of a better life. It now welcomes millions of tourists, many of whom head up to her crown for one of New York City's finest skyline and water views. Close by lies Ellis Island (p68), the American gateway for over 12 million new arrivals between 1892 and 1954. These days it's home to one of the city's most moving museums, paying tribute to these immigrants and their indelible courage.

⊙ *Lower Manhattan & the Financial District*

Food Scene (p39)

2 One of New York's greatest assets is the sheer variety of its restaurants. In a single neighborhood you'll find vintage-filled gastropubs, sushi counters, tapas bars, French bistros, barbecue joints, pizza parlors, vegan cafes and good old-fashioned delis whipping up toasted bagels with lox and cream cheese. And that's just the beginning. There's no wrong way to eat a meal, whether that means ordering from a food truck, nibbling your way through a market or sliding into that soft leather booth for a 4am feast after a night on the town.

✕ *Eating*

Central Park (p230)

3 London has Hyde Park. Paris has the Bois de Boulogne. And New York City has Central Park. One of the world's most renowned green spaces, it checks in with 843 acres of rolling meadows, boulder-studded outcrops, elm-lined walkways, manicured European-style gardens, a lake and a reservoir – not to mention an outdoor theater, a memorial to John Lennon, an idyllic waterside eatery (the Loeb Boathouse) and one very famous statue of Alice in Wonderland. The big challenge? Figuring out where to begin.

◉ *Upper West Side & Central Park*

Broadway & Times Square (p177)

4 Sizzling lights, electrifying energy: this is the America of the world's imagination. Broadway (p179) is NYC's dream factory – a place where romance, betrayal, murder and triumph come with dazzling costumes and stirring scores. The district's undisputed star is bright, blinding Times Square. More than the meeting point of Broadway and Seventh Ave, this is America in concentrate – an intense, intoxicating rush of Hollywood billboards, shimmering cola signs, and buffed topless cowboys. Welcome to the 'crossroads of the world'.

☆ *Midtown*

Empire State Building *(p180)*

5 The striking art-deco sky-scraper may no longer be New York's tallest building, but it remains one of its most recognizable icons. The ESB has appeared in dozens of films and still provides one of the best views in town – particularly around sunset when the twinkling lights of the city (and neighboring states) switch on. The beloved landmark hasn't stopped turning heads, especially since the addition of LED lights which create more than 16 million color possibilities. Keep your eye to the sky on big holidays, when dramatic displays light up the night sky.

◉ **Midtown**

8

Brooklyn Bridge
(p266)

6 Completed in 1883, this Gothic Revival masterpiece – crafted entirely from granite – has inspired poetry (Jack Kerouac's 'Brooklyn Bridge Blues'), music (Frank Sinatra's 'Brooklyn Bridge') and plenty of art (Walker Evans' photography). It is also the most scenic way to cross from Manhattan into Brooklyn. Go early in the morning (we're talking sun-up) to have the bridge largely to yourself. Come at sunset for romantic views as the amber skies form a magnificent backdrop to Lower Manhattan. Aside from strolling that plank path, you can also ride a bike across the bridge.

👁 *Brooklyn*

The High Line
(p132)

7 A resounding triumph of urban renewal, the High Line is – without a doubt – New York's proudest testament to the continuous effort to transform the scarring vestiges of the city's industrial past into eye-pleasing spaces. Once an unsightly elevated train track that snaked between slaughterhouses and low-end domestic dwellings, the High Line is today an unfurled emerald necklace of park space that encourages calm, crowds, and has – unsurprisingly – acted as a veritable real estate magnet luring world-class architects to the neighborhood to create gorgeous iterations of residential eye candy.

👁 *West Village, Chelsea & the Meatpacking District*

Metropolitan Museum of Art
(p214)

8 With more than two million objects in its collections, the Met is simply dazzling. Its great works span the world, from the chiseled sculptures of ancient Greece to the evocative tribal carvings of Papua New Guinea. The Renaissance galleries are packed with Old World masters, while the relics of ancient Egypt fire the imagination – particularly the Temple of Dendur, complete with its 2000-year-old stone walls covered in hieroglyphics and carvings of papyrus seemingly growing from a pond. After you think you've seen enough, head up to the rooftop for a sweeping view over Central Park.

👁 *Upper East Side*

Neighborhood Rambling
(p138)

9 One of the best ways to see New York is to pick a neighborhood, put on your walking shoes and spend the day exploring. Greenwich Village is a fine place to start, with picturesque cobblestone streets dotted with sunlit shops, narrow sidewalk cafes and quaint restaurants that beckon you inside. For a different take on New York, head over to the Bohemian East Village, overload your senses down in Chinatown, or take in the local scene in gallery-filled Chelsea. This is a city that invites endless wandering.

STREET ART IN GREENWICH VILLAGE

◉ *West Village, Chelsea & the Meatpacking District*

One World Observatory *(p71)*

10 New York's tallest and most anticipated skyscraper has arrived – a soaring 104-story landmark that looms like a beacon above Lower Manhattan. Take a high-speed ride in a 'sky pod' to the top for fabulous views over the city and surrounding states. Apart from the jaw-dropping panorama, a visit here gives insight into the workers who helped build the tower, and shows the very bedrock upon which the tower stands. There's also a virtual time-lapse that shows the evolution of the city skyline from the 1600s to the present.

◉ *Lower Manhattan & the Financial District*

National September 11 Memorial & Museum *(p68)*

11 Rising from the ashes of Ground Zero, the National September 11 Memorial & Museum is a beautiful, dignified response to the city's darkest chapter. Where the Twin Towers once soared, two reflecting pools now weep like dark, elegant waterfalls. Framing them are the names of those who lost their lives on September 11 and in the 1993 World Trade Center bombing. Deep below lies the Memorial Museum, a powerful, poignant exploration of these catastrophic events, the latter of which was the deadliest attack on American soil.

⊙ *Lower Manhattan & the Financial District*

Williamsburg (p270)

12 Retro cocktail lounges peddling a Depression-era vibe. Artsy eateries dishing out everything from barbecue ribs to Michelin-starred gastronomy. And enough music halls and rowdy beer gardens to keep the most dedicated night owls up for weeks. Prefer the daylight hours? Williamsburg is stocked with an array of designer homeware shops, in addition to fashion outposts of all stripes, from vintage thrift emporiums to high-design boutiques. It's not for nothing that this Brooklyn neighborhood – just one subway stop from downtown Manhattan – is the city's trendiest hangout.

⊙ *Brooklyn*

MoMA (p182)

13 Quite possibly the greatest hoarder of modern masterpieces on earth, the Museum of Modern Art (MoMA) is a cultural promised land. It's here that you'll see Van Gogh's *The Starry Night*, Cézanne's *The Bather,* Picasso's *Les Demoiselles d'Avignon,* Pollock's *One: Number 31,* and Warhol's *Campbell's Soup Cans.* Just make sure you leave time for Chagall, Dix, Rothko, de Kooning and Haring, a free film screening, a glass of vino in the Sculpture Garden, a little designer retail therapy, and a fine-dining feed at its lauded in-house restaurant, the Modern.

⊙ *Midtown*

Music & Nightlife
(p43)

14 Trendy all-night lounges tucked behind the walls of a Chinese restaurant; taco shops that clandestinely host late-night tranny cabarets; stadium-size clubs that clang to the thump of DJ'd beats; and after-after-after-parties on the roof as the sun rises. An alternate universe lurks between the cracks of everyday life, and it welcomes savvy visitors just as much as locals in the know. If New York doesn't turn into a pumpkin come midnight, why should you?

☆ *Drinking & Nightlife*

Shopping (p49)

15 Take it from the likes of Holly Golightly and Carrie Bradshaw, New York is a beacon of the material world. Hundreds of creators – both local and international – descend upon the city with alacrity to display their wares. You'll find dozens of ways to empty your coffers, but at the end of the day shopping in New York isn't about collecting a closet full of items, it's about accessing the city's myriad subcultures through their art and artifacts.

🔒 *Shopping*

Out on the Water (p75)

16 Step off the island of Manhattan onto a ferry and you'll have a new appreciation for those pedestrian-clogged streets as the city skyline rises slowly into view. Governors Island makes a fine destination, with new parkland, art exhibitions and peaceful, car-free lanes to stroll or cycle along. You can also hop across to Brooklyn aboard the East River Ferry (p388). The dock near the Brooklyn Bridge Park (p265) makes an excellent entry point to the borough. Meanwhile, the free Staten Island ferry (p82) provides superb views of the Statue of Liberty. GOVERNORS ISLAND (P75)

👁 *Lower Manhattan & the Financial District*

What's New

Queens

Long overshadowed by Manhattan and Brooklyn, Queens is on the rise, with much happening throughout its web of multi-ethnic neighborhoods. In recent years, the massive borough (biggest by size) has seen the opening of new microbreweries, thoughtfully designed boutique hotels (at half the price of Manhattan options), farm-to-table eateries and under-the-radar art galleries (in Ridgewood), plus an ever livelier seaside scene at Far Rockaway. If you haven't been, now's the time to go. (p302)

Downtown Nightlife

Despite news of its ever-imminent demise, nightlife in downtown Manhattan is still alive and well. Among other openings, a great new jazz bar (Mezzrow; p155) has landed in the West Village, while an underground club (Berlin; p119) harks back to pre-Giuliani days in the East Village.

Whitney Museum of American Art

At the southern end of the High Line, the Whitney Museum opened its brand new Renzo Piano–designed building. The gorgeous light-filled galleries bring more space and innovation to downtown's most impressive art center. (p136)

Mindful Dining

With increased awareness of the devastation of animal agriculture, growing numbers of New Yorkers are embracing a vegan diet. You'll find outstanding dishes at new hot spots like El Rey (p116), Dimes (p118) and vegan-only Peacefood (p139) downtown.

Market Madness

The love for food markets shows no signs of abating, with sprawling new Manhattan foodie halls, including Gansevoort Market (p148). There's more ahead, including

Anthony Bourdain's 155,000-sq-ft market opening in 2017, on a Hudson pier west of the Meatpacking District.

Brooklyn Flea & Smorgasburg

Speaking of markets, Brooklyn's big shopping and eating extravaganzas, Brooklyn Flea (p280) and Smorgasburg (p285), have only gotten bigger and better. There's also a Long Island City Flea (in Queens) that continues to expand.

National Sawdust Company

Williamsburg's newest performing arts theater stages a mix of genre-bending concerts and artist showcases. The futuristic hall has outstanding acoustics. (p295)

St Ann's Warehouse

Speaking of theaters, St Ann's Warehouse has opened its doors in its first ever permanent location under the Brooklyn Bridge. Expect to see cutting-edge programming, for which St Ann's is so well-known. (p296)

One World Trade Center

The tallest building in New York now looms high above Lower Manhattan. While you can admire its jewel-like facade from afar, the best view is up top from the magnificent observatory on the 102nd floor. (p70)

Uptown Allure

Downtown cool is finally arriving in both the Upper West and Upper East Sides, with a sprinkling of craft brew pubs (West End Hall; p241), creative cocktail dens (The Daisy; p225) and earth-friendly eateries (Birdbath Bakery; p236).

For more recommendations and reviews, see **lonelyplanet. com/usa/new-york-city**

Need to Know

For more information, see Survival Guide (p383)

Currency
US dollar (US$)

Language
English

Visas
The US Visa Waiver Program allows nationals of 38 countries to enter the US without a visa.

Money
ATMs widely available; credit cards accepted at most hotels, stores and restaurants. Farmers markets, food trucks and some restaurants and bars are cash-only.

Cell Phones
Most US cell phones, apart from the iPhone, operate on CDMA, not the European standard GSM; check compatibility with your phone service provider.

Time
Eastern Standard Time (GMT/UTC minus five hours)

Tourist Information
There are official NYC Visitor Information Centers throughout the city. The main office is in Midtown (☎212-484-1222; www.nycgo.com; Seventh Ave, at 44th St, Midtown West; ⌚9am-6pm; [S]N/Q/R, S, 1/2/3, 7 to Times Sq-42nd St).

Daily Costs

Budget: Less than $100
- Dorm bed: $40–70
- Slice of pizza: around $4
- Food-truck taco: from $3
- Bus or subway ride: $2.75

Midrange: $100–300
- Double room in a midrange hotel: from around $200
- Brunch for two at a midrange restaurant: $70
- Dinner for two at a midrange eatery: $130
- Craft cocktail at a lounge: $14–18
- Discount TKTS ticket to a Broadway show: $80
- Brooklyn Academy of Music orchestra seats: from $84

Top End: More than $300
- Luxury stay at the NoMad Hotel: $325–850
- Tasting menu at a top-end restaurant: $85–325
- A 1½-hour massage at the atmospheric Great Jones Spa: $200
- Metropolitan Opera orchestra seats: $100–390

Advance Planning

Two months before Book your hotel reservations as soon as possible – prices increase the closer you get to your arrival date. Snag tickets to your favorite Broadway blockbuster.

Three weeks before If you haven't done so already, score a table at your top-choice high-end restaurant.

One week before Surf the web and scan blogs and Twitter for the latest restaurant and bar openings, plus upcoming art exhibitions.

Useful Websites

Lonely Planet (www.lonelyplanet.com/usa/new-york-city) Destination information, hotel bookings, traveler forum and more.

NYC: The Official Guide (www.nycgo.com) New York City's official tourism portal.

Explore Brooklyn (www.explorebk.com) Brooklyn-specific events and listings.

New York Magazine (www.nymag.com) Comprehensive, current listings for bars, restaurants, entertainment and shopping.

New York Times (www.nytimes.com) Excellent local news coverage and theater listings.

WHEN TO GO

Summers can be scorching hot; winters cold and not without their blizzards. Spring or autumn are the best times to explore.

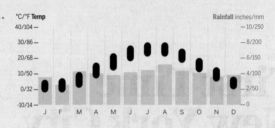

Arriving in New York

John F Kennedy International Airport (p384) The AirTrain ($5) links to the Metropolitan Transportation Authority's (MTA's) subway ($2.75), which makes the one-hour journey into Manhattan. Express bus to Grand Central or Port Authority costs $16. Shared vans to Manhattan hotels run $20 to $25. Taxis cost a flat rate of $52 excluding tolls and tip.

LaGuardia Airport (p384) This is the closest airport to Manhattan but least accessible by public transit: take the Q70 express bus from the airport to the 74th St–Broadway subway station (7 line, or the E, F, M and R lines at the connecting Jackson Heights Roosevelt Ave station). Express bus to Midtown costs $13. Taxis range from $26 to $48 (excluding tolls and tip) depending on traffic.

Newark Liberty International Airport (p385) Take the AirTrain to Newark Airport train station, and board any train bound for New York's Penn Station ($12.50). Express bus to Port Authority or Grand Central costs $16. Shared shuttle to Midtown costs $20 to $26. Taxis range from $60 to $80 (excluding the unavoidable $13 toll and tip).

 For much more on **arrival,** see p384.

Tipping

Tipping is *not* optional; only withhold tips in cases of outrageously bad service.

➡ **Restaurant servers** 18–20%, unless a gratuity is already charged on the bill (usually only for groups of five or more).

➡ **Bartenders** 15–20% per round, minimum per drink $1 for standard drinks, and $2 per specialty cocktail.

➡ **Taxi drivers** 10–15%, rounded up to the next dollar.

➡ **Airport & hotel porters** $2 per bag, minimum per cart $5.

➡ **Hotel maids** $2–4 per night, left in envelope or under the card provided.

 For much more on **money,** see p392.

Sleeping

In general, accommodations prices in New York City do not abide by any high-season or low-season rules; wavering rates usually reflect availability. With over 50 million visitors descending upon the city every year, you can expect that hotel rooms fill up quickly – especially in summer. Accommodations options range from boxy cookie-cutter rooms in Midtown high-rises to stylish boutique options downtown. You'll also find a few B&Bs set in residential neighborhoods.

Useful Websites

➡ **newyorkhotels.com** (www. newyorkhotels.com) The self-proclaimed official website for hotels in NYC.

➡ **NYC** (www.nycgo.com/ hotels) Loads of listings from the NYC Official Guide.

➡ **Lonely Planet** (www. lonelyplanet.com/usa/ new-york-city/hotels) Accommodation reviews and online booking service.

 For much more on **sleeping,** see p330.

First Time New York City

For more information, see Survival Guide (p383)

Checklist

➡ Ensure your passport is valid for at least six months past your arrival date.

➡ Check you meet all ESTA visa requirements for travel to the US.

➡ Check airline baggage restrictions.

➡ Arrange for appropriate travel insurance.

➡ Inform your credit-/debit-card company of your travels.

➡ Book popular restaurants, shows and accommodations well in advance.

What to Pack

➡ Good walking shoes – New York City is best seen on foot, so make sure your feet are super comfy.

➡ Dress shoes and a stylish outfit for smart restaurants and bars.

➡ If traveling with medications, ensure you bring enough for your trip.

➡ US electrical adapter.

Top Tips for Your Trip

➡ MetroCards are valid on subways, buses and the tramway to Roosevelt Island. If staying a while, buy a 7-Day Unlimited Pass.

➡ Subway lines run both local and express trains.

➡ If the number on a taxi's top light is lit, it's available.

➡ When giving an address, always include the nearest cross street/s (for example, 700 Sixth Ave *at* 22nd St).

➡ The TKTS Booth in Times Square sells half-price, same-day tickets to selected shows and musicals. The South Street Seaport and Downtown Brooklyn branches also sell next-day matinee tickets.

What to Wear

If visiting during New York's hot, humid summer, pack light garments. Fashionable shorts, T-shirts, summer dresses and skirts are all acceptable daywear, though higher-end restaurants and bars often call for more stylish attire, so bring at least one evening dress or long-sleeved shirt, pair of pants and dress shoes. Fluctuating temperatures in spring and fall call for layers: pants, jeans or warmer dresses, mixed with T-shirts, long-sleeve shirts, light sweaters, a smart blazer for men and a jacket for women. New York winters can be brutally cold, requiring gloves, scarf, hat, insulated, waterproof jacket and waterproof boots. In the evenings, 'dress to impress' remains the rule at many restaurants, bars and entertainment venues.

Be Forewarned

Crime rates in NYC are still at their lowest in years. There are few neighborhoods where you might feel apprehensive no matter what time of night it is (they're mainly in the outer boroughs). Subway stations are generally safe, too, though again, especially in the outer boroughs, some can be dicey. There's no reason to be paranoid, but it's better to be safe than sorry, so use common sense: don't walk around alone at night in sparsely populated areas, especially if you're a woman. Carry your daily money inside your clothing or in a front pocket rather than in a handbag or a back pocket, and be aware of pickpockets, particularly in mobbed areas, such as Times Square.

Taxes & Refunds

Restaurants and retailers never include the sales tax – 8.875% – in their prices, so beware of ordering the $4.99 lunch special when you only have $5 to your name. Several categories of so-called 'luxury items,' including rental cars and dry-cleaning, carry an additional city surcharge of 5%, so you wind up paying an extra 13.875% in total for these services. Clothing and footwear purchases under $110 are tax free; anything over that amount has a state sales tax of 4.5%. Hotel rooms in New York City are subject to a 14.75% tax, plus a flat $3.50 occupancy tax per night. Since the US has no nationwide value-added tax (VAT), there is no opportunity for foreign visitors to make 'tax-free' purchases.

Money Savers

New York City is expensive, but that doesn't mean you can't save some notes. If you plan on blitzing the major sights, consider buying one of the numerous multi-attraction passes (see www.nycgo.com/attraction-passes). Numerous museums are always free, while others offer weekly free admission times or pay-what-you-wish hours, among them MoMA and the Guggenheim. On the food front, numerous high-end restaurants offer cheaper, prix-fixe lunch menus, sometimes featuring dishes from the dinner menu.

Grand Central Terminal (p184)

Tackling Crowds

Avoid the ire of millions of harried New Yorkers by following some basic rules. When catching the subway, have your MetroCard at the ready (black stripe facing inward) before reaching the turnstile to avoid delays. If carrying a backpack, take it off on crowded trains. When walking on busy sidewalks, keep to the right. If you need to stop or slow down, move to the side to let others pass.

Getting Around

For more information, see Transportation (p384)

Check the Metropolitan Transportation Authority (www.mta.info/nyct) website for public transportation information (buses and subway), including a handy travel planner and regular notifications of delays and alternate travel routes during frequent maintenance.

Subway

Inexpensive, somewhat efficient and operates around the clock, though can be confusing to the uninitiated. Single ride is $2.75 with a MetroCard. A 7-Day Unlimited Pass costs $31.

Buses

Convenient during off hours – especially when transferring between the city's eastern and western sides. Uses the Metro-Card; same price as the subway.

Taxi

Meters start at $2.50 and increase roughly $5 for every 20 blocks. See www.nyc.gov/taxi for more information.

Inter-borough ferries

Hop-on, hop-off services are offered by New York Waterway (www.nywaterway.com) and New York Water Taxi (www.nywatertaxi.com). Journey across New York Harbor on the free, commuter Staten Island Ferry (www.siferry.com).

Key Phrases

Car service You can phone a car service (often a black sedan) to pick you up. Useful on return trips to the airport or if needing outer-borough transport (where taxis are in short supply).

Citi Bike The ubiquitous blue bikes that are part of NYC's bike-sharing scheme, with hundreds of quick-hire kiosks around town.

Express train/local train Express subway trains make limited stops, skipping many stations; local trains stop at every station. To switch between the two, often you just have to cross the platform.

LIRR The Long Island Rail Road, useful for speedy transport to JFK and for beach getaways.

MetroCard The flimsy yellow-and-blue card, which you load with credit, then swipe through for every ride on the subway or bus.

Uptown/Downtown Uptown means going north (Upper East Side, Harlem, etc), downtown means going south (Soho, Lower Manhattan, etc).

Key Routes

Scenic views Take the J, M or Z line over the Williamsburg Bridge or the B, D, N or Q line over the Manhattan Bridge for great views of Manhattan. There's also the Roosevelt Island Tramway (www.rioc.ny.gov/traintransportation).

Uptown bound The 4, 5 or 6 lines go to the Upper East Side; for the Upper West Side take the B, C, 1, 2 or 3 trains.

Taxi Etiquette

➡ To hail one of NYC's yellow cabs, look for one with its roof light lit (if it's not lit, the cab is taken).

➡ Stand in a prominent place on the side of the road and stick out your arm.

➡ Once inside the cab, tell them your destination (it's illegal for drivers to refuse you a ride somewhere).

➡ Pay your fare at the end, either with cash or credit card (via the touch screen in back). Don't forget to tip (typically 10% to 15%).

TOP TIPS

➡ Pay attention to 'Downtown' vs 'Uptown' subway station entrances. Sometimes there are separate entrances (usually across the street from one another) depending on which direction the train is going.

➡ Plan your route carefully. Sometimes walking a few blocks can get you to a faster or more direct subway line, thereby saving you time in the end.

➡ For short trips, consider hopping on a Citi Bike.

When to Travel

➡ Rush hour is never just an hour! On weekdays, from 8am to 9:30am and 4:30pm to 6:30pm, trains and buses are frustratingly packed.

➡ If it's not possible to avoid traveling at these peak times, allow extra time to get places (particularly to/from the airport).

➡ Hailing a cab can be difficult on weekdays from 4pm to 5pm when many drivers change shifts. And when it's raining, finding an available taxi can seem a monumental challenge.

Etiquette

➡ Have your MetroCard ready before you go through the gate. New Yorkers are skilled at moving through the ticket barriers without breaking stride.

➡ On subway platforms, stand to the side of the train doors and wait for passengers to exit before boarding.

➡ On escalators, stand on the right hand side or use the left if you want to walk down/up.

➡ When walking on the sidewalk, think of yourself as a car on the street: don't stop short, pay attention to the speed limit, and pull off to the side if you need to look at a map or dig through your bag for an umbrella.

Tickets & Passes

➡ The yellow-and-blue MetroCards are the swipe cards used for all of NYC's public transportation. You can purchase or add value at one of several easy-to-use automated machines at any station. Each ride on the subway or bus (except for express buses) deducts $2.75 from the card.

➡ Purchase the MetroCard itself for $1 at kiosks in subway stations, and load it with credit ($20, which will give you eight rides and change, is a good start). If you plan to ride a lot, buy a 7-day Unlimited Pass ($31). These cards are handy for travelers – particularly if you're jumping around town to a few different places in one day.

➡ The subway kiosks take credit or ATM cards (larger machines also take cash). When you need to add more credit, just insert your card and follow the prompts (tip: when it asks for your zip, input '99999' if you're not from the USA).

➡ Transfers from subway to bus, or bus to subway, are free. Just swipe/insert your card, and no extra charge will be deducted.

CITI BIKES

To use a Citi Bike, purchase a 24-hour or seven-day access pass (around $11 or $28 including tax) at any Citi Bike kiosk. You will then be given a five-digit code to unlock a bike. Return the bike to any station within 30 minutes to avoid incurring extra fees. Reinsert your credit card (you won't be charged) and follow the prompts to check out a bike again. You can make an unlimited number of 30-minute check-outs during those 24 hours or seven days.

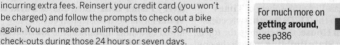

For much more on **getting around,** see p386

Top Itineraries

Day One

Upper West Side & Central Park (p228)

 Spend the morning exploring the wonders of **Central Park**, taking in the fortresslike walls of skyscrapers surrounding the green. Start at Columbus Circle, then head in the northeast direction passing the **Central Park Zoo**, the **Bethesda Fountain**, the **Conservatory Water** and **Strawberry Fields** on the western side. If you have the kids in tow, check out the dinosaur skeletons at the **American Museum of Natural History** then hit up the **Loeb Boathouse** to rent rowboats for a paddle around the lake.

 Lunch Pick up supplies at Zabar's (p236) for a picnic in Central Park.

Midtown (p175)

It's now time to uncover some of the city's architectural wonders: **Grand Central Terminal**, the **Chrysler Building**, the **New York Public Library** and **Rockefeller Center**. Round off the afternoon with a visit to the city's museum darling: **MoMA**.

Dinner For Broadway-goers, do an early dinner at ViceVersa (p199).

Midtown (p175)

Spend the evening under the starry lights of **Broadway**, checking out a blockbuster show or something distinctly ahead of the curve at **Playwrights Horizons** or **Signature Theatre**. Soak up the Las Vegas–like atmosphere of **Times Square** from the **TKTS Booth**, swig cocktails at **Rum House**, then climb to the top of the **Empire State Building** to wish the city goodnight.

Day Two

Upper East Side (p211)

 Start at the staggering **Metropolitan Museum of Art**. Wander through the Egyptian and Roman collections, take in European masters, then head up to the rooftop (in summer) for a view over Central Park. Afterwards, visit the nearby **Neue Galerie** for a feast of German and Austrian art in a 1914 mansion.

Lunch Lunch on Austrian specialties at elegant Café Sabarsky (p223).

SoHo & Chinatown (p83)

Head down to SoHo for an afternoon of shopping along **Prince** and **Spring Sts** amid crowds of tourists seeking the best brands in the world. Wander over to Chinatown's **Mulberry St**, which feels worlds away from mainstream consumerism, but is – in reality – only a few blocks over. Stroll by the neighborhood's **Buddhist temples**, stopping for custard tarts and almond ice cream.

Dinner Savor soup dumplings at Joe's Shanghai (p96), a Chinatown staple.

Upper West Side & Central Park (p228)

 If you have concert tickets, then skip dinner downtown and hit up **Barcibo Enoteca** for a preshow glass of expertly curated Italian wine. Then it's off to the **Lincoln Center** for opera at the **Metropolitan Opera House** or a symphony in **Avery Fisher Hall**. Later, dine at **Burke & Wills** for modern Australian cuisine, followed by drinks upstairs at the **Manhattan Cricket Club**.

Day Three

Brooklyn (p263)

 Catch the East River Ferry over to Dumbo, and admire the magnificent view of Manhattan from the lush new **Brooklyn Bridge Park**. Afterwards, stroll through the cobblestone streets of Dumbo, browsing bookshops, boutiques and cafes. Don't miss the vintage **Jane's Carousel** and more great views from the **Empire Fulton Ferry**.

Lunch Fill up on good-value lunch specials at atmospheric AlMar (p283).

Brooklyn (p263)

Travel up to the **Brooklyn Museum** for a look at fascinating works from Africa, the Americas and Ancient Egypt, plus excellent temporary shows. Afterwards take a stroll in **Prospect Park**, pausing for refreshments at the scenic new **Lakeside** complex.

Dinner Partake of Brooklyn's culinary renaissance at Marlow & Sons (p279).

Brooklyn (p263)

 Jump in a Boro Taxi up to **Williamsburg**, on the northern side of the borough, for oysters and bespoke cocktails at **Maison Premiere**. Head up to rooftop bar, the **Ides**, for a fabulous view over the city. End the night across the street at the **Brooklyn Bowl**, with a side of bowling and some groovy musical acts.

Day Four

Lower Manhattan & the Financial District (p62)

 Catch the **Staten Island Ferry** in the early morning and watch the sun come up over Lower Manhattan. Then head skyward for a marvelous view from the **One World Observatory**. Afterwards, visit the moving **National September 11 Memorial & Museum**.

Lunch Munch on gourmet goodies at the food-loving Chelsea Market (p148).

West Village, Chelsea & the Meatpacking District (p130)

Head up to the Meatpacking District and visit the gorgeous new **Whitney Museum of American Art**. Afterwards, take the nearby steps up to the **High Line** for a wander along a once abandoned rail line. Along the way stop for snacks, coffee breaks and intriguing views over the streetscape.

Dinner Dine on high-end bistro fare at the atmospheric Minetta Tavern (p148).

West Village, Chelsea & the Meatpacking District (p130)

 Stroll the lovely, meandering streets of Greenwich Village and delve into its soul-filed roots for an evening of intimate live jazz at **Mezzrow**, **Smalls** or the **Village Vanguard**. Afterwards, stop by for a craft cocktail at stylish **Employees Only**, then head over to **Cielo** for dancing in one of the city's best little clubs.

If You Like...

Skyline Views

Brooklyn Bridge Park Brooklyn's newest park has wide open views of downtown Manhattan and the Brooklyn and Manhattan Bridges. (p265)

Governors Island A lush and car-free space in the harbor with photogenic views of both Manhattan and Lady Liberty. (p75)

Top of the Strand Go one better than staring at Midtown's mix of scrapers and swig a drink while you're part of the view. (p201)

Le Bain Check out the downtown views from the rooftop perch of the very hip Standard Hotel. (p150)

Brooklyn Heights Promenade Staggering view of Manhattan, 24 hours a day. (p271)

Roosevelt Island River and skyscraper views from Louis Kahn's Franklin D Roosevelt Four Freedoms Park. (p219)

Metropolitan Museum Roof Garden Café & Martini Bar From late April through October, the rooftop garden at the Met offers incredible views of Central Park and the Midtown skyline. (p215)

East River State Park Take in an inspiring sweep of Midtown from the Williamsburg waterfront. (p270)

Old School New York

Coney Island An amusement center that dates back to the early days of the 20th century; don't forget the hot dogs at Nathan's Famous. (p269)

Brooklyn Bridge Park (p265)

Barney Greengrass After a century in the business, BG still serves up some of the best smoked fish in the city. (p240)

Russian & Turkish Baths Steam your stress away in this East Village classic, now over 120 years old. (p129)

Katz's Delicatessen Smoked meat that will please even the biggest kvetchers. (Map p418)

Marie's Crisis Show tunes and singing patrons at this legendary West Village gay bar. (p151)

Zabar's An emporium for all types of Upper West Side food-a-holics since the 1930s. (p236)

McSorley's Old Ale House Abraham Lincoln, Boss Tweed and Woody Guthrie are among the many who've raised a glass or two at this sawdust-on-the-floor pub. (p123)

Staying Up Late

Smalls Catch 1am 'after hours' shows at this atmospheric West Village jazz spot. (p154)

Veselka The go-to place when you've just got to have *pierogi* (homemade dumplings) and other Ukrainian fare at 4am. (p113)

IFC Center Watch midnight screenings of cult classics in the West Village. (p155)

Chinatown A secreted scatter of late-night lounges tucked behind the unassuming facades of hole-in-the-wall chow spots. (p85)

Verboten Get your groove on at this late-night dance club in Williamsburg. (p290)

Rue B This tiny late-night jazz den in the East Village is a great spot to end the night. (p119)

Slipper Room Catch a riotously fun burlesque show at this

cheeky den of debauchery on the Lower East Side. (p125)

Employees Only No need to eat sickening fast food after midnight. Head to this West Village gastrobar, which serves a good late-night menu till past 3am. (p149)

Museums

MoMA NYC's darling museum has brilliantly curated spaces boasting the best of the world's modern art. (p182)

Metropolitan Museum of Art The most incredible encyclopedic museum in the Americas comes stocked with its own Egyptian temple and the country's most famous canvas of George Washington. (p214)

Guggenheim Museum The exhibits can be uneven, but the architecture is the real star in this Frank Lloyd Wright–designed building. (p213)

Frick Collection This Gilded Age mansion has Vermeers, El Grecos and Goyas and a stunning courtyard fountain. (p218)

Cloisters Museum & Gardens Medieval treasures including a beguiling 16th-century tapestry that depicts a unicorn hunt. (p253)

Brooklyn Museum Ancient Egyptian treasures, a stellar collection of American painting and a cutting-edge feminist arts center. (p267)

Lower East Side Tenement Museum Fantastic insight into life as an immigrant during the 19th and early 20th centuries. (p107)

Whitney Museum of American Art Celebrated for cutting-edge contemporary and 20th-century works. See future American greats at the Whitney Biennial on even-numbered years. (p136)

For more top New York City spots, see the following:

➡ Eating (p39)
➡ Drinking & Nightlife (p43)
➡ Entertainment (p46)
➡ Shopping (p49)
➡ Sports & Activities (p53)
➡ Gay & Lesbian (p56)

Green Spaces

Central Park The city's most famous park has more than 800 acres of rolling meadows and boulder-topped hillocks. (p230)

Hudson River Park Manhattan's looking greener than ever thanks to new parkland running up its western side. (p137)

Brooklyn Bridge Park A brand new park lines the waterfront along Dumbo, all the way to the foot of Atlantic Ave. (p265)

The High Line A thin stripe of green with wild plants and surprising vantage points atop a former rail line. (p132)

Green-Wood Cemetery A lush oasis with great views and rambling paths that dates back to the 1830s. (p290)

Prospect Park Brooklyn's favorite outdoor space for picnics, kite-flying, running, cycling and ambling amid beautifully landscaped scenery. (p268)

Brooklyn Botanic Garden Three-season beauty with cherry blossoms in spring, vibrant summery blooms, and red, gold and yellow blazes in autumn. (p276)

Historic Sights

Ellis Island The gateway to freedom and opportunity for so many of America's immigrants. (p66)

Frick Collection A rare mansion from the Gilded Age survives to this day as a museum on the Upper East Side. (p218)

Gracie Mansion A graceful Federal-style structure now serves as the mayor's home. (p218)

Morgan Library & Museum Browse the exquisite interiors of the former home of industrialist JP Morgan. (p190)

Morris-Jumel Mansion Museum A Georgian-Federal structure is the oldest house in Manhattan. (p258)

Lower East Side Tenement Museum Get insight into how the early immigrants lived, on an eye-opening tour of a preserved tenement. (p107)

Castle Clinton This fort in Lower Manhattan built to defend New York Harbor during the war of 1812. (p74)

Venturing Off the Beaten Path

Flushing Go on a foodie safari deep in the heart of Queens and browse New York's biggest and best Chinatown. (p306)

Inwood Hill Park It's part of Manhattan, but it doesn't feel like it – this park remains wonderfully wild. (p256)

Queens Museum Excellent exhibits without the fanfare and crowds of some of Manhattan's other museum spaces. (p307)

Dyckman Farmhouse Museum Manhattan's last surviving Dutch farmhouse. (p256)

Gowanus An old industrial canal popular with urban decay types (and the Environmental Protection Agency; p275).

Ultimate Indulgences

Barneys The fashionista's aspirational closet comes with a hefty price tag. (p208)

Dough Head to Bed-Stuy for the best doughnuts on the planet (or find them at the Brooklyn Flea; p284).

Pegu Club Stylish lounge, with great ambience and a welcome lack of pretension (never mind the $15 cocktails; p98).

Brandy Library Nurse a glass of rare, amber-hued armagnac at this gentlemanly retreat. (p79)

Exhale Four-handed massage, beginner yoga classes, acupuncture: you'll find it all at this zen Upper East Side spa. (p227)

Bowery Hotel Treat yourself to a luxury stay in this beautifully designed downtown pad. (p336)

Hidden Hangouts

Beauty & Essex Hidden behind a pawnshop facade is an enchanting drinking den. (p123)

Bathtub Gin Slide behind a false wall at the back of a modest coffee shop for Prohibition-chic styling and retro cocktails. (p153)

Mulberry Project An unassuming set of stairs leads to the swank cocktail laboratory of the international owners and their coterie of server-friends. (p99)

Smith & Mills Push the unmarked door to find a kooky industrial interior (think 1900s factory) and smooth libations. (p80)

Freemans Walk down a tiny alley to find quaint cabinlike surrounds and legions of faithful brunchers. (p119)

Little Branch You'd never guess that great cocktails are crafted inside this seemingly abandoned West Village building. (p152)

Larry Lawrence Concealed drinking spot in Williamsburg with an old-time vibe. (p289)

Apothéke Apothecary turned cocktail lounge hidden deep in Chinatown. (p99)

Places of Worship

St Patrick's Cathedral A glorious neo-Gothic masterpiece – it's the largest cathedral in America. (p191)

Trinity Church This gorgeous Anglican church was the tallest building in NYC in the mid-1800s. (p72)

Cathedral Church of St John the Divine The largest house of worship in the US was begun in 1892 – and still isn't completely finished (hence its nickname, St John the Unfinished; p248).

Temple Emanu-El A Romanesque structure with gilded ceilings serves as one of New York's most beautiful synagogues. (p219)

Plymouth Church This Brooklyn Heights place of worship was a center of abolitionist activity in the 19th century. (p278)

Eldridge Street Synagogue Glittering after a multi-million-dollar restoration, the hallowed hall is now a museum space. (p112)

Month by Month

TOP EVENTS

Tribeca Film Festival, April

Cherry Blossom Festival, April or May

SummerStage, June to August

Independence Day, July

Village Halloween Parade, October

January

The winter doldrums arrive following the build-up of Christmas and New Year's Eve. Despite the long nights, New Yorkers take advantage of the frosty weather, with outdoor ice skating and weekend ski trips to the Catskills.

🏃 New Year's Day Swim

What better way to greet the new year than with an icy dip in the Atlantic? Join the Coney Island Polar Bear Club for this annual brrrr-fest.

🏃 No Pants Subway Ride

On the second Sunday in January, some 4000 New Yorkers spice things up with a bit of leg nudity on public transit. Anyone can join in, and there's usually an after-party for the cheeky participants. Check the website for meeting times and details.

☆ Winter Jazzfest

In mid-January, this four-day music fest brings over 100 acts playing at nearly a dozen venues around the city. Most of the action happens around the West Village.

February

The odd blizzard and below-freezing temperatures make February a good time to stay indoors nursing a drink or a warm meal at a cozy bar or bistro.

🎆 Lunar (Chinese) New Year Festival

One of the biggest Chinese New Year celebrations in the country, this display of fireworks and dancing dragons draws mobs of thrillseekers into the streets of Chinatown. The date of Chinese New Year fluctuates from year to year, but typically falls in early February.

🍴 Winter Restaurant Week

From late January to early February, celebrate the dreary weather with slash-cut meal deals at some of the city's finest eating establishments during New York's Winter Restaurant Week, which actually runs for about three weeks. A three-course lunch costs around $26 ($40 for dinner).

March

After months of freezing temperatures and thick winter coats, the odd warm spring day appears and everyone rejoices – though it's usually followed by a week of sub-zero drear as winter lingers on.

🎆 St Patrick's Day Parade

A massive audience, rowdy and wobbly from cups of green beer, lines Fifth Ave on March 17 for this popular parade of bagpipe blowers, sparkly floats and clusters of Irish-lovin' politicians. The parade, which was first held here in 1762, is the city's oldest and largest.

April

Spring finally appears: optimistic alfresco joints have a sprinkling of streetside chairs as the city squares overflow with bright tulips and blossom-covered trees.

Tribeca Film Festival

Created in response to the tragic events of September 11, Robert De Niro's downtown film festival has quickly become a star in the indie movie circuit. You'll have to make some tough choices: over 150 films are screened during the 10-day fest.

May

April showers bring May flowers in the form of brilliant bursts of blossoms adorning the flowering trees all around the city. The weather is warm and mild without the unpleasant humidity of summer.

Cherry Blossom Festival

Known in Japanese as Sakura Matsuri, this annual tradition, held on one weekend in late April or early May, celebrates the magnificent flowering of cherry trees in the Brooklyn Botanic Garden. It's complete with entertainment and activities (taiko drumming, folk dancing, origami workshops, ikebana flower displays, samurai sword showmanship), plus refreshments and awe-inspiring beauty.

TD Bank Five Boro Bike Tour

May is Bike Month, featuring two-wheelin' tours, parties and other events for pedal-pushing New Yorkers. TD Bank Five Boro Bike Tour, the main event, sees thousands of cyclists hit the pavement for a 42-mile ride, much of it on roads closed to traffic or on waterfront paths through each of the city's five boroughs.

Fleet Week

For one week at the end of May, Manhattan resembles a 1940s movie set as clusters of uniformed sailors go 'on the town' to look for adventures. For non-swabby visitors, this is a chance to take free tours of ships that have arrived from around the globe. See them docked off Manhattan (around Midtown) and Brooklyn (just south of Brooklyn Bridge Park's pier 6).

June

Summer's definitely here and locals emerge from of their office cubicles to relax in the city's green spaces. Parades roll down the busiest streets and portable movie screens are strung up in several parks.

SummerStage

Central Park's Summer-Stage, which runs from June through August, features an incredible lineup of music and dance throughout the summer. Django Django, Femi Kuti, Shuggie Otis and the Martha Graham Dance Company are among recent standouts. Most events are free. There's also a Summer-Stage Kids program just in case you've got the little ones in tow. Other parks throughout the city also host events.

Bryant Park Summer Film Festival

June through August, Bryant Park hosts free Monday-night outdoor screenings of classic Hollywood films, which kick off after sundown. Arrive early (the lawn area opens at 5pm and folks line up by 4pm).

NYC Pride

Gay Pride Month culminates in a major march down Fifth Ave on the last Sunday of the month. NYC Pride is a five-hour spectacle of dancers, drag queens, gay police officers, leathermen, lesbian soccer-moms and representatives of just about every other queer scene under the rainbow.

Mermaid Parade

Celebrating sand, sea and the beginning of summer is this quirky afternoon parade (www.coneyisland.com). It's a flash of glitter and glamour, as elaborately costumed folks display their fishy finery along the Coney Island boardwalk. It's even more fun to take part (all in costume are welcome). Held on the last Saturday of the month.

July

As the city swelters, locals flee to beachside escapes on Long Island. It's a busy month for tourism, however, as holidaying North Americans and Europeans fill the city.

Shakespeare in the Park

The much-loved Shakespeare in the Park pays

(Below) Christmas tree lighting ceremony, Rockefeller Center (p186)

(Bottom) St Patrick's Day Parade

THEO WARGO / GETTY IMAGES ©

JEWEL SAMAD / GETTY IMAGES ©

tribute to the Bard, with free performances in Central Park. The catch? You'll have to wait hours in line to score tickets, or win them in the online lottery (there's also an in-person lottery on performance days at noon at the Public Theater). Tickets are given out at noon on show days; arrive no later than 10am for a seat.

🎇 Independence Day

America's Independence Day is celebrated on the 4th of July with dramatic fireworks over the East River, starting at 9pm. Good viewing spots include the waterfronts of the Lower East Side and Williamsburg, Brooklyn, or any high rooftop or east-facing Manhattan apartment.

August

Thick waves of summer heat slide between skyscrapers as everyone heads to the seashore nearby or gulps cool blasts of air-conditioning when stuck in the city. Myriad outdoor events and attractions add life to the languid urban heat.

🎇 FringeNYC

The annual mid-August theater festival, FringeNYC, presents two weeks of performances by companies from all over the world. It's the best way to catch the edgiest, wackiest and most creative up-and-comers around.

September

Labor Day officially marks the end of the Hampton's share-house season as the blistering heat of summer

fades to more tolerable levels. As locals return to work, the cultural calendar ramps up.

☆ Electric Zoo

Celebrated over the Labor Day weekend, Electric Zoo is New York's electronic music festival held in sprawling Randall's Island Park. Past headliners have included Moby, Afrojack, David Guetta, Martin Solveig and The Chemical Brothers.

☆ BAM's Next Wave Festival

Celebrated for over 30 years, the Brooklyn Academy of Music's Next Wave Festival (p288), which runs through December, showcases world-class avantgarde theater, music and dance.

October

Brilliant bursts of orange, red and gold fill the trees in Central and Prospect Parks as temperatures cool and alfresco cafes finally shutter their windows. Along with May, October is one of the most pleasant and scenic months to visit NYC.

☆ Blessing of the Animals

In honor of the Feast Day of St Francis, which falls early in the month, pet owners flock to the grand Cathedral Church of St John the Divine for the annual Blessing of the Animals with their sidekicks – poodles, lizards, parrots, llamas, you name it – in tow. It's a wild and wonderful afternoon for participants and onlookers.

☆ Open House New York

The country's largest architecture and design event, Open House New York features architect-led tours, plus lectures, design workshops, studio visits and site-specific performances all over the city.

☆ Village Halloween Parade

October 31 brings riotous fun to the city, as New Yorkers don their wildest costumes for a night of revelry. See the most outrageous displays at the Village Halloween Parade that runs up Sixth Ave in the West Village. It's fun to watch, but even better to join in.

November

As the leaves tumble, light jackets are replaced by wool and down. A headliner marathon is tucked into the final days of prehibernation weather, then families gather to give thanks.

☆ New York Comedy Festival

Funny-makers take the city by storm during the New York Comedy Festival with stand-up sessions, improv nights and big-ticket shows hosted by the likes of Rosie O'Donnell and Ricky Gervais.

☆ New York City Marathon

Held in the first week of November, this annual 26-mile run draws thousands of athletes from around the world, and many more excited viewers line the streets to cheer the runners on.

☆ Thanksgiving Day Parade

Massive helium-filled balloons soar overhead, high-school marching bands rattle their snares and millions of onlookers bundle up with scarves and coats to celebrate Thanksgiving (the fourth Thursday in November) with Macy's world-famous 2.5-mile-long parade.

☆ Rockefeller Center Christmas Tree Lighting Ceremony

The flick of a switch ignites the massive Christmas tree in Rockefeller Center (p186), officially ushering in the holiday season. Bedecked with over 25,000 lights, it is NYC's unofficial Yuletide headquarters and a must-see for anyone visiting the city during December.

December

Winter's definitely here, but there's plenty of holiday cheer to warm the spirit. Fairy lights adorn most buildings and Fifth Ave department stores (as well as Macy's) create elaborate worlds within their storefront windows.

☆ New Year's Eve

The ultimate place to ring in the New Year in the northern hemisphere, Times Square swarms with millions of gatherers who come to stand squashed together like boxed sardines, swig booze, freeze in subarctic temperatures, witness the annual dropping of the ball made entirely of Waterford Crystal and chant the '10...9...8...' countdown in perfect unison.

With Kids

New York City has loads of activities for young ones, including imaginative playgrounds and leafy parks where kids can run free, plus lots of kid-friendly museums and sights. Other highs: carousel rides, puppet shows, and noshing at markets around town.

XINHUA NEWS AGENCY / GETTY IMAGES ©

American Museum of Natural History (p235)

Top Attractions

For many kids, some of New York City's top attractions are a world of fun.

Wildlife

The city has a number of zoos. The best, by far, is the **Bronx Zoo** (www.bronxzoo.com; 2300 Southern Blvd; tickets adult/child $26/19, suggested donation Wed; ⏰10am-5pm Mon-Fri, to 5:30pm Sat & Sun Apr-Oct, to 4:30pm Nov-Mar; [S] 2, 5 to West Farms Sq-E Tremont Ave). If you're pressed for time, the zoos in Central Park and Prospect Park are great for short visits.

Statue of Liberty

The boat ride to **Lady Liberty** (☎877-523-9849; www.statuecruises.com; adult/child from $18/9; ⏰varies, usually 8:30am-5pm; [S]4/5 to Bowling Green; R to Whitehall St; 1 to South Ferry) offers the opportunity to chug around New York Harbor and get to know an icon.

On Top of the World

A glass-roofed elevator leads to the Top of the Rock (p191), a lookout that offers glittering views of New York.

Coney Island

Hot dogs. Ice cream. Amusement-park rides. Coney Island (p269) is just the ticket if you want some low-brow entertainment.

Best Museums

The American Museum of Natural History (p235), with its dinosaurs, marine world, planetarium and IMAX films, should not be missed. Other big museums – the Metropolitan Museum of Art, the Museum of Modern Art and the Guggenheim Museum – all have kids' programs, but many smaller institutions are even more appealing for young visitors.

Toddler Time

For tots aged one to five, hit the Children's Museum of the Arts (p89) in West SoHo and the Brooklyn Children's Museum (p277) in Crown Heights. Both have story times, art classes and craft hours.

Five & Over

Bigger kids can clamber on vintage subway cars at the New York Transit Museum (p271), slide down a pole at the New York City Fire Museum (p87) and impose law

and order in a miniature cruiser at the New York City Police Museum. Book 'em.

Best Parks & Playgrounds

Central Park

Heckscher playground, near Seventh Ave and Central Park South, is the biggest and best of Central Park's (p230) 21 playgrounds.

Prospect Park

Brooklyn's hilly 585-acre Prospect Park (p268) has abundant amusement for kids, including a zoo and an ice-skating rink.

Brooklyn Bridge Park

Hit the fun water park in the summer on Pier 6 and nosh on pizza at waterfront Fornino (p266). Further north are the grassy hills of Pier 1 and Jane's Carousel.

Hudson River Park

Coursing along Manhattan's western side, this park (p137) offers loads of kiddy excitement, including mini-golf near Moore St and a fun playground near West St.

The High Line

NYC's celebrated elevated green space (p132) has food vendors, water features and warm-weather family events.

Riverside Park

This park (p235) on the Upper West Side has a bicycle trail with views of the Hudson River. Take a break at the River Run Playground (at W 83rd St).

South Street Seaport

The Imagination Playground (p75) features oversize foam building blocks, allowing kids to construct their own play spaces.

Kid-Friendly Theater

Tiny Puppetworks (p298) in Brooklyn's Park Slope has amusing weekend puppet shows throughout the year.

Market Snacks

Markets around NYC are great snack spots, particularly Brooklyn Flea (p280) and the Chelsea Market (p148).

Best Bets for a Rainy Day

Craft

Drop in to create ceramic masterpieces right on the spot at the **Craft Studio** (Map p434; ☎212-831-6626; www.craftstudionyc.com; 1657 Third Ave btwn 92nd & 93rd Sts; ⊙10am-6pm Mon-Sat, 11am-6pm Sun; ▮; ⓢ6 to 96th St).

Play

Let litte ones let off some steam at the colorful indoor playground, **Little Athletes Exploration Center** (Map p424; ☎212-336-6500, ext 0; www.chelseapiers.com; Chelsea Piers, Twelfth Ave at 23rd St; single session $12; ⊙9:30am-noon & 1-5pm; ▮; ⓢC/E to 23rd St).

Art

Visit the **Art Farm in the City** (Map p434; ☎212-410-3117; www.theartfarms.org; 419 E 91st St btwn First & York Aves; ▮; ⓢ4/5/6 to 86th St) for art supplies, craft sessions and a petting zoo.

Keep it Cheap

The Staten Island Ferry (p82) is free and offers spectacular views of New York Harbor and the Statue of Liberty.

The subway can be a great adventure. You can clatter across the bridges on the J, M or Z lines (Williamsburg Bridge) or B, D, N or Q lines across the Manhattan Bridge. For views of the Brooklyn Bridge and Lower Manhattan, take the N or Q train.

Online Resources

Baby Sitters' Guild (www.babysittersguild.com)

Mommy Poppins (www.mommypoppins.com)

Time Out New York Kids (www.timeout.com/new-york-kids)

Like a Local

New Yorkers have developed winning strategies when it comes to nightlife, dining out and partaking of the city's cultural calendar. From long weekend brunches to leisurely spring days in the park, there are plenty of ways to go local – without having to pay those ridiculous rents.

ce skating, Central Park (p230)

Dos & Don'ts: On the Street

➡ Hail a cab only if the roof light is on. If it's not lit, the cab is taken, so put your arm down already!

➡ You needn't obey 'walk' signs – simply cross the street when there isn't oncoming traffic.

➡ When negotiating pedestrian traffic on the sidewalk, think of yourself as a vehicle – don't stop short, follow the speed of the crowd around you and pull off to the side if you need to take out your map or umbrella. Most New Yorkers are respectful of personal space, but they will bump into you – and not apologize – if you get in the way.

➡ When boarding the subway, wait until the passengers disembark, then be aggressive enough when you hop on so that the doors don't close in front of you.

➡ In New York you wait 'on line' instead of 'in line'.

➡ Oh, and it's How-sten Street, not Hew-sten.

Eating & Drinking

The Culture of Brunch

Brunch in New York is deeply woven into the city's social fabric, much like teatime for British royals. It typically happens between 11am and 4pm on weekends (though some places, especially in Brooklyn, have begun serving brunch every day). The meal provides a perfect setting for friends to catch up on the week's events and the weekend's shenanigans over dishes constructed of breakfast materials and an indiscriminate mix of cocktails or coffee.

The Weekends Are for Amateurs

New Yorkers tend to avoid the big clubs, packed bars and certain neighborhoods (East Village, Lower East Side) on the weekends when you find yourself among a high proportion of less sophisticated types (some might unkindly use the word 'douchebags'). Instead, weeknights can be great for going out – with fewer crowds, fewer of the aforementioned types, and more creative folk who don't work the typical nine-to-five (actors, writers, artists). Plus, you'll be able to score happy-hour and early-in-the-week specials.

Bar Food

Many of New York's best bars blur the boundary between eating and drinking. Slide onto a bar stool, pick up a menu, and you'll often be faced with some surprising dining options. That could be oysters at the bar, small sharing plates (seared scallops, sliders, truffle-oil fries), cheese boards and charcuterie or anything else – roasted beet salads, gourmet sandwiches, braised artichokes, rack of lamb. When planning a meal, don't limit yourself to a sit-down restaurant: you can also eat and drink your way around a neighborhood by stopping in at gastropubs.

New York's Twitterati

Check out our favorite members of New York's Twitterati, who are always tweeting about the city's latest musts:

Everything NYC (@EverythingNYC) Hunting down the best things to see, do and eat in the Big Apple.

Pete Wells (@pete_wells) Restaurant critic of the *New York Times*.

Paper (@papermagazine) Art, culture and music news.

Guest of a Guest (@guestofaguest) In-the-know info on NYC parties, social and fashion scenes.

Gothamist (@gothamist) News and curiosities in NYC.

Hyperallergic (@Hyperallergic) Tweets from NYC's favorite art blogazine.

Colson Whitehead (@colsonwhitehead) Manhattan native, novelist and *New Yorker* contributor.

Paul Goldberger (@paulgoldberger) Pulitzer Prize–winning architecture critic.

Tom Colicchio (@tomcolicchio) Celebrity chef and owner of the popular Craft franchise.

Sam Sifton (@samsifton) Food editor at the *New York Times*.

Joining In

Truth be told, watching a parade can be a pretty dull affair. It's much more fun to take part. Along those lines, there are many ways you can join in the action. Don an outrageous costume for the Village Hal-loween Parade (p32) or the summertime Mermaid Parade (p30) in Coney Island. Sign up for an organized race in the city (New York Road Runners stages dozens of annual runs). Take a rock-climbing class at Brooklyn Boulders (p301) or The Cliffs (p316) in Queens. Polish up those old poems and take the stage at open-mic night at Nuyorican Poets Cafe (p126), or if there's music in you, try the open-mic at Sidewalk Cafe (p125). Whatever your passion – chess, hip-hop, drawing, architecture, beer-making – you'll find it in NYC, and be surrounded by plenty of like minds.

Seasonal Activities

Winter

Even dreary winter weather brings its delights – namely, ice skating! Beginning in November or December, the city's skating rinks provide ample amusement (and a good prequel to fireside drinks in a toasty bar afterwards). Locals skip tourist-swarmed Rockefeller Center and Bryant Park and instead head to Central Park, McCarren Park or Prospect Park for skating.

Spring

The city's blossoming parks are the place to be for spring picnics, sun-drenched strolls and lazy days lounging on the grass. Top spots for flower-gazing: the New York Botanical Garden and the Brooklyn Botanic Garden. The latter hosts a lovely Cherry Blossom Festival, much adored by Brooklynites.

Summer

Summer is the time for free open-air events: film screenings in Bryant Park, street festivals around town, and concerts in Central Park, Hudson River Park, Prospect Park and other green spaces around the city.

Fall

In fall the cultural calendar ramps up again as the city's premier performing arts halls open their seasons (which run from September through May) and galleries kick off their new shows (Thursday night, incidentally, is when the art openings happen).

For Free

The Big Apple isn't the world's cheapest destination. Nevertheless, there are many ways to kick open the NYC treasure chest without spending a dime – free concerts, theater and film screenings, pay-what-you-wish nights at legendary museums, city festivals, free ferry rides, plus loads of green space.

isters Museum & Gardens (p253)

Live Music, Theater & Dance

In summer there are scores of free events around town. From June through early September, SummerStage (p234) features over 100 free performances at 17 parks around the city, including Central Park. You'll have to be tenacious to get tickets to Shakespeare in the Park (p234), held also in Central Park, but it's well worth the effort. Top actors like Meryl Streep and Al Pacino have taken the stage in years past. Prospect Park has its own venerable open-air summer concert and events series: **Celebrate Brooklyn** (www.bricartsmedia.org/performing-arts/celebrate-brooklyn).

Summertime also brings free film screenings and events to the water's edge during the **River to River Festival** (www.rivertorivernyc.com; ☉Jun) at Hudson River Park in Manhattan and at Brooklyn Bridge Park. Another great option for film lovers is the free Bryant Park Summer Film Festival (p30) screenings on Monday nights.

A few places offer free music throughout the year. BAMcafé (p297) in Brooklyn has free concerts (world music, R&B, jazz, rock) on select Friday and Saturday nights. In Harlem, Marjorie Eliot (p262) opens her home for free jazz jams on Sunday.

On the Water

The free Staten Island Ferry (p388) provides magical views of the Statue of Liberty, and you can enjoy it with a cold beer (available on the boat). While it's not free, for just $4 you can sail from Lower Manhattan across to Brooklyn, Queens or up to 34th St on the East River Ferry (p388) – a great alternative to the subway. On summer weekends, you can also take a free ferry over to Governors Island (p75), a car-free oasis with priceless views.

For a bit more adventure, take out a free kayak, available in the Hudson River Park, Brooklyn Bridge Park and Red Hook (p301).

TV Tapings

Some of America's top evening shows are taped right here in New York City. *The Late Show with Stephen Colbert, The Daily Show with Trevor Noah* and *The Tonight*

Show starring Jimmy Fallon all give out free tickets to their shows. Go online to reserve seats.

Walking Tours

One of the best ways to experience the city is to have a local show you around. The highly recommended Big Apple Greeter (p388) provides free tours by locals who love showing off their neighborhoods.

For DIY adventures, check out our own walking tours of the following neighborhoods:

➡ Lower Manhattan (p78)

➡ Chinatown (p88)

➡ SoHo (p100)

➡ East Village (p117)

➡ Greenwich Village (p138)

➡ Chelsea (p142)

➡ Union Square (p172)

➡ Midtown (p198)

➡ Upper East Side (p224)

➡ Harlem (p257)

➡ Willliamsburg (p272)

➡ Brooklyn Heights (p278)

➡ South Brooklyn (p280)

Wi-Fi

If you're out for the day and need to get online, you'll find free wi-fi in public parks such as the High Line, Bryant Park, Battery Park, Tompkins Square Park and Union Square Park. Most cafes and many restaurants also offer free wi-fi.

NEED TO KNOW

Handy websites for tracking down free and discounted events in the city include **Club Free Time** (www.clubfreetime.com) and **Free in NYC** (www.freeinnyc.net). These have daily listings of free tours, concerts, workshops, talks, art openings, book readings and more.

Free Museums & Sites

Always Free

➡ The High Line (p132)

➡ National September 11 Memorial (p72)

➡ National Museum of the American Indian (p72)

➡ Hispanic Society of America Museum & Library (p256)

➡ Museum at FIT (p193)

➡ Hamilton Grange (p252)

➡ American Folk Art Museum (p235)

➡ Nicholas Roerich Museum (p236)

Admission by Donation

➡ Metropolitan Museum of Art (p214)

➡ American Museum of Natural History (p235)

➡ Cloisters Museum & Gardens (p253)

➡ Brooklyn Museum (p267)

➡ Museum of the City of New York (p222)

➡ Brooklyn Historical Society (p273)

Free or Pay-What-You-Wish on Certain Days

➡ MoMA (p182) 4–8pm Friday

➡ Guggenheim Museum (p213) 5:45–7:45pm Saturday

➡ Whitney Museum of American Art (p136) 7–10pm Friday

➡ Neue Galerie (p218) 6–8pm first Friday of month

➡ Frick Collection (p218) 11am–1pm Sunday

➡ New Museum of Contemporary Art (p108) 7–9pm Thursday

➡ New-York Historical Society (p235) 6–8pm Friday

➡ Jewish Museum (p219) 5–8pm Thursday and Saturday

➡ Rubin Museum of Art (p137) 6–10pm Friday

➡ Asia Society & Museum (p219) 6–9pm Friday

➡ Japan Society (p190) 6–9pm Friday

➡ Studio Museum in Harlem (p250) Sunday

➡ MoMA PS1 (p304) Free with your MoMA ticket

➡ National September 11 Memorial Museum (p68) 5–8pm Tuesday

Gansevoort Market (p148), Chelsea

Eating

From inspired iterations of world cuisine to quintessentially local nibbles, New York City's dining scene is infinite, all-consuming and a proud testament to the kaleidoscope of citizens that call the city home. So go ahead, take a bite out of the Big Apple – we promise you won't be sorry.

To Market, to Market

Don't let the concrete streets and buildings fool you – New York City has a thriving greens scene that comes in many shapes and sizes. At the top of your list should be the Chelsea Market (p134), which is packed with gourmet goodies of all kinds – both shops (where you can assemble picnics) and food stands (where you can eat on-site). Many other food halls have opened in recent years, including Gansevoort Market (p148) in the Meatpacking District and a trio of food halls at Brookfield Place (p77), in Lower Manhattan.

Many neighborhoods in NYC have their own greenmarket. One of the biggest is the Union Square Greenmarket (p174), open four days a week throughout the year. Check **Grow NYC** (www.grownyc.org/greenmarket) for a list of the other 50-plus markets around the city.

Out in Brooklyn, the best weekend markets for noshers (rather than cook-at-home types) are Smorgasburg (p285), with over 100 craft food vendors (there's also a smaller seasonal Smorgasburg in the Southstreet Seaport), and the Brooklyn Flea Market (p280), which has several dozen stalls.

Eating by Neighborhood

Harlem & Upper Manhattan
Comfort cuisine meets global flavours (p258)

Upper West Side & Central Park
A few top eats tucked between apartment blocks (p236)

Central Park

Upper East Side
Ladies-who-lunch meets cafe culture (p222)

Midtown
Fine dining, cocktail-literate bistros and old-school delis (p195)

Queens
A multicultural borough that cures all cravings (p309)

West Village, Chelsea & the Meatpacking District
See-and-be-seen brunch spots, wine bars and New American darlings (p139)

Union Square, Flatiron District & Gramercy
Everything from Michelin-starred meccas to parkside burgers (p166)

SoHo & Chinatown
Dirt-cheap noodles, hip cafes and fashionable foodie hangouts (p90)

East Village & Lower East Side
Unpretentious spectrum of eats, from Asia to the Middle East (p113)

Lower Manhattan & the Financial District
Celebrity-chef hot spots and a gourmet French marketplace (p76)

Brooklyn
Neighborhood pizzerias, Michelin-star dining and retro–New American fare (p277)

Also popular are high-end market-cum-grocers like Eataly (p166) and Dean & DeLuca (p100), where fresh produce and ready-made fare are given the five-star treatment. Whole Foods is another big draw, particularly its ecofriendly, locavore-focused Brooklyn outpost (p284).

And, in recent market gossip, at the time fo research, food-show host Anthony Bourdain was planning to open a massive international market (with more than 100 stalls) on a pier facing the Hudson River. Look for it on Pier 57 (off W 15th St) in 2017.

Food Trucks & Carts

Skip the bagel- and hot-dog-vending food carts. These days, there's a new mobile crew in town dishing up high-end treats and unique fusion fare. The trucks ply various routes, stopping in designated zones throughout the city – namely around Union Square, Midtown and the Financial District – so if you're looking for a particular grub wagon, it's best to follow them on Twitter. Here are a few of our favorites:

➜ **Kimchi Taco** (www.twitter.com/kimchitruck) Mouth-watering combo of Korean beef served in tacos.

➜ **Red Hook Lobster Pound** (twitter.com/lobstertruckny) You can't go wrong with succulent lobster rolls.

➜ **Calexico Cart** (www.calexico.net/locations) Hearty rich burritos, tacos and quesadillas.

➜ **Souvlaki GR** (www.souvlakigr.com/location/food-truck) A favorite for lovers of Greek fare.

➜ **Van Leeuwen Ice Cream** (www.twitter.com/VLAIC) Imaginative flavors of delectable (and addictive!) ice cream.

Tours & Courses

There's no better way to engage with the city's infinite dining scene than to link up with a savvy local for a food tour or cooking class. Check out the following winners:

➡ **Institute of Culinary Education** (p82) America's largest cooking school offers accessible, top-notch cooking courses, as well as foodie tours.

➡ **Urban Oyster** (www.urbanoyster.com) High-quality, themed foodie tours mostly in Lower Manhattan and Brooklyn.

➡ **Scott's Pizza Tours** (p282) Offbeat and always fun, Scott promises to unveil all of the secrets of the city's pizza-pie scene.

➡ **Joshua M Bernstein** (www.joshuambernstein.com) Respected food blogger and journalist who leads tours with a special focus on craft- and home-brewed beer.

➡ **Pizza A Casa** (www.pizzaacasa.com) Much-loved pie school on the Lower East Side specializing in rolling and decorating dough.

➡ **Chopsticks & Marrow** (www.chopsticksandmarrow.com) Fantastic Queens food blog by local Joe DiStefano, who also runs food tours.

➡ **League of Kitchens** (www.leagueofkitchens.com) Cooking classes taught by immigrant women in their own kitchens, in Brooklyn and Queens.

Vegetarians & Vegans

Though the city's herbivore scene has long lagged behind that of West Coast cities, and was for years mocked by serious foodies, many former naysayers are beginning to come around. That's thanks in part to the local-food movement, which has hit NYC like a ton of potatoes, as well as a slow but steady trickle of new eateries that have enticed skeptics by injecting big doses of cool ambience – and top-notch wine, liquor and dessert options – into the mix. But herbivore oases also dot the entire landscape, and even the most meat-heavy four-star restaurants are figuring out the lure of legume; the market-inspired *le potager* section on the menu at Café Boulud (p225) offers highbrow veggie dishes, while on Monday night Dovetail (p240) hosts a decadent prix-fixe vegetarian feast.

Vegans have much to celebrate with the arrival of excellent eateries serving up guilt-free goodness all around town. Top choices include Champs (p277), which serves up comfort fare out in Williamsburg,

NEED TO KNOW

Price Guide

The following price ranges refer to a main dish, exclusive of tax and tip:

$ under $15

$$ $15–25

$$$ more than $25

Websites

➡ **Yelp** (www.yelp.com) Comprehensive user-generated content and reviews.

➡ **Open Table** (www.opentable.com) Click-and-book reservation service for many restaurants.

➡ **Tasting Table** (www.tastingtable.com) Sign up for handy news blasts about the latest and greatest.

New Yorkers are famous for offering their opinion, so why not capitalize on their taste-bud experiences and click through scores of websites catering to the discerning diner. Some of our favorite blog-style rags include:

➡ **Eater** (ny.eater.com) Food news and restaurant round-ups.

➡ **Serious Eats** (www.newyork.seriouseats.com) Restaurant gossip and articles on the cuisine scene.

➡ **Grub Street** (http://newyork.grubstreet.com) In-the-know articles on NYC dining.

➡ **Restaurant Girl** (www.restaurantgirl.com) Blogger and restaurant critic eating her way around the city.

Tipping

New Yorkers tip between 18% and 20% of the final price of the meal. For takeaway, it's polite to drop a few dollars in the tip jar.

Reservations

Popular restaurants abide by one of two rules: either they take reservations and you need to plan in advance (weeks or months early for the real treasures) or they only seat patrons on a first-come basis, in which case you should arrive when it opens, and eat early. Otherwise, you might be looking at a two-hour wait.

and elegant Cafe Blossom (p149), with locations in Chelsea and elsewhere.

Lonely Planet's Top Choices

Pye Boat Noodle (p309) Outstanding Thai cooking in a quaint country-house setting in Astoria.

Battersby (p285) Farm-to-table brilliance on Brooklyn's restaurant-lined Smith St.

Gramercy Tavern (p167) Prime produce, culinary finesse and the choice of bustling tavern or fine-dining den.

RedFarm (p147) Savvy Sino-fusion dishes boast bold flavors but it doesn't take itself too seriously.

Dovetail (p240) Simplicity is key at this Upper West Side stunner – vegetarians unite on Monday for a divine tasting menu.

Foragers City Table (p147) A triumph of farm-to-table cooking with flavorful sustainable recipes.

Best by Budget

$

Taïm (p143) Outstanding falafel sandwiches at downtown locations.

Berg'n (p284) Market with craft brews in Crown Heights.

El Rey (p116) Daring combinations at a locavore haunt in the Lower East Side.

Le Grainne (p149) Good-value French restaurant in Chelsea.

$$

Upstate (p115) A seafood feast awaits in the East Village.

Jeffrey's Grocery (p145) Much-loved West Village neighborhood spot.

ViceVersa (p199) Elegant Italian in the shadow of the Theater District.

Cooklyn (p286) Small but beautifully executed menu in Propsect Heights.

$$$

Eleven Madison Park (p168) Arresting, cutting-edge cuisine laced with unexpected whimsy.

Blue Hill (p147) A West Village classic using ingredients sourced straight from the associated farm upstate.

Degustation (p116) A tiny East Village eatery where you can watch the chefs create edible works of art.

Best by Cuisine

Asian

Uncle Boons (p92) Zesty, Michelin-starred Thai with a generous serve of fun in Nolita.

Zenkichi (p279) Candlelit culinary temple of exquisite sushi in Williamsburg.

Lan Larb (p97) Real-deal northeastern Thai in a cheap and cheery hole in the wall on the edge of Chinatown.

Italian

Rosemary's (p145) A beautifully designed West Village spot with memorable cooking.

Roman's (p284) Changing seasonal menu of Italian invention in Fort Greene.

Morandi (p145) A West Village gem that invites lingering.

Vegetarian

Butcher's Daughter (p92) Inventive vegetarian menu in Nolita.

Hangawi (p195) Meat-free (and shoe-free) Korean restaurant in Koreatown.

Champs (p277) Comfort-food diner in East Williamsburg with outstanding vegan plates.

Best Brunch

Estela (p92) Seasonal plates in a buzzing Nolita wine bar.

Rabbit Hole (p281) Excellent brunch plates served daily till 5pm at this Williamsburg gem.

Cookshop (p145) Great indoor-outdoor dining spot in west Chelsea.

Peaches (p284) Southern perfection in less-traveled Bed-Stuy.

Cafe Mogador (p115) An icon of the East Village brunch scene.

Best Bakeries

Dough (p284) Probably NYC's best doughnut, in Brooklyn.

Four & Twenty Blackbirds (p285) Heavenly slices of homemade pies in Gowanus.

Dominique Ansel Kitchen (p143) Sweet magnificence from NYC's most famous pastry chef in the West Village.

Arcade Bakery (p76) One of the city's finest almond croissants in a Tribeca setting.

Best for Old-School NYC

Barney Greengrass (p240) Perfect plates of smoked salmon and sturgeon for over 100 years.

Russ & Daughters (p118) A celebrated Jewish deli in the Lower East Side.

Zabar's (p236) Upper West Side store selling gourmet, kosher foods since the 1930s.

El Margon (p199) Unfussy, unchanged Cuban lunch counter in Midtown.

Best Upscale Market Groceries

Sahadi's (p285) Assemble a picnic of Middle Eastern temptations.

Eataly (p166) A mecca for lovers of Italian food.

Whole Foods, Brooklyn (p284) Ecofriendly shopping in the reinvented Gowanus neighborhood.

Union Square Greenmarket (p174) Delicious veggies and bakery items from upstate.

Cocktail making

 # Drinking & Nightlife

Considering that 'Manhattan' is thought to be a derivation of the Munsee word manahactanienk ('place of general inebriation'), it shouldn't be surprising that New York lives up to its nickname: 'the city that never sleeps.' You'll find all species of thirst-quenching venues here, from cocktail lounges and dive bars to specialty tap rooms and Third Wave coffee shops. Then there's the city's legendary club scene, spanning everything from celebrity staples to gritty, indie hangouts.

Historic Cocktails, Crafty Beers

Here in the land where the term 'cocktail' was born, mixed drinks are still stirred with the utmost gravitas. From Jillian Vose at Dead Rabbit (p79) to Eben Freeman at Genuine Liquorette (p97), the city's top barkeeps are virtual celebrities, their deft precision creating some of the world's most sophisticated and innovative libations. Often, it's a case of history in a glass: New York's obsession with rediscovered recipes and Prohibition-era style continues to drive many a cocktail list.

The city's craft beer culture is equally dynamic, with an ever-expanding booty of breweries, bars and shops showcasing local artisanal brews. While Brooklyn may no longer be the major beer exporter of yesteryear, hipster breweries like Brooklyn Brewery (p270) and **Sixpoint** (www.sixpoint.com) have put it back on the map. Other boroughs are also making amber waves, with start-ups including **SingleCut Beersmiths** (www.singlecutbeer.com) and **Big Alice Brewery** (bigalicebrewing.com) in Queens, as well as Bronx Brewery (p366) and **Gun Hill Brewing Co** (www.gunhillbrewing.com) in the Bronx.

Clubbing

New Yorkers are always looking for the next big thing, so the city's club scene changes faster than a New York minute.

NEED TO KNOW

Websites

➜ **New York Magazine** (www.nymag. com/nightlife) Brilliantly curated nightlife options by the people who know best.

➜ **Thrillist** (www.thrillist.com) An on-the-ball round up of what's hot or coming soon on the NYC bar scene, including interviews with industry peeps.

➜ **Urbandaddy** (www.urbandaddy.com) More up-to-the-minute info and a handy 'hot right now' list.

➜ **Time Out** (www.timeout.com/new-york/nightlife) Reviews and on-the-ball listings of where to drink and dance.

➜ **partyearth** (www.partyearth.com/new-york) Detailed club reviews from some of the city's savviest party kids.

Opening Hours

Generally speaking, cafes (coffee shops) open from 7am to 7pm or 8pm. While some dive bars open as early as 8am, most drinking establishments get rolling around 5pm. Numerous bars stay open until 4am, while others close at around 1am early in the week and at 2am from Thursday to Saturday. Clubs generally operate from 10pm to 4am or 5pm.

How Much

Happy hour beers typically start at around $4; expect to pay about $7 or $8 for a regular draft, and slightly more for imported bottles. Glasses of wine start at around $9. Specialty cocktails run from $14 to well over $20. While bars don't usually have cover charges, you might find yourself paying between $5 and $30 to get into clubs. Cover charges are generally highest on the weekend.

Tipping

If you grab a beer at the bar, bartenders will expect at least a $1 tip *per drink;* tip $2 to $3 for fancier cocktails. Sit-down bars with waitstaff may expect more of a standard restaurant-style 18% to 20% tip, particularly if you snacked along with your boozing.

When clubbing it never hurts to plan ahead; having your name on a guest list can relieve unnecessary frustration and disappointment. If you're an uninitiated partier, dress the part. If you're fed the 'private party' line, try to bluff – chances are high that you've been bounced. Also, don't forget a wad of cash as many nightspots (even the swankiest ones) often refuse credit cards, and in-house ATMs scam a fortune in fees.

The Coffee Evolution

A boom in specialty coffee roasters is transforming New York's once-dismal caffeine culture. More locals are cluing-in on single-origin beans and different brewing techniques, with numerous roasters now offering cupping classes for curious drinkers. Many are transplants from A-list coffee cities, among them Portland's Stumptown (p201) and the Bay Area's Blue Bottle (p291). The Australian influence is especially notable, with antipodean mavericks including Little Collins (p201) and Bluestone Lane (p77).

Drinking & Nightlife by Neighborhood

➜ **Lower Manhattan & the Financial District** FiDi office slaves loosen their ties in everything from specialist beer and brandy bars to revered cocktail hot spots. In the warmer months, crowds pack pedestrianized Stone St.

➜ **East Village & Lower East Side** Proud home of the original-flavor dive bar, the East Village is brimming with options. In the cool 'n' edgy Lower East Side, hit Stanton and Rivington Sts.

➜ **West Village, Chelsea & the Meatpacking District** Jet setters flock to the Meatpacking District, with wine bars, backdoor lounges and gay hangouts radiating out into the West Village and Chelsea.

➜ **Union Square, Flatiron District & Gramercy** Vintage drinking dens packed with after-work ties, swinging cocktail bars jammed with slinky night owls and a string of fun student hangouts.

➜ **Midtown** Rooftop bars with skyline views, historic cocktail salons, and rough-n-ready dive bars.

➜ **Harlem & Upper Manhattan** A burgeoning mix of speakeasy-style bars, hipster hangouts pouring craft suds, and old-school dives. The heart of the action is Harlem.

➜ **Brooklyn** Brooklyn offers everything on the nightlife spectrum with Williamsburg as its heart.

Lonely Planet's Top Choices

Campbell Apartment (p201) Sip Kentucky Gingers in the lavish Grand Central office of a 1920s bigwig.

Little Branch (p152) Speakeasy-chic is all the craze, but no one does it quite like this West Village hideout.

Maison Premiere (p288) Absinthe, juleps and oysters shine bright at this Big Easy tribute in Williamsburg.

Bohemian Hall & Beer Garden (p315) Czech brews served with thick accents at NYC's favorite beer garden in underrated Queens.

Best Classic Date Bars

Pegu Club (p98) Made-from-scratch concoctions in a Burma-inspired SoHo hideaway.

Ten Bells (p124) Candlelit beauty with great drinks and tapas in the Lower East Side.

Buvette (p149) A buzzing, candlelit wine bar on a tree-lined West Village street.

Best Cocktails

Dead Rabbit (p79) Meticulously researched cocktails, punches and pop-inns – lightly hopped ales spiked with different flavors – in a snug FiDi den.

Employees Only (p149) Award-winning barkeeps and arresting libations in the timeless West Village.

Lantern's Keep (p202) Classic, elegant libations in a historic Midtown hotel.

Genuine Liquorette (p97) A Cali-style bodega in Little Italy, where innovative drinks meet playful irreverence.

Best Wine Selection

Terroir Tribeca (p79) An enlightened, encyclopedic wine list in trendy Tribeca.

La Compagnie des Vins Surnaturels (p98) A love letter to Gallic wines steps away from Little Italy.

Barcibo Enoteca (p241) Go-to spot for oenophiles before or after a show at the nearby Lincoln Center.

Immigrant (p122) Wonderful wines and service in a skinny East Village setting.

Best for Beer

Spuyten Duyvil (p288) A much-loved Williamsburg spot serving unique, high-quality crafts.

Astoria Bier & Cheese (p315) Artisanal suds meet gourmet cheeses in Astoria, Queens.

Birreria (p169) Unfiltered, unpasteurized Manhattan ales on a Flatiron rooftop.

Proletariat (p122) Tiny East Village bar serving up extremely uncommon brews.

Best for Spirits

Brandy Library (p79) Blue-blooded cognacs, brandies and more for Tribeca connoisseurs.

Rum House (p202) Unique, coveted rums and a pianist to boot in Midtown.

Mayahuel (p123) A sophisticated East Village temple to mescal and tequila.

Dead Rabbit (p79) NYC's finest collection of rare Irish whiskeys in the Financial District.

Best Dive Bars

Spring Lounge (p97) Soaks, ties and cool kids unite at this veteran Nolita rebel.

Sunny's (p294) Our favorite Red Hook dive, near the Brooklyn waterfront.

Best for Coffee

Stumptown Coffee Roasters (p201) Hipster baristas serving Portland's favorite cup o' joe.

Bluestone Lane (p77) Aussie brewing prowess in the shadow of Wall St.

Blue Bottle Coffee (p291) Specialty coffee roasted on-site in Brooklyn.

La Colombe (p79) Sucker-punch roasts for the downtown cognoscenti.

Little Collins (p201) A tribute to Melbourne coffee culture in Midtown East.

Matcha Bar (p291) Skip the traditional espresso and treat yourself to a rich, flavorful matcha latte.

Best Dance Clubs & House DJs

Cielo (p152) A thumping, modern classic in the Meatpacking District.

Le Bain (p152) Well-dressed crowds still pack this favorite near the High Line.

Verboten (p290) A big, industrial club in the heart of hiptastic Williamsburg.

Berlin (p119) Yesteryear's free-spirited dance days live on at this concealed East Village bolthole.

Bossa Nova Civic Club (p289) A hip little Bushwick haunt for those craving off-the-radar thrills.

Entertainment

Hollywood may hold court when it comes to the motion picture, but it's NYC that reigns supreme over the pantheon of other arts. Actors, musicians, dancers and artists flock to the bright lights of the Big Apple like moths to a flame. Like the old saying goes: if you can make it here, you can make it anywhere.

Theater

From the legendary hit factories of Broadway to the scruffy black-box theaters that dot countless downtown blocks, NYC boasts the full gamut of theater experiences. The most celebrated scene is, of course, that of Broadway. There's something truly magical about sitting in one of the ornate Broadway theaters and letting the show take you to another world as the lights dim.

The term 'off Broadway' is not a geographical one – it simply refers to theaters that are smaller in size (200 to 500 seats) and usually have less of a glitzy production budget than the Broadway big hitters. Off Broadway takes place in even smaller theaters, with shows that are often inexpensively produced and experimental in nature.

Live Music

NYC is the country's capital of live music, and just about every taste can be catered for here. You'll find big-band shindigs, jazz brunches and swank dress-up clubs on the Upper West Side and in Times Square, while Harlem and the West Village are the city's veritable jazz ghettos. Big name indie rockers earned their stripes downtown, but these days that scene has largely flocked to North Brooklyn.

Dance

Dance fans are spoiled for choice in this town, which is home to both the New York City Ballet (p241) and the **American Ballet Theatre** (Map p436; ☏212-477-3030; www.abt.org; David Koch Theater, Lincoln Center, 64th St, at Columbus Ave; Ⓢ1 to 66th St-Lincoln Center). Another key

venue dedicated to dance is the Joyce Theater (p156), which stages acclaimed contemporary productions by dance companies from every corner of the globe. There are also modern dance companies galore, including those of masters Alvin Ailey, Paul Taylor, Merce Cunningham, Martha Graham, Bill T Jones, Mark Morris and a slew of up-and-comers, which often take to the stage downtown and at the Brooklyn Academy of Music (p295).

Comedy

A good laugh is easy to find in the Big Apple, where comedians sharpen their stand-up and improv chops practising new material or hoping to get scouted by a producer or agent. The best spots for some chuckles are downtown, particularly around Chelsea and Greenwich Village. Several festivals, including Comic Con, draw big names throughout the year.

Film & TV

Feasting on films in NYC is quite a different experience to the traditional American blockbuster-at-the-multiplex scene. Filmgoing is a serious venture here, as evidenced by the preponderance of movie houses that show indie, classic, avant-garde, foreign and otherwise nonstandard fare. Frequent film festivals, such as the **Tribeca Film Festival** (☏212-941-2400; www.tribecafilm.com; ☺Apr), with different themes provide additional texture to the movie-going scene.

One of the least-known gems for films is Museum of Modern Art (p182), which has a rich collection of movies spanning all genres and corners of the world. The Film Society of Lincoln Center (p242) stages an incredible array of documentary and art house films. Also worth checking our is the BAM Rose Cinemas (p295), which does similar fare as well as revivals.

A handful of TV shows (p37) are taped in Midtown Manhattan, including *Saturday Night Live* and the *Late Show with Stephen Colbert*. You can be an audience member by signing up online or trying for standby tickets.

Opera & Classical Music

When thinking about opera, one name rules the roost: the Metropolitan Opera (p241), which stages lavish and exceptional productions. However, many other forms live within the city limits. The laudable downtown company **Amore Opera** (Map p412; www.facebook.com/AmoreOpera; Sheen Center, 18 Bleecker St, btwn Elizabeth & Mott Sts; tickets from $40; [S]F to 2nd Ave; 6 to Bleecker St) performs impressive works in the intimate 99-seat Connelly Theater. Other roving companies include **Opera on Tap** (www.operaontap.org/newyork), which stages performances not at grand theaters but bars around Brooklyn. Another creative Brooklyn outfit is LoftOpera (p296), which, true to name, performs condensed operas in a loft in Gowanus.

The choices for orchestras, chamber music and opera are abundant, with the more cutting-edge options often stealing center stage. For all things traditional on a grand scale, don't miss Lincoln Center (p234), the Brooklyn Academy of Music (p295) and the famously stunning Carnegie Hall (p204).

NEED TO KNOW

Calendars & Reviews

➡ **Playbill** (www.playbill.com) The publisher of that happy little yellow-and-white program provided by ushers at Broadway plays also has an online version, offering theater news, listings and a ticket-purchase system.

➡ **Talkin' Broadway** (www.talkingbroadway.com) A less formal site, with dishy reviews as well as a board for posting extra tickets to buy or sell.

➡ Print publications (plus their online equivalents) include *Time Out, New York Magazine, New York Times* and *Village Voice*.

Ticket Agencies

To purchase tickets for shows, you can either head directly to the venue's box office, or use one of several ticket agencies (most of which add a surcharge) to order by phone or online.

➡ **Broadway Line** (www.broadway.org) Provides descriptions and good prices for shows on the Great White Way.

➡ **SmartTix** (www.smarttix.com) A great source for practically anything but Broadway, with info on comedy, cabaret, performance art, music, dance and downtown theater.

➡ **Telecharge** (www.telecharge.com) Sells tickets for Broadway and off-Broadway shows.

➡ **Theatermania** (www.theatermania.com) For any form of theater; provides listings, reviews and ticketing.

➡ **Ticketmaster** (www.ticketmaster.com) An old chestnut, Ticketmaster sells tickets for every conceivable form of big-time entertainment.

➡ **TKTS Booths** Cut-price same-day tickets to Broadway shows, with locations in Midtown, South Street Seaport and Downtown Brooklyn.

Entertainment by Neighborhood

➡ **Lower Manhattan & the Financial District** Tribeca is home to the Flea Theatre and Soho Rep, two venerable theater companies.

➡ **East Village & Lower East Side** Experimental performance spaces, poetry slams and stand-up comics fill basements with laughter.

➡ **West Village, Chelsea & the Meatpacking District** Unofficial HQ of the world's jazz club scene, plus dance troupes galore in Chelsea.

➡ **Midtown** Razzle-dazzle extravaganzas, fresh American theater, world-class jazz sessions, stand-up comedy blue bloods: when the sun sinks, no neighborhood does 'classic New York' better than Midtown.

➡ **Upper West Side & Central Park** The Lincoln Center supplies an endless amount of high culture, while other venues (the Beacon Theatre and Cleopatra's Needle) provide more intimate settings for live music.

➡ **Brooklyn** There's a little bit of everything in America's fourth largest city, from the classical offerings at BAM and Theater for a New Audience to the indie rock bands in Williamsburg.

Lonely Planet's Top Choices

Book of Mormon (p204) Uproariously brilliant Broadway musical appreciated for its wit, charm and pitch-perfect performances.

Brooklyn Bowl (p295) Great line-up of funk, indie rock and global beats, plus beer and bowling!

Kinky Boots (p204) A feel-good tale of an old English shoe factory saved by a drag queen. Great costumes.

Jazz at Lincoln Center (p205) Glittering evening views of Central Park and world-class musical acts.

Carnegie Hall (p204) Legendary concert hall, blessed with perfect acoustics; hosts everything from opera to jazz.

Brooklyn Academy of Music (p295) This hallowed theater hosts cutting-edge works, particularly during its celebrated Next Wave Festival.

Hamilton (p203) A history lesson set to urban rhythms.

Best for Classical Music & Opera

Metropolitan Opera House (p241) Enchanting setting for seeing some of the best opera.

National Sawdust (p295) Cutting-edge contemporary composers that fuse classical, opera and global sounds.

Brooklyn Academy of Music (p295) Innovative works by Brooklyn's renowned hit-maker.

Best for Laughs

Upright Citizens Brigade Theatre (p154) Hilarious comedy sketches and improv.

Comedy Cellar (p156) A well-loved basement comedy joint in Greenwich Village.

Caroline's on Broadway (p207) The go-to spot for seeing famous comics perform.

Creek & the Cave (p315) Offbeat comedy clubhouse in Long Island City.

Best for Dance

Joyce Theater (p156) NY's best venue devoted solely to dance.

New York Live Arts (p155) Experimental leanings with performances by troupes from around the globe.

Brooklyn Academy of Music (p295) Catch Mark Morris Dance Group and many others.

Best for Film

Nitehawk Cinema (p295) Nibble great food and sip cocktails while watching first-run and foreign flicks in Williamsburg.

Anthology Film Archives (p125) East Village icon that screens obscure works and revivals.

BAM Rose Cinemas (p295) A good mix of first-run and foreign films in a landmark Fort Greene building.

Film Forum (p99) Another downtown film innovator with an excellent indie repertoire.

Best Broadway Shows

Book of Mormon (p204) Brilliantly funny, award-winning show by the creators of South Park.

Chicago (Map p432; 219 W 49th St, btwn Broadway & Eighth Ave, Midtown West) One of the most scintillating shows on Broadway.

Kinky Boots (p204) Book well ahead to score seats for this over-the-top musical.

An American in Paris (p205) Exuberant choreography, Gershwin tunes and a romantic Parisian setting.

Best for Theater (Non-Broadway)

Playwrights Horizons (p207) Showcase of powerfully written plays.

Signature Theatre (p207) Stages works by some of the world's top playwrights.

Soho Rep (p80) Some of the city's most powerful and inventive drama.

Theater for a New Audience (p296) Brooklyn's new theater opened to much fanfare in 2013.

Best for Jazz & Global Sounds

Jazz at Lincoln Center (p205) Innovative fare under the guidance of jazz luminary Wynton Marsalis.

Village Vanguard (p154) Legendary West Village jazz club.

Smalls (p154) Tiny West Village basement joint that evokes the feel of decades past.

Barbès (p296) Obscure but celebratory rhythms from around the globe in Park Slope.

Best for Rock

Bowery Ballroom (p126) Celebrated downtown concert hall.

Music Hall of Williamsburg (p297) Indie rock galore out in Brooklyn.

Rockwood Music Hall (p125) Music all the time at this Lower East Side spot.

Bell House (p295) South Brooklyn charmer with an innovative line-up of indie and folk sounds.

Barneys (p208), Madison Ave

Shopping

New York City is quite simply one of the best shopping destinations on the planet. Fashion boutiques, flea markets, booksellers, record stores, antique shops, Asian emporiums and gourmet grocers selling edibles from every corner of the globe are just a few places to begin the shopping adventure. And while it's quite easy to spend a fortune, sample sales and designer outlets yield some startlingly good deals.

Fashion Epicenter

One of the world's fashion capitals, NYC is ever setting trends for the rest of the country to follow. For checking out the latest designs hitting the streets, it's worth browsing some of the city's best-loved boutiques around town – regardless of whether you intend to spend. A few favorites include Opening Ceremony, Issey Miyake, Marc Jacobs, Steven Alan, Rag & Bone, John Varvatos, By Robert James and Piperlime.

If time is limited, or you simply want to browse a plethora of labels in one go, then head to those heady conglomerations known worldwide as department stores. New York has a special blend of alluring draws – in particular don't miss Barneys (p208), Bergdorf Goodman (p208), Macy's (p209) and Bloomingdale's (p208).

NYC Icons

A few stores in this city have cemented their status as NYC legends. This city just wouldn't quite be the same without them. For label hunters, Century 21 (p81) is a Big Apple institution, with wears by D&G, Prada, Marc Jacobs and many others at low prices. Other Music (p103) is a long-running

NEED TO KNOW

Websites

→ **Racked** (www.ny.racked.com) Informative shopping blog with its finger on the pulse.

→ **New York Magazine** (www.nymag.com) Trustworthy opinions on the Big Apple's best places to swipe your plastic.

→ **The Glamourai** (www.theglamourai.com) Glossy downtown fashion blog that's packed with cutting-edge style ideas.

Ones to Follow

→ **Bill Cunningham** (www.nytimes.com/video/on-the-street) Legendary fashion photographer who captures the zeitgeist in his work.

→ **Andre Leon Talley** (www.twitter.com/OfficialALT) Anna Wintour's top fashion editor in the know at *Vogue*.

→ **New York Times** (www.twitter.com/NYTFashion) Everything that's happening in the fashion industry.

Opening Hours

In general, most businesses are open from 10am to around 7pm on weekdays and 11am to around 8pm Saturdays. Sundays can be variable – some stores stay closed while others keep weekday hours. Stores tend to stay open later in the neighborhoods downtown. Small boutiques often have variable hours – many open at noon.

Sales Tax

Clothing and footwear that costs less than $110 is exempt from sales tax. For everything else, you'll pay 8.875% retail sales tax on every purchase.

Macy's (p209)

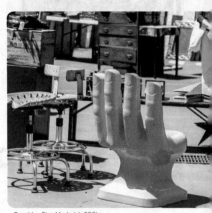
Brooklyn Flea Market (p280)

indie music store (CDs and some vinyl) that thrives despite the odds. Book lovers of the world unite at the Strand (p157), the city's biggest and best bookseller. Run by Hassidic Jews and employing mechanized whimsy, B&H Photo Video (p209) is a mecca for digital and audio geeks.

For secondhand clothing, home furnishings and books, good-hearted Housing Works (p160), with many locations around town, is a perennial favorite.

Sample Sales

While clothing sales happen year-round – usually when seasons change and old stock must be moved out – sample sales are held frequently, mostly in the huge warehouses in the Fashion District of Midtown or in SoHo. While the original sample sale was a way for designers to get rid of one-of-a-kind prototypes that weren't quite up to snuff, most sample sales these days are for high-end labels to get rid of overstock at wonderfully deep discounts. For the latest sample sales, check out **NY Racked** (http://ny.racked.com/sales). Consignment stores are another fine place to look for top (gently used) fashions at reduced prices.

Flea Markets & Vintage Adventure

As much as New Yorkers gravitate towards all that's shiny and new, it can be infinitely fun to rifle through closets of unwanted wares and threads. The most popular flea market is the Brooklyn Flea (p299), housed in all sorts of spaces throughout the year. The East Village is the city's de facto neighborhood for secondhand and vintage stores – the uniform of the unwavering legion of hipsters.

Shopping by Neighborhood

➡ **Lower Manhattan & the Financial District** While not a shopping hot spot per se, Lower Manhattan serves up a trickle of gems, from vintage film posters and hard-to-find vino to hipster-chic threads and hand-crafted artisanal axes.

➡ **SoHo & Chinatown** West Broadway is a veritable outdoor mall of encyclopedic proportions. It's like the UN of retail – if you can't find what you're looking for then it hasn't

been invented yet. Try Mott St for something a bit more something a little more idiosyncratic.

➡ **West Village, Chelsea & the Meatpacking District** Bleecker St, running off Abingdon Sq, is lined with boutiques with a handful on nearby W 4th St. Other high-end shops lurk around Washington St, Hudson St and W 14th St in the Meatpacking District.

➡ **East Village & Lower East Side** Hipster treasure trove of vintage wares and design goods. Go wild on E 9th St, St Marks Place and Orchard St.

➡ **Midtown** Epic department stores, global chains and the odd in-the-know treasure – window shoppers unite!

➡ **Upper East Side** The country's most expensive boutiques are found along Madison Ave, but plenty of price-conscious consignment shops can be scouted as well.

➡ **Brooklyn** A healthy mix of independent boutiques and thrift stores. Good shopping streets include Bedford Ave and Grand Ave in Williamsburg, Smith St in Boerum Hill and Fifth Ave in Park Slope.

PLAN YOUR TRIP SHOPPING

Window shopping, SoHo (p99)

Lonely Planet's Top Choices

Barneys (p208) Serious fashionistas shop (or at least browse) at Barneys, well-known for its spot-on collections of in-the-know labels.

Brooklyn Flea (p299) Brooklyn's collection of flea markets offers plenty of vintage furnishings, retro clothing and bric-a-brac, plus great food stalls.

ABC Carpet & Home (p173) Spread over six floors like a museum, ABC is packed with treasures large (furniture) and small (designer jewelry, gifts).

MoMA Design & Book Store (p209) The perfect one-stop shop for coffee-table tomes, art prints, edgy jewellery and 'Where-did-you-get?' that homewares.

Idlewild Books (p173) An inspiring place for travelers and daydreamers with titles (both fiction and nonfiction) spanning the globe.

Chelsea Market (p134) Culinary temptation in every shape and form at this wondrous food-focused market.

Best Fashion Boutiques

Steven Alan (p81) Stylish, heritage-inspired fashion, with branches around NYC, including downtown.

Marc by Marc Jacobs (p158) A downtown and uptown favorite particularly the West Village locations.

Rag & Bone (p102) Beautifully tailored clothes for men and women, in SoHo and elsewhere.

John Varvatos (p127) Rugged but worldly wearables in a former downtown rock club.

Opening Ceremony (p102) Head-turning, cutting-edge threads and kicks for the fashion avant-garde in SoHo.

Best for Women

Verameat (p127) Exquisite jewelry that treads between beauty and whimsy.

Beacon's Closet (p158) Valhalla for vintage lovers at multiple locations.

MIN New York (p100) Unique perfumes in an apothecary-like setting.

Best for Men

By Robert James (p129) Rugged menswear by a celebrated new local designer.

Nepenthes New York (p209) Japanese collective selling covetable, in-the-know labels.

Odin (p102) Tiny downtown men's boutique for one-of-a-kind pieces.

Best for Children

Dinosaur Hill (p127) Fun and creative toys, books and music that will inspire young minds.

Yoya (p157) Small clothing store in the Meatpacking District.

Books of Wonder (p173) Great gift ideas for kids, plus in-store readings.

Best for Unique Souvenirs & Gifts

De Vera (p102) Beautiful glasswares and art objects.

Obscura Antiques (p127) A cabinet of curiosities packed with strange and eerie objects.

Amé Amé (p209) Beautifully made umbrellas and rain gear, plus candy!

Top Hat (p129) Lovely collectible objects from around the globe.

Best Vintage Stores

Beacon's Closet (p158) Get a new outfit without breaking the bank at this great vintage shop.

Screaming Mimi's (p103) Lots of appealing clothes from decades past.

Resurrection (p103) Mint-condition pieces from couture labels.

Tokio 7 (p128) A fun place to browse high-end labels in the East Village.

Best Homewares & Design Stores

Shinola (p81) Unusual accessories from a cutting-edge Detroit design house in Tribeca.

A&G Merch (p298) Clever decorating ideas from this artful Williamsburg shop.

Magpie (p244) Ecofriendly curios to feather your nest, in the Upper West Side.

Best Bookshops

Strand Book Store (p157) Hands-down NYC's best used bookstore.

McNally Jackson (p102) Great SoHo spot for book browsing and author readings.

Housing Works Book Store (p103) Used books and a café in an atmospheric setting in Nolita.

192 Books (p159) The perfect neighborhood book shop in Chelsea.

Best Music Stores

Rough Trade (p298) Vinyl is far from dead at this sprawling new music shop/concert space in Williamsburg.

Other Music (p103) Great selection of rare grooves at this downtown icon.

A-1 Records (p126) Endless bins of records in the East Village.

Black Gold (p300) Rare vinyl (plus coffee and taxidermy).

Sports & Activities

Although hailing cabs in New York City can feel like a blood sport, and waiting on subway platforms in summer heat is steamier than a sauna, New Yorkers still love to stay active in their spare time. And considering how limited the green spaces are in the city, it's surprising for some visitors just how active the locals can be.

Spectator Sports

BASEBALL

New York is one of the last remaining corners of the USA where baseball reigns supreme over football and basketball. Tickets start around $15 – a great deal for seeing the home teams playing in their recently opened stadiums. The two Major League Baseball teams play 162 games during the regular season from April to October, when the playoffs begin.

➡ **New York Yankees** (p261) The Bronx Bombers are the USA's greatest dynasty, with over two dozen World Series championship titles since 1900.

➡ **New York Mets** (p316) In the National League since 1962, the Mets remain New York's 'new' baseball team, and won the pennant in 2015.

BASKETBALL

Two NBA (National Basketball Association) teams now play in New York City. The blue-and-orange **New York Knicks** (Map p432; www.nyknicks.com; Madison Sq Garden, Seventh Ave btwn 31st & 33rd Sts, Midtown West; tickets from $75.50; [S]A/C/E, 1/2/3 to 34th St-Penn Station) are loved by New Yorkers, occasional scandal aside, while the **Brooklyn Nets** (www.nba.com/nets; tickets from $15; 🚌351 from Port Authority), formerly the New Jersey Nets, is Brooklyn's new pro team (the first since the Dodgers left town) and has gained a strong local following. The season lasts from October to May or June.

FOOTBALL

Most of New York tunes into its NFL (National Football League) teams: the **New York Giants** (☎201-935-8222; www.giants.com; Meadowlands Stadium, Meadowlands Sports Complex, East Rutherford, NJ; 🚌351 from Port Authority, 🚆NJ Transit from PennStation to Meadowlands), one of the NFL's oldest teams, with four Super Bowl victories, most recently in 2011, and the **New York Jets** (☎800-469-5387; www.newyorkjets.com; Meadowlands Stadium, Meadowlands Sports Complex, East Rutherford, NJ; 🚌351 from Port Authority, 🚆NJ Transit from Penn Station to Meadowlands), whose games are always packed and new fans get swept away by the contagious 'J-E-T-S!' chants.

Both teams play at the new Metlife Stadium at the Meadowlands Sports Complex in New Jersey (from Manhattan take NJ Transit via Seacaucus Junction, $11 return). Metlife Stadium hosted the 2014 Super Bowl.

Football season runs from August to January or February. The NFL season has 16 regular-season games (held on Sunday or Monday night), then up to three playoffs before the Super Bowl.

HOCKEY

The NHL (National Hockey League) has three franchises in the greater New York area; each team plays three or four games weekly during the season from September to April.

➡ **New York Rangers** (www.nyrangers.com) Manhattan's favorite hockey squad.

➡ **New York Islanders** (www.newyorkislanders.com) New York City hasn't given much Islander

NEED TO KNOW

Websites

➤ **NYC Parks** (www.nycgovparks.org) Details on park services, including free pools and basketball courts, plus borough biking maps.

➤ **New York Road Runners Club** (www. nyrr.org) Organizes weekend runs and races citywide.

➤ **Central Park** (www.centralparknyc. org) Lists myriad activities and events inside NYC's best-loved green space.

➤ **NYC** (www.nycgo.com/sports) Lists all the major sporting events and activities happening in town.

Buying Tickets

With so many teams and overlapping seasons, a game is rarely a day away. Some teams' hotlines or box offices sell tickets directly (available under 'Tickets' on the relevant websites), but most go via **Ticket master** (www.ticketmaster.com). The other major buy/sell outlet is **StubHub** (☎866-788-2482; www.stubhub.com).

love since the unremarkable four-consecutive-year Stanley Cup streak in the '80s. Their stock is on the rise, however, since their move to Brooklyn's Barclay Center in 2015.

➤ **New Jersey Devils** (http://devils.nhl.com) The Devils may not be New Yorkers, but they've seen more wins combine than their neighbors.

Outdoor Sports

RUNNING & JOGGING

Central Park's loop roads are best during traffic-free hours, though you'll be in the company of many cyclists and in-line skaters. The 1.6-mile path surrounding the Jacqueline Kennedy Onassis Reservoir (where Jackie O used to run) is for runners and walkers only; access it between 86th and 96th Sts. Running along the Hudson River is a popular path, best from about 30th St

to Battery Park in Lower Manhattan. The Upper East Side has a path that runs along FDR Dr and the East River (from 63rd St to 115th St). Brooklyn's Prospect Park has plenty of paths (and a 3-mile loop), while 1.3-mile-long Brooklyn Bridge Park has incredible views of Manhattan (reach it via Brooklyn Bridge to up the mileage). The New York Road Runners Club organizes weekend runs citywide, including the New York City Marathon.

BICYCLING

NYC has taken enormous strides in making the city more bike-friendly, adding hundreds of miles of bike lanes in recent years. That said, we recommend that the uninitiated stick to the less hectic trails in the parks and along the waterways, such as Central Park, Prospect Park, the Manhattan Waterfront Greenway and the Brooklyn Waterfront Greenway.

The new **Citi Bike** (www.citibikenyc.com) is handy for quick jaunts, but for longer rides, you'll want a proper rental. **Bike & Roll** has loads of outdoor hire spots, including at Central Park (p244) by Columbus Circle.

Street Sports

With all that concrete around, New York has embraced a number of sports and events played directly on the streets themselves. Those with hoop dreams will find pick-up basketball games all over the city, the most famous courts being the West 4th Street Basketball Courts, known as 'the Cage'. Or try Holcombe Rucker Park up in Harlem – that's where many NBA bigshots cut their teeth. You'll also find pick-up games in Tompkins Square Park and Riverside Park. Hudson River Park has courts at Canal St and on W 11th Ave at 23rd St.

Lesser-known handball and stickball are also popular in NYC – you'll find one-wall courts in outdoor parks all over the city. For stickball, link up with the Bronx-based **Emperors Stickball League** (www.stickball. com) to check out its Sunday games during the warmer months.

Lonely Planet's Top Choices

Central Park (p230) The city's wondrous playground has rolling hills, forested paths, open green spaces and a beautiful lake.

New York Yankees (p261) Even if you don't follow baseball, it's well worth trekking out to the Bronx to experience the rabid fandom.

Chelsea Piers Complex (p160) Every activity imaginable – from kickboxing to ice hockey – under one gigantic roof, just a stone's throw from the High Line.

New York Spa Castle (p316) Bathing behemoth with wallet-friendly prices. Inspired by ancient Korean traditions of wellness. You'll want to stay for days.

Brooklyn Bridge Park (p265) This brand new green space is Brooklyn's pride and joy.

Prospect Park (p268) Escape the crowds at Brooklyn's gorgeous park, with trails, hills, a canal, lake and meadows.

Best Spectator Sports

New York Yankees (p261) One of the country's successful baseball teams.

New York Giants (p53) Football powerhouse that, despite the name, plays their home games in New Jersey.

New York Knicks (p53) See the Knicks sink a few three-pointers at Madison Square Garden.

Brooklyn Nets (p53) The hot new NBA team in town and symbol of Brooklyn's resurgence.

Brooklyn Cyclones (p297) See a minor league baseball game near Coney Island's boardwalk.

New York Mets (p316) NYC's other baseball team play their games at Citi Field in Queens.

Best Spas

New York Spa Castle (p316) An enchanting wonderland of waterfalls and steam rooms far out in Queens.

Russian & Turkish Baths (p129) An East Village icon since 1892.

Great Jones Spa (p104) Book a massage, then enjoy the steam room, hot tub and rock sauna.

Best Bowling

Brooklyn Bowl (p301) A Williamsburg classic that's equal parts hipster hangout, concert space and bowling alley.

Chelsea Piers Complex (p160) Take in a bit of bowling, followed by a stroll along the Hudson.

Lucky Strike (p210) A fun night of bowling in Midtown.

Best Out-of-the-Box Activities

Royal Palms (p294) A mecca for shuffleboard lovers, this place has shuffleboard courts, plus food trucks and microbrews.

New York Trapeze School (p160) Channel your inner circus star at this trapeze school with two locations.

Best Indoor Activities

The Cliffs (p316) Massive climbing center in Long Island City, Queens.

Brooklyn Boulders (p301) Another great spot for rock climbers – this one's in south Brooklyn.

Jivamukti (p174) Lavish yoga center near Union Square.

Area Yoga Center (p301) A great choice for yoga in health-minded Cobble Hill.

Best Urban Green Spaces

Governors Island (p75) Car-free island just a quick hop from Lower Manhattan or Brooklyn.

Bryant Park (p191) A small appealing oasis amid the skyscrapers of Midtown.

Madison Square Park (p165) A pretty little park between Midtown and downtown.

Gantry Plaza State Park (p305) A lovely riverside spot to relax in Long Island City, Queens.

Inwood Hill Park (p256) Serene setting of forest and salt marsh in Upper Manhattan.

Queens County Farm Museum (p314) Get a taste of barnyard life without leaving the metropolis.

Best Gardens

Brooklyn Botanic Garden (p276) Japanese gardens, native flora and photogenic springtime cherry blossoms.

New York Botanical Garden Fifty acres of old growth forest up in the Bronx.

Cloisters Museum & Gardens (p253) Pretty gardens next to a Medieval-esque building.

The High Line (p132) Wild plants and towering weeds steal the show.

Gay & Lesbian

From hand-locked married couples on the streets of Hell's Kitchen to a rainbow-hued Empire State Building at Pride, there's no doubt that New York City is one of the world's great gay cities. Indeed, few places come close to matching the breadth and depth of queer offerings here, from cabarets and clubs to festivals and readings.

School Night Shenanigans

Here in the Big Apple, any night of the week is fair game to paint the town rouge – especially for the gay community, who attack the weekday social scene with gusto. Wednesday and Thursday nights roar with a steady stream of parties, and locals love raging on Sunday (especially in summer). While there's undoubtedly much fun to be had on Friday and Saturday nights, weekend parties tend to be more 'bridge and tunnel' – Manhattanites often use these non-work days to catch up with friends, check out new restaurants and attend house parties.

Promoters

One of best ways to dial into the party hotline is to follow the various goings-on of your favorite promoter. Here are some of ours:

BoiParty (www.boiparty.com) Throws impressive weekly, monthly, and annual dance parties.

The Saint at Large (www.saintatlarge.com) Team behind the annual Black Party, a massive circuit event held in March.

Daniel Nardicio (www.danielnardicio.com) Party promoter famed for his often hedonistic events.

Josh Wood (www.joshwoodproductions.com) Known for gala events and philanthropic causes.

Spank (www.spankartmag.com) Art-themed parties.

Erich Conrad (Twitter @ZIGZAGLeBain) One of the city's veteran party producers.

Gay & Lesbian by Neighborhood

➡ **East Village & Lower East Side** Slightly grittier, sweatier, grungier versions of the west side haunts.

➡ **West Village, Chelsea & the Meatpacking District** Classic bars and clubs in the Village, with a wilting scene in high-rent Chelsea.

➡ **Union Square, Flatiron District & Gramercy** Hosts a small spillover of gay venues from the East Village, West Village and Chelsea.

➡ **Midtown** Hell's Kitchen is the city's 21st-century gay epicenter, with a plethora of gay and gay-friendly eateries, bars, clubs and shops.

➡ **Brooklyn** Multi-neighborhood borough with gays of every ilk, and diverse watering holes peppered throughout.

RESOURCES & SUPPORT

One of the largest centers of its kind in the world, the **LGBT Community Center** (☎212-620-7310; www.gaycenter.org; 208 W 13th St, btwn Seventh & Greenwich Aves; suggested donation $5; 🕐9am-10pm Mon-Sat, to 9pm Sun; [S]1/2/3 to 14th St) provides a ton of regional publications about gay events and nightlife, and hosts frequent special events – dance parties, art exhibits, Broadway-caliber performances, readings and political panels. Plus it's home to the National Archive for Lesbian, Gay, Bisexual & Transgender History (accessible to researchers by appointment); a small exhibition space, the Campbell-Soady Gallery; and a cyber center.

Lonely Planet's Top Choices

NYC Pride (p30) Rainbow-clad pomp and circumstance.

Leslie-Lohman Museum of Gay & Lesbian Art (p87) The world's first LGBT art museum.

Industry (p203) One of the best-loved bar-clubs in kicking Hell's Kitchen.

Duplex (p156) Camp quips, smooth crooners and a riotously fun piano bar define this Village veteran.

Cock (p124) Love-it-or-loathe-it debauchery in the fabled East Village.

Best Places to Slumber

Standard East Village (p336) Crisp, fresh, boutique chic in the funky East Village.

Chelsea Pines Inn (p337) Hollywood posters, diva-moniker rooms and a Chelsea address.

Hotel Gansevoort (p338) Jetsetter cool and a rooftop pool in the Meatpacking District.

Best for Dancing Queens

Industry (p203) As night deepens, this Hell's Kitchen hit turns from buzzing bar to thumping club.

Monster (p153) Cheeky go-go boys and cheekier drag queens keep the punters purring in the basement.

XL Nightclub (p203) A sprawling danceteria of hot, sweat-soaked muscle in where-it's-at Hell's Kitchen.

Best for Weeknights

Therapy (p203) Evening music, drag and showbiz guests give school nights some much-needed razzle dazzle.

Flaming Saddles (p203) Boot-scootin' barmen pouring liquor down your throat – who said weeknights were boring?

Boxers NYC (p169) From post-work to late-night, this sports bar sees dudes tackling the tighter ends on and off the field.

Best Old-School Hangouts

Marie's Crisis (p151) One-time hooker hangout turned Village showtune piano bar.

Stonewall Inn (p153) Scene of rioting drag queens during the Stonewall riots of '69.

Julius Bar (p151) The oldest gay in the village.

Cock (p124) Tongue-in-cheek sleaze in a former gay-punk hangout.

Best for Women

Ginger's (Map 444; 363 Fifth Ave at 5th St, Park Slope) Happy hour specials, karaoke and Sunday bingo pull the girls at Brooklyn's G-Spot.

Cubbyhole (p153) A no-attitude Village veteran with jukebox tunes and chatty regulars.

Henrietta Hudson (p152) A fun, classic dive packed with super-cool rocker chicks.

Best Daytime Scene

Brunch on Ninth Avenue Pick a sidewalk table and do your bit for Neighborhood Watch, Hell's Kitchen–style.

Shopping in Chelsea Style-up at Nasty Pig (p160) and other queer-centric Chelsea boutiques.

Pier 45 (Christopher Street Pier) (p136) Butt-hugging trunks and loved-up couples make this a summertime sunbaking staple.

Fire Island (p321) Mingle with the hot and rich at this sand-dune-swept playground.

NEED TO KNOW

There are tons of websites geared towards the goings-on of the city's gay community.

➡ **Next Magazine** (www.nextmagazine.com) Online version of the ubiquitous print guide to all things gay in NYC.

➡ **Get Out!** (www.getoutmag.com) Online version of another print guide to all things queer in town.

➡ **Gayletter** (www.gayletter.com) E-newsletter covering queer-related culture, musings and parties.

➡ **Gay City News** (www.gaycitynews.nyc) News and current affairs with a queer bent, as well as arts and travel reviews.

Best Events

NYC Pride (p30) A monthlong celebration in June, with parties, cultural events and the famous march down Fifth Ave.

NewFest NYC's premier queer film fest, with a weeklong program of homegrown and foreign flicks in September.

MIX New York Queer Experimental Film Festival Six days of avant-garde and political queer cinema in November.

Explore New York City

Grand Central Terminal (p184)

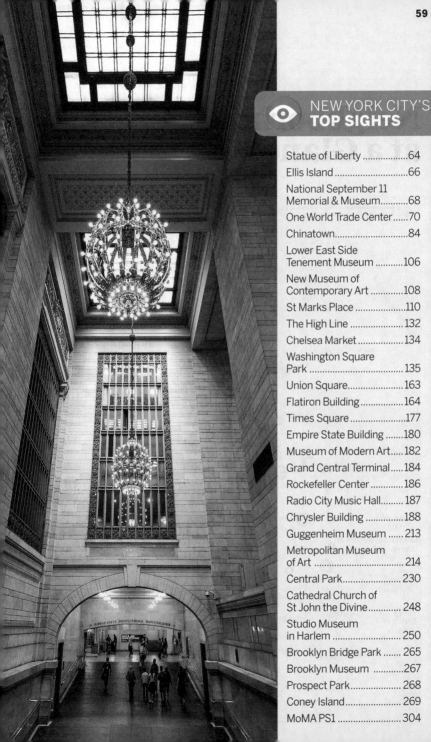

NEW YORK CITY'S TOP SIGHTS

Neighborhoods at a Glance

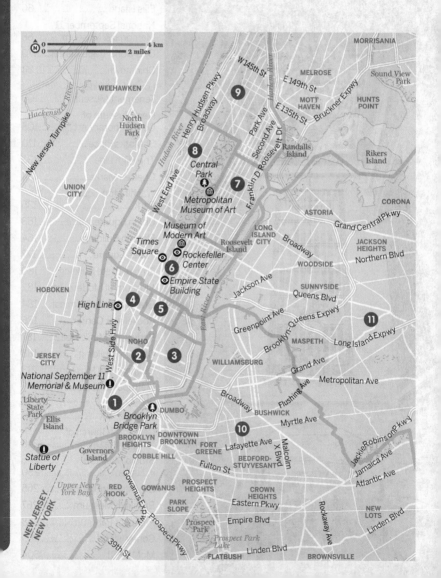

❶ Lower Manhattan & the Financial District (p62)

Home to icons such as Wall St, the National September 11 Memorial and Museum, and the Statue of Liberty, the southern end of Manhattan pulses with businesslike energy during the day before settling into quiet nights. Tribeca, however, continues to hum well after dark with its cache of restaurants and lounges.

❷ SoHo & Chinatown (p83)

Sacred temples, hawkers peddling bric-a-brac and steam-filled soup-dumpling parlors line the hurried streets of Chinatown, with SoHo, next door, providing the counterpoint with streamlined thoroughfares and storefronts representing all of the biggest–name brands in the world. Tucked somewhere in between is Little Italy (emphasis on the 'little').

❸ East Village & Lower East Side (p105)

Old meets new on every block of this downtown duo – two of the city's hottest 'hoods for nightlife and cheap eats that lure students, bankers and scruffier types alike.

❹ West Village, Chelsea & the Meatpacking District (p130)

Quaint, twisting streets and well-preserved townhouses offer endless options for intimate dining and drinking in the West Village. The Meatpacking District next door has trendy nightlife options galore; further up is Chelsea, home to hundreds of art galleries and a vibrant gay scene.

❺ Union Square, Flatiron District & Gramercy (p161)

Though short on sights, there's lots happening on and around Union Square, which bustles with a medley of protesters, buskers and businessfolk. North of there is grassy Madison Square Park, an elegant oasis en route to Midtown. The peaceful streets around Gramercy are mostly residential with a handful of high-end eating and drinking spots.

❻ Midtown (p175)

This is the home of the NYC found on postcards: Times Square, Empire State Building, Broadway theaters, canyons of skyscrapers, and bustling crowds. The Museum of Modern Art (MoMA), Bryant Park, the grand shops along Fifth Ave and the gay bars of Hell's Kitchen are also here.

❼ Upper East Side (p211)

High-end boutiques line Madison Ave and mansions run parallel along Fifth Ave, which culminates in an architectural flourish called Museum Mile – one of the most cultured strips in the city, if not the world.

❽ Upper West Side & Central Park (p228)

New York's antidote to the endless stretches of concrete, Central Park is a verdant escape from honking horns and sunless sidewalks. Lining the park with inspired residential towers, the Upper West Side is home to the Lincoln Center.

❾ Harlem & Upper Manhattan (p246)

Harlem and Hamilton Heights – a bastion of African American culture – offers good eats and jazz beats. Head up to Inwood for leafy park space, or try Morningside Heights to soak up some student life.

❿ Brooklyn (p263)

Brooklyn's sprawling checkerboard of distinct neighborhoods is over three times the size of Manhattan, not to mention more diverse and far-reaching. For skyline views and a pinch of history, try brownstone-studded Brooklyn Heights; or try Williamsburg for vintage wares and late-night bar crawls.

⓫ Queens (p302)

A patchwork of communities, Queens is trailblazer territory for return visitors and locals alike. Gorge at the ethnic delis of Astoria, ogle contemporary art in Long Island City, rip through steamed pork buns in Flushing, and ride the surf in Rockaway Beach.

Lower Manhattan & the Financial District

WALL STREET & THE FINANCIAL DISTRICT | NEW YORK HARBOR | BATTERY PARK CITY | EAST RIVER WATERFRONT | CITY HALL & CIVIC CENTER

Neighborhood Top Five

❶ Scaling the **Statue of Liberty** (p64), peering out from her crown and seeing the world's greatest city spread out before you. Prepare to pinch yourself.

❷ Reflecting on loss, hope and resilience at the **National September 11 Memorial & Museum** (p72) and **One World Observatory** (p70).

❸ Climbing the **One World Trade Center** (p72) for a knockout panorama of Manhattan and beyond.

❹ Taking in sunset-blazing skyscrapers from New York City's free-and-fantastic **Staten Island Ferry** (p82).

❺ Exploring the making of modern America at the country's most poignant, historically significant point of entry, **Ellis Island** (p66).

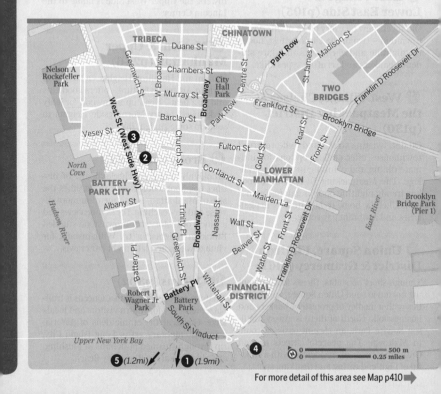

For more detail of this area see Map p410 ➡

Explore Lower Manhattan & the Financial District

A little planning will save you a lot of time in Lower Manhattan. Book tickets online to the unmissable Ellis Island and Statue of Liberty. Alternatively, catch the first ferry and avoid weekends, especially in summer. You'll need a good four or five hours to explore the two sights properly, and bring a picnic lunch – the food onsite is awful. Online ticket purchasing is also highly recommended for both the National September 11 Museum and the neighboring One World Observatory. To experience the Financial District's power-broking intensity, go during business hours. But to calmly contemplate the area's Federal homes, Greek Revival temples and early-modern skyscrapers, go after hours. To avoid the hordes at shopping mecca Century 21, raid the racks by 8am on weekdays. If the weather is on your side, soak up some rays and river views on Pier 15 at South Street Seaport, or walk across the Brooklyn Bridge for jaw-dropping views of Lower Manhattan. For an evening buzz on any night, head to Tribeca's string of renowned eateries and drinking dens, the former best reserved in advance.

Local Life

→ **Coffee** Ditch the chains for in-the-know Bluestone Lane (p77) and La Colombe (p79).

→ **Wine** Swill free vino on Sunday afternoons at Pasanella & Son (p81).

→ **Cocktails** Sip meticulous libations at top-of-the-class Dead Rabbit (p79).

→ **Culture** Catch encore-provoking drama at the Flea Theater (p80).

→ **Escape** Cycle, relax and eye-up art on the summer oasis that is Governors Island (p75).

Getting There & Away

→ **Subway** The Financial District is well serviced by subway lines, connecting the area to the rest of Manhattan, Brooklyn, Queens and the Bronx. Fulton St is the main interchange station, servicing the A/C, J/Z, 2/3 and 4/5 lines. The 1 train terminates at South Ferry, from where the Staten Island Ferry departs.

→ **Bus** From the Staten Island Ferry terminal, useful routes include the M15 (to East Village, Midtown East, Upper East Side and East Harlem) and the M20 (to Tribeca, West Village, Chelsea and Midtown West).

→ **Boat** The Staten Island Ferry Terminal is at the southern end of Whitehall St. Ferries to Governors Island leave from the adjacent Battery Maritime Building. Services to Liberty and Ellis Islands depart from nearby Battery Park.

Lonely Planet's Top Tip

After cheap tickets to Broadway shows? Ditch the TKTS Booth in Times Sq for the TKTS Booth at South Street Seaport. Queues usually move a little faster and you can purchase tickets for next-day matinees (something you can't do at the Times Sq outlet). The TKTS Smartphone app offers real-time listings of what's on sale.

Best Places to Eat

→ Locanda Verde (p77)

→ Bâtard (p77)

→ North End Grill (p77)

→ Brookfield Place (p77)

→ Da Mikele (p76)

For reviews, see p76

Best Places to Drink

→ Dead Rabbit (p79)

→ Ward III (p79)

→ Brandy Library (p79)

→ Smith & Mills (p80)

→ Bluestone Lane (p77)

For reviews, see p77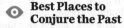

Best Places to Conjure the Past

→ Ellis Island (p66)

→ Trinity Church cemetery (p72)

→ Fraunces Tavern Museum (p72)

→ South Street Seaport (p75)

For reviews, see p72

JOSEPH MCNALLY / GETTY IMAGES ©

TOP SIGHT
STATUE OF LIBERTY

Lady Liberty has been gazing sternly towards 'unenlightened Europe' since 1886. Dubbed the 'Mother of Exiles,' the statue symbolically admonishes the rigid social structures of the old world. 'Give me your tired, your poor, your huddled masses yearning to breathe free, the wretched refuse of your teeming shore' she declares in Emma Lazarus' famous 1883 poem 'The New Colossus.'

From the Suez to the City

To the surprise of many, France's jumbo-sized gift to America was not originally conceived with the US in mind. Indeed, when sculptor Frédéric-Auguste Bartholdi began planning the piece, his vision was for a colossal sculpture to guard the entrance to the Suez Canal in Egypt, one of France's greatest 19th-century engineering achievements. Bartholdi's ode to Gallic ingenuity would incorporate elements of two of the Seven Wonders of the Ancient World: the Colossus of Rhodes and the lighthouse of Alexandria. Despite its appeal to human vanity, the ambitious monument failed to attract serious funding from either France or Egypt, and Bartholdi's dream seemed destined for the scrapheap. Salvation would come from Bartholdi's friend, Edouard René Lefèbvre de Laboulaye. A French jurist, writer and anti-slavery activist, de Laboulaye proposed a gift to America as a symbol of the triumph of Republicanism and of the democratic values that underpinned both France and the US. Seeing an opportunity too good to miss, Bartholdi quickly set to work, tweaking his vision and turning his Suez flop into 'Liberty Enlightening the World', an enviable gift to commemorate America's centennial of the Declaration of Independence.

DID YOU KNOW?

The Statue of Liberty weighs 225 tonnes and stretches 93m from ground to torch-tip.

PRACTICALITIES

- Map p410
- ☎212-363-3200, tickets 877-523-9849
- www.nps.gov/stli
- Liberty Island
- adult/child incl Ellis Island $18/9, incl crown $21/12
- 🕐8:30am-5:30pm, check website for seasonal changes
- ⛴to Liberty Island, [S]1 to South Ferry; 4/5 to Bowling Green

Creating The Lady

The artist spent most of 20 years turning his dream – to create the hollow monument and mount it in the New York Harbor – into reality. Along the way it was hindered by serious financial problems, but was helped in part by the fund-raising efforts of newspaper publisher Joseph Pulitzer. Lending a further hand was poet Emma Lazarus, whose ode to Lady Liberty was part of a fund-raising campaign for the statue's pedestal, designed by American architect Richard Morris Hunt. Bartholdi's work on the statue was also delayed by structural challenges – a problem resolved by the metal framework mastery of railway engineer Gustave Eiffel (yes, of the famous tower). The work of art was finally completed in France in 1884 (a bit off schedule for the centennial). It was shipped to NYC as 350 pieces packed into 214 crates, reassembled over a span of four months and placed on the US-made granite pedestal. Its spectacular October 1886 dedication included New York's first ticker-tape parade, and a flotilla of almost 300 vessels. Put under the administration of the National Park Service in 1933, a restoration of the Lady's oxidized copper began in 1984, the same year the monument made it onto the UN's list of World Heritage Sites.

Liberty Today

Folks who reserve their tickets in advance are able to climb the (steep) 393 steps to Lady Liberty's crown, from where the city and harbor are breathtaking. That said, crown access is extremely limited, and the only way in is to reserve your spot in advance; the further in advance you can do it, the better, as a six-month lead time is allowed. Each customer may only reserve a maximum of four crown tickets, and children must be at least 4ft tall to access the crown.

If you miss out on crown tickets, you may have better luck with tickets to the pedestal, which also offers commanding views. Like crown tickets, pedestal tickets are limited and should be reserved in advance, either online or by phone. Only crown and pedestal ticket holders have access to the Statue of Liberty museum in the pedestal.

If you don't have crown or pedestal tickets, don't fret. All ferry tickets to Liberty Island offer basic access to the grounds, including guided ranger tours or self-guided audio tours. The grounds also host a gift shop and cafeteria. (Tip: bring your own nibbles and enjoy them by the water, the Manhattan skyline stretched out before you.)

NEED TO KNOW

Although the ferry ride from Battery Park in Lower Manhattan lasts only 15 minutes, a trip to both the Statue of Liberty and Ellis Island is an all-day affair, and those setting out on the ferry at 2pm or later will only be allowed to visit one of the two sites. Security screening at the ferry terminal can take up to 90 minutes. Regardless of the ticket you're buying (Crown Access, Pedestal or Grounds Only), reservations to visit the Statue of Liberty are strongly recommended. Aside from guaranteeing you a specific time to visit, reserve tickets allow you to skip the often insanely long queues awaiting those *without* pre-purchased tickets.

The book of law in her left hand is inscribed with July IV MDC-CLXXVI (July 4 1776), the date of American Independence. The rays on her crown represent the seven seas and continents; the 25 windows adorning it symbolize gemstones. At her feet, chains and a broken shackle accentuate her status as free from oppression and servitude. The torch is a 1986 replacement of the original, which is now housed at the on-site museum.

TOP SIGHT
ELLIS ISLAND

Ellis Island is America's most famous and historically important gateway – the very spot where old-world despair met new-world promise. Between 1892 and 1924, over 12 million immigrants passed through this processing station, their dreams in tow. An estimated 40% of Americans today have at least one ancestor who was processed here, confirming the major role this tiny harbor island has played in the making of modern America.

Restoration

After a $160 million restoration, the island's Main Building was reopened to the public as the Ellis Island Immigration Museum in 1990. Now anybody who rides the ferry to the island can experience a cleaned-up, modern version of the historic new-arrival experience, the museum's interactive exhibits paying homage to the hope, jubilation and sometimes bitter disappointment of the millions who came here in search of a new beginning. Among them were Hungarian Erik Weisz (Harry Houdini), Rodolfo Guglielmi (Rudolph Valentino) and Brit Archibald Alexander Leach (Cary Grant).

Immigration Museum Exhibits

The museum's exhibits are spread over three levels. To get the most out of your visit, opt for the 50-minute self-guided audio tour (free with ferry ticket, available from the museum lobby). Featuring narratives from a number of sources, including historians, architects and the immigrants themselves, the tour brings to life the museum's hefty collection of personal objects, official documents, photographs and film footage. It's an evocative experience to relive personal memories – both good and bad – in the very halls and corridors in which they occurred.

The collection itself is divided into a number of permanent and temporary exhibitions. If you're very short on time, skip the 'Journeys: The Peopling of America 1550–1890' exhibit on the 1st floor and focus on 2nd floor. It's here that you'll find the two most fascinating exhibitions. The first, 'Through America's Gate,' examines the step-by-step process faced by the newly arrived, including the chalk-marking of those suspected of illness, a wince-inducing eye examination, and 29 questions in the beautiful, vaulted Registry Room. The second, 'Peak Immigration Years,' explores the motives behind the immigrants' journeys and the challenges they faced once free to begin their new American lives. Particularly interesting is the collection of old photographs, which offers intimate glimpses into the daily lives of these courageous new Americans.

For a history of the rise, fall and resurrection of the building itself, make time for the 'Restoring a Landmark' exhibition on the 3rd floor; its tableaux of trashed desks, chairs and other abandoned possessions are strangely haunting. Best of all, the audio tour offers optional, in-depth coverage for those wanting to delve deeper into the collections and the island's history. If you don't feel like opting for the audio tour, you can always pick up one of the phones in each display area and listen to the recorded, yet affecting memories of real Ellis Island immigrants, taped in the 1980s. Another option is the free, 45-minute guided tour with a park ranger. If booked three weeks in advance by phone, the tour is also available in American sign language.

DON'T MISS
➡ Immigration Museum exhibits
➡ Main Building architecture
➡ American Immigrant Wall of Honor & Fort Gibson ruins

PRACTICALITIES
➡ Map p410
➡ ☎212-363-3200, tickets 877-523-9849
➡ www.nps.gov/elis
➡ Ellis Island
➡ ferry incl Statue of Liberty adult/child $18/9
➡ ⏱8:30am-5:30pm, check website for seasonal changes
➡ 🚢to Ellis Island, Ⓢ1 to South Ferry; 4/5 to Bowling Green

Main Building Architecture

With their Main Building, architects Edward Lippincott Tilton and William A Boring created a suitably impressive and imposing 'prologue' to America. The designing duo won the contract after the original wooden building burnt down in 1897. Having attended the Ecole des Beaux Arts in Paris, it's not surprising that they opted for a beaux-arts aesthetic for the project. The building evokes a grand train station, with majestic triple-arched entrances, decorative Flemish bond brickwork, and granite quoins (cornerstones) and belvederes. Inside, it's the 2nd-floor, 338ft-long Registry Room (also known as the Great Hall) that takes the breath away. It was under its beautiful vaulted ceiling that the newly arrived lined up to have their documents checked, and that the polygamists, paupers, criminals and anarchists were turned back. The original plaster ceiling was severely damaged by an explosion of munition barges at nearby Black Tom Wharf. It was a blessing in disguise, the rebuilt version was adorned with striking, herringbone-patterned tiles by Rafael Guastavino. The Catalan-born engineer is also behind the beautiful tiled ceiling at the Grand Central Oyster Bar & Restaurant at Grand Central Terminal.

American Immigrant Wall of Honor & Fort Gibson Ruins

Accessible from the 1st-floor 'Journeys: The Peopling of America 1550–1890' exhibit is the outdoor American Immigrant Wall of Honor, inscribed with the names of over 700,000 immigrants. Believed to be the world's longest wall of names, it's a fund-raising project, allowing any American to have an immigrant relative's name recorded for the cost of a donation. Construction of the wall in the 1990s uncovered the remains of the island's original structure, Fort Gibson – you can see the ruins at the southwestern corner of the memorial. Built in 1808, the fortification was part of a harbor-defense system against the British that also included Castle Clinton in Battery Park and Castle Williams on Governors Island. During this time, Ellis Island measured a modest 3.3 acres of sand and slush. Between 1892 and 1934, the island expanded dramatically thanks to landfill brought in from the ballast of ships and construction of the city's subway system.

AN IRISH DEBUT

Ellis Island's very first immigrant arrival was 15-year-old Anna 'Annie' Moore. After a 12-day journey from County Cork, Ireland, on the steamship *Nevada*, the steerage passenger stepped onto the island on January 1 1892, accompanied by her brothers Phillip and Anthony. The three siblings had headed to America to join their parents, who had migrated to New York City four years earlier. After tying the knot with German immigrant Joseph Augustus Schayer, the Irish-American gave birth to at least 11 children, only five of whom survived. Annie died on December 6 1924 and was laid to rest at Calvary Cemetery, Queens.

HOSPITAL OF ALL NATIONS

At the turn of the 20th century, the since-defunct hospital on Ellis Island was one of the world's largest. Consisting of 22 buildings and dubbed the 'Hospital of all Nations,' it was America's front line in the fight against 'imported' diseases. The institution's fascinating history is vividly relayed in writer/producer Lorie Conway's documentary and accompanying book *Forgotten Ellis Island*.

The National September 11 Museum and Memorial is a dignified tribute to the victims of the worst terrorist attack on American soil. Titled *Reflecting Absence,* the memorial's two massive reflecting pools are symbols of hope and renewal as well as tributes to the thousands who lost their lives. Beside them stands the Memorial Museum, a striking, solemn space documenting that fateful fall day in 2001.

Reflecting Pools

Surrounded by a plaza planted with 400 swamp white oak trees, the September 11 Memorial's reflecting pools occupy the very footprints of the ill-fated twin towers. From their rim, a steady cascade of water pours 30ft down towards a central void. The flow of the water is richly symbolic, beginning as hundreds of smaller streams, merging into a massive torrent of collective confusion, and ending with a slow journey towards an abyss. Bronze panels frame the pools, inscribed with the names of those who died in the terrorist attacks of September 11, 2001, and in the World Trade Center car bombing on February 26, 1993. Designed by Michael Arad and Peter Walker, the pools are both striking and deeply poignant.

Memorial Museum

The contemplative energy of the monument is further enhanced by the National September 11 Memorial Museum. Standing between the reflective pools, the museum's glass entrance pavilion eerily evokes a toppled tower. Inside the entrance, an escalator leads down to the museum's main subterranean lobby. On the descent, visitors stand in the shadow of two steel tridents, originally embedded in the bedrock at the base of the North

DON'T MISS

➡ Reflecting Pools
➡ Memorial Museum
➡ Santiago Calatrava's oculus

PRACTICALITIES

➡ Map p410
➡ www.911memorial.org/museum
➡ 180 Greenwich St
➡ memorial free, museum adult/child $24/15, 5-8pm Tue free
➡ ⏲9am-8pm Sun-Thu, to 9pm Fri & Sat, last entry 2hr before close
➡ Ⓢ E to World Trade Center; R to Cortlandt St; 2/3 to Park Pl

Tower. Each over 80ft tall and 50 tons heavy, they once provided the structural support which allowed the towers to soar over 1360ft into the sky. In the subsequent sea of rubble, they remained standing, becoming immediate symbols of resilience.

The tridents are two of over 10,300 objects in the museum's collection. Among these are the Vesey Street Stairs. Dubbed the 'survivors staircase', they allowed hundreds of workers to flee the WTC site on the morning of September 11. At the bottom of these stairs is the moving In Memoriam gallery, its walls lined with the photographs and names of those who perished. Interactive touch screens and a central reflection room shed light on the victims' lives. Their humanity is further fleshed out by the numerous personal effects on display. Among these is a dust-covered wallet belonging to Robert Joseph Gschaar, an insurance underwriter working on level 92 of the South Tower. The wallet's contents include a photograph of Gschaar's wife, Myrta, and a $2 bill, given to Myrta by Gschaar as a symbol of their second chance at happiness.

Around the corner from the In Memoriam gallery is the New York City Fire Department's Engine Company 21. One of the largest artifacts on display, its burnt out cab is testament to the inferno faced by those at the scene. The fire engine stands at the entrance to the museum's main Historical Exhibition. Divided into three sections – Events of the Day, Before 9/11 and After 9/11 – its collection of videos, real-time audio recordings, images, objects and testimonies provides a rich, meditative exploration of the tragedy, the events that preceded it (including the WTC bombing of 1993), and the stories of grief, resilience and hope that followed.

The Historical Exhibition spills into the monumental Foundation Hall, flanked by a massive section of the original slurry wall, built to hold back the waters of the Hudson River during the towers' construction. It's also home to the last steel column removed during the clean-up, adorned with the messages and mementos of recovery workers, responders and loved ones of the victims.

CALATRAVA ARCHITECTURE

It was the image of a child releasing a dove that inspired Santiago Calatrava's dramatic oculus above the new WTC Transportation Hub. While budget-driven tweaks of the Spanish architect's design have led some to call it an 'immobilized stegosaurus', there's no doubt that the soaring creation is arresting. The structure will stream natural light into the WTC's $3.9 billion transit center, expected to serve 200,000 subway and PATH train commuters daily once completed in early 2016. A whopping 2.5 times bigger than Grand Central Terminal, the project features around 200,000 sq ft of retail and dining space for those who want to linger in Manhattan's latest architectural controversy.

One of the Memorial Museum's most curious (and famous) artifacts is the so-called 'Angel of 9/11', the eerie outline of a woman's anguished face on a twisted girder believed to originate from the point where American Airlines Flight 11 slammed into the North Tower. Experts have a more prosaic explanation: natural corrosion and sheer coincidence.

TOP SIGHT
ONE WORLD TRADE CENTER

Filling what was a sore and glaring gap in the Lower Manhattan skyline, One World Trade Center symbolizes rebirth, determination and a city's resilience. More than just another supertall, this tower is a richly symbolic giant, well aware of the past yet firmly focused on the future. For lovers of New York, it's also the hot new stop for dizzying, unforgettable urban views.

DON'T MISS

➡ A photo from the base looking up
➡ Sky Pod elevators
➡ Observatory views

PRACTICALITIES

➡ Map p410
➡ ☎ 844-696-1776
➡ www.oneworld-observatory.com
➡ cnr West & Vesey Sts
➡ adult/child $32/26
➡ ⊙9am-8pm, last ticket sold at 7:15pm
➡ Ⓢ E to World Trade Center; 2/3 to Park Pl; A/C, J/Z, 4/5 to Fulton St; R to Cortlandt St

The Building

Leaping up from the northwest corner of the World Trade Center site, the 104-floor tower is architect David M Childs' redesign of Daniel Libeskind's original 2002 concept. Not only the loftiest building in America, this tapered giant is currently the tallest building in the Western Hemisphere, not to mention the fourth tallest in the world by pinnacle height. The tower soars skywards with chamfered edges. The result is a series of isosceles triangles that, seen from the building's base, reach to infinity. Crowning the structure is a 408ft cabled-stayed spire. Co-designed by sculptor Kenneth Snelson, it brings the building's total height to 1776ft, a symbolic reference to the year of American independence. Indeed, symbolism feeds several aspects of the building: the tower's footprint is equal to those of the twin towers, while the observation decks match the heights of those in the old complex. Unlike the original towers, however, One WTC was built with a whole new level of safety in mind, its precautionary features including a 200ft-high blast-resistant base (clad in over 2000 pieces of glimmering prismatic glass) and 1m-thick concrete walls encasing all elevators, stairwells, and communication and safety systems. One thing that wasn't foreseen by the architects and engineers was the antenna's noisy disposition; the strong winds that race through its lattice design producing a haunting, howling sound known to keep some locals up at night.

One World Observatory

Not one to downplay its assets, the skyscraper is home to One World Observatory, the city's loftiest observation deck. While the observatory spans levels 100 to 102, the experience begins at the ground-floor Global Welcome Center, where an electronic world map highlights the homeland of visitors (data relayed from ticket scans). The bitter bickering that plagued much of the project's development is all but forgotten in the adjoining Voices exhibition, where architects and construction workers wax lyrically about the tower's formation on 144 video screens. After a quick rundown of the site's geology, the real thrills begin as you step inside one of five Sky Pod elevators, among the fastest in the world. As the elevators begin their 1250ft skyward journey, LED wall panels kick into action. Suddenly you're in a veritable time machine, watching Manhattan's evolution from forested island to teeming concrete jungle. Forty-seven seconds (and 500 years) later, you're on level 102, where another short presentation ends with a spectacular reveal. Skip the over-priced eateries on level 101 and continue down to the real highlight: level 100. Waiting for you is an epic, 360-degree panorama guaranteed to keep your index finger busy pointing out landmarks, from the Brooklyn and Manhattan Bridges, to Lady Liberty and the Woolworth, Empire State and Chrysler buildings. If you need a hand, interactive mobile tablets are available for hire ($15). As expected, the view is extraordinary (choose a clear day!), taking in all five boroughs and adjoining states. For a close-up view of the Midtown skyscrapers, however, you're better off scaling the Empire State Building or the Rockefeller Center's Top of the Rock.

FAMOUS RESIDENTS

VIP buildings demand VIP clients, and One World Trade Center delivers. It's most famous tenant is Condé Nast Publications, which made the move from 4 Times Square in 2014. The company's portfolio includes *Vogue* magazine, headed by the woman with the world's most famous bob, Anna Wintour. As to be expected, the company's headquarters are nothing short of fabulous, complete with dramatic spiral staircase and a glam-glam cafeteria with gourmet bites and a million-dollar view. How else can one expect to work, *darling*?

TICKETS & TIPS

Pre-purchase your tickets online (oneworld observatory.com/tickets) to avoid the longest queues. Tickets purchased online using a smartphone don't require a printout; simply take a screenshot of your ticket (including the bar code) and scan it on arrival. When purchasing your ticket, you will need to select a specific visiting time; head in by 9:15am for short waiting periods and thin crowds. Sunset is the busiest time. Whatever the hour, always arrive 15 minutes before your scheduled visiting time to avoid delays at security.

SIGHTS

Wall Street & the Financial District

★NATIONAL SEPTEMBER 11 MEMORIAL & MUSEUM MONUMENT, MUSEUM

See p68.

★ONE WORLD OBSERVATORY VIEWPOINT

See p70.

★ONE WORLD TRADE CENTER BUILDING

See p70.

FRAUNCES TAVERN MUSEUM MUSEUM

Map p410 (☎212-425-1778; www.frauncestavernmuseum.org; 54 Pearl St, btwn Broad St & Coenties Slip; adult/6-18yr/under 6yr $7/4/free; 🕐noon-5pm Mon-Fri, 11:30am-5pm Sat & Sun; [S]J/Z to Broad St; 4/5 to Bowling Green; R to Whitehall St-South Ferry; 1 to South Ferry) Combining five early-18th-century structures, this unique museum/restaurant/bar pays homage to the nation-shaping events of 1783, when the British relinquished control of New York at the end of the Revolutionary War, and General George Washington gave a farewell speech to the officers of the Continental Army in the 2nd-floor dining room on December 4.

The site was originally built as a tony residence for merchant Stephen Delancey's family; barkeeper Samuel Fraunces purchased it in 1762, turning it into a tavern in honor of the American victory in the Revolutionary War. After the war, when New York was the nation's first capital, the space was used by the Departments of War, Treasury and Foreign Affairs. The tavern was closed and fell into disuse in the 19th century – and soon after was damaged during several massive fires that destroyed most colonial buildings and Dutch-built structures in the area. In 1904, the Sons of the Revolution, a historical society, bought the building and returned it to an approximation of its colonial-era look – an act believed to be the first major attempt at historical preservation in the USA. Today, the museum hosts lectures, Revolutionary War paintings, occasional historical walking tours, and some surprising Washington relics, including a lock of hair and a fragment from his original coffin.

NATIONAL MUSEUM OF THE AMERICAN INDIAN MUSEUM

Map p410 (☎212-514-3700; www.nmai.si.edu; 1 Bowling Green; 🕐10am-5pm Fri-Wed, to 8pm Thu; 📶; [S]4/5 to Bowling Green; R to Whitehall St) [FREE] An affiliate of the Smithsonian Institution, this elegant tribute to Native American culture is set in Cass Gilbert's spectacular 1907 Custom House, one of NYC's finest beaux-arts buildings. Beyond a vast elliptical rotunda, sleek galleries play host to changing exhibitions documenting Native American art, culture, life and beliefs. The museum's permanent collection includes stunning decorative arts, textiles and ceremonial objects that document the diverse native cultures across the Americas.

The four giant female sculptures outside the building are the work of Daniel Chester French, who would go on to sculpt the seated Abraham Lincoln at Washington, DC's Lincoln Memorial. Representing (from left to right) Asia, North America, Europe and Africa, the figures offer a revealing look at America's world view at the beginning of the 20th century; Asia 'bound' by its religions, America 'youthful and virile,' Europe 'wise yet decaying' and Africa 'asleep and barbaric.' The museum also hosts a range of cultural programs, including dance and music performances, readings for children, craft demonstrations, films and workshops. The museum shop is well-stocked with Native American jewelry, books, CDs and crafts.

TRINITY CHURCH CHURCH

Map p410 (www.trinitywallstreet.org; Broadway, at Wall St; 🕐church 7am-6pm Mon-Fri, 8am-4pm Sat, 7am-4pm Sun, churchyard 7am-4pm Mon-Fri, 8am-3pm Sat, 7am-3pm Sun; [S]R to Rector St; 2/3, 4/5 to Wall St) New York City's tallest building upon completion in 1846, Trinity Church features a 280ft-high bell tower and a richly colored stained-glass window over the altar. Famous residents of its serene cemetery include Founding Father Alexander Hamilton, while its excellent music series includes Concerts at One (1pm Thursdays) and magnificent choir concerts, including an annual December rendition of Handel's *Messiah*.

The original Anglican parish church was founded by King William III in 1697 and once presided over several constituent chapels, including St Paul's Chapel at the corner of Fulton St and Broadway. Its huge landholdings in Lower Manhattan made it the country's wealthiest and most influential church throughout the 18th century. Burnt down in 1776, its second incarnation was demolished in 1839. The third and current church, designed by English architect Richard Upjohn, helped launch the picturesque neo-Gothic movement in America.

ST PAUL'S CHAPEL CHURCH

Map p410 (☎212-602-0800; www.trinitywallstreet.org; Broadway, at Fulton St; ⏰10am-6pm Mon-Sat, 7am-6pm Sun; [S]A/C, J/Z, 2/3, 4/5 to Fulton St; R to Cortlandt St; E to World Trade Center) After his inauguration in 1789, George Washington worshipped at this classic revival brownstone chapel, which found new fame in the aftermath of September 11. With the World Trade Center destruction occurring just a block away, the mighty structure became a spiritual support and volunteer center, movingly documented in its exhibition 'Unwavering Spirit: Hope & Healing at Ground Zero.'

Through photographs, personal objects and messages of support, the exhibition honors both the victims and the volunteers who worked round the clock, serving meals, setting up beds, doling out massages and counseling rescue workers.

FEDERAL HALL MUSEUM

Map p410 (www.nps.gov/feha; 26 Wall St, entrance on Pine St; ⏰9am-5pm Mon-Fri; 📶; [S]J/Z to Broad St; 2/3, 4/5 to Wall St) A Greek Revival masterpiece, Federal Hall houses a museum dedicated to postcolonial New York. Themes include George Washington's inauguration, Alexander Hamilton's relationship with the city, and the struggles of John Peter Zenger – jailed, tried and acquitted of libel on this site for exposing government corruption in his newspaper. There's also a visitor information hall with city maps and brochures.

Distinguished by a huge statue of George Washington, the building itself stands on the site of New York's original City Hall, completed in 1703. Remodeled by French engineer Pierre L'Enfant in 1788 and renamed Federal Hall, the building would see Washington taking the oath of office as the first US president on April 30, 1789. (The museum's artifacts include the very slab of stone on which Washington stood while taking that oath.) After that structure's demolition in 1812, the current building rose in its place between 1834 and 1842, serving as the US Customs House until 1862.

NEW YORK STOCK EXCHANGE NOTABLE BUILDING

Map p410 (www.nyse.com; 11 Wall St; ⏰closed to the public; [S]J/Z to Broad St; 2/3, 4/5 to Wall St) Home to the world's best-known stock exchange (the NYSE), Wall Street is an iconic symbol of US capitalism. Behind the portentous Romanesque facade about one billion shares change hands daily, a sight no longer accessible to the public due to security concerns. Feel free to gawk outside the building, protected by barricades and the hawk-eyed NYPD (New York Police Department).

BOWLING GREEN PARK

Map p410 (cnr Broadway & State St; 📶; [S]4/5 to Bowling Green; R to Whitehall St) New York's oldest – and possibly tiniest – public park is purportedly the spot where Dutch settler Peter Minuit paid Native Americans the equivalent of $24 to purchase Manhattan

BLAST FROM THE PAST

If you wander past the former headquarters of JP Morgan Bank on the southeast corner of Wall and Broad Sts, take a minute to examine its limestone facade on the Wall St side. The pockmarks you see are the remnants of the so-called Morgan Bank bombing – America's deadliest terrorist attack until the Oklahoma City bombing of 1995.

The fateful day was Thursday, September 16, 1920, when at exactly 12.01pm, 500 pounds of lead sash weights and 100 pounds of dynamite exploded from a horse-drawn carriage. Thirty-eight people were killed and around 400 injured. Among the latter was John F Kennedy's father, Joseph P Kennedy.

The bomb's detonation outside America's most influential financial institution at the time led many to blame anticapitalist groups, from Italian anarchists to stock-standard Bolsheviks. Yet the crime has yet to be solved, with the decision to reopen both the bank and New York Stock Exchange the following day leading to a swift clean-up of both debris and vital clues. Almost 100 years on, the shrapnel marks remain, purposely left by banker Jack Morgan as an act of remembrance and defiance.

Island. At its northern edge stands Arturo Di Modica's 7000lb bronze Charging Bull, placed here permanently after it mysteriously appeared in front of the New York Stock Exchange in 1989, two years after a market crash.

The tree-fringed triangle was leased by the people of New York from the English crown beginning in 1733, for the token amount of one peppercorn each. But an angry mob, inspired by George Washington's nearby reading of the Declaration of Independence, descended upon the site in 1776 and tore down a large statue of King George III; a fountain now stands in its place.

MUSEUM OF AMERICAN FINANCE MUSEUM

Map p410 (☎212-908-4110; www.moaf.org; 48 Wall St, btwn Pearl & William Sts; adult/child $8/free; ⏲10am-4pm Tue-Sat; [S]2/3, 4/5 to Wall St) Money makes this interactive museum go round. It focuses on historic moments in American financial history, and its permanent collections include rare historic currency (including Confederate currency used by America's southern states during the Civil War), stock and bond certificates from the Gilded Age, the oldest known photograph of Wall St and a stock ticker from circa 1875.

Once the headquarters for the Bank of New York, the building itself is a lavish spectacle, with 30ft ceilings, high-arched Palladian windows, a majestic staircase to the mezzanine, glass chandeliers, and murals depicting historic scenes of banking and commerce.

FEDERAL RESERVE BANK OF NEW YORK NOTABLE BUILDING

Map p410 (☎212-720-6130; www.newyorkfed.org; 33 Liberty St, at Nassau St, entrance at 44 Maiden Lane; reservation required; ⏲guided tours 1pm & 2pm Mon-Fri; [S]A/C, J/Z, 2/3, 4/5 to Fulton St) [FREE] The best reason to visit the Federal Reserve Bank is the chance to (briefly) ogle at its high-security vault – more than 10,000 tons of gold reserves reside here, 80ft below ground. You'll only see a small part of that fortune, but signing on to a free tour (the only way down; book several months ahead) is worth the effort.

While you don't need to join a guided tour to browse the bank's interactive museum, which delves into the bank's history and research, you will still need to book a time online. Bring your passport or other official ID.

◉ New York Harbor

★STATUE OF LIBERTY MONUMENT

See p64.

★ELLIS ISLAND LANDMARK, MUSEUM

See p66.

◉ Battery Park City

★MUSEUM OF JEWISH HERITAGE MUSEUM

Map p410 (☎646-437-4202; www.mjhnyc.org; 36 Battery Pl; adult/child $12/free, 4-8pm Wed free; ⏲10am-5:45pm Sun-Tue & Thu, to 8pm Wed, to 5pm Fri mid-Mar–mid-Nov, to 3pm Fri rest of yr; 📶👪; [S]4/5 to Bowling Green; R to Whitehall St) An evocative waterfront museum, exploring all aspects of modern Jewish identity and culture, from religious traditions to artistic accomplishments. The museum's core exhibition includes a detailed exploration of the Holocaust, with personal artifacts, photographs and documentary films providing a personal, moving experience. Outdoors is the Garden of Stones installation. Created by artist Andy Goldsworthy and dedicated to those who lost loved ones in the Holocaust, its 18 boulders form a narrow pathway for contemplating the fragility of life.

The building itself consists of six sides and three tiers to symbolize the Star of David and the six million Jews who perished in WWII. Exhibitions aside, the venue also hosts films, music concerts, ongoing lecture series and special holiday performances. Frequent, free workshops for families with children are also on offer, while the on-site kosher café serves light food.

BATTERY PARK PARK

Map p410 (www.nycgovparks.org; Broadway, at Battery Pl; ⏲sunrise-1am; [S]4/5 to Bowling Green; R to Whitehall St; 1 to South Ferry) Skirting the southern edge of Manhattan, this revamped, 12-acre oasis lures with public artworks, meandering walkways and perennial gardens. Its memorials include a Holocaust Memorial and the Irish Hunger Memorial. It was on this very part of the island that the Dutch settled in 1623. And it was right here that the first 'battery' of cannons was erected to defend the fledgling settlement of New Amsterdam. These days, the park is also where you'll find historic **Castle Clinton** (Map p410; www.nps.gov/cacl; Battery Park;

WORTH A DETOUR

GOVERNORS ISLAND

Off-limits to the public for 200 years, former military outpost **Governors Island** (☏212-825-3045; govisland.com; ☺10am-6pm Mon-Fri, 10am-7pm Sat & Sun; 🚇4, 5 to Bowling Green; 1 to South Ferry) FREE is now one of New York's most popular seasonal playgrounds. Each summer, free ferries make the seven-minute trip from Lower Manhattan to the 172-acre oasis. In 2014, 30 new acres of island parkland opened to the public, with features including the 6-acre, art-studded Liggett Terrace; the 10-acre Hammock Grove (complete with 50 hammocks); and the 14-acre Play Lawn, with a duo of natural-turf ball fields for adult softball and Little League baseball. Things get even better in 2017, with the completion of the Hills, an ambitious quartet of man-made hills offering spectacular city and harbor views.

Art is the focus at Figment (www.figmentproject.org), a one-weekend-only interactive art festival in June, while inspiring views are also on tap along the Great Promenade. Running for 2.2 miles along the island's perimeter, the path takes in everything from Lower Manhattan and Brooklyn, to Staten Island and New Jersey. Bike rental is available on the island.

Besides serving as a successful military fort in the Revolutionary War, the Union Army's central recruiting station during the Civil War, and the take-off point for Wilbur Wright's famous 1909 flight around the Statue of Liberty, Governors Island is where the 1988 Reagan-Gorbachev summit signaled the beginning of the end of the Cold War. You can visit the spot where that famous summit took place at the **Admiral's House**, a grand-colonnaded, 1843 military residence that's part of the elegant ghost-town area of Nolan Park. Other historic spots include **Fort Jay**, fortified in 1776 for what became a failed attempt to prevent the Brits from invading Manhattan; **Colonel's Row**, a collection of lovely, 19th-century brick officers' quarters; and the creepy **Castle Williams**, a 19th-century fort that was eventually used as a military penitentiary. The best way to explore it all is with the **National Park Service** (www.nps.gov/gois), whose rangers conduct guided tours of the historic district. See the website for specific days and times.

☺8am-5pm; 📷; 🚇4/5 to Bowling Green; R to Whitehall St; 1 to South Ferry) and the ferry service to Ellis Island and the Statue of Liberty.

SKYSCRAPER MUSEUM   MUSEUM
Map p410 (☏212-968-1961; www.skyscraper.org; 39 Battery Pl; admission $5; ☺noon-6pm Wed-Sun; 🚇4/5 to Bowling Green; R to Whitehall) Fans of phallic architecture will appreciate this compact, high-gloss gallery, examining skyscrapers as objects of design, engineering and urban renewal. Temporary exhibitions dominate the space, with past exhibitions exploring everything from New York's new generation of super-slim residential towers, to the world's new breed of supertalls. Permanent fixtures include information on the design and construction of the Empire State Building and World Trade Center.

The museum also hosts free, architecture-themed book talks and lectures; see the website for upcoming events.

IRISH HUNGER MEMORIAL   MEMORIAL
Map p410 (290 Vesey St, at North End Ave; 🚇2/3 to Park Place; E to World Trade Center; A/C to Chambers St) FREE Artist Brian Tolle's compact labyrinth of low limestone walls and patches of grass pays tribute to the Great Irish Famine and Migration (1845–52), which prompted hundreds of thousands of immigrants to leave Ireland for better opportunities in the New World. Representing abandoned cottages, stone walls and potato fields, the work was created with stones from each of Ireland's 32 counties.

◉ East River Waterfront

SOUTH STREET SEAPORT   NEIGHBORHOOD
Map p410 (www.southstreetseaport.com; 🚇A/C, J/Z, 2/3, 4/5 to Fulton St) This enclave of cobbled streets, maritime warehouses and shops combines the best and worst in historic preservation. It's not on the radar for most New Yorkers, but tourists are drawn to the nautical air, the frequent street performers and the mobbed restaurants.

The district incorporates the **South Street Seaport Museum** (www.southstreetseaportmuseum.org; 12 Fulton St; printing press & shop free), home to a vintage printing press and Bowne Stationers & Co (p81). The museum's booty extends to the iron-hulled Pioneer (p82) at Pier 16, a 19th-century vessel running spirit-lifting sailing journeys through the warmer months. Happy times also await at neighboring **Pier 15** (Map p410; South St, btwn Fletcher & John Sts; ⏲6am-dusk; [S]A/C, J/Z, 2/3, 4/5 to Fulton St), a breezy, soothing two-level pier with green spaces, deckchairs and spectacular city and water views. Also on the water is Pier 17, a revamped combo of boutiques, restaurants and a public rooftop terrace scheduled to open in 2017.

City Hall & Civic Center

WOOLWORTH BUILDING — NOTABLE BUILDING

Map p410 (☎203-966-9663; woolworthtours.com; 233 Broadway, at Park Pl; 30/60/90min tours $20/30/45; [S]R to City Hall; 2/3 to Park Pl; 4/5/6 to Brooklyn Bridge-City Hall) The world's tallest building upon completion in 1913, Cass Gilbert's 60-story, 792ft-tall Woolworth Building is a neo-Gothic marvel, elegantly clad in masonry and terracotta. Surpassed in height by the Chrysler Building in 1930, its landmarked lobby is a breathtaking spectacle of dazzling, Byzantine-like mosaics. The lobby is only accessible on prebooked guided tours, which also offer insight into the building's more curious original features, among them a dedicated subway entrance and a secret swimming pool.

At its dedication, the building was described as a 'cathedral of commerce'; though meant as an insult, FW Woolworth, head of the five-and-dime chain-store empire headquartered there, took the comment as a compliment and began throwing the term around himself.

AFRICAN BURIAL GROUND — MEMORIAL

Map p410 (☎212-637-2019; www.nps.gov/afbg; 290 Broadway, btwn Duane & Elk Sts; ⏲memorial 9am-5pm Mon-Sat, visitor center 10am-4pm Tue-Sat; [S]1/2/3, A/C, J/Z to Chambers St; R to City Hall; 4/5/6 to Brooklyn Bridge-City Hall) [FREE] In 1991, construction workers here uncovered over 400 stacked wooden caskets, just 16ft to 28ft below street level. The boxes contained the remains of enslaved Africans (nearby Trinity Church graveyard had banned the burial of Africans at the time). Today, a memorial and visitors center honors an estimated 15,000 Africans buried here during the 17th and 18th centuries.

The visitors center requires airportlike security screenings, so leave your nail files in the hotel.

🍴 EATING

The Financial District's food scene is enjoying new verve thanks to new arrivals Brookfield Place and Smorgasburg, perfect bedfellows to more established winners like North End Grill and Shake Shack. Further north, Tribeca is no stranger to cool, with a string of celeb-chef hot spots and one of New York's best (and most curiously located) bakeries.

SEAPORT SMORGASBURG — MARKET $

Map p410 (www.smorgasburg.com; Fulton St, btwn Front & South Sts; dishes $6-19; ⏲11am-8pm May-Sep; [S]A/C, J/Z, 2/3, 4/5 to Fulton St) Brooklyn's hipster food market has jumped the East River, injecting touristy South Street Seaport with some much-needed local cred. Cooking up a storm from May to late September, its offerings include anything from lobster rolls, ramen and pizza, to slow-smoked Texan-style brisket sandwiches. Add a splash of historic architecture and you have one of downtown's coolest cheap feeds.

ARCADE BAKERY — BAKERY $

Map p410 (☎212-227-7895; www.arcadebakery.com; 20 Church St, btwn Worth & Thomas Sts; pastries from $3, sandwiches $9, pizzas $9-13; ⏲8am-4pm Mon-Fri; [S]1 to Franklin St) It's easy to miss this little treasure, occupying the vaulted lobby of a 1920s office building. Where an ATM once stood, a counter now trades in beautiful, just-baked goods. Edibles include artful sandwiches and (between noon and 4pm) a small selection of puff-crust pizzas with combos like mushroom, caramelized onion and goat's cheese. Top of the lot is one of the city's finest almond croissants.

DA MIKELE — PIZZA $$

Map p410 (☎212-925-8800; luzzosgroup.com; 275 Church St, btwn White & Franklin Sts; pizzas

$17-21; noon-10:30pm Sun-Wed, to 11:30pm Thu-Sat; ⚑; **S**1 to Franklin St; A/C/E, N/Q/R, J/Z, 6 to Canal St) An Italo-Tribeca hybrid where pressed tin and recycled wood meet retro Vespa, Da Mikele channels the *dolce vita* (sweet life) with its weeknight *aperitivo* (5pm to 7pm), where your drink includes a complimentary spread of lip-smacking bar bites. The real reason to head here, however, is for the pizzas. We're talking light, beautifully charred revelations, simultaneously crisp and chewy, and good enough to make a Neapolitan weep.

BROOKFIELD PLACE   FAST FOOD, MARKET $$

Map p410 (📞212-417-7000; brookfieldplaceny. com; 200 Vesey St; ⚑; **S**E to World Trade Center; 2/3 to Park Place; R to Cortland St; A/C, 4/5, J/Z to Fulton St) World Financial Center is now Brookfield Place, a polished, high-end office and retail complex that's home to two fabulous food halls. For Gallic flavors, hit **Le District** (Map p410; 📞212-981-8588; ledistrict.com; Brookfield Place, 200 Vesey St; sandwiches $6-15; market mains $16-24, Beauborg dinner mains $18-45; 6:30am-11pm Mon-Fri, 8:30am-11pm Sat, 8:30am-10pm Sun; ⚑; **S**E to World Trade Center; 2/3 to Park Place; R to Cortland St; A/C, 4/5, J/Z to Fulton St), a sprawling wonderland of high-gloss pastries, stinky cheese, pretty tartines and lusty steak frites. One floor above is **Hudson Eats** (Map p410; 📞212-417-2445; brookfieldplaceny.com/directory/food; Brookfield Place, 200 Vesey St; dishes from $7; 10am-9pm Mon-Sat, noon-7pm Sun; ⚑; **S**E to World Trade Center; 2/3 to Park Place; R to Cortland St; A/C, 4/5, J/Z to Fulton St), a fashionable enclave of quality fast bites, from sushi and tacos to salads and burgers.

★ LOCANDA VERDE   ITALIAN $$$

Map p410 (📞212-925-3797; www.locandaverdenyc. com; 377 Greenwich St, at Moore St; mains lunch $19-29, dinner $29-36; 7am-11pm Mon-Thu, to 11:30pm Fri, 8am-11:30pm Sat, 8am-11pm Sun; **S**A/C/E to Canal St; 1 to Franklin St) Step through the velvet curtains into a scene of loosened button-downs, black dresses and slick barmen behind a long, crowded bar. This celebrated brasserie showcases modern, Italian-inspired fare like house-made pappardelle with lamb bolognese, mint and sheep's milk ricotta and Sicilian-style halibut with heirloom squash and almonds. Weekend brunch features no less creative fare: try scampi and grits or lemon ricotta pancakes with blueberries. Bookings recommended.

BÂTARD   MODERN AMERICAN $$$

Map p410 (📞212-219-2777; www.batardtribeca. com; 239 W Broadway, btwn Walker & White Sts; 2-/3-/4-courses $55/69/79; 5:30-10:30pm Mon-Sat; **S**1 to Franklin St; A/C/E to Canal St) Austrian chef Markus Glocker heads this warm, Michelin-starred hot spot, where a pared-back interior puts the focus squarely on the food. It's attention well deserved. Glocker's dishes are beautifully balanced and textured, whether it's sweet Maine lobster paired with salsify and gritty potato crisps, or tender venison wrapped in a skin of Swiss chard and golden filo pastry for added comfort. Service is gracious and the Francophile wine list stellar.

NORTH END GRILL   AMERICAN $$$

Map p410 (📞646-747-1600; www.northendgrill-nyc.com; 104 North End Ave, at Murray St; mains lunch $19-37, dinner $27-44; 11:30am-10pm Mon-Thu, to 10:30pm Fri, 11am-10:30pm Sat, 11am-9pm Sun; ⚑; **S**1/2/3, A/C to Chambers St; E to World Trade Center) Handsome, smart and friendly, this celeb haunt of chef Danny Meyer's take on the American grill. Top-tier produce (including herbs and vegetables from the restaurant's own rooftop garden) forms the basis for modern takes on comfort grub, happily devoured by suited silver foxes and a scattering of more casual passersby.

Dishes are given a kiss of smoke, either in the charcoal-fired oven or on the smokier wood-fired grill, with standouts including clam pizza with chili flakes and a feel-good roasted chicken for two. In true Meyer style, waitstaff are hawk-eyed and charming.

DRINKING & NIGHTLIFE

Corporate types don't always bolt for the 'burbs when 5pm hits, many loosening their ties in the smattering of wine bars and pubs around Stone St, Wall St and South Street Seaport. Tribeca keeps its cool with artisanal coffee shops and venerated cocktail dens. Thankfully, the drinks here tend to be stirred with a little more precision than over on the East Side.

★ BLUESTONE LANE   CAFE

Map p410 (📞646-684-3771; bluestonelaneny.com; 30 Broad St, entrance on New St; 7am-5pm Mon-Fri, 9am-3pm Sat & Sun; **S**J/Z to Broad St; 2/3,

Neighborhood Walk
Lower Manhattan Landmarks

START LA COLOMBE
END FEDERAL HALL
LENGTH 2.5 MILES; THREE HOURS

Intimate, circuitous and sometimes confusing side streets, Gothic churches and a fine collection of early-20th-century skyscrapers: Lower Manhattan is an area steeped in history.

Start with coffee at ❶ **La Colombe** (p79). In the 19th century, the site was a stop on the antislavery 'underground railway,' a secret network of routes and safe houses allowing African Americans to reach free states and Canada. A plaque on the Lispenard St side of the building commemorates the fact. Further west, the intersection of Varick and N Moore Sts is where you'll find ❷ **8 Hook & Ladder**, better known as ghost-control headquarters in '80s film *Ghostbusters*. Continue south on Varick St, turn left into Leonard St. On the southeast corner at the intersection with Church St stands the ❸ **Textile Building**, built in 1901. Its architect, Henry J Hardenbergh, subsequently designed Midtown's monumental Plaza Hotel. Further south on Church St, turn left into Park Pl and right into Broadway. Before you is the neo-Gothic ❹ **Woolworth Building** (p76), the world's tallest skycraper upon completion in 1913. Continue south on Broadway, cross Vesey St and you'll see ❺ **St Paul's Chapel** (p73) on your right – it's the only pre–Revolutionary War church left intact in the city. Directly behind it lies the World Trade Center site, now home to the ❻ **National September 11 memorial** (p72) and ❼ **museum** (p68). Soaring above them is the 1776ft One World Trade Center, whose sky-high ❽ **observatory** (p70) offers jaw-dropping views of the city and beyond. Further south on Broadway, ❾ **Trinity Church** (p72) was NYC's tallest building upon completion in 1846. Its cemetery is the final resting place of steamboat inventor Robert Fulton. Head east onto Wall St to the ❿ **New York Stock Exchange** (p73) and ⓫ **Federal Hall** (p73). You can visit the latter, in which John Peter Zenger was acquitted of seditious libel in 1735 – the first step, historians say, in establishing a democracy committed to a free press.

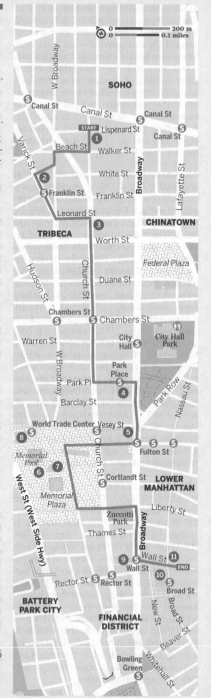

4/5 to Wall St) While the NYSE busies itself with stocks, its tiny Aussie neighbor does a roaring trade in killer coffee. Littered with retro Melbourne memorabilia and squeezed into the corner of an art-deco office block, it's never short of smooth suits and homesick antipodeans craving a cup of decent, velvety Joe. A small selection of edibles include pastries and Australian cafe standard 'avo smash' (mashed avocado on toast).

★DEAD RABBIT — COCKTAIL BAR

Map p410 (☎646-422-7906; www.deadrabbitnyc.com; 30 Water St; 🕒taproom 11am-4am; parlor 5pm-2am Mon-Wed, to 3am Thu-Sat; [S]R to Whitehall St; 1 to South Ferry) Named in honor of a dreaded Irish-American gang, this most-wanted rabbit is regularly voted one of the world's best bars. During the day, hit the sawdust-sprinkled taproom for specialty beers, historic punches and pop-inns (lightly hopped ale spiked with different flavors). Come evening, scurry upstairs to the cozy Parlor for over 70 meticulously researched cocktails. Tip: head in before 5:30pm to avoid a long wait for a Parlor seat.

LA COLOMBE — CAFE

Map p410 (☎212-343-1515; www.lacolombe.com; 319 Church St, at Lispenard St; 🕒7:30am-6:30pm Mon-Fri, from 8:30am Sat & Sun; [S]A/C/E to Canal St) Coffee and a few baked treats is all you'll get at this roaster but, man, are they good. Join cool kids and clued-in Continentals for dark, intense espresso and Third Wave offerings like draft latte, a naturally sweet iced caffè latte. Also on tap is La Colombe's cold-pressed Pure Black Coffee, steeped in oxygen-free stainless steel wine tanks for 16 hours.

WARD III — COCKTAIL BAR

Map p410 (☎212-240-9194; www.ward3tribeca.com; 111 Reade St, btwn Church St & W Broadway; 🕒4pm-4am Mon-Fri, 5pm-4am Sat, to 2am Sun; [S]A/C, 1/2/3 to Chambers St) Dark and bustling, Ward III channels old-school jauntiness with its elegant libations, vintage vibe (including old Singer sewing tables behind the bar), and gentlemanly house rules (No 2: 'Don't be creepy'). Reminisce over a Moroccan martini, or sample the bar's coveted collection of whiskeys. Top-notch bar grub is served till close.

BRANDY LIBRARY — BAR

Map p410 (☎212-226-5545; www.brandylibrary.com; 25 N Moore St, at Varick St; 🕒5pm-1am Sun-Wed, 4pm-2am Thu, 4pm-4am Fri & Sat; [S]1 to Franklin St) When sipping means serious business, settle in at this uber-luxe 'library', its club chairs facing floor-to-ceiling, bottle-lined shelves. Go for top-shelf cognac, malt scotch or vintage brandies, expertly paired with nibbles such as Gougeres (Gruyere-cheese puffs) and a wonderful tartare made to order. Saturday nights are generally quieter than weeknights, making it a civilized spot for a weekend evening tête-à-tête.

TERROIR TRIBECA — WINE BAR

Map p410 (☎212-625-9463; www.wineisterroir.com; 24 Harrison St, at Greenwich St; 🕒4pm-1am Mon-Sat, to 11pm Sun; [S]1 to Franklin St) Award-winning Terroir keeps oenophiles upbeat with its well-versed, well-priced wine list. Drops span the Old World and New, among them natural wines and inspired offerings from smaller producers. Best of all, there's a generous selection of wines by the glass, making a global wine tour a whole lot easier.

PIER A HARBOR HOUSE — BAR

Map p410 (☎212-785-0153; www.piera.com; 22 Battery Pl; 🕒11am-4am; 📶; [S]4/5 to Bowling Green; R to Whitehall St; 1 to South Ferry) Looking dashing after a major restoration, Pier A is now a super-spacious, casual eating and drinking house right on New York Harbor. If the weather's on your side, try for a seat on the waterside deck. Here, picnic benches, sun umbrellas and an eyeful of New York skyline make for a brilliant spot to sip craft beers or one of the house cocktails on tap.

If you're feeling peckish, stick to the burgers, sandwiches or raw bar options.

WEATHER UP — COCKTAIL BAR

Map p410 (☎212-766-3202; www.weatherupnyc.com; 159 Duane St, btwn Hudson St & W Broadway; 🕒5pm-late Mon-Sat; [S]1/2/3 to Chambers St) Softly lit subway tiles, amiable barkeeps and seductive cocktails make for a bewitching trio at Weather Up. Sweet talk the staff over a Whizz Bang (scotch whisky, dry vermouth, house-made grenadine, orange bitters and absinthe). Failing that, comfort yourself with some satisfying snacks.

KEG NO 229 — BEER HALL

Map p410 (☎212-566-2337; www.kegno229.com; 229 Front St, btwn Beekman St & Peck Slip;

Sean Muldoon, co-owner of award-winning bar **Dead Rabbit** (p79), gives the lowdown on his favorite downtown drinking holes.

Best Cocktails

My favorite bar is **Mayahuel** (p123) in the East Village. From the cocktails and bartenders, to the food and music, it's exactly what a tequila cocktail bar should be. They use a lot of mezcal, a smoky, tequila-like spirit. For New York's best negroni, reserve a spot at nearby **PDT** (p123).

Best Newcomers

Notable newbies include Alphabet City's **Pouring Ribbons** (p122; from the team behind the Death & Co) and the Lower East Side's **Attaboy** (p125).

Old Favorites

In the West Village, **Employees Only** (p149) offers a different take on the speakeasy bar, with interesting art-deco touches. The place was once only open to people in the hospitality industry, hence the name. While I don't necessarily love their drinks – I usually opt for a beer – the bartenders, music and vibe are brilliant.

Down in Tribeca, don't miss the decor at **Macao** (p80) and the effortless cool of **Weather Up** (p79).

⊘11:30am-midnight Sun-Wed, to 2am Thu-Sat; Ⓢ A/C, J/Z, 2/3, 4/5 to Fulton St; R to Cortlandt St) If you know that a Flying Dog Raging Bitch is a craft beer – not a nickname for your ex – this curated beer bar is for you. From Elysian Space Dust to Abita Purple Haze, its battalion of drafts, bottles and cans are a who's who of boutique American brews. Across the street, Bin No 220 is its wine-loving sibling.

MACAO COCKTAIL BAR

Map p410 (☑212-431-8642; www.macaonyc.com; 311 Church St, btwn Lispenard & Walker Sts; ⊘bar 5pm-2am Sun-Wed, to 4am Thu-Sat; Ⓢ A/C/E to Canal St) Though we love the '40s-style 'gambling parlor' bar/restaurant, it's the downstairs 'opium den' (open Thursday to Saturday) that gets our hearts racing. A Chinese-Portuguese fusion of grub and liquor, both floors are a solid spot for late-night sipping and snacking, especially if you've got a soft spot for sizzle-on-the-tongue libations.

SMITH & MILLS COCKTAIL BAR

Map p410 (☑212-226-2515; www.smithandmills.com; 71 N Moore St, btwn Hudson & Greenwich Sts; ⊘11am-2am Sun-Wed, to 3am Thu-Sat; Ⓢ1 to Franklin St) Petite Smith & Mills ticks all the cool boxes: unmarked exterior, kooky industrial interior and expertly crafted cocktails with a penchant for the classics. Space is limited so head in early if you fancy kicking

back on a plush banquette. A seasonal menu spans light snacks to a particularly notable burger pimped with caramelized onions.

 ENTERTAINMENT

SOHO REP THEATER

Map p410 (Soho Repertory Theatre; ☑212-941-8632; sohorep.org; 46 Walker St, btwn Church St & Broadway; Ⓢ A/C/E, N/Q/R, 6, J/Z to Canal St) This is one of New York's finest off-Broadway companies, wowing theater fans and critics with its annual trio of sharp, innovative new work. Kevin Spacey, Ed O'Neill and Kathleen Turner all made their professional debuts here, and the company's productions have garnered no shortage of Obie (Off-Broadway Theater) Awards. Check the website for current or upcoming shows.

FLEA THEATER THEATER

Map p410 (☑tickets 212-352-3101; www.theflea.org; 41 White St, btwn Church St & Broadway; Ⓢ1 to Franklin St; A/C/E, N/Q/R, J/Z, 6 to Canal St) One of NYC's top off-off-Broadway companies, Flea is famous for performing innovative, timely new works in its two performance spaces. Luminaries, including Sigourney Weaver and John Lithgow, have trodden the boards here, and the year-round program also includes music and dance performances.

🔒 SHOPPING

While the Financial District is not a shopping destination per se, it is where you'll find cut-price fashion mecca Century 21. Further north in Tribeca, hit the lower end of Hudson St and surrounding streets for high-end interior design, antiques and a handful of niche shops peddling everything from local threads to fetching axes.

★ CENTURY 21   FASHION

Map p410 (☎212-227-9092; www.c21stores. com; 22 Cortlandt St, btwn Church St & Broadway; ☺7:45am-9pm Mon-Fri, 10am-9pm Sat, 11am-8pm Sun; ⓢA/C, J/Z, 2/3, 4/5 to Fulton St; R to Cortlandt St) For penny-pinching fashionistas, this giant, cut-price department store is dangerously addictive. Raid the racks for designer duds at up to 65% off. Not everything is a knockout or a bargain, but persistence pays off. You'll also find accessories, shoes, cosmetics, homewares and toys.

SHINOLA   ACCESSORIES

Map p410 (☎917-728-3000; www.shinola.com; 177 Franklin St, btwn Greenwich & Hudson Sts; ☺11am-7pm Mon-Sat, noon-6pm Sun; ⓢ1 to Franklin St) Well known for its coveted wristwatches, Detroit-based Shinola branches out with a super-cool selection of Made-in-USA life props. Bag anything from leather iPad cases, journal covers and toiletry bags, to grooming products, jewelry and limited-edition bicycles with customized bags. Added bonuses include complimentary monogramming of leather goods and stationery, and an in-house espresso bar, **Smile** (Map p410; ☎917-728-3023; www. thesmilenyc.com; 177 Franklin St, btwn Greenwich & Hudson Sts; ☺7am-7pm Mon-Fri, 8am-7pm Sat, 8am-6pm Sun; ⓢ1 to Franklin St), to boot.

STEVEN ALAN   FASHION, ACCESSORIES

Map p410 (☎212-343-0692; www.stevenalan. com; 103 Franklin St, btwn Church St & W Broadway; ☺11:30am-7pm Mon-Wed, Fri & Sat, 11:30am-8pm Thu, noon-6pm Sun; ⓢA/C/E to Canal St; 1 to Franklin St) New York designer Steven Alan mixes his hip, heritage-inspired threads for men and women with a beautiful edit of clothes from indie-chic labels like France's Arpenteur and Scandinavia's Acne and Norse Projects. Accessories include hard-to-find fragrances, bags, jewelry and a selection of shoes by cognoscenti brands such as Common Projects and Isabel Marant Étoile.

PHILIP WILLIAMS POSTERS   VINTAGE

Map p410 (☎212-513-0313; www.postermuseum. com; 122 Chambers St, btwn Church St & W Broadway; ☺10am-7pm Mon-Sat; ⓢA/C, 1/2/3 to Chambers St) You'll find over half a million posters in this cavernous treasure trove, from oversized French advertisements for perfume and cognac to Soviet film posters and retro-fab promos for TWA. Prices range from $15 for small reproductions to a few thousand bucks for rare, showpiece originals. There is a second entrance at 52 Warren St.

PASANELLA & SON   WINE

Map p410 (☎212-233-8383; www.pasanellaand-son.com; 115 South St, btwn Peck Slip & Beekman St; ☺10am-9pm Mon-Sat, noon-7pm Sun; ⓢA/C, J/Z, 2/3, 4/5 to Fulton St; R to Cortlandt St) Oenophiles adore this savvy wine peddler, with its 400-plus drops both inspired and affordable. The focus is on small producers, with a number of biodynamic and organic winemakers in the mix. It offers an impressive choice of American whiskeys, free wine tastings of the week's new arrivals on Sundays, and themed wine and cheese tastings throughout the year.

BOWNE STATIONERS & CO   GIFTS

Map p410 (☎646-315-4478; 211 Water St, btwn Beekman & Fulton Sts; ☺11am-7pm; ⓢ2/3, 4/5, A/C, J/Z to Fulton St) Suitably set in cobbled South Street Seaport, this 18th-century veteran stocks vintage reproduction New York posters, city-themed notepads, pencil cases, cards, stamps and more. You can even bag New York–themed wrapping paper to wrap them in. Next door is the printing workshop, where you can order customized business cards or hone your printing skills at one of the monthly workshops.

CITYSTORE   SOUVENIRS

Map p410 (☎212-386-0007; a856-citystore. nyc.gov; Municipal Bldg, North Plaza, 1 Centre St; ☺10am-5pm Mon-Fri; ⓢJ/Z to Chambers St; 4/5/6 to Brooklyn Bridge-City Hall) Score all manner of New York memorabilia, from authentic taxi medallions, manhole coasters and subway-themed socks to NYPD baseball caps and wine totes featuring Manhattan and Brooklyn themes. Topping it off is a great collection of city-themed books.

SPORTS & ACTIVITIES

★STATEN ISLAND FERRY — FERRY

Map p410 (www.siferry.com; Whitehall Terminal, 4 South St, at Whitehall; 🕒24hr; 📶; [S]1 to South Ferry) [FREE] Staten Islanders know these hulking, dirty-orange ferryboats as commuter vehicles, while Manhattanites like to think of them as their secret, romantic vessels for a spring-day escape. Yet many a tourist is clued into the charms of the Staten Island Ferry, whose 5.2-mile journey between Lower Manhattan and the Staten Island neighborhood of St George is one of NYC's finest free adventures.

In service since 1905, the ferry service carries around 20 million passengers each year. Whether you choose to simply ride it to Staten Island and back in one run – enjoying cinematic views of the city skyline, the Verrazano-Narrows Bridge (which connects Staten Island to Brooklyn) and the Statue of Liberty – or stay and explore New York's least-known borough before catching a later return ferry, you're guaranteed a memorable experience. Alas, not all ferryboats in the fleet have extensive outdoor side decks (your best bet for a clear view of the skyline); some only offer an open section at the very front and back of the vessel, with most people taking in the views through dirty ferry windows.

Services from Manhattan depart from the Whitehall Terminal, located right above South Ferry subway station on the 1 line.

INSTITUTE OF CULINARY EDUCATION — COOKING COURSE

Map p410 (ICE; ☎212-847-0700; recreational.ice.edu; Brookfield Place, 225 Liberty St; courses $70-605; [S]E to World Trade Center; 2/3 to Park Place; R to Cortland St; A/C, 4/5, J/Z to Fulton St) Release your inner Jean Jacques with a cooking course at the Institute of Culinary Education (ICE). The center runs the country's biggest program of cooking, baking and wine-appreciation courses, from 90-minute classes to multiday sessions. The varied themes range from Tuscan cooking and American comfort food, to classic gin cocktails. Restless foodies can choose from numerous culinary tours of the city.

BIKE & ROLL BIKE RENTALS — BICYCLE RENTAL

Map p410 (☎212-260-0400; www.bikenewyorkcity.com; State & Water Sts; rentals per day from $44, tours from $50; 🕒varies, check website; [S]4/5 to Bowling Green; 1 to South Ferry) Located just northwest of the Staten Island Ferry terminal, this is one of several Bike & Roll Bike Rental outlets in the city. The outfit also leads bike tours, including across the Brooklyn Bridge and along the Hudson River.

PIONEER — SAILING

Map p410 (☎212-742-1969; southstreetseaportmuseum.org; Pier 16, South Street Seaport; adult/child $45/35; 🕒varies; [S]2/3, 4/5, A/C, J/Z to Fulton St) In the warmer months, break free with a salty sail aboard one of the South Street Seaport's historic schooners, the *Pioneer*. Tickets can be purchased via the South Street Seaport Museum website or directly at Pier 16.

SoHo & Chinatown

SOHO, NOHO & NOLITA | CHINATOWN & LITTLE ITALY

Neighborhood Top Five

❶ Maxing out the credit cards on SoHo's big-name fashion streets, followed by cool-hunting and lesser-known labels on the cognoscenti sidewalks of nearby Nolita and NoHo. (p99)

❷ Slurping soup dumplings and haggling for designer wares of ambiguous authenticity amid the sizzling lights of **Chinatown**. (p85)

❸ Snooping around the time-jarred **Merchant's House Museum** (p91), imagining NYC life in the wild and dusty 1800s.

❹ Re-imagining **Little Italy's** action-packed past, with prized *porchetta* (roast pork) sandwich from **Di Palo** (p97) in hand.

❺ Nighttime conversation, drinks and the chance of comedy, cabaret or live tunes at modern classic **Joe's Pub** (p99).

For more detail of this area see Map p412 and p415 ➡

Lonely Planet's Top Tip

Serious shopaholics should consult the city's in-the-know retail blogs (p18) before hitting SoHo and surrounds – there's always some sort of 'sample sale' or offer going on, not to mention the opening of yet another boutique stocking fresh, emerging design talent.

Best Places to Eat

➡ Uncle Boons (p92)

➡ Dutch (p93)

➡ Public (p93)

➡ Estela (p92)

➡ Prince Street Pizza (p90)

For reviews, see p90 ➡

Best Places to Drink

➡ Pegu Club (p98)

➡ Spring Lounge (p97)

➡ Genuine Liquorette (p97)

➡ Joe's Pub (p99)

➡ Apothéke (p99)

For reviews, see p97 ➡

Best Places to Shop

➡ MoMA Design Store (p102)

➡ Rag & Bone (p102)

➡ MiN New York (p100)

➡ Will Leather Goods (p100)

➡ United Nude (p102)

For reviews, see p99 ➡

Explore

Like a colorful quilt of subneighborhoods sewn together in mismatched patches, the areas orbiting SoHo (SOuth of HOuston) feel like a string of mini republics. Style-mavens boutique hop in booming Nolita (NOrth of LIttle ITAly), Italo-Americans channel Napoli in ever-shrinking Little Italy, and Chinese extended families gossip over *xiao long bao* (soup dumplings) in hyperactive Chinatown.

Lower-rise buildings inject these streets with a cozy, village-like vibe (main drags Broadway and Canal St excepted). Celebrities, cast-iron lofts and A-list boutiques stud SoHo's cobbled side streets, while humbler 19th-century tenements and quirkier one-off boutiques flavor neighboring Nolita.

In Chinatown, an 'anything goes' spirit wafts up like stall smoke, with frenzied crowds and hawkers mingling and haggling under faded billboards. The best way to weave your way around here is on foot. And don't bother planning your route of attack. It's all about letting your senses guide you. Whether you're following your nose down an alleyway for freshly baked pork buns, or your ears to a prayer gong in a heady Buddhist temple, unexpected surprises are always at the ready.

Local Life

➡ **Family style** Hit Chinatown's bustling dining dens with a handful of friends and eat 'family style' (order a ton of dishes and sample spoonfuls of each). You'll think the waiter left a zero off the bill.

➡ **Side streets** The stretch of Broadway cutting through SoHo is reserved for the legions of tourists – you'll find New Yorkers scouring the one-of-a-kind boutiques on the side streets for idiosyncratic buys and slashed prices.

➡ **Cultural breaks** It's not all retail therapy in SoHo. Take time to explore the area's artistic legacy at spaces such as Drawing Center (p87), Artists Space (p87) and the Leslie-Lohman Museum of Gay & Lesbian Art (p87).

Getting There & Away

➡ **Subway** The subway lines dump off along various points of Canal St (J/Z, N/Q/R and 6). Once you arrive it's best to explore on foot. The neighborhood's downtown location makes it easy to access from Midtown and Brooklyn.

➡ **Bus & Taxi** Avoid taking cabs or buses – especially in Chinatown, as the traffic is full-on. For SoHo, have your taxi let you off along Broadway if you aren't fussed about your final destination. Don't take cabs south of Canal St if you're simply planning to wander around Chinatown.

TOP SIGHT
CHINATOWN

Endless exotic moments await in New York City's most colorfully cramped community, where a walk through the neighborhood is never the same, no matter how many times you pass through. Catch the whiff of fresh fish and ripe persimmons, hear the clacking of mah-jongg tiles on makeshift tables, drool over dangling duck roasts swinging in store windows, and shop for everything imaginable, from rice-paper lanterns and 'faux-lex' watches to tire irons and a pound of pressed nutmeg. America's largest congregation of Chinese immigrants is your oyster – dipped in piquant soy sauce, of course.

DON'T MISS

- A family-style meal at a bustling, back-alley dive
- Museum of Chinese in America
- Canal St vendors and street life
- Mahayana Temple

PRACTICALITIES

- Map p415
- www.explorechinatown.com
- south of Canal St & east of Broadway
- [S]N/Q/R, J/Z, 6 to Canal St; B/D to Grand St; F to East Broadway

Canal Street

Walking down Canal St is like a game of Frogger played on the streets of Shanghai. This is Chinatown's spine, where you'll dodge oncoming human traffic as you scurry into side streets to scout treasures from the Far East. You'll pass stinky seafood stalls hawking slippery fish; mysterious herb shops peddling a witch's cauldron's worth of roots and potions; storefront bakeries with steamy windows and the tastiest 80-cent pork buns you've ever had; restaurants with whole, roasted ducks and pigs hanging by their skinny necks in the windows; produce markets piled high with fresh lychee, bok choy and Asian pears; and street vendors selling every iteration of knock-off, from Gucci sunglasses to Prada bags.

Buddhist Temples

Chinatown is home to Buddhist temples large and small, public and obscure. They are easily stumbled upon during a full-on stroll of the neighborhood, and at least two such temples are considered landmarks. The **Eastern States Buddhist Temple** (Map p415;

HISTORY

The history of Chinese immigrants in New York City is a long and tumultuous one. The first Chinese people to arrive in America came to work under difficult conditions on the Central Pacific Railroad; others were lured to the West Coast in search of gold. When prospects dried up, many moved east to NYC to work in factory assembly lines and in the laundry houses of New Jersey.

CHINESE EXCLUSION ACT

A rising racist sentiment gave way to the Chinese Exclusion Act (1882–1943), which made naturalization an impossibility, and largely squashed the opportunity for mainland Chinese to find work in the US. When the ban was lifted, the Chinese were given a limited immigration quota that eventually expanded and grew. Today it's estimated that over 150,000 citizens fill the bursting, tenement-like structures orbiting Mott St.

(☎212-966-6229; 64 Mott St, btwn Bayard & Canal Sts; ⏲8.30am-6pm; [S]J/Z, 6 to Canal St) is filled with hundreds of Buddhas, while the Mahayana Temple (p89) holds one golden, 16ft-high Buddha, sitting on a lotus and edged with offerings of fresh oranges, apples and flowers. Mahayana is the largest Buddhist temple in Chinatown, and its entrance, which overlooks the frenzied vehicle entrance to the Manhattan Bridge, is guarded by two proud and handsome golden lions. Step inside and you'll find a simple interior of wooden floor and red paper lanterns, dramatically upstaged by the temple's magnificent Buddha, thought to be the largest in the city.

Food Glorious Food

The most rewarding experience for Chinatown neophytes is to access this wild and wonderful world through their taste buds. More than any other area of Manhattan, Chinatown's menus sport wonderfully low prices, uninflated by ambience, hype or reputation. But more than cheap eats, the neighborhood is rife with family recipes passed across generations and continents. Food displays and preparation remain unchanged and untempered by American norms; it's not unusual to walk by storefronts sporting a tangled array of lacquered animals – chickens, rabbit and duck, in particular – ready to be chopped up and served at a family banquet. Steaming street stalls clang down the sidewalk serving pork buns and other finger-friendly food. Don't forget to wander down the back alleys for a Technicolor assortment of spices and herbs to perfect your own Eastern dishes.

Museum of Chinese in America

Map p415 (☎212-619-4785; www.mocanyc.org; 215 Centre St, btwn Grand & Howard Sts; adult/child $10/free, first Thu of month free; ⏲11am-6pm Tue, Wed & Fri-Sun, to 9pm Thu; 📶; [S]N/Q/R, J/Z, 6 to Canal St) In a space designed by architect Maya Lin (designer of the famed Vietnam Memorial in Washington DC), the Museum of Chinese in America is a multifaceted space whose engaging permanent and temporary exhibitions shed light on Chinese American life, both past and present. Browse through interactive multimedia exhibits, maps, timelines, photos, letters, films and artifacts. The museum's anchor exhibit, 'With a Single Step: Stories in the Making of America', provides an often intimate glimpse into topics including immigration, cultural identity and racial stereotyping.

SIGHTS

SoHo, NoHo & Nolita

DRAWING CENTER GALLERY

Map p412 (☎212-219-2166; www.drawingcenter.org; 35 Wooster St, btwn Grand & Broome Sts; adult/child $5/free; 🕐noon-6pm Wed & Fri-Sun, to 8pm Thu; [S]A/C/E, 1 to Canal St) America's only nonprofit institute focused solely on drawings, the Drawing Center uses work by masters as well as unknowns to juxtapose the medium's various styles. Historical exhibitions have included work by Michelangelo, James Ensor and Marcel Duchamp, while contemporary shows have showcased heavyweights such as Richard Serra, Ellsworth Kelly and Richard Tuttle. As to the themes themselves, expect anything from the whimsical to the politically controversial.

Artist lectures and performance-art programs are hot tickets here; check the website for upcoming events.

NEW YORK CITY FIRE MUSEUM MUSEUM

Map p412 (☎212-691-1303; www.nycfiremuseum.org; 278 Spring St, btwn Varick & Hudson Sts; adult/child $8/5; 🕐10am-5pm; 📶👪; [S]C/E to Spring St) In a grand old firehouse dating from 1904, this ode to firefighters includes a fantastic collection of historic equipment and artifacts. Eye up everything from horse-drawn firefighting carriages and early stovepipe firefighter hats to Chief, a four-legged fire-fighting hero from Brooklyn. Exhibits trace the development of the NYC firefighting system, and the museum's friendly staff (and the heavy equipment) make this a great spot to bring kids.

The New York Fire Department (FDNY) lost half of its members in the collapse of the World Trade Center on September 11, 2001, and memorials and exhibits have become a permanent part of the collection. Fans can stock up on books about firefighting history and official FDNY clothing and patches in the gift shop.

NEW YORK EARTH ROOM GALLERY

Map p412 (☎212-989-5566; www.earthroom.org; 141 Wooster St, btwn Prince & W Houston Sts; 🕐noon-3pm & 3:30-6pm Wed-Sun, closed mid-Jun–mid-Sep; [S]N/R to Prince St) [FREE] Since 1980 the oddity of the New York Earth Room, the work of artist Walter De Maria, has been wooing the curious with something not easily found in the city: dirt (250 cu yd, or 280,000lb, of it, to be exact). Walking into the small space is a heady experience, as the scent will make you feel like you've entered a wet forest; the sight of such beautiful, pure earth in the midst of this crazy city is surprisingly moving.

A short walk away is De Maria's equally arresting **Broken Kilometer** (Map p412; ☎212-989-5566; 393 W Broadway, btwn Spring & Broome Sts; 🕐noon-3pm & 3:30-6pm Wed-Sun, closed mid-Jun–mid-Sep; [S]N/R to Prince St) [FREE].

LESLIE-LOHMAN MUSEUM OF GAY & LESBIAN ART MUSEUM

Map p412 (☎212-431-2609; www.leslielohman.org; 26 Wooster St, btwn Grand & Canal Sts; 🕐noon-6pm Tue, Wed & Fri-Sun, to 8pm Thu; [S]A/C/E, N/Q/R, 1 to Canal St) [FREE] Expected to double in size in 2016, the world's first museu m dedicated to LGBT themes stages six to eight annual exhibitions of both homegrown and international art. Offerings have included solo-artist retrospectives as well as themed shows exploring the likes of art and sex along the New York waterfront. Much of the work on display is from the museum's own collection, which consists of over 24,000 works. The space also hosts queer-centric lectures, readings, film screenings and performances; check the website for updates.

ARTISTS SPACE GALLERY

Map p412 (☎212-226-3970; www.artistsspace.org; 38 Greene St, 3rd fl, btwn Grand & Broome Sts; 🕐vary; [S]A/C/E, N/Q/R, 1 to Canal St) [FREE] One of the first alternative spaces in New York, Artists Space made its debut in 1972. Its mission was to support contemporary artists working in the visual arts, from video, electronic media and performance, to architecture and design. More than 40 years on, it remains a solid choice for those seeking crisp, provocative and experimental creativity. Check the website for upcoming exhibitions.

INTERNATIONAL CENTER OF PHOTOGRAPHY GALLERY

Map p412 (ICP; www.icp.org; 250 Bowery, btwn Houston & Prince; adult/child $14/free, by donation Fri 5-8pm; 🕐10am-6pm Tue-Thu, Sat & Sun, to 8pm Fri; 📶; [S]F to Second Ave; J/Z to Bowery) ICP is New York's paramount platform for photography, with a strong emphasis on photojournalism and changing exhibitions

Neighborhood Walk
Chinatown

START CHATHAM SQ
END MUSEUM OF CHINESE IN AMERICA
LENGTH 0.9 MILES, 1½ HOURS

Begin exploring at ❶ **Chatham Sq**, home to the Kim Lau Memorial Arch, erected in 1962 to honor the Chinese Americans who have fallen in battle. There's also a statue of Lin Ze Xu, a Qing-dynasty scholar whose anti-drug trafficking stance largely lead to the First Opium War in 1839.

From Chatham Sq head northwest on Worth St until you hit ❷ **Colombus Park**, Chinatown's unofficial living room. In the 19th century, this was NYC's notorious Five Points slum, about which Charles Dickens wrote: 'Debauchery has made the very houses prematurely old'. To the east, slip into ❸ **Mosco St**, known in the 19th century as Bandits Roost, a menacing hangout for Irish gangs. Turn left into Mott St, right into Pell St, then right into ❹ **Doyers St**, a crooked lane dubbed 'Barbers Row' for its bounty of hair snippers. The lane's popularity with feuding tongs (secret societies) early

last century earned it the nickname Bloody Angle. American composer and lyricist Irving Berlin practiced upstairs at number 10, while at number 12 stands the neighborhood's oldest Chinese restaurant, wokking since 1920.

Turn left into Bowery and head north. At the southwest corner of Pell St and Bowery stands ❺ **Edward Mooney House**, NYC's oldest townhouse, built in 1785 by butcher Edward Mooney. This Georgian-Federal–style veteran has housed a store, hotel, billiards parlor and Chinese social club; it's now a bank. Continue north on Bowery to Canal St, where you'll see Manhattan Bridge and, just beyond that, the ❻ **Mahayana Buddhist Temple** (p89). See the massive golden Buddha inside, then dive into ❼ **Canal St**, Chinatown's hyperactive spine and NYC's one-time Jewish Diamond District. Make a right on Mott St for superlative steamed *bao* at ❽ **Golden Steamer** (p97). Turn left into Grand St and left again at Centre St, delving into the Chinese-American experience at the ❾ **Museum of Chinese in America** (p89).

on a wide range of themes. Past shows have included work by Sebastião Salgado, Henri Cartier-Bresson, Man Ray and Robert Capa. Its new 11,000-sq-ft home on the Bowery places it close to the epicenter of the downtown art scene.

The center is also a school, offering coursework (for credit) and a public lecture series. Stop by the excellent gallery shop, great for instant cameras and photography tomes, cool little gifts and NYC souvenirs.

CHILDREN'S MUSEUM OF THE ARTS MUSEUM

Map p412 (☎212-274-0986; www.cmany.org; 103 Charlton St, btwn Greenwich & Hudson Sts; admission $12, 4-6pm Thu by donation; ⏰noon-5pm Mon, noon-6pm Thu & Fri, 10am-5pm Sat & Sun; 📶👪; [S]1 to Houston St; C/E to Spring St) This small but worthy stop encourages kids aged 10 months to 15 years to view, make and share art. Rotating exhibitions aside, the center offers a vast program of daily activities for fledgling artists, from sculpture and collaborative mural painting, to songwriting and children's book design. It also runs movie nights and other special treats. See the website for upcoming offerings.

ST PATRICK'S OLD CATHEDRAL CHURCH

Map p412 (☎212-226-8075; www.oldsaintpatricks.com; 263 Mulberry St, entrance on Mott St; ⏰6am-9pm; [S]N/R to Prince St; B/D/F/M to Broadway-Lafayette St; 6 to Bleecker St) Though St Patrick's Cathedral is now famously located on Fifth Ave in Midtown, its first congregation was housed here, in this recently restored Gothic Revival church. Designed by Joseph-François Mangin and constructed between 1809 and 1815, the church was once the seat of religious life for the Archdiocese of New York, as well as an important community center for new immigrants, mainly from Ireland.

When the church was built, the city hadn't yet spread this far north, the building's calculated isolation a welcome relief from the hostility of New York's Protestant majority. Anti-Catholic sentiments also led to the construction of the church grounds' brick wall, an attempt to hinder stone-throwers.

The church and its beautiful graveyard feature in Martin Scorsese's celluloid classic *Mean Streets* (1973). It's a spot well-known to the Italian-American auteur, who grew up in nearby Elizabeth St.

👁 Chinatown & Little Italy

★CHINATOWN NEIGHBORHOOD

See p85.

MUSEUM OF CHINESE IN AMERICA MUSEUM

See p85.

MAHAYANA TEMPLE TEMPLE

Map p415 (☎212-925-8787; en.mahayana.us; 133 Canal St, at Manhattan Bridge Plaza; ⏰8.30am-6pm; [S]B/D to Grand St, J/Z; 6 to Canal St) Mahayana is the biggest Buddhist temple in Chinatown and its magnificent 16ft-high Buddha – sitting on a lotus and edged with offerings of fresh oranges, apples and flowers – is believed to be the largest in town. The temple itself faces the frenzied vehicle entrance to the Manhattan Bridge, and its entrance is guarded by two giant golden lions – symbols of protection.

MULBERRY STREET STREET

Map p415 ([S]N/Q/R, J/Z, 6 to Canal St; B/D to Grand St) Named for the mulberry farms that once stood here, Mulberry St is now better known as the meat in Little Italy's sauce. It's an animated strip, packed with smooth-talking restaurant hawkers (especially between Hester and Grand Sts), wisecracking baristas and a healthy dose of kitschy souvenirs.

Despite the neighborhood's many changes over the years, history looms large. It was inside restaurant **Da Gennaro** (Map p415; ☎212-431-3934; www.dagennarorestaurant.com; 129 Mulberry St, at Hester St; pizzas $13.50-15, mains $17-28; ⏰10am-1am; [S]N/Q/R, J/Z, 6 to Canal St; B/D to Grand St), formerly Umberto's Clam House, that 'Crazy Joe' Gallo was gunned down on 2 April 1972, an unexpected birthday surprise for the Brooklyn-born mobster. One block further north stands fourth-generation **Alleva** (Map p415; ☎212-226-7990; www.allevadairy.com; 188 Grand St, at Mulberry St; ⏰8.30am-6pm Mon-Sat, to 3pm Sun; [S]J/Z, N/Q/R, 6 to Canal St; B/D to Grand St), one of the city's original cheese shops and famed for its mozzarella. Across the street on Grand lies another veteran, **Ferrara Cafe & Bakery** (Map p415; ☎212-226-6150; www.ferraracafe.com; 195 Grand St, btwn Mulberry & Mott Sts; pastries $5; ⏰8am-midnight; [S]J/Z, N/Q/R, 6 to Canal St, B/D to Grand St), celebrated for its classic Italian pastries and gelati. Back on Mulberry, old-time **Mulberry Street Bar** (Map p415; ☑212-226-9345; www.mulberrystreetbar.com; 176 Mulberry St, at Broome St; ☺11am-2am Sun-Thu, to 4am Fri & Sat; ⓢB/D to Grand St; J/Z to Bowery) was a favorite haunt of the late Frank Sinatra; its own TV cameos include *Law & Order* and the *Sopranos*.

Alcohol was openly traded on the corner of Mulberry and Kenmare Sts during Prohibition, leading to its nickname, the 'Curb Exchange.' That the police headquarters at the time were only a block away at 240 Centre St is testament to the power of good old-fashioned bribes. From this point north, the old-school delis and restaurants of Little Italy give way to the new-school boutiques, galleries and restaurants of Nolita. Take a gander at what was once the **Ravenite Social Club** (Map p412; 247 Mulberry St; ⓢ6 to Spring St; N/R to Prince St) to see how things have really changed around here. Now a designer shoe store, it was once a mobster hangout (originally known as the Alto Knights Social Club). Indeed, it was right here that big hitters such as Lucky Luciano and John Gotti (as well as the FBI, who kept a watchful eye from the building across the street) logged time. Only the shop's tile floor remains from the day, the shop windows once an intimidating brick wall.

COLUMBUS PARK
PARK

Map p415 (Mulberry & Bayard Sts; ⓢJ/Z, N/Q/R, 6 to Canal St) Mah-jongg meisters, slow-motion tai-chi practitioners and old aunties gossiping over homemade dumplings: it might feel like Shanghai, but this leafy oasis is core to NYC history. In the 19th century, this was part of the infamous Five Points neighborhood, the city's first tenement slums and the inspiration for Martin Scorsese's *Gangs of New York*.

The 'five points' were the five streets that used to converge here; now you'll find the intersection of only Mosco, Worth and Baxter Sts. Aside from serving up an intriguing slice of multicultural life, the park's other perk these days is its public bathroom, making it the perfect place for a pit stop.

CHURCH OF THE TRANSFIGURATION
CHURCH

Map p415 (☑212-962-5157; www.transfiguration nyc.org; 29 Mott St, btwn Bayard & Mosco Sts; donations welcome; ☺English-language services 12:10pm daily, 6pm Sat, 11:30am Sun; ⓢJ/Z, N/Q/R, 6 to Canal St) It's been serving New York's immigrant communities since 1801,

and the Church of the Transfiguration doesn't stop adapting. First it was the Irish, then Italians and now Chinese. Indeed, the sermons here are delivered in Cantonese, Mandarin and English. This small landmark is not far from Pell and Doyers Sts, two winding paths worth exploring.

✖ EATING

In the land of acronyms there are only three letters you need to know: Y.U.M. Though the area may not have a plethora of headliners like the East and West Villages just beyond, it has no shortage of worthy options, from cult-status delis to Michelin-starred Thai and New American restaurants. The 99 percenters are spoiled for choice in Chinatown, where heaping portions are served up for pennies.

✖ SoHo, NoHo & Nolita

★ PRINCE STREET PIZZA
PIZZA $

Map p412 (☑212-966-4100; 27 Prince St, btwn Mott & Elizabeth Sts; pizza slices from $2.95; ☺11am-11pm Sun-Thu, to 2am Fri & Sat; ⓢN/R to Prince St; 6 to Spring St) It's a miracle the oven door hasn't come off its hinges at this classic slice joint, its brick walls hung with shots of B-list celebrity fans. Ditch the average cheese slice for the exceptional square varieties (the pepperoni will blow your socks off, Tony). The sauces, mozzarella and ricotta are made in-house and while the queues can get long, they usually move fast.

RUBY'S
CAFE $

Map p412 (☑212-925-5755; www.rubyscafe.com; 219 Mulberry St, btwn Spring & Prince Sts; mains $10-15; ☺9:30am-11pm; ⓢ6 to Spring St, N/R to Prince St) Almost always packed, this minute, cash-only cafe has all the bases covered: 'breakie' friendly avo toast (mashed avocado on ciabatta or eight-grain toast), buttermilk pancakes, competent pastas and salads, and (above all else) lusty burgers named after Australian surf beaches. Flat-white coffees and Aussie beers complete your Down Under dining adventure.

TOP SIGHT
MERCHANT'S HOUSE MUSEUM

Built in 1832 and purchased by merchant magnate Seabury Tredwell three years later, this red-brick mansion remains the most authentic Federal house (of which there are about 300) in town. It's an antiquarian's dream, as much about the city's mercantile past as it is a showcase of 19th-century high-end domestic furnishings. Everything in the house is testament to what money could buy, from the mahogany pocket doors, bronze gasoliers and marble mantelpieces, to the elegant parlor chairs, attributed to noted furniture designer Duncan Phyfe. Even the elaborate system of multilevel call bells for the servants works to this day.

Many believe that the ghost of Gertrude Tredwell – Seabury's youngest child and the building's last resident – haunts the old mansion, making cameo appearances late in evenings and sometimes at public events. At a Valentine's Day concert a few years back several attendees witnessed the shadow of a woman walk up to the performers and take a seat in the parlor chairs. Appropriately, the museum offers ghost tours after dark (usually in late October), as well as lectures, special events and historical walking tours of NoHo. Check the website.

DON'T MISS

➡ Chairs attributed to Duncan Phyfe
➡ Servant call bells
➡ Maid's quarters
➡ Ghost tours

PRACTICALITIES

➡ Map p412
➡ 212-777-1089
➡ www.merchantshouse.org
➡ 29 E 4th St, btwn Lafayette St & Bowery
➡ adult/child $10/free
➡ noon-5pm Fri-Mon, to 8pm Thu, guided tours 2pm Thu-Mon & 6.30pm Thu

CAFÉ GITANE MEDITERRANEAN $

Map p412 (212-334-9552; www.cafegitanenyc.com; 242 Mott St, at Prince St; salads $9.50-16, mains $14-17; 8:30am-midnight Sun-Thu, to 12.30am Fri & Sat; N/R to Prince St, 6 to Spring St) Clear the Gauloise smoke from your eyes and blink twice if you think you're in Paris: bistroesque Gitane has that kind of louche vibe. This is a classic see-and-be-seen haunt, popular with salad-picking models and the odd Hollywood regular. Join them for a nibble on the likes of blueberry and almond friands (small French cake), heart-of-palm salad or Moroccan couscous with organic chicken. Cash only.

TWO HANDS CAFE $

Map p415 (www.twohandsnyc.com; 164 Mott St, btwn Broome & Grands Sts; dishes $6-15; 8am-6pm; B/D to Grand St, J/Z to Bowery) Named after the crime-com film starring Heath Ledger, Two Hands encapsulates Australia's relaxed, sophisticated cafe culture. Dream of Byron Bay over small-batch specialty coffee and out-of-the-box grub such as sweet corn fritters with spinach, avocado, sour cream, pickled beets and chili, or a healthier-than-

thou Acai Bowl (berries, cocoa and acai powder, almond milk, gluten-free granola, coconut, cocoa nibs, hemp and chia seeds).

TACOMBI MEXICAN $

Map p412 (917-727-0179; www.tacombi.com; 267 Elizabeth St, btwn E Houston & Prince Sts; tacos $4-6; 11am-midnight Mon-Wed, 11am-1am Thu & Fri, 10am-1am Sat, 10am-midnight Sun; F to Second Ave, 6 to Bleecker St) Festively strung lights, foldaway chairs and Mexican men flipping tacos in an old VW Kombi: if you can't make it to the Yucatan shore, here's your Plan B. Casual, convivial and ever-popular, Tacombi serves up fine, fresh tacos, including a fine barbacoa (roasted black Angus beef). Wash down the goodness with a pitcher of sangria and start plotting that south-of-the-border getaway.

AB BIAGI ICE CREAM $

Map p412 (212-219-8094; abbiagi.com; 235 Elizabeth St, at Prince St; ice cream from $4.75; 10am-10pm Sun-Thu, to 11pm Fri & Sat; 6 to Spring St; N/R to Prince St) Precious things come in small packages, including this tiny, bright gelateria. Squeeze in for some of the finest gelato in town, made fresh on-site using first-rate ingredients. A rotating cast of eight outstanding flavors usually includes Bronte pistachio and mint chocolate chip that actually tastes like just-picked mint.

★UNCLE BOONS
THAI $$

Map p412 (☎646-370-6650; www.uncleboons.com; 7 Spring St, btwn Elizabeth St & Bowery; small plates $12-16, large plates $21-28; ⏲5:30-11pm Mon-Thu, to midnight Fri & Sat, to 10pm Sun; 📶; [S]J/Z to Bowery; 6 to Spring St) New York's new favorite uncle, Boons serves up Michelin-star Thai in a fun, tongue-in-cheek combo of retro wood panels, Thai film posters and old family snaps. Spanning the old and the new, zesty, tangy dishes include fantastically crunchy *mieng kum* (betel leaf wrap with ginger, lime, toasted coconut, dried shrimp, peanuts and chili), *kao pat puu* (crab fried rice) and banana blossom salad.

Book ahead or head in either before 6pm or after 10pm.

BUTCHER'S DAUGHTER
VEGETARIAN $$

Map p412 (☎212-219-3434; www.thebutchersdaughter.com; 19 Kenmare St, at Elizabeth St; salads & sandwiches $12-14, dinner mains $16-18; ⏲8am-10pm Sun-Thu, to 11pm Fri & Sat; 📶🌱; [S]J to Bowery; 6 to Spring St) The butcher's daughter certainly has rebelled, peddling nothing but fresh herbivorous fare in her white-washed cafe. While healthy it is, boring it's not: everything from the soaked organic muesli, to the spicy kale Caesar salad with almond Parmesan, to the dinnertime Butcher's burger (vegetable and black-bean patty with cashew cheddar cheese) is devilishly delish.

Add glow to your halo with a juice spritzer, or get buzzy with a craft beer or biodynamic vino. Warning: service can be painfully slow.

SIGGI'S
CAFE $$

Map p412 (☎212-226-5775; www.siggysgoodfood.com; 292 Elizabeth St, btwn E Houston & Bleecker Sts; dishes $11-22; ⏲11am-10.30pm Mon-Sat; 🌱; [S]6 to Bleecker St; B/D/F/M to Broadway-Lafayette St) Organic deliciousness awaits at this casual, art-slung cafe (bonus points for the wintertime fireplace). All bases are covered, from soups and salads to made-from-scratch burgers, sandwiches, even vegetarian lasagna. Virtuous libations include smoothies and freshly squeezed juices, with optional health-boosting supplements. Vegan and gluten-free diners won't go hungry either.

BOQUERIA SOHO
TAPAS $$

Map p412 (☎212-343-4255; www.boquerianyc.com; 171 Spring St, btwn West Broadway & Thompson St; tapas $6-18; ⏲noon-10.30pm Sun-Thu, to 11.30pm Fri & Sat; [S]C/E to Spring St) Channeling Barcelona, this expansive, welcoming tapas joint serves both classic and classic-with-a-twist morsels, dexterously assembled in the open kitchen. Order a beer-and-pear sangria and feast on standouts such as *abondigas* (Colorado lamb meatballs with tomato sauce and sheep's milk cheese), mushroom and Serrano ham croquettes, and a fine selection of hard and soft cheeses.

You'll find another branch of Boqueria (p167) in the Flatiron district.

LA ESQUINA
MEXICAN $$

Map p412 (☎646-613-7100; www.esquinanyc.com; 114 Kenmare St, at Petrosino Sq; tacos from $3.25, mains cafe $15-25, brasserie $18-34; ⏲taqueria 11am-1:45am daily, cafe noon-midnight Mon-Fri, from 11am Sat & Sun, brasserie 6pm-2am daily; [S]6 to Spring St) This mega-popular and quirky little spot combines three places really: a stand-while-you-eat taco window, a casual Mexican cafe (entrance on Lafayette St) and a dim, slinky, cavernous brasserie downstairs requiring reservations. Standouts include the *elotes callejeros* (grilled corn with queso Cotija cheese, mayo and chili powder), pulled pork tacos and mango-jicama salad.

★ESTELA
MODERN AMERICAN $$$

Map p412 (☎212-219-7693; www.estelanyc.com; 47 E Houston St, btwn Mulberry & Mott Sts; dishes $15-37; ⏲5:30-11pm Sun-Thu, to 11:30pm Fri & Sat; [S]B/D/F/M to Broadway-Lafayette St, 6 to Bleecker St) Estela might be hopeless at hide-and-seek (its location up some nondescript stairs hardly tricks savvy gourmands), but this busy, skinny wine-bar kicks butt on the food and vino front. Graze from a competent string of market-driven sharing plates, from phenomenal beef tartare (spiked with beef heart for added complexity) to moreish mussels *escabeche* on toast, to an impossibly sexy endive salad with walnuts and anchovy.

Another highlight is the delicate, smooth ricotta dumplings, lavished with earthy mushrooms and *pecorino sardo* (firm Italian sheep-milk cheese). Book ahead or head in early for a seat at the bar.

★DUTCH MODERN AMERICAN $$$

Map p412 (☎212-677-6200; www.thedutchnyc.com; 131 Sullivan St, at Prince St; mains lunch $18-29, dinner $29-58; ⏲11:30am-11pm Mon-Thu, 11:30am-11:30pm Fri, 10am-11:30pm Sat, 10am-11pm Sun; [S]C/E to Spring St; N/R to Prince St; 1 to Houston St) Whether perched at the bar or dining snugly in the back room, you can always expect smart, farm-to-table comfort grub at this see-and-be-seen stalwart. Flavors traverse the globe, from sweet potato tempura with Thai basil and fermented chili sauce to ricotta ravioli with Swiss chard and walnut pesto. Reservations are recommended, especially for dinner and all day on weekends.

★PUBLIC MODERN AMERICAN $$$

Map p412 (☎212-343-7011; www.public-nyc.com; 210 Elizabeth St, btwn Prince & Spring Sts; mains $21-34; ⏲6pm-10pm Mon, to 11pm Tue-Fri, 10:30am-3:30pm & 6-11pm Sat, 10:30am-3:30pm & 6-10pm Sun; [S]6 to Spring St; N/R to Prince St) What was once a muffin factory is now a svelte culinary hot spot, complete with sultry bar, industrial touches and masterfully textured dishes deserving of their Michelin star. Global twists surprise and delight, whether it's ricotta *cavatelli* schmoozing with candied sunflower seeds and Thai basil, or Berkshire pork matched with carrot-pineapple puree and *chimichurri*.

The Australian provenance of chef de cuisine Alan Wise sneaks through in dishes such as kangaroo carpaccio, not to mention what is one of the city's most extensive selections of antipodean wines.

IL BUCO ALIMENTARI & VINERIA ITALIAN $$$

Map p412 (☎212-837-2622; www.ilbucovineria.com; 53 Great Jones St, btwn Bowery & Lafayette St; sandwiches $12-16, dinner mains $32-34; ⏲cafe 7am-late Mon-Fri, from 9am weekends, restaurant noon-3pm & 5:30-late Mon- Fri, 11am-3pm & 5:30pm-late weekends; 📶; [S]6 to Bleecker St; B/D/F/M to Broadway-Lafayette St) Whether it's wham-bam espresso at the front bar, a panino to go from the deli, or long-and-lazy Italian feasting in the sunken dining room, Il Buco's trendier spin-off delivers the goods. Brickwork, hessian and giant industrial lamps set a hip-n-rustic tone, echoed in the menu's bold, nostalgic flavors.

Whet the appetite with crunchy Casareccio bread, linger over beautiful pasta dishes, and ponder the adage 'less is more' over mains such as whole roasted branzino (European sea bass) with fennel pollen and charred lemons.

BALTHAZAR FRENCH $$$

Map p412 (☎212-965-1414; www.balthazarny.com; 80 Spring St, btwn Broadway & Crosby St; mains $19-45; ⏲7:30am-midnight Sun-Thu, 7:30am-1am Fri, 8am-1am Sat; [S]6 to Spring St; N/R to Prince St) Still the king of bistros, bustling (OK, *loud*) Balthazar is never short of a mob. That's all thanks to three winning details: its location in SoHo's shopping-spree heartland; the uplifting Paris-meets-NYC ambience; and, of course, the something-for-everyone menu. Highlights include the outstanding raw bar, steak frites, salade Niçoise, as well as the roasted beet salad.

The kitchen stays open till 1am Friday and Saturday, and weekend brunch here is a very crowded production. For a decadent treat to go, grab a pastry from the Balthazar bakery next door.

CHERCHE MIDI AMERICAN, FRENCH $$$

Map p412 (☎212-226-3055; www.cherchemidiny.com; 282 Bowery, at E Houston St; lunch 2-course prix-fixe $25, dinner mains $19-39; ⏲noon-3:30pm & 5:30-11pm Mon-Wed, to midnight Thu & Fri, 10am-3:30pm & 5:30pm-midnight Sat, 10am-3:30pm & 5:30pm-11pm Sun; 📶; [S]F to Second Ave) Chipped subway tiles, red banquettes and a nostalgic amber glow: Montparnasse meets Manhattan at this studiously vintage newcomer. Stay pure with lunchtime salade Niçoise or tartine, or salute Franco-American fraternity with the all-day prime-rib burger, pimped with cognac-spiked bacon marmalade, aged Gruyère and perfect fries. If it's on the dinner menu, make sure someone orders the lobster ravioli in ginger *beurre blanc*. Consider booking ahead for dinner and the popular weekend brunch.

🍴 Chinatown & Little Italy

BÁNH MÌ SAIGON BAKERY VIETNAMESE $

Map p415 (☎212-941-1541; www.banhmisaigonnyc.com; 198 Grand St, btwn Mulberry & Mott Sts; sandwiches $3.50-5.75; ⏲8.30am-7pm; [S]N/Q/R, J/Z, 6 to Canal St) This no-frills storefront doles out some of the best *bánh mì* in town – we're talking crisp, toasted baguettes generously stuffed with hot peppers, pickled

PAUL DE GREGORIO / GETTY IMAGES ©

1. Cannoli
Indulge in traditional Italian cuisine in Little Italy (p93).

2. Mahayana Temple (p89)
Pay respects to the giant golden Buddha in Chinatown.

3. La Esquina (p92)
Join the crowds at this popular Mexican brasserie and cafe.

4. SoHo shopping (p99)
Browse high-end boutiques or fossick for a vintage gem.

5. SoHo streets (p87)
Wander through SoHo's cobbled streets and towering apartment blocks.

TOP SIGHT
LITTLE ITALY

In the last 50 years, New York's Little Italy has shrunk from a big, brash boot to an ultra-slim sandal. A mid-century exodus to the suburbs of Brooklyn and beyond has seen this once-strong Italian neighborhood turn into a micro pastiche of its former self. Indeed, Little Italy is little more than **Mulberry St** (p89) these days, an endearingly kitsch strip of gingham-tablecloths, mandolin muzak and nostalgia for the old country.

Come late September, the street turns into a raucous, 11-day block party for the **San Gennaro Festival**, a celebration honoring the patron saint of Naples. It's a loud, convivial affair, with food and carnival stalls, free entertainment, and more big hair than *Jersey Shore*.

It's also on Mulberry St that you'll find the tiny **Italian American Museum** (Map p415; ☎212-965-9000; www.italianamericanmuseum.org; 155 Mulberry St, at Grand St; suggested donation $7; 🕘noon-6pm Fri-Sun; [S]J/Z, N/Q/R, 6 to Canal St; B/D to Grand St), a random mishmash of historical objects documenting early Italian life in NYC, from Sicilian marionettes to old Italian comics starring mafia-busting cop, Giuseppe 'Joe' Petrosino. Between 1885 and 1932, the building was occupied by the Banca Stabile, which helped immigrants sort their monetary needs and provided a lifeline back to the homeland.

DON'T MISS

- ➡ Mulberry St
- ➡ San Gennaro Festival in September
- ➡ Pizza by the slice

PRACTICALITIES

- ➡ Map p415
- ➡ [S]N/Q/R, J/Z, 6 to Canal St; B/D to Grand St

carrots, daikon, cucumber, cilantro and your choice of meat. Top billing goes to the classic BBQ pork version. Tip: head in by 3pm as the *bánh mì* sometimes sell out, leading the place to close early.

XI'AN FAMOUS FOODS CHINESE $

Map p415 (xianfoods.com; 67 Bayard St, btwn Mott & Elizabeth Sts; dishes $2.75-10.25; 🕘11:30am-9pm Sun-Thu, to 9:30pm Fri & Sat; [S]J/Z, N/Q, 6 to Canal St) Food bloggers short-circuit their keyboards at the mere thought of this small, no-fuss Chinatown joint. Star turn here is the spicy cumin lamb burger – tender lamb sautéed with ground cumin, toasted chili seeds, long-horn peppers, red onions and scallions, and stuffed into a crispy, flat-bread bun. The hand-pulled noodles also enjoy a cult following.

BAZ BAGELS JEWISH $

Map p415 (☎212-335-0609; bazbagel.com; 181 Grand St, btwn Baxter & Mulberry Sts; bagels $10-16; 🕘7am-4pm Mon-Fri, 8am-5pm Sat & Sun; [S]J/Z, N/Q/R, 6 to Canal St; B/D to Grand St) A shamelessly flamboyant combo of pink, palm prints and portraits of Dolly and Barbra, New York's campest diner keeps things fabulous with its hand-rolled, kettle-boiled bagels. Star of the show is the Mooch, an epic concoction that's half Scottish salmon, half cold-smoked sable and utterly scrumptious. Bagels aside, other standouts include blintzes and latkes, the latter made to the owner's grandmother's recipe.

JOE'S SHANGHAI CHINESE $

Map p415 (☎212-233-8888; www.joeshanghairestaurants.com; 9 Pell St, btwn Bowery & Doyers St; dishes $5.25-20.25; 🕘11am-11pm; [S]N/Q/R, J/Z, 6 to Canal St; B/D to Grand St) This Flushing transplant has no shortage of loyal fans, descending *en masse* for Joe's cult-status crab-meat *xiao long bao*. Frankly, you can find better soup dumplings in town, but the place is still a safe bet for a cheap, cheerful Chinatown feed. Chomp outside the box with dishes such as string beans Szechuan-style with pork and spicy buffalo carp fish belly. Cash only.

NICE GREEN BO CHINESE $

Map p415 (New Green Bow; ☎212-625-2359; www.nicegreenbo.com; 66 Bayard St, btwn Elizabeth & Mott Sts; mains $5.95-19.95; 🕘11am-11pm Sun-Thu, to midnight Fri & Sat; [S]N/Q/R, J/Z, 6 to Canal St; B/D to Grand St) Not a shred of effort – not even a new sign (you'll see!) – has been made to spruce up Nice Green Bo, and that's the way we like it. It's all about the food here: gorgeous *xiao long bao* served in steaming drums, heaping portions of noodles and gleaming plates of salubrious, sautéed spinach. Cash only.

GOLDEN STEAMER
CHINESE $

Map p415 (☑212-226-1886; 143a Mott St, btwn Grand & Hester Sts; buns from $0.80; ⊙7am-7:30pm; S B/D to Grand St; N/Q/R, 6 to Canal St; J/Z to Bowery) Squeeze into this hole-in-the-wall for some of the fluffiest, tastiest *bao* (steamed buns) in Chinatown. Made on-site by bellowing Chinese cooks, fillings include succulent roast pork, Chinese sausage, salt-ed egg and the crowd favorite – pumpkin. For something a little sweeter, try the egg custard tart.

LAN LARB
THAI $

Map p415 (☑646-895-9264; 227 Centre St, at Grand St; dishes $9-21; ⊙11:30am-10:15pm; S N/Q/R, J/Z, 6 to Canal St) Food fiends flock to Lan Larb's plastic tables for cheap, flavor-packed Thai. The place specializes in *larb*, a spicy, minced-meat salad from Thailand's northeast (Isan) region (opt for the duck version). Other top choices include sucker-punch *som tam* (green papaya salad) and a delicate *kui teiw nam tok nuer* (dark noodle soup with beef, morning glory, scallion, cilantro and bean sprouts).

DI PALO
DELI $

Map p415 (☑212-226-1033; www.dipaloselects. com; 200 Grand St, at Mott St; sandwich from $7; ⊙9am-6:30pm Mon-Sat, to 4pm Sun; S B/D to Grand St; N/Q/R, J/Z, 6 to Canal St) Food bloggers revere the *porchetta* sandwich from this family-run deli; a crusty baguette stuffed with melt-in-your-mouth roast pork seasoned with garlic, fennel and herbs. Not only is it sinfully good, it's huge, so opt for just one slice of *porchetta* when asked. Normally available from 1:30pm (though this can vary), the prized meat sells out in 20 minutes. Get there at 1:15pm or call ahead. Not available Mondays.

ORIGINAL CHINATOWN ICE CREAM FACTORY
ICE CREAM $

Map p415 (☑212-608-4170; www.chinatownice creamfactory.com; 65 Bayard St; ice cream from $4.35; ⊙11am-10pm Sun-Thu, to 10:30pm Fri &

Sat; S N/Q/R, J/Z, 6 to Canal St) Chinatown's favorite ice-cream peddler keeps it local with flavors such as green tea, pandan, durian and lychee sorbet. The Factory also sells ridiculously cute, trademark T-shirts with an ice-cream–slurping happy dragon on them.

NYONYA
MALAYSIAN $$

Map p415 (☑212-334-3669; www.ilovenyonya. com; 199 Grand St, btwn Mott & Mulberry Sts; mains $7-24; ⊙11am-11:30pm Mon-Thu & Sun, to midnight Fri & Sat; S N/Q/R, J/Z, 6 to Canal Street; B/D to Grand St) Take your palate to steamy Melaka at this bustling temple to Chinese-Malay Nyonya cuisine. Savor the sweet, the sour and the spicy in classics such as tangy Assam fish-head casserole, rich beef *rendang* (spicy dry curry) and refreshing *rojak* (savory fruit salad tossed in a piquant tamarind dressing). Vegetarians should be warned: there's not much on the menu for you. Cash only.

DRINKING & NIGHTLIFE

GENUINE LIQUORETTE
COCKTAIL BAR

Map p415 (genuineliquorette.com; 191 Grand St, at Mulberry St; ⊙6pm-midnight Tue & Wed, to 2am Thu-Sat; S J/Z, N/Q/R, 6 to Canal St; B/D to Grand St) What's not to love about a jamming basement bar with Cha-Chunkers (canned cocktails) and a Farah Fawcett–themed restroom? Hell, you're even free to grab the bottles and mixers and make your own drinks (bottles are weighed before and after you're done). At the helm is prolific mixologist Eben Freeman, who regularly invites New York's finest barkeeps to create cocktails using less-celebrated hooch.

Retro-hip bites come from the playful upstairs eatery, including burgers, fries and a buttermilk battered chicken sandwich.

SPRING LOUNGE
BAR

Map p412 (☑212-965-1774; www.thespring lounge.com; 48 Spring St, at Mulberry St; ⊙8am-4am Mon-Sat, from noon Sun; S 6 to Spring St; N/R to Prince St) This neon-red rebel has never let anything get in the way of a good time. In Prohibition days, it peddled buckets of beer. In the '60s its basement was a gambling den. These days, it's best known for its kooky stuffed sharks, early-start regulars and come-one, come-all late-night revelry.

LOCAL KNOWLEDGE

DRINKING IN THE CITY

Eben Freeman, mixology meister behind **Genuine Liquorette** (p97), talks liquor and New York City.

Crowning Achievement

While I'm very happy with my Cha-Chunker at Genuine Liquorette, it would probably be my smoked Coke and bourbon cocktail, the Waylon. The idea was inspired by pastry chef Sam Mason, who was playing around with smoking the milk and cream that he was making ice cream with. It was the first time I realised that you could smoke liquids.

Bar Scene Trends

Greater technical precision combined with a more playful attitude. Take Genuine Liquorette, where serious technique takes place in what is a fun, casual, high-volume environment. Other good examples include the **Happiest Hour** (p150) and Slowly Shirley. One standout mixologist is Kenta Goto. After a successful run at **Pegu Club**, he's now making very Japanese-style drinks at his own place, **Bar Goto**.

A Taste of Old New York

Head to **Bemelmans Bar** (p226), a beautiful space with murals by Ludwig Bemelmans and good martinis. **Fanelli's Cafe** has one of the city's first liquor licences. It hasn't changed in years and you can really get a sense of the old New York there. Another spot is Capri Social Club in Brooklyn. You can still see the once-separate sections for men and women, and the carved wooden bar is beautiful.

Barkeep Peeves

People coming in and saying 'I've been dying to come here and try this thing' and then wanting to modify it. Another trend is younger people asking for sugarless cocktails. I understand what sugar can do to a body, but it's just gotten a bit ridiculous. One bar recently reacted by putting on a cocktail named 'Not Too Sweet'.

Fueling the fun are cheap drinks and free grub (hot dogs on Wednesdays from 5pm, bagels on Sundays from noon, while they last). Bottoms up, baby!

PEGU CLUB   COCKTAIL BAR
Map p412 (📞212-473-7348; www.peguclub.com; 77 W Houston St, btwn W Broadway & Wooster St; ⏰5pm-2am Sun-Thu, to 4am Fri & Sat; 🚇B/D/F/M to Broadway-Lafayette St; C/E to Spring St) Dark, elegant Pegu Club (named after a legendary gentleman's club in colonial-era Rangoon) is an obligatory stop for cocktail connoisseurs. Sink into a velvet lounge and savor seamless libations such as the silky smooth Earl Grey MarTEAni (tea-infused gin, lemon juice and raw egg white). Grazing options are suitably Asianesque, among them sloppy duck (braised duck with tropical fruit BBQ sauce on toasted mini-brioche buns).

LA COMPAGNIE DES
VINS SURNATURELS   WINE BAR
Map p415 (📞212-343-3660; www.compagnie nyc.com; 249 Centre St, btwn Broome & Grand

Sts; ⏰5pm-1am Mon-Wed, to 2am Thu-Sat; 🚇6 to Spring St; N/R to Prince St) A snug melange of Gallic-themed wallpaper, svelte armchairs and tea lights, La Compagnie des Vins Surnaturels is an offshoot of a Paris bar by the same name. Head sommelier Caleb Ganzer steers an impressive, French-heavy wine list, with some 600 drops and no shortage of arresting drops by the glass. A short, sophisticated menu of bites includes housemade charcuterie and (if you're lucky) buffalo chicken rillettes.

The good-value happy hour (5pm to 7pm Wednesday to Saturday, to 8pm Tuesday) offers house wines and snacks at $5 a serve.

CAFÉ INTEGRAL   CAFE
Map p412 (📞646-801-5747; www.cafeintegral. com; 135 Grand St, btwn Crosby & Lafayette Sts; ⏰8:30am-6pm Mon-Fri, 11am-5pm Sat; 🚇N/Q/R, J/Z, 6 to Canal St) Refuel with exceptional single-origin coffee at Café Integral, a teeny-tiny espresso bar inside kooky shop-cum-gallery American Two Shot. You'll probably find owner César Martin Vega

at the machine, a 20-something obsessed with Nicaraguan coffee beans. A must for the coffee cognoscenti.

MADAM GENEVA COCKTAIL BAR

Map p412 (☎212-254-0350; www.madamgenevanyc.com; 4 Bleecker St, at Bowery; 🕒6pm-2am; [S]6 to Bleecker St; B/D/F/M to Broadway-Lafayette St) Hanging lanterns, leather couches and flouncy wallpaper echo colonial Nanyang at this dark and sultry cocktail den. Gin-based cocktails dominate, meticulously crafted and suitably paired with Asian-inspired bites such as sambal deviled eggs, duck steamed buns, and chicken wings with Korean chili sauce. Next door lies hotspot sibling restaurant **Saxon + Parole** (Map p412; ☎212-254-0350; www.saxonandparole.com; 316 Bowery, at Bleecker St; mains $20-32; 🕒5-10pm Mon, to 11pm Tue-Fri, 10am-11pm Sat, 10am-10pm Sun; 📶; [S]6 to Bleecker S; B/D/F/M to Broadway-Lafayette St).

MULBERRY PROJECT COCKTAIL BAR

Map p415 (☎646-448-4536; www.mulberryproject.com; 149 Mulberry St, btwn Hester & Grand Sts; 🕒5pm-2am Sun-Thu, to 4am Fri & Sat; [S]N/Q/R, J/Z, 6 to Canal St) Lurking behind an unmarked door is this intimate, cavernous cocktail den, with its festive, 'garden-party' backyard one of the best spots to chill in the hood. Bespoke, made-to-order cocktails are the specialty, so disclose your preferences and let the barkeep do the rest. If you're peckish, choose from a competent list of bites that might include peach salad with pecorino cheese.

APOTHÉKE COCKTAIL BAR

Map p415 (☎212-406-0400; www.apothekenyc.com; 9 Doyers St; 🕒6:30pm-2am Mon-Sat, 8pm-2am Sun; [S]J/Z to Chambers St; 4/5/6 to Brooklyn Bridge-City Hall) It takes a little effort to track down this former opium-den-turned-apothecary bar on Doyers St. Inside, skilled barkeeps work like careful chemists, using local, seasonal produce from greenmarkets to produce intense, flavorful 'prescriptions.' Toast to your health with the likes of MVO Negative, a smoky concoction of Lapsang tea–infused gin, Antica Formula, Campari and Peychauds Bitters.

FANELLI'S CAFE BAR

Map p412 (☎212-226-9412; 94 Prince St, at Mercer St; 🕒10am-12:30am Mon-Thu, to 4am Fri & Sat, to midnight Sun; [S]N/R to Prince St) Snug, convivial Fanelli's is the consummate soak, pouring drinks on this corner since 1874. And while SoHo may have changed over the years, Fanelli's remains true to its earthy roots – tinted mirrors, hanging pugilists and all. Skip the average food; you're here to swill and reminisce.

☆ ENTERTAINMENT

★JOE'S PUB LIVE MUSIC

Map p412 (☎212-539-8500, tickets 212-967-7555; www.joespub.com; Public Theater, 425 Lafayette St, btwn Astor Pl & 4th St; [S]6 to Astor Pl; R/W to 8th St-NYU) Part bar, part cabaret and performance venue, intimate Joe's serves up both emerging acts and top-shelf performers. Performers have included caustic comic Sandra Bernhard and British songstress Adele. In fact, it was right here that Adele gave her very first American performance back in 2008.

FILM FORUM CINEMA

Map p412 (☎212-727-8110; www.filmforum.com; 209 W Houston St, btwn Varick St & Sixth Ave; [S]1 to Houston St) This three-screen cinema screens an astounding array of independent films, revivals and career retrospectives from greats such as Sidney Lumet. Theaters are small, as are the screens, so get there early for a good viewing spot. Showings are often combined with director talks or other film-themed discussions.

SHOPPING

SoHo bursts at its fashionable seams with stores, big and small. Hit Broadway for Main St chains, or the streets to the west of it for higher-end fashion and accessories. Over on Lafayette, shops cater to the DJ and skate crowds with indie labels and vintage shops thrown into the mix. If indie-chic is your thing, continue east to Nolita, home of tiny jewel-box boutiques selling unique threads, kicks and accessories. Mott St is best for browsing, followed by Mulberry and Elizabeth. For medicinal herbs, exotic Eastern fruits, woks and Chinese teapots, scour the frenetic streets of Chinatown.

WILL LEATHER GOODS ACCESSORIES

Map p412 (☎212-925-2824; www.willleathergoods.com; 29 Prince St, at Mott St; 🕒10am-8pm Mon-Sat, 11am-7pm Sun; [S]N/R to Prince St; 6

to Spring St) Beautifully crafted, classically styled leather goods fill this family-owned Oregon import. While you'll find everything from wallets and belts to pet leashes, it's the bags that take the breath away. Made using American and Italian leathers, products include erudite satchels, briefcases, messenger bags, jet-setter duffles, clutches and cross-body bags. The store also sells vintage pieces: US Postal Service mail bag, anyone?

3X1 FASHION
Map p412 (☎212-391-6969; www.3x1.us; 15 Mercer St, btwn Howard & Grand Sts; ⏲11am-7pm Mon-Sat, noon-6pm Sun; [S]N/Q/R, J/Z, 6 to Canal St) Design your most flattering pair of jeans at this bespoke denim factory/showroom, which offers three levels of service. Quick, on-the-spot 'ready-to-wear service' lets you choose the hem for ready-to-wear denim (women's from $195, men's from $245); 'custom service' sees you choosing the fabric and detailing for an existing fit ($525 to $750); while the 'full bespoke service' ($1200) designs your perfect pair from scratch. Ready-to-go accessories include totes, shirts and skirts.

MIN NEW YORK BEAUTY
Map p412 (☎212-206-6366; www.min.com; 117 Crosby St, btwn Jersey & Prince Sts; ⏲11am-7pm Tue-Sat, noon-6pm Mon & Sun; [S]B/D/F/M to Broadway-Lafayette St; N/R to Prince St) This chic, library-like apothecary curates an extraordinary, rotating collection of rare and exclusive perfumes, grooming products and scented candles. Esteemed and historic European lines aside, look out for artisanal American fragrances from the likes of Strangelove NYC and the Vagabond Prince, as well as MiN's own line of coveted hair products. Prices span affordable to astronomical, and there's no vulgar pressure to buy.

SATURDAYS FASHION, ACCESSORIES
Map p412 (www.saturdaysnyc.com; 31 Crosby St, btwn Broome & Grand Sts; ⏲store 10am-7pm, coffee bar 8am-7pm Mon-Fri, 10am-7pm Sat & Sun; 📶; [S]N/Q/R, J/Z, 6 to Canal St) SoHo's version of a surf shop sees boards and wax paired up with designer grooming products, graphic art and surf tomes, and Saturdays' own line of high-quality, fashion-literate threads for dudes. Styled-up, grab a coffee from the in-house espresso bar, hang in the back garden and fish for some crazy, shark-dodging

Local Life
An Artisanal Afternoon in SoHo

Shopaholics across the world lust for SoHo and its sharp, trendy whirlwind of flagship stores, coveted labels and strutting fashionistas. Look beyond the giant global brands, however, and you'll discover a whole other retail scene, one where talented artisans and independent, one-off enterprises keep things local, unique and utterly inspiring. Welcome to SoHo at its homegrown best.

A Shop with Single Origin

Charge up with a cup of single-origin coffee from [1] **Café Integral** (p98), a tiny espresso bar where you'll probably find coffee-obsessed owner César Martin Vega behind the machine. It's in shop-cum-gallery American Two Shot.

Perfect Jeans

[2] **3x1** lets you design your perfect pair of jeans. Choose hems for ready-to-wear pairs, customize fabric and detailing on existing cuts, or create your most flattering pair from scratch.

Curbside Culture

The [3] sidewalk engraving on the northwest corner of Prince St and Broadway is the work of Japanese-born sculptor Ken Hiratsuka, who has carved almost 40 sidewalks since moving to NYC in 1982. While this engraving took five or so actual hours of work, its completion took two years (1983–84), as Hiratsuka's illegal nighttime chiseling was often disrupted by police.

A Gourmet Nibble

NYC loves its luxe grocers and [4] **Dean & DeLuca** is one of the biggest names around town. If you're feeling peckish, ready-to-eat delectables include freshly baked cheese sticks, gourmet quesadillas and sugar-dusted almond croissants.

Sweets on display at Dean & DeLuca

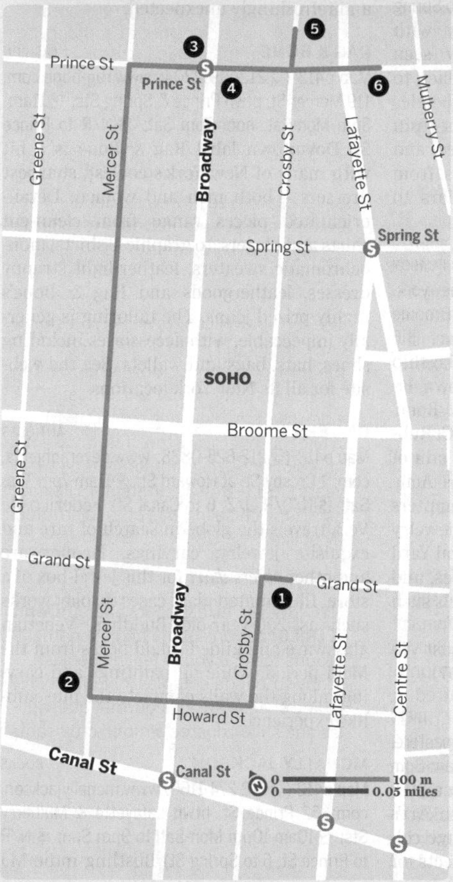

Fragrance Flights

Drop into library-like apothecary **5 MiN New York** and request a free 'fragrance flight,' a guided exploration of the store's extraordinary collection of rare, exclusive perfumes and grooming products. Look out for homegrown fragrances from the likes of Strangelove NYC and The Vagabond Prince.

Books & Conversation

If MiN ignites a passion for fragrance, scan the shelves at **6 McNally Jackson** (p102) for a title on the subject. This is one of the city's best-loved independent bookstores, stocked with cognoscenti magazines and books, and an in-house cafe for quality downtime and conversation. In short, a pleasing downtown epilogue.

tales. There's a second branch in the West Village (p159).

UNITED NUDE SHOES

Map p412 (☎212-420-6000; www.unitednude.com; 25 Bond St, btwn Lafayette St & Bowery; ⏰noon-7pm Mon, 11am-7pm Tue-Thu, 11am-8pm Fri & Sat, noon-6pm Sun; [S]6 to Bleecker St; B/D/F/M to Broadway-Lafayette St) United Nude's flagship store is stocked with improbably beautiful, statement-making footwear – flamboyant, classic, business-savvy and sporty. Whether you want strappy sandals, towering stilettos or a solid pair of wedge-heeled pumps, you'll score here. The line of men's shoes is smaller, but no less eye-catching.

EVOLUTION GIFTS

Map p412 (☎212-343-1114; www.theevolutionstore.com; 120 Spring St, btwn Mercer & Greene Sts; ⏰11am-8pm; [S]N/R to Prince St; 6 to Spring St) Evolution keeps things quirky with natural-history collectibles usually seen in museum cabinets. This is the place to buy – or simply gawk at – framed beetles and butterflies, bugs frozen in amber-resin cubes, stuffed parrots, zebra hides and shark teeth, as well as stony wonders, from meteorites and fragments from Mars to 100-million-year-old fossils.

ODIN FASHION

Map p412 (☎212-966-0026; www.odinnewyork.com; 199 Lafayette St, btwn Kenmare & Broome Sts; ⏰11am-8pm Mon-Sat, noon-7pm Sun; [S]6 to Spring St; N/R to Prince St) Odin's flagship men's boutique carries hip downtown labels such as Thom Browne, Rag & Bone, Duckie Brown and Public School NYC. Rubbing shoulders with them is a select edit of imports, among them Nordic labels Acne and Won Hundred. Other in-store tempters include Odin candles, fragrances, jewelry from Brooklyn creatives such as Naval Yard and Uhuru, Oliver Peoples sunglasses, and street-smart footwear from cult labels such as Common Projects.

You'll find other branches in the East Village (p128) and the West Village (p157).

MOMA DESIGN STORE GIFTS

Map p412 (☎646-613-1367; www.momastore.org; 81 Spring St, at Crosby St; ⏰10am-8pm Mon-Sat, 11am-7pm Sun; [S]N/R to Prince St; 6 to Spring St) The Museum of Modern Art's downtown retail space carries a huge collection of sleek, smart and clever objects for the home, office and wardrobe. You'll find modernist alarm clocks, sculptural vases and jewelry, surreal lamps, svelte kitchenware, plus brainy games, hand puppets, fanciful scarves, coffee-table tomes and loads of other unique gift ideas.

OPENING CEREMONY FASHION, SHOES

Map p412 (☎212-219-2688; www.openingceremony.us; 35 Howard St, btwn Broadway & Lafayette St; ⏰11am-8pm Mon-Sat, noon-7pm Sun; [S]N/Q/R, J/Z, 6 to Canal St) Unisex Opening Ceremony is famed for its never-boring edit of A-list indie labels. The place showcases a changing roster of names from across the globe, both established and emerging. Complimenting them is Opening Ceremony's own avant-garde creations. No matter who is hanging on the racks, you can always expect show-stopping, 'where-did-you-get-that?!' threads that are street-smart, bold and refreshingly unexpected.

RAG & BONE FASHION

Map p412 (☎212-219-2204; www.rag-bone.com; 119 Mercer St, btwn Prince & Spring Sts; ⏰11am-8pm Mon-Sat, noon-7pm Sat; [S]N/R to Prince St) Downtown label Rag & Bone is a hit with many of New York's coolest, sharpest dressers – both men and women. Detail-orientated pieces range from clean-cut shirts and blazers, to graphic T-shirts, monochromatic sweaters, feather-light strappy dresses, leathergoods and Rag & Bone's highly prized jeans. The tailoring is generally impeccable, with accessories including shoes, hats, bags and wallets. See the website for all its New York locations.

DE VERA ANTIQUES

Map p412 (☎212-625-0838; www.deveraobjects.com; 1 Crosby St, at Howard St; ⏰11am-7pm Tue-Sat; [S]N/Q/R, J/Z, 6 to Canal St) Federico de Vera travels the globe in search of rare and exquisite jewelry, carvings, lacquerware and other *objets d'art* for this jewel-box of a store. Illuminated glass cases display works such as 200-year-old Buddhas, Venetian glassware and gilded inlaid boxes from the Meiji period, while oil paintings and carvings along the walls complete the museum-like experience.

MCNALLY JACKSON BOOKS

Map p412 (☎212-274-1160; www.mcnallyjackson.com; 52 Prince St, btwn Lafayette & Mulberry Sts; ⏰10am-10pm Mon-Sat, to 9pm Sun; [S]N/R to Prince St; 6 to Spring St) Bustling indie MJ stocks an excellent selection of magazines and books covering contemporary fiction, food writing, architecture and design, art and history. The in-store cafe is a fine spot to settle in with some reading material or to catch one of the frequent readings and book signings held here.

FILLMORE & 5TH
VINTAGE

Map p412 (646-791-5458; fillmore5th.com; 398 Broome St, at Centre St; 11am-7pm Mon-Sat, noon-6pm Sun; 6 to Spring St; N/R to Prince St) Fashion is a fickle affair, as the racks at this Californian consignment store reveal. Near-new designer pieces are delivered daily and sold at mere-mortal prices, whether it's a Maison Kitsuné men's sweat top for $90, a Burberry blazer for $150, or a killer pair of Manolo Blahnik stilettos for $200. Always check the dedicated sale rack for the biggest savings.

INA MEN
VINTAGE

Map p412 (www.inanyc.com; 19 Prince St, at Elizabeth St; noon-8pm Mon-Sat, to 7pm Sun; 6 to Spring St; N/R to Prince St) Male style-meisters love INA for pre-loved, luxury clothes, shoes and accessories. Edits are high quality across the board, with sought-after items including the likes of Rag & Bone jeans, Alexander McQueen wool pants, Burberry shirts and Church's brogues. Next door is the women's store. You'll find unisex branches in **NoHo** (Map p412; 212-228-8511; 15 Bleecker St, at Elizabeth St; noon-8pm Mon-Sat, to 7pm Sun; 6 to Bleecker St; B/D/F/M to Broadway-Lafayette St) and Chelsea (p160), as well as another women's-only store in **SoHo** (Map p412; 212-941-4757; 101 Thompson Street, btwn Prince & Spring Sts; noon-8pm Mon-Sat, to 7pm Sun; C/E to Spring St).

RESURRECTION
VINTAGE

Map p412 (212-625-1374; www.resurrection vintage.com; 217 Mott St, btwn Prince & Spring Sts; 11am-7pm Mon-Fri; 6 to Spring St; N/R to Prince St) Boudoir-red Resurrection gives new life to cutting-edge designs from past decades. Striking, mint-condition pieces cover the eras of mod, glam-rock and new-wave design, and design deities such as Marc Jacobs have dropped by for inspiration. Top picks include Halston dresses and Courrèges coats and jackets.

SCREAMING MIMI'S
VINTAGE

Map p412 (212-677-6464; www.screaming mimis.com; 382 Lafayette St, btwn E 4th & Great Jones Sts; noon-8pm Mon-Sat, 1-7pm Sun; 6 to Bleecker St; B/D/F/M to Broadway-Lafayette St) If you dig vintage threads, you may just scream too. This funtastic shop carries an excellent selection of yesteryear pieces – organized, ingeniously, by decade, from the '50s to the '90s (ask to see the small, stashed-away collection of clothing from the '20s, '30s and '40s).

From prim, beaded wool cardigans to suede minidresses and white leather go-go boots, the stock is in great condition. A selection of accessories and jewelry completes any back-to-the-future look.

UNIQLO
FASHION

Map p412 (877-486-4756; www.uniqlo.com; 546 Broadway, btwn Prince & Spring Sts; 10am-9pm Mon-Sat, 11am-8pm Sun; N/R to Prince St; 6 to Spring St) This enormous three-story Japanese emporium owes its popularity to good looking, good quality apparel at discount prices. You'll find Japanese denim, Mongolian cashmere, graphic T-shirts, svelte skirts, high-tech thermals and endless racks of colorful ready-to-wear items – with most things falling below the $100 mark.

OTHER MUSIC
MUSIC

Map p412 (212-477-8150; www.othermusic.com; 15 E 4th St, btwn Lafayette St & Broadway; 11am-8pm Mon-Wed, 11am-9pm Thu & Fri, noon-8pm Sat, noon-7pm Sun; 6 to Bleecker St; B/D/F/M to Broadway-Lafayette St) This indie-run CD store feeds its loyal fan base with a clued-in selection of, well, other types of music: offbeat lounge, psychedelic, electronica, indie rock etc, available new and used. Friendly staffers like what they do, and may be able to help translate your inner musical whims and dreams to actual CD reality. OM also stocks a small but excellent selection of new and used vinyl.

HOUSING WORKS BOOK STORE
BOOKS

Map p412 (212-334-3324; www.housingworks. org/usedbookcafe; 126 Crosby St, btwn E Houston & Prince Sts; 9am-9pm Mon-Fri, 10am-5pm Sat & Sun; B/D/F/M to Broadway-Lafayette St; N/R to Prince St) Relaxed, earthy and featuring a great selection of secondhand books, vinyl, CDs and DVDs you can buy for a good cause (proceeds go to the city's HIV-positive and AIDS homeless communities), this creaky hideaway is a very local place to while away a few quiet afternoon hours (there's an in-house cafe).

Check the website for regular events, which include highly entertaining Moth StorySLAM competitions.

ADIDAS ORIGINALS SHOES, FASHION

Map p412 (☎212-673-0398; www.adidas.com; 136 Wooster St, btwn Prince & W Houston Sts; 🕐10am-9pm Mon-Sat, 11am-8pm Sun; [S]N/R to Prince St) Iconic triple-striped sneakers, many referencing Adidas' halcyon days from the '60s to the '80s, is what you get here. Kicks aside, pimp your look with hoodies, track wear, T-shirts and accessories including eye wear, watches and retro-funky bags.

For the big-box retail experience, head to the 29,500-sq-ft **Adidas** (Map p412; ☎212-529-0081; www.adidas.com; 610 Broadway, at Houston St; 🕐10am-7pm Mon-Thu, 10am-8pm Fri & Sat, 11am-7pm Sun; [S]B/D/F/M to Broadway-Lafayette St; N/R to Prince St) sneaker emporium a few blocks back.

SPORTS & ACTIVITIES

GREAT JONES SPA SPA

Map p412 (☎212-505-3185; www.greatjonesspa.com; 29 Great Jones St, btwn Lafayette St & Bowery; 🕐9am-10pm; [S]6 to Bleecker St; B/D/F/M to Broadway-Lafayette St) Don't skimp on the services at this downtown feng shui master, whose offerings include Moroccan rose sea salt scrubs and stem-cell facials. If you spend over $100 per person (not hard: hour-long massages start at $145, hour-long facials start at $135), you get three-hour access to the water lounge and its thermal hot tub, river rock sauna, chakra-light steam room and cold plunge pool. Swimwear is essential.

DOWNTOWN BOATHOUSE KAYAKING

Map p410 (www.downtownboathouse.org; Pier 26, near N Moore St; 🕐9am-4:30pm Sat & Sun mid-May–mid-Oct, 5-6:30pm Mon-Fri Jul & Aug; [S]1 to Houston St) New York's most active public boathouse offers free walk-up 20-minute kayaking sessions (including equipment) in a protected embayment in the Hudson River on weekends and some weekday evenings. For more activities – kayaking trips, stand-up paddle boarding and classes, check out www.hudsonriverpark.org for the four other kayaking locations on the Hudson River. There's also a summer-only kayaking location on Governors Island (p75).

East Village & Lower East Side

EAST VILLAGE | LOWER EAST SIDE

Neighborhood Top Five

❶ Admiring the off-white webbing of the boxy facade of the **New Museum of Contemporary Art** (p108), then wandering in to appreciate mind-bending iterations of art across myriad media.

❷ Witnessing the shockingly cramped conditions of early immigrants at the brilliantly curated **Lower East Side Tenement Museum** (p107).

❸ Passing knickknack shops and sake bars on **St Marks Place** (p110), then heading to the neighboring streets for a quieter round of nibbling and boutique-ing.

❹ Pub-crawling through **Alphabet City**, stopping en route at **Rue B** (p119) for jazz and **Wayland** (p122) for moonshine cocktails.

❺ Snacking on a tantalizing array of global dishes such as upscale Indian street food at **Babu Ji** (p115).

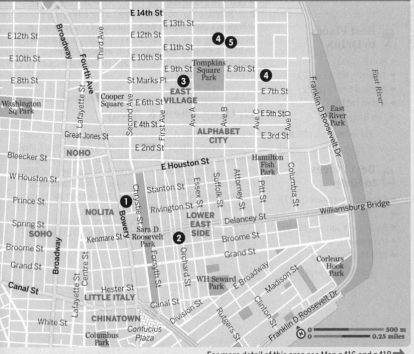

For more detail of this area see Map p416 and p418 ➡

Lonely Planet's Top Tip

A lot of the restaurants in this neck of the woods don't take reservations, so stop by the restaurant of your choosing in the early afternoon (2pm should do the trick) and place your name on the roster for the evening meal – chances are high that they'll take your name and you'll get seated right away when you return for dinner later on.

 Best Places to Eat

➡ Upstate (p115)
➡ Degustation (p116)
➡ El Rey (p116)
➡ Fung Tu (p119)
➡ Momofuku Noodle Bar (p114)

For reviews, see p113 ➡

 Best Places to Drink

➡ Rue B (p119)
➡ Jimmy's No 43 (p122)
➡ Angel's Share (p122)
➡ Berlin (p119)
➡ Ten Bells (p124)

For reviews, see p119 ➡

 Best Places to Shop

➡ Obscura Antiques (p127)
➡ A-1 Records (p127)
➡ By Robert James (p129)
➡ Verameat (p127)
➡ Still House (p127)

For reviews, see p127 ➡

Explore the East Village & Lower East Side

If you've been dreaming of those quintessential New York City moments – graffiti on crimson brick, skyscrapers rising overhead, punks and grannies walking side by side, and cute cafes with rickety tables spilling out onto the sidewalks – then the East Village is your Holy Grail. Stick to the area around Tompkins Square Park, and the lettered avenues (known as Alphabet City) to its east, for interesting little nooks in which to eat and drink – as well as a collection of great little community gardens that provide leafy respite and the occasional live performance. The streets below 14th St and east of First Ave are packed with cool boutiques and excellent snack-food spots, offering styles and flavors from around the world. It's a mixed bag, indeed, and perhaps one of the most emblematic of today's city.

Local Life

➡ **One block over** Famed St Marks Place draws swarms of people shopping and carousing – though it's a bit of a circus most days. Hop a block over in either direction for some great retail and restaurant finds with half the crowds.

➡ **Taste the rainbow** The East Village and the Lower East Side are like no other place in the city when it comes to sampling the finest spread of ethnic cuisine. Many of the area's restaurants don't take reservations, so have a wander and grab an open table to eat-pray-love your way through Italy, India, Indonesia or anywhere in between.

Getting There & Away

➡ **Subway** Trains don't go far enough east to carry you to most East Village locations, but it's a quick walk (and even quicker cab or bus ride) from the 6 at Astor Pl, the F, V at Lower East Side-Second Ave or the L at First or Third Aves. The subway's F line (Lower East Side-Second Ave or Delancey St stops) will let you off in the thick of the Lower East Side.

➡ **Bus** If you're traveling from the west side, it's convenient to take the M14 (across 14th St) or the M21 (down Houston).

TOP SIGHT
LOWER EAST SIDE TENEMENT MUSEUM

There's no museum in New York that humanizes the city's colorful past quite like the Lower East Side Tenement Museum, which puts the neighborhood's heartbreaking but inspiring heritage on full display in several re-creations of former tenements. Always evolving and expanding, the museum has a variety of tours and talks beyond the museum's walls – a must for anyone interested in old New York.

Inside the Tenement
A wide range of tenement tours lead visitors into the building where hundreds of immigrants lived and worked over the years. Hard Times, one of the most popular tours, visits apartments from two different time periods – the 1870s and the 1930s. There you'll see the squalid conditions tenants faced – in the early days there was a wretched communal outhouse, and no electricity or running water – and what life was like for the families who lived there. Other tours focus on Irish immigrants and the harsh discrimination they faced, sweatshop workers and 'shop life' (with a tour through a re-created 1870s German beer hall).

Neighborhood Tours
A great way to understand the immigrant experience is on a walking tour around the neighborhood. These tours, ranging from 75 minutes to two hours, explore a variety of topics. Foods of the Lower East Side looks at the ways traditional foods have shaped American cuisine; Then & Now explores the way the neighborhood has changed over the decades; Outside the Home looks at life beyond the apartment – where immigrants stored (and lost) their life savings, the churches and synagogues so integral to community life, and the meeting halls where poorly paid workers gathered to fight for better conditions.

Meet Victoria
Travel back to 1916 and meet Victoria Confino, a 14-year-old girl from a Greek Sephardic family. Played by a costumed interpreter, Victoria interacts with visitors answering questions about what her life was like in those days. It's especially recommended for kids, as visitors are free to handle household objects. This one-hour tour is held on weekends year-round, and daily during the summer.

103 Orchard St
The visitor center at 103 Orchard St has a museum shop and a small screening room that plays an original film. Several evenings a month, the museum hosts talks here, often relating to the present immigrant experience in America. The building itself was, naturally, a tenement too – ask the staff about the interesting families of East European and Italian descent that once dwelled here.

DON'T MISS
- Themed walks around the neighborhood
- A peek into the 1870s and the 1930s on the Hard Times tour
- The free 30-minute film shown in the visitor center
- The outhouses

PRACTICALITIES
- Map p418
- ☎877-975-3786
- www.tenement.org
- 103 Orchard St, btwn Broome & Delancey Sts
- adult/student from $25/20
- ⏲tours 10:15am-5pm Fri-Wed, to 6:30pm Thu
- [S]B/D to Grand St; J/M/Z to Essex St; F to Delancey St

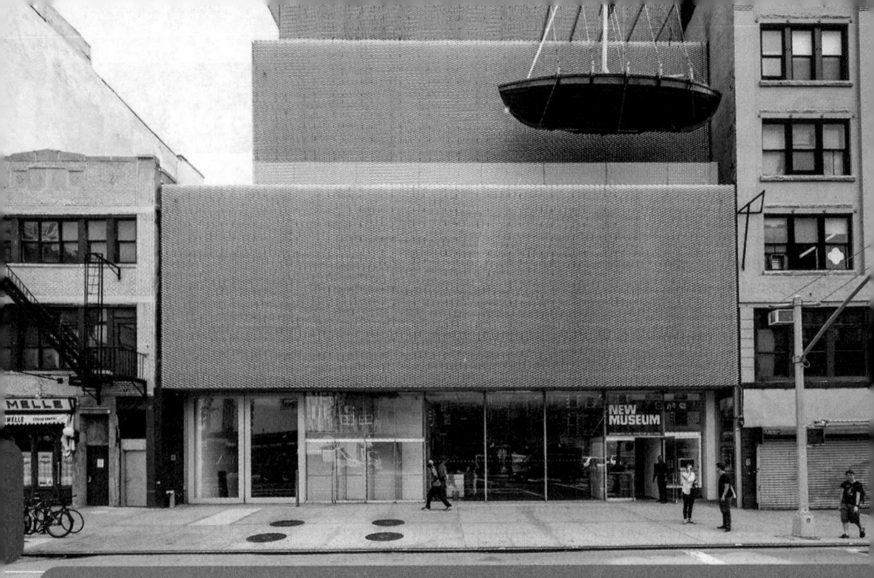

TOP SIGHT
NEW MUSEUM OF CONTEMPORARY ART

For any modern-day museum worth its salt, the structure makes just as much of a statement as the artwork inside. The New Museum of Contemporary Art's Lower East Side avatar accomplishes just that and more with its inspired design by noted Japanese architecture firm SANAA. The Lower East Side has seen its fair share of physical changes over the last two decades as the sweeping hand of gentrification has cleaned up slummy nooks and replaced them with glittering residential blocks. The New Museum manages to punctuate the neighborhood with something unique, and its cache of artistic work will dazzle and confuse just as much as its facade.

A Museum With a Mission

Founded in 1977 by Marcia Tucker and housed in five different locations over the years, the museum's mission statement is simple: 'New art, new ideas.' The institution gave gallery space to artists Keith Haring, Jeff Koons, Joan Jonas, Mary Kelly and Andres Serrano at the beginning of their careers, and continues to show contemporary heavy hitters. The city's sole museum dedicated to contemporary art has brought a steady menu of edgy works in new forms, such as seemingly random, discarded materials fused together and displayed in the middle of a vast room.

The museum also houses the New Museum Cafe, a great spot for sampling the gourmet goodies of NYC purveyors, including baked goods by Cafe Grumpy, teas by McNulty, coffee by Intelligentsia and sandwiches by Duck's Eatery.

DON'T MISS

- The facade from across the street
- Pay-what-you-wish Thursday evening
- New Museum Cafe
- New Museum Store

PRACTICALITIES

- Map p418
- ☎ 212-219-1222
- www.newmuseum.org
- 235 Bowery, btwn Stanton & Rivington Sts
- adult/child $16/free, 7-9pm Thu by donation
- 🕒 11am-6pm Wed & Fri-Sun, to 9pm Thu
- [S] N/R to Prince St; F to Second Ave; J/Z to Bowery; 6 to Spring St

In Orbit

It's now been several years since the New Museum has taken hold, inspiring nearby structures to adopt similarly ethereal designs. Perhaps most interestingly the museum has become somewhat of a magnetic force attracting a clutch of small workshops and creative spaces (p113) to its orbit.

SANAA's Vision

While exhibits rotate through the museum, regularly changing the character of the space within, the shell – an inspired architectural gesture – remains a constant, acting as a unique structural element in the diverse cityscape, while also simultaneously fading into the background and allowing the exhibits to shine.

The building's structure is the brainchild of the hot Japanese firm SANAA – a partnership between two great minds, Kazuyo Sejima and Ryue Nishizawa. In 2010 SANAA won the coveted Pritzker Prize (think the Oscars of architecture) for their contributions to the world of design. Their trademark vanishing facades are known worldwide for abiding by a strict adherence to a form-follows-function design aesthetic, sometimes taking the land plot's footprint into the overall shape of the structure. The box-atop-box scheme provides a striking counterpoint to the clusters of crimson brick and iron fire escapes outside, while alluding to the geometric exhibition chasms within.

DISCOUNTED ADMISSION

To save cash, stop by on Thursday evening between 7pm and 9pm, when admission is pay what you wish. Depending on the show, the crowds can be sizable. We recommend lining up by 6:45pm.

MUSEUM SHOP

If you aren't so keen on the current exhibits, it's still worth stopping by the museum's store to peruse some of the excellent coffee-table books – sometimes the take-homes include savvy collaborations with showcased artists. The shop has the same hours of operation as the museum.

FIRST SATURDAYS

On the first Saturday of the month, the New Museum hosts special events for budding artists, with hands-on crafts and activities for kids aged four to 15. Free museum admission is included for adults (it's always free for kids).

EAST VILLAGE & LOWER EAST SIDE NEW MUSEUM OF CONTEMPORARY ART

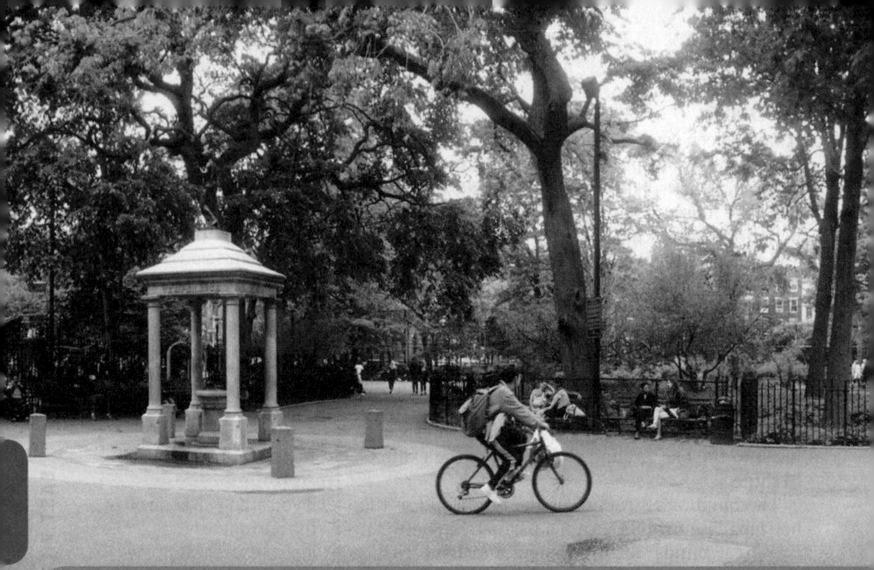

MICHAEL MARQUAND / GETTY IMAGES ©

TOP SIGHT
ST MARKS PLACE

One of the most magical things about New York is that every street tells a story, from the action unfurling before your eyes to the dense history hidden behind colorful facades. St Marks Place is one of the best strips of pavement in the city for story telling, as almost every building on these hallowed blocks is rife with tales from a time when the East Village embodied a far more lawless spirit. Technically St Marks Place is 8th St between Third Ave and Ave A; it earned its saintly moniker from the like-named church nearby on 10th St.

Astor Place

To the west of St Marks Place is **Astor Place** (8th St, btwn Third & Fourth Aves; [S]N/R to 8th St-NYU; 6 to Astor Pl), a crowded crisscrossing of streets anchored by a curious square sculpture that's affectionately (and appropriately) known by locals as *The Cube*. A favorite meeting spot for neighborhood dwellers, this work of art – actually named *Alamo* – weighs over 1800 pounds and is made entirely of Cor-Tensteel.

Originally Astor Place was the home of the Astor Opera House (now gone), which attracted the city's wealthy elite for regular performances in the mid-1800s. The square was also the site of the notorious Astor Place riots, in which the city's protesting Irish population caused such a stir about their homeland potato famine that the police fired shots into the masses, injuring hundreds and killing at least 18 people.

Today the square is largely known as the home of the Village Voice and the **Cooper Union** (Foundation Building, Great Hall; www.cooper.edu; 7 E 7th St, btwn Third & Fourth Aves; [S]6 to Astor Pl, N/R to 8th St-NYU) design institute.

DON'T MISS

- The *Physical Graffiti* buildings made famous by Led Zeppelin (numbers 96 and 98)
- Brunch at one of the tasty cafes
- Tompkins Square Park at the end of the street
- Sake bombs at one of the basement Japanese bars
- Shopping for knick-knacks and odd souvenirs

PRACTICALITIES

- Map p416
- St Marks Pl, Ave A to Third Ave
- [S]N/R/W to 8th St-NYU; 6 to Astor Pl

Third Ave to Ave A

Easily one of NYC's most famous streets, St Marks Place is also one of the city's smallest, occupying only three blocks between Astor Pl and Tompkins Square Park. The road, however, is jam-packed with historical tidbits that would delight any trivia buff. Number 2 St Marks Place is known as the St Mark's Ale House, but for a time it was the famous Five-Spot, where jazz fiend Thelonious Monk got his start in the 1950s. A cast of colorful characters have left their mark at 4 St Marks Place: Alexander Hamilton's son built the structure, James Fenimore Cooper lived here in the 1830s and Yoko Ono's Fluxus artists descended upon the building in the 1960s. The buildings at 96 and 98 St Marks Place are immortalized on the cover of Led Zepellin's *Physical Graffiti* album. Though it closed in the 1990s, number 122 St Marks Place was the location of a popular cafe called Sin-é, where Jeff Buckley and David Gray often performed.

Tompkins Square Park

St Marks Place terminates at a welcome clearing of green deep in the heart of the East Village. The 10.5-acre **Tompkins Square Park** (www.nycgovparks. org; E 7th & 10th Sts, btwn Aves A & B; ⊘6am-midnight; S6 to Astor Pl) honors Daniel Tompkins, who served as governor of New York from 1807 to 1817 (and as the nation's vice president after that, under James Monroe). It's like a friendly town square for locals, who gather for chess at concrete tables, picnics on the lawn on warm days and spontaneous guitar or drum jams on various grassy knolls. It's also the site of basketball courts, a fun-to-watch dog run (a fenced-in area where humans can unleash their canines), frequent summer concerts and an always-lively kids' playground. The park, which recently underwent a facelift, wasn't always a place for such clean fun, however. In the '80s it was a dirty, needle-strewn homeless encampment, unusable for folks wanting a place to stroll or picnic. A contentious turning point came when police razed the band shell and evicted more than 100 squatters living in a tent city in the park in 1988 (and again in 1991). That first eviction turned violent; the Tompkins Square Riot, as it came to be known, ushered in the first wave of yuppies in the dog run, fashionistas lolling in the grass and undercover narcotics agents trying to pass as druggie punk kids. There's not much drama here these days, unless you count the annual Howl! Festival of East Village Arts, which brings Allen Ginsberg–inspired theater, music, film, dance and spoken-word events to the park each September.

TOP BRUNCH SPOTS

In addition to all of its quirky and historical landmarks, St Marks has some wonderful places to stop for a bite. Weekend brunches in the East Village are a great bet, as the local restaurants are typically less expensive (and less scene-y) than the hotspots in neighboring 'hoods. Try Cafe Mogador (p115), which fuses American favorites with an assortment of Middle Eastern plates.

PUNK ROCK SHOPS

The East Village was once the home base for emerging punk rock acts – many would frequent the clothing shops along St Marks to assemble their trademark looks. Although most joints have gone the way of the dodo in favor of more tourist-friendly wares, there are still a few spots that remain.

SIGHTS

East Village

★ST MARKS PLACE STREET

See p110.

TOMPKINS SQUARE PARK PARK

See p111

ST MARK'S IN THE BOWERY CHURCH

Map p416 (☎212-674-6377; www.stmarksbowery.org; 131 E 10th St, at Second Ave; 🕘10am-6pm Mon-Fri; [S]L to Third Ave; 6 to Astor Pl) Though it's most popular with East Village locals for its cultural offerings – such as poetry readings hosted by the Poetry Project or cutting-edge dance performances from Danspace and the Ontological Hysteric Theater – St Mark's is also a historic site. This Episcopal church stands on the site of the farm, or *bouwerij*, owned by Dutch Governor Peter Stuyvesant, whose crypt lies under the grounds.

EAST RIVER PARK PARK

Map p416 (www.nycgovparks.org/parks/east-river-park; FDR Dr & E Houston St; 🕘sunrise to 1am; [S]F to Delancey-Essex Sts) In addition to the great ballparks, running and biking paths, 5000-seat amphitheater that hosts concerts and expansive patches of green, this park has cool, natural breezes and fine views of the Williamsburg, Manhattan and Brooklyn Bridges.

Although flanked by a looming housing project and the clogged FDR Dr on one side and the less-than-pure East River on the other, it's a fine spot for a stroll or a morning run.

Lower East Side

★LOWER EAST SIDE TENEMENT MUSEUM MUSEUM

See p107.

★NEW MUSEUM OF CONTEMPORARY ART MUSEUM

See p108.

ANASTASIA PHOTO GALLERY

Map p418 (www.anastasia-photo.com; 143 Ludlow St, btwn Stanton & Rivington Sts; 🕘11am-7pm Tue-Sun; [S]F to Delancey St; J/M/Z to Essex St) This small gallery specializes in documentary photography and photojournalism. Expect evocative, thought-provoking works covering subjects such as poverty in rural America, the ravages of war and disappearing cultures in Africa. Works are beautifully shot, and the staff member on hand can give a meaningful context to the images.

MUSEUM AT ELDRIDGE STREET SYNAGOGUE MUSEUM

Map p418 (☎212-219-0302; www.eldridgestreet.org; 12 Eldridge St, btwn Canal & Division Sts; adult/child $12/8, Mon free; 🕘10am-5pm Sun-Thu, 10am-3pm Fri; [S]F to East Broadway) This landmark house of worship, built in 1887, was once the center of Jewish life, before falling into squalor in the 1920s. Left to rot, the synagogue was restored following a 20-year-long, $20-million restoration that was completed in 2007, and it now shines with original splendor. Museum admission includes a tour of the synagogue, which departs hourly, with the last one starting at 4pm.

KEHILA KEDOSHA JANINA SYNAGOGUE & MUSEUM SYNAGOGUE

Map p418 (☎212-431-1619; www.kkjsm.org; 280 Broome St, at Allen St; 🕘11am-4pm Sun, service 9am Sat; [S]F, J/M/Z to Delancey-Essex Sts) This small synagogue is home to an obscure branch of Judaism, the Romaniotes, whose ancestors were slaves sent to Rome by ship but rerouted to Greece by a storm. This is their only synagogue in the Western Hemisphere, and includes a small museum bearing artifacts such as hand-painted birth certificates, an art gallery, a Holocaust memorial for Greek Jews and costumes from Janina, the Romaniote capital of Greece.

SARA D ROOSEVELT PARK PARK

Map p418 (Houston St, at Chrystie St; [S]F to Delancey-Essex Sts) Spiffed up in recent years, this three-block-long park is a hive of activity on weekends, with basketball courts, a small soccer pitch (with synthetic turf) and a well-loved playground (just north of Hester St). Tai-chi practitioners, vegetable sellers (on the nearby cross streets) and strollers of all ages and ethnic backgrounds add to the ever-evolving scene.

LOWER EAST SIDE GALLERIES

Though Chelsea may be the heavy hitter when it comes to the New York gallery scene, the Lower East Side has dozens of quality showplaces. One of the early pioneers, the **Sperone Westwater** (Map p418; www.speronewestwater.com; 257 Bowery; ⏰10am-6pm Tue-Sat; [S]F to 2nd Ave) gallery (opened in 1975) represents heavy hitters such as William Wegman and Richard Long, and its new home was designed by the famed Norman Foster, who's already made a splash in NYC with his Hearst Building and Avery Fisher Hall designs. Nearby the avant-garde **Salon 94** has two Lower East Side outposts: one secreted away on **Freeman Alley** (Map p418; www.salon94.com; 1 Freeman Alley, off Rivington; ⏰11am-6pm Wed-Sat; [S]F to 2nd Ave; J/Z to Bowery) and another on **Bowery** (Map p418; www.salon94.com; 243 Bowery, cnr Stanton St; ⏰11am-6pm Tue-Sat, from 1pm Sun; [S]F to 2nd Ave; J/Z to Bowery) near the New Museum of Contemporary Art. The latter has a 20ft LCD video wall that broadcasts video art out into the street. A few blocks north is the 4000-sq-ft **Hole** (theholenyc.com; 312 Bowery, at Bleecker; ⏰noon-7pm Wed-Sun; [S]6 to Bleeker St; B/D/F/M to Broadway-Lafayette St) – known as much for its art as it is for its rowdy openings that gather both scenesters of the downtown art circuit and well-known faces such as Courtney Love and Salman Rushdie.

Broome St between Chrystie and Bowery is quickly becoming the nexus of the Lower East Side art scene, with galleries such as White Box, Canada and Jack Hanley right next door to one another. Another buzzing strip of galleries runs down Orchard St between Rivington and Canal St.

Other popular, contemporary spaces include **Lehmann Maupin** (Map p418; ☎212-254-0054; www.lehmannmaupin.com; 201 Chrystie St; ⏰11am-6pm Wed-Sun; [S]F to Delancey-Essex Sts), **Mark Miller Gallery** (Map p418; www.markmillergallery.com; 92 Orchard St, btwn Delancey & Broome; ⏰noon-6pm Wed-Sun; [S]F to Delancey St; J/M/Z to Essex St), **Mesler Feuer** (Map p418; meslerfeuer.com; 30 Orchard St, btwn Canal & Hester; ⏰11am-6pm Wed-Sun; [S]F to East Broadway; B/D to Grand St) and **Lesley Heller** (Map p418; www.lesleyheller.com; 54 Orchard St, btwn Grand & Hester; ⏰11am-6pm Wed-Sat, from noon Sun; [S]B/D to Grand St; F to East Broadway).

🍴 EATING

Here lies the epitome of what is beautiful in New York's dining scene: mind-blowing variety – which can cover the full spectrum of continents and budgets – in just a single city block. You'll find every type of taste-bud tantalizer from Ukrainian *pierogi* (dumpling) palaces and dozens of sushi joints to pizza parlors and falafel huts. There's tons of Indian fare too, especially on the carnival-esque strip of E 6th St between First and Second Aves, otherwise known as Curry Row, where cheap, decent restaurants from the subcontinent are a dime a dozen.

🍴 East Village

VESELKA — EASTERN EUROPEAN $

Map p416 (☎212-228-9682; www.veselka.com; 144 Second Ave, at 9th St; mains $10-19; ⏰24hr; [S]L to Third Ave; 6 to Astor Pl) A bustling tribute to the area's Ukrainian past, Veselka dishes out *varenyky* (handmade dumplings) and veal goulash amid the usual suspects of greasy comfort food. The cluttered spread of tables is available to loungers and carbo-loaders all night long, though it's a favorite any time of day.

TACOS MORELOS — MEXICAN $

Map p416 (☎347-772-5216; 438 E 9th St, btwn First Ave & Ave A; tacos from $3; ⏰noon-midnight Sun-Thu, to 1:30am Fri & Sat; [S]L to First Ave) This famed food truck put down roots in a no-frills East Village storefront in 2013, quickly becoming one of downtown's favorite taco joints. Order yours with chicken, steak, roast pork, beef tongue or vegetarian. Tip: pay the $0.50 extra for the home-made tortilla.

MUD — CAFE $

Map p416 (☎212-228-9074; www.onmud.com; 307 E 9th St, btwn Second & First Aves; mains $8-14; ⏰8am-midnight; [S]L to Third Ave; L to First Ave; 4/6 to Astor Pl) Offering trustworthy beans and an all-day breakfast that hits the spot after a late night out, this 9th St nook is a favorite among East Villagers looking for a quick caffeine fix or a friendly place to chat with old friends. The everyday brunch (coffee, craft beer or mimosa and any main course) is a deal at $18.

Keep an eye out for the MUD trucks that roam the city streets; there's also a handy kiosk in the tiny plaza (that's been rechristened 'Mud Park') on First Ave and 1st St.

PORCHETTA SANDWICHES $

Map p416 (☎212-777-2151; www.porchettanyc.com; 110 E 7th St; sandwiches $10-12; ⏲11:30am-10pm Sun-Thu, to 11pm Fri & Sat; [S]6 to Astor Pl; F to second Ave) This tiny white-tiled storefront serves tender, boneless roasted pork that's been wrapped in a pork belly and seasoned with fennel pollen, rosemary, sage, thyme and garlic, available in sandwich or platter-with-sides versions.

MIGHTY QUINN'S BARBECUE $

Map p416 (☎212-677-3733; www.mightyquinnsbbq.com; 103 Second Ave, at 6th St; mains $8-10; ⏲11:30am-11pm Sun-Thu, to midnight Fri & Sat; [S]6 to Astor Pl; F to Second Ave) Grab yourself a tray and join hordes of barbecue lovers at this buzzing, very popular meat eatery. Tender brisket, smoky spare ribs, juicy piles of pulled pork and ample portions of sides (coleslaw, sweet potato casserole, baked beans) add up to a decadent carnivorous feast. There's also a location in the West Village.

RAI RAI KEN RAMEN $

Map p416 (☎212-477-7030; 218 E 10th St, btwn First & Second Aves; ramen $10-13; ⏲noon-midnight Mon-Thu, to 2am Fri & Sat; [S]L to First Ave; 6 to Astor Pl) Rai Rai Ken's storefront may only be the size of its door, but it's pretty hard to miss since there's usually a small congregation of hungry locals lurking out the front. Inside, low-slung wooden stools are arranged around the noodle bar, where the cooks busily churn out piping-hot portions of tasty pork-infused broth.

★**MOMOFUKU NOODLE BAR** NOODLES $$

Map p416 (☎212-777-7773; noodlebar-ny.momofuku.com; 171 First Ave, btwn 10th & 11th Sts; mains $17-28; ⏲noon-11pm Sun-Thu, to 1am Fri & Sat; [S]L to First Ave; 6 to Astor Pl) With just 30 stools and a no-reservations policy, you will always have to wait to cram into this tiny phenomenon. Queue up for the namesake special: homemade ramen noodles in broth, served with poached egg, pork belly and pork shoulder or some interesting combos. The menu changes daily and includes buns (such as brisket and horseradish), snacks (smoked chicken wings) and desserts.

The open kitchen creates quite a bit of smoke, but the crowd remains unfazed.

COMMUNITY GARDENS

After a stretch of arboreal abstinence in New York City, the community gardens of Alphabet City are breathtaking. A network of gardens was carved out of abandoned lots to provide low-income neighborhoods with a communal backyard. Trees and flowers were planted, sandboxes were built, found-art sculptures erected and domino games played – all within green spaces wedged between buildings or even claiming entire blocks. And while some were destroyed – in the face of much protest – to make way for the projects of developers, plenty of green spots have held their ground. You can visit most on weekends, when the gardens tend to be open to the public; many gardeners are activists within the community and are a good source of information about local politics.

Le Petit Versailles (Map p416; alliedproductions.org; 346 E Houston St, at Ave C; ⏲2-7pm Thu-Sun; [S]F to Delancey St; J/M/Z to Essex St) is a unique marriage of a verdant oasis and an electrifying arts organization, offering a range of quirky performances and screenings to the public. The **6th & B Garden** (Map p416; www.6bgarden.org; E 6th St & Ave B; ⏲1-6pm Sat & Sun Apr-Oct; [S]6 to Astor Pl; L to 1st Ave) is a well-organized space that hosts free music events, workshops and yoga sessions; check the website for details. Three dramatic weeping willows, an odd sight in the city, grace the twin plots of **9th St Garden & La Plaza Cultural** (Map p416; www.laplazacultural.com; E 9th St, at Ave C; ⏲10am-7pm Sat & Sun Apr-Oct; [S]F to 2nd Ave; L to 1st Ave). Also check out the **All People's Garden** (Map p416; www.allpeoplesgarden.org; 293 E 3rd St, btwn Aves C & D; ⏲1-5pm Sat & Sun Apr-Oct; [S]F to 2nd Ave) and **Brisas del Caribe** (Map p416; 237 E 3rd St; ⏲1-5pm Sat & Sun Apr-Oct; [S]F to 2nd Ave).

Momofuku is part of David Chang's crazy popular restaurant empire (www.momofuku.com) that includes two-Michelin-starred Momofuku Ko, which serves up pricey ($175) tasting menus and has a prohibitive, we-dare-you-to-try reservations scheme; Momofuku Ssäm Bar, which features large and small meat-heavy dishes; and Momofuku Milk Bar with its decadent desserts and snacks.

UPSTATE SEAFOOD $$

Map p416 (☎212-460-5293; www.upstatenyc.com; 95 First Ave, btwn 5th & 6th Sts; mains $15-30; 🕐5-11pm; [S]F to Second Ave) Upstate serves outstanding seafood dishes and craft beers. The small, always-changing menu features the likes of beer-steamed mussels, seafood stew, scallops over mushroom risotto, soft-shell crab and wondrous oyster selections. There's no freezer – seafood comes from the market each day, so you know you'll be getting only the freshest ingredients. Lines can be long, so go early.

BABU JI INDIAN $$

Map p416 (☎212-951-182; www.babujinyc.com; 175 Ave B, btwn 11th & 12 Sts; mains $16-25; 🕐6pm-late Mon-Sat; [S]L to First Ave) A playful spirit marks this excellent Australian-run Indian restaurant in Alphabet City. You can assemble a meal from street-food–style dishes such as *papadi chaat* (chickpeas, pomegranate and yogurt chutney) and potato croquettes stuffed with lobster, or feast on heartier dishes such as tandoori lamb chops or scallop coconut curry.

It all happens beneath the benevolent gaze of *babujis* (respected elders), whose photos adorn the walls.

LAVAGNA ITALIAN $$

Map p416 (☎212-979-1005; www.lavagnanyc.com; 545 E 5th St, btwn Aves A & B; mains $19-35; 🕐6-11pm Mon-Thu, to midnight Fri, noon-midnight Sat & Sun; 🥕👪; [S]F to Second Ave) Dark wood, flickering candles and a fiery glow from a somewhat open kitchen help make homey Lavagna a late-night hideaway for lovers. But it's laid-back enough to make it appropriate for children, at least in the early hours before the smallish space fills up. Delicious pastas, thin-crust pizzas and hearty mains, such as baby rack of lamb, are standard fare. Come early (6pm to 7pm nightly) for a $35 three-course prix-fixe special.

CAFE MOGADOR MOROCCAN $$

Map p416 (☎212-677-2226; www.cafemogador.com; 101 St Marks Pl; mains lunch $8-14, dinner $17-21; 🕐9am-midnight; [S]6 to Astor Pl) Family-run Mogador is a long-running NYC classic serving fluffy piles of couscous, char-grilled lamb and merguez sausage over basmati rice, as well as satisfying mixed platters of hummus and baba ganoush. The standouts, however, are the tagines – traditionally spiced, long-simmered chicken or lamb dishes served up five different ways.

A garrulous young crowd packs the space, spilling out onto the small cafe tables on warm days. Brunch (served weekends from 9am to 4pm) is excellent.

LUZZO'S PIZZA $$

Map p416 (☎212-473-7447; www.luzzosgroup.com; 211 First Ave, btwn 12th & 13th Sts; pizzas $18-26; 🕐noon-11pm Sun-Thu, to midnight Fri & Sat; [S]L to First Ave) Fan-favorite Luzzo's occupies a thin sliver of real estate in the East Village, which gets stuffed to the gills each evening as discerning diners feast on thin-crust pies, kissed with ripe tomatoes and cooked in a coal-fired stove.

MOTORINO PIZZA $$

Map p416 (☎212-777-2644; www.motorinopizza.com; 349 E 12th St, btwn First & Second Aves; individual pizza $15-18; 🕐11am-midnight Sun-Thu, to 1am Fri & Sat; 🥕; [S]L to First Ave; 4/5/6 to 14th St-Union Sq) On a restaurant-lined strip of the East Village, this intimate eatery serves up excellent pizzas with perfect pillowy crusts.

REDHEAD SOUTHERN $$

Map p416 (☎212-533-6212; www.theredheadnyc.com; 349 E 13th St, btwn First & Second Aves; mains $15-25; 🕐5:30pm-1am Mon-Sat, 5-10pm Sun; [S]L to First Ave; L to Third Ave; 6 to Astor Pl) Cozy corners of exposed brick and warm smiles from the staff mirror the home-style comfort food, which has a distinctly Southern bent. There are stacks of fried chicken and rounds of pucker-inducing cocktails on everyone else's table – you should follow suit.

ANGELICA KITCHEN VEGETARIAN $$

Map p416 (☎212-228-2909; www.angelicakitchen.com; 300 E 12th St, btwn First & Second Aves; mains $17-21; 🕐11:30am-10:30pm; 🥕; [S]L to First Ave) This enduring herbivore classic has a calming vibe – candles, tables both intimate and communal, and mellow, long-time staff – and enough creative options to make your head spin. Some dishes get too-cute names

(Goodnight Mushroom, Thai Mee Up), but all do wonders with tofu, seitan, spices and soy products, and sometimes an array of raw ingredients. There's brunch on weekends.

IPPUDO NY NOODLES **$$**

Map p416 (☎212-388-0088; www.ippudo.com/ny; 65 Fourth Ave, btwn 9th & 10th Sts; ramen $15; 🕐11am-3:30pm & 5pm-11:30pm Mon-Fri, 11am-11:30pm Sat, 11am-10:30pm Sun; [S]N/R to 8th St-NYU; 4/5/6 to 14th St-Union Sq; 6 to Astor Pl) The good folks from Ippudo have kicked things up a notch here – they've taken their mouthwatering ramen recipe (truly, it's delicious) and spiced it up with sleek surrounds (hello shiny black surfaces and streamers of cherry red) and blasts of rock and roll on the overhead speakers.

DEGUSTATION MODERN EUROPEAN **$$$**

Map p416 (☎212-979-1012; degustation-nyc.com; 239 E 5th St btwn Second & Third Aves; small plates $12-22, tasting menu $85; 🕐6pm-11:30pm Mon-Sat, to 10pm Sun; [S]6 to Astor Pl) Blending Iberian, French and new world recipes, Degustation does a beautiful array of tapas-style plates at this narrow 19-seat eatery. It's an intimate setting, with guests seated around a long wooden counter, and chef Nicholas Licata and team at center stage firing up crisp octopus, lamb belly with soft poached egg and paella with blue prawns and chorizo.

For the full experience, opt for the seven-course tasting menu.

PRUNE AMERICAN **$$$**

Map p416 (☎212-677-6221; www.prunerestaurant.com; 54 E 1st St, btwn First & Second Aves; mains brunch $14-22, dinner $25-32; 🕐10am-3:30pm Sat & Sun, 5:30-11pm daily; [S]F/V to Lower East Side-Second Ave) Expect lines around the block on the weekend, when the hungover show up to cure their ills with Prune's brunches and excellent Bloody Marys (in 11 varieties). The small room is always busy as diners pour in for grilled trout with mint and almond salsa, seared duck breast and rich sweetbreads. Reservations available for dinner only.

🍴 Lower East Side

EL REY CAFE **$**

Map p418 (☎212-260-3950; elreynyc.com; 100 Stanton St, btwn Orchard & Ludlow; small plates $7-17; 🕐7am-10:30pm Mon-Fri, from 8am Sat & Sun; ✎; [S]F to Second Ave) This white, minimalist space on Stanton feels more SoCal than LES, and has earned a huge following for its delectably inventive (and fairly priced) farm-to-table plates with plenty of vegan options. Stop by at lunchtime for a frittata with shaved fennel salad or roasted beets with granola and yogurt, or come at evening for octopus salad with black-bean puree. Microbrews, good coffees (pulled from a Strada espresso machine) and wine round out the menu. On the downside, this place is always crowded, and there isn't much space.

MEATBALL SHOP ITALIAN **$**

Map p418 (☎212-982-8895; www.themeatballshop.com; 84 Stanton St, btwn Allen & Orchard Sts; mains around $12; 🕐11:30am-2am Sun-Thu, to 4am Fri-Sat; [S]Second Ave; F to Delancey St; J/M/Z to Essex St) Elevating the humble meatball to high art, the Meatball Shop serves up five varieties of juiciness (including a tasty mushroom and lentil vegetarian option). Order those balls on a hero, add mozzarella and spicy tomato sauce, and voila, you have a tasty, if happily down-market, meal. The Lower East Side branch boasts a rock-and-roll vibe, with tattooed waitstaff and prominent beats. There are five other branches in NYC. Check the website for details.

SPAGHETTI INCIDENT ITALIAN **$**

Map p418 (☎646-896-1446; www.spaghettiincidentnyc.com; 231 Eldridge St, btwn Stanton & E Houston Sts; mains $9-12; 🕐5:30-11:30pm Mon-Fri, from noon Sat & Sun; [S]F to Second Ave) Grab a seat at the marble-topped bar or one of the side tables and watch the cooks whip up tasty dishes of spaghetti beautifully topped with fresh ingredients such as kale pesto, chopped salmon and asparagus in a light cream sauce, or Italian sausage and broccoli rabe. The flavors (and prices!) are quite good. Salads, arancini (rice balls) and affordable wines round out the menu.

ESSEX STREET MARKET MARKET **$**

Map p418 (☎212-312-3603; www.essexstreetmarket.com; 120 Essex St, btwn Delancey & Rivington Sts; 🕐8am-7pm Mon-Sat, 10am-6pm Sun; [S]F to Delancey St; J/M/Z to Essex St) Founded in 1940, this market is the local place for produce, seafood, butcher-cut meats, cheeses, Latino grocery items, and even a barber's shop. Although the interior is fairly bland, there are some excellent gourmet goodies here. Stop in Rainbo's for smoked

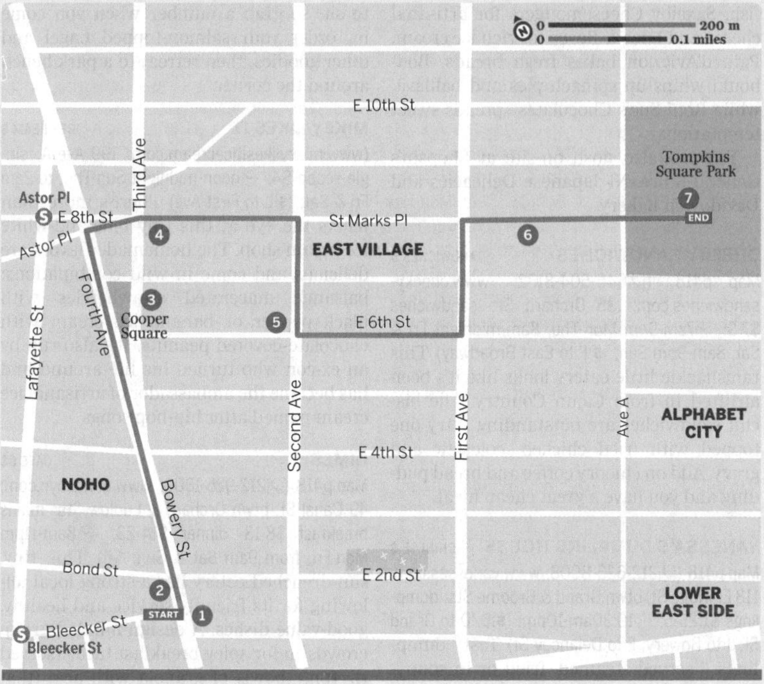

Neighborhood Walk
East Village Nostalgia

START CBGB
END TOMPKINS SQUARE PARK
LENGTH 1.5 MILES; 1.5 HOURS

From the Bleecker St subway station, head east along the leafy like-named street for a few blocks until you reach the former 1 **CBGB**, a famous music venue that opened in 1973 and launched punk rock via the Ramones. Today, it's a John Varvatos boutique (p127) selling rock-inspired leather jackets – the old walls of fading posters and wild graffiti remain untouched. The corner just north of here marks the block-long 2 **Joey Ramone Place**, named after the Ramones' singer who succumbed to cancer in 2001. Head north on the Bowery to Astor Pl. Turn right and head east through the square to come to 3 **Cooper Union** (p110), where in 1860 presidential hopeful Abraham Lincoln rocked a skeptical New York crowd with a rousing anti-slavery speech that ensured his candidacy. Continue east on St Marks Pl, a block full of tattoo parlors and cheap eateries that haven't changed much at all since the 1980s. Poke your head into 4 **Trash & Vaudeville**, a landmark goth-and-punk shop. Head south down Second Ave to the site of the long-defunct 5 **Fillmore East**, a 2000-seat live-music venue run by promoter Bill Graham from 1968 to 1971. In the '80s the space was transformed into the Saint – the legendary, 5000-sq-ft dance club that kicked off a joyous, drug-laden, gay disco culture. Cross Second Ave at 6th St and head down the block-long strip of Indian restaurants and curry shops. At First Ave, turn left, rejoin St Marks Pl and turn right. The row of tenements is the site of Led Zeppelin's 6 **Physical Graffiti cover** (96–98 St Marks Pl), where Mick and Keith sat in 1981 in the Rolling Stones' hilarious video for 'Waiting on a Friend.' End your stroll at the infamous 7 **Tompkins Square Park** (p112), where drag queens started the Wigstock summer festival at the bandshell where Jimi Hendrix played in the 1960s.

fish, Saxelby Cheesemongers for artisanal cheese and Luca & Bosco for rich ice cream. Pain d'Avignon bakes fresh breads, Boubouki whips up spinach pies and baklava, while Roni-Sue's Chocolates spreads sweet temptations.

You can also nosh on-site at Shopsin's General Store, Ni Japanese Delicacies and Davidovich Bakery.

CHEEKY SANDWICHES SANDWICHES $

Map p418 (646-504-8132; www.cheeky-sandwiches.com; 35 Orchard St; sandwiches $7-9; ⏰7am-9pm Mon-Thu, 8am-midnight Fri & Sat, 8am-9pm Sun; ⓢF to East Broadway) This ramshackle little eatery looks like it's been airlifted in from Cajun Country. The biscuit sandwiches are outstanding – try one topped with fried chicken, coleslaw and gravy. Add on chicory coffee and bread pudding and you have a great cheap meal.

VANESSA'S DUMPLING HOUSE CHINESE $

Map p418 (212-625-8008; www.vanessas.com; 118 Eldridge St, btwn Grand & Broome Sts; dumplings $1.25-5; ⏰10:30am-10pm; ⓢB/D to Grand St; J to Bowery; F to Delancey St) Tasty dumplings – served steamed, fried or in soup – are whipped together in iron skillets at light speed and tossed into hungry mouths at unbeatable prices.

PROHIBITION BAKERY BAKERY $

Map p418 (www.prohibitionbakery.com; 9 Clinton St, btwn Houston & Stanton Sts; 3/12 mini-cupcakes $5/20; ⏰11am-8pm Tue-Thu, to 9pm Fri & Sat, noon-6pm Sun; ⓢJ/M/Z TO Essex St; F to Delancey St) Can't decide whether to swig a shot of rum or munch down an eclair? Prohibition Bakery has you covered, with its boozy cupcakes melding two essential but somehow neglected food groups: alcohol and dessert. Try flavors such as the Car Bomb (whiskey, Baileys, stout and chocolate) or the Bee's Knees (lemon, honey and gin) and you'll wonder why no one thought of this sooner.

RUSS & DAUGHTERS DELI $

Map p418 (www.russanddaughters.com; 179 E Houston St, btwn Orchard & Allen Sts ; mains $10-14; ⏰8am-7pm Mon-Sat, to 5:30pm Sun; ⓢF to Second Ave) In business since 1914, this landmark establishment serves up Eastern European Jewish delicacies such as caviar, herring and lox, and, of course, a smear of cream cheese on a bagel. There's nowhere to sit, so grab a number when you come in, order your salmon-topped bagel and other goodies, then retreat to a park bench around the corner.

MIKEY LIKES IT ICE CREAM $

(www.mikeylikesiticecream.com; 199 Ave A; single scoop $4; ⏰noon-midnight Sun-Thu, to 2am Fri & Sat; ⓢL to First Ave) There's more than meets the eye at this tiny blue-and-white ice-cream shop. The homemade flavors are delicious and come in wild combinations: balsamic macerated strawberries with black pepper or banana ice cream with chocolate-covered peanuts. It's also run by an ex-con who turned his life around and has become the ambassador of artisanal ice cream named after hip-hop songs.

DIMES CAFE $$

Map p418 (212-925-1300; www.dimesnyc.com; 49 Canal St, btwn Orchard & Ludlow Sts; mains breakfast $8-13, dinner $14-23; ⏰8am-11pm Mon-Fri, from 9am Sat & Sun; ⓙ) This tiny, sun-drenched eatery has a strong local following for its friendly service and healthy, good-value dishes. A design-minded group crowds in for spicy breakfast tacos (served til 4pm), bowls of granola with açaí (that strongly flavored, vitamin-rich Amazonian berry), creative salads (with sunchokes, anchovies, goat cheese) and heartier dishes for dinner (striped bass with green curry, pulled pork with jasmine rice).

RUSS & DAUGHTERS
CAFE EASTERN EUROPEAN $$

Map p418 (212-475-4881; 127 Orchard St, btwn Delancey & Rivington Sts; mains $13-20; ⏰10am-10pm Mon-Fri, from 8am Sat & Sun; ⓢF to Delancey St; J/M/Z to Essex St) Sit down and feast on bagels and lox in the comfort of an old-school diner. Aside from rich slices of smoked fish, you can nibble on potato latkes, warm up over a bowl of borscht or feast on eggs Benny (poached eggs with smoked salmon, sauteed spinach and hollandaise sauce).

ANTIBES FRENCH $$

Map p418 (212-533-6088; www.antibesbistro. com; 112 Suffolk St, btwn Delancey & Rivington Sts; mains $17-24; ⏰11am-4:30pm Sat & Sun, 5pm-11:30pm daily ; ⓢJ/M/Z to Essex St; F to Delancey St) Named after a seaside town on the Côte d'Azur, this petite bistro exudes effortless charm, with its rustic chandeliers and cozy, low-lit dining room. It also remains somewhat undiscovered, despite serving excellent French-Mediterranean dishes at fair prices. Start off with grilled octopus with crushed chickpeas or seared foie gras, then move onto braised short ribs or wild mushroom risotto. There's also a decent wine list, with glasses starting at $8.

CLINTON STREET BAKING COMPANY
AMERICAN $$

Map p418 (☎646-602-6263; www.clintonstreet baking.com; 4 Clinton St, btwn Stanton & Houston Sts; mains $12-20; ☺8am-4pm & 6-11pm Mon-Sat, 9am-6pm Sun; ⓈJ/M/Z to Essex St; F to Delancey St; F to Second Ave) Mom-and-pop shop extraordinaire, Clinton Street Baking Company gets the blue-ribbon in so many categories – best pancakes (blueberry! swoon!), best muffins, best po'boys (southern-style sandwiches), best biscuits etc – that you're pretty much guaranteed a stellar meal no matter what time you stop by. In the evenings, you can opt for 'breakfast for dinner' (pancakes, eggs Benedict), fish tacos or the excellent buttermilk fried chicken.

Half-priced bottles of wine sweeten the deal on Monday and Tuesday.

BOIL
SEAFOOD $$

Map p418 (☎212-925-8815; www.theboilny.com; 139 Chrystie St, btwn Delancey & Broome Sts; shrimp/crab/crab legs per pound from $13/35/18; ☺5-11pm Mon-Fri, from 4pm Sat & Sun; ⓈJ/Z to Bowery; B/D to Grand St) When the waitstaff asks if you'd care for rubber gloves and a bib, you know you're in for a dining adventure. Crustaceans, of course, are the reason you're here and you'll make an ungodly mess tearing into succulent Dungeness crab, lobster, crawfish, shrimp and clams (hence the gloves). Craft beers go down nicely with the proceedings. Cash only.

FUNG TU
FUSION $$$

Map p418 (☎212-219-8785; www.fungtu.com; 22 Orchard St, btwn Hester & Canal Sts; small plates $13-18, mains $24-32; ☺6pm-midnight Tue-Sat, 4pm-10pm Sun; ⓈF to East Broadway) Celebrated chef Jonathan Wu brilliantly blends Chinese cooking with global accents at this elegant little eatery on the edge of Chinatown. The complex sharing plates are superb (try scallion pancakes with cashew salad and smoked chicken or crepe roll stuffed with braised beef, pickled cucumbers and watercress) and pair nicely with creative cocktails like the Fung Tu Gibson.

FREEMANS
AMERICAN $$$

Map p418 (☎212-420-0012; www.freemansres taurant.com; end of Freeman Alley; mains lunch $14-22, dinner $23-32; ☺11am-11:30pm Mon-Fri, from 10am Sat & Sun; ⓈF to Second Ave) Tucked down a back alley, the charmingly located Freeman's draws a mostly hipster crowd who let their chunky jewelry clang on the wooden tables as they lean over to sip overflowing cocktails. Potted plants and taxidermic antlers lend an endearing hunting-cabin vibe – a charming escape from the bustle (when there isn't a crowd inside).

The seasonal menu features the likes of whole grilled trout (from upstate NY), Colorado lamb stew, and roasted squash with wild mushrooms.

FAT RADISH
MODERN BRITISH $$$

Map p418 (☎212-300-4053; www.thefatrad ishnyc.com; 17 Orchard St, btwn Hester & Canal Sts; mains lunch $12-17, dinner $20-31; ☺noon-3:30pm daily, 5:30pm-midnight Mon-Sat, to 10pm Sun; ⓈF to East Broadway; B/D to Grand St) The young and fashionable pack into this dimly lit dining room with exposed white brick and industrial touches. There's a loud buzz and people checking each other out but the mains, typical of the local, seasonal, haute-pub-food fad, are worth your attention. Start off with big briny oysters before moving on to heritage pork chop with glazed squash or Montauk diver scallops with sweet potato mash.

DRINKING & NIGHTLIFE

🍸 East Village

RUE B
BAR

Map p416 (www.ruebnyc188.com; 188 Ave B, btwn 11th & 12th Sts; ☺noon-4am; ⓈL to First Ave) There's live jazz (and the odd rockabilly group) every night from about 8:30pm at this tiny, amber-lit drinking den on a bar-dappled stretch of Avenue B. It draws a young, celebratory crowd, and the space is quite small, so mind the tight corners, lest the trombonist end up in your lap.

BERLIN
CLUB

Map p416 (25 Ave A, btwn First & Second Aves; ☺10pm-4am; ⓈF to Second Ave) Like a secret bunker hidden beneath the ever-gentrifying

BARRY WINIKER / GETTY IMAGES ©

1. Cocktail hour at Cienfuegos (p123)
Bar hop through the East Village (p119), where the cocktail was born.

2. Museum at Eldridge Street Synagogue (p112)
Tour the fully restored synagogue, once the thriving center of Jewish life in the city.

3. Tompkins Square Park (p111)
Pull up a bench and take in the East Village atmosphere.

4. Almost-secret bars
Enter through the downstairs phone booth and enjoy a drink and the novelty factor of bar PDT (Please Don't Tell; p123).

LIFESTOCK / GETTY IMAGES ©

streets of the East Village, Berlin is a throwback to the neighborhood's more riotous days of wildness and dancing. Once you find the unmarked entrance, head downstairs to the grotto-like space with vaulted brick ceilings, a long bar and tiny dance floor, with funk and rare grooves spilling all around.

It draws a fun, bohemian crowd, a mix of class and trash, with little pretension.

WAYLAND BAR

Map p416 (☎212-777-7022; www.thewaylandnyc.com; 700 E 9th St, cnr Ave C; ⌚5pm-4am; [S]L to First Ave) Whitewashed walls, weathered floorboards and salvaged lamps give this urban outpost a Mississippi flair, which goes well with the live music (bluegrass, jazz, folk) played on Monday to Wednesday nights. The drinks, though, are the real draw – try the 'I hear banjos', made of Apple pie moonshine, rye whiskey and applewood smoke, which tastes like a campfire (but slightly less burning).

Decent drink specials and $1 oysters from 5 to 7pm on weekdays.

IMMIGRANT BAR

Map p416 (☎646-308-1724; 341 E 9th St, btwn First & Second Aves; ⌚5pm-1am Sun-Wed, to 2am Thu-Sat; [S]L to First Ave; 4/6 to Astor Pl) Wholly unpretentious, these twin boxcar-sized bars could easily become your neighborhood local if you decide to stick around town. The staff are knowledgeable and kind, mingling with faithful regulars while dishing out tangy olives and topping up glasses with imported snifters.

Enter the right side for the wine bar, with an excellent assortment of wines by the glass. The left entrance takes you into the tap room, where the focus is on unique microbrews. Both have a similar design – chandeliers, exposed brick, vintage charm.

JIMMY'S NO 43 BAR

Map p416 (☎212-982-3006; www.jimmysno43.com; 43 E 7th St, btwn Third & Second Aves; ⌚5pm-1am Mon-Thu, 1pm-4am Fri & Sat, 1pm-1am Sun; [S]N/R to 8th St-NYU; F to Second Ave; 4/6 to Astor Pl) Barrels and stag antlers line the walls up to the ceiling of this cozy basement beer hall as locals chug their drinks. Select from over 50 imported favorites (a dozen on draft) to go with a round of delectable, locally sourced bar nibbles.

PROLETARIAT BAR

Map p416 (☎212-777-6707; proletariatny.com; 102 St Marks Pl, btwn First Ave & Ave A; ⌚5pm-2am; [S]L to First Ave) The cognoscente of NYC's beer world pack this tiny, 10-stool bar just west of Tompkins Square Park. Promising 'rare, new and unusual beers,' Proletariat delivers the goods with a changing lineup of brews you won't find elsewhere. Recent hits have included drafts from artisanal brewers such as Hitachino Nest of Japan, Swiss-based BFM and Mahrs Bräu from Germany.

ANGEL'S SHARE BAR

Map p416 (☎212-777-5415; 2nd fl, 8 Stuyvesant St, near Third Ave & E 9th St; ⌚6pm-1:30am Sun-Thu, to 2:30am Fri & Sat; [S]6 to Astor Pl) Show up early and snag a seat at this hidden gem, behind a Japanese restaurant on the same floor. It's quiet and elegant with creative cocktails, but you can't stay if you don't have a table or a seat at the bar, and they tend to go fast.

OST CAFE CAFE

Map p416 (☎212-477-5600; www.ostcafenyc.com; 441 E 12th St, cnr Ave A; ⌚7:30am-10pm Mon-Fri, from 8:30am Sat & Sun; [S]L to First Ave) If you seek a charming spot to drink a frothy latte this is the place. With exposed brick walls, pressed tin ceiling, velvety armchairs and marble-topped cafe tables, Ost Cafe has class. It also has excellent coffee drinks (the kind that are topped with foam art) and wines by the glass (around $12).

POURING RIBBONS COCKTAIL BAR

Map p416 (☎917-656-6788; www.pouringribbons.com; 2nd fl, 225 Avenue B; ⌚6pm-2am; [S]L to First Ave) From the team behind Death & Co, Pouring Ribbons keeps the gimmicks and pretension low and the flavors exceptional. The encyclopedic cocktail menu could sate any appetite and includes a handy 'drink-decider' listing flavors such as 'refreshing' to 'comforting' on different axes. There is also possibly the largest collection of Chartreuse in NYC.

DEATH + CO LOUNGE

Map p416 (☎212-388-0882; www.deathandcompany.com; 433 E 6th St, btwn First Ave & Ave A; ⌚6pm-1am Sun-Thu, to 2am Fri & Sat; [S]F to Second Ave; L to First Ave; 6 Astor Pl) Relax amid dim lighting and thick wooden slatting and let the bartenders – with their PhDs in mixology – work their magic as they shake, rattle and roll some of the most perfectly concocted cocktails (from $15) in town.

ABC BEER CO BAR

Map p416 (☎646-422-7103; www.abcbeer.co; 96 Ave C, btwn 6th & 7th Sts; 🕒noon-midnight Sun-Thu, to 2am Fri & Sat; [S]F to Second Ave; L to First Ave) At first glance, ABC looks like a dimly lit beer shop (indeed bottles are available for purchase), but venture deeper inside and you'll find a small indie-rock–playing gastropub in back, with a long communal table, a few plush leather sofas and chairs set against the brick walls. The generally young crowd come for craft beer (350 by the bottle and 12 constantly rotating selections on draft), plus cheese plates, smoked meats and delicious 'brown bag' sandwiches (good value at $9 each). There's also a small patio out the back.

AMOR Y AMARGO BAR

Map p416 (☎212-614-6818; amoryamargony.com; 443 E 6th St, btwn Ave A & First Ave; 🕒5pm-1am Mon-Fri, noon-3am Sat, noon-1am Sun; [S]F to 2nd Ave; L to 1st Ave; 6 to Astor Pl) 'Love and Bitters' is a tiny but powerful specialist in crafty cocktails, showcasing its namesake selection of bitters. Ask the knowledgeable barkeeps for advice on flavors; you won't be disappointed.

TEN DEGREES BAR WINE BAR

Map p416 (☎212-358-8600; www.10degreesbar.com; 121 St Marks Pl, btwn First Ave & Ave A; 🕒noon-4am; [S]F to Second Ave; L to First Ave; L to Third Ave) This small, candlelit St Marks charmer is a great spot to start out the night with leather couches, friendly bartenders and an excellent wine and cocktails list. Come from noon to 8pm for two-for-one drink specials (otherwise, it's $11 to $15 for cocktails), or get half-priced bottles of wine on Monday night. Go for the couches up front or grab a tiny table in the back nook.

MAYAHUEL COCKTAIL BAR

Map p416 (☎212-253-5888; www.mayahuelny.com; 304 E 6th St, at Second Ave; 🕒6pm-2am; [S]L to Third Ave; L to First Ave; 6 to Astor Pl) About as far from your typical Spring Break tequila bar as you can get, Mayahuel is more like the cellar of a monastery. Devotees of the fermented agave can seriously indulge themselves experimenting with dozens of varieties (all cocktails $15); in between drinks, snack on quesadillas and tamales.

CIENFUEGOS BAR

Map p416 (☎212-614-6818; www.cienfuegosny.com; 95 Ave A, btwn 6th & 7th Sts; 🕒5pm-1am Sun-Thu, to 2am Fri & Sat ; [S]F to Second Ave; L to First Ave; 4/6 to Astor Pl) Cienfuegos channels the old-fashioned style of its colonial-era Cuban namesake inside an upstairs rum-punch joint. A sampler of tasty Cuban dishes makes the perfect midnight snack. If you like this place, then make a pit stop around the corner at Amor y Amargo – Cienfuegos' tiny bitters-centric brother.

PDT BAR

Map p416 (☎212-614-0386; www.pdtnyc.com; 113 St Marks Pl, btwn First Ave & Ave A; 🕒6pm-2am Sun-Thu, to 4am Fri & Sat; [S]L to First Ave) PDT, which stands for 'Please Don't Tell', scores high on novelty. You enter through the phone booth at the hot dog snack shop (Crif Dogs) next door. Once you're given the OK (reservations are recommended to avoid being turned away), you'll step into an intimate lowlit bar with the odd animal head on the wall.

First-rate cocktails, high prices and a (sometimes) snooty attitude from the hostess come standard with the experience.

BEAUTY & ESSEX BAR

Map p418 (☎212-614-0146; www.beautyandessex.com; 146 Essex St, btwn Stanton & Rivington Sts; 🕒5pm-1am; [S]F to Delancey St; J/M/Z to Essex St) Venture behind a tawdry pawnshop front space for a world of glamour. Beyond lies 10,000-sq-ft of sleek lounge space, complete with leather sofas and banquettes, dramatic amber-tinged lighting and a curved staircase that leads to yet another lounge and bar area. The exuberance, high prices and pretentious crowd give the place a Gatsby-esque vibe.

Ladies in need of a drink might want to bypass the bar and pay a visit to the powder room, where there's complimentary champagne (sorry, fellas).

MCSORLEY'S OLD ALE HOUSE BAR

Map p416 (☎212-473-9148; www.facebook.com/McSorleysOldAleHouse; 15 E 7th St, btwn Second & Third Aves; 🕒noon-12:30am; [S]6 to Astor Pl) Around since 1854, McSorley's feels far removed from the East Village veneer of cool: you're more likely to drink with frat boys, tourists and the odd fireman. It's hard to beat the cobwebs, sawdust floors and flip waiters who slap down two mugs of the house's ale for every one ordered.

COCK GAY

Map p416 (www.cockbar.com; 93 Second Ave; ⏰11pm-4am; [S]F/V to Lower East Side-Second Ave) A dark, dank spot that's proud of its sleazy-chic reputation, this is the place to join lanky hipster boys and rage until you're kicked out at 4am. Varying theme nights present popular parties with live performers, DJs, drag-queen hostesses, nearly naked go-go boys and porn videos on constant loops. It's wild and friendly.

EASTERN BLOC GAY

Map p416 (☎212-777-2555; www.easternblocnyc.com; 505 E 6th St, btwn Aves A & B; ⏰7pm-4am; [S]F to Second Ave) Though the theme may be 'Iron Curtain,' the drapery is most definitely velvet and taffeta at this East Village gay bar. Spring forth into the crowded sea of boys – some flirting with the topless barkeeps, others pretending not to stare at the retro '70s porno playing on the TVs.

Lower East Side

TEN BELLS BAR

Map p418 (☎212-228-4450; www.tenbellsnyc.com; 247 Broome St, btwn Ludlow & Orchard Sts; ⏰5pm-2am Mon-Fri, from 3pm Sat & Sun; [S]F to Delancey St; J/M/Z to Essex St) This charmingly tucked-away tapas bar has a grotto-like design, with flickering candles, dark tin ceilings, brick walls and a U-shaped bar that's an ideal setting for a conversation with a new friend.

The chalkboard menu hangs on both walls and features excellent wines by the glass, which go nicely with *boquerones* (marinated anchovies), *txipirones en su tinta* (squid in ink sauce) and regional cheeses. Come for happy hour when oysters are $1 each, and a carafe of wine costs $15. The unsigned entrance is easy to miss. It's right next to the shop Top Hat.

BARRIO CHINO COCKTAIL BAR

Map p418 (☎212-228-6710; www.barriochinonyc.com; 253 Broome St, btwn Ludlow & Orchard Sts; ⏰11:30am-4:30pm & 5:30pm-1am; [S]F, J/M/Z to Delancey-Essex Sts) An eatery that spills easily into a party scene, with an airy Havana-meets-Beijing vibe and a focus on fine sipping tequilas. Or stick with fresh blood-orange or black-plum margaritas, guacamole and chicken tacos.

BAR GOTO BAR

(☎212-475-4411; bargoto.com; 245 Eldridge St, btwn E Houston & Stanton Sts; ⏰5pm-midnight Tue-Thu & Sun, to 2am Fri & Sat; [S]F to Second Ave) Maverick mixologist Kenta Goto has cocktail connoisseurs spellbound at his eponymous hot spot. Expect meticulous, elegant drinks that revel in Koto's Japanese heritage (the sake-spiked Sakura Martini is utterly smashing), paired with authentic, Japanese comfort bites such as *okonomiyaki* (savory pancakes).

JADIS WINE BAR

Map p418 (☎212-254-1675; jadisnyc.com; 42 Rivington St, btwn Eldridge & Forsyth Sts; ⏰5pm-2am; [S]F to Second Ave; J/Z to Bowery) French for 'in olden days', Jadis channels a bit of European nostalgia with its worn brick walls, antique fixtures and warmly lit interior. You'll find around two dozen or so wines by the glass, with French labels taking pride of place. Snacks include escargots, salads, pressed sandwiches, homemade quiches and rich cheeses. Start the evening early with $5 wines from 5pm to 7pm.

CAKE SHOP BAR

Map p418 (☎212-253-0036; www.cake-shop.com; 152 Ludlow St, btwn Stanton & Rivington Sts; ⏰noon-2am Sun-Wed, to 4am Thu-Sat; [S]F to Second Ave; F to Delancey St; J/M/Z to Essex St) This little cafe and bar has a downtown bohemian vibe, with a small selection of vinyl for sale up front and a few tables in back, fine for nursing an evening beer or pastry (it's not called Cake Shop for nothing), while admiring your neighbor's intriguing tattoos. There's a stage downstairs where indie bands play ($10 cover) throughout the week, but the small space can get cramped quickly.

ROUND K CAFE

Map p418 (roundk.com; 99 Allen St, btwn Delancey & Broome Sts; ⏰9am-8pm Sun-Wed, to 10pm Thu-Sat; [S]B/D to Grand St; F to Delancey St; J/M/Z to Essex St) There's something special about this charmingly hidden Korean-run cafe. Step inside and smell the coffee roasting, admire some antique-looking machinery, then order a perfectly made latte – and perhaps some 'Mom's Toast (a waffle with bourbon-infused bananas) – take your delicate porcelain and pull back the curtain to reveal a quiet seating area lit with Tiffany-style glass lamps.

You never know who you may bump into; we chatted with a Serbian painter trying to break into the gallery scene when last we passed through.

CASA MEZCAL
BAR

Map p418 (☎212-777-2600; www.casamezcalny. com; 86 Orchard St, btwn Broome & Grand Sts; ⊗noon-11pm; ⓢF to Delancey St; J/M/Z to Essex St; B/D to Grand St) This festive three-story arts space celebrates the rich eating, drinking and musical traditions of Mexico – and Oaxaca in particular. The tall-ceilinged main room is decorated with colorful paper streamers, masks, Day-of-the-Dead skulls, and other folk art. Downstairs is the cocktail lounge and performance venue Botanic Lab. Upstairs is a small space called The Gallery, which hosts the odd art exhibition.

ATTABOY
COCKTAIL BAR

Map p418 (134 Eldridge St, btwn Delancey & Broome Sts; ⊗6:45pm-4am; ⓢB/D to Grand St) One of those no-door-sign, speakeasy-vibe bars that are two-a-penny these days, this one is a notch above, serving knockout artisanal cocktails – that will set you back $17 each. There is no menu, so let the expert bartenders guide you.

 ENTERTAINMENT

ROCKWOOD MUSIC HALL
LIVE MUSIC

Map p418 (☎212-477-4155; www.rockwoodmusic hall.com; 196 Allen St, btwn Houston & Stanton Sts; ⊗6pm-2am Mon-Fri, from 3pm Sat & Sun; ⓢF/V to Lower East Side-Second Ave) Opened by indie rocker Ken Rockwood, this breadbox-sized concert space has three stages that see a rapid-fire flow of bands and singer/songwriters. If cash and time are limited, head to stage 1, which has free shows, with a maximum of one hour per band (diehards can see five or more performances a night). Music kicks off at 3pm on weekends and 6pm on weeknights.

NEW YORK THEATRE WORKSHOP
THEATER

Map p416 (☎212-460-5475; www.nytw.org; 79 E 4th St, btwn Second & Third Aves; ⓢF to Second Ave) Recently celebrating its 25th year, this innovative production house is a treasure to those seeking cutting-edge, contemporary plays with purpose. It was the originator of two big Broadway hits, *Rent* and *Urine-*

town, and offers a constant supply of high-quality drama.

SIDEWALK CAFÉ
LIVE MUSIC

Map p416 (☎212-473-7373; www.sidewalkmusic. net; 94 Ave A, at 6th St; ⊗11am-1am Sun-Thu, to 4am Fri & Sat; ⓢF/V to Lower East Side-Second Ave; 6 to Astor Pl) Anti-folk forever! Never mind the Sidewalk's burger-bar appearance outside – inside is the home of New York's 'anti-folk' scene, where the Moldy Peaches carved out their legacy before Juno got knocked up. The open-mic 'anti-hootenanny' is Monday night. Other nights host a wide range of sounds: garage rock, indie pop, bluesy piano, and all things anti-folk.

SLIPPER ROOM
LIVE PERFORMANCE

Map p418 (☎212-253-7246; www.slipperroom. com; 167 Orchard St, entrance on Stanton St; admission $10-20; ⊗8pm-3am; ⓢF to Second Ave) The Slipper Room is back, and looking better than ever thanks to a major renovation. The two-story club hosts a wide range of performances, including Seth Herzog's (sethherzog.tumblr.com) popular variety show Sweet at 9pm on Tuesday (admission $5 to $7) and several weekly burlesque shows, which feature a mash-up of acrobatics, sexiness, comedy and absurdity – generally well worth the admission. Tickets available online.

PS 122
THEATER

Map p416 (☎212-477-5829; www.ps122.org; 150 First Ave, at E 9th St; ⓢL to First Ave; 6 to Astor Pl) This theatre set in a former schoolhouse has been committed to fostering new artists and their far-out ideas since its inception in 1979. Its two stages have hosted such now-known performers as Meredith Monk, Eric Bogosian and the late Spalding Gray, and it's also home to dance shows, film screenings and various festivals for up-and-coming talents. At the time of writing PS 122 was undergoing a massive transformation as it creates new state-of-the-art performance spaces and adds additional artist studios, a new lobby and a roof deck. There will also be an outdoor light installation called *Inhale/Exhale* that will give a gentle pulse to the building, making it appear alive. PS 122 is scheduled to reopen in mid-2016.

ANTHOLOGY FILM ARCHIVES
CINEMA

Map p416 (☎212-505-5181; www.anthologyfilm-archives.org;32 Second Ave, at 2nd St; ⓢF to Second Ave) Opened in 1970, this theater is dedicated to the idea of film as an art form. It screens indie works by new filmmakers and revives classics and obscure oldies, from Luis Buñuel to Ken Brown's psychedelia.

STONE LIVE MUSIC

Map p416 (www.thestonenyc.com; Ave C, at 2nd St; admission $10-20; ⏲shows 8pm & 10pm; [S]F/V to Lower East Side-Second Ave) Created by renowned downtown jazz cat John Zorn, the Stone is about the music and nothing but the music, in all its experimental and avant-garde forms. There's no bar or frills of any kind – just folding chairs in a dark space on a concrete floor.

PIANOS LIVE MUSIC

Map p418 (☎212-505-3733; www.pianosnyc.com; 158 Ludlow St, at Stanton St; cover $8-12; ⏲2pm-4am; [S]F to Second Ave) Nobody's bothered to change the sign at the door, a leftover from the location's previous incarnation as a piano shop. Now it's dedicated to a musical mix of genres and styles, leaning more toward pop, punk and new wave, but throwing in some hip-hop and indie for good measure. Sometimes you get a double feature – one act upstairs and another below.

ABRONS ARTS CENTER THEATER

Map p418 (☎212-598-0400; www.abronsartscenter.org; 466 Grand St, cnr Pitt St; 👪; [S]F, J, M, Z to Delancey St-Essex St) This venerable cultural hub has three theaters, the largest being the Playhouse Theater (a national landmark), with its own lobby, fixed seats on a rise, a large, deep stage and good visibility. A mainstay of the downtown Fringe Festival, Abrons Art Center is also your best bet to catch experimental and community productions.

Not afraid of difficult subjects, Abrons sponsors plays, dance and photography exhibits that don't get much play elsewhere.

LANDMARK SUNSHINE CINEMA CINEMA

Map p418 (☎212-260-7289; www.landmarktheatres.com; 143 E Houston St, btwn Forsyth & Eldridge Sts; [S]F/V to Lower East Side-Second Ave) A renovated Yiddish theater, the wonderful Landmark shows foreign and first-run mainstream art-house films on massive screens. It also has much-coveted stadium-style seating, so it doesn't matter what giant sits in front of you after the lights go out.

NUYORICAN POETS CAFÉ LIVE PERFORMANCE

Map p416 (☎212-780-9386; www.nuyorican.org; 236 E 3rd St; cover $8-25; ⏲shows 9pm or 10pm; [S]F to Lower East Side-Second Ave) Still going strong after 40-plus years, the legendary Nuyorican is home to poetry slams, hip-hop performances, plays, and film and video events. It's a piece of East Village history, but also a vibrant and still-relevant non-profit arts organization. Buy tickets online for the more popular weekend shows.

BOWERY BALLROOM LIVE MUSIC

Map p418 (☎212-533-2111; www.boweryballroom.com; 6 Delancey St, at Bowery St; [S]J/Z to Bowery; B/D to Grand St) This terrific, medium-sized venue has the perfect sound and feel for well-known indie-rock acts such as The Shins, Stephen Malkmus and Patti Smith.

LA MAMA ETC THEATER

Map p416 (☎646-430-5374; www.lamama.org; 74A E 4th St; admission $25; [S]F to Second Ave) A long-standing home for onstage experimentation (the ETC stands for Experimental Theater Club), La MaMa is now a three-theater complex with a cafe, an art gallery and a separate studio building that features cutting-edge dramas, sketch comedy and readings of all kinds. Ten $10 tickets are available for each show. Book early to score a deal!

MERCURY LOUNGE LIVE MUSIC

Map p418 (☎212-260-4700; www.mercuryloungenyc.com; 217 E Houston St, btwn Essex & Ludlow Sts; cover charge $10-15; ⏲6pm-3am; [S]F/V to Lower East Side-Second Ave) The Mercury dependably pulls in a cool new or comeback band everyone downtown wants to see – such as Dengue Fever or the Slits. The sound is good, with an intimate seating area and dance space.

SHOPPING

East Village

A-1 RECORDS MUSIC

Map p416 (☎212-473-2870; www.a1recordshop.com; 439 E 6th St, btwn First Ave & Ave A; ⏲1-9pm; [S]F/V to Lower East Side-Second Ave) One of the last of the many record stores that once graced the East Village, A-1 has an excellent selection of jazz, funk and soul, and the cramped aisles draw vinyl fans from far and wide.

STILL HOUSE HOMEWARES

Map p416 (☎212-539-0200; www.stillhousenyc.com; 117 E 7th St; ⏲noon-8pm; [S]6 to Astor Pl) Step into this petite, peaceful boutique to browse sculptural glassware and pottery: handblown vases, geometric tabletop objects, ceramic bowls and cups, and other finery for the home. You'll also find minimalistic jewelry, delicately bound notebooks and small framed artworks for the wall.

Still House has lots of great gift ideas, and the objects are small enough to bring home. They are quite delicate, so make sure they're well wrapped.

OBSCURA ANTIQUES ANTIQUES

Map p416 (☎212-505-9251; www.obscuraantiques.com; 207 Ave A, btwn 12th & 13th Sts; ⏲noon-8pm Mon-Sat, to 7pm Sun; [S]L to First Ave) This small cabinet of curiosities pleases both lovers of the macabre and inveterate antique hunters. Here you'll find taxidermied animal heads, tiny rodent skulls and skeletons, butterfly displays in glass boxes, photos of dead people, disturbing little (dental?) instruments, German landmine flags (stackable so tanks could see them), old poison bottles and glass eyes.

Dig deeper to find cane toad purses (sure to please the Aussie crowd), Zippos from Vietnam soldiers, anatomical drawings, a two-headed calf, a stuffed hyena and other items not currently available at the local department store.

VERAMEAT JEWELRY

Map p416 (☎212-388-9045; www.verameat.com; 315 E 9th St, btwn First & Second Aves; ⏲noon-8pm; [S]6 to Astor Pl; F to Second Ave) Designer Vera Balyura creates exquisite little pieces with a dark sense of humor in this delightful little shop on 9th St. Tiny, artfully wrought pendants, rings, earrings and bracelets appear almost too precious, until a closer inspection reveals zombies, godzilla robots, animal heads, dinosaurs and encircling claws – bringing a whole new level of miniaturized complexity to the realm of jewelry.

DINOSAUR HILL CHILDREN

Map p416 (☎212-473-5850; www.dinosaurhill.com; 306 E 9th St; ⏲11am-7pm; [S]6 to Astor Pl) A small, old-fashioned toy store that's inspired more by imagination than Disney movies, this shop has loads of great gift ideas: Czech marionettes, shadow puppets, micro building blocks, calligraphy sets, toy pianos, art and science kits, kids' music CDs from around the globe, and wooden blocks in half-a-dozen different languages, plus natural-fiber clothing for infants.

JOHN VARVATOS FASHION

Map p416 (☎212-358-0315; www.johnvarvatos.com; 315 Bowery, btwn 1st & 2nd Sts; ⏲noon-8pm Mon-Sat, to 6pm Sun; [S]F to Second Ave; 6 to Bleecker St) Set in the hallowed halls of former punk club CBGB (p381), the John Varvatos Bowery store goes to great lengths to tie fashion with rock-and-roll, with records, '70s audio equipment and even electric guitars for sale alongside JV's denim, leather boots, belts and graphic tees.

JOHN DERIAN HOMEWARES

Map p416 (☎212-677-3917; www.johnderian.com; 6 E 2nd St, btwn Bowery & Second Ave; ⏲11am-7pm Tue-Sun; [S]F/V to Lower East Side-Second Ave) John Derian is famed for its decoupage – pieces from original botanical and animal prints stamped under glass. The result is a beautiful collection of one-of-a-kind plates,

DOWNTOWN SHOPPING 101

The downtown fashion crowd looking for that edgy, experimental or 'old-school hip-hop' look heads to the shops in the Lower East Side. Here dozens of stores sell vintage apparel, vegan shoes, old-fashioned candy, sex toys, left-wing books and more. Swing by the Essex Street Market for bagels, smoked salmon and other edible temptations.

In NYC's ever-ephemeral shopping scene, boutiques – like style trends – come and go on a whim. The shops Reformation (p128), Yumi Kim (p128), and Assembly (p128) are a great starting point in seeking hot new downtown fashions.

In the East Village – once known as the archetype of underground downtown style – you'll find urban and outsider fashion. New local designers, sleeker shops and chain stores have also moved into the area, taking away some of its former edginess.

paperweights, coasters, lamps, bowls and vases.

ODIN (EAST VILLAGE) FASHION

Map p416 (☎212-475-0666; www.odinnewyork.com; 328 E 11th St; ⏰noon-9pm Mon-Sat, to 7pm Sun; [S]L to First Ave; L, N/Q/R, 4/5/6 to 14th St-Union Sq) Named after the mighty Norse god, Odin offers a bit of magic for men seeking a new look. The large boutique carries stylish downtown labels such as Phillip Lim, Band of Outsiders and Edward, and is a great place to browse for up-and-coming designers. Other eye candy at the minimalist store includes Comme des Garçons wallets, sleek sunglasses, Sharps grooming products and Taschen coffee-table books.

Other branches are in SoHo (p102) and the West Village (p157).

TOKIO 7 FASHION

Map p416 (☎212-353-8443; www.tokio7.net; 83 E 7th St, near First Ave; ⏰noon-8pm; [S]6 to Astor Pl) This revered, hip consignment shop, on a shady stretch of E 7th St, has good-condition designer labels for men and women at some fairly hefty prices. The Japanese-owned store often features lovely pieces by Issey Miyake and Yohji Yamamoto, as well as a well-curated selection of Dolce & Gabbana, Prada, Chanel and other top labels.

Watch out for the giant alien-samurai thing out front (made of repurposed machine parts).

NO RELATION VINTAGE VINTAGE

Map p416 (☎212-228-5201; norelationvintage.com; 204 First Ave, btwn 12th & 13th Sts; ⏰noon-8pm; [S]L to First Ave) Among the many vintage shops of the East Village, No Relation is a winner for its wide-ranging collections that run the gamut from denim and leather jackets to flannels, sneakers, plaid shirts, candy-colored T-shirts, varsity jackets, clutches and more. Sharpen your elbows: hipster crowds flock here on weekends.

KIEHL'S BEAUTY

Map p416 (☎212-677-3171; 109 Third Ave, btwn 13th & 14th Sts; ⏰10am-9pm Mon-Sat, 11am-7pm Sun; [S]L to 3rd Ave) Making and selling skincare products since it opened in NYC as an apothecary in 1851, this Kiehl's flagship store has doubled its shop size and expanded into an international chain, but its personal touch remains – as do the coveted, generous sample sizes.

Lower East Side

ECONOMY CANDY FOOD

Map p418 (☎212-254-1531; www.economycandy.com; 108 Rivington St, at Essex St; ⏰9am-6pm Sun & Tue-Fri, 10am-6pm Sat & Mon; [S]F, J/M/Z to Delancey St-Essex St) Bringing sweetness to the 'hood since 1937, this candy shop is stocked with floor-to-ceiling goods in package and bulk, and is home to some beautiful antique gum machines. You'll find everything from the kid-worthy jelly beans, lollipops, gum balls, Cadbury imports, gummy worms and rock candy to more adult delicacies such as halvah, green tea bonbons, hand-dipped chocolates, dried ginger and papaya.

There's also an eye-catching assortment of collectible Pez dispensers.

REFORMATION CLOTHING

Map p418 (☎646-448-4925; www.thereformation.com; 156 Ludlow St, btwn Rivington & Stanton Sts; ⏰noon-8pm Mon-Sat, to 7pm Sun; [S]F to Delancey St; F to 2nd Ave; J/M/Z to Essex St) 🍃 This stylish boutique sells beautifully designed garments with minimal environmental impact. Aside from their green credentials, they sell unique tops, blouses, sweaters and dresses, with fair prices in comparison to other Lower Eeast Side boutiques.

Clothes are manufactured in California using renewable energy and shipped in 100% recycled packaging – plus they tick other boxes: fair labor practices, support for volunteer organizations and other policies unusual for a clothing company.

ASSEMBLY FASHION

Map p418 (☎212-253-5393; www.assemblynewyork.com; 170 Ludlow St, btwn Stanton & Houston Sts; ⏰noon-8pm; [S]F to Second Ave) Whitewashed floorboards and an air of stylish whimsy define this dapper men's and women's shop in the Lower East Side. There's lots of covet-worthy wares on display, showcasing obscure designers from East and West. Look for canvas high tops by Shoes Like Pottery, satchels by Le Bas, chunky jewelry by Open House and outerwear by the shop's in-house label Assembly.

YUMI KIM CLOTHING

Map p418 (☎212-420-5919; www.yumikim.com; 105 Stanton St, btwn Ludlow & Essex Sts; ⏰noon-7pm; [S]F to Delancey St; F to Second Ave; J/M/Z to

Essex St) To add a burst of color to your wardrobe, head to Yumi Kim, a delightful little boutique selling fun dresses, blouses, skirts, jumpsuits and accessories all adorned with bright floral and tropical prints. The cuts are quite flattering, and most are made of 100% silk – making them good, lightweight options for travel.

EDITH MACHINIST VINTAGE

Map p418 (☎212-979-9992; www.edithmachinist.com; 104 Rivington St, at Ludlow St; 🕒noon-7pm Tue-Sat, to 6pm Sun & Mon; [S]F to Delancey St; J/M/Z to Essex St) To properly strut about the Lower East Side, you've got to dress the part. Edith Machinist can help you get that rumpled but stylish look in a hurry – a bit of vintage glam via knee-high soft suede boots, 1930s silk dresses and ballet-style flats.

MOO SHOES SHOES

Map p418 (☎212-254-6512; www.mooshoes.com; 78 Orchard St, btwn Broome & Grand Sts; 🕒11:30am-7:30pm Mon-Sat, noon-6pm Sun; [S]F to Delancey St; J/M/Z to Essex St) This earth- and animal-friendly boutique sells surprisingly stylish microfiber (faux leather) shoes, handbags and wallets. Look for elegant ballet flats from Love Is Mighty, rugged men's Oxfords by Novacos, and sleek Matt & Nat wallets.

BY ROBERT JAMES FASHION

Map p418 (☎212-253-2121; www.byrobertjames.com; 74 Orchard St; 🕒noon-8pm Mon-Sat, to 6pm Sun; [S]F to Delancey St; J/M/Z to Essex St) Rugged, beautifully tailored menswear is the mantra of Robert James, who sources and manufactures right here in NYC (the design studio is just upstairs). The racks are lined with slim-fitting denim, handsome button-downs, and classic-looking sports coats. Lola, James' black labrador, sometimes roams the store. He also has a store in Williamsburg.

TOP HAT ACCESSORIES

Map p418 (☎212-677-4240; www.tophatnyc.com; 245 Broome St, btwn Ludlow & Orchard Sts; 🕒noon-8pm; [S]B/D to Grand St) Sporting curios from around the globe, this whimsical little shop is packed with intrigue: from vintage Italian pencils and handsomely miniaturized leather journals to beautifully carved wooden bird whistles. If you're looking for an endless rain album, a toy clarinet, Japanese fabrics, a crumpled map of the night sky or geometric Spanish cups and saucers, you'll find all these and more at fanciful Top Hat.

BLUESTOCKINGS BOOKS

Map p418 (☎212-777-6028; www.bluestockings.com; 172 Allen St, btwn Stanton & Rivington Sts; 🕒11am-11pm; [S]F/V to Lower East Side-Second Ave) This independent bookstore, which first opened with a lesbian bent, has now expanded its turf to encompass a wide range of topics, including feminism, globalism and African American studies. It's also the site of a vegan, organic, fair-trade cafe, as well as myriad readings and speaking events.

SPORTS & ACTIVITIES

RUSSIAN & TURKISH BATHS BATHHOUSE

Map p416 (☎212-674-9250; www.russianturkishbaths.com; 268 E 10th St, btwn First Ave & Ave A; per visit $40; 🕒noon-10pm Mon-Tue & Thu-Fri, from 10am Wed, from 9am Sat, from 8am Sun; [S]L to First Ave; 6 to Astor Pl) Since 1892, this has been the spa for anyone who wants to get naked (or stay in their swimsuit) and romp in steam baths, an ice-cold plunge pool, a sauna or on the sundeck. The baths are open to both men and women most hours (wearing shorts is required at these times), though at some times it's men or women only. Check the website for more detailed opening hours.

West Village, Chelsea & the Meatpacking District

WEST VILLAGE & THE MEATPACKING DISTRICT | CHELSEA

Neighborhood Top Five

1 Packing a picnic lunch from Chelsea Market and having a uniquely pastoral moment on the thin strand of green along the **High Line** (p132) as it soars above the gridiron.

2 Checking out the brightest art stars at the top galleries in **Chelsea** (p142).

3 Walking through **Washington Square Park** (p135), pausing under the signature arch, then loitering at the fountain to eavesdrop on gossiping NYU kids.

4 Exploring fascinating exhibitions from the Himalayas and beyond at the **Rubin Museum of Art** (p137).

5 Sipping lattes alfresco on cobblestone corners and browsing the latest boutiques in the **West Village**.

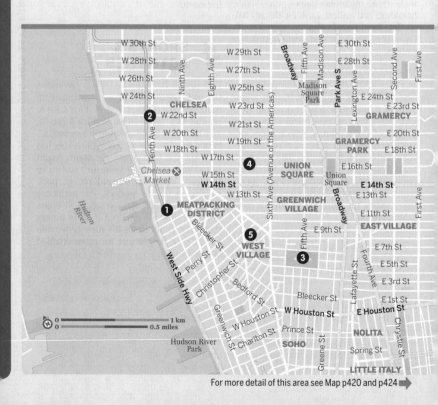

For more detail of this area see Map p420 and p424 ➡

Explore West Village, Chelsea & the Meatpacking District

There's a very good reason why this area is known as the Village: it actually looks like one! Quaint, quiet lanes carve their way between brown-brick townhouses offering endless strolling for locals appreciating good weather, or tourists coming to see what all the fuss is about. The Village is indeed picturesque, and the best way to uncover its treasures is to simply have a wander. When your feet grow tired of negotiating the cobbled streets, plunk yourself down at a cafe with a frothy cappuccino or a glass of wine.

Stroll through the Meatpacking District – once filled with slaughterhouses and now brimming with sleek boutiques and roaring nightclubs – to reach Chelsea just to the north. Chelsea bridges the gap between the West Village and Midtown, importing bits and bobs from both. It's the de facto neighborhood for the city's sociable gay community, and its broad avenues are lined with breezy cafes, themed bars and sweaty clubs. The neighborhood's massive gallery scene can be found in the West 20s.

Local Life

➡ **Eighth Ave brunch** If you're a dude looking to meet (or at least look at) other dudes, but the cruisey bar scene isn't your style, then opt for the weekend brunch scene along Eighth Ave. You'll spot piles of friendly Chelsea boys drinking their hangovers off in tight jeans and even tighter T-shirts.

➡ **West Village cafes** The quizzes and surveys can't be wrong – the West Village is the most desirable residential neighborhood in Manhattan, so do as the locals do and make the most of this quaint district stacked to the brim with cute cafes. Grab a book and a latte and hunker down for a blissful afternoon of people-watching.

➡ **Gallery hopping** Join the fashionable, art-minded crowds at the latest gallery shows in Chelsea. Thursday night, when some galleries have openings (and free wine), is a good time to roam.

Getting There & Away

➡ **Subway** Sixth Ave, Seventh Ave and Eighth Ave are graced with convenient subway stations, but public transportation slims further west. Take the A/C/E or 1/2/3 lines to reach this colorful clump of neighborhoods – disembark at 14th St (along either service) if you're looking for a good place to make tracks.

➡ **Bus** Try M14 or the M8 if you're traveling across town and want to access the westernmost areas of Chelsea and the West Village by public transportation. It's a shame, however, to use the bus or a taxi to get around the West Village – the charming cobblestone streets are perfect for a stroll.

Lonely Planet's Top Tip

It's perfectly acceptable to arm yourself with a map (or rely on your smartphone) to get around the West Village's charming-but-challenging side streets. Even some locals have a tricky time finding their way! Just remember that 4th St makes a diagonal turn north – breaking away from usual east-west street grid – and you'll quickly become a Village pro.

Best Places to Eat

➡ Jeffrey's Grocery (p145)
➡ Gansevoort Market (p148)
➡ RedFarm (p147)
➡ Chelsea Market (p148)
➡ Blue Hill (p147)

For reviews, see p139 ➡

Best Places to Drink

➡ Employees Only (p149)
➡ Buvette (p150)
➡ Frying Pan (p153)
➡ Smalls (p154)
➡ Duplex (p156)

For reviews, see p149 ➡

Best Bookshops

➡ Printed Matter (p160)
➡ Strand Book Store (p157)
➡ Three Lives & Company (p158)
➡ Posman Books (p160)

For reviews, see p157 ➡

WEST VILLAGE, CHELSEA & THE MEATPACKING DISTRICT

TOP SIGHT
THE HIGH LINE

It's hard to believe that the High Line – a shining example of brilliant urban renewal – was once a dingy rail line that anchored a rather unsavory district of slaughterhouses. Today, this eye-catching attraction is one of New York's best loved green spaces, drawing visitors far and wide who come to stroll, sit and picnic 30ft above the city, while enjoying fabulous views of Manhattan's ever-changing urban landscape.

Industrial Past

The tracks that would one day become the High Line were commissioned in the 1930s when the municipal government decided to raise the street-level tracks after years of accidents that gave Tenth Ave the nickname 'Death Avenue.' The project drained over $150 million in funds (equivalent to around $2 billion by today's dime) and took roughly five years to complete. After two decades of effective use, a rise in truck transportation led to the eventual decrease in usage, and finally, in the 1980s, the rails became obsolete. Petitions were signed by local residents to remove the eyesores, but in 1999 a committee called the Friends of the High Line – founded by Joshua David and Robert Hammond – was formed to save the rusting iron and transform the tracks into a unique elevated green space.

A Green Future

On a warm spring day in 2009, the High Line – full of blooming flowers and broad-leaved trees – opened to the public, the first of three phases that today link the

DON'T MISS

- The amphitheater-style viewing platforms at 17th and 26th Sts
- Spencer Finch's art installation *The River That Flows Both Ways* between 15th and 16th Sts

PRACTICALITIES

- Map p420
- ☎212-206-9922
- www.thehighline.org
- Gansevoort St
- admission free
- 🕐7am-11pm Jun-Sep, to 10pm Apr, May, Oct & Nov, to 7pm Dec-Mar
- 🚌M11 to Washington St; M11, M14 to Ninth Ave; M23, M34 to Tenth Ave, [S]L, A/C/E to 14th St-Eighth Ave; C/E to 23rd St-Eighth Ave

Meatpacking District and Midtown. Section 1 starts at Gansevoort St and runs parallel to Tenth Ave up to W 20th St. Full of sitting space in various forms – from giant chaises longues to bleacher-like benching – the first part quickly became the setting for various public works and activities, many geared towards the neighborhood's growing population of families. Two years later, Section 2 opened, adding another 10 blocks of green-ified tracks. The final section opened in 2014. Here the High Line meanders from 30th up to 34th St, going up to and around the West Side Rail Yards in a U-like fashion. As it veers west toward Twelfth Ave, the path widens, and you have open views of the Hudson, with the rusting, weed-filled rail road tracks running alongside the walkway (the designers wanted to evoke the same sense of over-grown wilderness in the heart of the metropolis that greeted visitors who stumbled upon the tracks prior to the park's creation). This section also features a dedicated children's play area – a jungle gym made up of exposed beams covered in a soft play surface.

To reach the High Line, there are numerous stairways along the park, including Gansevoort, 14th, 16th, 18th, 20th, 23rd, 26th, 28th, 30th and 34th Sts. There are also strategically placed elevators at Gansevoort, 14th, 16th, 23rd, 30th and 34th.

More than just a Public Space

The High Line's civic influence extends far beyond being the trendsetter in the island's re-greenification. As the West Village and Chelsea continue to embrace their new-found residential nature, the High Line is making a dedicated move towards becoming more than just a public place but an inspired meeting point for families and friends. As you walk along the High Line you'll find staffers wearing shirts with the signature double-H, logo who can point you in the right direction or offer you additional information about the converted rails.

GASTRONOMIC DELIGHTS

The High Line invites various gastronomic establishments from around the city to set up vending carts and stalls so that strollers can enjoy to-go items on the green. Expect a showing of the finest coffee and ice-cream establishments during the warmer months.

PUBLIC ART

In addition to being a haven of hovering green, the High Line is also an informal art space featuring a variety of installations, both site-specific and standalone. For detailed information about the public art on display at the time of your visit, check out www.art.thehighline.org.

TOP SIGHT CHELSEA MARKET

In a shining example of redevelopment and preservation, the Chelsea Market has transformed a former factory into a shopping concourse that caters to foodies.

National Biscuit Company

The long brick edifice occupied by Chelsea Market was built in the 1890s to house a massive bakery complex that became the headquarters of the National Biscuit Company (makers of Saltines, Fig Newtons and Oreos). The market, which opened in the 1990s, is now a base camp for gourmet outlets and apparel boutiques.

Foodie Hub

More than two dozen food vendors ply their temptations including Mokbar (ramen with Korean accents), Takumi tacos (mixing Japanese and Mexican ingredients), Tuck Shop (Aussie-style savory pies), Bar Suzette (crepes), Num Pang (Cambodian sandwiches), Ninth St Coffee (perfect lattes), Doughnuttery (piping hot mini-donuts) and L'Arte de Gelato (rich ice cream). If you're after something more indulgent, linger over a meal at the Green Table, which serves farm-fresh organic ingredients; sample the first-rate seafood and raw bar at Cull & Pistol; or stop by Friedman's Lunch for upscale American comfort food.

Beyond the Cuisine

Browse the various nonfood offerings at Imports from Marrakesh, which specializes in Moroccan art and design; check out the latest literary hits at Posman Books; search for a new outfit or home accessory at Anthropologie; or pick up a bottle at the expert-staffed Chelsea Wine Vault. The market only takes up the lower part of a larger, million-sq-ft space, occupying a full city block, which is the current home of TV channels the Food Network, Oxygen Network, Google offices and NY1, the local news channel. Cellists and bluegrass players fill the main walkway with music, and the new High Line passes right by the rear of the building.

DON'T MISS

- Takumi
- Lobster Place
- The High Line out back

PRACTICALITIES

- Map p424
- www.chelseamarket.com
- 75 Ninth Ave, at 15th St
- ⏲7am-9pm Mon-Sat, 8am-8pm Sun
- [S]A/C/E to 14th St; L to Eighth Ave

TOP SIGHT
WASHINGTON SQUARE PARK

What was once a potter's field and a square for public executions is now the unofficial town square of the Village. Encased in perfectly manicured brownstones and gorgeous twists of modern architecture (all owned by NYU), Washington Square Park is one of the most striking garden spaces in the city – especially as you are welcomed by the iconic Stanford White Arch on the north side of the green.

DON'T MISS

➡ Stanford White Arch
➡ Central fountain
➡ Greek Revival houses surrounding the park

PRACTICALITIES

➡ Map p420
➡ Fifth Ave at Washington Sq N
➡ S A/C/E, B/D/F/M to W 4th St-Washington Sq; N/R to 8th St-NYU

History

Although quite ravishing today, Washington Square Park had a long and sordid history before finally blossoming into the paradigm of public space we see today (thanks largely to a $30 million renovation completed in 2014).

When the Dutch settled Manhattan to run the Dutch East India Company, they gave what is now the park to their freed black slaves. The land was squarely between the Dutch and Native settlements, so, in a way, the area acted as a buffer between enemies. Though somewhat marshy, it was arable land and farming took place for around 60 years.

At the turn of the 19th century, the municipality of New York purchased the land for use as a burial ground straddling the city's limit. At first the cemetery was mainly for indigent workers, but the space quickly reached capacity during an outbreak of yellow fever. Over 20,000 bodies remain buried under the park today.

By 1830 the grounds were used for military parades, and then quickly transformed into a park for the wealthy elite who were constructing lavish townhouses along the surrounding streets.

Stanford White Arch

The iconic Stanford White Arch, colloquially known as the Washington Square Arch, dominates the park with its 72ft of beaming white Dover marble. Originally designed in wood to celebrate the centennial of George Washington's inauguration in 1889, the arch proved so popular that it was replaced with stone six years later and adorned with statues of the general in war and peace. In 1916 artist Marcel Duchamp famously climbed to the top of the arch by its internal stairway and declared the park the 'Free and Independent Republic of Washington Square.'

A Political Stage

Washington Square Park has long provided a stage for political activity, from local protests against proposed changes to the shape and usage of the park, to issues of national importance such as the 1912 protests for better working conditions.

In 2007, Democratic Party candidate Barack Obama led a rally here to drum up support for his successful presidential bid. Turnout was, unsurprisingly, overwhelming.

SIGHTS

West Village & the Meatpacking District

★THE HIGH LINE PARK

See p132.

★WASHINGTON SQUARE PARK PARK

See p135.

★WHITNEY MUSEUM OF AMERICAN ART MUSEUM

Map p420 (☎212-570-3600; www.whitney.org; 99 Gansevoort St; adult/child $22/free; ⏰10:30am-6pm Mon, Wed & Sun, to 10pm Thu-Sat; [S]L to Eighth Ave) After years of construction, the Whitney's new downtown location opened to much fanfare in 2015. Perched near the foot of the High Line, this architecturally stunning building – designed by Renzo Piano – makes a suitable introduction to the museum's superb collection. Inside the spacious, light-filled galleries, you'll find works by all the great American artists, including Edward Hopper, Jasper Johns, Georgia O'Keeffe and Mark Rothko.

In addition to rotating exhibits, there is a biennial on even-numbered years, an ambitious survey of contemporary art that rarely fails to generate controversy.

NEW YORK UNIVERSITY UNIVERSITY

Map p420 (NYU; ☎212-998-4550; www.nyu.edu; information center 50 W 4th St; [S]A/C/E, B/D/F/M to W 4th St-Washington Sq; N/R to 8th St-NYU) In 1831 Albert Gallatin, formerly Secretary of the Treasury under President Thomas Jefferson, founded an intimate center of higher learning open to all students, regardless of race or class background. He'd scarcely recognize the place today, as it's swelled to a student population of around 50,000, with more than 16,000 employees, and schools and colleges at six Manhattan locations.

It just keeps growing, too – to the dismay of landmark activists and business owners, who have seen buildings rapidly bought out by the academic giant (or destroyed through careless planning, such as with the historic Provincetown Playhouse) and replaced with ugly dormitories or administrative offices. Still, some of its crevices are charming, such as the leafy courtyard at its School of Law, or impressively modern, like the Skirball Center for the Performing Arts, where top-notch dance, theater, music, spoken-word and other performers wow audiences at the 850-seat theater. NYU's academic offerings are highly regarded and wide-ranging, especially its film, theater, writing, medical and law programs. For a unique experience that will put you on the fast track to meeting locals, sign up for a weekend or one-day class – from American history to photography – offered by the School of Professional Studies and Continuing Education, and open to all.

GRACE CHURCH CHURCH

Map p420 (☎212-254-2000; www.gracechurchnyc.org; 802 Broadway, at 10th St; ⏰10am-5pm, services daily; [S]N/R to 8th St-NYU; 6 to Astor Pl) This Gothic Revival Episcopal church, designed in 1843 by James Renwick Jr, was made of marble quarried by prisoners at 'Sing Sing,' the state penitentiary in the town of Ossining, 30 miles up the Hudson River (which, legend has it, is the origin of the expression 'being sent upriver'). After years of neglect, Grace Church has been beautifully restored.

It's now a National Landmark, whose elaborate carvings, towering spire and verdant, groomed yard are sure to stop you in your tracks as you make your way down this otherwise ordinary stretch of the Village. The stained-glass windows inside are stunning, and the soaring interior makes a perfect setting for the frequent organ and choir concerts. Free guided tours are offered at 1pm on Sundays.

ABINGDON SQUARE SQUARE

Map p420 (Hudson St, at 12th St; [S]A/C/E to 14th St; L to Eighth Ave) This historical dot on the landscape (just a quarter-acre) is a lovely little patch of green, home to grassy knolls, beds of perennial flowers and winding bluestone paths, as well as a popular Saturday green market. It's a great place to enjoy a midday picnic or rest after an afternoon of wandering the winding West Village streets.

After getting horizontal, look up at the southern end of the park and you'll see the Abingdon Doughboy, a bronze statue dedicated to servicemen from the neighborhood who gave their lives in WWI (when soldiers were commonly known as 'doughboys').

PIER 45 OUTDOORS

Map p420 (W 10th St, at Hudson River; [S]1 to Christopher St-Sheridan Sq) Still known to many as the Christopher Street Pier, this is an 850ft-

TOP SIGHT
HUDSON RIVER PARK

The High Line may be all the rage these days, but one block away there stretches a five-mile-long ribbon of green that has dramatically transformed the city over the past 10 years. Covering 550 acres, and running from Battery Park at Manhattan's southern tip to 59th St in Midtown, the Hudson River Park is Manhattan's wondrous backyard. The long riverside path is a great spot for running, strolling and cycling, and the **Waterfront Bicycle Shop** (Map p420; ☎212-414-2453; www.bikeshopny.com; 391 West St, btwn W 10th & Christopher Sts; rental per 1/4hrs $13/25; ⏰10am-7pm; [S]1 to Christopher St) is a convenient place to rent bikes; several boathouses (p104) offer kayak hire and longer excursions for the more experienced. There's also beach volleyball, basketball courts, a skate park and tennis courts. Families with kids have loads of options including four sparkling new playgrounds, a carousel (off W 22nd St) and minigolf (Pier 25 off West St near N Moore St).

Those who simply need a break from the city come here to loll on the grass, while those seeking something less sedate can join the sangria- and sun-loving crowds at the dockside Frying Pan (p153). The park is also a fine spot to come and watch the sunset. And, of course, on the Fourth of July, there's no better place in the city to be.

DON'T MISS

- Kayaking on the river
- Sunset strolls
- Summertime drinks at Frying Pan

PRACTICALITIES

- Map p420
- www.hudsonriverpark.org

long finger of concrete, spiffily renovated with a grass lawn, flowerbeds, a comfort station, an outdoor cafe, tented shade shelters and a stop for the New York Water Taxi.

Now part of the Hudson River Park, it's a magnet for downtowners of all stripes, from local families with toddlers in daylight to mobs of young gay kids who flock here at night from all over the city (and beyond) thanks to the pier's long-established history as a gay cruising hangout. The spot offers sweeping views of the Hudson and cool, relieving breezes in the thick of summer.

Chelsea

CHELSEA MARKET MARKET

See p134.

★**RUBIN MUSEUM OF ART** GALLERY

Map p424 (☎212-620-5000; www.rmanyc.org; 150 W 17th St , btwn Sixth & Seventh Aves; adult/child $15/free, 6-10pm Fri free; ⏰11am-5pm Mon & Thu, to 9pm Wed, to 10pm Fri, to 6pm Sat & Sun; [S]1 to 18th St) The Rubin is the first museum in the Western world to dedicate itself to the art of the Himalayas and surrounding regions. Its impressive collections include embroidered textiles from China, metal sculptures from Tibet, Pakistani stone sculptures and intricate Bhutanese paintings, as well as ritual objects and dance masks from various Tibetan regions, spanning from the 2nd to the 19th centuries.

Rotating exhibitions have included the enlightening 'Red Book of CJ Jung' and 'Victorious Ones,' which comprised sculptures and paintings of Jinas, the founding teachers of Jainism. The Cafe Serai serves traditional Himalayan foods and features live music on Wednesday nights, from 5pm onwards. Later in the week, the cafe transforms into the K2 Lounge, where you can sip wine and martinis after visiting the galleries on free Friday evenings.

GENERAL THEOLOGICAL SEMINARY RELIGIOUS SITE

Map p424 (☎212-243-5150; www.gts.edu; 440 W 21st St, btwn Ninth & Tenth Aves; ⏰10am-5:30pm Mon-Fri; [S]C/E to 23rd St) [FREE] Founded in 1817, this is the oldest seminary of the Episcopal Church in America. The school, which sits in the midst of the beautiful Chelsea historic district, has been working hard lately to

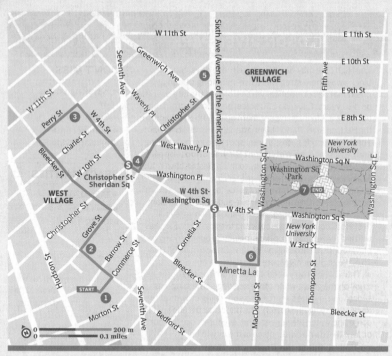

🏃 Neighborhood Walk
It Takes a Village

START COMMERCE ST
END WASHINGTON SQUARE PARK
LENGTH 1 MILE; ONE HOUR

Of all the neighborhoods in New York City, Greenwich Village is the most pedestrian-friendly, with its cobbled corners that stray from the signature gridiron that unfurls across the rest of the island. Start your walkabout at the ❶ **Cherry Lane Theater** (p156). Established in 1924, the small theater is the city's longest continuously running off-Broadway establishment, and was the center of creative activity during the 1940s. Make a left on Bedford and you'll find ❷ **90 Bedford** on the right-hand side at the corner of Grove St. You might recognize the apartment block as the fictitious home of the cast of *Friends* (sadly, Central Perk was just a figment of the writers' imaginations). For another iconic TV landmark, wander up Bleecker St and make a right on Perry St, stopping at ❸ **66 Perry St**, which was used as the facade and stoop of the city's 'It Girl', Carrie Bradshaw, in *Sex and the City*.

Make a right on W 4th St until you reach ❹ **Christopher Park**, where two white, life-sized statues of same-sex couples stand guard. On the north side of the green space is the legendary Stonewall Inn, where a clutch of fed-up drag queens rioted for their civil rights in 1969, signaling the start of what would become the gay revolution. Follow Christopher St to Sixth Ave to find the ❺ **Jefferson Market Library** straddling a triangular plot of land. The 'Ruskinian Gothic' spire was once a fire lookout tower. In the 1870s the building was used as a courthouse but today it houses a branch of the public library. Stroll down Sixth Ave taking in the flurry of passersby, then make a left on Minetta Lane to swing by ❻ **Cafe Wha?**, the notorious institution where many young musicians and comedians – such as Bob Dylan and Richard Pryor – got their start. End your wandering further along MacDougal St in ❼ **Washington Square Park** (p135), the Village's unofficial town square, which plays host to loitering NYU students, buskers and a regular crowd of protestors chanting about various global and municipal injustices.

make sure it can preserve its best asset – the garden-like campus snuggled in the middle of its full block of buildings – even as Chelsea development sprouts up all around it.

This peaceful haven is the perfect spot for finding respite, either before or after your neighborhood gallery crawl. To visit, ring the buzzer at the garden gate, located halfway down 21st St between Ninth and Tenth Aves.

CHELSEA HOTEL   HISTORIC BUILDING

Map p424 (222 W 23rd St, btwn Seventh & Eighth Aves; S1, C/E to 23rd St) This red-brick hotel, built in the 1880s and featuring ornate iron balconies and no fewer than seven plaques declaring its literary landmark status, has played a major role in pop-culture history. It's where the likes of Mark Twain, Thomas Wolfe, Dylan Thomas and Arthur Miller hung out; Jack Kerouac allegedly crafted *On the Road* during one marathon session here, and it's where Arthur C Clarke wrote *2001: A Space Odyssey*.

Dylan Thomas died of alcohol poisoning while staying here in 1953, and Nancy Spungen died here after being stabbed by her Sex Pistols boyfriend Sid Vicious in 1978. Among the many celebs who have logged time living at the Chelsea are Joni Mitchell, Stanley Kubrick, Dennis Hopper, Edith Piaf, Bob Dylan and Leonard Cohen, whose song 'Chelsea Hotel' recalls a romp with Janis Joplin (who spent time here, too).

Sadly, the hotel's days of artistry and intrigue are long gone. At the time of writing a developer was converting the property into a luxury hotel, set to open in late 2016.

 EATING

While the West Village is known for its classy, cozy and intimate spots, the adjacent Meatpacking District's dining scene is a bit more ostentatious, complete with nightclub-like queues behind velvet ropes, bold decor and swarms of trend-obsessed patrons. Chelsea strikes a balance between the two with a brash assortment of très gay eateries along the uber-popular Eighth Ave (a must for see-and-be-seen brunch), and more cafes lining Ninth Ave further west. In the warmer months expect windows and doors to fling open and plenty of alfresco seating to spill out onto the streets, be they the concrete of Chelsea or the cobblestone of the Village. New York is no longer a second-string city when it comes to great coffee. Celebrated brewmasters, bringing technical wizardry and high-quality single-source coffee beans, have reinvented the simple cup of joe. For experiencing a mix of both classic and cutting-edge cafes, the West Village is a great place to start.

✖ West Village & the Meatpacking District

MOUSTACHE   MIDDLE EASTERN $

Map p420 (☏212-229-2220; moustachepitza. com; 90 Bedford St, btwn Grove & Barrow Sts; mains $10-17; ⊙noon-midnight; S1 to Christopher St-Sheridan Sq) Small and delightful Moustache serves up rich, flavorful sandwiches (leg of lamb, merguez sausage, falafel), thin-crust pizzas, tangy salads and hearty specialties such as *ouzi* (filo stuffed with chicken, rice and spices) and moussaka. The best start to a meal: a platter of hummus or baba ghanoush, served with fluffy, piping hot pitas. It's a warm, earthy space with copper-topped tables and brick walls.

PEACEFOOD   VEGAN $

Map p420 (☏212-979-2288; www.peacefoodcafe. com; 41 E 11th St, btwn University Pl & Broadway; mains $12-18; ⊙10am-10pm; ☏; S4/5/6, L, N/Q/R to Union Sq-14th St) Eating vegan can be a pretty powerful way to do good for the environment and one's health (not to mention abstaining from the often cruel business of animal agriculture). That said, cutting back on meat is a lot easier when you can dine at places like Peacefood, with its tasty pizzas, roasted vegetable dishes, pan-seared dumplings and other delicacies.

UMAMI   BURGERS $

Map p420 (☏212-677-8626; www.umamiburger. com; 432 Sixth Ave, btwn 9th & 10th Sts; burgers $10-15; ⊙11:30am-11pm Sun-Thu, to midnight Fri & Sat; S1 to Christopher St-Sheridan Sq; F/M to 14th St; L to Sixth Ave) That mysterious fifth taste sensation will be more than satisfied at this stylish burger bar. Combos such as the Truffle (truffled aioli and housemade truffle cheese) and the bacon-topped Manly are first-rate as is the veg-friendly Black Bean. With creative cocktails, microbrews on draft and tasty sides (including beet salad and tempura onion rings), you're clearly not in the burger land of your childhood.

DENNIS K JOHNSON / GETTY IMAGES ©

1. Washington Square Park (p135)
People-watch in the Village's unofficial town square.

2. Rubin Museum of Art (p137)
Check out this museum dedicated to the art of the Himalayas.

3. The Spotted Pig (p148)
Enjoy a hearty meal at this Michelin-starred Village favorite.

4. Pier 45 (p136)
Take in the views of the Hudson at Pier 45 (aka the Christopher Street Pier).

STEVEN GREAVES / GETTY IMAGES ©

LONELY PLANET / GETTY IMAGES ©

LONELY PLANET / GETTY IMAGES ©

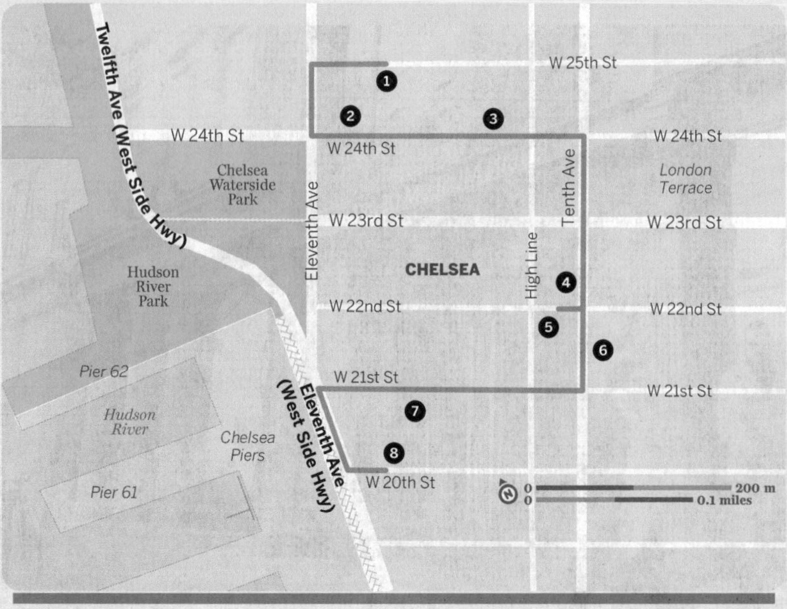

Local Life
Chelsea Galleries

Chelsea is home to the highest concentration of art galleries in the entire city. Most lie in the 20s, on the blocks between Tenth and Eleventh Aves, and openings for their new shows are typically held on Thursday evenings. Pick up Art Info's *Gallery Guide* (with map) available for free at most galleries, or visit www.westchelseaarts.com.

1 Pace Gallery
In a dramatically transformed garage, the **Pace Gallery** (Map p424; ☎212-929-7000; www.pacegallery.com; 534 W 25th St, btwn Tenth & Eleventh Aves; 🕐10am-6pm Tue-Sat; [S]C/E to 23rd St) has worked with some of the leading artists of recent years including Sol LeWitt, David Hockney, Chuck Close and Robert Rauschenberg. It has three locations on W 25th St, and one in Midtown.

2 Gagosian
The **Gagosian** (Map p424; ☎212-741-1111; www.gagosian.com; 555 W 24th St; 🕐10am-6pm Tue-Sat; [S]C/E to 23rd St) offers a different vibe from most of the one-off galleries, as it's part of a constellation of showrooms that spreads well across the globe. Also check out the 21st St location, which easily rivals some of the city's museums with its large-scale installations.

3 Barbara Gladstone
The curator of the eponymous **Barbara Gladstone Gallery** (Map p424; ☎212-206-9300; www.gladstonegallery.com; 515 W 24th St, btwn Tenth & Eleventh Aves; 🕐10am-6pm Tue-Sat; [S]C/E, 1 to 23rd St) has learned a thing or two in her 30 years in the Manhattan art world. Ms Gladstone consistently puts together the most talked-about and well-critiqued displays around.

4 Refuel, Spanish-Style
Wielding Spanish tapas amid closet-sized surrounds, Tía Pol (p148) is the real deal, as the hordes of swarming locals can attest.

5 Matthew Marks
Famous for exhibiting big names such as Jasper Johns and Ellsworth Kelly, **Matthew Marks** (522 W 22nd St) is a true Chelsea pioneer. There are three other nearby locations (on 22nd and 24th Sts) besides this one.

6 192 Books
This small delightful **bookshop** (p159) makes a fine reprieve from the big gallery experience. Inside, you'll find an edifying selection of

Gagosian

literary works covering many genres, plus artist monographs and children's books.

❼ Paula Cooper

An icon of the art world, **Paula** (Map p424; 📞212-255-1105; www.paulacooper gallery.com; 534 W 21st St, btwn Tenth & Eleventh Aves; ⏰10am-6pm Tue-Sat; 🚇C/E to 23rd St) was one of the first to move from SoHo to Chelsea. She continues to push boundaries and draw crowds, as she did for her 2011 exhibition *The Clock* when the gallery stayed open 24 hours a day on weekends.

❽ David Zwirner

One of the major players in the art world, **David Zwirner** (Map p424; 📞212-517-8677; www.davidzwirner.com; 537 W 20th St, btwn Tenth & Eleventh Aves; ⏰10am-6pm Tue-Sat; 🚇C/E to 23rd St) opened a five-story, LEED-certified gallery with 30,000 sq ft of exhibition space in 2013. He stages some of New York's best gallery shows. *Infinity Mirrored Room* was a major recent event which drew three-hour lines to see Yayoi Kutsuma's otherworldly light installations. He also has a location at 525 W 19th St.

DOMINIQUE ANSEL KITCHEN BAKERY $

Map p420 (📞212-242-5111; dominiqueanselkitchen.com; 137 Seventh Ave, btwn Charles & W 10th Sts; pastries $4-8; ⏰9am-9pm; 🚇1 to Christopher St-Sheridan Sq) The famed creator of the cronut owns this small sun-lit bakery in the West Village where you can nibble on perfectly flaky croissants, raspberry passion-fruit pavlova, blueberry shortcake and many other heavenly treats (but no cronuts). There's also light savory fare such as turkey pot pie with foie gras gravy and edamame avocado toast.

The stadium-style seating allows you to peak into the kitchen and see the chefs whipping up the creamy desserts.

TAÏM ISRAELI $

Map p420 (📞212-691-1287; www.taimfalafel.com; 222 Waverly Pl, btwn Perry & W 11th Sts; sandwiches $7-8; ⏰11am-10pm; 🚇1/2/3, A/C/E to 14th St) This tiny joint whips up some of the best falafels in the city. You can order them Green (traditional style), Harissa (with Tunisian spices) or Red (with roasted peppers). Whichever you choose, you'll get them stuffed into pita bread with creamy tahini sauce and a generous dose of Israeli salad.

There are also mixed platters, zesty salads and delicious smoothies (try the date, lime and banana).

OTTO ENOTECA PIZZERIA PIZZA $

Map p420 (📞212-995-9559; www.ottopizzeria.com; 1 Fifth Ave, near 8th St; pizzas $9-15; ⏰11:30am-midnight; 📞; 🚇A/C/E, B/D/F/M to W 4th St-Washington Sq) Just north of Washington Square Park, this is a refreshingly affordable part of Mario Batali's empire, a pizza palace where thin pizzas are cooked on flat-iron griddles till they crackle perfectly. They come topped with items far beyond your standard pizza joint – asparagus, goat's cheese, egg, fresh chilies, capers, the best fresh mozzarella – and sauce that has the perfect balance of smoky and sweet.

Pasta dishes (for just 11 bucks!) veer toward the exotic, such as penne with Tuscan kale, dried lemon and walnuts. And don't even think of leaving without trying the housemade gelato.

HAMILTON'S LUNCHEONETTE AMERICAN $

Map p420 (www.hamiltonsoda.com; 51 Bank St, at W 4th St; mains $7-16; ⏰6am-midnight Mon-Sat, to 11pm Sun; 🚇A/C/E, 1/2/3 to 14th St) Like a blast from the past, this quaint soda fountain and luncheonette channels 1940s New York with bow-tie-wearing clerks, plates of

LOCAL KNOWLEDGE

PARK IN THE SKY

Robert Hammond, co-founder of Friends of the High Line, talks about what, in his opinion, makes the 'park in the sky' and its surrounding neighborhood so special.

High Line Highlights

To me, the West Village is a reminder of New York's industrial past and residential future. What I love most about the High Line are its hidden moments, like at the Tenth Ave cut-out near 17th St. Most people sit on the bleachers, but if you turn the other way you can see the Statue of Liberty far away in the harbor. Architecture buffs will love looking down 18th St, and up on 30th is my favorite moment – a steel cut-out where you can see the cars underneath.

Stop-Offs

For lunch near the High Line, I recommend **Hector's Café & Diner** (Map p420; ☎212-206-7592; 44 Little W 12th St; mains $7-12; ⏲2am-10pm Mon-Sat; [S]A/C/E to 14th St; L to Eighth Ave). It's cheap, untouristy and not at all a see-and-be-seen spot – the cookies are great. If you're in the area, you have to visit the galleries in Chelsea – there are over 300, and check out **Printed Matter** (p160), with its artist-made books. For an evening out on the town, head to the Boom Boom Room at the **Top of the Standard** (p152) – go early and book ahead.

Family-Friendly Activities

The High Line is also great for children with scheduled programming for kids on Saturdays and Wednesdays.

corned beef and cabbage, and frothy egg creams. Never mind that it opened in 2014, Hamilton's is a fine dose of nostalgia in a city ever on the cusp of reinvention.

THELEWALA — INDIAN $

Map p420 (☎212-614-9100; thelewalany.com; 112 MacDougal St, btwn Bleecker & W 3rd Sts; rolls $4-6; ⏲11:30am-2am Sun-Thu, to 5am Fri & Sat; [S]A/C/E, B/D/F/M to W 4th St) This small, rockin' place serves up Calcutta-style street food: delicious rolls filled with the likes of minced lamb, paneer cheese, crispy okra and other ingredients. There are also *chaats* (savory snacks) and dishes such as chickpea curry. Seating options – just a few stools at the counter – are limited, so get it to go and devour your rolls (you'll want more than one) in nearby Washington Square Park.

BONSIGNOUR — SANDWICHES $

Map p420 (☎212-229-9700; 35 Jane St, at Eighth Ave; sandwiches $8-10; ⏲7:30am-10pm Mon-Sat, to 8pm Sun; [S]L to Eighth Ave; A/C/E, 1/2/3 to 14th St) Nestled on a quiet Village street, this shop offers dozens of delicious sandwich choices as well as salads, panini, empanada and desserts. Get a roasted turkey with brie sandwich or a chicken curry salad to go and wander down the street to Abingdon Square for alfresco dining.

SAIGON SHACK — VIETNAMESE $

Map p420 (☎212-228-0588; saigonshacknyc.com; 114 MacDougal St, btwn Bleecker & 3rd Sts; mains $7-10; ⏲11am-11pm Sun-Thu, to 1am Fri & Sat; [S]A/C, B/D/F/M to W 4th St) Steaming bowls of *pho* (noodle soup), tangy *båhn mì* (baguette) sandwiches and crunchy spring rolls await at this bustling wood-lined eatery just a few strides from Washington Square Park. The prices are fair and the food arrives in a hurry; the only downside: you might have to wait for a table, as it's a popular draw for the NYU crowd.

GROUNDED ORGANIC COFFEE & TEA HOUSE — CAFE $

Map p420 (☎212-647-0943; www.groundedcoffee.com; 28 Jane St; sandwiches $7-9; ⏲7:30am-9pm; 🌿; [S]A/C/E, L to 14th St) We won't blame you for having flashbacks to your '90s grunge look when you step into this coffeehouse, which seems to have been encased in amber since *Reality Bites*. In addition to brag-worthy coffee blends and loose teas, Grounded also serves up wraps (scrambled eggs, vegan tofu) for breakfast, and salads and tasty sandwiches (try the portobello with gorgonzola) for lunch.

VICTORY GARDEN · ICE CREAM $

Map p420 (📞212-206-7273; www.victorygarden nyc.com; 31 Carmine St, btwn Bleecker & Bedford Sts; ice cream $4-7; ☺noon-11pm Mon-Sat, to 10pm Sun; ⓢA/C/E, B/D/F/M to W 4th St) If you've never tried goat's milk ice cream, you're in for a treat. This small, charming cafe doles out delectable soft-serve ice cream in flavors such as salted caramel, chocolate made from Mexican stoneground cocoa, and seasonal selections (including watermelon, lemon poppy and roasted plum). The flavors change weekly, with four or so available each day.

JOE'S PIZZA · PIZZA $

Map p420 (📞212-366-1182; www.joespizzanyc. com; 7 Carmine St, btwn Sixth Ave & Bleecker St; slices from $3; ☺10am-4am; ⓢA/C/E, B/D/F/M to W 4th St; 1 to Christopher St-Sheridan Sq or Houston St) No-frills pies are served up indiscriminately to students, tourists and celebrities alike – everyone's stopped by for a bite, from Kirsten Dunst to Bill Murray.

★JEFFREY'S GROCERY · MODERN AMERICAN $$

Map p420 (📞646-398-7630; jeffreysgrocery.com; 172 Waverly Pl, at Christopher St; mains $25-39; ☺8am-11pm Mon-Fri, from 9:30am Sat & Sun ; ⓢ1 to Christopher St-Sheridan Sq) A West Village classic, Jeffrey's is a lively eating and drinking spot that hits all the right notes. Seafood is the focus: there's an oyster bar and beautifully executed seafood selections such as razor clams with caviar and dill, whole roasted dourade with curry, and seafood platters to share. Meat dishes come in the shape of roasted chicken with Jerusalem artichoke, and a humble but juicy pastrami burger.

The scene: exposed brick, oversized windows, wood floors and a buzzing bar scene that draws more drinkers than diners as the night wears on. Brunch is fantastic. From midnight to 1am on Thursday to Saturday nights, Jeffrey's serves a late-night menu of grilled oysters, Old Bay fries and other satisfying snacks.

ROSEMARY'S · ITALIAN $$

Map p420 (📞212-647-1818; rosemarysnyc.com; 18 Greenwich Ave, at W 10th St; mains $15-32; ☺8am-midnight Mon-Fri, from 10am Sat & Sun; ⓢ1 to Christopher St-Sheridan Sq) One of the West Village's hottest restaurants, Rosemary's serves high-end Italian fare that more than lives up to the hype. In a vaguely farmhouse-like setting, diners tuck into generous portions of housemade pastas, rich salads, and cheese and *salumi* (cured meat) boards. Current favorites include the *acqua pazza* (seafood stew) and smoked lamb with roasted vegetables.

Some of the produce is grown in-house, or rather over the house, with a state-of-the-art roof garden producing crisp dandelion greens, plump zucchinis and mouth-watering tomatoes. Plan for crowds (no reservations) or arrive early.

CAFE CLUNY · BISTRO $$

Map p420 (📞212-255-6900; www.cafecluny.com; 284 W 12th St; mains lunch $15-32, dinner $29-35; ☺8am-11pm Mon-Fri, 9am-4pm & 5:30-11pm Sat & Sun; ⓢL to Eighth Ave; A/C/E, 1/2/3 to 14th St) Café Cluny brings the charm of Paris to the West Village, with woven bistro-style bar chairs, light wooden upholstery, and a selection of *joie-de-vivre*-inducing platters such as wagyu sirloin *steak frites*, white-wine-braised hake, pasta with porcini and chanterelle ragout, fragrant cheese plates, mixed green salads and, for dessert, profiteroles or housemade biscotti.

MORANDI · ITALIAN $$

Map p420 (📞212-627-7575; www.morandiny.com; 211 Waverly Place, btwn Seventh Ave & Charles St; mains $18-38; ☺8am-midnight Mon-Fri, from 10am Sat & Sun; ⓢ1 to Christopher St-Sheridan Sq) Run by celebrated restaurateur Keith McNally, Morandi is a warmly lit space where the hubbub of garrulous diners resounds amid brick walls, wide plank floors and rustic chandeliers. Squeeze into a table for the full-meal experience – hand-rolled spaghetti with lemon and parmesan; meatballs with pine nuts and raisins; and grilled whole sea bream.

You can also grab a seat at the copper-topped bar for wine, well-made cocktails and lighter fare such as stuffed olives, mixed antipasti and minestrone with pesto.

COOKSHOP · MODERN AMERICAN $$

Map p424 (📞212-924-4440; www.cookshopny. com; 156 Tenth Ave, btwn 19th & 20th Sts; mains brunch $14-20, lunch $16-24, dinner $22-38; ☺8am-11:30pm Mon-Fri, from 10am Sat, 10am-10pm Sun; ⓢL to Eighth Ave; A/C/E to 23rd St) A brilliant brunching pit stop before (or after) tackling the verdant High Line across the street, Cookshop is a lively place that knows its niche and does it oh so well. Excellent service, eye-opening cocktails (good morning, bacon-infused BLT Mary!), a perfectly baked breadbasket and a selection of inventive egg mains make this a favorite in Chelsea on a Sunday afternoon.

Dinner is a surefire win as well. There's ample outdoor seating on warm days.

COTENNA ITALIAN $$

Map p420 (21 Bedford St, btwn Downing & W Houston Sts ; mains $12-24; ⌚noon-midnight ; [S]1 to Houston St) Tucked away on a picturesque corner of the Village, this intimate, attractively designed eatery is a favorite on date night. It has a small menu of affordable pastas (from $12), bruschetta and grilled dishes, though you can also come for wine or cocktails and sharing plates, including salumi and cheese boards.

CAFE MINERVA CAFE $$

Map p420 (☎212-242-4800; 302 W 4th St, btwn W 12th & Bank; mains $11-27; ⌚8am-11pm; 📶; [S]A/C/E, 1/2/3 to 14th St; L to Eighth Ave) On a peaceful stretch of W 4th St, this neighborhood charmer makes a great setting for a catch up with a friend or a fine spot to linger over a light meal (panini, mussels, salads) when you're solo. The small tables and wrap-around marble-topped bar draws a cappuccino-sipping and snacking crowd by day and wine drinkers by night.

ALTA TAPAS $$

Map p420 (☎212-505-7777; www.altarestaurant.com; 64 W 10th St, btwn Fifth & Sixth Aves; small plates $10-23; ⌚5:30-11pm Mon-Thu, 5pm-midnight Fri & Sat, 5:30-10:30pm Sun; [S]A/C/E, B/D/F/V to W 4th St-Washington Sq) This gorgeous townhouse highlights the neighborhood's quaintness, with plenty of exposed brick, wood beams, flickering candles, massive mirrors and romantic fireplace glows. A small-plates menu of encyclopedic proportions cures indecision with the likes of succulent lamb meatballs, roasted scallops with sunchoke puree, Japanese eggplant with feta, fried goat cheese, and braised short rib. The wine list is outstanding, too.

MALAPARTE ITALIAN $$

Map p420 (☎212-255-2122; www.malapartenyc.com; 753 Washington St, at Bethune St; mains $14-26; ⌚7:30am-midnight Mon-Fri, from 10:30am Sat & Sun; [S]A/C/E to 14th St; L to Eighth Ave) Tucked away on a peaceful stretch of the West Village, Malaparte is a charming neighborhood trattoria serving simple, beautifully executed Italian dishes – *garganelli* (tubular pasta) with porcini mushrooms and truffle oil, chewy crust pizzas, fennel and arugula salads, roasted cornish hen, and tiramisu (of course) for dessert. The focaccia bread basket, which arrives after you sit down, is a nice touch. Cash only.

SNACK TAVERNA GREEK $$

Map p420 (☎212-929-3499; www.snacktaverna.com; 63 Bedford St; small plates $12-14, large plates $22-28, lunch mains $15-18; ⌚7:15am-11pm Mon-Fri, 11am-11pm Sat, to 10pm Sun; [S]A/C/E, B/D to W 4 St; 1 to Christopher St-Sheridan Sq) So much more than your usual Greek restaurant, Snack Taverna eschews gyros for a seasonal selection of scrumptious small plates to accompany the flavorful selection of market mains. The regional wines are worth a miss, but the Med beers are surprisingly refreshing.

WESTVILLE MODERN AMERICAN $$

Map p420 (☎212-741-7971; westvillenyc.com; 210 W 10th St, btwn 4th & Bleecker Sts; mains $12-24; ⌚11:30am-11pm Mon-Fri, from 10am Sat & Sun; [S]1/2 Christopher St-Sheridan Sq; A/C/E, B/D/F, M to W 4th St; 1/2/3 to 14th St) With four downtown locations, Westville has earned many admirers for its reasonably priced market-fresh fare. Set on a peaceful, tree-lined stretch of 10th St, the tiny West Village branch is a cozy setting for beer-battered fish and chips, kale salad and daily specials such as almond-crusted trout or crispy buttermilk chicken sandwich.

MURRAY'S CHEESE BAR CHEESE $$

Map p420 (☎646-476-8882; www.murrayscheesebar.com; 246 Bleecker St; mains $12-26, cheese platters $14-22; ⌚noon-10pm Tue-Sun, from 5pm Mon; [S]A/C/E, B/D/F/M to W 4th St) Lovers of fine cheeses no longer have to settle for take-out orders from Murray's famed West Village *fromagerie*. Gourmet mac and cheese, melted cheese sandwiches, fondue and other cheese-centric dishes dominate the menu at this tile-lined eat-and-drinkery, though the cheese platters (especially the Cheesemongers Choice with five to eight cheeses, plus charcuterie items) are the things to order.

There's a nicely curated wine list, and suggested wine pairings for the cheese platters. Brunch is served on weekends from 11am.

EMPELLÓN TAQUERIA MEXICAN $$

Map p420 (☎212-367-0999; www.empellon.com; 230 W 4th St, at W 10th St; mains $14-26; ⌚11:45am-3pm Thu-Sun & 5:30-11pm daily; [S]1 to Christopher St-Sheridan Sq; A/C/E, B/D/F, M to W 4th St; 1/2/3 to 14th St) Chef Alex Stupak has transformed the all-important avocado into the most inventive and flavorful guacamole in town. He's also dropped the 'Tex' from Tex-Mex, creating imaginative south-of-the-border fare that is wholly elegant and beautifully presented. The white-brick walls further accentuate the mural of luscious red petals behind the bar.

CAFE BLOSSOM VEGAN $$

Map p420 (☎646-438-9939; blossomnyc.com; 41 Carmine St, btwn Bleecker & Bedford Sts; mains lunch $15-22, dinner $19-24; ⏲11am-10:30pm Mon-Fri, 10am-11pm Sat, 10am-10pm Sun; 🥕; [S]A/C/E, B/D/F/M to W 4th St) This candlelit eatery serves first-rate organic vegan cuisine. The menu is small but features comfort fare that puts tofu to creative uses in dishes such as 'salmon' tofu, seitan steak au poivre and flatbread pizza with sauteed kale. There are also organic wines, beers and cocktails, plus luscious desserts.

DOMINIQUE BISTRO FRENCH $$

Map p420 (☎646-756-4145; www.dominiquebistro.nyc; 14 Christopher St, at Gay St; mains $21-31; ⏲8am-midnight Sun-Thu, to 1am Fri-Sat; [S]1 to Christopher St-Sheridan Sq) On one of the prettiest corners in the West Village you'll find this airy space with soaring ceilings, oversized oil canvases and big windows for watching the city stroll past. Chef Dominick Pepe serves classic French bistro fare: start off with foie gras or escargots with parsley butter, before moving on to bouillabaisse, duck cassoulet or vegetarian-friendly ratatouille. You can dine to live music downstairs in the cozy Piano Room. Check the website for the schedule.

FATTY CRAB ASIAN $$

Map p420 (☎212-352-3592; www.fattycrab.com; 643 Hudson St, btwn Gansevoort & Horatio Sts; mains $19-34; ⏲noon-11pm Sun-Wed, to midnight Thu-Sat; [S]L to Eighth Ave; A/C/E, 1/2/3 to 14th St) This small Malaysian-inspired joint is super hip and always teeming with locals who swing by in droves to devour fish curries and pork belly accompanied by a signature selection of cocktails.

BARBUTO MODERN AMERICAN $$

Map p420 (☎212-924-9700; www.barbutonyc.com; 775 Washington St, btwn 12th & Jane Sts; mains $22-28; ⏲noon-3:30pm & 5:30-11pm; [S]L to Eighth Ave; A/C/E to 14th St; 1 to Christopher St-Sheridan Sq) Occupying a cavernous garage space with sweeping see-through doors that roll up and into the ceiling during the warmer months, Barbuto slaps together a delightful assortment of nouveau Italian dishes such as pork loin with polenta and apple, and bruschetta smeared with duck liver, pistachio and balsamic.

★BLUE HILL AMERICAN $$$

Map p420 (☎212-539-1776; www.bluehillfarm.com; 75 Washington Pl, btwn Sixth Ave & Washington Sq W; prix-fixe menu $88-98; ⏲5-11pm; [S]A/C/E, B/D/F/M to W 4th St-Washington Sq) A place for slow-food junkies with deep pockets, Blue Hill was an early crusader in the local-is-better movement. Gifted chef Dan Barber, who hails from a farm family in the Berkshires, Massachusetts, uses harvests from that land, as well as from farms in upstate New York, to create his widely praised fare.

Expect barely seasoned, perfectly ripe vegetables that highlight centerpieces of cod in almond broth, Berkshire pork stewed with four types of beans, and grass-fed lamb with white beans and new potatoes. The space itself, slightly below street level and housed in a landmark former speakeasy on a quaint Village block, is sophisticated and serene.

★REDFARM FUSION $$$

Map p420 (☎212-792-9700; www.redfarmnyc.com; 529 Hudson St, btwn 10th & Charles Sts; mains $22-46, dim sum $10-16; ⏲11am-2:30pm Sat & Sun, 5pm-11pm daily; [S]A/C/E, B/D/F/M to W 4th St; 1 to Christopher St-Sheridan Sq) RedFarm transforms Chinese cooking into pure, delectable artistry at this small, buzzing space on Hudson St. Fresh crab and eggplant bruschetta, juicy rib steak (marinated overnight in papaya, ginger and soy) and pastrami egg rolls are among the many creative dishes that brilliantly blend east with west. Other hits include the spicy crispy beef, pan-fried lamb dumplings and the grilled jumbo shrimp red curry.

Waits can be long, so arrive early as reservations are not accepted.

★FORAGERS CITY TABLE MODERN AMERICAN $$$

Map p424 (☎212-243-8888; www.foragerscitygrocer.com; 300 W 22nd St, cnr Eighth Ave; mains $25-36; ⏲10:30am-2:30pm Sat & Sun, 5:30-10pm daily; 🥕; [S]C/E, 1 to 23rd St) The owners of this excellent restaurant in Chelsea run a 28-acre farm in the Hudson Valley, from which much of their menu is sourced. The menu, which showcases seasonal hits, changes frequently. Recent temptations include squash soup with Jerusalem artichokes and black truffles, roasted chicken with polenta, heritage pork loin, and the season's harvest with toasted quinoa and a flavorful mix of vegetables.

Next door is the gourmet market, where you can browse many goodies, from organic produce to heavenly desserts. There's also a wine shop with reasonably priced bottles from small producers.

MINETTA TAVERN   BISTRO $$$

Map p420 (☎212-475-3850; www.minettata vernny.com; 113 MacDougal St; mains $22-36; ☺noon-3pm Wed-Sun, 5:30pm-midnight daily; ⓈA/C/E, B/D/F/M to W 4th St) Book in advance, or come early to snag a table on a weeknight, because Minetta Tavern is often packed to the rafters. The snug red-leather banquettes, dark-paneled walls with black-and-white photos, and glowing yellow bistro lamps will lure you in. The flavor-filled bistro fare – pan-seared marrow bones, roasted free-range chicken, mussels and foie gras – will have you wishing you lived upstairs.

SPOTTED PIG   PUB FOOD $$$

Map p420 (☎212-620-0393; www.thespottedpig. com; 314 W 11th St, at Greenwich St; mains lunch $17-26, dinner $22-36; ☺noon-2am Mon-Fri, from 11am Sat & Sun; ☝ ➍; ⓈA/C/E to 14th St; L to 8th Ave) This Michelin-starred gastro-pub is a favorite with Villagers, serving an upscale blend of hearty Italian and British dishes. Its two floors are bedecked with old-timey trinkets that give the whole place an air of relaxed elegance. There are no reservations, so there is often a wait for a table. Lunch on weekdays is less crowded.

✕ Chelsea

★CHELSEA MARKET   MARKET $

Map p424 (www.chelseamarket.com; 75 9th Ave, btwn 15th & 16th Sts; ☺7am-9pm Mon-Sat, 8am-8pm Sun; ⓈA/C/E to 14th St) A factory formerly owned by cookie giant Nabisco (creator of Oreo) is now an 800ft-long foodie haven. Taking the place of the old factory ovens that churned out massive numbers of biscuits are eclectic eateries that fill the renovated hallways of this food-lovers hub (for more on the market see p134).

GANSEVOORT MARKET   MARKET $

Map p420 (www.gansmarket.com; 52 Gansevoort, btwn Greenwich & Washington Sts; mains $5-20; ☺8am-8pm; ⓈA/C/E to 14th St; L to Eighth Ave) Inside a brick building in the heart of the Meatpacking District, this sprawling market is the latest and greatest food emporium to land in NYC. Inside a raw, industrial space lit by skylights, several dozen gourmet vendors sling tapas, arepas, tacos, pizzas, meat pies, ice cream, pastries and more.

There's a communal seating area, and several food counters where you can sit around and watch the cooks in action while munching your meal.

JUN-MEN   RAMEN $

Map p424 (☎646-852-6787; www.junmenramen. com; 249 Ninth Ave, btwn 25th & 26th Sts; ramen $14-18; ☺11:30am-3pm & 5-10pm Mon-Thu, to 11pm Fri & Sat; ⓈC/E to 23rd St) This tiny, ultra-modern ramen joint whips up delectably flavored noodle bowls, in variants of pork shoulder, spicy miso or uni mushroom (with sea urchin). Don't skip the appetizers: the yellowtail ceviche and barbecue pork buns are outstanding. Service is speedy, and it's fun to watch the adroit prep team in action in the tiny kitchen at center stage.

The wait can be long – go early to beat the crowds.

TÍA POL   TAPAS $$

Map p424 (☎212-675-8805; www.tiapol.com; 205 Tenth Ave, btwn 22nd & 23rd Sts; small plates $5-14; ☺noon-11pm Tue-Sun, from 5:30pm Mon; ⓈC/E to 23rd St) Wielding Spanish tapas in closet-sized surrounds, Tía Pol is the real deal, as the hordes of locals swarming the entrance can attest. There's a great wine list and a tantalizing array of small plates: fried chickpeas, squid and ink with rice, cockles in white wine and garlic, and Navarran-style trout with serrano ham.

It's the perfect post-gallery-opening pit stop. Come on the early side to take your best stab at grabbing one of the handful of tables in the back.

CO   PIZZA $$

Map p424 (☎212-243-1105; www.co-pane.com; 230 Ninth Ave, at 24th St; pizza $17-21; ☺5-11pm Mon, 11:30am-11pm Tue-Sat, 11am-10pm Sun; ⓈC/E to 23rd St) Masterfully prepared pizza is served in trim wooden surrounds that have a Scandinavian farmhouse vibe. Expect a faithful reproduction of the trademark Neapolitan thin-crust pies topped with an assortment of fresh-from-the-farm items such as fennel and buffalo mozzarella. Salads of escarole, beet or radicchio – as well as global wines and a sprinkling of sweets – round out the offerings.

BLOSSOM VEGAN $$

Map p424 (☎212-627-1144; www.blossomnyc.com; 187 Ninth Ave, btwn 21st & 22nd Sts; mains lunch $15-19, dinner $20-25; 🕐noon-2:45pm & 5-9:30pm; 🌱; [S]C/E to 23rd St) This Chelsea veg oasis – with a sinful wine and chocolate bar attached – is a peaceful, romantic dining room that offers imaginative tofu, seitan and vegetable creations, some raw, all kosher. The stellar Autumn Sweet Potato Rolls have raw strips of the orange root wrapped around tangy strips of coconut, carrots and peppers, and will leave your taste buds reeling.

Seitan *scaloppini* perfectly blends richness with a light lemony zing, while the hickory-roasted tempeh gets tempered with creamy horseradish *crème fraîche*. Desserts are so rich, you'll swear they're filled with butter and cream.

LE GRAINNE FRENCH $$

Map p424 (☎646-486-3000; www.legrainnecafe.com; 183 Ninth Ave, btwn 21st & 22nd Sts; mains $11-30; 🕐8am-midnight; [S]C/E, 1 to 23rd St; A/C/E to 14th St) Tap the top of your French onion soup as you dream of ingenue Amélie cracking open her crème brulée; Le Grainne transports the senses from the busy blocks of Chelsea to the backstreets of Paris. The tin-topped eatery excels at lunch time, when baguette sandwiches and savory crepes are scarfed down amid cramped quarters.

Come for dinner to breathe in the wafting garlic as hearty pastas are tossed in the kitchen.

HEATH SUPPER CLUB $$

Map p424 (☎212-564-1622; mckittrickhotel.com/theheath; 542 W 27th St, btwn Tenth & Eleventh Aves; mains $23-39; 🕐6pm-11pm Wed & Thu, to 2am Fri & Sat, 11:30am-4:30pm Sat & Sun; [S]C/E to 23rd St) The creators of hit interactive theater piece *Sleep No More* operate this atmospheric restaurant next door to their warehouse venue. Like the fictional McKittrick Hotel in the drama, the Heath is set in another place and time (vaguely Britain, 1920s), with suspenders-wearing barkeeps, period furnishings and (fake) smoke wafting over the dining room, as a jazz band performs on stage.

Actors disguised as waitstaff interact with the diners, and soon you become part of the whole theatrical experience. The menu features heritage English recipes – roasted Amish chicken, summer vegetable stew, grilled sea scallops – and is fairly solid. But the ambience and entertainment are the real draws. Prepare for a memorable evening, marked with a touch of drama.

DRINKING & NIGHTLIFE

The key word in the West Village is 'west' – the further towards the Hudson you go, the more likely you are to sidestep the frat party scene found around the NYU campus. Generally the going gets good around the crooked lanes west of Sixth Ave. Just to the north, the Meatpacking District is strictly contemporary in vibe, with sprawling, modern spaces boasting long cocktail lists, velvet-roped entrances and dins that'll rattle your brain. Chelsea is still very much the territory for gay men, but there's a handful of options for all tastes, from speakeasy-chic digs to well-worn dive bars.

West Village & the Meatpacking District

EMPLOYEES ONLY BAR

Map p420 (☎212-242-3021; www.employeesonlynyc.com; 510 Hudson St, near Christopher St; 🕐6pm-4am; [S]1 to Christopher St-Sheridan Sq) Duck behind the neon 'Psychic' sign to find this hidden hangout. The bar gets busier as the night wears on. Bartenders are ace mixologists, fizzing up crazy, addictive libations such as the Ginger Smash and the Mata Hari. Great for late-night drinking and eating, courtesy of the on-site restaurant that serves till 3:30am.

BUVETTE WINE BAR

Map p420 (☎212-255-3590; www.ilovebuvette.com; 42 Grove St, btwn Bedford & Bleecker Sts; 🕐9am-2am; [S]1 to Christopher St-Sheridan Sq; A/C/E, B/D/F/M to W 4th St) The rustic-chic decor here (think delicate tin tiles and a swooshing marble counter) make it the perfect place for a glass of wine – no matter the time of day. For the full experience at this self-proclaimed *gastrotèque,* grab a seat at one of the surrounding tables, and nibble on small plates while enjoying the old-world wines (mostly from France and Italy).

HAPPIEST HOUR COCKTAIL BAR

(☎212-243-2827; www.happiesthournyc.com; 121 W 10th St, btwn Greenwich St & Avenue of the Americas (Sixth Ave); ⏲5pm-late Mon-Fri, from 2pm Sat & Sun; [S]A/C/E, B/D/F/M to W 4th St; 1 to Christopher St-Sheridan Sq) A super-cool, tiki-licious cocktail bar splashed with palm prints, 60s pop and playful mixed drinks. Below it sits serious sibling, Slowly Shirley, a subterranean temple to beautifully crafted, thoroughly researched libations.

ARIA WINE BAR

Map p420 (☎212-242-4233; 117 Perry St, btwn Greenwich & Hudson Sts; ⏲noon-midnight; [S]1 to Christopher St-Sheridan Sq) In the western reaches of the Village, Aria is an inviting music-filled space, with a mix of brick and tile walls and rustic wood tables. There's a good selection of wines by the glass, particularly organic labels, with prices starting around $8 a (small) glass. Recommended *cicchetti* (bite-sized plates, good for sharing) include gorgonzola-stuffed dates, crab cakes and stewed calamari.

It attracts a lively crowd most nights, and the small space can get a bit cramped.

STANDARD BAR

Map p420 (☎877-550-4646, 212-645-4646; www.standardhotels.com; 848 Washington St; [S]A/C/E to 14th St; L to 8 Eighth Ave) Rising on concrete stilts over the High Line, the Standard attracts an A-list crowd, with a chichi lounge and nightclub on the upper floors – the Top of the Standard (p152) and Le Bain (p152). There's also a grill, an eating-and-drinking plaza (that becomes a skating rink in winter) and an open-air beer garden with a classic German menu and frothy drafts.

HIGHLANDS BAR

Map p420 (☎212-229-2670; www.highlands-nyc.com; 150 W 10th St; ⏲5:30pm-1am Sun-Wed, to 2am Thu-Sat; [S]1 to Christopher St-Sheridan Sq) This handsome Scottish-inspired drinkery is a fine place to while away an evening. Exposed brick, a fireplace and a mix of animal heads, pheasant wallpaper, oil paintings and Edinburgh tartans on the walls bring in more than a touch of the old country. Scottish beers and spirits, plus haggis, scotch eggs, shepherd's pie and other traditional bites round out the menu.

ART BAR BAR

Map p420 (☎212-727-0244; www.artbar.com; 52 Eighth Ave, near Horatio St; ⏲4pm-4am, happy hour 4-7pm; [S]L to Eighth Ave-14th St; A/C/E to 14th St) A decidedly bohemian crowd favors Art Bar, which doesn't look like much up front (the booths are crowded too close to the wooden bar), but has a bit more going on in the back. Grab your beer or one of the house specials (usually martinis) and head for the couches, placed under a huge *Last Supper*-esque mural featuring Jimmy Dean and Marilyn Monroe, among others.

There's a roaring fire in the winter.

TROY LIQUOR BAR LOUNGE

Map p420 (☎212-699-2410; www.troyliquorbar.com; 675 Hudson St, at W 13th St (entrance on W 13th St); ⏲6pm-midnight Tue & Wed, to 3am Thu-Sat ; [S]L to Eighth Ave; 1/2/3, A/C/E to 14th St) Tucked under Bill's Bar & Burger in the Meatpacking District is this indie-rock–loving, graffiti-scrawled hangout. Come for a game of foosball or hide away with your retro cocktail in one of the cave-like nooks.

JANE BALLROOM LOUNGE

Map p420 (☎212-924-6700; www.thejanenyc.com; 113 Jane St, cnr West St; ⏲5pm-2am Sun-Wed, to 4am Thu-Sat; [S]L to Eighth Ave; A/C/E, 1/2/3 to 14th St) Inside the Jane Hotel, this spacious high-ceilinged lounge is an explosion of wild design: beneath an oversized disco ball is a mish-mash of leather sofas and velour chairs, animal print fabrics, potted palms and various taxidermied creatures (a peacock, a ram's head over the flickering fireplace).

Head up to the balcony to take in the scene, which remains low-key and lounge-like during the week and morphs into a full-blown party on weekends, when revelers sometimes dance on the furniture (you've been warned). The Jane Hotel also has an elegant rooftop bar – an unbeatable spot for a sundowner.

BELL BOOK & CANDLE BAR

Map p420 (☎212-414-2355; www.bbandcnyc.com; 141 W 10th St, btwn Waverley Pl & Greenwich Ave; ⏲5:30pm-2am Sun-Wed, to 4am Thu-Sat; [S]A/B/C, B/D/F/M to W 4th St; 1 to Christopher St-Sheridan Sq) Step down into this candelit gastropub for strong, inventive libations (try the canela margarita, with cinnamon-infused tequila) and hearty pub grub. A 20-something crowd gathers around the small, packed bar (for $1 oysters and happy hour drink specials early in the night), though there's a lot more seating hidden in the back, with big booths ideal for larger groups.

KETTLE OF FISH BAR

Map p420 (☎212-414-2278; www.kettleoffishnyc.com; 59 Christopher St, near Seventh Ave; ⏲3pm-4am Mon-Fri, 2pm-4am Sat & Sun; [S]1 to Christopher St-Sheridan Sq) Step into this dimly lit spot, full of couches and plump chairs, and prepare to stay for a while because the crowd is simply beguiling. It's a dive bar, a sports bar and a gay bar in one, and everyone mixes happily.

There are stacks of board games, including Monopoly and checkers, to while away the time, as well as a dart board. And if you get hungry, the barkeeps can offer menus from nearby restaurants that deliver here. The owner is a Packers fan, so expect raucous activity on game days.

124 OLD RABBIT CLUB BAR

Map p420 (☎212-254-0575; 124 MacDougal St; ⏲6pm-2am Sun-Thu, to 4am Fri & Sat; [S]A/C/E, B/D/F/M to W 4th St; 1 to Houston St) You'll wanna pat yourself on the back when you find this well-concealed bar (hint: look for the tiny word 'Rabbit' over the door). Once you're inside the narrow, cavern-like space with its low-key vibe, grab a seat at the dimly lit bar and reward yourself with a quenching stout or one of the dozens of imported brews.

JOE THE ART OF COFFEE CAFE

Map p420 (☎212-924-6750; www.joetheartofcoffee.com; 141 Waverly Pl; ⏲7am-8pm Mon-Fri, from 8am Sat & Sun; [S]A/C/E, B/D/F/M to W 4th St-Washington Sq) Superb coffee is served at this always-bustling joint sitting squarely on bucolic Waverly Place in the heart of the Village. Some say this is the best cup of joe in town.

STUMPTOWN COFFEE ROASTERS (GREENWICH VILLAGE) CAFE

Map p420 (☎347-414-7802; stumptowncoffee.com; 30 W Eighth St, at MacDougal St; ⏲7am-8pm; [S]A/C/E, B/D/F/M to W 4th St) This renowned Portland roaster is helping to reinvent the NYC cafe scene with its exquisitely made brews. It has an elegant interior with coffered ceiling and walnut bar, though its few tables are often overtaken by the laptop-toting crowd.

VIN SUR VINGT WINE BAR

Map p420 (☎212-924-4442; www.vinsur20nyc.com; 201 W 11th St, btwn Seventh Ave & Waverly Pl; ⏲3pm-2am Mon-Fri, from 11:30am Sat & Sun; [S]1/2/3 to 14th St; 1/2 to Christopher St-Sheridan Sq; L to Eighth Ave) A cozy spot just off Seventh Ave's bustle, Vin Sur Vingt is a slender wine bar with a strip of bar seating and a quaint row of two-seat tables, perfect for a first date. Warning: if you come for a pre-dinner drink, you'll inevitably be charmed into staying through dinner as you munch on the excellent selection of bar bites.

The reasonably priced all-French wine list (with over 50 options by the glass) keeps locals coming back for seconds.

MARIE'S CRISIS BAR

Map p420 (☎212-243-9323; 59 Grove St, btwn Seventh Ave & Bleecker St; ⏲4pm-4am; [S]1 to Christopher St-Sheridan Sq) Ageing Broadway queens, wide-eyed out-of-town gay boys, giggly tourists and various other fans of musical theater assemble around the piano here and take turns belting out campy show tunes, often joined by the entire crowd – and the occasional celebrity (Jimmy Fallon joined in singing 'Summer Nights' from *Grease* in 2015).

It's old-school fun, no matter how jaded you were when you went in.

JULIUS BAR GAY

Map p420 (☎212-243-1928; www.juliusbarny.com; 159 W 10th St, at Waverly Pl; ⏲noon-4am; [S]A/C/E, B/D/F/M to W 4th St; 1 to Christopher St-Sheridan Sq) One of the infamous originals – in fact, it's the oldest operating gay bar in NYC – Julius is a dive bar through and through. The only hint of its homo roots is the clientele, a mixed bag of faithful locals and the occasional newbie. It's refreshingly unpretentious, and just steps away from the better known Stonewall (p153) and Duplex (p156).

BRASS MONKEY BAR

Map p420 (☎212-675-6686; www.brassmonkeynyc.com; 55 Little W 12th St, at Washington St; ⏲11am-4am; [S]A/C/E to 14th St; L to Eighth Ave) While most Meatpacking District bars tend toward the chic, the Monkey is more for beer lovers than those worrying about what shoes to wear. The multifloor place is at ease and down-to-earth, with squeaking wood floors and a nice long list of beers and Scotch. The roof deck is a fine destination in warm weather.

LITTLE BRANCH COCKTAIL BAR

Map p420 (☎212-929-4360; 20 Seventh Ave, at Leroy St; 🕒7pm-3am; [S]1 to Houston St) If it weren't for the doorman, you'd never guess that a charming drinking den lurked beyond the plain metal door positioned at this triangular intersection. When you get the go-ahead to enter, you'll find a basement bar that feels like a kickback to Prohibition times. Old-time jazz tunes waft overhead as locals clink glasses and sip inventive, artfully prepared cocktails.

CIELO CLUB

Map p420 (☎212-645-5700; www.cieloclub.com; 18 Little W 12th St; cover charge $15-25; 🕒10pm-5am Mon & Wed-Sat; [S]A/C/E, L to Eighth Ave-14th St) This long-running club boasts a largely attitude-free crowd and an excellent sound system. Join dance lovers on Deep Space Monday when DJ François K spins dub and underground beats. Other nights feature various DJs from Europe who mix entrancing, seductive sounds that pull everyone to their feet.

TOP OF THE STANDARD LOUNGE

Map p420 (☎212-645-7600; standardhotels.com/high-line; 848 Washington St, btwn 13th & Little W 12th Sts; 🕒4pm-midnight Mon, to 9pm Tue-Sat, noon-midnight Sun; [S]L to Eighth Ave; 1/2/3, A/C/E to 14th St) Smooth beige surrounds, soft music and plenty of room to swig your top-shelf tipple, the Top of the Standard is strictly VIP and the favored hangout for the vogue elite (and *Vogue* elite) – expect models, their photographers and the occasional celeb sighting. Sunset is the best time to be here.

Dress your best and book ahead – that's the only way to gain access if you're not a cornerstone of New York's social scene.

LE BAIN CLUB

Map p420 (☎212-645-7600; www.standardculture.com/lebain.com; 848 Washington St, btwn 13th & Little W 12th Sts; 🕒4pm-midnight Mon, to 4am Tue-Thu, 2pm-4am Fri-Sun; [S]L to Eighth Ave; 1/2/3, A/C/E to 14th St) The sweeping rooftop venue at the tragically hip Standard Hotel, Le Bain sees a garish parade of party promoters who do their thang on any day of the week. Brace yourself for skyline views, a dance floor with a giant Jacuzzi built right into it and an eclectic crowd getting wasted on pricey snifters.

When hunger strikes, you can hit up the rooftop crepe stand, which is open all night.

FAT CATS BAR

Map p420 (☎212-675-6056; www.fatcatmusic.org; 75 Christopher St, near Seventh Ave; cover $3; 🕒2pm-5am Mon-Thu, noon-5am Fri-Sun; [S]1 to Christopher St-Sheridan Sq; A/C/E, B/D/F/M to W 4th St) If $16 cocktails and fancy-schmancy Village boutiquery are getting you down, maybe it's time to pay a visit to this run-down little Ping-Pong hall. Fat Cats is a basement dive that draws a young, unpretentious crowd who want to hang out, shoot some pool, play a little shuffleboard, and maybe even get a Ping-Pong game going. You'll also find cheap beers and live music nightly.

HENRIETTA HUDSON LESBIAN

Map p420 (☎212-924-3347; www.henriettahudson.com; 438 Hudson St; 🕒 5pm-2am Mon & Tue, 4pm-4am Wed-Fri, 2pm-4am Sat & Sun; [S]1 to Houston St) All sorts of cute young women, many from neighboring New Jersey and Long Island, storm this sleek lounge, where varying theme nights bring in spirited DJs, who stick to particular genres (hip-hop, house, rock). The owner, Brooklyn native Lisa Canistraci, is a favorite promoter in the world of lesbian nightlife, and is often on hand to mix it up with her fans.

VOL DE NUIT PUB

Map p420 (☎212-982-3388; voldenuitbar.com; 148 W 4th St; 🕒4pm-1am Sun-Thu, to 3am Fri & Sat; [S]A/C/E, B/D/F/M to W 4th St-Washington Sq) Even all the NYU students can't ruin this: a cozy Belgian beer bar with Delirium Tremens on tap and a few dozen bottle options, including Duvel and Lindemans Framboise (raspberry beer!). You can order *moules* (mussels) and *frites* (fries) to share at the front patio seats, the lounge, the communal wood tables or under the dangling red lights at the bar.

WHITE HORSE TAVERN BAR

Map p420 (☎212-989-3956; 567 Hudson St, at 11th St; 🕒11am-2am Sun-Thu, to 4am Fri & Sat; [S]1 to Christopher St-Sheridan Sq) It's a bit on the tourist trail, but that doesn't dampen the century-old, pubby, dark-wood, tin-ceiling atmosphere of this bar, where Dylan Thomas had his last drink (too many beers led to his 1953 death) and a tipsy Jack Kerouac got kicked out. Sit at the long oak bar inside or on sidewalk tables.

MONSTER GAY

Map p420 (☎212-924-3558; www.monsterbarnyc.com; 80 Grove St, at Sheridan Sq; 🕒4pm-4am Sun-Thu, from 2pm Fri & Sat; [S]1 to Christopher St-Sheridan Sq) It's old-school gay-man heaven in here, with a small dance floor downstairs as well as a piano bar and cabaret space. Spirited theme nights range from Latino parties to drag-queen–hosted soirees.

STONEWALL INN GAY

Map p420 (☎212-488-2705; www.thestonewallinnnyc.com; 53 Christopher St; 🕒2pm-4am; [S]1 to Christopher St-Sheridan Sq) Site of the Stonewall riots in 1969, this historic bar was losing its fan base to trendier spots until new owners came along several years back, gave it a facelift and opened it to a new and welcoming crowd. Since then, it's been pulling in varied crowds nightly for parties catering to everyone under the gay rainbow.

CUBBYHOLE GAY & LESBIAN

Map p420 (☎212-243-9041; www.cubbyholebar.com; 281 W 12th St; 🕒4pm-4am Mon-Fri, from 2pm Sat & Sun; [S]A/C/E to 14th St; L to 8th Ave) If you can handle all the crazy kitsch covering the walls and ceiling, this no-attitude neighborhood watering hole is a good spot for a drink. It has a truly rare mix of lesbians and gay men who are out to make friends rather than hit the road with the first trick they find. It's got a great jukebox, friendly bartenders and plenty of regulars.

🍷 Chelsea

BATHTUB GIN COCKTAIL BAR

Map p424 (☎646-559-1671; www.bathtubginnyc.com; 132 Ninth Ave, btwn 18th & 19th Sts; 🕒6pm-1:30am Sun-Tue, to 3:30am Wed-Sat; [S]A/C/E to 14th St; L to Eighth Ave; A/C/E to 23rd St) Amid New York City's obsession with speakeasy-styled hangouts, Bathtub Gin manages to poke its head above the crowd with its super-secret front door hidden on the wall of an unassuming cafe (the Stone Street Coffee Company). Once inside, chill seating, soft background beats and kindly staff make it a great place to sling back bespoke cocktails with friends.

PETER MCMANUS TAVERN BAR

Map p424 (☎212-929-9691; www.petermcmanuscafe.com; 152 Seventh Ave, at 19th St; 🕒10am-4am Mon-Sat, noon-4am Sun; [S]A/C/E to 14th St) Pouring drafts since the 1930s, this family-run dive is something of a museum to the world of the McManuses: photos of yesteryear, an old telephone booth and Tiffany glass. There's also greasy bar food to eat at the comfy green booths.

FRYING PAN BAR

Map p424 (☎212-989-6363; www.fryingpan.com; Pier 66, at W 26th St; 🕒noon-midnight May-Oct; [S]C/E to 23rd St) Salvaged from the bottom of the sea (or at least the Chesapeake Bay), the Lightship *Frying Pan* and the two-tiered dockside bar where it's parked are fine go-to spots for a sundowner. On warm days, the rustic open-air space brings in the crowds, who come to laze on deck chairs and drink ice-cold beers ($7 for a microbrew; $25 for a pitcher).

You can also come for burgers, cooked up on the sizzling grill, or just sit back and admire the fine views across the water to, uh, New Jersey.

GALLOW GREEN BAR

Map p424 (☎212-564-1662; mckittrickhotel.com/gallowgreen; 542 W 27th St, btwn Tenth & Eleventh Aves; 🕒5pm-midnight Mon-Fri, from noon Sat & Sun; [S]C/E to 23rd St; 1 to 28th St) Run by the creative team behind Sleep No More (p154) theatre, Gallow Green is a rooftop bar festooned with vines, potted plants and fairy lights. It's a great add-on before or after experiencing the show, with waitstaff in period costume, a live band most nights and tasty rum-filled cocktails.

When the cold weather arrives, Gallow Green sets up 'the Lodge', a cozy chalet, with various astonishingly filled rooms, complete with books, bunk beds, fur rugs, a rocking chair and a fireplace. For a woodsy escape without leaving Midtown, this is it.

G LOUNGE GAY

Map p424 (☎212-929-1085; www.glounge.com; 225 W 19th St, btwn Seventh & Eighth Aves; 🕒4pm-4am; [S]1 to 18th St) Glossy and unpretentious, this gay bar is as friendly as they come, and it's really all about the music. Check out the website to find out who's spinning while you're in town. For heavy drinking and dancing with no cover, you can't beat G – although you may have to wait in line to get in.

The occasional burlesque or drag show adds to the good fun. Cash only

EAGLE NYC GAY

Map p424 (☎646-473-1866; www.eaglenyc.com; 554 W 28th St, btwn Tenth & Eleventh Aves; 🕐10pm-4am Mon-Fri, 5pm-4am Sat & Sun; [S]C/E to 23rd St) A bi-level club full of hot men in leather, the Eagle is the choice for out-and-proud fetishists. Its two levels, plus roof deck, offer plenty of room for dancing and drinking, which are done with abandon. Thursdays are Code nights, meaning everyone must meet the dress code (wear leather or nothing at all).

Located in a renovated 19th-century stable, the inside joke is that 'the studs keep coming.'

BARRACUDA GAY

Map p424 (☎212-645-8613; www.facebook.com/BarracudaLounge; 275 W 22nd St, btwn Seventh & Eighth Aves; 🕐4pm-4am; [S]C/E to 23rd St) This old standby holds its own even as newer, slicker places come and go. That's because it's got a simple, winning formula: affordable cocktails, a cozy rec-room vibe and free entertainment from some of the city's top drag queens.

BLUE BOTTLE CAFE

Map p424 (450 W 15th St, btwn Ninth & Tenth Aves; 🕐7am-6pm Mon-Fri, from 8am Sat & Sun; [S]A/C/E to 14th St; L to Eighth Ave) Blue Bottle may have originated in Oakland, but New Yorkers have happily embraced this high-quality third-wave roaster. Blue Bottle's small outpost across from the Chelsea Market does beautiful pour-overs and pulls rich lattes. Grab one of the few window seats, or head to one of the mezzanine tables above the baristas.

ENTERTAINMENT

★UPRIGHT CITIZENS BRIGADE THEATRE COMEDY

Map p424 (☎212-366-9176; www.ucbtheatre.com; 307 W 26th St, btwn Eighth & Ninth Aves; admission free-$10; 🕐7pm-midnight; [S]C/E to 23rd St) Pros of comedy sketches and outrageous improvisations reign at this popular 74-seat venue, which gets drop-ins from casting directors. Getting in is cheap, and so is the beer and wine. You may recognize pranksters on stage from late-night comedy shows. It's free on Sundays after 9:30pm and on Mondays after 11pm, featuring up-and-coming comics. You'll find quality shows happening nightly, from about 7:30pm, though the Sunday night Asssscat Improv session is always a riot.

There's also an Upright Citizens Brigade outpost in the East Village. Check the website for popular classes on sketch and improv, which happen in a studio at 520 Eighth Ave.

SLEEP NO MORE THEATER

Map p424 (www.sleepnomorenyc.com; McKittrick Hotel, 530 W 27th St; tickets from $91; 🕐7pm-midnight Mon-Sat; [S]C/E to 23rd St) One of the most immersive theater experiences ever conceived, *Sleep No More* is a loosely based retelling of *Macbeth* set inside a series of Chelsea warehouses that have been redesigned to look like an abandoned hotel.

It's a choose-your-own adventure kind of experience where audience members are free to wander the elaborate rooms (ballroom, graveyard, taxidermy shop, lunatic asylum) and interact with the actors who perform a variety of scenes that border on the bizarre to the risqué. Be prepared: you must check-in everything when you arrive (jackets, handbag, cell phone), and you will wear a mask, à la *Eyes Wide Shut*.

SMALLS JAZZ

Map p420 (☎212-252-5091; www.smallslive.com; 183 W 10th St; cover from 7:30pm-12:30am $20, after 12:30am $10; 🕐7:30pm-4am Mon-Thu, from 4pm Fri-Sun; [S]1 to Christopher St-Sheridan Sq) Living up to its name, this cramped but appealing basement jazz den offers a grab-bag collection of jazz acts who take the stage nightly. Cover for the evening is $20, with a come-and-go policy if you need to duck out for a bite.

BLUE NOTE JAZZ

Map p420 (☎212-475-8592; www.bluenote.net; 131 W 3rd St, btwn Sixth Ave & MacDougal St; [S]A/C/E, B/D/F/M to W 4th St-Washington Sq) This is by far the most famous (and expensive) of the city's jazz clubs. Most shows are $30 at the bar or $45 at a table, but can rise for the biggest jazz stars. There are also a few cheaper $20 shows, as well as jazz brunch on Sundays at 11:30am. Go on an off night, and be quiet – all attention is on the stage!

VILLAGE VANGUARD JAZZ

Map p420 (☎212-255-4037; www.villagevanguard.com; 178 Seventh Ave, at 11th St; cover around $33; 🕐7:30pm-12:30am; [S]1/2/3 to 14th St) Possibly the city's most prestigious jazz club, the

Vanguard has hosted literally every major star of the past 50 years. It started as a home to spoken-word performances and occasionally returns to its roots, but most of the time it's just big, bold jazz all night long.

Mind your step on the steep stairs, and close your eyes to the signs of wear and tear – acoustically, you're in one of the greatest venues in the world. There's a one-drink minimum.

MEZZROW JAZZ

Map p420 (☎646-476-4346; www.mezzrow.com; 163 W 10th St, at Seventh Ave; 🕐7:30pm-12:30am Sun-Thu, to 2am Fri & Sat; [S]1 to Christopher St-Sheridan Sq) A new jazz bar opening in NYC is a rare thing, especially in the pricey West Village. All the more reason music fans should celebrate the arrival of this intimate basement jazz club, which opened its doors in 2014. It's run by the same folks behind nearby Smalls, and admission (generally $20) gets you same-night admission to Smalls.

It's all about the music here (boisterous chattering is not tolerated), with quality acts playing throughout the week. Book upcoming gigs online.

IRISH REPERTORY THEATER THEATER

Map p424 (☎212-727-2737; www.irishrep.org; 132 W 22nd St, btwn Sixth & Seventh Aves; [S]1/2, F/M to 23 St; 1/2 to 18th St) This repertory troupe, based in a Chelsea warehouse, showcases the finest contributions to the theater world from the Irish and Irish-American community. At the time of writing the theatre was undergoing a $13 million restoration, expected to be completed in late 2016.

BARROW STREET THEATER THEATER

Map p420 (☎212-868-4444; www.barrowstreettheatre.com; 27 Barrow St, btwn Seventh Ave & W 4th St; [S]1/2 to Christopher St-Sheridan Sq; A/C/E, B/D/F/M to W 4th St; 1/2 to Houston St) A fantastic off-Broadway space in the heart of the West Village showcasing a variety of local and international theater.

ATLANTIC THEATER COMPANY THEATER

Map p424 (☎212-691-5919; www.atlantictheater.org; 336 W 20th St, btwn Eighth & Ninth Aves; [S]C/E to 23rd St; 1 to 18th St) Founded by David Mamet and William H Macy in 1985, the Atlantic Theater is a pivotal anchor for the off-Broadway community, hosting many Tony Award and Drama Desk winners over the last three decades.

CORNELIA ST CAFÉ LIVE MUSIC

Map p420 (☎212-989-9319; www.corneliastreetcafe.com; 29 Cornelia St, btwn Bleecker & W 4th Sts; [S]A/C/E, B/D/F/M to W 4th St-Washington Sq) This small cafe is known for its intimate music performances with innovative jazz trios, genre-bending vocalists and other musical and visual arts combos. Cornelia St also has a literary component with monthly storytelling gatherings and open-mic poetry nights and readings.

CHELSEA BOW TIE CINEMA CINEMA

Map p424 (☎212-691-4744; www.bowtiecinemas.com; 260 W 23rd St, btwn Seventh & Eighth Aves; [S]C/E to 23rd St) In addition to showing first-run films, this multiscreen complex hosts weekend midnight showings of the *Rocky Horror Picture Show,* as well as a great Thursday-night series, Chelsea Classics, which has local drag star Hedda Lettuce hosting old-school camp fare from Joan Crawford, Bette Davis, Barbra Streisand and the like.

IFC CENTER CINEMA

Map p420 (☎212-924-7771; www.ifccenter.com; 323 Sixth Ave, at 3rd St; tickets $14; [S]A/C/E, B/D/F/M to W 4th St-Washington Sq) This art-house cinema in NYU-land has a solidly curated lineup of new indies, cult classics and foreign films. Catch shorts, documentaries, '80s revivals, director-focused series, weekend classics and frequent special series, such as cult favorites (*The Shining, Taxi Driver, Aliens*) at midnight.

KITCHEN THEATER, DANCE

Map p424 (☎212-255-5793; www.thekitchen.org; 512 W 19th St, btwn Tenth & Eleventh Aves; [S]A/C/E to 14th St; L to Eighth Ave) A loft-like experimental space in west Chelsea that also produces edgy theater, readings and music performances, Kitchen is where you'll find new, progressive pieces and works-in-progress from local movers and shakers.

NEW YORK LIVE ARTS DANCE

Map p424 (☎212-691-6500; www.newyorklivearts.org; 219 W 19th St, btwn Seventh & Eighth Aves; [S]1 to 18th St) You'll find a program of more than 100 experimental, contemporary performances annually at this sleek dance center, led by artistic director Carla Peterson. International troupes from Serbia, South Africa, Korea and beyond bring fresh works to the stage, with shows that will often include pre- or post-show discussions with choreographers or dancers.

LE POISSON ROUGE LIVE MUSIC

Map p420 (☎212-505-3474; www.lepoissonrouge.com; 158 Bleecker St; [S]A/C/E, B/D/F/M to W 4th St-Washington Sq) This high-concept art space hosts a highly eclectic lineup of live music, with the likes of Deerhunter, Marc Ribot and Cibo Matto performing in past years. There's a lot of experimentation and cross-genre pollination between classical, folk music, opera and more.

GOTHAM COMEDY CLUB COMEDY

Map p424 (☎212-367-9000; www.gothamcomedyclub.com; 208 W 23rd St, btwn Seventh & Eighth Aves; [S]1, C/E to 23rd St) Fancying itself as a NYC comedy hall of fame, and backing it up with regular big names and Gotham All-Stars shows, this expanded club provides space for comedians who've cut their teeth on HBO, *The Tonight Show with Jimmy Fallon* and *The Late Show with Stephen Colbert*.

DUPLEX CABARET

Map p420 (☎212-255-5438; www.theduplex.com; 61 Christopher St; cover $5-15; ⏲4pm-4am; [S]1 to Christopher St-Sheridan Sq) Cabaret, karaoke and campy dance moves are par for the course at the legendary Duplex. Pictures of Joan Rivers line the walls, and the performers like to mimic her sassy form of self-deprecation, while getting in a few jokes about audience members as well. It's a fun and unpretentious place, and certainly not for the bashful.

At the downstairs piano bar (from 9pm onwards), you can sing a tune, or simply watch some extremely talented regulars (including Broadway performers) and staff belt out the hits. There's a two-drink minimum.

CHERRY LANE THEATER THEATER

Map p420 (☎212-989-2020; www.cherrylanetheater.org; 38 Commerce St; [S]1 to Christopher St-Sheridan Sq) A theater with a distinctive charm hidden in the West Village, Cherry Lane has a long and distinguished history. It was started by poet Edna St Vincent Millay and has given a voice to numerous playwrights and actors over the years. It remains true to its mission of creating 'live' theater that's accessible to the public. Readings, plays and spoken-word performances rotate frequently.

BAR NEXT DOOR LIVE MUSIC

Map p420 (☎212-529-5945; lalanternacaffe.com; 129 MacDougal St, btwn W 3rd & W 4th Sts; cover $12-15; ⏲6pm-2am Sun-Thu, to 3am Fri & Sat; [S]A/C/E, B/D/F/M to W 4th St) One of the loveliest hangouts in the neighborhood, the basement of this restored townhouse is all low ceilings, exposed brick and romantic lighting. You'll find mellow, live jazz nightly, as well as the tasty Italian menu of the restaurant next door, La Lanterna di Vittorio.

Admission is free for the emerging artist sets, held from 6:30pm to 7:45pm Monday through Thursday.

JOYCE THEATER DANCE

Map p424 (☎212-691-9740; www.joyce.org; 175 Eighth Ave; [S]C/E to 23rd St; A/C/E to Eighth Ave-14th St; 1 to 18th St) A favorite among dance junkies thanks to its excellent sight lines and offbeat offerings, this is an intimate venue, seating 472 in a renovated cinema. Its focus is on traditional modern companies such as Pilobolus, Stephen Petronio Company and Parsons Dance as well as global stars, such as Dance Brazil, Ballet Hispanico and MalPaso Dance Company.

COMEDY CELLAR COMEDY

Map p420 (☎212-254-3480; www.comedycellar.com; 117 MacDougal St, btwn W 3rd & Minetta Ln; cover $12-24; [S]A/C/E, B/D/F/M to W 4th St-Washington Sq) This long-established basement comedy club in Greenwich Village features mainstream material and a good list of regulars (Colin Quinn, *Saturday Night Live's* Darrell Hammond, Wanda Sykes), plus an occasional high-profile drop-in like Dave Chappelle. Its success continues: Comedy Cellar now boasts another location around the corner on W 3rd St.

55 BAR LIVE MUSIC

Map p420 (☎212-929-9883; www.55bar.com; 55 Christopher St, at Seventh Ave; cover $10; ⏲1pm-4am; [S]1 to Christopher St-Sheridan Sq) Dating back to the Prohibition era, this friendly basement dive is great for low-key shows without high covers or dressing up. There are regular performances twice nightly by quality artists-in-residence, some blues bands and Miles Davis' super '80s guitarist Mike Stern. There's a two-drink minimum.

ANGELIKA FILM CENTER CINEMA

Map p420 (☎212-995-2570; www.angelikafilmcenter.com; 18 W Houston St, at Mercer St; tickets $15; 👪; [S]B/D/F/M to Broadway-Lafayette St)

Angelika specializes in foreign and independent films and has some quirky charms (the rumble of the subway, long lines and occasionally bad sound). But its roomy cafe is a great place to meet and the beauty of its Stanford White–designed, beaux-arts building is undeniable.

13TH ST REPERTORY COMPANY THEATER
Map p420 (☎212-675-6677; www.13thstreetrep.org; 50 W 13th St, btwn Fifth & Sixth Aves; [S]L to Sixth Ave; F/M, 1/2/3 to 14th St) Founded in 1972, this rep theater offers regular shows throughout the year, including children's theater and the New Works Reading Series on weekends. The company is also home to the longest-running off-off-Broadway show, *Line*.

SHOPPING

The picturesque, tranquil streets of the West Village are home to some lovely boutiques, with a few antique dealers, bookstores, record stores, and quirky gift and curio shops adding a bit of eclecticism to an otherwise fashion-focused 'hood. High-end shoppers stick to top-label stores along Bleecker St between Bank and W 10th. There's much more color along Christopher St, with its stores selling leather play gear and rainbow-colored T-shirts.

The Meatpacking District is all about that sleek, high-ceilinged industrial-chic vibe, with ultramodern designers reigning at expansive boutiques that are among the most fashionable haunts in town (some stores indeed look like sets for futuristic and beautifully stylized Kubrick films).

West Village & the Meatpacking District

★STRAND BOOK STORE BOOKS
Map p420 (☎212-473-1452; www.strandbooks.com; 828 Broadway, at 12th St; ⏲9:30am-10:30pm Mon-Sat, from 11am Sun; [S]L, N/Q/R, 4/5/6 to 14th St-Union Sq) Book fiends (or even those who have casually skimmed one or two) shouldn't miss New York's most loved and famous bookstore. In operation since 1927, the Strand sells new, used and rare titles, spreading an incredible 18 miles of books (over 2.5 million of them) among three labyrinthine floors.

Check out titles in foreign languages in the basement and browse eye-catching merchandise (iPhone covers, tote bags, paratrooper messenger bags). Or sell off your own tomes before you get back on the plane – the Strand buys or trades books at a side counter Monday through Saturday.

ODIN (WEST VILLAGE) CLOTHING
Map p420 (☎212-243-4724; odinnewyork.com; 106 Greenwich Ave; ⏲noon-8pm Mon-Sat, to 7pm Sun; [S]1/2/3 to 14th St) Named after the mighty Norse god, Odin offers a bit of magic for men seeking a new look. The large boutique carries stylish downtown labels such as Phillip Lim, Band of Outsiders and Edward, and is a great place to browse for up-and-coming designers. Other eye candy at the minimalist store includes Comme des Garçons wallets, sleek sunglasses, Sharps grooming products and Taschen coffee-table books.

AEDES DE VENUSTAS BEAUTY
Map p420 (☎212-206-8674; www.aedes.com; 7 Greenwich Ave; ⏲noon-8pm Mon-Sat, 1-7pm Sun; [S]A/C/E, B/D/F/M to W 4th St; 1 to Christopher St-Sheridan Sq) Plush and inviting, Aedes de Venustas ('Temple of Beauty' in Latin) provides more than 40 brands of luxury European perfumes, including Hierbas de Ibiza, Mark Birley for Men, Costes, Odin and Shalini. They also have skincare products created by Susanne Kaufmann and Acqua di Rose, and everyone's favorite scented candles from Diptyque.

YOYA CHILDREN
Map p420 (☎646-336-6844; www.yoyanyc.com; 605 Hudson St; ⏲11am-7pm Mon-Sat, noon-5pm Sun; [S]A/C/E to 14th St; L to Eighth Ave) For well-made kiddy clothes and accessories visit Yoya, which stocks high-end brands such as Bobo Choses and 1+ in the family.

FLAT 128 ACCESSORIES
Map p420 (☎646-707-0673; flat128.com; 15 Christopher St, btwn Waverly Pl & Greenwich Ave; ⏲11am-7pm Mon-Sat, noon-6pm Sun; [S]1 to Christopher St-Sheridan Sq) In a small, handsomely curated shop on tree-lined Christopher St, Flat 128 brings a dose of British craftiness to the Big Apple. You'll find rare, unusual jewelry (such as Alice Menter's metallic cuffs), vintage print cushion covers, vibrantly hued scarves by Age of Reason and a few curios (mini model of Battersea power station anyone?).

PERSONNEL OF NEW YORK
FASHION, ACCESSORIES

Map p420 (212-924-0604; personnelofnew york.com; 9 Greenwich Ave btwn Christopher & W 10th St; 11am-8pm Mon-Sat, noon-7pm Sun; A/C/E, B/D/F/M to W 4th St; 1 to Christopher St-Sheridan Sq) This small, delightful indie shop sells women's designer clothing from unique labels from the East and West Coasts and beyond. Look for easy-to-wear Sunja Link dresses, soft pullover sweaters by Ali Golden, statement-making jewelry by Marisa Mason, comfy canvas sneakers by Shoes Like Pottery, and couture pieces by Rodebjer.

You'll also find a few housewares and crafty gifts including eye-catching Tadahiro bird-shaped bottle openers.

MARC BY MARC JACOBS
FASHION

Map p420 (212-924-0026; www.marcjacobs. com; 403 Bleecker St; 11am-7pm Mon-Sat, noon-6pm Sun; A/C/E to 14th St; L to Eighth Ave) With five small shops sprinkled around the West Village, Marc Jacobs has established a real presence in this well-heeled neighborhood. Large front windows allow easy peeking – assuming there's not a sale, during which you'll only see hordes of fawning shoppers.

Here's the layout: on Bleecker St, you'll find the women's line at No 403, the higher-end handbags and skincare products at No 385 Bleecker, and the men's collection at No 382. There's also BookMarc (for books, stationery and knickknacks) at No 400. One block over, you'll find the children's line (Little Marc) at 298 W 4th St. For men's and women's apparel from the Marc Jacobs Collection (the priciest stuff of all), head to the SoHo **Marc Jacobs** (Map p412; 212-343-1490; www.marcjacobs.com; 163 Mercer St, btwn W Houston & Prince Sts; 11am-7pm Mon-Sat, noon-6pm Sun; B/D/F/M to Broadway-Lafayette St; N/R to Prince St).

STORY
GIFTS

Map p424 (thisisstory.com; 144 Tenth Ave, btwn 18th & 19th Sts; 11am-8pm Mon-Fri, from 10am Sat & Sun; C/E to 23rd St; 1 to 18th St) This high concept shop near the High Line functions like a gallery, showcasing new themes and products every month or two. The 2000-sq-ft space covers all the bases from crafty jewelry and eye-catching accessories to lovely stationery, imagination-inspiring toys for kids, thick coffee table books, environmentally friendly soaps and whimsical souvenirs.

THREE LIVES & COMPANY
BOOKS

Map p420 (212-741-2069; www.threelives.com; 154 W 10th St, btwn Seventh Ave & Waverly Pl; noon-7pm Sun-Tue, 11am-8:30pm Wed-Sat; 1 to Christopher St-Sheridan Sq; A/C/E, B/D/F/M to W 4th St; 1/2/3 to 14th St) Your neighborhood bookstore extraordinaire, Three Lives & Company is a wondrous spot that's tended by a coterie of exceptionally well-read individuals. A trip here is not just a pleasure, it's an adventure into the magical world of words.

BEACON'S CLOSET
THRIFT STORE

Map p420 (917-261-4863; www.beaconscloset. com; 10 W 13th St, btwn Fifth & Sixth Aves; 11am-8pm; L, N/R, 4/5/6 to Union Sq) You'll find a good selection of gently used clothing (which is of a decidedly downtown/Brooklyn hipster aesthetic) at only slightly higher prices than Beacon's sister store in Williamsburg. Thrift shops are thin on the ground in this area, which makes Beacon's even more of a draw. Come mid-week or be prepared to brave the crowds.

LOMOGRAPHY GALLERY STORE
SOUVENIRS

Map p420 (lomography.com; 41 W 8th St, btwn Fifth & Sixth Aves; 11am-9pm Mon-Sat, to 7pm Sun; A/C, B/D, F/M to West 4th St) Photography fans and those just craving a bit of old-fashioned analogue beauty should pay a visit to this colorful store. You can buy old-fashioned Lomo 110 film cameras, score a new fish-eye lens or browse photo snapshot books. Unfortunately, service is decidedly lackluster here.

FLIGHT 001
TRAVEL

Map p420 (212-989-0001; www.flight001. com; 96 Greenwich Ave; 11am-8pm Mon-Sat, noon-6pm Sun; A/C/E to 14th St; L to Eighth Ave) Travel is fun, sure – but getting travel gear is even more fun. Check out Flight 001's range of luggage and smaller bags by brands ranging from Bree to Rimowa, kitschy 'shemergency' kits (breath freshener, lip balm, stain remover, etc), pin-up-girl flasks, brightly colored passport holders and leather luggage tags, travel guidebooks, toiletry cases and a range of mini toothpastes, eye masks, pillboxes and the like.

MONOCLE
ACCESSORIES, FASHION

Map p420 (212-229-1120; monocle.com/shop; 535 Hudson St, at Charles St; 11am-7pm Mon-Sat, noon-6pm Sun; 1 to Christopher St-Sheridan Sq) Tyler Brûlé, the man behind one of the great magazines of the 21st century, founded this tiny bento-box-sized shop in 2010, featuring stylish, well-made products for both the urbanite and the global traveler. Stock includes leather-bound journals, elegant stationery, Japanese body soaps, passport holders and swimming trunks.

If by chance you haven't heard of *Monocle* magazine, pick up a copy (or even back issues) here.

FORBIDDEN PLANET BOOKS

Map p420 (☎212-473-1576; www.fpnyc.com; 832 Broadway; 🕐9am-10pm Sun-Tue, to midnight Wed-Sat; [S]L, N/Q/R, 4/5/6 to 14th St-Union Sq) Indulge your inner sci-fi and fantasy nerd with heaps of comics, manga, graphic novels, posters and figurines ranging from *Star Trek* to *Doctor Who*. Stop in, or check the website for upcoming book signings and other events.

GREENWICH LETTERPRESS GIFTS

Map p420 (☎212-989-7464; www.greenwichletterpress.com; 39 Christopher St, btwn Seventh Ave & Waverly Pl; 🕐noon-6pm Sat-Mon, 11am-7pm Tue-Fri; [S]1 to Christopher St-Sheridan Sq; A/C/E, B/D/F/M to W 4th St; 1/2/3 to 14th St) Founded by two sisters, this cute card shop specializes in wedding announcements and other specially made letterpress endeavors, so skip the stock postcards of the Empire State Building and send your loved ones a bespoke greeting card from this stalwart stationer.

SATURDAYS (WEST VILLAGE) FASHION, ACCESSORIES

Map p420 (☎347-246-5830; www.saturdaysnyc.com; 17 Perry St; 🕐10am-7pm ; [S]1/2/3 to 14th St) For a strange sight in the West Village, stop by this eye-catching surf shop, complete with pricey boards by Tudor, Fowler and Haydenshapes. Of course, shopping here is more about buying into the surfing lifestyle – with stylish shades, boardshorts, colorful tees and grooming products – for both you and your surfboard. There's also an on-site cafe that opens at 8am on weekdays.

CO BIGELOW CHEMISTS BEAUTY

Map p420 (☎212-533-2700; 414 Sixth Ave, btwn 8th & 9th Sts; 🕐7:30am-9pm Mon-Fri, 8:30am-7pm Sat, 8:30am-5:30pm Sun; [S]1 to Christopher St-Sheridan Sq; A/C/E, B/D/F/M to W 4th St-Washington Sq) The 'oldest apothecary in America' is now a slightly upscale fantasyland for the beauty-product obsessed, though there's still an actual pharmacy for prescriptions and standard drugstore items for sale on the premises, too.

In addition to its own CO Bigelow label products, including lip balms, hand and foot salves, shaving creams and rosewater, you can browse through lotions, shampoos, cosmetics and fragrances from makers including Weleda, Yu-Be, Vichy and many more.

MURRAY'S CHEESE FOOD & DRINK

Map p420 (☎212-243-3289; www.murrayscheese.com; 254 Bleecker St, btwn Morton & Leroy Sts; 🕐8am-9pm Mon-Sat, 9am-7pm Sun; [S]1 to Christopher St-Sheridan Sq; A/C/E, B/D/F/V to West 4th St) Founded in 1914, this is one of New York's best cheese shops. Owner Rob Kaufelt is known for his talent for sniffing out devastatingly delicious varieties from around the world. You'll find (and be able to taste) all manner of *fromage*, be it stinky, sweet or nutty, from European nations and from small farms in Vermont and upstate New York.

MCNULTY'S TEA & COFFEE CO, INC FOOD & DRINK

Map p420 (☎212-242-5351; mcnultys.com; 109 Christopher St; 🕐10am-9pm Mon-Sat, 1-7pm Sun; [S]1 to Christopher St-Sheridan Sq) Just down from a few sex shops, sweet McNulty's, with worn wooden floorboards, fragrant sacks of coffee beans and large glass jars of tea, flaunts a different era of Greenwich Village. It's been selling gourmet teas and coffees here since 1895.

🛍 Chelsea

Better known for its dining and nightlife scenes, Chelsea has a decent selection of antiques, discount fashion, chain stores and kitsch, along with a hidden bookstore and well-edited thrift shop. The neighborhood standout is the beloved Chelsea Market (p134), a huge concourse packed with shops selling freshly baked goods, wines, veggies, imported cheeses and other temptations.

192 BOOKS BOOKS

Map p424 (☎212-255-4022; www.192books.com; 192 Tenth Ave, btwn 21st & 22nd Sts; 🕐11am-7pm; [S]C/E to 23rd St) Located right in the gallery district is this small indie bookstore, with sections on fiction, history, travel, art and criticism. Its rotating art exhibits are a special treat, during which the owners organize special displays of books that relate thematically to the featured show or artist. Weekly book readings feature acclaimed (often NY-based) authors.

HOUSING WORKS THRIFT SHOP VINTAGE

Map p424 (☎718-838-5050; 143 W 17th St, btwn Sixth & Seventh Aves; ⏰10am-7pm Mon-Fri, to 6pm Sat, noon-6pm Sun; [S]1 to 18th St) This shop, with its swank window displays, looks more boutique than thrift, but its selections of clothes, accessories, furniture, books and records are great value. All proceeds benefit the charity serving the city's HIV-positive and AIDS homeless communities. There are 11 other branches around town.

INA (CHELSEA) VINTAGE

Map p424 (☎212-334-6572; inanyc.com; 207 West 18th St; ⏰noon-8pm Mon-Sat, to 7pm Sun; [S]1 to 18th St) This small but elegantly designed consignment store carries high-quality, gently used apparel and accessories. The prices are high and some of the staff can be rude, but you can occasionally unearth one-of-a-kind finds here.

POSMAN BOOKS BOOKS

Map p424 (☎212-627-0304; www.posmanbooks.com; 75 Ninth Ave, btwn 15th & 16th Sts; ⏰9am-9pm Mon-Sat, to 8pm Sun; [S]A/C/E to 14th St; L to Eighth Ave; 1 to 18th St) Inside Chelsea Market, family-run Posman is a sleekly designed reading hub and an inviting social space that hosts talks and activities for the little ones. Definitely worth stopping by for a gander.

NASTY PIG CLOTHING

Map p424 (☎212-691-6067; 265 W 19th St, btwn Seventh & Eighth Aves; ⏰noon-8pm Mon-Sat, from 1pm Sun; [S]A/C/E to 14th St; 1 to 18th St) T-shirts, socks and underwear bearing the store's namesake, along with a bit of rubber and leather fetish wear, make this an ideal stop for Chelsea boys and their admirers.

PRINTED MATTER BOOKS

Map p424 (☎212-925-0325; printedmatter.org; 231 Eleventh Ave, btwn 25th & 26th Sts ; ⏰11am-7pm Sat & Mon-Wed, to 8pm Thu & Fri; [S]7 to 34th St-Hudson Yards; 1 to 28th St) Printed Matter is a wondrous little shop dedicated to limited-edition artist monographs and strange little zines. Here you will find nothing carried by mainstream bookstores; instead, trim little shelves hide call-to-arms manifestos, critical essays about comic books, flip books that reveal Jesus' face through barcodes and how-to guides written by prisoners.

SPORTS & ACTIVITIES

CHELSEA PIERS COMPLEX HEALTH & FITNESS

Map p424 (☎212-336-6666; www.chelseapiers.com; Hudson River, at end of W 23rd St; [S]C/E to 23rd St) This massive waterfront sports center caters to the athlete in everyone. You can set out to hit a bucket of golf balls at the four-level driving range, ice skate on the complex's indoor rink or rack up a few strikes in a jazzy bowling alley. There's Hoop City for basketball, a sailing school for kids, batting cages, a huge gym facility with an indoor pool (day passes for non-members are $50), indoor rock-climbing walls – the works.

NEW YORK TRAPEZE SCHOOL SPORTS

Map p420 (☎212-242-8769; www.newyork.trapezeschool.com; Pier 40, at West Side Hwy; per class $50-60; [S]1 to Houston St) Fulfill your circus dreams, flying trapeze to trapeze in this open-air tent by the river. It's open from May to September, on top of Pier 40. The school also has an indoor facility inside the Circus Warehouse in Long Island City, Queens, that's open from October to April. There's a one-time $22 registration fee.

SCHOONER ADIRONDACK BOATING

Map p424 (☎212-913-9991; www.sail-nyc.com; Chelsea Piers, Pier 62 at W 22th St; tours $48-78; [S]C, E to 23rd St) The two-masted *'Dack* hits the New York Harbor with four two-hour sails daily from May to October. The 1920s-style, 80ft *Manhattan* yacht sails daily at 3:30pm and 6pm, with other tours throughout the week.

WEST 4TH STREET BASKETBALL COURTS BASKETBALL

Map p420 (Sixth Ave, btwn 3rd & 4th Sts; [S]A/C/E, B/D/F/V to W 4th St-Washington Sq) Also known as 'the Cage,' this small basketball court enclosed within chain-link fencing is home to some of the best streetball in the country. Though it's more touristy than its counterpart, Rucker Park in Harlem, that's also part of its charm, as the games held here in the center of the Village draw massive, excitable crowds, who often stand five-deep to hoot and holler for the skilled, competitive guys who play here. Prime time is summer, when the W 4th St Summer Pro-Classic League, with daily high-energy games, hits the scene.

Union Square, Flatiron District & Gramercy

Neighborhood Top Five

1 Mentally configuring your fantasy loft while perusing floor after floor of wildly priced but uber-gorgeous home goods at **ABC Carpet & Home** (p174).

2 Prodding fresh produce and sampling artisanal treats at **Union Square Greenmarket** (p174), which

transforms into a delightful Christmas market.

3 Slurping on seamless, happy-hour cocktails at the dark and deco-licious **Flatiron Lounge** (p168).

4 Walking square around elegant **Gramercy Park** (p167), enjoying one of the city's most intimate urban moments.

5 Snacking on coveted burgers from **Shake Shack** (p166) while taking in art installations and the iconic Flatiron Building at Madison Square Park.

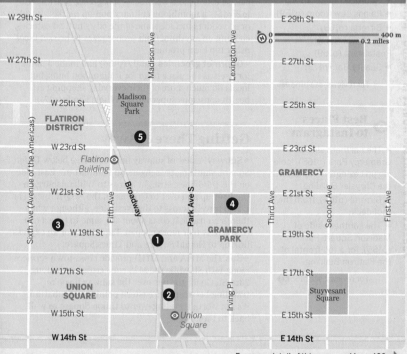

Lonely Planet's Top Tip

Human traffic can be overwhelming in Union Square, especially along 14th St. If you're in a rush, or trying to hoof it on foot, then switch over to 13th St and you'll cover a lot more ground in much less time.

🍴 Best Places to Eat

- Eleven Madison Park (p168)
- Gramercy Tavern (p167)
- Maialino (p167)
- The Clocktower (p168)
- Cosme (p168)

For reviews, see p166 ➡

🍷 Best Places to Drink

- Flatiron Lounge (p168)
- Raines Law Room (p169)
- Birreria (p169)
- Old Town Bar & Restaurant (p169)
- Beauty Bar (p173)

For reviews, see p168 ➡

👁 Best Places to Instagram

- The northern side of Gramercy Park (p165), looking up Lexington Ave toward the Chrysler Building.
- Birreria (p169), from the roof deck.
- The southern side of Madison Square Park (p165), for a full-frontal of the Flatiron Building.

For reviews, see p165 ➡

Explore Union Square, Flatiron District & Gramercy

Union Square unifies many disparate parts of the city, acting as a veritable urban pragmatist linking unlikely cousins. Some may criticize the area for not having a distinct personality of its own, but upon closer inspection, Union Square and the Flatiron District borrow rather cautiously and selectively from their neighbors.

There's not a lot of ground to cover, so the best plan of attack is to use the two major public spaces – Union Square and Madison Square Park – as your anchors. From Union Square you'll feel the Village vibe spilling over with quirky cafes, funky store fronts and buskers in the square itself. Up towards 23rd St you'll find the namesake Flatiron Building looming over the commercial quarter, replete with crowded lunch spots and after-work watering holes. East of both public spaces is Gramercy, its distinctly residential vibe tempered with noted, buzzing restaurants.

Local Life

➡ **Mad Sq Eats** Each spring and fall, foodies flock to tiny General Worth Square – wedged between Fifth Ave and Broadway, opposite Madison Square Park – for Mad Sq Eats (Map p426; www.madisonsquarepark.org/tag/mad-sq-eats; General Worth Sq; ⏲spring & fall; [S]N/R, F/M, 6 to 23rd St), a monthlong culinary pop-up market. Its 30 or so vendors include some of the city's hottest eateries, cooking up anything from proper pizza to brisket tacos using top local produce.

➡ **Gourmet groceries** Eataly (p166) had made a name for itself as the place to go for Italian food buffs, but locals do much more of their everyday shopping at health-conscious supermarket Whole Foods (p174).

Getting There & Away

➡ **Subway** A slew of subway lines converge below Union Square, shuttling passengers up Manhattan's East Side on the 4/5/6 lines, straight across to Williamsburg on the L, or up and over to Queens on the N/Q/R lines. The L also travels across to the West Side, although when there's no traffic it costs about the same to take a cab (if you're two or more people). Take the Q for an express link up to Herald Square and Times Square.

➡ **Bus** The M14A and M14D provide cross-town services along 14th St, while the M23 runs cross-town along 23rd St. Go for the bus over the subway if you're traveling between two eastern points in Manhattan – it's not worth traveling over to Union Square to walk back to First Ave.

TOP SIGHT
UNION SQUARE

Union Square is like the Noah's Ark of New York, rescuing at least two of every kind from the curling seas of concrete. In fact, one would be hard-pressed to find a more eclectic cross-section of locals gathered in one public place. Amid the tapestry of stone steps and fenced-in foliage it's not uncommon to find denizens of every ilk: suited businessfolk gulping fresh air during their lunch breaks, dreadlocked loiterers tapping beats on their tabla, and skateboarders flipping tricks on the southeastern stairs.

Riches & Rags

Opened in 1831, Union Square quickly became the central gathering place for those who lived in the mansions nearby. Concert halls and artist societies further enhanced the cultured atmosphere, and high-end shopping quickly proliferated along Broadway, which was dubbed 'Ladies' Mile.'

When the Civil War broke out, the vast public space (large by New York standards, of course) was center stage for protesters of all sorts – from union workers to political activists. By the height of WWI, the area had fallen largely into disuse, allowing politically and socially driven organizations like the American Civil Liberties Union, the Communist and Socialist Parties, and the Ladies' Garment Workers Union to move in. Many decades later, the square remains a popular site for political and social protests.

For an unforgettable, sweeping view of Union Square and the Empire State Building beyond, hit DSW (p174), a 3rd-floor discount shoe store at the southern end of the square.

The Factory

After over a century of the continuous push-and-pull between dapper-dom and political protest, a third – artistic, if not thoroughly hippie-ish – ingredient was tossed into the mix when Andy Warhol moved his Factory to the 6th floor of the Decker Building at 33 Union Sq West. It was here, on 3 June, 1968, that disgruntled writer Valerie Solanas shot Warhol three times, seriously wounding him. The ground floor of the building is now occupied by a candy store chain – a telling sign of the times.

Metronome

A walk around Union Square will reveal a string of whimsical, temporary sculptures. Of the permanent offerings is an imposing equestrian statue of George Washington (one of the first public pieces of art in New York City) and a statue of peacemaker Mahatma Gandhi. Trumping both on the southeastern side of the square is a massive art installation that either earns confused stares or simply gets overlooked by passersby. A symbolic representation of the passage of time, *Metronome* has two parts – a digital clock with a puzzling display of numbers, and a wand-like apparatus with smoke puffing out of concentric rings. We'll let you ponder the latter while we give you the skinny on what exactly the winking orange digits denote: the 14 numbers must be split into two groups of seven – the seven from the left tell the current time (hour, minute, second, tenth-of-a-second) and the seven from the right are meant to be read in reverse order; they represent the remaining amount of time in the day.

DON'T MISS

- Union Square Greenmarket
- *Metronome* art installation
- The view from DSW shoe store
- Eclectics, sit-ins and buskers

PRACTICALITIES

- Map p426
- www.unionsquarenyc.org
- 17th St, btwn Broadway & Park Ave S
- [S]4/5/6, N/Q/R, L to 14th St-Union Sq

TOP SIGHT
FLATIRON BUILDING

Designed by Daniel Burnham and built in 1902, the 20-story Flatiron Building has a uniquely narrow triangular footprint that resembles the prow of a massive ship. It also features a traditional beaux-arts limestone and terra-cotta facade that gets more complex and beautiful the longer you stare at it. Until 1909 it was the world's tallest building.

The Immortal Tower

Publisher Frank Munsey was one of the building's first tenants. From his 18th-floor offices he published *Munsey's Magazine,* which featured the work of short-story writer William Sydney Porter, whose pen name was 'O Henry.' His musings (in popular stories such as 'The Gift of the Magi'), the paintings of John Sloan and photographs of Alfred Stieglitz best immortalized the Flatiron back in the day – along with a famous comment by actress Katharine Hepburn, who quipped that she'd like to be admired as much as the grand old building.

Today & Tomorrow

While there are plans to transform the Flatiron into a luxurious five-star hotel, progress is on hold until the final business tenants willingly vacate the premises. In the meantime, the ground floor of the building's 'prow' has been transformed into a glassed-in art space showcasing the work of guest artists. Past installations have included a life-size 3-D-cut-out replica of Edward Hopper's 1942 painting *Nighthawks,* its angular diner remarkably similar to the Flatiron's distinctive shape.

DON'T MISS

➡ The view of the facade from Madison Square Park

➡ An up-close-and-personal look to appreciate the fine exterior detail

➡ Flatiron Prow art space

PRACTICALITIES

➡ Map p426

➡ Broadway, cnr Fifth Ave & 23rd St

➡ Ⓢ N/R, F/M, 6 to 23rd St

SIGHTS

★UNION SQUARE — SQUARE

See p163.

★FLATIRON BUILDING — HISTORIC BUILDING

See p164.

MADISON SQUARE PARK — PARK

Map p426 (☎212-520-7600; www.madisonsquarepark.org; 23rd to 26th Sts, btwn Fifth & Madison Aves; ⏰6am-midnight; 📶👪; [S]N/R, F/M, 6 to 23rd St) This park defined the northern reaches of Manhattan until the island's population exploded after the Civil War. These days it's a much-welcome oasis from Manhattan's relentless pace, with a popular children's playground, dog-run area and Shake Shack (p166) burger joint. It's also one of the city's most cultured parks, with specially commissioned art installations and (in the warmer months) activities ranging from literary discussions to live music gigs.

The park is also the perfect spot from which to gaze up at the landmarks that surround it, including the Flatiron Building to the southwest, the moderne Metropolitan Life Tower to the southeast and the New York Life Insurance Building, topped with a gilded spire, to the northeast.

Between 1876 and 1882 the torch-bearing arm of the Statue of Liberty was on display here, and in 1879 the first Madison Square Garden arena was constructed at Madison Ave and 26th St. At the southeastern corner of the park, you'll find one of the city's few self-cleaning, coin-operated toilets.

METROPOLITAN LIFE TOWER — HISTORIC BUILDING

Map p426 (1 Madison Ave; [S]N/R, F/M, 6 to 23rd St) Completed in 1909, this 700ft-high clock tower soaring above Madison Square Park's southeastern corner is the work of Napoleon LeBrun, a Philadelphia-born architect of French stock. Italophiles may feel a certain déjà vu gazing at the tower. After all, LeBrun's inspiration was Venice's world-famous *campanile* (bell tower) in Piazza San Marco. Ironically, LeBrun's New World version is now older than its muse: the original Venetian tower collapsed in 1902, with its replacement not completed until 1912.

Despite being upstaged by taller skyscrapers these days, the 41-level building remains one the largest four-dial timepieces in the world, each of its four clock faces measuring a big-is-better 26.5ft in diameter.

TIBET HOUSE — CULTURAL CENTER

Map p426 (☎212-807-0563; www.tibethouse.us; 22 W 15th St, btwn Fifth & Sixth Aves; suggested donation $5; ⏰11am-6pm Mon-Fri, to 4pm Sun; [S]F/M to 14th St, L to sixth Ave) With the Dalai Lama as the patron of its board, this non-profit cultural space is dedicated to presenting Tibet's ancient traditions through art exhibits, a research library and various publications. Programs on offer include educational workshops, open meditations, retreat weekends and docent-led tours to Tibet, Nepal and Bhutan.

Exhibits span a variety of subjects, from traditional Tibetan tangka painting and sculpture to contemporary views of Tibetan Buddhist and Hindu tantric art.

THEODORE ROOSEVELT BIRTHPLACE — HISTORIC SITE

Map p426 (☎212-260-1616; www.nps.gov/thrb; 28 E 20th St, btwn Broadway & Park Ave S; ⏰40min guided tours 10am, 11am, 1pm, 2pm, 3pm & 4pm Tue-Sat; [S]N/R, 6 to 23rd St) [FREE] Scheduled to reopen in 2016 after restoration work, this National Historic Site is a bit of a cheat, since the physical house where the 26th president was actually born was demolished in his own lifetime. But this building is a worthy reconstruction by his relatives, who joined it with another family residence next door.

If you're interested in Roosevelt's extraordinary life, which has been somewhat overshadowed by the enduring legacy of his younger cousin Franklin D, the site is worth visiting – especially if you don't have the time to see his spectacular summer home in Long Island's Oyster Bay. Check the website for updates on the building's reopening.

NATIONAL ARTS CLUB — CULTURAL CENTER

Map p426 (☎212-475-3424; www.nationalartsclub.org; 15 Gramercy Park S; drawing classes $15-25; [S]N/R, 6 to 23rd St) Founded in 1898 to promote public interest in the arts, the National Arts Club holds art exhibitions, usually open to the public from 10am to 5pm Monday to Friday (check the website for upcoming shows). Calvert Vaux – one of the creators of Central Park – designed the building itself, its picture-lined front parlor adorned with a beautiful, vaulted, stained-glass ceiling. The place was once home to Samuel J Tilden, governor of New York and failed presidential candidate in 1876.

It also hosts evening life drawing classes, usually on Monday, Wednesday and Friday from 7pm to 9pm.

🍴 EATING

TACOMBI CAFÉ EL PRESIDENTE MEXICAN $

Map p426 (☎212-242-3491; http://tacombi.com; 30 W 24th St, btwn Fifth & Sixth Aves; tacos $3.50-5.50, quesadillas $8-9; 🕐11am-midnight Mon-Sat, to 10:30pm Sun; [S]F/M, N/R to 23rd St) Channeling the cafes of Mexico City, pink-and-green Tacombi covers numerous bases, from juice and liquor bar to taco joint. Score a table, order a margarita and hop your way around a menu of Mexican street-food deliciousness. Top choices include *esquites* (grilled corn with *cotija* cheese and chipotle mayonnaise, served in a paper cup) and succulent *carnitas michoacan* (beer-marinated pork) tacos.

ARTICHOKE BASILLE'S PIZZA PIZZA $

Map p426 (☎212-228-2004; www.artichokepizza.com; 328 E 14th St, btwn First & Second Aves; slice from $4.75; 🕐11am-5am; [S]L to First Ave) Run by two Italian guys from Staten Island, this place has authentic pizza piled high with all sorts of toppings. The signature pie is a rich, cheesy treat with artichokes and spinach; the plain Sicilian is thinner, with emphasis solely on the crisp crust and savory sauce. Lines usually form fast. Cash only.

SHAKE SHACK BURGERS $

Map p426 (☎646-747-2606; www.shakeshack.com; Madison Square Park, cnr 23rd St & Madison Ave; burgers $4.20-9.50; 🕐11am-11pm; [S]N/R, F/M, 6 to 23rd St) The flagship of chef Danny Meyer's gourmet burger chainlet, Shake Shack whips up hyper-fresh burgers, hand-cut fries and a rotating line-up of frozen custards. Veg-heads can dip into the crisp portobello burger. Lines are long, but it's worth it.

DOS TOROS TAQUERIA MEXICAN $

Map p426 (☎212-677-7300; www.dostoros.com; 137 Fourth Ave, btwn 13th & 14th Sts; burritos from $7.35, quesadillas from $6.20; 🕐11:30am-10:30pm Mon & Sun, to 11pm Tue-Sat; [S]4/5/6, N/Q/R, L to 14th St-Union Sq) Skip the national Mexican-food chain in favor of this city-wide favorite that promises high-quality meats tucked safely in a sea of thick guacamole and refried beans. Lines can be long (so you know it's good) but efficient staffers whip up your Tex-Mex treat in minutes.

EATALY ITALIAN $$

Map p426 (www.eataly.com; 200 Fifth Ave, at 23rd St; 🕐8am-11pm; 🌿; [S]N/R, F/M, 6 to 23rd St) Mario Batali's sleek, sprawling temple to Italian gastronomy is a veritable wonderland. Feast on everything from vibrant *crudo* (raw fish) and *fritto misto* (tempura-style vegetables) to steamy pasta and pizza at the emporium's string of sit-down eateries. Alternatively, guzzle espresso at the bar and scour the countless counters and shelves for a DIY picnic hamper *nonna* would approve of.

Eataly's other assets include its rooftop beer garden, Birreria (p169), and a busy schedule of onsite cooking and culinary appreciation classes. See the website for details.

JAVELINA TEX-MEX $$

Map p426 (☎212-539-0202; http://javelinatexmex.com; 119 E 18th St, btwn Park Ave S & Irving Pl; tacos $12-16, dinner mains $19-23; 🕐11:30am-3:30pm & 5:30-11pm Mon-Thu, to 11:30pm Fri & Sat, to 10pm Sun; 📶; [S]4/5/6, N/Q/R, L to 14th St-Union Sq) Guarded by a gang of cacti, easy, affable Javelina gives Tex-Mex some much-needed culinary cred. It's especially great for brunch, when prickly-pear mimosas help wash down your peaches and cream French toast or the standout Red Headed Stranger breakfast taco – a hangover-busting combo of scrambled eggs, brisket, black beans avocado, cheese and piquant ranchero sauce.

BAR JAMÓN TAPAS $$

Map p426 (☎212-253-2773; http://casamononyc.com; 125 E 17th St, btwn Irving Pl & Third Ave; tapas $5-15; 🕐5pm-2am Mon-Fri, noon-2am Sat & Sun; [S]4/5/6, N/Q/R, L to 14th St-Union Sq) Around the corner from its big brother, Casa Mono, lies Mario Batali's fun, communal Bar Jamón. Sniff, swill and sip your way across Spain's wine terroirs while grazing on superb, Catalan-inspired tapas like pickled sardines, duck liver with apricots and *fuet catalán* (cured pork sausage) with lentils.

DHABA INDIAN $$

Map p428 (☎212-679-1284; www.dhabanyc.com; 108 Lexington Ave, btwn 27th & 28th Sts; mains $11-24; 🕐noon-midnight Mon-Thu, noon-1am Fri & Sat, 4-10pm Sun; 🌿; [S]6 to 28th St) Murray Hill (aka Curry Hill) has no shortage

TOP SIGHT
GRAMERCY PARK

To Manhattan's early Dutch settlers, the area now known as Gramercy was *Krom Moerasje*, named for the 'little crooked swamp' that once straddled part of the district. The swamp would meet its end in 1831, when lawyer and public official Samuel Ruggles purchased the land from a descendant of Peter Stuyvesant. Ruggles had the swamp drained and the land carved into 108 lots. Forty-two of these were set aside for an English-style private park, to be held in perpetuity by the residents of its surrounding 66 lots.

Almost two centuries later, Gramercy Park remains a private oasis for surrounding residents, birds and squirrels. Only once has it been made accessible to nonresidents, when Union soldiers were permitted during the Draft Riots of 1863.

Many of the original townhouses facing the park were replaced by high-rise apartment buildings through the 1920s. Of those that did survive, many found new purpose as apartments or private clubs. Among the latter is the **National Arts Club** (p165), whose elegance attests to the district's desirable pedigree. Indeed, Gramercy Park has had its fair share of illustrious residents: the townhouse at 4 Gramercy Park W was home to American publisher and former Mayor James Harper from 1847 to 1869.

DON'T MISS

- The view of elegant townhouses surrounding the park
- Eye-catching 'mayor's lights' at 4 Gramercy Park
- A peak through the wrought-iron gates

PRACTICALITIES

- Map p426
- E 20th St, btwn Park & Third Aves
- [S]N/R, 6 to 23rd St

of subcontinental bites, but funky Dhaba packs one serious flavor punch. Mouthwatering standouts include the crunchy, tangy *lasoni gobi* (fried cauliflower with tomato and spices) and the insanely flavorful *murgh bharta* (minced chicken cooked with smoked eggplant).

Concessions to the mostly Punjabi menu include a string of British curry-house classics. There's also a good-value lunch buffet to boot ($12 Monday to Saturday, $14 Sunday).

BOQUERIA FLATIRON TAPAS $$

Map p426 (☎212-255-4160; www.boquerianyc.com; 53 W 19th St, btwn Fifth & Sixth Aves; tapas $6-18; ⏰noon-10:30pm Sun-Thu, to 11:30pm Fri & Sat; 📶; [S]1 to 18th St, F/M, N/R to 23rd St) A holy union between Spanish-style tapas and market-fresh fare, Boqueria woos the after-work crowd with a brilliant line up of small plates and larger *raciones*. Lick lips and fingers over the likes of garlicky shrimp with brandy and guindilla pepper, or bacon-wrapped dates stuffed with almonds and Valdeón blue cheese. A smooth selection of Spanish wines tops it all off. *¡Buen provecho!*

★MAIALINO ITALIAN $$$

Map p426 (☎212-777-2410; www.maialinonyc.com; Gramercy Park Hotel, 2 Lexington Ave, at 21st St; mains lunch $21-34, dinner $27-42; ⏰7:30am-10:30pm Mon-Thu, to 11pm Fri, 10am-11pm Sat, 10am-10:30pm Sun; [S]6, N/R to 23rd St) Fans reserve tables up to four weeks in advance at this Danny Meyer classic, but the best seats in the house are at the walk-in bar, manned by sociable, knowledgeable staffers. Wherever you're plonked, take your taste buds on a Roman holiday, Maialino's lip-smacking, rustic Italian fare created using produce from the nearby Union Square Greenmarket.

A solid wine list and good-value $40 prix-fixe lunch seals the deal.

★GRAMERCY TAVERN MODERN AMERICAN $$$

Map p426 (☎212-477-0777; www.gramercytavern.com; 42 E 20th St, btwn Broadway & Park Ave S; tavern mains $19-24, dining room 3-course menu $98, tasting menus $105-120; ⏰tavern noon-11pm Sun-Thu, to midnight Fri & Sat; dining room noon-2pm & 5:30-10pm Mon-Thu, to 11pm Fri, noon-1:30pm & 5.30-11pm Sat, 5:30-10pm Sun; 📶✍; [S]N/R, 6 to 23rd St) 🌿 Seasonal, local ingredients drive this perennial favorite, a vibrant, country-chic institution aglow with copper sconces, murals and dramatic floral arrangements. Choose from two spaces: the walk-in-only tavern and its à la carte menu, or the swankier dining room and its fancier prix-fixe and degustation feasts. Tavern highlights include a show-stopping duck meatloaf with mushrooms, chestnuts and brussels sprouts.

Desserts are suitably decadent and the wine list one of the city's best.

★CRAFT
NEW AMERICAN $$$

Map p426 (☎212-780-0880; www.craftrestaurantsinc.com/craft-new-york; 43 E 19th St, btwn Broadway & Park Ave S; lunch $15-35, dinner mains $31-45; ⏰5:30-10pm Sun-Thu, to 11pm Fri & Sat; 📶; [S]4/5/6, N/Q/R, L to 14th St-Union Sq) 🍃 Humming, high-end Craft flies the flag for small, family-owned farms and food producers, their bounty transformed into pure, polished dishes. Whether nibbling on flawlessly charred braised octopus, pillowy scallops, or pumpkin mezzaluna pasta with sage, brown butter and Parmesan, expect every ingredient to sing with flavor. Book ahead Wednesday to Saturday or head in by 6pm or after 9:30pm.

★ELEVEN MADISON PARK
MODERN AMERICAN $$$

Map p426 (☎212-889-0905; www.elevenmadisonpark.com; 11 Madison Ave, btwn 24th & 25th Sts; tasting menu $225; ⏰noon-1pm Thu-Sat, 5.30-10pm daily; [S]N/R, 6 to 23rd St) Fine-dining Eleven Madison Park came in at number five in the 2015 San Pellegrino World's 50 Best Restaurants list. Frankly, we're not surprised: this revamped poster child of modern, sustainable American cooking is also one of only six NYC restaurants sporting three Michelin stars.

Driving the buzz is young-gun co-owner and chef Daniel Humm, whose insane attention to detail is matched by intense creativity and whimsy. The result is dishes like honey lavender duck with apple and rutabaga. Reserve a table a few weeks in advance and dress to impress.

THE CLOCKTOWER
MODERN BRITISH $$$

Map p426 (☎212-413-4300; http://theclocktowernyc.com; 5 Madison Ave, btwn 23rd & 24th Sts; 3-course prix-fixe lunch $40, dinner mains $23-43; 📶; [S]N/R, F/M, 6 to 23rd St) Brits do it best at Jason Atherton's clubby, new A-lister, hidden away inside the landmark Metropolitan Life Tower. This is the latest venture for the Michelin-starred British chef, its wood-and-stucco dining rooms setting a handsome scene for high-end comfort grub like pan-fried gnocchi with market peas, favas, asparagus, seasonal mushrooms and Parmesan cream, or heavenly Amish chicken breast with lemon yogurt and bulgur wheat.

Book ahead, dress sharply, and consider opting for the good-value prix-fixe lunch.

COSME
MEXICAN $$$

Map p426 (☎212-913-9659; http://cosmenyc.com; 35 E 21st St, btwn Broadway & Park Ave S; dinner dishes $15-35; ⏰5:30-11pm Mon-Thu, to midnight Fri, 11:30am-2:30pm & 5:30pm-midnight Sat, 11:30am-2:30pm & 5:30-11pm Sun; 📶; [S]N/R, 6 to 23rd St) Mexican gets haute at this slinky, charcoal-hued newcomer, home to chef Enrique Olvera and his innovative takes on south-of-the-border flavors. Subvert culinary stereotypes with the likes of delicate, invigorating scallop *aguachile* with poached jicama and fresh wasabi-cucumber-lime; an intriguing roasted eggplant with cauliflower, sesame seed salsa and preserved lemon; or Cosme's cult-status duck *carnitas*. Book ahead or try your luck at the walk-in bar.

ABC KITCHEN
MODERN AMERICAN $$$

Map p426 (☎212-475-5829; www.abckitchennyc.com; 35 E 18th St, at Broadway; pizzas $17-20, dinner mains $24-40; ⏰noon-3pm & 5:30-10:30pm Mon-Wed, to 11pm Thu, to 11:30pm Fri, 11am-3pm & 5:30-11:30pm Sat, 11am-3pm & 5:30-10pm Sun; ✍; [S]4/5/6, N/Q/R, L to 14th St-Union Sq) 🍃 Looking part gallery, part rustic farmhouse, sustainable ABC Kitchen is the culinary avatar of the chi-chi home goods department store ABC Carpet & Home (p174). Organic gets haute in dishes like tuna sashimi with ginger and mint, or crispy pork confit with smoked bacon marmalade and braised turnips. For a more casual bite, try the scrumptious whole-wheat pizzas.

🍷 DRINKING & NIGHTLIFE

★FLATIRON LOUNGE
COCKTAIL BAR

Map p426 (☎212-727-7741; www.flatironlounge.com; 37 W 19th St, btwn Fifth & Sixth Aves; ⏰4pm-2am Mon-Wed, to 3am Thu, to 4am Fri, 5pm-4am Sat, 5pm-2am Sun; 📶; [S]F/M, N/R, 6 to 23rd St) Head through a dramatic archway and into a dark, swinging, deco-inspired fantasy of lipstick-red booths, racy jazz tunes and sassy grown-ups downing seasonal drinks. The Beijing Mule (Jasmine vodka, lime juice, ginger syrup and pomegranate molasses) is scrumptious, while the genial Flight of the Day (a trio of mini-sized cocktails) is head-spinning enlightenment. Happy hour cocktails go for $10 a pop (4pm to 6pm weekdays).

RAINES LAW ROOM COCKTAIL BAR

Map p426 (www.raineslawroom.com; 48 W 17th St, btwn Fifth & Sixth Aves; ⏲5pm-2am Mon-Wed, to 3am Thu-Sat, 7pm-1am Sun; [S]F/M to 14th St; L to 6th Ave, 1 to 18th St) A sea of velvet drapes and overstuffed leather lounge chairs, the perfect amount of exposed brick, and expertly crafted cocktails using meticulously aged spirits – these guys are about as serious as a mortgage payment when it comes to amplified atmosphere. Reservations (recommended) are only possible Sunday to Tuesday. Whatever the night, style up for the taste of a far more sumptuous era.

BIRRERIA BEER HALL

Map p426 (☎212-937-8910; www.eataly.com; 200 Fifth Ave, at 23rd St; mains $17-37; ⏲11:30am-11pm Sun-Thu, to midnight Fri & Sat; [S]N/R, F/M, 6 to 23rd St) The crown jewel of Italian food emporium Eataly (p166) is its rooftop beer garden tucked betwixt the Flatiron's corporate towers. A beer menu of encyclopedic proportions offers drinkers some of the best suds on the planet. If you're hungry, the signature beer-braised pork shoulder is your frosty one's soul mate.

The sneaky access elevator is near the checkouts on the 23rd St side of the store.

OLD TOWN BAR & RESTAURANT BAR

Map p426 (☎212-529-6732; www.oldtownbar.com; 45 E 18th St, btwn Broadway & Park Ave S; ⏲11:30am-1am Mon-Fri, noon-2am Sat, 1pm-midnight Sun; [S]4/5/6, N/Q/R, L to 14th St-Union Sq) It still looks like 1892 in here, with the original tile floors and tin ceilings – the Old Town is an 'old world' drinking-man's classic (and woman's: Madonna lit up at the bar here, when lighting up was still legal, in her 'Bad Girl' video). There are cocktails around, but most come for beers and a burger (from $12.50).

PETE'S TAVERN BAR

Map p426 (☎212-473-7676; www.petestavern.com; 129 E 18th St, at Irving Pl; ⏲11am-2am; [S]4/5/6, N/Q/R, L to 14th St-Union Sq) Adorned with its original 19th-century mirrors, pressed-tin ceiling and rosewood bar, this dark, atmospheric watering hole has all the earmarks of a New York classic. You can get a respectable prime-rib burger here and choose from 17 draft beers. The bar draws in everyone from post-theater couples and Irish expats to no-nonsense NYU students and the odd celebrity (see photos by the restrooms).

FLATIRON ROOM COCKTAIL BAR

Map p426 (☎212-725-3860; www.theflatironroom.com; 37 W 26th St, btwn Sixth Ave & Broadway; ⏲4pm-2am Mon-Fri, 5pm-2am Sat, 5pm-midnight Sun; [S]N/R to 28th St; F/M to 23rd St) Vintage wallpaper, a glittering chandelier and hand-painted coffer ceilings make for a suitably elegant scene at this grown-up drinking den, its artfully lit cabinets graced with rare whiskeys. Fine cocktails pair nicely with high-end sharing plates, from citrus-marinated olive tapenade to flatbread with guanciale and fig. Most nights also feature live music, including bluegrass and jazz. Reservations are highly recommended.

TOBY'S ESTATE CAFE, COFFEE

Map p426 (☎646-559-0161; www.tobysestate.com; 160 Fifth Ave, btwn 20th & 21st Sts; ⏲7am-9pm Mon-Fri, 8:30am-9pm Sat, 8:30am-8pm Sun; [S]N/R, F/M, 6 to 23rd St) Sydney-born, Williamsburg-roasting Toby's Estate is part of Manhattan's evolving artisanal coffee culture. Loaded with a custom-made Strada espresso machine, you'll find it tucked away in the Club Monaco store. Join coffee geeks for thick, rich brews, among them a geo-specific Flatiron Espresso Blend. Nibbles include pastries and sandwiches from local bakeries.

BOXERS NYC GAY

Map p426 (☎212-255-5082; www.boxersnyc.com; 37 W 20th St, btwn Fifth & Sixth Aves; ⏲4pm-2am Mon-Thu, to 4am Fri, 1pm-4am Sat, 1pm-2am Sun; [S]F/M, N/R, 6 to 23rd St) Dave & Busters meets David Bowie at this self-proclaimed gay sports bar in the heart of the Flatiron District. There's football on TV, buffalo wings at the bar, and topless wait staff keeping the pool cues polished. And in case you think Boxers is all brawn, think again: Tuesday's popular Trivia Night gives brains a good, hard workout.

While there's a second Boxers branch in **Hell's Kitchen** (Map p432; ☎212-951-1518; www.boxersnyc.com; 742 Ninth Ave, at 50th St, Midtown West; ⏲4pm-2am Mon-Thu, to 4am Fri, noon-4am Sat, noon-2am Sun; [S]C/E, 1 to 50th St), nothing beats the original.

HUW JONES / GETTY IMAGES ©

Eataly (p166)
ample gourmet produce or take part in a cooking
ass in this 50,000-sq-ft market.

Union Square Greenmarket (p174)
heck out the produce in the city's most famous
armers market, which offers everything from
resh fruit and vegetables to local honey.

Flatiron District (p161)
aze up at the district's namesake building
ooming over the commercial hub.

Metronome (p163)
eflect on the passing of time at the art
nstallation, *Metronome*, by Kristin Jones and
ndrew Ginzel, in Union Square.

BARRY WINIKER / GETTY IMAGES ©

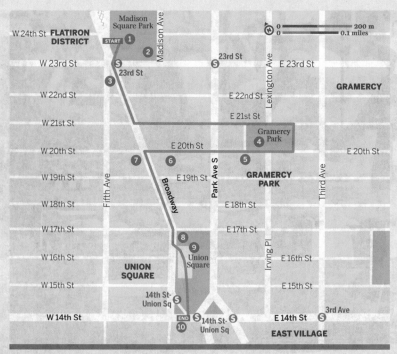

Neighborhood Walk
Be There, Be Square

START MADISON SQUARE PARK
END DSW
LENGTH 2 MILES; TWO HOURS

Start off in the leafy oasis of **1 Madison Square Park** (p165), dotted with historic statues and contemporary installations. If you're peckish, hit up **2 Shake Shack** (p166) for a gourmet burger and fries. Before exiting the park, stand at its southwestern corner and take in the arresting **3 Flatiron Building** (p164), Chicago architect Daniel Burnham's clever response to the awkward space where Fifth Ave and Broadway meet. Follow Broadway south to 21st St and take a left. Past Park Ave S you'll find yourself alongside **4 Gramercy Park** (p165), a private garden reminiscent of those found in Britain. Legendary 19th-century actor Edwin Booth spent the final years of his life living at 16 Gramercy Park S, while actor Margaret Hamilton (best known as the Wicked Witch of the West in the MGM classic *The Wizard of Oz*) was a long-term resident of 34 Gramercy Park E. At 15 Gramercy Park S stands the **5 National Arts Club**

(p165), whose own film cameos include Martin Scorsese's *The Age of Innocence* and Woody Allen's *Manhattan Murder Mystery*.

Head back west along 20th St and stop at the reconstructed version of **6 Theodore Roosevelt's Birthplace** (p165), which offers hourly tours. On the southwestern corner of Broadway and E 20th St stands the old **7 Lord & Taylor Building**, former home of the famous Midtown department store. A Gothic-inspired creation, it stands in an area formerly nicknamed 'Ladies' Mile' for its once-abundant emporiums.

Continue south on Broadway and you'll find yourself at the northwestern corner of **8 Union Square** (p163). Check out the produce, baked goods and flowers of the **9 Greenmarket**, seek out Gandhi near the southwest corner, or grab some food at one of the surrounding eateries for a picnic in the park. If you have any residual energy, cross Union Sq South (14th St) and dive into **10 DSW** (p174), a massive warehouse dedicated to heavily discounted designer shoes and accessories.

71 IRVING PLACE
CAFE, COFFEE

Map p426 (Irving Farm Coffee Company; ☎212-995-5252; www.irvingfarm.com; 71 Irving Pl, btwn 18th & 19th Sts; ⏰7am-10pm Mon-Fri, 8am-10pm Sat & Sun; [S]4/5/6, N/Q/R, L to 14th St-Union Sq) From keyboard-tapping scribes to gossiping friends and academics, this bustling cafe is never short of a crowd. Hand-picked beans are lovingly roasted on a farm in the Hudson Valley (about 90 miles from NYC), and served alongside tasty edibles like Balthazar-baked croissants, granola, egg dishes, bagels and pressed sandwiches.

BEAUTY BAR
BAR

Map p426 (☎212-539-1389; www.thebeautybar.com/home-new-york; 231 E 14th St, btwn Second & Third Aves; ⏰5pm-4am Mon-Fri, 2pm-4am Sat & Sun; [S]L to Third Ave) A kitschy favorite since the mid-'90s, this homage to old-fashioned beauty parlors pulls in a cool local crowd with its retro soundtrack, nostalgic vibe and $10 manicures (with a free Blue Rinse margarita thrown in) from 6pm to 11pm on weekdays, and 3pm to 11pm on weekends. Nightly events range from comedy to burlesque.

ENTERTAINMENT

PEOPLES IMPROV THEATER
COMEDY

Map p426 (PIT; ☎212-563-7488; www.thepit-nyc.com; 123 E 24th St, btwn Lexington & Park Aves; 📶; [S]6, N/R, F/M to 23rd St) Aglow in red neon, this bustling comedy club serves up top-notch laughs at dirt-cheap prices. The string of nightly acts ranges from stand-up to sketch and musical comedy, playing in either the main stage theater or the basement lounge. PIT also runs courses, including three-hour, drop-in improv workshops at its Midtown venue, **Simple Studios** (Map p432; ☎212-273-9696; simplestudiosnyc.com; 134 W 29th St, btwn Sixth & Seventh Aves, Midtown West; [S]1, N/R to 28th St). See the website for all classes and schedules.

IRVING PLAZA
LIVE MUSIC

Map p426 (☎212-777-6817; www.irvingplaza.com; 17 Irving Pl, at 15th St; [S]4/5/6, N/Q/R, L to 14th St-Union Sq) Rocking since 1978, Irving Plaza has seen them all: the Ramones, Bob Dylan, U2, Pearl Jam, you name it. These days it's a great in-between stage for quirkier rock and pop acts – from indie chicks Sleater-Kinney to hard rockers Disturbed. There's a cozy floor around the stage, and good views from the mezzanine.

SHOPPING

BEDFORD CHEESE SHOP
FOOD

Map p426 (☎718-599-7588; www.bedfordcheeseshop.com; 67 Irving Pl, btwn 18th & 19th Sts; ⏰8am-9pm Mon-Sat, to 8pm Sun; [S]4/5/6, N/Q/R, L to 14th St-Union Sq) Whether you're after local, raw cow's-milk cheese washed in absinthe or garlic-infused goat's-milk cheese from Australia, chances are you'll find it among the 200-strong selection at this outpost of Brooklyn's most celebrated cheese vendor. Pair the cheesy goodness with artisanal charcuterie, deli treats, ready-to-eat sandwiches ($9 to $11), as well as a proud array of Made-in-Brooklyn edibles.

The shop runs regular on-site classes, from wine and European cheese pairings to Knife Skills 101. Check the website.

IDLEWILD BOOKS
BOOKS

Map p426 (☎212-414-8888; www.idlewildbooks.com; 12 W 19th St, btwn Fifth & Sixth Aves; ⏰noon-7.30pm Mon-Thu, to 6pm Fri & Sat, to 5pm Sun; [S]4/5/6, N/Q/R, L to 14th St-Union Sq) Named after JFK Airport's original moniker, this indie travel bookshop gets feet seriously itchy. Books are divided by region, and cover guidebooks as well as fiction, travelogues, history, cookbooks and other stimulating fare for delving into different corners of the world. The store also runs popular language classes in French, Italian, Spanish and German; see the website for details.

BOOKS OF WONDER
BOOKS

Map p426 (☎212-989-3270; www.booksofwonder.com; 18 W 18th St, btwn Fifth & Sixth Aves; ⏰10am-7pm Mon-Sat, 11am-6pm Sun; 👪; [S]F/M to 14th St; L to 6th Ave) Devoted to children's and young-adult titles, this wonderful bookstore is a great place to take young ones on a rainy day, especially when a kids' author is giving a reading or a storyteller is on hand. There's an impressive range of NYC-themed picture books, as well as a section dedicated to rare and vintage children's books and limited-edition children's book artwork.

ABC CARPET & HOME
HOMEWARES

Map p426 (☎212-473-3000; www.abchome.com; 888 Broadway, at 19th St; ⏰10am-7pm Mon-Wed, Fri & Sat, to 8pm Thu, 11am-6:30pm Sun; [S]4/5/6, N/Q/R, L to 14th St-Union Sq) A mecca for home designers and decorators brainstorming ideas, this beautifully curated, seven-level temple to good taste heaves with all sorts of furnishings, small and large. Shop for easy-to-pack knickknacks, textiles and jewelry, as well as statement furniture, designer lighting, ceramics and antique carpets. Come Christmas season the shop is a joy to behold.

UNION SQUARE GREENMARKET MARKET

Map p426 (www.grownyc.org; Union Square, 17th St btwn Broadway & Park Ave S; ⏰8am-6pm Mon, Wed, Fri & Sat; [S]4/5/6, N/Q/R, L to 14th St-Union Sq) Don't be surprised if you spot some of New York's top chefs prodding the produce here: Union Square's greenmarket is arguably the city's most famous. Whet your appetite trawling the stalls, which peddle anything and everything from upstate fruit and vegetables to artisanal breads, cheeses and cider.

WHOLE FOODS FOOD & DRINK

Map p426 (☎212-673-5388; www.wholefoods market.com; 4 Union Sq S, btwn University Place & Broadway; ⏰7am-11pm; 📶; [S]4/5/6, N/Q/R, L to 14th St-Union Sq) One of several locations of the popular, healthy food emporium, Whole Foods is an excellent place to fill the picnic hamper. Drool over endless rows of gorgeous produce, both organic and nonorganic, plus a butcher, a bakery, ready-to-eat dishes, a health and beauty section, and aisles packed with natural packaged goods.

DSW SHOES

Map p426 (☎212-674-2146; www.dsw.com; 4 Union Sq S, btwn University Pl & Broadway; ⏰10am-9:30pm Mon-Sat, to 8pm Sun; [S]4/5/6, N/Q/R, L to 14th St-Union Sq) If your idea of paradise involves a great selection of cut-price kicks, make a bee line for this sprawling, unisex chain. Shoes range from formal to athletic, with no shortage of popular and higher-end labels.

ABRACADABRA ACCESSORIES

Map p426 (☎212-627-5194; www.abracadabra superstore.com; 19 W 21st St, btwn Fifth & Sixth Aves; ⏰11am-7pm Mon-Sat, noon-5pm Sun; [S]N/R, F/M to 23rd St) It's not just a Steve Miller Band song, it's also an emporium of horror, costumes and magic. Those who like this sort of thing will be hard-pressed to leave without racking up some credit-card bills.

SPORTS & ACTIVITIES

JIVAMUKTI YOGA

Map p426 (☎212-353-0214; www.jivamuktiyoga.com; 841 Broadway, btwn 13th & 14 Sts; classes $15-22; ⏰classes 7am-9pm Mon-Thu, 7am-8pm Fri, 8am-8pm Sat & Sun; [S]4/5/6, N/Q/R, L to 14th St-Union Sq) *The* yoga spot in Manhattan, Jivamukti – in a 12,000-sq-ft locale on Union Sq – is a posh place for Vinyasa, Hatha and Ashtanga classes. The center's 'open classes' are suitable for both rookies and experienced practitioners, and there's an organic, vegan cafE on-site too. Gratuitous celebrity tidbit: Uma's little bro Dechen Thurman teaches classes here.

SOUL CYCLE CYCLING

Map p426 (☎212-208-1300; www.soul-cycle.com; 12 E 18th St, btwn Fifth Ave & Broadway; classes $34; ⏰classes 6am-8:30pm Mon-Thu, to 7pm Fri, 7:30am-6pm Sat, 8:30am-7pm Sun; [S]4/5/6, N/Q/R, L to 14th St-Union Sq) Soul Cycle's wellness recipe (one part spinning class, one part dance party, one part therapy session) makes exercise an easy pill to swallow. There are no membership fees, so locals and tourists alike are welcome. You may even spot a celeb – Jake Gyllenhaal is known to take a class from time to time.

Midtown

MIDTOWN EAST | FIFTH AVENUE | MIDTOWN WEST & TIMES SQUARE |

Neighborhood Top Five

1 Playing spot the landmark at the jaw-dropping Top of the Rock, the **Rockefeller Center's** (p186) observation deck, or sipping cocktails at grown-ups-only SixtyFive five floors down.

2 Hanging out with Picasso, Warhol and Rothko at the blockbuster **Museum of Modern Art** (p182).

3 Conducting **shopping** (p208) sorties on and around Fifth and Madison Aves.

4 Slurping martinis, gazing at the skyline and dabbling in a little hot evening sax at **Jazz at Lincoln Center** (p205).

5 Adding a little sparkle to life with a toe-tapping, soul-lifting **Broadway show** (p179).

For more detail of this area see Map p428 and p432 ➡

Lonely Planet's Top Tip

Savoring Midtown's A-list restaurants without mortgaging the house is possible if you go for the prix-fixe lunch menu where available. Participants include Michelin-starred **Le Bernardin** (p200) and **Betony** (p200), which offer dishes featured in their evening menus. How far ahead you should book depends on the restaurant. While you can usually secure a lunch table at Betony with a few days' notice, it can sometimes be a one-month wait at Le Bernardin. Both offer online reservations.

✕ Best Places to Eat

➡ Le Bernardin (p200)
➡ Betony (p200)
➡ Modern (p183)
➡ Totto Ramen (p199)

For reviews, see p195 ➡

🍷 Best Places to Drink

➡ SixtyFive (p202)
➡ Campbell Apartment (p201)
➡ Rum House (p202)
➡ Jimmy's Corner (p202)
➡ Flaming Saddles (p203)

For reviews, see p201 ➡

◉ Best Places for a Skyline View

➡ Top of the Rock (p191)
➡ SixtyFive (p202)
➡ Empire State Building (p180)
➡ Robert (p193)

For reviews, see p190 ➡

Explore Midtown

Midtown is big, brazen and best seen on foot, so slice it up and enjoy it bit by bit. The top end of Fifth Ave (around the 50s) makes for a fabled introduction, home to Tiffany & Co, the Plaza Hotel, the Museum of Modern Art (MoMA), and the Rockefeller Center's Top of the Rock observation decks. A day in Midtown East could easily incorporate rare manuscripts at the Morgan Library & Museum, beaux-arts architecture at Grand Central Terminal, the art-deco lobby of the Chrysler Building and a tour of the United Nations. If it's a rainy day, explore the gilded New York Public Library.

In Midtown West, design and fashion buffs head to the Museum of Arts & Design and the Museum at FIT. Between the two is blinding Times Square, most spectacular at night. Its residents include a TKTS Booth selling cut-price Broadway tickets. The queues are usually shortest after 5:30pm, though clever cookies buy their tickets at the less crowded South Street Seaport branch. Further west is Hell's Kitchen, packed with great eateries and gay venues.

Local Life

➡**Dive bars** Stiff drinks, loosened ties and the whiff of nostalgia await at no-bull bars such as Jimmy's Corner (p202) and Rudy's Bar & Grill (p203).

➡**Theater** Look beyond the glitz and kitsch of Broadway for innovative drama at Playwrights Horizons (p207) and Second Stage Theatre (p207).

➡**Food** Join all walks of life at time-warped Cuban diner El Margon (p199).

Getting There & Away

➡**Subway** Times Sq-42nd St, Grand Central-42nd St and 34th St-Herald Sq are Midtown's main interchange stations. A/C/E and 1/2/3 lines run north–south through Midtown West. The 4/5/6 lines run north–south through Midtown East. The central B/D/F/M lines run up Sixth Ave, while N/Q/R lines follow Broadway. The 7, E and M lines offer some crosstown service.

➡**Bus** Useful for the western and eastern extremes of Midtown. Routes include the M11 (north on Tenth Ave and south on Ninth Ave), the M101, M102 and M103 (north on Third Ave and south on Lexington Ave) and the M15 (north on First Ave and south on Second Ave). Crosstown buses run along 34th and 42nd Sts.

➡**Train** Long-distance Amtrak and Long Island Rail Road (LIRR) trains terminate at Penn Station (p386). Jersey's PATH trains stop at 33rd St, while Metro-North commuter trains terminate at Grand Central Terminal (p184).

TOP SIGHT
TIMES SQUARE

'I had traveled eight thousand miles around the American continent and I was back on Times Square; and right in the middle of a rush-hour, too, seeing with my innocent road-eyes the absolute madness and fantastic hoorair of New York with its millions and millions hustling forever for a buck among themselves, the mad dream...' Jack Kerouac, *On the Road.*

Hyperactive Heart

Love it or hate it, the intersection of Broadway and Seventh Ave (better known as Times Square) is New York City's hyperactive heart. It's a restless, hypnotic torrent of glittering lights, bombastic billboards and raw urban energy. It's not hip, fashionable or in-the-know, and it couldn't care less. It's too busy pumping out iconic, mass-marketed NYC, from yellow cabs and golden arches to razzle-dazzle Broadway marquees. This is the New York of collective fantasies – the place where Al Jolson 'makes it' in the 1927 film *The Jazz Singer,* where photojournalist Alfred Eisenstaedt famously captured a sailor and nurse lip-locked on V-J Day in 1945, and where Alicia Keys and Jay-Z waxed lyrically about this 'concrete jungle where dreams are made.'

For several decades, the dream here was a sordid, wet one. The economic crash of the early 1970s led to a mass exodus of corporations from Times Square. Billboard niches went dark, stores shut and once-grand hotels were converted into SRO (single-room occupancy) dives. While the adjoining Theater District survived, its respectable playhouses shared the streets with porn cinemas and strip clubs. That all changed with tough-talking Mayor Rudolph Giuliani, who, in the 1990s, boosted police numbers and lured a wave of 'respectable' retail chains, restaurants and attractions. By the new millennium, Times Square had gone from 'X-rated' to 'G-rated,' drawing almost 40 million visitors annually.

DON'T MISS

- Taking in Times Square from the TKTS Booth steps
- Discount tickets to a Broadway show
- A drink at R Lounge, the Renaissance Hotel

PRACTICALITIES

- Map p433
- www.timessquarenyc.org
- Broadway, at Seventh Ave
- [S]N/Q/R, S, 1/2/3, 7 to Times Sq-42nd St

BRILL BUILDING

Standing at the northwest corner of Broadway and 49th St, the **Brill Building** (Map p432; Broadway, at 49th St, Midtown West; [S]N/Q/R to 49th St; 1, C/E to 50th St) is widely considered the most important generator of popular songs in the western world. By 1962, more than 160 music businesses were based here, from songwriters and managers to record companies and promoters. It was a one-stop shop for artists, who could craft a song, hire musicians, cut a demo and convince a producer without leaving the building. Among the legends who did were Carol King, Bob Dylan, Joni Mitchell and Paul Simon. When they did leave the building, no doubt many would have headed to W 48th St, a street so packed with music stores it was famously dubbed Music Row.

KISS-IN

Alfred Eisenstaedt's famous 1945 photograph of a smooching US sailor and nurse is the inspiration behind the Times Square Kiss-In. Conducted every five years on the anniversary of the end of World War II, it sees hundreds of couples fill the square to recreate the scene famously captured on the cover of *LIFE* magazine. The next reenactment is set for August 2020.

For a panoramic overview over the square, order a drink at the Renaissance Hotel's **R Lounge** (Map p432; ☎212-261-5200; www.rloungetimessquare.com; Two Times Square, 714 Seventh Ave, at 48th St, Midtown West; ⏰5-11pm Mon, to 11:30pm Tue-Thu, to midnight Fri, 7:30am-midnight Sat, 7:30am-11pm Sun; [S]N/Q/R to 49th St), which offers floor-to-ceiling glass windows of the neon-lit spectacle below. It might not be the savviest spot for a sip in town, but with a view like this, who's judging?

A Subway, A Newspaper & A Very Famous Dropping Ball

At the turn of last century, Times Square was known as Longacre Sq, an unremarkable intersection far from the commercial epicenter of Lower Manhattan. This would change with a deal made between subway pioneer August Belmont and *New York Times* publisher Adolph Ochs. Heading construction of the city's first subway line (from Lower Manhattan to the Upper West Side and Harlem), Belmont astutely realized that a Midtown business hub along 42nd St would maximize profit and patronage on the route. On his mission to draw business into the area, Belmont approached Ochs, who had recently turned around the fortunes of the *New York Times*. Belmont argued that moving the newspaper's operations to the intersection of Broadway and 42nd St would be a win-win for Ochs, for not only would an in-house subway station mean faster distribution of the newspaper around town, the influx of commuters to the square would also mean more sales right outside its headquarters. Belmont even convinced New York Mayor George B McClellan Jr to rename the square in honor of the broadsheet. It was an irresistible offer, and in the winter of 1904–05, both subway station and the *Times'* new headquarters at One Times Square made their debut.

In honor of the move, the *Times* hosted a New Year's Eve party in 1904, setting off fireworks from its skyscraper rooftop. By 1907, the square had become so built-up that fireworks were deemed a safety hazard, forcing the newspaper to come up with alternative crowd-puller. It came in the form of a 700-pound, wood-and-iron ball, lowered from the roof of One Times Square to herald the arrival of 1908.

While the *Times* may have left the building (it's now in a Renzo Piano–designed skyscraper at 620 Eighth Ave), around one million people still gather in Times Square every New Year's Eve to watch a Waterford crystal ball descend from the building at midnight. It's a mere 90-second spectacle that is arguably one of NYC's greatest anticlimaxes. Looking up, it's easy to forget that behind the current armor of billboards, the One Times Square building still exists. To see what it looked like in the days of Adolph Ochs, pay a visit to the beautiful DeWitt Wallace Periodical Room at the New York Public Library (p191), whose large-scale paintings by muralist Richard Haas include a depiction of Times Square in the time of streetcars.

On Broadway

By the 1920s, Belmont's dream for Times Square had kicked into overdrive. Not only was it the heart of a growing commercial district, but it had overtaken Union Square as New York's theater hub. The neighborhood's first playhouse was the long-gone Empire, opened in 1893 and located on Broadway between 40th and 41st Sts. Two years later, cigar manufacturer and part-time comedy scribe Oscar Hammerstein opened the Olympia, also on Broadway, before opening the Republic – now children's theater **New Victory** (Map p432; ☑646-223-3010; www.newvictory. org; 209 W 42nd St, btwn Seventh & Eighth Aves, Midtown West; 🚻; ⓈN/Q/R, S, 1/2/3, 7 to Times Sq-42nd St; A/C/E to 42nd St-Port Authority Bus Terminal) – in 1900. This lead to a string of new venues, among them the still-beating **New Amsterdam Theatre** (Map p432; ☑212-282-2900; www.new-amsterdam-theatre.com; 214 W 42nd St, btwn Seventh & Eighth Aves, Midtown West; 🚻; ⓈN/Q/R, S, 1/2/3, 7 to Times Sq-42nd St; A/C/E to 42nd St-Port Authority Bus Terminal) and **Lyceum Theatre** (Map p432; www.shubert.nyc/theatres/lyceum; 149 W 45th St, btwn Sixth & Seventh Aves, Midtown West; ⓈN/Q/R to 49th St).

The Broadway of the 1920s was well known for its lighthearted musicals, commonly fusing vaudeville and music-hall traditions, and producing classic tunes such as Cole Porter's 'Let's Misbehave'. At the same time, Midtown's theater district was evolving as a platform for new American dramatists. One of the greatest was Eugene O'Neill. Born in Times Square at the long-gone Barrett Hotel (1500 Broadway) in 1888, the playwright debuted many of his works here, including Pulitzer Prize–winners *Beyond the Horizon* and *Anna Christie*. O'Neill's success on Broadway paved the way for other American greats including Tennessee Williams, Arthur Miller and Edward Albee – a surge of serious talent that led to the establishment of the annual Tony Awards in 1947.

These days, New York's Theater District covers an area stretching roughly from 40th St to 54th St between Sixth and Eighth Aves, with dozens of Broadway and off-Broadway theaters spanning blockbuster musicals to new and classic drama. Unless there's a specific show you're after, the best – and cheapest – way to score tickets in the area is at the TKTS Booth, where you can line up and get same-day discounted tickets for top Broadway and off-Broadway shows. Smartphone users can download the free TKTS app, which offers rundowns of both Broadway and off-Broadway shows, as well as real-time updates of what's available on that day. Always have a back-up choice in case your first preference sells out, and never buy from scalpers on the street.

The TKTS Booth is an attraction in its own right, its illuminated roof of 27 ruby-red steps rising a panoramic 16ft 1in above the 47th St sidewalk.

TOP SIGHT
EMPIRE STATE BUILDING

The Chrysler Building may be prettier and One World Trade Center and 432 Park Avenue may be taller, but the Queen Bee of the New York skyline remains the Empire State Building. NYC's tallest star, it has enjoyed close-ups in around 100 films, from *King Kong* to *Independence Day*. And heading up to the top is as quintessential an experience as pastrami, rye and pickles at Katz's Delicatessen.

By the Numbers

The statistics are astounding: 10 million bricks, 60,000 tons of steel, 6400 windows and 328,000 sq ft of marble. Built on the original site of the Waldorf-Astoria, construction took a record-setting 410 days, using seven million hours of labor and costing a mere $41 million. It might sound like a lot, but it fell well below its $50 million budget (just as well, given it went up during the Great Depression). Coming in at 102 stories and 1472ft from top to bottom, the limestone phallus opened for business on May 1, 1931. Generations later, Deborah Kerr's words to Cary Grant in *An Affair to Remember* still ring true: 'It's the nearest thing to heaven we have in New York.'

DON'T MISS

- Observation decks at sunset
- Live jazz Thursday to Saturday nights

PRACTICALITIES

- Map p429
- www.esbnyc.com
- 350 Fifth Ave, at 34th St
- 86th-fl observation deck adult/child $32/26, incl 102nd-fl observation deck $52/46
- 🕘8am-2am, last elevators up 1:15am
- [S]B/D/F/M, N/Q/R to 34th St-Herald Sq

Observation Decks

Unless you're Ann Darrow (the unfortunate blonde caught in King Kong's grip), heading to the top of the Empire State Building should leave you beaming. There are two observation decks. The open-air 86th-floor deck offers an alfresco experience, with coin-operated telescopes for close-up glimpses of the metropolis in action. Further up, the enclosed 102nd-floor deck is New York's second-highest observation deck, trumped only by the observation deck at One World Trade Center. Needless to say, the views over the city's five boroughs (and five neighboring states, weather permitting) are quite simply exquisite. The views from both decks are especially spectacular at sunset, when the city dons its nighttime cloak in dusk's afterglow. For a little of that *Arthur's Theme* magic, head to the 86th floor between 9pm and 1am from Thursday to Saturday, when the twinkling sea of lights is accompanied by a soundtrack of live sax (yes, requests are taken). Alas, the passage to heaven will involve a trip through purgatory: the queues to the top are notorious. Getting here very early or very late will help you avoid delays – as will buying your tickets online, ahead of time, where an extra $2 convenience fee is well worth the hassle it will save you.

An Ambitious Antenna

A locked, unmarked door on the 102nd-floor observation deck leads to one of New York's most outrageous pie-in-the-sky projects to date: a narrow terrace intended to dock zeppelins. Spearheading the dream was Alfred E Smith, who went from failed presidential candidate in 1928 to head honcho of the Empire State Building project. When architect William Van Alen revealed the secret spire of his competing Chrysler Building, Smith went one better, declaring that the top of the Empire State Building would sport an even taller mooring mast for transatlantic airships. While the plan looked good on paper, there were two (major) oversights: dirigibles require anchoring at both ends (not just at the nose as planned) and passengers (traveling in the zeppelin's gondola) cannot exit the craft through the giant helium-filled balloon. Regardless, it didn't stop them from trying. In September 1931, the *New York Evening Journal* threw sanity to the wind, managing to moor a zeppelin and deliver a pile of newspapers fresh out of Lower Manhattan. Years later, an aircraft met up with the building with less success: a B-25 bomber crashed into the 79th floor on a foggy day in 1945, killing 14 people.

LANGUAGE OF LIGHT

Since 1976, the building's top 30 floors have been floodlit in a spectrum of colors each night, reflecting seasonal and holiday hues. Famous combos include orange, white and green for St Patrick's Day; blue and white for Chanukah; white, red and green for Christmas; and the rainbow colors for Gay Pride weekend in June. For a full rundown of the color schemes, check the website.

SIBLING COMPARISONS

The Empire State Building was designed by the prolific architectural firm Shreve, Lamb and Harmon. According to legend, the skyscraper's conception began with a meeting between William Lamb and building co-financier John Jakob Raskob, during which Raskob propped up a No 2 pencil and asked, 'Bill, how high can you make it so that it won't fall down?' Shreve, Lamb and Harmon's other projects include the skyscraper at 500 Fifth Ave. To compare the soaring siblings, head to the northeast corner of Fifth Ave and 40th St.

TOP SIGHT
MUSEUM OF MODERN ART

MoMA boasts more A-listers than an Oscars after-party: Van Gogh, Matisse, Picasso, Warhol, Rothko, Pollock and Bourgeois. Since its founding in 1929, the museum has amassed almost 200,000 artworks, documenting the creative ideas and movements of the late 19th century through to those dominating today. For art buffs, it's Valhalla. For the uninitiated, it's a crash course in all that is addictive about art.

Collection Highlights

MoMA's permanent collection spans four levels. From time to time, major temporary exhibitions may alter the order slightly, but prints, illustrated books and the unmissable Contemporary Galleries are usually on level two; architecture, design, drawings and photography are on level three; and painting and sculpture are on levels four and five. Many of the big hitters are on these last two levels, so tackle the museum from the top down before fatigue sets in. Must-sees include Van Gogh's *Starry Night,* Cézanne's *The Bather,* Picasso's *Les Demoiselles d'Avignon,* and Henri Rousseau's *The Sleeping Gypsy,* not to mention iconic American works like Warhol's *Campbell's Soup Cans* and *Gold Marilyn Monroe,* Lichtenstein's equally poptastic *Girl with Ball,* and Hopper's haunting *House by the Railroad.* Generally speaking, Mondays and Tuesdays are the best (least-crowded) days to visit, except on public holidays. Friday evenings and weekends can be incredibly crowded and frustrating.

DON'T MISS

- Van Gogh's *Starry Night*
- Edward Hopper's *House by the Railroad*
- Andy Warhol's *Gold Marilyn Monroe*
- Dining at Modern

PRACTICALITIES

- MoMA
- Map p432
- ☎212-708-9400
- www.moma.org
- 11 W 53rd St, btwn Fifth & Sixth Aves
- adult/child $25/free, 4-8pm Fri free
- ⏲10:30am-5:30pm Sat-Thu, to 8pm Fri, to 8pm Thu Jul & Aug
- [S] E, M to 5th Ave-53rd St

Abby Aldrich Rockefeller Sculpture Garden

With architect Yoshio Taniguchi's acclaimed reconstruction of the museum in 2004 came the restoration of the Sculpture Garden to the original, larger vision of Philip Johnson's 1953 design. Johnson described the space as a 'sort of outdoor room,' and on warm, sunny days, it's hard not to think of it as a soothing alfresco lounge. One resident that can't seem to get enough of it is Aristide Maillol's *The River*, a larger-than-life female sculpture that featured in Johnson's original garden. She's in fine company too, with fellow works from greats including Matisse, Miró and Picasso. Sitting sneakily above the garden's eastern end is *Water Tower*, a translucent resin installation by British artist Rachel Whiteread. The Sculpture Garden is open free of charge from 9:30am to 10:15am daily, except in inclement weather and during maintenance.

The Eateries

MoMA's eateries have a stellar reputation. For communal tables and a super-casual vibe, nosh on Italian-inspired panini, pasta dishes, salads, salumi and cheeses at **Cafe 2** (Map p432; ☑212-333-1299; www.moma.org; sandwiches & salads $12-14; mains $19; ☺11am-5pm, to 7:30pm Fri; ☎). For table service, à la carte options and Danish design, opt for **Terrace Five** (Map p432; ☑212-333-1288; www.moma.org; mains $14-18; ☺11am-5pm Sat-Thu, to 7:30pm Fri; ☎), which features an outdoor terrace overlooking the Sculpture Garden. If you're after a luxe feed, however, book a table at the Michelin-starred **Modern** (Map p432; ☑212-333-1220; www.themodernnyc.com; 9 W 53rd St, btwn Fifth & Sixth Aves; 3-/4-course lunch $80/90, 4-course dinner $118; ☺restaurant noon-2pm & 5-10:30pm Mon-Fri, 5-10:30pm Sat, bar 11:30am-10:30pm Mon-Sat, to 9:30pm Sun). Fans of *Sex and the City* might know that it was here that scribe-about-town Carrie announced her impending marriage to 'Mr Big.' (If you're on a *real* writer's wage, you can always opt for simpler, cheaper bites in the adjacent Bar Room.)

Film Screenings

Not only a palace of visual art, MoMA screens an incredibly well-rounded selection of celluloid gems from its collection of more than 22,000 films, including the works of the Maysles Brothers and every Pixar animation film ever produced. Expect anything from Academy Award–nominated documentary shorts and Hollywood classics to experimental works and international retrospectives. Best of all, your museum ticket will get you in for free.

GALLERY CONVERSATIONS

To delve a little deeper into MoMA's collection, join one of the museum's lunchtime talks and readings, which offer thought-provoking insight into specific works and exhibitions on view. The talks take place daily at 11:30am and 1:30pm. To check upcoming topics, click the 'Learn' link on the MoMA website, followed by the 'Lectures & Events' and 'Gallery Sessions' links.

ABSTRACT EXPRESSIONISM

One of the greatest strengths of MoMA's collections is abstract expressionism, a radical movement that emerged in New York in the 1940s and boomed a decade later. Defined by its penchant for irreverent individualism and monumentally scaled works, this so-called 'New York School' helped turn the metropolis into *the* epicenter of western contemporary art. Among the stars are Rothko's *Magenta, Black, Green on Orange*, Pollock's *One (Number 31, 1950)* and de Kooning's *Painting*.

TOP SIGHT
GRAND CENTRAL TERMINAL

Threatened by the opening of the original Penn Station, transport magnate Cornelius Vanderbilt transformed his 19th-century Grand Central Depot into a 20th-century showpiece. The fruit of his envy is Grand Central Terminal, New York's most breathtaking beaux-arts building. Grand Central's swirl of chandeliers, marble, and historic bars and restaurants is a porthole into an era where train travel and romance were not mutually exclusive.

DON'T MISS

- Main beaux-arts facade
- Paul César Helleu's celestial mural
- Oysters under Rafael Guastavino's vaulted ceiling
- Cocktails at Campbell Apartment
- A foodie trawl of Grand Central Market

PRACTICALITIES

- Map p429
- www.grandcentralterminal.com
- 42nd St, at Park Ave, Midtown East
- ⏲5:30am-2am
- [S] S, 4/5/6, 7 to Grand Central-42nd St

42nd St Facade

Clad in Connecticut Stony Creek granite at its base and Indiana limestone on top, Grand Central's showpiece facade is crowned by America's greatest monumental sculpture, *The Glory of Commerce*. Designed by the French sculptor Jules Félix Coutan, the piece was executed in Long Island City by local carvers Donnely and Ricci. Once completed, it was hoisted up, piece by piece, in 1914. Its protagonist is a wing-capped Mercury, the Roman god of travel and commerce. To the left is Hercules in an unusually placid stance, while looking down on the mayhem of 42nd St is Minerva, the ancient guardian of cities. The clock beneath Mercury's foot contains the largest example of Tiffany glass in the world.

Main Concourse

Grand Central's trump card is more akin to a glorious ballroom than a thoroughfare. The marble floors are Tennessee pink, while the vintage ticket counters are Italian Bottocino marble. The vaulted ceiling is (quite literally) heavenly, its turquoise and gold-leaf mural depicting eight constellations...backwards. A mistake?

Apparently not. Its French designer, painter Paul César Helleu, wished to depict the stars from God's point of view – from the out, looking in. The original, frescoed execution of Helleu's design was by New York–based artists J Monroe Hewlett and Charles Basing. Moisture damage saw it faithfully repainted (alas, not in fresco form) by Charles Gulbrandsen in 1944. By the 1990s, however, the mural was in ruins again. Enter renovation architects Beyer Blinder Belle, who restored the work, but left a tiny patch of soot (in the northwest corner) as testament to just what a fine job they did.

Whispering Gallery, Oyster Bar & Restaurant & Campbell Apartment

The vaulted landing directly below the bridge linking the Main Concourse and Vanderbilt Hall harbors one of Grand Central's quirkier features, the so-called Whispering Gallery. If you're in company, stand facing the walls diagonally opposite each other and whisper something. If your partner proposes (it happens a lot down here), chilled champagne is just through the door at the Grand Central Oyster Bar & Restaurant (p195). It's hugely atmospheric (with a vaulted tiled ceiling by Catalan-born engineer Rafael Guastavino), and you're best to stick to what it does exceptionally well: oysters. An elevator beside the restaurant leads up to another historic gem: the deliciously snooty bar Campbell Apartment (p201).

Grand Central Market

More drooling awaits at the **Grand Central Market** (Map p428; Grand Central Terminal, Lexington Ave, at 42nd St, Midtown East; 🕗7am-9pm Mon-Fri, 10am-7pm Sat, 11am-6pm Sun; [S]S, 4/5/6, 7 to Grand Central-42nd St), a 240ft corridor lined with fresh produce and artisan treats. Stock up on anything from crusty bread and fruit tarts to artisanal cheese, chicken pot pies, Spanish quince paste, fruit and vegetables, and roasted coffee beans.

GUIDED TOURS

The **Municipal Art Society** (Map p432; ☎212-935-3960; www.mas.org; tours adult/child $20/15; [S]F to 57th St) runs 75-minute walking tours through Grand Central daily at 12.30pm. Tours start at the information booth in the Main Concourse. The Grand Central Partnership (p210) leads free, 90-minute tours of the terminal and the surrounding neighborhood on Fridays at 12:30pm. Tours commence on the southwest corner of E 42nd St and Park Ave.

THE PRESIDENT'S SECRET

Hidden away under the Waldorf-Astoria hotel is Grand Central's little-known Platform 61. One person who did know it well was polio-afflicted President Franklin D Roosevelt. Determined to hide his affliction from public view, Roosevelt made good use of the platform's freight elevator. Upon arrival at the station, the president would be driven straight out of his train carriage, along the platform and into the elevator...his public none the wiser.

TOP SIGHT
ROCKEFELLER CENTER

This 22-acre 'city within a city' debuted at the height of the Great Depression. Taking nine years to build, it was America's first multiuse retail, entertainment and office space – a modernist sprawl of 19 buildings (14 of which are the original art-deco structures), outdoor plazas and big-name tenants. Developer John D Rockefeller Jr may have sweated over the cost (a mere $100 million), but it was all worth it: the Center was declared a National Landmark in 1987.

Top of the Rock

There are views, and then there's *the* view from the Top of the Rock (p191). Crowning the GE Building, 70 stories above Midtown, its blockbuster vista includes one icon that you won't see from atop the Empire State Building – *the* Empire State Building. If possible, head up just before sunset to see the city transform from day to glittering night (if you're already in the area and the queues aren't long, purchase your tickets in advance to avoid the late-afternoon rush). Alternatively, if you don't have under-21s in tow, ditch Top of the Rock for the 65th-floor cocktail bar (p202), where the same spectacular views come with well-mixed drinks...at a cheaper price than the Top of the Rock admission.

DON'T MISS

- Sky-high views from the observation deck
- Sunset cocktails at SixtyFive
- José Maria Sert's *American Progress* mural
- *Saturday Night Live* set (NBC Studio Tour)

PRACTICALITIES

- Map p428
- www.rockefellercenter.com
- Fifth to Sixth Aves & 48th to 51st Sts
- [S]B/D/F/M to 47th-50th Sts-Rockefeller Center

Public Artworks

Rockefeller Center features the work of 30 great artists, commissioned around the theme 'Man at the Crossroads Looks Uncertainly But Hopefully at the Future.' Paul Manship contributed *Prometheus,* overlooking the sunken plaza, and *Atlas,* in front of the International Building (630 Fifth Ave). Isamu Noguchi's *News* sits above the entrance to the Associated Press Building (50 Rockefeller Plaza), while José Maria Sert's oil *American Progress* awaits in the lobby of the GE Building. The latter work replaced Mexican artist Diego Rivera's original painting, rejected by the Rockefellers for containing 'communist imagery.'

NBC Studio Tour

TV comedy *30 Rock* gets its name from the GE Building, and the tower is the real-life home of NBC TV. One-hour NBC Studio Tours (p210) (enter from 1250 Sixth Ave) usually include a visit to Studio 8H, home of the iconic *Saturday Night Live* set. Tours have a strict 'no bathrooms policy ' (empty your bladder beforehand!) and advanced online reservations are strongly recommended. Across 49th St, opposite the plaza, is the glass-enclosed NBC *Today Show* studio, broadcasting live from 7am to 11am on weekdays. If you fancy some screen time, head in by 6am to be at the front of the crowd.

Rockefeller Plaza

Come the festive season, Rockefeller Plaza is where you'll find New York's most famous Christmas tree. Ceremoniously lit just after Thanksgiving, it's a tradition that dates back to the 1930s, when construction workers set up a small tree on the site. In its shadow, **Rink at Rockefeller Center** (Map p428; ☎212-332-7654; http:therinkatrockcenter.com; Rockefeller Center, Fifth Ave, btwn 49th & 50th Sts; adult $25-32, child $15, skate rental $12; ⏰8:30am-midnight mid-Oct–Apr; 👪; [S]B/D/F/M to 47th-50th Sts-Rockefeller Center) is the city's most famous ice-skating rink. Incomparably magical, it's also undeniably small and crowded. Opt for the first skating period (8.30am) to avoid a long wait. Come summer, the rink becomes a cafe.

TOP SIGHT
RADIO CITY MUSIC HALL

Ladies and gentleman, boys and girls, welcome to the one and only Radio City Music Hall. A spectacular art-deco diva, this 5901-seat movie palace was the brainchild of vaudeville producer Samuel Lionel 'Roxy' Rothafel. Roxy launched his venue in 1932 with an extravaganza that included a *Symphony of the Curtains* (starring...the curtains), and the high-kick campness of the Roxyettes (mercifully renamed the Rockettes).

Heyday & Decline

By the 1940s, Radio City had become the greatest single attraction in New York, its red carpet well worn with a string of movie premieres. Alas, the good times didn't last, with dwindling popularity and soaring rents forcing the theater's closure in 1978. In true showbiz style, however, the venue escaped demolition with a last-minute reprieve, its interior declared a landmark worthy of a $5 million restoration.

A Great Stage

For a real treat, join a 75-minute guided tour of the sumptuous interiors, designed by Donald Deskey. But first, eye-up the building's 50th St facade, where Hildreth Meière's brass rondels represent (from left to right) dance, drama and song. Celebrated artists also lavished the interiors. Among them was Lithuanian-born William Zorach, whose nude sculpture *Spirit of the Dance* sparked enough controversy to have the work temporarily removed. Less scandalous gems include Stuart Davies' abstract wall mural *Men Without Women* in the Smoking Room, and Witold Gordon's classically inspired *History of Cosmetics* in the Women's Downstairs Lounge. The adjoining restroom (open to all) sports the world's first modern hand dryers.

While the original, wood-paneled elevators are sublime, the pièce de résistance is the main auditorium, its radiating arches evoking a setting sun. Here you'll see Radio City Music Hall's legendary pipe organ (the biggest built for a movie palace) and the landmark-listed Great Stage, famed for its still-sophisticated hydraulics. Much smaller but très exclusive is the VIP Roxy Suite, lavished with rich cherrywood walls, 20ft-high domed ceilings and an acoustically clever dining area.

The Show Must Go On

As far as catching a show here goes, be warned: the vibe doesn't quite match the theater's splendor now that it's managed by the folks from Madison Square Garden. Latecomers are allowed, disrupting performances, and glow-in-the-dark cocktails often create an ugly sea of purple drinks that's more akin to a stadium rock concert than a sophisticated show in an elegant theater. Still, there are often some fabulous talents in the lineup, with past performers including Rufus Wainwright, Aretha Franklin and Dolly Parton. And while the word 'Rockettes' provokes eye rolling from most self-consciously cynical New Yorkers, fans of glitz and kitsch might just get a thrill from the precision dance troupe's annual Christmas Spectacular.

Same-day tickets are available at the candy store beside the Sixth Ave entrance, though it's worth considering paying the extra $5 to book your ticket online given that tours can sell out quickly, particularly on rainy days.

DON'T MISS

- Artworks
- Main auditorium
- Roxy Suite
- Vintage hand dryers

PRACTICALITIES

- Map p432
- www.radiocity.com
- 1260 Sixth Ave, at 51st St
- tours adult/child $26.95/19.95
- ⏰tours 10am-5pm
- [S]B/D/F/M to 47th-50th Sts-Rockefeller Center

TOP SIGHT
CHRYSLER BUILDING

The 77-floor Chrysler Building makes most other skyscrapers look like uptight geeks. Designed by Willian Van Alen in 1930, it's a dramatic fusion of art deco and Gothic aesthetics, adorned with stern steel eagles and topped by a spire that screams *Bride of Frankenstein*. Constructed as the headquarters for Walter P Chrysler and his automobile empire, the ambitious $15 million building remains one of New York's most poignant symbols.

The Lobby

Although the Chrysler Building has no restaurant or observation deck, its lobby is a lavish consolation prize. Bathed in an amber glow, its Jazz Age vintage is echoed in its architecture – dark, exotic African wood and marble, contrasted against the brash, man-made steel of industrial America. The elaborately veneered elevators are especially beautiful, their Egyptian lotus motifs made of inlaid Japanese ash, Oriental walnut and Cuban plum-pudding wood. When the doors open, you almost expect Bette Davis to strut on out. Above you is painter Edward Trumbull's ceiling mural *Transport and Human Endeavor*. Purportedly the world's largest mural at 97ft by 100ft, its depiction of buildings, airplanes and industrious workers on Chrysler assembly lines shows the golden promise of industry and modernity.

DON'T MISS

- *Transport and Human Endeavor* lobby ceiling mural
- William Van Alen's spire
- Facade ornamentation
- View from Third Ave–44th St and the Empire State Building
- René Chambellan and Jacques Delamarre's reliefs, Chanin Building

PRACTICALITIES

- Map p429
- 405 Lexington Ave, at 42nd St, Midtown East
- 🕒lobby 8am-6pm Mon-Fri
- [S]S, 4/5/6, 7 to Grand Central-42nd St

The Spire

Composed of seven radiating steel arches, the Chrysler Building's 185ft spire was as much a feat of vengeance as it was of modern engineering. Secretly constructed in the stairwell, the 200ft creation (dubbed 'the vertex') was raised through a false roof and anchored into place in an impressive 1½ hours. The novel reveal shocked and outraged architect H Craig Severance, who had hoped that his Manhattan Company skyscraper on Wall Street would become the world's tallest building. The fait accompli was especially humiliating given that Severance had personally fallen out with architect William Van Alen, a former colleague. Karmic retribution may have been served with the 1931 debut of the even-taller Empire State Building, but Van Alen's crowning glory endures as a showstopping symbol of 20th-century daring.

The Gargoyles

If the spire is the building's diva, the gargoyles are its supporting cast. Pairs of gleaming steel American eagles look ready to leap from the corners of the 61st floor, giving the building a brooding, Gothic edge. Further down on the 31st floor, giant winged hubcaps echo the Chrysler radiator caps of the late 1920s. For a dramatic view of the gargoyles from street level, head to the corner of Lexington Ave and 43rd St and look up.

Two Impressive Views

For a great view of the Chrysler Building, head to the corner of Third Ave and 44th St, from where you can appreciate the building's slimline profile, gargoyles and spire in one hit. If you have binoculars, bring them for a close-up view of the facade's detailing, which includes basket-weave motifs and a band of abstract automobiles. Alternatively, head to the top of the Chrysler Building's taller rival, the Empire State Building, where pay-per-view telescopes will get you up close and personal with that gleaming steel spire.

Chanin Building A Neighboring Gem

Across the street from the Chrysler Building, on the southwest corner of Lexington Ave and 42nd St, stands another art-deco gem: the **Chanin Building** (Map p428; 122 E 42nd St, at Lexington Ave, Midtown East; [S]S, 4/5/6, 7 to Grand Central-42nd St). Completed in 1929, the 56-story brick and terra-cotta tower is the work of unlicensed architect Irwin S Chanin, who teamed up with the legally recognized firm Sloan & Robertson to achieve his dream. Yet the star attraction here is the work of René Chambellan and Jacques Delamarre, creators of the exquisite bands of relief at the building's base. While birds and fish create a sense of whimsy in the lower band, the upper band of terra-cotta steals the show with its rich botanical carvings.

THE CLOUD CLUB

Nestled at the top of the Chrysler Building between 1930 and 1979 was the famed Cloud Club. Its regulars included tycoon John D Rockefeller, publishing magnate Condé Montrose and boxing legend Gene Tunney. The art-deco-meets-Hunting-Lodge hangout from floors 66 to 68 featured a lounge and dining rooms (including a private room for Walter Chrysler), as well as kitchens, a barber shop and a locker room with sneak cabinets for hiding booze during Prohibition. Chrysler merrily boasted about having the highest toilet in town.

CREMASTER 3

The Chrysler Building's lobby and crown feature in *Cremaster 3* (2002), an avant-garde film by award-winning visual artist and filmmaker Matthew Barney. The third installment of an epic five-part film project, it delivers a surreal take on the skyscraper's construction, fusing Irish mythology with genre elements from both zombie and gangster films. To read more about the project, check out www.cremaster.net.

SIGHTS

Midtown East

★CHRYSLER BUILDING HISTORIC BUILDING

See p187.

★GRAND CENTRAL TERMINAL HISTORIC BUILDING

See p184.

★MORGAN LIBRARY & MUSEUM MUSEUM

Map p428 (www.morganlibrary.org; 29 E 36th St, at Madison Ave, Midtown East; adult/child $18/12; ⏲10:30am-5pm Tue-Thu, to 9pm Fri, 10am-6pm Sat, 11am-6pm Sun; [S]6 to 33rd St) Incorporating the mansion once owned by steel magnate JP Morgan, this sumptuous cultural center houses a phenomenal array of manuscripts, tapestries and books (with no fewer than three Gutenberg Bibles). Adorned with Italian and Dutch Renaissance artworks, Morgan's personal study is only trumped by his personal library (East Room), an extraordinary, vaulted space adorned with walnut bookcases, a 16th-century Dutch tapestry and zodiac-themed ceiling. The center's rotating exhibitions are often superb, as are its regular cultural events.

UNITED NATIONS HISTORIC BUILDING

Map p428 (☎212-963-4475; http:visit.un.org; visitors' gate First Ave at 46th St, Midtown East; guided tour adult/child $20/11, children under 5yr not admitted, grounds Sat & Sun free; ⏲tours 9am-4:30pm Mon-Fri, visitor center 10am-4:30pm Sat & Sun; 📶; [S]S, 4/5/6, 7 to Grand Central-42nd St) Welcome to the headquarters of the UN, a worldwide organization overseeing international law, international security and human rights. While the Le Corbusier-designed Secretariat building is off-limits, one-hour guided tours do cover the recently restored General Assembly Hall, Security Council Chamber, Trusteeship Council Chamber and Economic and Social Council (ECOSOC) Chamber, as well as exhibitions about the UN's work and artworks given by member states. Weekday tours must be booked online and photo ID is required to enter the site.

Free walk-in access to the visitor center only is permitted on weekends (enter at 43rd St). To the north of the UN complex, which technically stands on international territory, is a serene park featuring Henry Moore's *Reclining Figure* as well as several other peace-themed sculptures.

JAPAN SOCIETY CULTURAL CENTER

Map p428 (www.japansociety.org; 333 E 47th St, btwn First & Second Aves, Midtown East; adult/child $12/free, 6-9pm Fri free; ⏲11am-6pm Tue-Thu, to 9pm Fri, to 5pm Sat & Sun; 📶; [S]S, 4/5/6, 7 to Grand Central-42nd St) Elegant exhibitions of both traditional and contemporary Japanese art, textiles and design are the main draw at this calming cultural center, complete with indoor gardens and water features. Its theater hosts a range of films and dance and theatrical performances, while those wanting to dig deeper can browse through 14,000 volumes in the research library or attend one of its myriad lectures or workshops.

Founded in 1907 by a group of NYC businesspeople with a deep admiration for Japan, this nonprofit society has played a large role in strengthening American-Japanese relations. Its expansion into a full arts and cultural center was thanks in no small part to philanthropist John D Rockefeller III, an ardent fan of the country.

MUSEUM OF SEX MUSEUM

Map p428 (☎212-689-6337; www.museumofsex.com; 233 Fifth Ave, at 27th St; adult $17.50; ⏲10am-8pm Sun-Thu, to 9pm Fri & Sat; [S]N/R to 23rd St) Get the lowdown on anything from online fetishes to homosexual necrophilia in the mallard duck at this slick ode to all things hot and sweaty. The rotating program of temporary exhibitions has included explorations of cyber sex and retrospectives of controversial artists, while the permanent collection showcases the likes of erotic lithographs and awkward anti-onanism devices.

Stock up on erotic books, gifts and ergonomic sex toys in the design-savvy museum shop, or kiss a cocktail in the bar-cum-lounge.

Fifth Avenue

★EMPIRE STATE BUILDING HISTORIC BUILDING

See p180.

★ROCKEFELLER CENTER HISTORIC BUILDING

See p186.

TOP OF THE ROCK VIEWPOINT

Map p428 (☎212-698-2000; www.topoftherocknyc.com; 30 Rockefeller Plaza, at 49th St, entrance on W 50th St btwn Fifth & Sixth Aves; adult/child $32/26, sunrise/sunset combo $47/36; ⏰8am-midnight, last elevator at 11pm; [S]B/D/F/M to 47th-50th Sts-Rockefeller Center) Designed in homage to ocean liners and first opened in 1933, this 70th-floor, open-air observation deck sits atop the GE Building, the tallest skyscraper at the Rockefeller Center. Top of the Rock trumps the Empire State Building on several levels: it's less crowded, has wider observation decks (both outdoor and indoor) and actually offers a view of the Empire State Building itself.

NEW YORK PUBLIC LIBRARY HISTORIC BUILDING

Map p428 (Stephen A Schwarzman Building; ☎917-275-6975; www.nypl.org; Fifth Ave, at 42nd St; ⏰10am-6pm Mon & Thu-Sat, to 8pm Tue & Wed, 1-5pm Sun, guided tours 11am & 2pm Mon-Sat, 2pm Sun; 📶; [S]B/D/F/M to 42nd St-Bryant Park, 7 to 5th Ave) [FREE] Loyally guarded by 'Patience' and 'Fortitude' (the marble lions overlooking Fifth Ave), this beaux-arts show-off is one of NYC's best free attractions. When dedicated in 1911, New York's flagship library ranked as the largest marble structure ever built in the US, and to this day, its Rose Main Reading Room steals the breath away with its lavish, coffered ceiling. While the room may be closed for restoration until early 2017, it's only one of several glories, among them the DeWitt Wallace Periodical Room.

This extraordinary building is home to precious manuscripts by just about every author of note in the English language, including an original copy of the Declaration of Independence and a Gutenberg Bible. The Map Division is equally astounding, with a collection that holds some 431,000 maps, 16,000 atlases and books on cartography, dating from the 16th century to the present. To properly explore this mini-universe of books, art and architectural flourishes, join a free guided tour (departing from Astor Hall) or grab a free audio guide from the information desk (also in Astor Hall).

BRYANT PARK PARK

Map p428 (☎212-768-4242; www.bryantpark.org; 42nd St, btwn Fifth & Sixth Aves; ⏰7am-midnight Mon-Fri, to 11pm Sat & Sun Jun-Sep, shorter hr rest of yr; 📶; [S]B/D/F/M to 42nd St-Bryant Park, 7 to Fifth Ave) European coffee kiosks, alfresco chess games, summer film screenings and winter ice-skating: it's hard to believe that this leafy oasis was dubbed 'Needle Park' in the '80s. Nestled behind the beaux-arts New York Public Library building, it's a whimsical spot for a little time-out from the Midtown madness.

Among the park's attractions is the French-inspired, Brooklyn-made **Le Carrousel** (W 40th St, at Sixth Ave, Midtown West; ride $3; ⏰11am-9pm Jan, to 8pm Jun-Oct, reduced hr rest of yr; [S]B/D/F/M to 42nd St-Bryant Park, 7 to 5th Ave) offering rides, as well as frequent special events. These include the Bryant Park Summer Film Festival, popular with postwork crowds lugging cheese-and-wine picnics. Come Christmastime, the place becomes a winter wonderland, with holiday gift vendors lining the park's edge and a popular ice-skating rink sprouting in its middle. Lovely **Bryant Park Grill** (☎212-840-6500; www.arkrestaurants.com/bryant_park.html; Bryant Park, 25 W 40th St, btwn Fifth & Sixth Aves; mains $18.50-42; ⏰11:30am-11pm; [S]B/D/F/M to 42nd St-Bryant Park; 7 to 5th Ave) is the site of many a New York wedding come springtime, and when it's not closed for a private event, the patio bar is a perfect spot for a twilight cocktail. Next door you'll find its more casual alfresco sibling **Bryant Park Café** (☎212-840-6500; www.arkrestaurants.com; Bryant Park; ⏰7am-10pm mid-Apr–Nov; [S]B/D/F/M to 42nd St-Bryant Park, 7 to 5th Ave), a much-loved spot for after-five catch-ups.

ST PATRICK'S CATHEDRAL CHURCH

Map p428 (www.saintpatrickscathedral.org; Fifth Ave, btwn 50th & 51st Sts; ⏰6:30am-8:45pm; [S]B/D/F/M to 47th-50th Sts-Rockefeller Center; E/M to 5th Ave-53rd St) Fresh from a major restoration, America's largest Catholic cathedral graces Fifth Ave with its Gothic Revival splendor. Built at a cost of nearly $2 million during the Civil War, the building did not originally include the two front spires; those were added in 1888. Step inside to appreciate the Louis Tiffany-designed altar and Charles Connick's stunning Rose Window, the latter gleaming above a 7000-pipe church organ.

A basement crypt behind the altar contains the coffins of every New York cardinal and the remains of Pierre Touissant, a champion of the poor and the first African American up for sainthood.

PALEY CENTER FOR MEDIA CULTURAL CENTRE
Map p428 (☎212-621-6800; www.paleycenter.org; 25 W 52nd St, btwn Fifth & Sixth Aves; adult/child $10/5; 🕒noon-6pm Wed & Fri-Sun, to 8pm Thu; [S]E, M to 5th Ave-53rd St) Pop culture repository Paley Center offers more than 160,000 TV and radio programs from around the world on its computer catalog. Reliving your favorite TV shows on one of the center's consoles is sheer bliss on a rainy day, as are the excellent, regular screenings, festivals, speakers and performers.

Midtown West & Times Square

★**MUSEUM OF MODERN ART** MUSEUM
See p182.

★**RADIO CITY MUSIC HALL** HISTORIC BUILDING
See p189.

HELL'S KITCHEN NEIGHBORHOOD
Map p432 (Clinton; 34th to 59th Sts & Eighth to Twelfth Aves, Midtown West; [S]C/E to 50th St) For years, the far west side of Midtown was a working-class jumble of tenements and food warehouses known as Hell's Kitchen – supposedly its name was muttered by a cop in reaction to a riot in the neighborhood in 1881. A 1990s economic boom seriously altered its character and the area is now best known for its plethora of eateries (especially along Ninth and Tenth Aves between about 37th and 55th Sts) and heaving gay bars and clubs.

Antique-lovers should check out the weekend Hell's Kitchen Flea Market (p209), its stalls packed with vintage clothing, antique jewelry, period furniture and other finds.

MUSEUM OF ARTS & DESIGN MUSEUM
Map p432 (MAD; www.madmuseum.org; 2 Columbus Circle, btwn Eighth Ave & Broadway; adult/child $16/free, by donation 6-9pm Thu; 🕒10am-6pm Tue, Wed, Sat & Sun, to 9pm Thu & Fri; 📶👪; [S]A/C, B/D, 1 to 59th St-Columbus Circle) MAD offers four floors of superlative design and handicrafts, from blown glass and carved wood to elaborate metal jewelry. Its temporary exhibitions are top notch and innovative; one past show explored the art of scent. Usually on the first Sunday of the month, professional artists lead family-friendly explorations of the galleries, followed by hands-on workshops inspired by the current exhibitions. The museum gift shop sells some fantastic contemporary

WORTH A DETOUR

FOUR FREEDOMS PARK

Dramatic design, presidential inspiration and a refreshing perspective on the New York skyline make for an arresting trio at the **Franklin D Roosevelt Four Freedoms Park** (Map p428; ☎212-204-8831; www.fdrfourfreedomspark.org; Roosevelt Island; 🕒9am-7pm Wed-Mon Apr-Sep, to 5pm Wed-Mon Oct-Mar; [S]F to Roosevelt Island, 🚋Roosevelt Island) [FREE]. Clinging to the southern tip of sinuous Roosevelt Island on the East River, this remarkable monument honors America's 32nd president and his State of the Union speech of 1941. In it, Franklin D Roosevelt addressed his desire for a world based upon four essential human freedoms: freedom of speech, freedom of worship, freedom from want and freedom from fear. Designed by renowned architect Louis Kahn in 1973, the monument would only reach completion in 2012, 38 years after Kahn's death.

The wait was worth it. Kahn's luminous granite vision is breathtakingly cinematic in its scale and effect. A sweep of grand, stark steps lead up to a sloping triangular lawn. Fringed by linden trees, the lawn gently spills down to a bronze bust of Roosevelt by American sculptor Jo Davidson. Framing the sculpture is a granite wall, hand engraved with Roosevelt's rousing speech. The wall also serves to separate the bust from 'The Room,' a contemplative granite terrace clinging to the very tip of the island. The combination of lapping waves and hovering skyline are utterly mesmerizing.

Although the F subway line will get you to Roosevelt Island, it's much more fun catching the aerial **tramway** (p219) car, which glides above the East River, offering eagle-eye views of the Manhattan skyline. The monument is a 15-minute walk south of both the Roosevelt Island tramway car and subway stations.

jewelry, while the 9th-floor restaurant-bar **Robert** (☎212-299-7730; www.robertnyc.com; ⏰11:30am-10pm Mon & Sun, to 11pm Tue, to midnight Wed-Sat) is perfect for panoramic cocktails.

DIAMOND DISTRICT STREET

Map p432 (www.diamonddistrict.org; 47th St, btwn Fifth & Sixth Aves; [S]B/D/F/M to 47th-50th Sts-Rockefeller Center) Like Diagon Alley in *Harry Potter*, the Diamond District is a world unto itself. Best experienced on weekdays, it's an industrious whirl of Hasidic Jewish traders, pesky hawkers and lovestruck couples looking for the perfect rock. It's home to over 2600 businesses, at street level and on upper floors, cutting, polishing, appraising or showcasing all manner of diamonds. In fact, the strip handles approximately 90% of the cut diamonds sold in the country. Marilyn, eat your heart out!

GARMENT DISTRICT NEIGHBORHOOD

Map p432 (Seventh Ave, btwn 34th St & Times Sq, Midtown West; [S]N/Q/R, S, 1/2/3 & 7 to Times Sq-42nd St) Otherwise known as the Fashion District, this thread-obsessed territory might look like an unremarkable stretch of designers' offices and wholesale and retail shops, but it's where you'll find a huge selection of fabrics, sequins, lace and, chances are, those day-glo velvet buttons you've been missing since 1986.

In the lead up to Fashion Week (February and September), the area swarms with portfolio-clutching models on their way from one casting to the next. Whatever the time of year, look down at the sidewalk when you hit Seventh Avenue and 39th St and you'll catch the Fashion Walk of Fame, honoring the likes of Betsey Johnson, Marc Jacobs, Geoffrey Beene, Halston and other fashion visionaries. It's on the same corner as Claes Oldenburg's sculpture of the world's largest button, held upright by a 31ft-tall steel needle.

HERALD SQUARE SQUARE

Map p432 (cnr Broadway, Sixth Ave & 34th St; [S]B/D/F/M, N/Q/R to 34th St-Herald Sq) This crowded convergence of Broadway, Sixth Ave and 34th St is best known as the home of mammoth department store Macy's (p209), where you can still ride some of the original wooden elevators. As part of the city's 'traffic-free Times Square' plan, you can also (try to) relax in a lawn chair outside the store, slap-bang in the middle of Broadway.

Herald Square gets its name from a long-defunct newspaper, the *New York Herald* (1835–1924), and the small, leafy park here bustles during business hours thanks to a much-needed facelift. Skip the indoor malls south of Macy's on Sixth Ave, packed with dull, suburban chains.

KOREATOWN (KOREA WAY) NEIGHBORHOOD

Map p428 (31st to 36th Sts & Broadway to Fifth Ave; [S]B/D/F/M, N/Q/R to 34th St-Herald Sq) Centered on W 32nd St between Fifth Ave and the intersection of Sixth Ave and Broadway, this Seoul-ful jumble of Korean-owned restaurants, shops, salons and spas will satiate any kimchi pangs.

MUSEUM AT FIT MUSEUM

Map p432 (☎212-217-4558; www.fitnyc.edu/museum; 227 W 27th St, at Seventh Ave, Midtown West; ⏰noon-8pm Tue-Fri, 10am-5pm Sat; [S]1 to 28th St) [FREE] The Fashion Institute of Technology (FIT) lays claim to one of the world's richest collections of garments, textiles and accessories. At last count, there were more than 50,000 items spanning the 18th century to the present day. The school's museum features innovative, rotating exhibitions showcasing both permanent-collection items and on-loan curiosities. Exhibitions aside, the museum also hosts film screenings and talks, including with prolific fashion designers and critics.

INTREPID SEA, AIR & SPACE MUSEUM MUSEUM

Map p432 (☎877-957-7447; www.intrepidmuseum.org; Pier 86, Twelfth Ave, at 46th St, Midtown West; Intrepid & Growler submarine adult/child $24/19, incl Space Shuttle Pavilion $31/24; ⏰10am-5pm Mon-Fri, to 6pm Sat & Sun Apr-Oct, 10am-5pm daily Nov-Mar; 👪; 🚌M42, M50 westbound, [S]A/C/E to 42nd St-Port Authority Bus Terminal) The USS *Intrepid* survived both a WWII bomb and kamikaze attacks. Thankfully, this hulking aircraft carrier is now a lot less stressed, playing host to a multimillion-dollar interactive military museum that tells its tale through videos, historical artifacts and frozen-in-time living quarters. The flight deck features fighter planes and military helicopters, which might inspire you try the museum's high-tech flight simulators.

The rides include the G Force Encounter, allowing you to experience the virtual thrill of flying a supersonic jet plane, and the

MIDTOWN SKYSCRAPERS: BEST OF THE REST

Midtown's skyline is more than just the Empire State and Chrysler Buildings, with enough modernist and postmodernist beauties to satisfy the wildest of high-rise dreams. Celebrate all things phallic with six of Midtown's finest.

➡ **Seagram Building (1956–58; 514ft)** A textbook regular, the 38-floor **Seagram Building** (Map p428; 100 E 53rd St, at Park Ave, Midtown East; [S]6 to 51st St, E, M to Fifth Ave-53rd St) is one of the world's finest examples of the international style. Its lead architect, Ludwig Mies van der Rohe, was recommended for the project by Arthur Drexler, then-curator of architecture at MoMA. With its low podium, colonnade-like pillars and bronze cladding, Mies cleverly references classical Greek influences.

➡ **Lever House (1950–52; 306ft)** Upon its debut, 21-story **Lever House** (Map p428; 390 Park Ave, btwn 53rd & 54th Sts, Midtown East; [S]E, M to Fifth Ave-53rd St) was on the cutting edge. The UN Secretariat Building was the only other skyscraper to feature a glass skin, an innovation that would redefine urban architecture. The building's form was equally bold: two counter-posed rectangular shapes consisting of a slender tower atop a low-rise base. The open courtyard features marble benches by Japanese American sculptor Isamu Noguchi, while the lobby exhibits specially commissioned contemporary art.

➡ **Citigroup Center (1974–77; 915ft)** With its striking triangular roof and candy-like striped facade, Hugh Stubbins' 59-story **Citigroup Center** (Map p428; 139 E 53rd St, at Lexington Ave, Midtown East; [S]6 to 51st St; E, M to Lexington Ave-53rd St) signaled a shift from the flat-roof sobriety of the international style. Even more dramatic is the building's base, which is cut away at the four corners, leaving the tower to perch dramatically on a cross-shaped footing. This unusual configuration allowed for the construction of St Peter's Lutheran Church on the site's northwest corner, replacing the original neo-Gothic church demolished during construction.

➡ **Hearst Tower (2003–06; 597ft)** The diagonal grid of trusses defining Foster & Partners' **Hearst Tower** (Map p432; 949 Eighth Ave, btwn 56th & 57th Sts, Midtown West; [S]A/C, B/D, 1 to 59th St-Columbus Circle) evokes a jagged glass-and-steel honeycomb. The tower rises above the hollowed-out core of John Urban's 1928 cast-stone Hearst Magazine Building, itself originally envisioned as a skyscraper. The 46-floor structure is also one of the city's greenest creations: around 90% of its structural steel is from recycled sources. In the lobby you'll find Richard Long's mural *Riverlines*, created with mud from New York's Hudson River and England's River Avon.

➡ **Bank of America Tower (2004–09; 1200ft)** Topped by a 255ft spire, the crystal-shaped **Bank of America Tower** (Map p432; Sixth Ave, btwn 42nd & 43rd Sts; [S]B/D/F/M to 42nd St-Bryant Park) also boasts enviable green credentials. A clean-burning, on-site cogeneration plant provides around 65% of the tower's annual electricity requirements; CO_2-detecting air filters channel filtered air where needed; and destination-dispatch elevators avoid empty car trips. Designed by Cook & Fox Architects, the 58-floor role model was awarded Best Tall Building in America at the Council on Tall Buildings & Urban Habitat awards in 2010.

➡ **432 Park Avenue (2011–15; 1396ft)** It's a case of 'thin is in' with the arrival of super-skinny, $1.3-billion **432 Park Avenue** (Map p428; 432 Park Ave, btwn 56th & 57th Sts, Midtown East; [S]N/Q/R to Lexington Ave-59th St), a residential tower by Uruguayan architect Rafael Viñoly. With a crisp, white, cubic facade inspired by a 1905 trash can by Austrian designer Josef Hoffman, the tower rises above the Midtown skyline like a thin, square tube. It's currently the city's second-tallest building, upstaged only by One World Trade Center. Measured to actual roof height, however, it's actually 28ft taller than its spire-crowned downtown rival.

Transporter FX, a flight simulator promising six full minutes of a 'complete sensory overload.' The museum is also home to the guided-missile submarine *Growler*, (not for the claustrophobic), a decommissioned Concorde, and the former NASA space shuttle *Enterprise*.

🍴 Midtown East & Fifth Avenue

ESS-A-BAGEL DELI $

Map p428 (☎212-980-1010; www.ess-a-bagel.com; 831 Third Ave, at 51st St, Midtown East; bagels sandwiches from $3; ⏲6am-9pm Mon-Fri, to 5pm Sat & Sun; [S]6 to 51st St, E/M to Lexington Ave-53rd St) Fresh, toothsome bagels have made this kosher deli a veritable institution. Tell the bagel monger your preference of bagel, then choose from a sprawling counter of cream cheeses and other sandwich fillings. For a classic, opt for scallion cream cheese with lox (salmon), capers, tomato and red onion. If the weather's fine, turn right into 51st St and lunch in pretty Greenacre Park. Warning: deli queues can get insanely long on weekends.

HANGAWI KOREAN $$

Map p428 (☎212-213-0077; www.hangawirestaurant.com; 12 E 32nd St, btwn Fifth & Madison Aves; mains lunch $11-30, dinner $19-30; ⏲noon-2:30pm & 5:30-10:15pm Mon-Fri, 1-10:30pm Sat, 5-9:30pm Sun; 🌿; [S]B/D/F/M, N/Q/R to 34th St-Herald Sq) Meat-free Korean is the draw at high-achieving Hangawi. Leave your shoes at the entrance and slip into a soothing, Zen-like space of meditative music, soft low seating and clean, complex dishes. Showstoppers include the leek pancakes and a seductively smooth tofu claypot in ginger sauce.

Organic and gluten-free options add to the holistic vibe, while the $22 prix-fixe lunch is good value. Book ahead for dinner.

SMITH AMERICAN $$

Map p428 (☎212-644-2700; www.thesmithnyc.com; 956 Second Ave, at 51st St, Midtown East; mains $17-32; ⏲7:30am-midnight Mon-Wed, to 1am Thu & Fri, 9:30am-1am Sat, 9:30am-midnight Sun; 📶; [S]6 to 51st St) This cool, bustling brasserie has sexed-up Midtown's far east with its industrial-chic interior, sociable bar and well-executed grub. Much of the food is made from scratch, the seasonal menus a mix of nostalgic American and Italian inspiration (we're talking hot potato chips with blue-cheese fondue, chicken pot pie with cheddar chive biscuit, and Sicilian baked eggs with artichokes, spinach and spicy tomato sauce). Book ahead for weekend brunch or prepare to wait.

ARTISANAL FRENCH $$$

Map p428 (☎212-725-8585; www.artisanalbistro.com; 2 Park Ave S, btwn 32nd & 33rd Sts, Midtown East; mains $24-50 ; ⏲10am-midnight Mon-Fri, from 9am Sat & Sun; 🌿; [S]6 to 33rd St) Artisanal is Valhalla for *fromage* fiends. From spicy Italian Canestrato to pungent French Livarot, you'll find more than 200 varieties of cheese at what is a modern take on an old Parisian bistro. Experiment with a cheese-and-wine flight or throw caution to the wind with one of a string of fondues. Beyond them is a cast of bistro standbys, from onion soup *gratinée* (with a three-cheese blend, naturally) to bouillabaisse.

JOHN DORY OYSTER BAR SEAFOOD $$$

Map p428 (☎212-792-9000; www.thejohndory.com; 1196 Broadway, at 29th St; plates $10-38; ⏲noon-midnight; [S]N/R to 28th St) Anchored to the Ace Hotel (p343) lobby, John Dory is a fine spot to sip some bubbles and slurp on an oyster or three. Top billing goes to happy hour (5pm to 7pm weekdays, noon to 3pm on weekends), when both oysters and clams beckon at $2 a pop (minimum of six).

CANNIBAL BEER & BUTCHER AMERICAN $$$

Map p428 (☎212-686-5480; www.cannibalnyc.com; 113 E 29th St, btwn Park Ave S & Lexington Ave, Midtown East; small plates $11-18, mains $15-42.50; ⏲11am-11:30pm; [S]6 to 28th St) The stuff of red-blooded dreams, this hip, hybrid eatery/bar/butcher peddles more than 200 craft beers and a sharp, seasonal menu of mostly carnivorous sharing plates. Graze on competent, house-made charcuterie and sausages, creative pâtés (think: chicken liver with beer, shallot jam and cocoa nibs), all tempered by beautifully textured sides like smokey kale salad with walnuts, Armenian string cheese and bacon.

Famished, pork-loving duos shouldn't miss the the General Tso's pig's head, served with broccoli, scallion salad and Chinese *moo shu* pancakes. The place gets super-busy, so head in by 7pm, or on a Monday or Sunday, to shorten the wait.

GRAND CENTRAL OYSTER BAR & RESTAURANT SEAFOOD $$$

Map p428 (☎212-490-6650; www.oysterbarny.com; Grand Central Terminal, 42nd St, at Park Ave; mains $13-39; ⏲11:30am-9:30pm Mon-Sat; [S]S, 4/5/6, 7 to Grand Central-42nd St) This buzzing bar and restaurant within Grand Central is hugely atmospheric, with a vaulted tiled ceiling by Catalan-born engineer Rafael

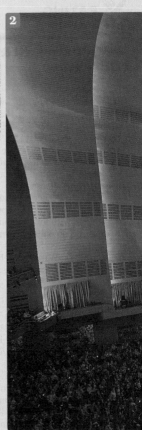

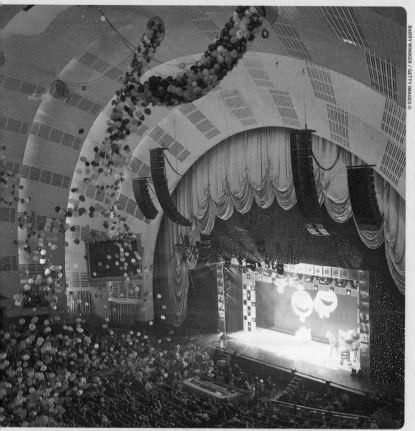

BARRY WINIKER / GETTY IMAGES ©

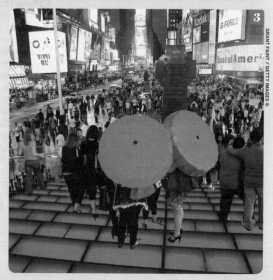

GRANT FAINT / GETTY IMAGES ©

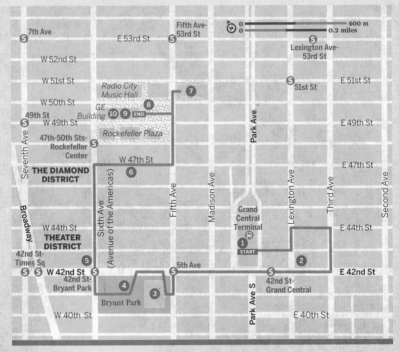

Neighborhood Walk
A Midtown Meander

START GRAND CENTRAL TERMINAL
END ROCKEFELLER CENTER
LENGTH 1.8 MILES; 3½ HOURS

Start your Midtown saunter at beaux-arts marvel ❶ **Grand Central Terminal** (p184). Star gaze at the Main Concourse ceiling, share sweet nothings at the Whispering Gallery and pick up a gourmet treat at the Grand Central Market. Exit onto Lexington Ave and walk one block east along 44th St to Third Ave for a view of William Van Alen's 1930 masterpiece, the ❷ **Chrysler Building** (p187). Walk down Third Ave to 42nd St, turn right and slip into the Chrysler Building's sumptuous art-deco lobby with purportedly the world's largest ceiling mural. At the corner of 42nd St and Fifth Ave stands the stately ❸ **New York Public Library** (p191). On this very site, between the 1840s and 1890s, stood the Croton Distributing Reservoir, an aboveground, 4-acre lake supplying drinking water to the city. Step inside the library to peek at its spectacular Rose Reading Room,

then nibble on your market treat in neighboring ❹ **Bryant Park** (p191). On the northwest corner of 42nd St and Sixth Ave soars the ❺ **Bank of America Tower** (p194), NYC's fourth-tallest building and one of its most ecofriendly. Head north along Sixth Ave to 47th St. Here, between Sixth and Fifth Aves, is the ❻ **Diamond District** (p193), home to more than 2600 independent businesses selling diamonds, gold, pearls, gemstones and watches. Walk towards Fifth Ave, taking in its swirl of Jewish traders. Turn left into Fifth Ave and admire the splendor of ❼ **St Patrick's Cathedral** (p191). Your last stop is ❽ **Rockefeller Center** (p186), a magnificent complex of art-deco skyscrapers and sculptures. Enter between 49th and 50th Sts to the main plaza and its golden statue of Prometheus. Then, either head to the 70th floor of the GE Building for an unforgettable vista at the ❾ **Top of the Rock** (p191) observation deck (book your tickets online to avoid the longest queues), or, if it's after 5pm, head straight up to cocktail bar ❿ **SixtyFive** (p202).

Guastavino. While the extensive menu covers everything from clam chowder and seafood stews to pan-fried softshell crab, the real reason to head here is for the two-dozen oyster varieties. Get slurping.

🍴 Midtown West & Times Square

★TOTTO RAMEN JAPANESE $

Map p432 (☎212-582-0052; www.tottoramen.com; 366 W 52nd St, btwn Eighth & Ninth Aves, Midtown West; ramen from $10; 🕐noon-4:30pm & 5:30pm-midnight Mon-Sat, 4-11pm Sun; [S]C/E to 50th St) There might be another two branches in Midtown, but purists know that neither beats the tiny 20-seat original. Write your name and the number of guests on the clipboard and wait your turn. Your reward: extraordinary ramen. Skip the chicken and go for the pork, which sings in dishes like miso ramen (with fermented soybean paste, egg, scallion, bean sprouts, onion and homemade chili paste).

Behind the counter, ramen masters tackle bubbling vats of fragrant broth and char the melt-in-your-mouth pork with a blowtorch. While there's never any guarantee, 3pm on Tuesdays and Wednesday seem to be the 'quietest' times. Avoid the place on weekends as waiting times are particularly excruciating.

WHOLE FOODS SUPERMARKET $

Map p432 (☎212-823-9600; www.wholefoodsmarket.com; Time Warner Center, 10 Columbus Circle; 🕐7am-11pm; [S]A/C, B/D, 1 to 59th St-Columbus Circle) Load up on freshly baked bread, cheeses, sushi, rotisserie chicken or items off the sprawling buffet counters, then stroll across the road for a memorable picnic in the park.

LARB UBOL THAI $

Map p432 (☎212-564-1822; www.larbubol.com; 480 Ninth Ave, at 37th St, Midtown West; 11:30am-10pm Sun-Thu, to 11pm Fri & Sat; 🕐dishes $6-22; [S]A/C/E to 34th St-Penn Station) Petite pastel parasols are among the few design concessions at this low-frills joint. But you're here for the fresh, jumping flavors of northeastern Thailand. Drool over *larb* (spicy, ground-meat salad), brilliant *nam tok nuer* (grilled beef with lime, fish sauce and palm sugar), and unexpected concoctions like *pla dook pad ped* (stir-fried catfish with Thai eggplant, peppercorn, basil, ginger and spicy curry paste). Lunch specials run between $8 and $9.

EL MARGON CUBAN $

Map p432 (☎212-354-5013; www.margonnyc.com; 136 W 46th St, btwn Sixth & Seventh Aves, Midtown West; sandwiches $4-8, mains from $10; 🕐6am-5pm Mon-Fri, from 7am Sat; [S]B/D/F/M to 47th-50th Sts-Rockefeller Center) It's still 1973 at this ever-packed Cuban lunch counter, where orange Laminex and greasy goodness never went out of style. Go for gold with its legendary cubano sandwich (a pressed panino jammed with rich roast pork, salami, cheese, pickles, mojo and mayo). It's obscenely good.

BURGER JOINT BURGERS $

Map p432 (☎212-708-7414; www.burgerjointny.com; Le Parker Meridien, 119 W 56th St, btwn Sixth & Seventh Aves, Midtown West; burgers from $8.50; 🕐11am-11:30pm Sun-Thu, to midnight Fri & Sat; [S]F to 57th St) With only a small neon burger as your clue, this speakeasy-style burger hut lurks behind the lobby curtain in the Le Parker Meridien hotel. Though it might not be as 'hip' or as 'secret' as it once was, it still delivers the same winning formula of graffiti-strewn walls, retro booths and attitude-loaded staff slapping up beef 'n' patty brilliance.

The choice is easy: hamburger or cheeseburger, cooked to your liking and pimped with your choice of garnishes. Order a side of golden fries, a pitcher of beer and scan the walls for celebrity scribbles. Head in early or late, or prepare to wait.

★VICEVERSA ITALIAN $$

Map p432 (☎212-399-9291; www.viceversanyc.com; 325 W 51st St, btwn Eighth & Ninth Aves, Midtown West; 2-course lunch $25, dinner mains $24-32; 🕐noon-2:30pm & 4:30-11pm Mon-Fri, 4:30-11pm Sat, 11:30am-3pm & 4:30-10pm Sun; [S]C/E to 50th St) ViceVersa is the quintessential Italian: suave and sophisticated, affable and scrumptious. Scan the menu for refined, cross-regional dishes like arancini with black truffle and fontina cheese. For a celebrated classic, order the *casoncelli alla bergamasca* (ravioli-like pasta filled with minced veal, raisins and amaretto cookies and seasoned with sage, butter, pancetta and Grana Padano), a nod to chef Stefano Terzi's Lombard heritage.

The bar seating is perfect for solo diners, while the leafy courtyard is a fun spot for a see-and-be-seen Sunday brunch.

KOREAN $$

2 (☎212-586-2880; www.danjinyc.com; nd St, btwn Eighth & Ninth Aves, Midtown West; dishes $13-26; ⏰noon-2:30pm & 5-11pm Mon-Thu, noon-2:30pm & 5pm-midnight Fri, 5pm-midnight Sat; [S]C/E to 50th St) Young-gun Hooni Kim woos palates with his Korean creations, served in a snug, slinky, white-washed space. The simpler lunch menu includes *bibimbap* (a traditional Korean rice dish), while the more expansive dinner list offers small, medium and large plates. Thankfully, both lunch and dinner menus offer Danji's cult-status *bulgogi* beef sliders, made with heavenly, butter-grilled buns. Head in early or wait.

DON ANTONIO
PIZZA $$

Map p432 (☎646-719-1043; www.donantoniopizza.com; 309 W 50th St, btwn Eighth & Ninth Aves, Midtown West; pizzas $9-25; ⏰11:30am-11pm Mon-Thu, to midnight Fri & Sat, to 10:30pm Sun; [S]C/E, 1 to 50th St) A top spot for authentic Neapolitan-style pizza, this hopping eatery is the offspring of Naples' historic pizzeria Starita. While New York concessions include a cocktail-shaking, solo-diner-friendly bar, the pies here are pure Napoli: chewy, thin-crust wonders with charred edges and sweet, ripe *sugo* (tomato sauce). All pizzas can be made using a wholewheat base, and there's a good selection of gluten-free pizzas too.

★BETONY
MODERN AMERICAN $$$

Map p432 (☎212-465-2400; www.betony-nyc.com; 41 W 57th St, btwn Fifth & Sixth Aves; 2-course lunch prix fixe $38, 4-/10-course dinner $95/195; ⏰noon-2pm & 5:30-10pm Mon-Thu, noon-2pm & 5:30-10.30pm Fri, 5:30-10:30pm Sat; [S]F to 57th St) Thrilling menus, seamless service and a slinky downtown vibe keep this Michelin-starred Midtowner in the black books of New York gastronomes. While industrial windows, exposed brickwork and a soaring bar make Betony's front section perfect for after-five cocktails, request a table in the intimate, baroque-esque back dining room to savor chef Bryce Shuman's sophisticated (albeit playful) dishes.

Here, smoked pork hock bursts through seared foie gras; roasted eggplant dallies with liquorice and amaranth; and a string of *amuse-bouches* (appetizers) provides no shortage of whimsical punctuation. Book ahead.

★LE BERNARDIN
SEAFOOD $$$

Map p432 (☎212-554-1515; www.le-bernardin.com; 155 W 51st St, btwn Sixth & Seventh Aves, Midtown West; prix fixe lunch/dinner $80/140, tasting menus $170-205; ⏰noon-2:30pm & 5:15-10:30pm Mon-Thu, to 11pm Fri, 5:15-11pm Sat; [S]1 to 50th St; B/D, E to 7th Ave) The interiors may have been subtly sexed-up for a 'younger clientele' (the stunning storm-themed triptych is by Brooklyn artist Ran Ortner), but triple Michelin-starred Le Bernardin remains a luxe, fine-dining holy grail. At the helm is French-born celebrity chef Éric Ripert, whose deceptively simple-looking seafood often borders on the transcendental.

The menu works simply: three lunch courses for $80 or four dinner courses for $140, with ample choices per course, and two tasting menus for those with more time and money. The dishes themselves are divided into three categories (Almost Raw, Barely Touched, Lightly Cooked), and while most shine with delicious complexity, Ripert's signature tuna and foie gras creation is especially outstanding. Book at least three weeks ahead for dinner and two weeks ahead for lunch.

TABOON
MEDITERRANEAN $$$

Map p432 (☎212-713-0271; www.taboononline.com; 773 Tenth Ave, at 52nd St, Midtown West; meze dishes $11-20, mains $26-38; ⏰5-11pm Mon-Fri, to 11:30pm Sat, 11am-3:30pm & 5-10pm Sun; [S]C/E to 50th St) Taboon is Arabic for stone oven, and it's the first thing you'll see when stepping through the curtain into this warm, casually chic hot spot. Join urbane theater-goers and Hell's Kitchen muscle boys for Med-inspired dishes like sizzling shrimp with garlic and lemon or truffle-oil-drizzled egg *burek* (soft-poached egg in crispy phyllo dough). Reservations recommended...as are the oven-fresh breads.

NOMAD
NEW AMERICAN $$$

Map p432 (☎212-796-1500; www.thenomadhotel.com; NoMad Hotel, 1170 Broadway, at 28th St; 2-course lunch prix fixe $29, dinner mains $23-41; ⏰noon-2pm & 5:30-10:30pm Mon-Thu, to 11pm Fri, 11am-2:30pm & 5:30-11pm Sat, 11am-2:30pm & 5:30-10pm Sun; [S]N/R, 6 to 28th St; F/M to 23rd St) Sharing the same name as the 'It kid' hotel it inhabits, NoMad has become one of Manhattan's culinary highlights. Carved up into a series of distinctly different spaces – including a see-and-be-seen Atrium, an elegant Parlour and a snacks-only Library – the restaurant serves delicacies ranging from roasted quail with plums, kale and chanterelle, to suckling pig confit with pears and bitter greens.

While the snacks can be a little hit-and-miss, both appetizers and mains are generally outstanding, whether it's slow-poached egg with pumpkin, cotechino and wild mushrooms, or NoMad's thrilling 'chicken for two,' roasted in a wood-burning oven and served with foie-gras-rich brioche under its crackly skin. Book ahead.

DRINKING & NIGHTLIFE

Midtown East & Fifth Avenue

CAMPBELL APARTMENT — COCKTAIL BAR

Map p428 (☎212-953-0409; www.hospitalityholdings.com; Grand Central Terminal, 15 Vanderbilt Ave, at 43rd St; ⏰noon-1am Mon-Thu, to 2am Fri & Sat, to midnight Sun; Ⓢ S, 4/5/6, 7 to Grand Central-42nd St) Party like it's 1928! This sublime, deliciously buttoned-up gem in Grand Central was once the office of a '20s railroad magnate fond of Euro eccentricities: think Florentine-style carpets, decorative wooden ceiling beams and a soaring leaded glass window. Suitably tucked away from the hordes, reach it from the lift beside the Oyster Bar or the stairs to the West Balcony.

A (somewhat arbitrary) dress code applies. Play it safe and leave the shorts, ripped jeans, T-shirts and sneakers in your wardrobe.

LITTLE COLLINS — CAFE

Map p428 (☎212-308-1969; http:littlecollinsnyc.com; 667 Lexington Ave, btwn 55th & 56th Sts, Midtown East; ⏰7am-5pm Mon-Fri, 8am-4pm Sat & Sun; Ⓢ E, M to 53rd St; 4/5/6 to 59th St) Co-owned by Aussie expat Leon Unglik, Little Collins emulates the celebrated cafes of his hometown, Melbourne: understatedly cool, welcoming spaces serving superlative coffee and equally tasty grub. The cafe is home to NYC's very first Modbar: high-tech, under-the-counter brewers that look like sleek chrome taps.

CULTURE ESPRESSO — CAFE

Map p428 (☎212-302-0200; www.cultureespresso.com; 72 W 38th St, at Sixth Ave; ⏰7am-7pm Mon-Fri, from 8am Sat & Sun; 📶; Ⓢ B/D/F/M to 42nd St-Bryant Park) Culture peddles single-origin espresso that's nutty, complex and creamy, as well as Third Wave options like Chemex and cold-brew varieties (we're addicted to the Kyoto-style iced coffee). Tasty edibles include baked treats from local artisans, and Culture's very own super-gooey choc-chip cookies.

STUMPTOWN COFFEE ROASTERS — CAFE

Map p428 (☎347-414-7805; www.stumptowncoffee.com; 18 W 29th St, btwn Broadway & Fifth Ave; ⏰6am-8pm Mon-Fri, from 7am Sat & Sun; Ⓢ N/R to 28th St) Hipster baristas in fedora hats brewing killer coffee? No, you're not in Williamsburg, you're at the Manhattan outpost of Portland's cult-status coffee roaster. The queue is a small price to pay for proper espresso, so count your blessings. It's standing-room only, though weary punters might find a seat in the adjacent Ace Hotel (p343) lobby.

There's a second branch in Greenwich Village (p151).

TOP OF THE STRAND — COCKTAIL BAR

Map p428 (www.topofthestrand.com; Strand Hotel, 33 W 37th St, btwn Fifth & Sixth Aves; ⏰5pm-midnight Mon & Sun, to 1am Tue-Sat; Ⓢ B/D/F/M to 34th St) For that 'Oh my God, I'm in New York' feeling, head to the Strand hotel's rooftop bar, order a martini (extra dirty) and drop your jaw (discreetly). Sporting comfy cabana-style seating, a refreshingly mixed-age crowd and a sliding glass roof, its view of the Empire State Building is simply unforgettable.

MIDDLE BRANCH — COCKTAIL BAR

Map p428 (☎212-213-1350; www.facebook.com/MiddleBranch; 154 E 33rd St, btwn Lexington & Third Aves, Midtown East; ⏰5pm-2am; Ⓢ 6 to 33rd St) Brainchild of the late cocktail deity Sasha Petraske, bi-level Middle Branch injects some much-needed drinking cred in beer-and-margarita-centric Murray Hill. Eye-candy bartenders whip up some of Midtown's sharpest libations, from faithful classics to playful reinterpretations like the Enzoni (a lemon-and-grape-laced twist on the classic Negroni).

PJ CLARKE'S — BAR

Map p428 (☎212-317-1616; www.pjclarkes.com; 915 Third Ave, at 55th St, Midtown East; ⏰11:30am-4am; Ⓢ E, M to Lexington Ave-53rd St) A bastion of old New York, this lovingly worn wooden saloon has been straddling the scene since 1884; Buddy Holly proposed to his fiancée here and Ol' Blue Eyes pretty much owned table 20. Choose a jukebox tune, order the knockout burger and settle in with a come-one-and-all crowd of collar-and-tie colleagues, college students and nostalgia-craving urbanites.

🍸 Midtown West & Times Square

★ SIXTYFIVE
COCKTAIL BAR

Map p428 (📞212-632-5000; www.rainbowroom. com; 30 Rockefeller Plaza, entrance on W 49th St; ⏰5pm-midnight Mon-Fri; ⓢB/D/F/M to 47th-50th Sts-Rockefeller Center) Not to be missed, sophisticated SixtyFive sits on level 65 of the GE Building at Rockefeller Center. Dress well (no sportswear or guests under 21) and arrive by 5pm for a seat with a multimillion-dollar view. Even if you don't score a table on the balcony or by the window, head outside to soak up that sweeping New York panorama.

At the other end of the corridor is the revamped Rainbow Room, a legendary, elite nightclub turned swanky nosh spot serving Sunday brunch as well as dinner on select evenings (see the website).

WAYLON
BAR

Map p432 (📞212-265-0010; www.thewaylon. com; 736 Tenth Ave, at 50th St, Midtown West; ⏰2pm-4am Mon-Fri, from noon Sat & Sun; ⓢC/E to 50th St) Slip on your spurs, partner, there's a honky-tonk in Hell's! Celebrate Dixie at this saloon-style watering hole, where the jukebox keeps good folk dancing to Tim McGraw's broken heart, where the barkeeps pour American whiskeys and tequila, and where the bar bites include Texan-style Frito pie and country-fried steak sandwiches. For live country-and-western sounds, head in on Thursdays between 8pm and 11pm.

RUM HOUSE
COCKTAIL BAR

Map p432 (📞646-490-6924; www.therumhouse-nyc.com; 228 W 47th St, btwn Broadway & Eighth Ave, Midtown West; ⏰1pm-4am; ⓢN/Q/R to 49th St) This sultry, revamped slice of old New York is revered for its cognoscenti rums and whiskeys. Savor them straight up or mixed in impeccable cocktails like a classic Dark & Stormy (rum, ginger beer and lime). Adding to the magic is nightly live music, spanning solo piano tunes to jaunty jazz trios and sentimental torch divas.

LANTERN'S KEEP
COCKTAIL BAR

Map p432 (📞212-453-4287; www.thelanterns-keep.com; Iroquois Hotel, 49 W 44th St, btwn Fifth & Sixth Aves; ⏰5-11:30pm Mon-Fri, 7pm-12:30am Sat; ⓢB/D/F/M to 42nd St-Bryant Park) Can you keep a secret? If so, cross the lobby of the **Iroquois Hotel** (Map p432; 📞212-840-3080; www.iroquoisny.com; 49 W 44th St, btwn Fifth & Sixth Aves, Midtown West; r from $509; ✱❄🛜; ⓢB/D/F/M to 42nd St-Bryant Park) and slip into this dark, intimate cocktail salon. Its specialty is classic drinks, shaken and stirred by passionate, personable mixologists. If you're feeling spicy, request a Gordon's Breakfast, a fiery mélange of gin, Worcestershire sauce, hot sauce, muddled lime and cucumber, salt and pepper. Reservations are recommended.

BAR CENTRALE
BAR

Map p432 (📞212-581-3130; www.barcentralenyc. com; 324 W 46th St, btwn Eighth & Ninth Aves, Midtown West; ⏰5pm-late; ⓢA/C/E to 42nd St-Port Authority) Set in an old brownstone, this unmarked bar is a favorite of Broadway stars, often seen here post-curtain debriefing and unwinding to sultry jazz. It's an intimate spot with a no-standing policy, so consider calling ahead (reservations are taken up to a week in advance). If you're having trouble finding it, it's just up the stairs to the left of Joe Allen's.

RUSSIAN VODKA ROOM
BAR

Map p432 (📞212-307-5835; www.russianvodka room.com; 265 W 52nd St, btwn Eighth Ave & Broadway, Midtown West; ⏰4pm-2am Mon-Thu, to 4am Fri & Sat; ⓢC/E to 50th St) Long for Mother Russia at this swank, affable drinking hole, pouring a head-spinning list of flavored vodkas, from cranberry to horseradish. When the room starts spinning, slow it down with stoic grub like borscht, *pirozhki* (stuffed buns), smoked fish and schnitzel.

JIMMY'S CORNER
BAR

Map p432 (📞212-221-9510; 140 W 44th St, btwn Sixth & Seventh Aves, Midtown West; ⏰11am-4am Mon-Fri, from 12:30pm Sat, from 3pm Sun ; ⓢN/Q/R, 1/2/3, 7 to 42nd St-Times Sq, B/D/F/M to 42nd St-Bryant Park) This welcoming, completely unpretentious dive off Times Square is run by an old boxing trainer – as if you wouldn't guess by all the framed photos of boxing greats (and lesser-known fighters, too). The jukebox covers Stax to Miles Davis (plus Lionel Ritchie's most regretful moments), kept low enough for after-work gangs to chat away.

RUDY'S BAR & GRILL BAR

Map p432 (☎646-707-0890; www.rudysbarnyc.com; 627 Ninth Ave, at 44th St, Midtown West; ⏰8am-4am Mon-Sat, noon-4am Sun; [S]A/C/E to 42nd St-Port Authority Bus Terminal) The big pantless pig in a red jacket out front marks Hell's Kitchen's best divey mingler, with cheap pitchers of Rudy's two beers, half-circle booths covered in red duct tape, and free hot dogs. A mix of folks come to flirt or watch muted Knicks games as classic rock plays.

FLAMING SADDLES GAY

Map p432 (☎212-713-0481; flamingsaddles.com/nyc; 793 Ninth Ave, btwn 52nd & 53rd Sts, Midtown West; ⏰3pm-4am Mon-Fri, noon-4am Sat & Sun; [S]C/E to 50th St) Butter my butt and call me a biscuit, a country-and-western gay bar in Midtown! *Coyote Ugly* meets *Calamity Jane* at this Hell's Kitchen hangout, complete with studly bar-dancing barmen, aspiring urban cowboys and a rough 'n' ready vibe. So slip on them Wranglers and hit the Saddle, partner. You're in for a wild and boozy ride.

INDUSTRY GAY

Map p432 (☎646-476-2747; www.industry-bar.com; 355 W 52nd St, btwn Eighth & Ninth Aves, Midtown West; ⏰4pm-4am; [S]C/E, 1 to 50th St) What was once a parking garage is now one of the hottest gay bars in Hell's Kitchen – a slick 4000-sq-ft watering hole with handsome lounge areas, a pool table and a stage for top-notch drag divas. Head in between 4pm and 9pm for the two-for-one drinks special or squeeze in later to party with the eye-candy party hordes. Cash only.

THERAPY GAY

Map p432 (☎212-397-1700; www.therapy-nyc.com; 348 W 52nd St, btwn Eighth & Ninth Aves, Midtown West; ⏰5pm-2am Sun-Thu, to 4am Fri & Sat; [S]C/E, 1 to 50th St) Multilevel Therapy was the first gay man's lounge-club to draw throngs to Hell's Kitchen, and it still pulls a crowd with its nightly shows (from music to interviews with Broadway stars) and decent grub Sunday to Friday (the quesadillas are especially popular). Drink monikers match the theme: Oral Fixation and Size Queen, to name a few.

XL NIGHTCLUB GAY

Map p432 (☎212-239-2999; www.xlnightclub.com; 512 W 42nd St, btwn Tenth & Eleventh Aves, Midtown West; ⏰10pm-4am; [S]A/C/E to 42nd St-Port Authority Bus Terminal) Muscle boys pack this mega dance club, a hedonistic playpen featuring two dance floors, cabaret theater, lounge bar, and the prerequisite quota of go-go boys and pin-up bartenders. The venue hosts some great themed nights, from cheeky drag revues to lip-sync battles.

☆ ENTERTAINMENT

☆ Midtown East & Fifth Avenue

JAZZ STANDARD JAZZ

Map p428 (☎212-576-2232; www.jazzstandard.com; 116 E 27th St, btwn Lexington & Park Aves; [S]6 to 28th St) One of the city's great jazz clubs is the Jazz Standard. The service is impeccable. The food is great. There's no minimum and it's programmed by Seth Abramson, a guy who really knows his stuff.

NEW YORK PUBLIC LIBRARY LECTURES, WORKSHOPS

Map p428 (www.nypl.org/events/calendar; 42nd St, at Fifth Ave; [S]B/D/F/M to 42nd St-Bryant Park; 7 to 5th Ave) Across its branches, the NYPL keeps brains lubricated with its string of lectures, seminars and workshops, with topics ranging from contemporary art to the writings of Jane Austen. You'll find some of the best at the main branch on 42nd St. You can search all happenings at the library's website.

☆ Midtown West & Times Square

★HAMILTON THEATER

Map p432 (Richard Rodgers Theatre; ☎tickets 877-250-2929; www.hamiltonbroadway.com; 226 W 46th St, btwn Seventh & Eighth Aves, Midtown West; [S]N/Q/R to 49th St) Lin-Manuel Miranda's acclaimed new musical is Broadway's hottest ticket, using contemporary hip-hop beats to recount the story of America's founding father, Alexander Hamilton. Inspired by Ron Chernow's biography *Alexander Hamilton*, the musical has won a swath of awards, including Outstanding Musical at the Drama Desk Awards and Best Musical at the New York Drama Critics' Circle Awards.

Book tickets at least six months in advance. Alternatively, head to the theater 2.5 hours before the performance to enter your name in the ticket lottery (bring photo ID). Winners – announced two hours before showtime – are able to purchase two $10 front row tickets.

★BOOK OF MORMON — THEATER

Map p432 (Eugene O'Neill Theatre; ☎tickets 212-239-6200; www.bookofmormonbroadway.com; 230 W 49th St, btwn Broadway & Eighth Ave, Midtown West; [S]N/Q/R to 49th St; 1 to 50th St; C/E to 50th St) Subversive, obscene and ridiculously hilarious, this cutting musical satire is the work of *South Park* creators Trey Parker and Matt Stone and *Avenue Q* composer Robert Lopez. Winner of nine Tony Awards, it tells the story of two naive Mormons on a mission to 'save' a Ugandan village.

Book at least three months ahead for the best choice of prices and seats, or pay a premium at shorter notice. Alternatively, head to the theater 2½ hours before the show to enter the lottery. Winners – announced two hours before curtain – get in for a bargain $32. Once the winners are called, a limited number of standing room tickets are sold at $27 subject to availability.

★KINKY BOOTS — THEATER

Map p432 (Hirschfeld Theatre; ☎tickets 212-239-6200; www.kinkybootsthemusical.com; 302 W 45th St, btwn Eighth & Ninth Aves, Midtown West; [S]A/C/E to 42nd St-Port Authority Bus Terminal) Adapted from a 2005 British indie film, Harvey Fierstein and Cyndi Lauper's smash hit tells the story of a doomed English shoe factory unexpectedly saved by Lola, a business-savvy drag queen. Its solid characters and electrifying energy have not been lost on critics, the musical winning six Tony Awards, including Best Musical in 2013.

If booking last minute, consider attending a matinee for cheaper tickets. If you're feeling particularly lucky, the show's website runs a daily ticket lottery, which offers $37 tickets for that day's performance. Winners are notified via email three hours before showtime. A limited number of standing-room tickets ($27) may also be offered at the box office subject to availability.

★CARNEGIE HALL — LIVE MUSIC

Map p432 (☎212-247-7800; www.carnegiehall.org; W 57th St, at Seventh Ave, Midtown West; ⏲tours 11:30am, 12:30pm, 2pm & 3pm Mon-Fri, 11:30am & 12:30pm Sat, 12:30pm Sun Oct-Jun; [S]N/Q/R to 57th St-7th Ave) This legendary music hall may not be the world's biggest, nor grandest, but it's definitely one of the most acoustically blessed venues around. Opera, jazz and folk greats feature in the Isaac Stern Auditorium, with edgier jazz,

ℹ BROADWAY BARGAINS

Unless booked many months in advance, must-see Broadway musicals can be prohibitively expensive. Discount ticket agent **TKTS** (www.tdf.org/nyc/7/TKTS) offers great deals daily, though rarely to the most in-demand shows. For these, your best bet for last-minute discounts is at the theater box office itself.

Many of the hottest shows – including **Hamilton** (p203), **Kinky Boots** and **Book of Mormon** – run ticket lotteries, entered at the theater 2½ hours before the performance. If your name is drawn, the show is yours for a steal. The bad news: tickets are limited and in high demand.

Other shows offer a limited number of general rush tickets, available each morning when the box office opens. Again, tickets are limited and in high demand, translating into early-morning queues and long waits.

Several shows also offer Standing Room Only (SRO) tickets, allowing patrons to stand through the performance in numbered spaces the width of a standard seat, usually at the back of the orchestra. Commonly between $27 and $40, SRO tickets can be especially tricky to land, as they are generally only available if the show is sold out. While there's no foolproof way to predict a sold-out show in advance, shows that do often include *Hamilton, Book of Mormon, Kinky Boots* and *Matilda*. Policies can change, so always check the specific show's website before hitting the theater, toes and fingers crossed.

THE NEW YORK STAGE

Charles Isherwood, theater critic for the *New York Times*, shares his tips on New York's vibrant theater scene.

Don't-Miss Musicals

Musical of the moment is **Hamilton** (p203). The book and score by Lin-Manuel Miranda, who also portrays Alexander Hamilton in the show, have caused more excitement than any musical in recent seasons. Also terrific is the ebullient stage version of **An American in Paris** (p205).

Best Back-Up Shows

Matilda (p206) makes for a fun evening, though the dense lyrics and British accents can make it difficult for non-English speakers to understand. **Aladdin** (New Amsterdam Theatre; Map p432; 212-827-5400, tickets 866-870-2717; www.aladdinthemusical.com; 214 W 42nd St, btwn Seventh & Eights Aves, Midtown West; ; N/Q/R, S, 1/2/3, 7 to Times Sq-42nd St; A/C/E to 42nd St-Port Authority Bus Terminal) is surprisingly good fun for both adults and children (especially if you've already seen **The Lion King** (Minskoff Theatre; Map p432; 212-869-0550, tickets 866-870-2717; www.lionking.com; 200 W 45th St, at Seventh Ave, Midtown West; ; N/Q/R, S, 1/2/3, 7 to Times Sq-42nd St)). Anyone with a tween or teenage girl might want to check out **Wicked** (Gershwin Theatre; Map p432; 212-586-6510, tickets 877-250-2929; www.wickedthemusical.com; 222 W 51st St, btwn Broadway & Eighth Ave, Midtown West; ; C/E, 1 to 50th St).

For Contemporary American Theater

Off Broadway is where most of the really interesting and innovative new work can be found. Reliably good companies include **Playwrights Horizons** (p207), **New York Theatre Workshop** (p125) and the **Roundabout Theatre Company** (212-719-1300; www.roundabouttheatre.org), whose off-Broadway offerings are often better than its Broadway shows. For adventurous theater, see what's playing at **Soho Rep** (p80) or the **Brooklyn Academy of Music** (p295).

Homegrown Stars

A list of the most exciting playwrights working in the American theater today would include Annie Baker (whose play *The Flick* won a Pulitzer Prize), Stephen Karam, Sarah Ruhl, Will Eno, Lynn Nottage and Amy Herzog.

For a Post-Show Tipple

Head to **Bar Centrale** (p202). It has no sign and is something of a theater-industry hangout where you'll usually see a boldface name or two after theater. Hint: if you go up the stairs to the left of the entrance of the restaurant Joe Allen on 46th St you'll find it.

pop, classical and world music in the hugely popular Zankel Hall. The intimate Weill Recital Hall hosts chamber-music concerts, debut performances and panel discussions.

From October to June, Carnegie Hall runs one-hour guided tours of the building, shedding light on the venue's storied history. **Guided tours** (adult/child $17/12) are subject to performance and rehearsal schedules, so check the website before heading in.

★**JAZZ AT LINCOLN CENTER** JAZZ
Map p432 (tickets to Dizzy's Club Coca-Cola 212-258-9595, tickets to Rose Theater & Appel Room 212-721-6500; www.jazz.org; Time Warner Center, Broadway, at 60th St, Midtown West; A/C, B/D, 1 to 59th St-Columbus Circle)

Perched high atop the Time Warner Center, Jazz at Lincoln Center consists of three state-of-the-art venues: the mid-sized Rose Theater; the panoramic, glass-backed Appel Room; and the intimate, atmospheric Dizzy's Club Coca-Cola. It's the last of these that you're most likely to visit given its nightly shows. The talent is often exceptional, as are the dazzling Central Park views.

AN AMERICAN IN PARIS THEATER
Map p432 (Palace Theatre; 212-730-8200, tickets 877-250-2929; www.anamericaninparisbroad-way.com; 1564 Broadway, at 47th St, Midtown West; N/Q/R to 49th St) Adapted from the 1951 film starring Gene Kelly, this elegant, critically acclaimed stage musical tells the

TV TAPINGS

Wanna be part of a live studio audience for the taping of one of your favorite shows? NYC is the place to do it. Follow the instructions below to gain access to some of TV's big-ticket tapings.

Saturday Night Live (www.nbc.com/saturday-night-live) One of the most popular NYC-based shows, and known for being difficult to get into. That said, you can try your luck by getting your name into the mix in the fall, when seats are assigned by lottery. Simply send an email in August, or line up by 7am the day of the show on the 48th St side of Rockefeller Plaza for standby lottery tickets. You can choose a standby ticket for either the 8pm dress rehearsal or the 11:30pm live broadcast. The tickets are limited to one per person and are issued on a first-come, first-served basis. You will need to bring valid photo ID when the ticket is issued, as well as to the show later that day. Audience members must be 16 or over.

The Late Show with Stephen Colbert (www.showclix.com/event/thelateshowwith-stephencolbert; Ed Sullivan Theater, 1697 Broadway, btwn 53rd & 54th Sts) Tickets for this hugely popular late-night show are available at online, but they commonly sell out on the day of their release. Check *The Late Show*'s official Twitter account (@colbert-lateshow) and Facebook page for release date announcements, usually made one to two months in advance. If you do manage to reserve tickets, you will need to line up outside the Ed Sullivan Theater no later than 3:15pm on the day of taping. Given that the show is intentionally overbooked to ensure capacity, consider arriving by 2.30pm to increase your chance of actually getting in. *The Late Show* tapes Monday through Friday at 5pm. Audience members must be 18 or over.

The Daily Show with Trevor Noah (www.showclix.com/event/thedailyshowwithtrevor-noah; 733 Eleventh Ave, btwn W 51st and W 52nd Sts) Sign up online to catch this popular news parody show. Reservations for shows are released on a gradual basis a few weeks before, so it pays to keep visiting the website. Tapings take place at 6pm and around 7:15pm Monday through Thursday. Check-in begins at 2:30pm, at which time the actual tickets are distributed. Consider arriving early as there is no guarantee of entry. Upon collecting your tickets at the venue you will be given a time to return (usually around 4:30pm). Audience members must be aged 18 or over.

Last Week Tonight with John Oliver (www.lastweektickets.com; CBS Broadcast Center, 528 W 57th St, btwn Tenth & Eleventh Aves) Tickets to this biting British comedian's news recap show are available at www.lastweektickets.com up to 2.5 weeks in advance of taping dates. The show is taped at 6:15pm on Sundays and audience members are requested to arrive at least 40 minutes in advance. Minimum age of admission is 18.

For more show ticket details, visit the websites of individual TV stations, or try www.tvtickets.com.

story of an American ex-GI in post-war Paris, following his artistic dreams and falling head over heels for an alluring dancer. Packed with toe-tapping Gershwin tunes (including rarer numbers), it's directed by renowned English choreographer Christopher Wheeldon.

A (very) limited number of cheaper rush tickets ($32) are available for purchase at the box office at opening each day (cash only).

MATILDA THEATER

Map p432 (Shubert Theatre; ☎tickets 212-239-6200; http://us.matildathemusical.com; 225 W 44th St, btwn Seventh & Eighth Aves, Midtown West; ; Ⓢ N/Q/R, S, 1/2/3, 7 to Times Sq-42nd St; A/C/E to 42nd St-Port Authority Bus Terminal) Giddily subversive, this multi-award-winning musical is an adaptation of Roald Dahl's classic children's tale. Star of the show is a precocious five-year-old who uses wit, intellect and a little telekinesis to tackle parental neglect, unjust punishment, even the Russian mafia.

The nightly ticket lottery – held at the theater 2½ hours before showtime – offers a limited number of $27 tickets. Discounted standing-room tickets are also offered at sold-out shows.

PLAYWRIGHTS HORIZONS THEATER

Map p432 (☎212-279-4200; www.playwrightshorizons.org; 416 W 42nd St, btwn Ninth & Tenth Aves, Midtown West; [S]A/C/E to 42nd St-Port Authority Bus Terminal) An excellent place to catch what could be the next big thing, this veteran 'writers' theater' is dedicated to fostering contemporary American works. Notable past productions include Bruce Norris' Tony Award–winning *Clybourne Park*, as well as *I Am My Own Wife* and *Grey Gardens*, both of which moved on to Broadway.

SIGNATURE THEATRE THEATER

Map p432 (☎tickets 212-244-7529; www.signaturetheatre.org; 480 W 42nd St, btwn Ninth & Tenth Aves, Midtown West; [S]A/C/E to 42nd St-Port Authority Bus Terminal) Looking good in its Frank Gehry–designed home – complete with three theaters, bookshop and cafe – Signature Theatre is devoted to the work of its playwrights-in-residence, both past and present. To date, featured dramatists have included Tony Kushner, Edward Albee, Athol Fugard and Kenneth Lonergan. Shows aside, the theater also runs talks with playwrights, directors, designers and actors. Aim to book performances one month in advance.

SECOND STAGE THEATRE THEATER

Map p432 (Tony Kiser Theatre; ☎tickets 212-246-4422; www.2st.com; 305 W 43rd St, at Eighth Ave, Midtown West; [S]A/C/E to 42nd St-Port Authority Bus Terminal) This is the main of two venues run by Second Stage Theatre, a non-profit theater company famed for debuting the work of talented emerging writers as well as that of the country's more established names. If you're after well-crafted contemporary American theater, this is a good place to find it.

The company purchased the Helen Hayes Theatre on W 44th St, with plans to use it as a second Midtown venue from 2017–18.

MAGNET THEATER COMEDY

Map p432 (☎tickets 212-244-8824; www.magnettheater.com; 254 W 29th St, btwn Seventh & Eighth Aves, Midtown West; [S]1/2 to 28th St; A/C/E to 23rd St; 1/2/3 to 34th St-Penn Station) Tons of comedy in several incarnations (mostly improv) lures the crowds at this theater-cum-training-ground for comics. Performances vary weekly, though regular favorites include Megawitt (featuring the theater's resident ensembles) and the Friday Night Sh*w, the latter using the audience's written rants and confessions to drive the evening's shenanigans.

BIRDLAND JAZZ, CABARET

Map p432 (☎212-581-3080; www.birdlandjazz.com; 315 W 44th St, btwn Eighth & Ninth Aves, Midtown West; admission $20-50; ⏰5pm-1am; 📶; [S]A/C/E to 42nd St-Port Authority Bus Terminal) This bird's got a slick look, not to mention the legend – its name dates from bebop legend Charlie Parker (aka 'Bird'), who headlined at the previous location on 52nd St, along with Miles, Monk and just about everyone else (you can see their photos on the walls). Covers run from $20 to $50 and the lineup is always stellar.

Regular highlights include David Ostwald's Louis Armstrong Eternity Band on Wednesdays and the Arturo O'Farrill Afro-Cuban Orchestra on Sundays. Dress to impress.

CAROLINE'S ON BROADWAY COMEDY

Map p432 (☎212-757-4100; www.carolines.com; 1626 Broadway, at 50th St, Midtown West; [S]N/Q/R to 49th St; 1, C/E to 50th St) You may recognize this big, bright, mainstream classic from comedy specials filmed here on location. It's a top spot to catch US comedy big guns and sitcom stars.

DON'T TELL MAMA CABARET

Map p432 (☎212-757-0788; www.donttellmamanyc.com; 343 W 46th St, btwn Eighth & Ninth Aves, Midtown West; ⏰4pm-3am Mon-Thu, to 4am Fri-Sun; [S]N/Q/R, S, 1/2/3, 7 to Times Sq-42nd St) Piano bar and cabaret venue extraordinaire, Don't Tell Mama is an unpretentious little spot that's been around for more than 30 years and has the talent to prove it. Its regular roster of performers aren't big names, but true lovers of cabaret who give each show their all.

AMC EMPIRE 25 CINEMA

Map p432 (www.amctheatres.com/empire; 234 W 42nd St, at Eighth Ave, Midtown West; [S]N/Q/R, S, 1/2/3, 7 to 42nd St-Times Sq) It's pretty cool to gaze out over illuminated 42nd St at this massive cinema complex, and even more thrilling to settle into the stadium-style seating. While it's not the best place to catch mainstream Hollywood flicks (crowds can be massive and rowdy), it's the perfect off-the-radar spot for indies, which screen frequently to civilized numbers.

MADISON SQUARE GARDEN STADIUM

Map p432 (www.thegarden.com; Seventh Ave, btwn 31st & 33rd Sts, Midtown West; [S]A/C/E, 1/2/3 to 34th St-Penn Station) NYC's major performance venue – part of the massive complex housing Penn Station and the Theater at Madison Square Garden – hosts big-arena performers, from Kanye West to Madonna. It's also a sports arena, with New York Knicks and New York Rangers games, as well as boxing and events like the Annual Westminster Kennel Club Dog Show.

SHOPPING

Midtown East & Fifth Avenue

BLOOMINGDALE'S DEPARTMENT STORE

Map p428 (☎212-705-2000; www.bloomingdales.com; 1000 Third Ave, at E 59th St, Midtown East; ⏰10am-8:30pm Mon & Tue, to 10pm Wed-Sat, to 9pm Sun; 📶; [S]4/5/6 to 59th St; N/Q/R to Lexington Ave-59th St) Blockbuster Bloomie's is something like the Metropolitan Museum of Art of the shopping world: historic, sprawling, overwhelming and packed with bodies, but you'd be sorry to miss it. Raid the racks for clothes and shoes from a who's who of US and global designers, including a number of 'new-blood' collections. Refuel pitstops include a branch of cupcake heaven Magnolia Bakery.

BERGDORF GOODMAN DEPARTMENT STORE

Map p428 (☎212-753-7300; www.bergdorfgoodman.com; 754 Fifth Ave, btwn 57th & 58th Sts; ⏰10am-8pm Mon-Sat, 11am-7pm Sun; [S]N/Q/R to 5th Ave-59th St; F to 57th St) Not merely loved for its Christmas windows (the city's best), plush BG leads the fashion race, its fashion director Linda Fargo considered an Anna Wintour of sorts. A mainstay of ladies who lunch, its drawcards include exclusive collections of Tom Ford and Chanel shoes and a coveted women's shoe department. The men's store is across the street.

BARNEYS DEPARTMENT STORE

Map p428 (www.barneys.com; 660 Madison Ave, at 61st St, Midtown East; ⏰10am-8pm Mon-Fri, to 7pm Sat, 11am-7pm Sun; [S]N/Q/R to 5th Ave-59th St) Serious fashionistas swipe their plastic at Barneys, respected for its spot-on collections of top-tier labels like Isabel Marant Étoile, Mr & Mrs Italy and Lanvin. For (slightly) less expensive deals geared to a younger market, shop street-chic labels on the 8th floor. Coveted threads aside, other in-store highlights include a basement cosmetics department and Genes, a futuristic cafe with touch-screen communal tables for online shopping.

You'll find other branches in Upper West Side (p244) and on Atlantic Avenue in Brooklyn.

SAKS FIFTH AVE DEPARTMENT STORE

Map p428 (☎212-753-4000; www.saksfifthavenue.com; 611 Fifth Ave, at 50th St; ⏰10am-8:30pm Mon-Sat, 11am-7pm Sun; [S]B/D/F/M to 47th-50th Sts-Rockefeller Center; E/M to 5th Ave-53rd St) Graced with vintage elevators, Saks' 10-floor flagship store is home to the 'Shoe Salon,' NYC's biggest women's shoe department (complete with express elevator and zip code). Other fortes include the cosmetics and men's departments, the latter home to destination grooming salon John Allan's and a sharply edited offering of fashion-forward labels. The store's January sale is legendary.

DYLAN'S CANDY BAR FOOD

Map p428 (www.dylanscandybar.com; 1011 Third Ave, at 60th St, Midtown East; ⏰10am-9pm Mon-Thu, to 11pm Fri & Sat, 11am-9pm Sun; [S]N/Q/R to Lexington Ave-59th St) Willy Wonka has nothing on this dental nightmare of giant swirly lollipops, crunchy candy bars, glowing jars of jelly beans, softball-sized cupcakes, and sugar-free and kosher treats, not to mention a luminescent staircase embedded with scrumptious, unattainable sweets. There's even a cafe on the 2nd floor if you need an instant sugar rush.

ARGOSY BOOKS, MAPS

Map p428 (www.argosybooks.com; 116 E 59th St, btwn Park & Lexington Aves, Midtown East; ⏰10am-6pm Mon-Fri, to 5pm Sat; [S]4/5/6 to 59th St; N/Q/R to Lexington Ave-59th St) Since 1925, this landmark used bookstore has stocked fine antiquarian items such as leatherbound books, old maps, art monographs and other classics picked up from high-class estate sales and closed antique shops. There's also an interesting booty of Hollywood memorabilia, from personal letters and signed books, to contracts and autographed publicity stills. Prices range from costly to clearance.

TIFFANY & CO
JEWELRY, HOMEWARES

Map p428 (☎212-755-8000; www.tiffany.com; 727 Fifth Ave, at 57th St; ☺10am-7pm Mon-Sat, noon-6pm Sun; ⓢF to 57th St; N/Q/R to 5th Ave-59th St) Ever since Audrey Hepburn gazed longingly through its windows, Tiffany & Co has won countless hearts with its glittering diamond rings, watches, silver Elsa Peretti heart necklaces, crystal vases and glassware. But wait, there's more, including handbags and travel-friendly gifts like letter openers. Swoon, drool, but whatever you do, don't harass the elevator attendants with tired 'Where's the breakfast?' jokes.

🏠 Midtown West & Times Square

★MOMA DESIGN & BOOK STORE
GIFTS, BOOKS

Map p432 (☎212-708-9700; www.momastore.org; 11 W 53rd St, btwn Fifth & Sixth Aves; ☺9:30am-6:30pm Sat-Thu, to 9pm Fri; ⓢE, M to 5th Ave-53rd St) The flagship store at the Museum of Modern Art is a fab spot to souvenir shop in one fell swoop. Aside from stocking gorgeous books (from art and architecture tomes to pop culture readers and kids' picture books), you'll find art prints and posters, and one-of-a-kind knick-knacks. For furniture, lighting, homewares, jewelry, bags, and MUJI merchandise, head to the MoMA Design Store across the street.

NEPENTHES NEW YORK
FASHION

Map p432 (☎212-643-9540; www.nepenthesny.com; 307 W 38th St, btwn Eighth & Ninth Aves, Midtown West; ☺noon-7pm Mon-Sat, to 5pm Sun; ⓢA/C/E to 42nd St-Port Authority Bus Terminal) Occupying an old sewing shop in the Garment District, this cult Japanese collective stocks edgy menswear from the likes of Engineered Garments and Needles, known for their quirky detailing and artisanal production value (think tweed lace-up hem pants). Accessories include bags and satchels, gloves, eyewear and footwear.

HELL'S KITCHEN FLEA MARKET
MARKET

Map p432 (☎212-243-5343; www.annexmarkets.com; 39th St, btwn Ninth & Tenth Aves, Midtown West; ☺9am-5pm Sat & Sun; ⓢA/C/E to 42nd St) This weekend flea market lures both collectors and the common curious with its wonderful booty of vintage furnishings, accessories, clothing and unidentifiable objects from past eras.

MACY'S
DEPARTMENT STORE

Map p432 (☎212-695-4400; www.macys.com; 151 W 34th St, at Broadway; ☺9:30am-10pm Mon & Wed-Fri, to 9:30pm Tue, 10am-10pm Sat, 11am-9pm Sun; ⓢB/D/F/M, N/Q/R to 34th St-Herald Sq) Fresh from a much-needed facelift, the world's largest department store covers most bases, with fashion, furnishings, kitchenware, sheets, cafes, hair salons and even a branch of the Metropolitan Museum of Art gift store. It's more 'mid-priced' than 'exclusive,' with mainstream labels and big-name cosmetics. The store also houses a NYC Information Center (p394) with information desk and free city maps.

B&H PHOTO VIDEO
ELECTRONICS

Map p432 (☎212-444-6615; www.bhphotovideo.com; 420 Ninth Ave, btwn 33rd & 34th Sts, Midtown West; ☺9am-7pm Mon-Thu, to 2pm Fri, 10am-6pm Sun, closed Sat; ⓢA/C/E to 34th St-Penn Station) Visiting NYC's most popular camera shop is an experience in itself – it's massive and crowded, and bustling with black-clad (and tech-savvy) Hasidic Jewish salesmen. Your chosen item is dropped into a bucket, which then moves up and across the ceiling to the purchase area (which requires a second queue).

It's all very orderly and fascinating, and the selection of cameras, camcorders, computers and other electronics is outstanding.

AMÉ AMÉ
ACCESSORIES

Map p432 (☎646-867-2342; www.amerain.com; 17 W 29th St, at Broadway; ☺noon-7pm; ⓢN/R to 28th St) Rain gear and candy? Kindly owner Teresa will explain what Amé Amé means if you're perplexed by this unusual juxtaposition. She'll also set you straight on the fallacy of buying cheap disposable umbrellas. Only well-crafted, long-lasting rain gear is sold here, from perfectly fitting Aigle boots and handsome Barbour coats, to elegant scarves and hats, and whimsical, out-of-the-ordinary gifts.

HOUSING WORKS
VINTAGE

Map p432 (☎646-963-2665; www.housingworks.org; 730-732 Ninth Ave, btwn 49th & 50th Sts, Midtown West; ☺11am-8pm Mon-Sat, to 6pm Sun; ⓢC/E to 50th St) As one shopper put it: 'They have some fabulous shit in here.' Welcome to the Hell's Kitchen branch of this much-loved thrift store, where Paul Smith shirts go for $35 and Bottega Veneta heels are yours for $75. While it's all about luck, the daily consignments mean a sterling find is never far off. Profits go to helping homeless people living with HIV/AIDS.

TIME WARNER CENTER   MALL

Map p432 (📞212-823-6300; www.theshopsat columbuscircle.com; Time Warner Center, 10 Columbus Circle; ⊘10am-9pm Mon-Sat, 11am-7pm Sun; Ⓢ A/C, B/D, 1 to 59th St-Columbus Circle) A great add-on to an adventure in Central Park, the swank Time Warner Center has a fine lineup of largely upscale vendors including Coach, Eileen Fisher, Williams-Sonoma, True Religion, Sephora and J Crew. For salubrious picnic fare, visit the enormous Whole Foods (p199) in the basement.

SPORTS & ACTIVITIES

NBC STUDIO TOURS   WALKING TOUR

Map p428 (📞212-664-3700; www.thetourat nbcstudios.com; 30 Rockefeller Plaza, entrance at 1250 Sixth Ave; tours adult/child $33/29, children under 6yr not admitted; ⊘8:30am-2pm Mon-Fri, to 5pm Sat & Sun; Ⓢ B/D/F/M to 47th-50th Sts-Rockefeller Center) Peppered with interesting anecdotes, this revamped, one-hour tour takes TV fans through parts of the NBC Studios, home to iconic TV shows *Saturday Night Live* and *The Tonight Show Starring Jimmy Fallon*. Stops usually include the beautifully restored art-deco Rotunda, two studios and the NBC Broadcast Operations Center. Things get interactive in the Tour Studio, where you get to 'star' or 'produce' your own talk show segment. Book online to avoid the queues.

GRAND CENTRAL PARTNERSHIP   WALKING TOUR

Map p428 (www.grandcentralpartnership.com) FREE The Grand Central Partnership leads free, 90-minute tours of both the Grand Central Terminal and the surrounding neighborhood on Fridays at 12:30pm. Tours depart from the southwest corner of E 42nd Street and Park Avenue.

CENTRAL PARK BIKE TOURS   BICYCLE RENTAL

Map p432 (📞212-541-8759; www.centralpark biketours.com; 203 W 58th St, at Seventh Ave, Midtown West; rentals per 2hr/day $14/28, 2hr tours $49; ⊘8am-9pm Apr-Dec, to 8pm Jan-Mar; Ⓢ A/C, B/D, 1 to 59th St-Columbus Circle) This place rents good bikes and leads two-hour guided tours of Central Park and the Brooklyn Bridge area. It also offers themed movie-location and architecture tours in season. See the website for tour times.

MANHATTAN COMMUNITY BOATHOUSE   KAYAKING

Map p432 (www.manhattancommunityboat house.org; Pier 96 at W 56th St; ⊘10am-6pm Sat & Sun mid-Jun–mid-Oct, 5:30-7:30pm Mon-Wed mid-Jun–Aug; Ⓢ A/C, B/D, 1 to 59th St-Columbus Circle) Fancy a quick glide on the mighty Hudson? Manhattan Community Boathouse offers free, seasonal kayaking at Pier 96 on a first-come, first-served basis. Expect to get wet while paddling, so dress appropriately or bring a change of clothes (there are changing rooms and lockers at the pier). The non-profit organization also conducts summertime kayaking lessons – check the website for dates.

LUCKY STRIKE   BOWLING

Map p432 (📞646-829-0170; www.bowllucky strike.com; 624-660 W 42nd St, btwn Eleventh & Twelfth Aves, Midtown West; individual games from $10, shoe rental $6; ⊘noon-midnight Sun-Wed, to 1am Thu, to 2am Fri & Sat; 📶; Ⓢ A/C/E to 42nd St-Port Authority Bus Terminal) One of the world's few bowling alleys with a dress code, Lucky Strike has pricey drinks, plush lounge fittings and a fashion-conscious crowd – which makes the whole experience more akin to a nightclub than a bowling alley. Book ahead.

Upper East Side

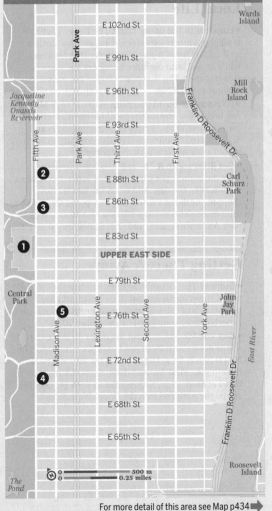

Neighborhood Top Five

1 Spending a few hours (or weeks) wandering amid the priceless treasures, from mesmerizing Egyptian artifacts to Renaissance masterpieces, at the **Metropolitan Museum of Art** (p214).

2 Walking the spiral ramps of Frank Lloyd Wright's architectural masterpiece, the **Guggenheim Museum** (p215).

3 Gazing at the gilded masterpieces of Gustav Klimt at the **Neue Galerie** (p218).

4 Listening to Sunday classical music in a beaux-arts mansion at **Frick Collection** (p226).

5 Sipping an early evening cocktail at the elegant, mural-lined **Bemelmans Bar** (p226).

For more detail of this area see Map p434 ➡

Lonely Planet's Top Tip

The Upper East Side is ground zero for all things luxurious, especially the area that covers the blocks from 60th to 86th Sts between Park and Fifth Aves. If you're looking for eating and drinking spots that are easier on the wallet, head east of Lexington Ave. First, Second and Third Aves are lined with less pricey neighborhood spots.

 Best Places to Eat

- Tanoshi (p223)
- Café Boulud (p225)
- Boqueria (p222)
- Café Sabarsky (p223)
- Beyoglu (p223)

For reviews, see p222

Best Places to Drink

- The Daisy (p225)
- The Penrose (p226)
- Drunken Munkey (p226)
- Uva (p225)
- Vinus & Marc (p225)

For reviews, see p225

Best Museums

- Metropolitan Museum of Art (p214)
- Guggenheim Museum (p215)
- Frick Collection (p218)
- Neue Galerie (p218)
- Cooper-Hewitt National Design Museum (p218)
- Jewish Museum (p219)

For reviews, see p218

Explore Upper East Side

There are infinite ways to tackle this large, well-moneyed neighborhood. Begin with a walk south down Fifth Ave, starting at about 96th St. This will take you down storied Museum Mile, which is studded with vintage mansions and prestigious museums. At 72nd St, scoot east to Madison Ave and head south, where you can then enjoy the sight of some of the country's most extravagant flagship boutiques (Cartier, Prada and Oscar de la Renta, to name a few). The path is strewn with Old World cafes and opulent restaurants. Welcome to the rarefied air of uptown.

Local Life

⇒ **Lunch with the upper crust** The Upper East Side is all about lunch – specifically ladies who lunch, a well-coiffed breed known for dispensing air kisses while armed with designer handbags the size of steam trunks. The best places to see 'em include Sant Ambroeus (p225) and Café Boulud (p225), on weekdays.

⇒ **(Window) shop 'til you drop** Skip the ritzy Madison Ave boutiques, and hit the neighborhood's high-end consignment shops. Places like Encore (p227) and Michael's (p227) offer good deals on mildly worn frocks tossed aside by New York society types.

⇒ **Get jittery with it** The neighborhood seems to have the highest per capita ratio of coffee emporiums anywhere in the city. And when the locals aren't shopping or doing Pilates, they're sipping steamy skim-milk macchiatos at cafes like Via Quadronno (p223), Sant Ambroeus (p225) and Oslo Coffee Roasters (p225).

Getting There & Away

⇒ **Subway** The sole subway lines here are the 4/5/6 which travel north and south on Lexington Ave. A new stretch of subway track underneath Second Ave is expected to be completed by December 2016.

⇒ **Bus** The M1, M2, M3 and M4 buses all make the scenic drive down Fifth Ave beside Central Park. The M15 is handy for getting around the far eastern side, traveling up First Ave and down Second. Cross-town buses at 66th, 72nd, 79th, 86th and 96th Sts take you across the park and into the Upper West Side.

GUGGENHEIM MUSEUM

A sculpture in its own right, architect Frank Lloyd Wright's building almost overshadows the collection of 20th-century art that it houses. Completed in 1959, the inverted ziggurat structure was derided by some critics but hailed by others, who welcomed it as a beloved architectural icon. Since it first opened, this unusual structure has appeared on countless postcards, TV programs and films.

DON'T MISS

➡ Permanent Collection Galleries

➡ Lunch at The Wright

➡ Exterior views of the facade

PRACTICALITIES

➡ Map p434

➡ ☎212-423-3500

➡ www.guggenheim.org

➡ 1071 Fifth Ave, at 89th St

➡ adult/child $25/free, by donation 5:45-7:45pm Sat

➡ ⏱10am-5:45pm Sun-Wed & Fri, to 7:45pm Sat, closed Thu

➡ Ⓢ4/5/6 to 86th St

Abstract Roots

The Guggenheim came out of the collection of Solomon R Guggenheim, a New York mining magnate who began acquiring abstract art in his 60s at the behest of his art adviser, an eccentric German baroness named Hilla Rebay. In 1939, with Rebay serving as director, Guggenheim opened a temporary museum on 54th St titled Museum of Non-Objective Painting. (Incredibly, it had grey velour walls, piped-in classical music and burning incense.) Four years later, the pair commissioned Wright to construct a permanent home for the collection.

Years in the Making

Like any development in New York City, the project took forever to come to fruition. Construction was delayed for almost 13 years due to budget constraints, the outbreak of WWII and outraged neighbors who weren't all that excited to see an architectural spaceship land in their midst. Construction was completed in 1959, after both Wright and Guggenheim had passed away.

Bring on the Critics

When the Guggenheim opened its doors in October 1959, the ticket price was 50¢ and the works on view included pieces by Kandinsky, Alexander Calder and abstract expressionists Franz Kline and Willem de Kooning. The structure was savaged by the *New York Times,* which lambasted it as 'a war between architecture and painting in which both come out badly maimed.' But others quickly celebrated it as 'the most beautiful building in America.' Whether Wright intended to or not, he had given the city one of its most recognizable landmarks.

To the Present

A renovation in the early 1990s added an eight-story tower to the east, which provided an extra 50,000 sq ft of exhibition space. These galleries show the permanent collection and other exhibits, while the ramps are occupied by rotating exhibits. The museum's holdings include works by Kandinsky, Picasso and Jackson Pollock. Over time, other key additions have been made, including paintings by Monet, Van Gogh and Degas, photographs by Robert Mapplethorpe, and key surrealist works donated by Guggenheim's niece Peggy.

Visiting the Museum

The museum's ascending ramp is occupied by rotating exhibitions of modern and contemporary art. Though Wright intended visitors to go to the top and wind their way down, the cramped, single elevator doesn't allow for this. Exhibitions, therefore, are installed from bottom to top.

METROPOLITAN MUSEUM OF ART (MET)

This sprawling encyclopedic museum, founded in 1870, houses one of the biggest art collections in the world. Its permanent collection has more than two million individual objects, from Egyptian temples to American paintings. Known colloquially as 'The Met,' the museum attracts more than six million visitors a year to its 17 acres of galleries – making it the largest single-site attraction in New York City. In other words, plan on spending some time here.

Egyptian Art

The museum has an unrivaled collection of ancient Egyptian art, some of which dates back to the Paleolithic era. Located to the north of the Great Hall, the 39 Egyptian galleries open dramatically with one of the Met's prized pieces: the Mastaba Tomb of Perneb (c 2300 BC), an Old Kingdom burial chamber crafted from limestone. From here, a web of rooms is cluttered with funerary stele, carved reliefs and fragments of pyramids. (Don't miss the intriguing Models of Meketre, clay figurines meant to help in the afterlife, in Gallery 105.) These eventually lead to the Temple of Dendur (Gallery 131), a sandstone temple to the goddess Isis that resides in a sunny atrium gallery with a reflecting pool – a must-see for the first-time visitor.

European Paintings

Want Renaissance? The Met's got it. On the museum's 2nd floor, the European Paintings galleries display a stunning collection of masterworks. This includes more than 1700 canvases from the roughly 500-year-period starting in the 13th century, with works by every important painter from Duccio to Rembrandt. In fact, everything here is, literally,

DON'T MISS

➡ The Temple of Dendur

➡ Paintings by Caravaggio, El Greco, Vermeer and other old masters.

➡ The Damascus Room inside the Islamic Art galleries

➡ Roof Garden Café & Martini Bar

PRACTICALITIES

➡ Map p434

➡ 212-535-7710

➡ www.metmuseum.org

➡ 1000 Fifth Ave, at 82nd St

➡ suggested donation adult/child $25/free

➡ ⏰10am-5.30pm Sun-Thu, to 9pm Fri & Sat

➡ 🚇4/5/6 to 86th St

a masterpiece. In Gallery 621 are several Caravaggios, including the masterfully painted *The Denial of St Peter*. Gallery 611, to the west, is packed with Spanish treasures, including El Greco's famed *View of Toledo*. Continue south to Gallery 632 to see various Vermeers, including the *Young Woman with a Water Pitcher*. Nearby, in Gallery 634, gaze at several Rembrandts, including a 1660 *Self-Portrait*. And that's just the beginning. You could spend hours exploring these many powerful works.

Art of the Arab Lands

On the 2nd floor you'll find the Islamic galleries with 15 incredible rooms showcasing the museum's extensive collection of art from the Middle East and Central and South Asia. In addition to garments, secular decorative objects and manuscripts, you'll find gilded and enameled glassware (Gallery 452) and a magnificent 14th-century *mihrab* (prayer niche) lined with elaborately patterned polychrome tilework (Gallery 455). There is also a superb array of Ottoman textiles (Gallery 459), a medieval-style Moroccan court (Gallery 456) and an 18th-century room from Damascus (Gallery 461).

American Wing

In the northwestern corner, the American galleries showcase a wide variety of decorative and fine art from throughout US history. These include every-thing from colonial portraiture to Hudson River School masterpieces to John Singer Sargent's unbearably sexy *Madame X* (Gallery 771) – not to mention Emanuel Leutze's massive canvas of *Washington Crossing the Delaware* (Gallery 760).

Greek & Roman Art

The 27 galleries devoted to classical antiquity are another Met doozy. From the Great Hall, a passageway takes viewers through a barrel-vaulted room flanked by the chiseled torsos of Greek figures. This spills right into one of the Met's loveliest spaces: the airy Roman sculpture court (Gallery 162), full of marble carvings of gods and historical figures. The statue of a bearded Hercules from AD 68–98, with a lion's skin draped about him, is particularly awe-inspiring.

THE ROOF GARDEN

One of the best spots in the entire museum is the roof garden, which features rotating sculpture installations by contemporary and 20th-century artists. (Jeff Koons, Andy Goldsworthy and Imran Qureshi have all shown here.) But its best features are the views it offers of the city and Central Park. It's also home to the Roof Garden Café & Martini Bar an ideal spot for a drink – especially at sunset. The roof garden is open from April to October.

THE MET FOR KIDS

The most popular galleries with children are generally the Egyptian, African and Oceania galleries (great masks) and the collection of medieval arms and armor. The Met hosts plenty of kid-centric happenings (check the website) and distributes a special museum brochure and map made specifically for the tykes.

SEEING THE MUSEUM

A desk inside the Great Hall has audio tours in several languages ($7), though you can also access audio tours for free if you have a smartphone. Docents also offer guided tours of specific galleries (free with admission).

Metropolitan Museum of Art

PLAN OF ATTACK

Standing in the aptly named Great Hall, past the main entrance, head into the Egyptian galleries and make your way to the dramatic ❶ Temple of Dendur.

Stroll through the Charles Engelhard Court, a soaring sunlit atrium packed with American sculptures, and dip into the Arms and Armor galleries. See the meticulous craftsmanship of the 16th-century ❷ Armor of Henry II of France. The next room (Gallery 371) has four fully armored, mounted horsemen..

Head back into the American Wing and up to the 2nd floor for a look at the ❸ Washington Crossing the Delaware. Also on the 2nd floor is a jaw-dropping collection of European masters. Don't miss the Caravaggios in Gallery 621, in particular ❹ The Denial of Saint Peter.

Staying on the 2nd floor, wind your way over to the Islamic Art galleries, where you'll find an elaborate ❺ Mihrab, it's right next to a medieval-style Moroccan court with gurgling fountain (Gallery 456).

Nearby you'll find works by Monet, Renoir, Van Gogh and Gauguin. There are several masterpieces by Picasso, including ❻ The Blind Man's Meal.

Head downstairs and into Oceania exhibition halls for vivid tribal art from New Guinea and beyond. Have a look at tribal costumes such as the ❼ Asmat Body Mask; overhead is a ceiling lined with shields.

The Met has a trove of ancient Greek and Roman works. In the largest gallery you'll find the intricate marble sarcophagus, ❽ Triumph of Dionysos and the Seasons.

The Denial of Saint Peter
Gallery 621
Painted in the final months of Caravaggio's short, tempestuous life, this magnificent work is a masterpiece of storytelling.

The Blind Man's Meal **Gallery 830**
Picasso's painting of a blind man at a table alludes to human suffering in general; the bread and wine also have undertones of Christian symbolism.

Mihrab (prayer niche) **Gallery 455**
One of the world's finest religious architectural decorations, this 8th-century piece from Iran was created by joining cut glazed tiles into a richly ornate mosaic.

Asmat Body Mask **Gallery 354**
A New Guinea costume like this was worn to represent the spirit of someone who recently died, and featured in ritual dances of the Asmat people.

Triumph of Dionysos and the Seasons **Gallery 162**
On this marble sarcophagus, you'll see the god Dionysos seated on a panther, joined by four figures representing (from left to right) winter, spring, summer and fall.

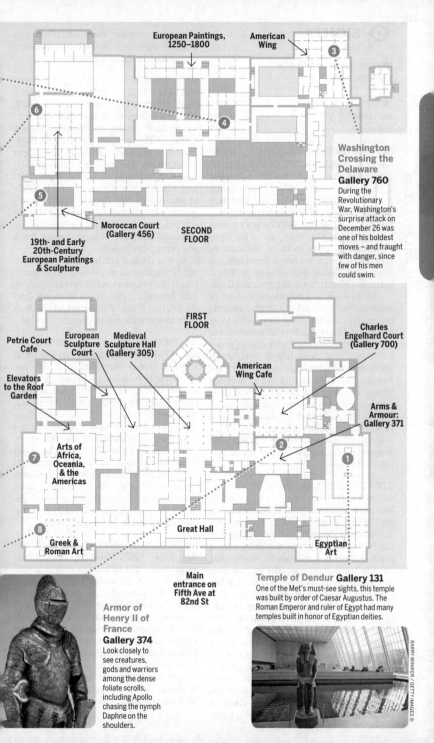

European Paintings, 1250–1800

American Wing

③

⑥

④

⑤

19th- and Early 20th-Century European Paintings & Sculpture

Moroccan Court (Gallery 456)

SECOND FLOOR

Washington Crossing the Delaware
Gallery 760
During the Revolutionary War, Washington's surprise attack on December 26 was one of his boldest moves – and fraught with danger, since few of his men could swim.

FIRST FLOOR

Petrie Court Cafe

European Sculpture Court

Medieval Sculpture Hall (Gallery 305)

Charles Engelhard Court (Gallery 700)

American Wing Cafe

Elevators to the Roof Garden

Arms & Armour: Gallery 371

Arts of Africa, Oceania, & the Americas

⑦

②

Great Hall

①

Egyptian Art

⑧

Greek & Roman Art

Main entrance on Fifth Ave at 82nd St

Armor of Henry II of France
Gallery 374
Look closely to see creatures, gods and warriors among the dense foliate scrolls, including Apollo chasing the nymph Daphne on the shoulders.

Temple of Dendur Gallery 131
One of the Met's must-see sights, this temple was built by order of Caesar Augustus. The Roman Emperor and ruler of Egypt had many temples built in honor of Egyptian deities.

BARRY WINIKER / GETTY IMAGES ©

SIGHTS

★GUGGENHEIM MUSEUM — MUSEUM

See p213.

★METROPOLITAN MUSEUM OF ART — MUSEUM

See p214.

★FRICK COLLECTION — GALLERY

Map p434 (☎212-288-0700; www.frick.org; 1 E 70th St, at Fifth Ave; admission $20, by donation 11am-1pm Sun, children under 10 not admitted; 🕐10am-6pm Tue-Sat, 11am-5pm Sun; [S]6 to 68th St-Hunter College) This spectacular art collection sits in a mansion built by prickly steel magnate Henry Clay Frick, one of the many such residences that made up Millionaires' Row. The museum has over a dozen splendid rooms that display masterpieces by Titian, Vermeer, Gilbert Stuart, El Greco and Goya.

The museum is a treat for a number of reasons. One, it resides in a lovely, rambling beaux-arts structure built from 1913–14 by Carrère and Hastings. Two, it's generally not crowded (one exception being during popular shows). And, three, it feels refreshingly intimate, with a trickling indoor courtyard fountain and gardens that can be explored on warmer days. A demure Portico Gallery displays decorative works and sculpture. A worthwhile audio tour (available in several languages) is included in the price of admission. Classical-music fans will enjoy the frequent piano and violin concerts that take place on Sunday.

COOPER-HEWITT NATIONAL DESIGN MUSEUM — MUSEUM

Map p434 (☎212-849-8400; www.cooperhewitt.org; 2 E 91st St, at Fifth Ave; adult/student/child $18/9/free, by donation 6-9pm Sat; 🕐10am-6pm Sun-Fri, to 9pm Sat; [S]4/5/6 to 86th St) Part of the Smithsonian Institution in Washington, DC, this house of culture is the only museum in the country that's dedicated to both historic and contemporary design. The collection is housed in the 64-room mansion built by billionaire Andrew Carnegie in 1901. The 210,000-piece collection is exquisite, with artful displays spanning 3000 years spread across four floors of the building. An extensive three-year renovation, completed in 2014, brings novelty to its exhibitions with interactive touch screens and wild technology.

There's also more exhibition space, a problem-solving Process Lab and an eye-popping Immersion Room, where you can project images onto the walls from patterns dating back to the 18th century.

NEUE GALERIE — MUSEUM

Map p434 (☎212-628-6200; www.neuegalerie.org; 1048 Fifth Ave, cnr E 86th St; admission $20, 6-8pm 1st Fri of the month free, children under 12 not admitted; 🕐11am-6pm Thu-Mon; [S]4/5/6 to 86th St) This restored Carrère and Hastings mansion from 1914 is a resplendent showcase for German and Austrian art, featuring works by Paul Klee, Ernst Ludwig Kirchner and Egon Schiele. In pride of place on the 2nd floor is Gustav Klimt's golden 1907 portrait of Adele Bloch-Bauer – which was acquired for the museum by cosmetics magnate Ronald Lauder for a whopping $135 million.

This is a small but beautiful place with winding staircases and wrought-iron banisters. It also boasts a lovely, street-level eatery, Café Sabarsky (p223). Avoid weekends (and the free first Friday of the month) if you don't want to deal with gallery-clogging crowds.

GRACIE MANSION — HISTORIC BUILDING

Map p434 (www.nyc.gov/gracie; East End Ave, at E 88th St; 🕐tours 10am, 11am, 2pm & 3pm Tue; [S]4/5/6 to 86th St) This Federal-style home served as the country residence of merchant Archibald Gracie in 1799. Since 1942, it has been where New York's mayors have lived – with the exception of Mayor Michael Bloomberg, who preferred his own plush, Upper East Side digs. The house has been added to and renovated over the years. To peer inside, you'll have to go online to reserve a spot on one of the 45-minute house tours held once a week (less frequently during the holiday season). The home is bordered by the pleasant, riverside Carl Schurz Park.

NATIONAL ACADEMY MUSEUM — GALLERY

Map p434 (☎212-369-4880; www.nationalacademy.org; 1083 Fifth Ave, at 89th St; admission by donation; 🕐11am-6pm Wed-Sun; [S]4/5/6 to 86th St) Co-founded by painter and inventor Samuel Morse in 1825, the National Academy Museum comprises an incredible permanent collection of paintings by figures such as Will Barnet, Thomas Hart Benton and George Bellows. (This includes some highly compelling self-portraits.) It's housed in a beaux-arts structure designed by Ogden Codman Jr and featuring a marble foyer and spiral staircase.

WORTH A DETOUR

ROOSEVELT ISLAND

Roosevelt Island, the tiny sliver of land that sits in the middle of the East River, has never had much to offer in the way of sights. For much of the 19th century, when it was known as Welfare Island, it was cluttered with hospitals, including a mental hospital and a crenelated small-pox ward. In the 1970s, a series of cookie-cutter apartment buildings were built along the island's only road. For years, the only thing Roosevelt Island really had going for it were the good views of Manhattan and the picturesque ruins of the old small-pox hospital (which is under restoration and will eventually be open to the public).

But the island hit the architectural map in 2012, when a 5-acre **memorial** (p192) to President Franklin D Roosevelt opened on the southern tip. Designed by architect Louis Kahn in the 1960s, construction of the 4½-acre park stalled in the 1970s when Kahn died and New York City almost went into bankruptcy. William vanden Heuvel, chairman of the Four Freedoms Park Conservancy and a former diplomat, kept the dream alive, and spent years raising funds and lobbying for the park's completion.

Remarkably, it was built as Kahn had originally envisioned with only minor tweaks. A tapered lawn lined with linden trees leads down to the island's southern tip. As visitors walk toward the end of V-shaped lawn, they arrive at a small viewing platform, anchored with huge slabs of North Carolina granite. This final space perched over the river is 'the room,' offering views of Manhattan through the narrow openings, with the UN building among the most prominently featured landmarks – a clear reference point between the president and one of his crowning achievements. It's a peaceful and sober monument, with many subtle hidden details.

The best way to get to Roosevelt Island is to take the picturesque four-minute aerial tram across the East River. Trams leave from the **Roosevelt Island Tramway Station** (www.rioc.ny.gov/traintransportation; 60th St at Second Ave; 1-way fare $2.50; every 15 minutes v6am-2am Sun-Thu, to 3am Fri & Sat). Otherwise, take the F train to the Roosevelt Island stop.

ASIA SOCIETY & MUSEUM — MUSEUM

Map p434 (☎212-288-6400212-288-6400; www.asiasociety.org; 725 Park Ave, at E 70th St; adult/child $12/free, 6-9pm Fri mid-Sep–Jun free; 🕒11am-6pm Tue-Sun, to 9pm Fri mid-Sep–Jun; [S] 6 to 68th St-Hunter College) Founded in 1956 by John D Rockefeller (an avid collector of Asian Art), this cultural center hosts fascinating exhibits (pre-Revolutionary art of Iran, retrospectives of leading Chinese artists, block prints of Edo-era Japan), as well as Jain sculptures and Nepalese Buddhist paintings. There are daily tours (free with admission) at 2pm Tuesday through Sunday year-round and at 6:30pm Friday (excluding summer months).

The Society part of the equation brings abundant cultural fare: concerts, film screenings, lectures and culinary events (tea tastings, ramen-making demos). You'll also find great gift ideas at the small museum shop, with its silk scarves, delicate jewelry, children's stories and music from the Near and Far East.

JEWISH MUSEUM — MUSEUM

Map p434 (☎212-423-3200; www.thejewishmuseum.org; 1109 Fifth Ave, btwn 92nd & 93rd Sts; adult/child $15/free, Sat free, by donation 5-8pm Thu; 🕒11am-6pm Sat-Tue, to 8pm Thu, to 4pm Fri, closed Wed; 👪; [S] 6 to 96th St) This New York City gem is tucked into a French-Gothic mansion from 1908, housing 30,000 items of Judaica, as well as sculpture, painting and decorative arts. It hosts excellent temporary exhibits, featuring retrospectives on influential figures such as Art Spiegelman, as well as world-class shows on the likes of Marc Chagall, Édouard Vuillard and Man Ray among other past luminaries.

There are frequent lectures and events, as well as an array of activities and concerts for children. Every January, the museum collaborates with the Film Society of Lincoln Center to present the New York Jewish Film Festival.

TEMPLE EMANU-EL — SYNAGOGUE

Map p434 (☎212-744-1400; www.emanuelnyc.org; 1 E 65th St, cnr Fifth Ave; 🕒10am-4:30pm Sun-Thu; [S] 6 to 68th St-Hunter College) Founded in 1845 as the first Reform synagogue in New York, this temple, completed in 1929, is now one of the largest Jewish houses of worship in the world. An imposing Romanesque structure, it is more than 175ft

ROOSEVELT ISLAND

PANORAMIC IMAGES / GETTY IMAGES ©

1. Metropolitan Museum of Art (p214)
Get lost in the Met's 17 acres of galleries.

2. Fifth Avenue
Brace yourself for the hustle and bustle of iconic Fifth Ave.

3. Madison Avenue (p227)
Witness the extravagance of fashion's high-end flagship stores.

4. Roosevelt Island (p219)
Take the aerial tram for a scenic ride across the East River to the island.

long and 100ft tall, with a brilliant, hand-painted ceiling with gold details.

The structure also boasts 60 stained-glass windows and a massive rose window whose dozen panels represent the 12 tribes of Israel. Other stained-glass elements pay tribute to notable synagogues, including the Altneuschul in Prague (the oldest continually used Jewish house of worship in the world). The ark containing the Torah scrolls, on the eastern wall, is surrounded by a glittering glass-and-marble mosaic arch.

The temple is home to the small **Herbert & Eileen Bernard Museum of Judaica**, with more than 650 pieces that date back to the 14th century.

MUSEUM OF THE CITY OF NEW YORK — MUSEUM

Map p434 (☎212-534-1672; www.mcny.org; 1220 Fifth Ave, btwn 103rd & 104th Sts; suggested admission adult/child $14/free; ⏰10am-6pm; [S]6 to 103rd St) Situated in a colonial Georgian-style mansion, this local museum focuses solely on New York City's past, present and future. Don't miss the 22-minute film *Timescapes* (on the 2nd floor), which charts NYC's growth from tiny native trading post to burgeoning metropolis.

One of the museum's star attractions is the 12-room mansion dollhouse fabricated by Carrie Stettheimer over 25 years at the turn of the 20th century – replete with tiny art works (including miniatures of pieces by Marcel Duchamp and Gaston Lachaise).

🍴 EATING

★EARL'S BEER & CHEESE — AMERICAN $

Map p434 (☎212-289-1581; www.earlsny.com; 1259 Park Ave, btwn 97th & 98th Sts; grilled cheese $8; ⏰11am-midnight Sun-Thu, to 2am Fri & Sat; [S]6 to 96th St) Chef Corey Cova's tiny comfort-food outpost channels a hipster hunting vibe, complete with a giant deer in the woods mural and a mounted buck's head. Basic grilled cheese is a paradigm shifter, served with pork belly, fried egg and kimchi. There is also mac 'n' cheese (with goat's cheese and crispy rosemary) and tacos (featuring braised pork shoulder and *queso fresco*).

Earl's has great craft beers and a fine brunch menu (eggs Benedict, yogurt and house-made granola) too.

LEXINGTON CANDY SHOP — DINER $

Map p434 (☎212-288-0057; www.lexingtoncandyshop.net; 1226 Lexington Ave, at 83rd St; mains $9-17; ⏰7am-7pm Mon-Sat, 8am-6pm Sun; [S]4/5/6 to 86th St) Founded in 1925, this picture-perfect diner feels like a bygone slice of NYC. Slip into a booth or grab a seat at the long counter amid the clatter of forks and the chatter of old-timers. Breakfast is served all day, and there are plenty of other reliable standards: burgers, tuna melts, milkshakes, plus egg creams pulled from the old-fashioned soda fountain.

JG MELON — PUB FOOD $

Map p434 (☎212-744-0585; 1291 Third Ave, at 74th St; mains $11-18; ⏰11:30am-4am; [S]6 to 77th St) JG's is a loud, old-school pub that has been serving juicy burgers on tea plates since 1972. It's a local favorite for both eating and drinking (the Bloody Marys are excellent) and it gets crowded in the after-work hours.

WILLIAM GREENBERG DESSERTS — BAKERY $

Map p434 (☎212-861-1340; www.wmgreenbergdesserts.com; 1100 Madison Ave, btwn E 82nd & 83rd Sts; baked goods from $3; ⏰8am-6:30pm Mon-Fri, to 6pm Sat, 10am-4pm Sun; 👪; [S]4/5/6 to 86th St) Make a pit stop here for New York City's finest black-and-white cookies – soft vanilla discs dipped in white sugar and dark chocolate glazes. Take-out only.

BOQUERIA — SPANISH $$

Map p434 (☎212-343-2227; www.boquerianyc.com; 1460 Second Ave, btwn 76th & 77th Sts; tapas $6-16, paella for two $38-46; ⏰noon-11pm Mon-Fri, 11am-11pm Sat & Sun; [S]6 to 77th St) This lively, much-loved tapas place brings a bit of downtown cool to the Upper East Side, with nicely spiced *patatas bravas*, tender slices of *jamon ibérico* and rich *pulpo a gallega* (grilled octopus). Head chef Marc Vidal, who hails from Barcelona, also creates an exquisite seafood paella.

It's a great place to pop in for a glass of wine, with unusual selections from the Balearic and Canary Islands.

UP THAI — THAI $$

Map p434 (☎212-256-1199; www.upthainyc.com; 1411 Second Ave, btwn 73rd & 74th Sts; mains $15-30; ⏰noon-10:30pm Sun-Thu, to 11:30pm Fri & Sat; 🌿; [S]6 to 77th St) Hands down the best Thai place in the Upper East Side, this narrow but artfully designed restaurant serves a mix of traditional and innovative recipes.

Standouts here include creamy rich Tom Kah soup (with coconut broth and vegetables), pillowy steamed chive dumplings and crispy duck breast with tamarind sauce. It's not a bad date spot, with wood-paneled walls, flickering candles, and colorful lamps hanging overhead.

BEYOGLU TURKISH **$$**

Map p434 (☎212-650-0850; 1431 Third Ave, at 81st St; mains $16-18, sharing plates $6-8; ⏲noon-10pm Sun-Thu, to 11pm Fri & Sat; 🌿; [S]6 to 77th St, 4/5/6 to 86th St) A long-time favorite of Mediterranean-craving Upper East Siders, Beyoglu whips up meze (appetizers) platters that are ideal for sharing. Creamy rich hummus, juicy lamb kebabs, tender grape leaves and lemon-scented char-grilled octopus. On sunny days you can head to one of the sidewalk tables in front.

ABV MODERN AMERICAN **$$**

Map p434 (☎212-722-8959; www.abvny.com; 1504 Lexington Ave, at 97th St; mains $17-24; ⏲5pm-midnight Mon-Fri, 11am-midnight Sat & Sun; 📶; [S]6 to 96th St) On the borderline of East Harlem, ABV draws a young, laid-back crowd who come for eclectic sharing plates (wild morels and ramps, chicken liver mousse), heartier mains (roasted Maine scallops, buttermilk-brined fried chicken), wine ($9 to $14 per glass) and craft beers. Tall ceilings and brick walls invite lingering, and it's not a bad spot to catch the game.

JONES WOOD FOUNDRY BRITISH **$$**

Map p434 (☎212-249-2700; www.joneswoodfoundry.com; 401 E 76th St, btwn First & York Aves; mains lunch $16-20, dinner $19-26; ⏲11am-11pm; 📶; [S]6 to 77th St) Inside a narrow brick building that once housed an ironworks, the Jones Wood Foundry is a British-inspired gastropub serving first-rate beer-battered fish and chips, bangers and mash, lamb and rosemary pie and other hearty temptations. On warm days, grab a table on the enclosed courtyard patio.

VIA QUADRONNO CAFE **$$**

Map p434 (☎212-650-9880; www.viaquadronno.com; 25 E 73rd St, btwn Madison & Fifth Aves; sandwiches $8-15, mains $23-38; ⏲8am-11pm Mon-Fri, 9am-11pm Sat, 10am-9pm Sun; 🌿; [S]6 to 77th St) A little slice of Italy that looks like it's been airlifted into New York, this cozy cafe-bistro has exquisite coffee, as well as a mind-boggling selection of sandwiches – piled high with delectable ingredients such as prosciutto and Camembert. There are soups, pastas and a very popular daily lasagna. If you're pressed for time, belly up to the granite counter for a quick macchiato and a cookie snack.

CANDLE CAFE VEGAN **$$**

Map p434 (☎212-472-0970; www.candlecafe.com; 1307 Third Ave, btwn 74th & 75th Sts; mains $15-22; ⏲11:30am-10:30pm Mon-Sat, to 9:30pm Sun; 🌿; [S]6 to 77th St) The moneyed, yoga set piles into this attractive vegan cafe serving a long list of sandwiches, salads, comfort food and market-driven specials. The specialty here is the house-made seitan. There is a juice bar and a gluten-free menu.

For a more upscale take on the subject, check out its sister restaurant, Candle 79, two blocks away.

CANDLE 79 VEGAN **$$**

Map p434 (☎212-537-7179; www.candle79.com; 154 E 79th St, at Lexington Ave; mains $21-24; ⏲noon-3:30pm & 5:30-10:30pm; 🌿; [S]6 to 77th St) Head to this high-end organic vegan restaurant to enjoy a feast without the guilt in an elegant setting: seaweed salads, cornmeal poppers, portobello steaks and wild mushroom crepes.

CAFÉ SABARSKY AUSTRIAN **$$**

Map p434 (☎212-288-0665; www.kg-ny.com/cafe-sabarsky; 1048 Fifth Ave, cnr E 86th St; mains $18-30; ⏲9am-6pm Mon & Wed, to 9pm Thu-Sun; 🌿👪; [S]4/5/6 to 86th St) The lines get long at this popular café, which evokes opulent turn-of-the-century Vienna. But the well-rendered Austrian specialties make the wait worth it. Expect crepes with smoked trout, goulash soup and roasted bratwurst. There's also a long list of specialty sweets, including a divine Sacher torte (dark chocolate cake with apricot confiture).

★TANOSHI SUSHI **$$$**

Map p434 (☎917-265-8254; www.tanoshisushinyc.com; 1372 York Ave, btwn 73rd & 74th Sts; chef's sushi selection around $80; ⏲6-10:30pm Mon-Sat; [S]6 to 77th St) It's not easy to snag one of the 20 stools at Tanoshi, a wildly popular sushi spot. The setting may be humble, but the flavors are simply magnificent, which might include Hokkaido scallops, Atlantic shad, seared salmon belly or mouthwatering *uni* (sea urchin). Only sushi is on offer and only *omakase* – the chef's selection of whatever is particularly outstanding that day. BYO beer, sake or whatnot. Reserve well in advance.

Neighborhood Walk
Memorable Manhattan Movies

START BLOOMINGDALE'S
END METROPOLITAN MUSEUM OF ART
LENGTH 1.5 MILES; TWO HOURS

An exploration of Manhattan's most storied film sites takes you past film locations big and small. Start outside ❶ **Bloomingdale's**, where Darryl Hannah and Tom Hanks shattered televisions in *Splash* (1984) and Dustin Hoffman hailed a cab in *Tootsie* (1982). West of here, 10 E 60th St is the site of the now defunct ❷ **Copacabana**, a nightclub (now a Michelin-starred restaurant) that hosted Ray Liotta and Lorraine Bracco in *Goodfellas* (1990) and a coked-up lawyer played by Sean Penn in *Carlito's Way* (1993). Continue west to ❸ **Central Park** (p230), which has appeared in *The Royal Tenenbaums* (2001), *Ghostbusters* (1983), *The Muppets Take Manhattan* (1983), *Barefoot in the Park* (1967) and the cult classic *The Warriors* (1979). From here, head east to Park Ave. At 620 Park Ave at E 65th St, you'll find the building that served as ❹ **John Malkovich's apartment** in Charlie Kaufman's *Being John Malkovich* (1999). And to the north at 114 E 72nd St is the ❺ **high-rise** where Sylvia Miles lured Jon Voight in *Midnight Cowboy* (1969). One block to the east and south is 171 E 71st St, a townhouse featured in one of the most famous movies to star New York: this was ❻ **Holly Golightly's apartment** in *Breakfast at Tiffany's* (1961). Continuing east to Third Ave, you'll find ❼ **JG Melon** (p222) at the corner of E 74th St, a good spot for beer and burger – plus the site of a meeting between Dustin Hoffman and Meryl Streep in *Kramer vs Kramer* (1979). Heading west to Madison Ave, the tony ❽ **Carlyle** hotel stands at 35 76th St where Woody Allen and Dianne Wiest had a date from hell in *Hannah and Her Sisters* (1986). From the Carlyle, it's a short jaunt west to the ❾ **Metropolitan Museum of Art** (p214) at E 82nd St and Fifth Ave, where Angie Dickinson had a fatal encounter in *Dressed to Kill* (1980) and Billy Crystal chatted up Meg Ryan in *When Harry Met Sally* (1989).

CAFÉ BOULUD FRENCH $$$

Map p434 (☎212-772-2600; www.cafeboulud.com/nyc; 20 E 76th St, btwn Fifth & Madison Aves; mains around $45; 🕐7am-10:30am, noon-2:30pm & 5:30-10:30pm Mon-Fri, from 8am Sat & Sun; ✎; [S]6 to 77th St) This Michelin-starred bistro – part of Daniel Boulud's gastronomic empire – attracts a staid crowd with its globe-trotting French cuisine. Seasonal menus include classic dishes such as coq au vin, as well as more inventive fare such as scallop *crudo* (raw) with white miso. Foodies on a budget will be interested in the three-course, $43 prix-fixe lunch.

The adjacent 40-seat **Bar Pleiades** (Map p434; ☎212-772-2600; www.barpleiades.com; 20 E 76th St, btwn Fifth & Madison Aves; 🕐noon-midnight; [S]6 to 77th St) serves seasonal cocktails, along with a full bar menu (think beef sliders and grilled baby octopus), plus live jazz on Monday and Friday nights (9pm to midnight).

SANT AMBROEUS CAFE, ITALIAN $$$

Map p434 (☎212-570-2211; www.santambroeus.com; 1000 Madison Ave, btwn 77th & 78th St; panini $13-18, mains $23-66; 🕐7am-11pm Mon-Fri, 8am-11pm Sat & Sun; ✎; [S]6 to 77th St) Behind a demure facade lies this dressy Milanese bistro and cafe that oozes Old World charm. Up front, a long granite counter dispenses rich cappuccinos, pastries and panini (grilled with the likes of parma ham and fontina), while the elegant dining room in the back dishes up northern Italian specialties such as breaded veal chop and saffron risotto. Don't bypass the famed gelato.

DRINKING & NIGHTLIFE

The choices here have traditionally been extreme: luxury lounges or frat-house vomitoriums. Times are changing, however, with Brooklyn-style cocktail lounges and gastropubs opening their doors in recent years.

OSLO COFFEE ROASTERS CAFE, COFFEE

Map p434 (www.oslocoffee.com; 422 E 75th St, btwn York & First Aves; coffee from $3; 🕐7am-6pm Mon-Fri, 8am-6pm Sat & Sun; [S]6 to 77th St) Headquartered in Williamsburg (where they do their roasting), Oslo whips up magnificent brews, espressos and lattes – all fair trade and organic, of course. Minuses: limited seating, though there is bench-type seating out front.

THE DAISY BAR

Map p434 (☎646-964-5756; 1641 Second Ave, at 85th St; 🕐4pm-1am Sun-Wed, to 2am Thu-Sat; [S]4/5/6 to 86th St) Billing itself as an 'agave gastropub,' the Daisy serves up mescal cocktails and creative Latin-inspired drinks (Michelada) and dishes (rice with duck) alongside bistro fare like duck-fat fries and grilled octopus. Unlike most other UES bars, there are no TVs or bros here – it's a laid-back, low-lit spot, with good grooves, skilled bartenders and a friendly crowd.

UVA WINE BAR

Map p434 (☎212-472-4552; www.uvanyc.com; 1486 Second Ave, btwn 77th & 78th Sts; 🕐4pm-1am Mon-Fri, 11am-4pm Sat & Sun; [S]6 to 77th St) Rustic brick walls, low-lit chandeliers and worn floorboards give the feel of an old European tavern at this lively eating and drinking spot. There are dozens of wines by the glass (from $9) plus wine flights (before 7pm), allowing you to sample a range of varietals – both Old World (particularly Italian) and New.

Food is an equally important part of the Uva experience, and you can nibble on wild mushroom bruschetta, thick focaccia covered in tomatoes and mozzarella, cheese boards and cured meats, as well as heartier fare such breaded calamari, sea scallops and baked eggplant.

BONDURANTS BAR

Map p434 (☎212-249-1509; http://bondurantsnyc.com; 303 E 85th St, btwn First & Second Aves; 🕐4pm-2am Mon-Fri, 11am-2am Sat & Sun; [S]4/5/6 to 86th St) Ticking all the boxes, Bondurants is a craft beer and bourbon bar with creative cocktails and a winning pub menu (Gruyère mac and cheese, applewood smoked wings, flame-seared shishito peppers). It has a wraparound bar, vintage fixtures and TVs for the sports-minded.

VINUS & MARC LOUNGE

Map p434 (☎646-692-9105; www.vinusandmarc.com; 1825 Second Ave, btwn 95th & 94th Sts; 🕐noon-2am Mon-Fri, 10am-3am Sat, 10am-1am Sun; [S]6 to 96th St) Red walls, gilt-edge mirrors, vintage fixtures and a long dark-wood bar sets the stage at this inviting new lounge in Yorkville. The cocktails range from elegant inventions like the spicy Baby Vamp (tequila, mescal, strawberry and habanero bitters) to Prohibition-era classics like the Scofflaw (rye whiskey, dry vermouth and house-made grenadine).

There's also good bistro fare (organic beet salad, shrimp and grits, steak frites).

DRUNKEN MUNKEY LOUNGE

Map p434 (☎646-998-4600; www.drunkenmunkeynyc.com; 338 E 92nd St, btwn First & Second Aves; ⏲11am-2am Mon-Thu, to 3am Fri-Sun; [S]6 to 96th St) This playful lounge channels colonial-era Bombay with vintage wallpaper, cricket-ball door handles and jauntily attired waitstaff. The monkey chandeliers may be pure whimsy, but the cocktails and tasty curries (small, meant for sharing) are serious business. Gin, not surprisingly, is the drink of choice. Try the Bramble (Bombay gin, blackberry liqueur and fresh lemon juice and blackberries).

THE PENROSE BAR

Map p434 (☎212-203-2751; www.penrosebar.com; 1590 Second Ave, btwn 82nd & 83rd Sts; ⏲noon-4am Mon-Fri, 10am-4am Sat & Sun; [S]4/5/6 to 86th St) The Penrose brings a dose of style to the Upper East Side, with craft beers, exposed brick walls, vintage mirrors, floral wallpaper, reclaimed wood details and friendly bartenders setting the stage for a fine evening outing among friends.

There's Duvel and Murphy's on draft, a decent selection of Irish whiskeys (no surprise, given the owners hail from Cork) and plenty of good pub fare: fish and chips, portobello dip sandwich, oyster sliders and fried chicken, among other bites.

AUCTION HOUSE BAR

Map p434 (☎212-427-4458; www.auctionhousenyc.com; 300 E 89th St, at Second Ave; ⏲7:30pm-2am Sun-Thu, to 4am Fri & Sat; [S]4/5/6 to 86th St) Dark maroon doors lead into a candlelit hangout that's perfect for a relaxing drink. Victorian-style couches and fat, overstuffed easy chairs are strewn about the wood-floored rooms. Take your well-mixed cocktail to a seat by the fireplace and admire the scene reflected in the gilt-edged mirrors propped up on the walls.

SEAMSTRESS BAR

Map p434 (☎212-288-8033; www.seamstressny.com; 339 E 75th St, btwn First & Second Aves; ⏲5pm-2am Sun-Wed, to 4am Thu-Sat; [S]6 to 77th St) This rare uptown gem serves craft cocktails and seasonal pub fare in a screen-free environment that feels more downtown than uptown. Grab a seat at the bar or arrive early and sink into a dark leather banquette. Nibble on oysters, raw field greens or a mutton burger, while sipping complex libations made of rye whiskey, pomegranate liqueur and other unusual spirits.

BEMELMANS BAR LOUNGE

Map p434 (☎212-744-1600; www.rosewoodhotels.com/en/the-carlyle-new-york; Carlyle Hotel, 35 E 76th St, at Madison Ave; ⏲noon-1am; [S]6 to 77th St) Sink into a chocolate leather banquette and take in the glorious 1940s elegance of this fabled bar – the sort of place where the waiters wear white jackets, a baby grand is always tinkling and the ceiling is 24-carat gold leaf. Note the charming murals by Ludwig Bemelman (famed creator of *Madeline*).

Show up before 9pm if you don't want to pay a cover (per person $15 to $35).

☆ ENTERTAINMENT

COMIC STRIP LIVE COMEDY

Map p434 (☎212-861-9386; www.comicstriplive.com; 1568 Second Ave, btwn 81st & 82nd Sts; cover charge $15-30, plus 2-drink min; ⏲shows 8:30pm Sun-Thu, 8:30pm, 10:30pm & 12:30am Fri, 8pm, 10:30pm & 12:30am Sat; [S]4/5/6 to 86th St) Chris Rock, Adam Sandler, Jerry Seinfeld and Eddie Murphy have all performed at this club. Not recently, but you're sure to find somebody stealing their acts here most nights. Reservations required.

FRICK COLLECTION CLASSICAL MUSIC

Map p434 (☎212-288-0700; www.frick.org; 1 E 70th St, at Fifth Ave; admission $40; [S]6 to 68th St-Hunter College) Once a month this opulent mansion-museum hosts a Sunday concert that brings world-renowned performers such as cellist Yehuda Hanani and violinist Thomas Zehetmair.

92ND STREET Y CULTURAL CENTER

Map p434 (☎212-415-5500; www.92y.org; 1395 Lexington Ave, at 92nd St; 👪; [S]6 to 96th St) In addition to its wide spectrum of concerts, dance performances and literary readings, this nonprofit cultural center hosts an excellent lecture and conversation series. Playwright Edward Albee, cellist Yo-Yo Ma, funnyman Steve Martin and novelist Salman Rushdie have all taken the stage here.

CAFÉ CARLYLE JAZZ

Map p434 (☎212-744-1600; www.thecarlyle.com/dining/cafe_carlyle; Carlyle Hotel, 35 E 76th St, at

Madison Ave; cover $110-185; S 6 to 77th St) This swanky spot at the Carlyle Hotel draws top-shelf talent, including Woody Allen, who plays his clarinet here with the Eddy Davis New Orleans Jazz Band on Monday at 8:45pm (September through May). Bring bucks: the cover doesn't include food or drinks.

SHOPPING

The Upper East Side isn't for amateurs. Madison Ave (from 60th St to 72nd St) features one of the globe's glitziest stretches of retail: the flagship boutiques of some of the world's top designers, including Gucci, Prada and Cartier. The neighborhood is also a good spot to hunt down designer deals at consignment shops.

MARIMEKKO   CLOTHING
Map p434 (212-628-8400; http://kiitosmarimekko.com; 1262 Third Ave, btwn 72nd & 73rd Sts; 10am-7pm Mon-Sat, noon-5pm Sun; S 6 to 68th St) This adorable store sells beautiful clothing and accessories adorned with colorful prints for which the Finnish designer is famed. Aside from dresses, skirts and tops, there's much eye candy here, including towels, umbrellas, bags, pillows, hats and fabric (designers may go weak in the knees).

LA MAISON DU CHOCOLAT   FOOD
Map p434 (212-744-7118; www.lamaisonduchocolat.us; 1018 Madison Ave, btwn 78th & 79th Sts; 10am-7pm Mon-Sat, 11am-6pm Sun; S 6 to 77th St) The US flagship store of the famed Parisian chocolatier is a dangerous place for chocoholics. Dark sweet decadence comes in many forms here, from powdery, cocoa-dusted truffles to intensely rich bars sourced from the finest beans on the planet. There's also a cafe in back where you can sink your teeth into creamy chocolate éclairs or sip a cup of steaming hot chocolate.

ENCORE   CLOTHING
Map p434 (212-879-2850; www.encoreresale.com; 1132 Madison Ave, btwn 84th & 85th Sts; 10:30am-6:30pm Mon-Sat, noon-6pm Sun; S 4/5/6 to 86th St) An exclusive consignment store has been emptying out Upper East Side closets since the 1950s. (Jacqueline Kennedy Onassis used to sell her clothes here.) Expect to find a gently worn selection of name brands such as Louboutin, Fendi and Dior.

MICHAEL'S   CLOTHING
Map p434 (212-737-7273; www.michaelsconsignment.com; 2nd fl, 1041 Madison Ave, btwn 79th & 80th Sts; 9:30am-6pm Mon-Sat, to 8pm Thu; S 6 to 77th St) In operation since the 1950s, this is a vaunted Upper East Side re-sale store that is strong on high-end labels, including Chanel, Gucci and Prada. Almost everything on display is less than two years old. It's pricey but cheaper than shopping the flagship boutiques on Madison Ave.

BLUE TREE   FASHION, HOMEWARES
Map p434 (212-369-2583; www.bluetreenyc.com; 1283 Madison Ave, btwn 91st & 92nd Sts; 10am-6pm Mon-Fri, 11am-6pm Sat; S 4/5/6 to 86th St) This charming (and expensive) little boutique, owned by actress Phoebe Cates Kline (of *Fast Times at Ridgemont High*) sells a dainty array of women's clothing, cashmere scarves, Lucite objects, whimsical accessories and quirky home design.

CRAWFORD DOYLE BOOKSELLERS   BOOKS
Map p434 (212-288-6300; http://crawforddoyle.com; 1082 Madison Ave, btwn 81st & 82nd Sts; 10am-6pm Mon-Sat, noon-5pm Sun; S 6 to 77th St) This genteel bookstore invites browsing, with stacks devoted to art, literature and the history of New York – not to mention plenty of first editions. A wonderful place to while away a chilly afternoon.

SPORTS & ACTIVITIES

EXHALE   SPA
Map p434 (212-561-6400; www.exhalespa.com; 980 Madison Ave, btwn 76th & 77th Sts; classes $25-37, 1hr massage around $150; 7:30am-9pm Mon-Sat, to 8pm Sun; S 6 to 77th St) This Zen-like spa offers all the standard treatments, including massages, facials and scrubs, plus acupuncture, cupping and Reiki. The spa offers yoga, cardio and barre classes.

ASPHALT GREEN   SWIMMING
Map p434 (212-369-8890; www.asphaltgreen.org; 555 E 90th St, btwn York & East End Aves; gym & pool pass $35; 5:30am-10:30pm Mon-Fri, 7am-8pm Sat & Sun; ; S 4/5/6 to 86th St) Not to be confused with the 1973 Charlton Heston sci-fi film *Soylent Green*, the Asphalt Green fitness center is set in a former municipal asphalt plant. There's an excellent 50m pool, as well as a smaller pool for classes.

Upper West Side & Central Park

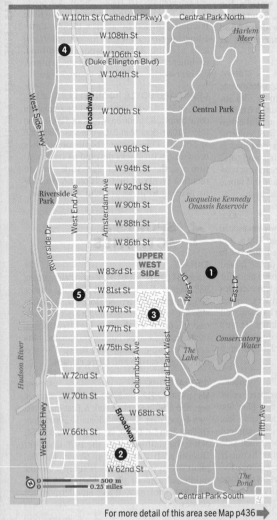

Neighborhood Top Five

1 Escaping the city's frantic urban madness with a day spent picnicking on Sheep's Meadow, row-boating on the lake and strolling the grand Literary Walk in **Central Park** (p230).

2 Wallowing in the operatic trials of Rigoletto, Carmen and Figaro at the **Metropolitan Opera House** (p241).

3 Walking among the world's largest dinosaurs at the **American Museum of Natural History** (p235).

4 Taking a pilgrimage to Tibet without leaving New York City at the **Nicholas Roerich Museum** (p236).

5 Strolling, jogging or cycling along the Hudson waterfront in **Riverside Park** (p235).

Map labels

W 110th St (Cathedral Pkwy)
Central Park North
Harlem Meer
W 108th St
W 106th St (Duke Ellington Blvd)
W 104th St
Broadway
W 100th St
Central Park
Fifth Ave
W 96th St
W 94th St
W 92nd St
Jacqueline Kennedy Onassis Reservoir
West End Ave
Amsterdam Ave
W 90th St
Riverside Park
W 88th St
Riverside Dr
West Side Hwy
W 86th St
UPPER WEST SIDE
W 83rd St
W 81st St
West Dr
East Dr
W 79th St
W 77th St
W 75th St
Conservatory Water
Central Park West
Columbus Ave
The Lake
Hudson River
W 72nd St
W 70th St
Broadway
W 68th St
W 66th St
W 62nd St
Central Park South
The Pond
Fifth Ave

0 500 m
0 0.25 miles

For more detail of this area see Map p436 ➡

Explore Upper West Side & Central Park

Manhattan's midsection has a lot of ground to cover – and the best plan of attack will depend on your flavor. Traveling with tykes? Then dazzle their budding brains with a visit to the American Museum of Natural History, followed by a journey through the sprawling wonderland that is Central Park. If the high arts are your pleasure, then make for the Lincoln Center – where the Metropolitan Opera, the New York Philharmonic and the New York City Ballet all inject the city with vibrant doses of culture. And, if your idea of a good time is just ambling around, then take in the sights in and off Broadway in the 70s, an area cluttered with bustling shops and fine architecture.

Local Life

➡ **Go fishing** Wood-smoked lox. Briny pickled herring. Meaty sturgeon. It doesn't get more Upper West Side than examining the seafood treats at Zabar's (p236) and Barney Greengrass (p240).

➡ **Central chill** You can pick out the tourists in Central Park (p230) because they're rushing to see sights. Make like a local by picking out a patch of green with good views and letting the world come to you.

➡ **Catch a flick** Manhattan's die-hard film buffs can be found taking in quality cinema courtesy of the Film Society of Lincoln Center (p242).

➡ **Late-night munchies** Nothing is more New York than soaking up the evening's liquor damage with a 2am hot dog from Gray's Papaya (p237).

Getting There & Away

➡ **Subway** On the Upper West Side, the 1, 2 and 3 subway lines are good for destinations along Broadway and points west, while the B and C trains are best for points of interest and access to Central Park. The park can be accessed from all sides, making every subway that travels north–south through Manhattan convenient. The A, C, B, D and 1 all stop at Columbus Circle at Central Park's southwestern edge, while the N, R or Q will leave you at the southeast corner. The 2 or 3 will deposit you at the northern gate in Harlem.

➡ **Bus** The M104 bus runs north–south along Broadway, and the M10 plies the scenic ride along the western edge of the park. Cross-town buses at 66th, 72nd, 79th, 86th and 96th Sts take you through the park to the Upper East Side. Note that these pick up and drop off passengers at the edge of the park – not inside.

Lonely Planet's Top Tip

The best way to cover 840 acres of Central Park is to rent a bicycle. **Bike & Roll** (p244) and the **Loeb Boathouse** (p244) both offer rentals. If starting at the Loeb Boathouse, pedal north along East Dr to see the Great Lawn, the reservoir, the Conservatory Garden and Harlem Meer. From the Great Hill you can coast down West Dr, past the Delacorte Theater and end up at Strawberry Fields (weather permitting).

UPPER WEST SIDE & CENTRAL PARK

 ### Best Places to Eat

➡ Jacob's Pickles (p237)
➡ Burke & Wills (p237)
➡ Peacefood Cafe (p236)
➡ Kefi (p237)
➡ Dovetail (p240)

For reviews, see p236 ➡

Best Places to Drink

➡ West End Hall (p241)
➡ Dead Poet (p241)
➡ Barcibo Enoteca (p241)
➡ Manhattan Cricket Club (p241)
➡ West 79th St Boat Basin Café (p235)

For reviews, see p240 ➡

 ### Best Places for Music

➡ Metropolitan Opera House (p241)
➡ SummerStage (p234)
➡ Smoke (p243)
➡ Cleopatra's Needle (p243)
➡ Beacon Theatre (p243)

For reviews, see p241 ➡

TOP SIGHT
CENTRAL PARK

Comprising more than 800 acres of picturesque meadows, ponds and woods, it might be tempting to think that Central Park represents Manhattan in its raw state. It does not. Designed by Frederick Law Olmsted and Calvert Vaux, the park is the result of serious engineering: thousands of workers shifted 10 million cartloads of soil to transform swamp and rocky outcroppings into the 'people's park' of today.

DON'T MISS

- The Mall
- The Reservoir
- Conservatory Garden
- Central Park Zoo

PRACTICALITIES

- Map p436
- www.centralparknyc.org
- 59th & 110th Sts, btwn Central Park West & Fifth Ave
- 🕒6am-1am

Birth of a Park

In the 1850s, the area was occupied by pig farms, a garbage dump, a bone-boiling operation and an African American village. It took 20,000 laborers 20 years to transform this terrain into a park. Today, Central Park has more than 24,000 trees, 136 acres of woodland, 21 playgrounds and seven bodies of water. It attracts more than 38 million visitors a year.

Strawberry Fields

This tear-shaped **garden** (72nd St on the west side; 👪; [S]A/C, B to 72nd St) serves as a memorial to former Beatle John Lennon. The garden is composed of a grove of stately elms and a tiled mosaic that reads, simply, 'Imagine.'

Bethesda Terrace & the Mall

The arched walkways of **Bethesda Terrace**, crowned by the magnificent Bethesda Fountain at the level of 72nd St, have long been a gathering area for New Yorkers of all flavors. To the south is **the Mall** (featured in countless movies), a promenade shrouded in mature North American elms. The southern stretch, known as **Literary Walk** (Central Park, btwn 67th & 72nd Sts; [S]N/Q/R to 5th Ave-59th St), is flanked by statues of famous authors.

Central Park Zoo

Officially known as Central Park Wildlife Center (no one calls it that), this small **zoo** (☎212-439-6500; www.centralparkzoo.com; 64th St, at Fifth Ave; adult/child $12/7; ⏰10am-5:30pm May-Oct, to 4:30pm Nov-Apr; 👪; [S]N/Q/R to 5th Ave-59th St) is home to penguins, snow leopards, dart poison frogs and red pandas. Feeding times in the sea lion and penguin tanks make for a rowdy spectacle. (Check the website for times.) The attached **Tisch Children's Zoo** (www.centralparkzoo.com/animals-and-exhibits/exhibits/tisch-childrens-zoo.aspx; Central Park, at 65th & Fifth Ave; adult/child $12/7; ⏰10am-5:30pm May-Oct, to 4:30pm Nov-Mar; [S]N/Q/R to 5th Ave-59th St), a petting zoo, has alpacas and mini-Nubian goats and is perfect for small children.

Conservatory Water & Alice in Wonderland

North of the zoo at the level of 74th St is Conservatory Water, where model sailboats drift lazily and kids scramble about on a toadstool-studded statue of Alice in Wonderland. There are Saturday story hours (www.hcastorycenter.org) at 11am from June to September at the Hans Christian Andersen statue to the west of the water.

Great Lawn & the Ramble

The **Great Lawn** (btwn 79th & 86th Sts; [S]B, C to 86th St) is a massive emerald carpet at the center of the park and is surrounded by ball fields and London plane trees. (This is where Simon & Garfunkel played their famous 1981 concert.) Immediately to the southeast is **Delacorte Theater** (enter at W 81st St; [S]B, C to 81st St), home to an annual Shakespeare in the Park festival, as well as Belvedere Castle (p245), a bird-watching lookout. Further south is the leafy **Ramble** (mid-park from 73rd to 79th Sts; [S]B,C to 81st St), a popular birding destination. On the southeastern end is the Loeb Boathouse (p244), home to a waterside restaurant that offers rowboat and bicycle rentals.

Jacqueline Kennedy Onassis Reservoir

The reservoir takes up almost the entire width of the park at the level of 90th St and serves as a gorgeous reflecting pool for the city skyline. It is surrounded by a 1.58-mile track that draws legions of joggers in the warmer months. Nearby, at Fifth Ave and 90th St, is a statue of New York City Marathon founder Fred Lebow, peering at his watch.

CONSERVATORY GARDEN

If you want a little peace and quiet (as in, no runners, cyclists or buskers), the 6-acre **Conservatory Garden** ([S]6 to 103rd St) serves as one of the park's official quiet zones. And it's beautiful, to boot: bursting with crab-apple trees, meandering boxwood and, in the spring, lots of flowers. It's located at 105th St off Fifth Ave. Otherwise, you can catch maximum calm (and max bird life) in all areas of the park just after dawn.

NORTH WOODS & BLOCKHOUSE

The North Woods, on the west side between 106th and 110th Sts, is home to the park's oldest structure, **the Blockhouse**, a military fortification from the War of 1812.

VISITING THE PARK

Free and custom walking tours are available via the **Central Park Conservancy** (☎212-310-6600; www.centralparknyc.org/tours; 14 E 60th St; [S]N/Q/R to 5th Ave-59th St), a non-profit organization that supports park maintenance.

Central Park

THE LUNGS OF NEW YORK

The rectangular patch of green that occupies Manhattan's heart began life in the mid-19th century as a swampy piece of land that was carefully bulldozed into the idyllic nature-scape you see today. Since officially becoming Central Park, it has brought New Yorkers of all stripes together in interesting and unexpected ways. The park has served as a place for the rich to show off their fancy carriages (1860s), for the poor to enjoy free Sunday concerts (1880s) and for activists to hold be-ins against the Vietnam War (1960s).

Since then, legions of locals – not to mention travelers from all kinds of faraway places – have poured in to stroll, picnic, sunbathe, play ball and catch free concerts and performances of works by Shakespeare.

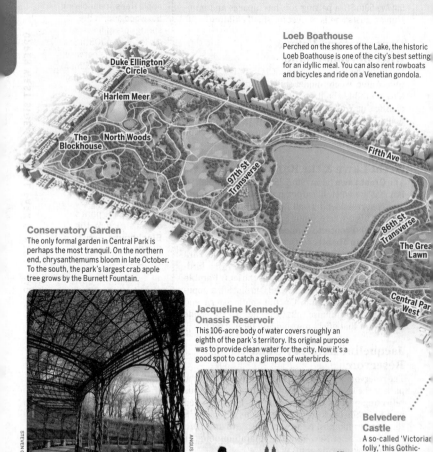

Loeb Boathouse
Perched on the shores of the Lake, the historic Loeb Boathouse is one of the city's best settings for an idyllic meal. You can also rent rowboats and bicycles and ride on a Venetian gondola.

Duke Ellington Circle

Harlem Meer

The Blockhouse North Woods

97th St Transverse

Fifth Ave

86th St Transverse

The Great Lawn

Central Park West

Conservatory Garden
The only formal garden in Central Park is perhaps the most tranquil. On the northern end, chrysanthemums bloom in late October. To the south, the park's largest crab apple tree grows by the Burnett Fountain.

Jacqueline Kennedy Onassis Reservoir
This 106-acre body of water covers roughly an eighth of the park's territory. Its original purpose was to provide clean water for the city. Now it's a good spot to catch a glimpse of waterbirds.

Belvedere Castle
A so-called 'Victorian folly,' this Gothic-Romanesque castle serves no other purpose than to be a very dramatic lookout point. It was built by Central Park co-designer Calvert Vaux in 1869.

STEVEN GREAVES / GETTY IMAGES ©

ANGUS OSBORN / GETTY IMAGES ©

The park's varied terrain offers a wonderland of experiences. There are quiet, woodsy knolls in the north. To the south is the reservoir, crowded with joggers. There are European gardens, a zoo and various bodies of water. For maximum flamboyance, hit the Sheep Meadow on a sunny day, when all of New York shows up to lounge.

Central Park is more than just a green space. It is New York City's backyard.

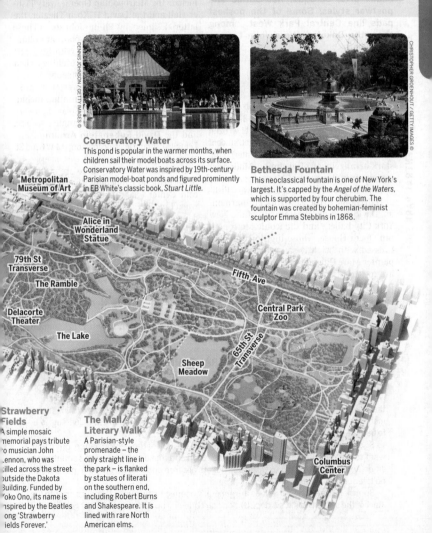

Conservatory Water
This pond is popular in the warmer months, when children sail their model boats across its surface. Conservatory Water was inspired by 19th-century Parisian model-boat ponds and figured prominently in EB White's classic book, *Stuart Little*.

Bethesda Fountain
This neoclassical fountain is one of New York's largest. It's capped by the *Angel of the Waters*, which is supported by four cherubim. The fountain was created by bohemian-feminist sculptor Emma Stebbins in 1868.

Metropolitan Museum of Art

Alice in Wonderland Statue

79th St Transverse

The Ramble

Delacorte Theater

The Lake

Fifth Ave

Central Park Zoo

65th St Transverse

Sheep Meadow

Columbus Center

Strawberry Fields
A simple mosaic memorial pays tribute to musician John Lennon, who was killed across the street outside the Dakota Building. Funded by Yoko Ono, its name is inspired by the Beatles song 'Strawberry Fields Forever.'

The Mall / Literary Walk
A Parisian-style promenade – the only straight line in the park – is flanked by statues of literati on the southern end, including Robert Burns and Shakespeare. It is lined with rare North American elms.

⊙ SIGHTS

The stretch of Manhattan west of Central Park was once a lively mix of African American, Latino and German Jewish immigrant communities. (This is where you'll find some of the best smoked fish in town.) In more recent decades, it has been a base for well-to-do artsy types, young professionals and the stroller set. While long stretches of Broadway are lined with charmless chain stores, the rest of the neighborhood is an architectural bonanza featuring beaux arts, baroque, neo-Gothic and postwar styles. Some of the poshest pads line Central Park West, among them the Dakota, where John Lennon once lived.

★CENTRAL PARK   PARK
See p230.

★LINCOLN CENTER   CULTURAL CENTER
Map p436 (☑212-875-5456, tours 212-875-5350; www.lincolncenter.org; Columbus Ave btwn 62nd & 66th Sts; public plazas free, tours adult/student $18/15; ⌖; Ⓢ1 to 66th St-Lincoln Center) This stark arrangement of gleaming Modernist temples contains some of Manhattan's most important performance spaces: Avery Fisher Hall (home to the New York Philharmonic), David H Koch Theater (site of the New York City ballet), and the iconic Metropolitan Opera House, whose interior walls are dressed with brightly saturated murals by painter Marc Chagall. Various other venues are tucked in and around the 16-acre campus, including a theater, two film-screening centers and the renowned Juilliard School.

Built in the 1960s, this imposing campus replaced a group of tenements called San Juan Hill, a predominantly African American neighborhood where the exterior shots for the movie *West Side Story* were filmed. In addition to being a controversial urban planning move, Lincoln Center wasn't exactly well received on an architectural level – it was relentlessly criticized for its conservative design, fortress-like aspect and poor acoustics. For the center's 50th anniversary (2009–10), Diller Scofidio + Renfro and other architects gave the complex a much-needed and critically acclaimed freshening up.

A survey of the three classic buildings surrounding Revson Fountain is a must. These include the Metropolitan Opera, Avery Fisher Hall and the David H Koch Theater, the latter designed by Philip Johnson. (These are all located on the main plaza at Columbus Ave, between 62nd and 65th Sts.) The fountain is spectacular in the evenings when it puts on Las Vegas–like light shows.

Of the refurbished structures, there are a number that are worth examining, including Alice Tully Hall, now displaying a very contemporary translucent, angled facade, and the **David Rubenstein Atrium** (☑212-721-6500; atrium.lincolncenter.org; 61 W 62nd St, at Broadway; Ⓢ1 to 66th St-Lincoln Center).

On any given night, there are at least 10 performances happening throughout Lincoln Center – and even more in summer, when Lincoln Center Out of Doors (a series of dance and music concerts) and Midsummer Night Swing (ballroom dancing under the stars) lure those who love parks and culture. For details on seasons, tickets and programming – which runs the gamut from opera to dance to theater to ballet – check the website.

Daily tours of the complex explore the Metropolitan Opera House, Revson Fountain and Alice Tully Hall and are a great way to get acquainted with the complex.

SUMMER HAPPENINGS IN CENTRAL PARK

During the warm months, Central Park is home to countless cultural events, many of which are free. The two most popular are: **Shakespeare in the Park** (www.public theater.org), which is managed by the Public Theater, and **SummerStage** (www.summerstage.org; Rumsey Playfield, Central Park, access via Fifth Ave & 69th St; ☺Jun-Aug; Ⓢ6 to 68th St-Hunter College) FREE, a series of free concerts.

Shakespeare tickets are given out at 1pm on the day of the performance, but if you want to lay your hands on a seat, line up by 8am and make sure you have something to sit on and your entire group with you. Tickets are free and there's only one per person; no latecomers are allowed in line.

SummerStage concert venues are generally opened to the public 1½ hours prior to the start of the show. But if it's a popular act, start queuing up early or you're not getting in.

TOP SIGHT
AMERICAN MUSEUM OF NATURAL HISTORY

Founded in 1869, this classic museum contains a veritable wonderland of some 30 million artifacts, as well as a cutting-edge planetarium. From September through May, it's home to the Butterfly Conservatory, featuring 500-plus butterflies from around the globe. But the museum is perhaps best known for its Fossil Halls, which contain nearly 600 specimens including the skeletons of a massive mammoth and a fearsome Tyrannosaurus Rex.

There are plentiful animal exhibits, galleries devoted to gems, and an IMAX theater. The Hall of Ocean Life contains dioramas devoted to ecologies, weather and conservation, as well as a beloved 94ft replica of a blue whale. At the 77th St Lobby Gallery, visitors are greeted by a 63ft 19th-century canoe, carved by the Haida people of British Columbia.

For the space set, the Rose Center for Earth & Space is the star of the show. Its mesmerizing glass-box facade – home to space-show theaters and the planetarium – is an otherworldly setting. Dark Universe, which screens every half-hour between 10:30am and 4:30pm, explores the mysteries and wonders of the cosmos.

The museum is understandably a hit with kids and is therefore swamped on weekends. Aim to go early on a weekday.

DON'T MISS

- Tyrannosaurus Rex (4th fl)
- Hall of Ocean Life (1st fl)
- Big Bang Theater (1st fl)

PRACTICALITIES

- Map p436
- www.amnh.org
- Central Park West, at 79th St
- suggested donation adult/child $22/12.50
- ⏲10am-5:45pm, Rose Center to 8:45pm Fri
- [S]B, C to 81st St-Museum of Natural History, 1 to 79th St

RIVERSIDE PARK OUTDOORS
Map p436 (☎212-870-3070; www.riversideparknyc.org; Riverside Dr, btwn 68th & 155th Sts; ⏲6am-1am; 👪; [S]1/2/3 to any stop btwn 66th & 157th Sts) A classic beauty designed by Central Park creators Frederick Law Olmsted and Calvert Vaux, this waterside spot, running north on the Upper West Side and banked by the Hudson River from 59th to 158th Sts, is lusciously leafy. Plenty of bike paths and playgrounds make it a family favorite.

From late March through October (weather permitting), lively waterside restaurant **West 79th Street Boat Basin Café** (☎212-496-5542; www.boatbasincafe.com; W 79th St, at Henry Hudson Parkway; sandwiches $10-17; ⏲noon-11pm Mon-Sat, to 10pm Sun Apr-Oct, weather permitting; [S]1 to 79th St) serves a light menu at the level of 79th St. **Pier i Café** (☎212-362-4450; www.piericafe.com; at W 70th St & Riverside Blvd; mains $12-22; ⏲8am-midnight May–mid-Oct; 👪; [S]1/2/3 to 72nd St), an outdoor cafe nine blocks south on the waterfront, is another option.

AMERICAN FOLK ART MUSEUM MUSEUM
Map p436 (☎212-595-9533; www.folkartmuseum.org; 2 Lincoln Sq, Columbus Ave, at 66th St; ⏲11:30am-7pm Tue-Thu & Sat, noon-7:30pm Fri, noon-6pm Sun; [S]1 to 66th St-Lincoln Center) [FREE] This tiny institution contains a couple of centuries' worth of folk and outsider art treasures, including pieces by Henry Darger (known for his girl-filled battlescapes) and Martín Ramírez (producer of hallucinatory *caballeros* on horseback). There is also an array of wood carvings, paintings, hand-tinted photographs and decorative objects. On Wednesday there are guitar concerts, and there's free music on Friday.

During November and December the museum also opens on Mondays from 11:30am to 7pm.

NEW-YORK HISTORICAL SOCIETY MUSEUM
Map p436 (www.nyhistory.org; 170 Central Park West, at 77th St; adult/child $20/6, by donation 6-8pm Fri, library free; ⏲10am-6pm Tue-Thu & Sat, to 8pm Fri, 11am-5pm Sun; [S]B, C to 81st St-Museum of Natural History) As the antiquated hyphenated name implies, the Historical Society is the city's oldest museum, founded in 1804 to preserve the city's historical and cultural artifacts. Its collection of more than 60,000 objects is quirky and fascinating and includes everything from George

Washington's inauguration chair to a 19th-century Tiffany ice-cream dish (gilded, of course).

Other treasures include a leg brace worn by President Franklin D Roosevelt, a 19th-century mechanical bank in which a political figure slips coins into his pocket and photographer Jack Stewart's graffiti-covered door from the 1970s (featuring tags by known graffiti writers such as Tracy 168). In the lobby, be sure to look up: the ceiling mural from Keith Haring's 1986 'Pop Shop' hangs above the admissions desk.

NICHOLAS ROERICH MUSEUM MUSEUM

Map p436 (☎212-864-7752; www.roerich.org; 319 W 107th St, btwn Riverside Dr & Broadway; 🕐noon-5pm Tue-Fri, from 2pm Sat & Sun; [S]1 to Cathedral Pkwy) [FREE] This compelling little museum, housed in a three-story townhouse from 1898, is one of the city's best-kept secrets. It contains more than 200 paintings by the prolific Nicholas Konstantinovich Roerich (1874–1947), a Russian-born poet, philosopher and painter. His most remarkable works are his stunning depictions of the Himalayas, where he often traveled.

While the collection includes early modern figure paintings and religious scenes (the latter of which are quite forgettable), his mountainscapes are truly a wonder to behold: icy Tibetan peaks in shades of blue, white, green and purple, channeling a Georgia O'Keeffe/Rockwell Kent vibe. This is a curious and intriguing place. Check the calendar for periodic classical concerts – always free.

ZABAR'S MARKET

Map p436 (☎212-787-2000; www.zabars.com; 2245 Broadway, at 80th St; 🕐8am-7:30pm Mon-Fri, to 8pm Sat, 9am-6pm Sun; [S]1 to 79th St) A bastion of gourmet Kosher foodie-ism, this sprawling local market has been a neighborhood fixture since the 1930s. And what a fixture it is! It features a heavenly array of cheeses, meats, olives, caviar, smoked fish, pickles, dried fruits, nuts and baked goods, including pillowy, fresh-out-of-the-oven *knishes* (Eastern European–style potato dumplings wrapped in dough).

🍴 EATING

Though not known for its dining scene, this huge swathe of neighborhood nonetheless manages to serve up everything from chewy bagels to fancy French cassoulets to the latest in New American cooking. It is also ground zero for off-the-hook picnic fixings: head to Zabar's or Whole Foods (in the basement of the Time Warner Center to pick up delicacies for an alfresco meal in Central Park.

PEACEFOOD CAFE VEGAN $

Map p436 (☎212-362-2266; www.peacefoodcafe.com; 460 Amsterdam Ave, at 82nd St; mains $12-18; 🕐10am-10pm; 🍼; [S]1 to 79th St) 🌿 This bright and airy vegan haven dishes up a popular fried seitan panino (served on homemade focaccia and topped with cashew cheese, arugula, tomatoes and pesto), as well as pizzas, roasted vegetable plates and an excellent quinoa salad. There are daily raw specials, energy-fueling juices and rich desserts. Healthy and good – for you, the animals and the environment.

JIN RAMEN JAPANESE $

Map p436 (☎646-657-0755; www.jinramen.com; 462 Amsterdam Ave, btwn 82nd & 83rd St; mains $12-16; 🕐11:30am-3:30pm & 5-11pm Mon-Sat, to 10pm Sun; 🍼; [S]1 to 79th St) This buzzing little joint off Amsterdam Ave serves up delectable bowls of piping hot ramen. *Tonkotsu* (pork broth) ramen is a favorite though vegetarians also have options. Don't neglect the appetizers: *shishito* peppers, pork buns and *hijiki* salad. The mix of rustic wood elements, exposed bulbs and red industrial fixtures give the place a cozy vibe.

BIRDBATH BAKERY BAKERY $

Map p436 (☎646-722-6562; http://thecitybakery.com/birdbath-bakery; 274 Columbus Ave, at 72nd St; mains $10-14; 🕐8am-7pm; 🍼; [S]1/2/3, B, C to 72nd St) 🌿 Aside from the lack of seating inside, it's hard to find fault with this delightful cafe. The menu changes daily and features excellent sandwiches, vitamin-rich juices and salads (try the chicken, kale and corn salad). The bakery items are outstanding. Birdbath also has an ecofriendly ethos implemented through the use of green building materials, recycled woods, and deliveries made on bicycle.

TUM & YUM THAI $

Map p436 (☎212-222-1998; www.tumyumnyc.com; 917 Columbus Ave, at 105th St; mains $10-19; 🕐11am-11pm; [S]B, C to 103rd St) This small neighborhood Thai eatery whips up excellent curries, crispy roast duck and steaming bowls of rich Tom Yum shrimp soup –

best washed down with fresh coconut juice or a sweet Thai iced coffee. The rustic wooden interior makes a cozy retreat when the weather sours.

GRAY'S PAPAYA HOT DOGS $

Map p436 (☎212-799-0243; 2090 Broadway, at 72nd St, entrance on Amsterdam Ave; hot dog $2; ⏲24hr; [S]A/B/C, 1/2/3 to 72nd St) It doesn't get more New York than bellying up to this classic stand-up joint in the wake of a beer bender. The lights are bright, the color palette is 1970s and the hot dogs are unpretentiously good. Granted, the papaya drink is more 'drink' than papaya, but you can't go wrong with Gray's famous 'Recession Special' – $5.95 for two grilled dogs and a beverage. Deal.

JACOB'S PICKLES AMERICAN $$

Map p436 (☎212-470-5566; www.jacobspickles.com; 509 Amsterdam Ave, btwn 84th & 85th; mains $15-26; ⏲10am-2am Mon-Thu, to 4am Fri, 9am-4am Sat, to 2am Sun; [S]1 to 86th St) Jacob's elevates the humble pickle to exalted status at this inviting and warmly lit eatery on a restaurant-lined stretch of Amsterdam Ave. Aside from briny cucumbers and other preserves, you'll find heaping portions of upscale comfort food, such as catfish tacos, wine-braised turkey leg dinner, and mushroom mac and cheese. The biscuits are top notch. The two dozen or so craft beers on tap showcase unique brews from New York, Maine and beyond.

KEFI GREEK $$

Map p436 (☎212-873-0200; michaelpsilakis.com/kefi; 505 Columbus Ave, btwn 84th & 85th Sts; small sharing plates $7-14, mains $15-24; ⏲noon-10pm Mon-Fri, from 11am Sat & Sun; 🍷 👪; [S]B, C to 86th St) This homey, whitewashed eatery run by chef Michael Psilakis channels a sleek taverna vibe while dispensing excellent rustic Greek dishes. Expect favorites such as spicy lamb sausage, sheep-milk dumplings and creamy sun-dried tomato hummus. You can also assemble a feast with the meze (sharing plates), including crispy calamari, meatballs and tzatziki, and grilled octopus and bean salad. The wine list features a comprehensive selection of Greek vintages (from $24 per bottle).

THE SMITH MODERN AMERICAN $$

Map p436 (☎212-496-5700; thesmithrestaurant.com; 1900 Broadway, btwn 63rd & 64th Sts; mains $17-44; ⏲7:30am-midnight Mon-Fri, from 9am Sat & Sun; [S]1, A/C, B/D to 59th-St-Columbus Circle) On a restaurant-lined strip across from Lincoln Center, this always buzzing bistro serves up high-end comfort food with seasonal accents. Braised short ribs with butternut squash, pastrami spiced salmon with roasted cauliflower, and chicken pot pie are a few recent selections. There's also a raw bar and myriad drink selections. On warm days, there's open-air seating in front.

LAND THAI $$

Map p436 (☎212-501-8121; www.landthaikitchen.com; 450 Amsterdam Ave, btwn 81st & 82nd St; mains $12-22; ⏲noon-3:30pm & 5-10pm; [S]1 to 79th St) It's no secret that good Thai food is hard to find in Manhattan – Queens is where the real-deal eateries reside. Although Land serves up Americanized versions of Thai recipes, the dishes are quite good, with zesty green papaya salad, crispy wonton-wrapped shrimp parcels and juicy pan-seared duck breast. It's a small, narrow space that's often crowded, so go early to avoid a long wait.

BURKE & WILLS MODERN AUSTRALIAN $$

Map p436 (☎646-823-9251; www.burkeandwillsny.com; 226 W 79th St, btwn Broadway & Amsterdam Ave; mains lunch $19-26, dinner $20-45; ⏲noon-3pm & 5:30pm-11pm Mon-Fri, from 11am Sat & Sun; [S]1 to 79th St) This ruggedly attractive bistro and bar brings a touch of the outback to the Upper West Side. The menu leans toward Modern Australian pub grub: juicy kangaroo burgers with triple-fried chips, grilled prawns, kale cobb salad, braised pork belly with apple and celery slaw, and seafood platters with oysters, clams and crab claws.

Vintage framed artwork on the walls pays tribute to Oz, in particular those ill-fated European explorers (who died in the outback) for whom the restaurant is named. After the meal, head upstairs and sink into a Chesterfield while nursing a cocktail at the gilded Manhattan Cricket Club (p241).

GASTRONOMÍA CULINARIA ITALIAN $$

Map p436 (☎212-663-1040; 53 W 106th St, btwn Columbus & Manhattan Aves; mains $14-26; ⏲5-10pm Mon-Fri, 11:30am-11pm Sat & Sun; [S]B, C, 1 to 103rd St) For locals, this tongue-twister of a restaurant is more often known as 'that great Italian restaurant on 106th St'. Run by a Roman chef, GC feels like a charming old-world trattoria, its narrow brick-walled dining room the backdrop to richly prepared dishes at reasonable prices. Unfortunately, the service can be a bit disappointing.

1. Strawberry Fields (p230)
Remember John Lennon at the tiled mosaic in this memorial garden.

2. Upper West Side (p228)
Wander streets lined with beaux-arts, baroque, neo-Gothic and postwar-style architecture.

3. Central Park (p230)
Spend an afternoon getting lost in the 800 acres of the 'people's park'.

4. American Museum of Natural History (p235)
Visit a 94ft replica of a blue whale, just one of 30 million artifacts on display at the museum.

Top selections: Tuscan kale salad with anchovies and pecorino, crispy Jewish-style artichokes, pappardelle with lamb ragu and thin-crust pizza covered in mozzarella and San Daniele prosciutto. There's a small but original wine list with equally fair prices.

PJ CLARKE'S AMERICAN **$$**

Map p436 (☎212-957-9700; www.pjclarkes.com; 44 W 63rd St, cnr Broadway; burgers $13-16, mains $20-26; ⏰11:30am-2am; [S]1 to 66th St-Lincoln Center) Across the street from Lincoln Center, this spot has red-checked tablecloths, a buttoned-down crowd, friendly bartenders and a solid menu. If you're in a rush, belly up to the bar for a Black Angus burger and a Brooklyn Lager. A raw bar offers fresh Long Island Little Neck and Cherry Stone clams, as well as jumbo shrimp cocktails.

BARNEY GREENGRASS DELI **$$**

Map p436 (☎212-724-4707; www.barneygreengrass.com; 541 Amsterdam Ave, at 86th St; mains $12-22; ⏰8:30am-4pm Tue-Fri, to 5pm Sat & Sun; [S]1 to 86th St) The self-proclaimed 'King of Sturgeon' Barney Greengrass serves up the same heaping dishes of eggs and salty lox, luxuriant caviar, and melt-in-your-mouth chocolate babkas that first made it famous when it opened a century ago. Pop in to fuel up in the morning or for a quick lunch; there are rickety tables set amid the crowded produce aisles.

In addition to an array of Jewish delicacies (seriously, try the smoked sturgeon), you can, of course, get a perfect New York bagel. On weekends, it has fresh garlic *bialys* (a type of chewy, baked roll).

SALUMERIA ROSI PARMACOTTO ITALIAN **$$**

Map p436 (☎212-877-4800; www.salumeriarosi.com; 283 Amsterdam Ave, at 73rd St; mains $14-19; ⏰11am-11pm; [S]1/2/3 to 72nd St) At this intimate little meat-loving nook you can dip into tasting plates that feature cheeses, salami, slow-roasted pork loin, sausages, cured hams and every other piece of the pig you care to imagine. There are other tasty Tuscan-inspired offerings, too, including homemade lasagna, savory leek tart, escarole-anchovy salad, and hand-rolled ricotta and goat's cheese gnocchi.

DOVETAIL MODERN AMERICAN **$$$**

Map p436 (☎212-362-3800; www.dovetailnyc.com; 103 W 77th St, cnr Columbus Ave; tasting menu $58-135; ⏰5:30-10pm Mon-Thu, to 11pm Fri & Sat, 5-10pm Sun; 🌿; [S]A/C, B to 81st St-Museum of Natural History, 1 to 79th St) This Michelin-starred restaurant showcases its Zen-like beauty in both its decor (exposed brick, bare tables) and its delectable seasonal menus. Think striped bass with sunchokes and burgundy truffle, and venison with bacon, golden beets and foraged greens. Each evening there are two seven-course tasting menus: one for omnivores ($135) and one for vegetarians ($108).

On Mondays, chef John Fraser offers a four-course vegetarian tasting menu ($58) that is winning over carnivores with dishes such as plump hen of the woods mushrooms with d'anjou pears and green peppercorns. An excellent wine list (from around $14 per glass) features top vintages from all over the world, with charming anecdotes about some of the vineyards.

LOEB BOATHOUSE AMERICAN **$$$**

Map p436 (☎212-517-2233; www.thecentralparkboathouse.com; Central Park Lake, Central Park, at 74th St; mains $25-36; ⏰restaurant noon-4pm Mon-Fri, 9:30am-4pm Sat & Sun year-round, 6pm-9:30pm daily Apr-Nov; [S]A/C, B to 72nd St, 6 to 77th St) Perched on the northeastern tip of the Central Park Lake, the Loeb Boathouse, with its views of the Midtown skyline in the distance, provides one of New York's most idyllic spots for a meal. That said, what you're paying for is the setting. While the food is generally good (the crab cakes are the standout), we've often found the service to be indifferent.

If you want to experience the location without having to lay out the bucks, a better bet is to hit the adjacent open-air bar, where you can enjoy cocktails on the lake.

DRINKING & NIGHTLIFE

A noted family neighborhood, the Upper West Side isn't exactly the number-one destination for hard-core drinkers. But it has its moments, with some good beer halls, cocktail lounges and wine bars.

EARTH CAFE CAFE

Map p436 (☎917-363-8867; 2850 Broadway, at 97th St; ⏰7am-11pm Mon-Fri, from 8am Sat & Sun; 📶; [S]1/2/3 to 96th St) This charming neighborhood cafe fairly beckons you inside with its cheery, sunny interior of whitewashed brick walls and the scent of fresh-roasted coffee beans lingering in the air. Order an expertly poured almond latte, take a seat beside the oversized world map and watch the city glide past.

MANHATTAN CRICKET CLUB COCKTAIL LOUNGE

Map p436 (☎646-823-9252; www.mccnew-york.com; 226 W 79th St, btwn Amsterdam Ave & Broadway; 🕐6pm-2am; [S]1 to 79th St) Above an Australian bistro (p237), this elegant drinking lounge is modeled on the classy Anglo-Aussie cricket clubs of the early 1900s. Sepia-toned photos of batsmen adorn the gold brocaded walls, while mahogany bookshelves and Chesterfield sofas create a fine setting for quaffing well-made, but pricey, cocktails. It's a guaranteed date pleaser.

JOE'S BAR

Map p436 (☎646-918-6510; joesbarnyc.com; 480 Amsterdam Ave, btwn 83rd & 84th Sts; 🕐4pm-4am Mon-Fri, from noon Sat & Sun; [S]1 to 86th St) Joe's brings a bit of Brooklyn to the Upper West Side, with a changing lineup of craft beers, creative cocktails and moustached barkeeps. Exposed brick walls and wide plank floors give an old-fashioned jauntiness to the place, and the long wooden bar is a fine place to nosh on juicy burgers.

WEST END HALL BEER GARDEN

Map p436 (☎212-662-7200; www.westendhall.com; 2756 Broadway, btwn 105th & 106th Sts; 🕐4pm-1am Mon-Fri, from 11am Sat & Sun; [S]1 to 103rd St) Beer drinkers of the UWS have much to celebrate with the arrival of this grand beer hall that showcases craft brews from around Belgium, Germany, the US and beyond. There are around 20 drafts on rotation along with another 30 bottle choices, most of which go nicely with the meaty menu of sausages, schnitzel, pork sliders and an excellent truffle burger.

The interior sports a mix of communal tables, exposed brick walls and a long wooden bar where you can watch the barkeeps in action (or sports if the game is on). Head to the backyard garden on warm nights.

BARCIBO ENOTECA WINE BAR

Map p436 (☎212-595-2805; www.barciboenoteca.com; 2020 Broadway, cnr 69th St; 🕐4:30-11:30pm Tue-Fri, from 3:30pm Sat-Mon; [S]1/2/3 to 72nd St) Just north of Lincoln Center, this casual chic marble-table spot is ideal for sipping, with a long list of vintages from all over Italy, including 40 different varieties sold by the glass. There is a short menu of small plates and light meals. The staff is knowledgeable; ask for recommendations.

DEAD POET BAR

Map p436 (☎212-595-5670; www.thedeadpoet.com; 450 Amsterdam Ave, btwn 81st & 82nd Sts; 🕐noon-4am; [S]1 to 79th St) This skinny, mahogany-paneled pub has been a neighborhood favorite for over a decade, with a mix of locals and students nursing pints of Guinness. There are cocktails named after dead poets, including a Walt Whitman Long Island iced tea ($11) and a Pablo Neruda spiced rum sangria ($9). Funny, because we always pegged Neruda as a pisco sour kind of guy.

☆ ENTERTAINMENT

NEW YORK CITY BALLET DANCE

Map p436 (☎212-496-0600; www.nycballet.com; David H Koch Theater, Lincoln Center, Columbus Ave, at 62nd St; 👪; [S]1 to 66th St-Lincoln Center) This prestigious ballet company was first directed by renowned Russian-born choreo-grapher George Balanchine back in the 1940s. Today, the company has 90 dancers and is the largest ballet organization in the US, performing 23 weeks a year at Lincoln Center's David H Koch Theater. During the holidays the troop is best known for its annual production of *The Nutcracker*.

Depending on the ballet, ticket prices can range from $30 to $170. Rush tickets for those under age 30 are available for $29. There are also select one-hour Family Saturday performances, appropriate for young audiences ($22 per ticket)

METROPOLITAN OPERA HOUSE OPERA

Map p436 (☎tickets 212-362-6000, tours 212-769-7028; www.metopera.org; Lincoln Center, 64th St, at Columbus Ave; [S]1 to 66th St-Lincoln Center) New York's premier opera company, the Metropolitan Opera is the place to see classics such as *Carmen*, *Madame Butterfly* and *Macbeth*, not to mention Wagner's *Ring Cycle*. The Opera also hosts premieres and revivals of more contemporary works, such as Peter Sellars' *Nixon in China*. The season runs from September to April.

Ticket prices start at $25 and can get close to $500. Note that the box seats can be a bargain, but unless you're in boxes right over the stage, the views are dreadful. Seeing the

LOCAL KNOWLEDGE

NYC'S BEST SPOTS FOR LIVE MUSIC

A jazz and pop music critic who writes for *JazzTimes* and the *New York Times*, Nate Chinen covers the music scene in New York City and beyond. (You can follow him at @natechinen on Twitter.) He gives us a list of his favorite music venues.

Village Vanguard (p154) The Vanguard is run by Lorraine Gordon, an authentic New York character with a real take-no-nonsense attitude. It's the oldest jazz club in the city and is sort of bare bones, but the acoustics are perfect and the vibe is terrific. This is my favorite room for music in the world.

Jazz Standard (p203) One of the city's other great jazz clubs is the Jazz Standard in Midtown. The service is impeccable. The food is great. There's no minimum and it's programmed by Seth Abramson, a guy who really knows his stuff.

Bowery Ballroom (p126) For rock and pop, this is my favorite space. The Bowery Ballroom is a room with history (it was built in the 1920s), and it has really good sound and strong bookings. This is where bigger acts will sometimes do their small shows.

Brooklyn Bowl (p295) Brooklyn Bowl is kind of a weird venue because people are also bowling, but it's where you'll find plenty of groovier gigs, including jam bands. Questlove, the drummer for The Roots, DJs every Thursday night.

Joe's Pub (p99) The room here feels cozy and elegant. Joe's Pub in NoHo has a high concentration of tongue-in-cheek cabaret, and the sensibility is pretty young. (It's attached to the Public Theater, located in NoHo, so there's a performance aspect to it a lot of the time.)

Beacon Theatre The Beacon generally skews to classic rock. But it's a great concert hall, and the renovation was spectacular. It's like a mini–Radio City Music Hall: it doesn't swallow the artist.

stage requires sitting with your head cocked over a handrail – a literal pain in the neck.

For last-minute ticket-buyers there are other deals. You can get bargain-priced standing-room tickets ($20 to $25) starting at 10am on the day of the performance. (You won't see much, but you'll hear everything.) Monday through Friday at noon and Saturdays at 2pm, a number of rush tickets are put on sale for starving artist types – just $25 for a seat. These are available online only. Matinee tickets go on sale four hours before curtain.

Don't miss the gift shop, which is full of operatic bric-a-brac, including Met curtain cufflinks and Rhinemaidens soap. (Seriously.)

For a behind-the-scenes look at the Opera House, tours ($25) are offered weekdays at 3pm and Sundays at 10:30am and 1:30pm during the performance season.

FILM SOCIETY OF LINCOLN CENTER — CINEMA

Map p436 (☎212-875-5610; www.filmlinc.com; [S]1 to 66th St-Lincoln Center) The Film Society is one of New York's cinematic gems, providing an invaluable platform for a wide gamut of documentary, feature, independent, foreign and avant-garde art pictures. Films screen in one of two facilities at Lincoln Center: the **Elinor Bunin Munroe Film Center** (☎212-875-5232; www.filmlinc.com; Lincoln Center, 144 W 65th St; [S]1 to 66 St-Lincoln Center), a more intimate, experimental venue, or the **Walter Reade Theater** (☎212-875-5601; www.filmlinc.com; Lincoln Center, 165 W 65th St; [S]1 to 66th St-Lincoln Center), with wonderfully wide, screening room–style seats.

Every September both venues host the New York Film Festival, featuring plenty of New York and world premieres. In March you'll find the New Directors/New Films series on view. It's highly recommended for cinephiles.

NEW YORK PHILHARMONIC — CLASSICAL MUSIC

Map p436 (☎212-875-5656; www.nyphil.org; Avery Fisher Hall, Lincoln Center, cnr Columbus Ave & 65th St; 👪; [S]1 to 66 St-Lincoln Center) The oldest professional orchestra in the US (dating back to 1842) holds its season every year at Avery Fisher Hall. Directed by Alan Gilbert, the son of two Philharmonic musicians, the orchestra plays a mix of classics (Tchaikovsky, Mahler, Haydn) and contemporary works, as well as concerts geared towards children.

Tickets run in the $29 to $125 range. If you're on a budget, check out its open rehearsals held several times a month (starting at 9:45am) on the day of the concert for only $20. In addition, students with a valid school ID can pick up rush tickets for $16 up to 10 days before an event.

SYMPHONY SPACE LIVE MUSIC

Map p436 (☎212-864-5400; www.symphonyspace.org; 2537 Broadway, btwn 94th & 95th Sts; [S]1/2/3 to 96th St) Symphony Space is a multidisciplinary gem supported by the local community. It often hosts three-day series that are dedicated to one musician, and has an affinity for world music, theater, film, dance and literature (with appearances by acclaimed writers).

MERKIN CONCERT HALL CLASSICAL MUSIC

Map p436 (☎212-501-3330; www.kaufman-center.org/mch; 129 W 67th St, btwn Amsterdam Ave & Broadway; [S]1 to 66th St-Lincoln Center) Just north of Lincoln Center, this 450-seat hall, part of the Kaufman Center, is one of the city's more intimate venues for classical music, as well as jazz, world music and pop. The hall hosts Tuesday matinees (a deal at $19) that highlight emerging classical solo artists.

BEACON THEATRE LIVE MUSIC

Map p436 (☎212-465-6500; www.beacontheatre.com; 2124 Broadway, btwn 74th & 75th Sts; [S]1/2/3 to 72nd St) This historic 1929 theater is a perfect medium-size venue with 2600 seats (not a terrible one in the house) and a constant flow of popular acts from Nick Cave to Bryan Adams. A recent restoration has left the gilded interiors – a mix of Greek, Roman, Renaissance and rococo design elements – totally sparkling.

SMOKE JAZZ

Map p436 (☎212-864-6662; www.smokejazz.com; 2751 Broadway, btwn 105th & 106th Sts; ⏲5:30pm-3am Mon-Sat, 11am-3am Sun; [S]1 to 103rd St) This swank but laid-back lounge – with good stage views from plush sofas – brings out old-timers and local faves, such as George Coleman and Wynton Marsalis. Most nights there's a $10 cover, plus a $20 to $30 food and drink minimum. On Sundays there's a soulful jazz brunch from 11am to 4pm. Purchase tickets online for weekend shows. Late nights, you can stop by for free shows (no cover but $20 minimum spend applies) that kick off around 11:30pm.

CLEOPATRA'S NEEDLE CLUB

Map p436 (☎212-769-6969; www.cleopatrasneedleny.com; 2485 Broadway, btwn 92nd & 93rd Sts; ⏲3:30pm-late; [S]1/2/3 to 96th St) Named after an Egyptian obelisk that resides in Central Park, this somewhat dated venue is small and narrow like its namesake. There's no cover, but there's a $10 minimum spend. Come early and you can enjoy happy hour (3:30pm to 7pm daily; Sunday until 6pm), when select cocktails are half-price. Be prepared to stay late: Cleopatra's is famous for late-night jam sessions that hit their peak after midnight.

SHOPPING

The Upper West Side is chain-store central, so local flavor can be hard to find. That said, there are some good shopping stops.

GREENFLEA MARKET

Map p436 (☎212-239-3025; www.greenfleamarkets.com; 100 W 77th St, near Columbus Ave; ⏲10am-5:30pm Sun; [S]B, C to 81st St-Museum of Natural History, 1 to 79th St) One of the oldest open-air shopping spots in the city, browsing this friendly, well-stocked flea market is a perfect activity for a lazy Upper West Side Sunday morning. You'll find a little bit of everything here, including vintage and contemporary furnishings, antique maps, custom eyewear, hand-woven scarves, handmade jewelry and so much more. The market is also open on occasional Saturdays in warm months; call ahead to check.

SHISHI CLOTHING

Map p436 (☎646-692-4510; shishiboutique.com; 2488 Broadway, btwn 92nd & 93rd Sts; ⏲11am-8pm Mon-Sat, to 7pm Sun; [S]1/2/3 to 96th St) A welcome addition to a fashion-challenged hood, Shishi is a delightful boutique stocking an ever-changing selection of stylish but affordable apparel. Recent finds include felt hats, elegant sweaters, eye-catching jewelry and soft flannels. It's a fun place to browse – the chandelier and vintage nude prints on the wall remind you this is no TJ Maxx. The friendly young staff offer helpful guidance.

UNIQUE BOUTIQUE VINTAGE

Map p436 (487 Columbus Ave, btwn 83rd & 84th Sts; ⏲10am-8pm; [S]B, C to 86th St) A first-rate vintage store on the Upper West Side is something of a rarity, so it's worth stopping in if you need to freshen up your wardrobe. The prices are excellent, though the sheer quantity of clothing means you'll have to dig. Aside from designer labels and friendly staff, you'll also find an extensive collection of CDs and books (hardbacks for a buck).

MAGPIE CRAFTS

Map p436 (☎646-998-3002; magpienewyork.com; 488 Amsterdam Ave, btwn 83rd & 84th Sts; 🕐11am-7pm Tue-Sat, to 6pm Sun; [S]1 to 86th St) 🍃 When you're short of gift ideas, stop in this charming little outpost, where you'll find a wide range of ecofriendly objects. Elegant stationery, beeswax candles, hand-painted mugs, organic cotton scarves, recycled resin necklaces, hand-dyed felt journals and wooden earth puzzles are a few things that may catch your eye. Most products are fair-trade, made of sustainable materials or are locally designed and made.

DSW SHOES

Map p436 (☎917-746-9422; www.dsw.com; 2220 Broadway, btwn 79th & 80th Sts; 🕐10am-9pm Mon-Sat, 11am-7pm Sun; [S]1 to 79th St) Shoe-lovers pack this multi-story emporium, which offers some of the best deals on footwear in the city...aside from its other locations around town, that is. All the major labels are here – Steve Madden, Nine West, Cole Haan, UGG, Converse, Clarks – plus a few luxury brands, including Miu Miu, Prada and Salvatore Ferragamo. All are sold at discounted – sometimes heavily – prices.

WEST SIDE KIDS TOYS

Map p436 (☎212-496-7282; www.westsidekidsnyc.com; 498 Amsterdam Ave; 🕐10am-7pm Mon-Sat, 11am-6pm Sun; [S]1 to 86th St) A great place to pick up a gift for that little someone special, no matter their age. Stocks lots of hands-on activities and fun but educational games, as well as puzzles, mini musical instruments, science kits (carnivorous creations? indeed), magic sets, snap circuits, old-fashioned wooden trains and building kits.

BARNEYS DEPARTMENT STORE

Map p436 (☎646-335-0978; www.barneys.com; 2151 Broadway; 🕐10am-8pm Mon-Fri, to 7pm Sat, 11am-7pm Sun; [S]1/2/3 to 72nd St) An anchor of fashion in NYC, Barneys has a well-curated collection of women's apparel and accessories from luxury brands such as Alexander Wang, Stella McCartney and Band of Outsiders. Prices are high so look for sales.

CENTURY 21 DEPARTMENT STORE

Map p436 (☎212-518-2121; www.c21stores.com; 1972 Broadway, btwn 66th & 67th Sts; 🕐10am-10pm Mon-Sat, 11am-8pm Sun; [S]1 to 66th St-Lincoln Center) Exceedingly popular with fashionable locals and foreign travelers, the Century 21 chain is a bounty of season-old brand name and designer labels sold at steeply discounted prices. Featuring everything from Missoni to Marc Jacobs, prices may sometimes seem high, but compared to retail, they're a steal.

WESTSIDER BOOKS BOOKS

Map p436 (☎212-362-0706; www.westsiderbooks.com; 2246 Broadway, btwn 80th & 81st Sts; 🕐10am-10pm; [S]1 to 79th St) This great little shop is packed to the gills with rare and used books, including a good selection of fiction and illustrated tomes. There are first editions and a smattering of vintage vinyl.

SPORTS & ACTIVITIES

LOEB BOATHOUSE KAYAKING, CYCLING

Map p436 (☎212-517-2233; www.thecentralparkboathouse.com; Central Park, btwn 74th & 75th Sts; boating per hr $15, bike rental per hr $9-15; 🕐10am-6pm Apr-Nov; 👪; [S]B, C to 72nd St, 6 to 77th St) Central Park's boathouse has a fleet of 100 rowboats as well as a Venetian-style gondola that seats up to six if you'd rather someone else do the paddling. Bicycles are also available, weather permitting. Rentals require ID and a credit card, and helmets are included.

BIKE & ROLL CYCLING

Map p436 (☎212-260-0400; www.bikeandroll.com/newyork; Columbus Circle, at Central Park West; per 2hr/half-day/full day from $28/39/44; 🕐8am-10pm; 👪; [S]A/C, B/D, 1/2 to 59th St-Columbus Circle) At the southwestern entrance to the park, a small pop-up kiosk dispenses beach cruisers and 10-speed bicycles for rides around Central Park. It also has child seats and tandem bikes.

CHARLES A DANA DISCOVERY CENTER FISHING

Map p436 (☎212-860-1370; www.centralparknyc.org; Central Park, at 110th St, btwn Fifth & Lenox Aves; 🕐10am-3pm Mon-Sat, to 1pm Sun mid-

Apr–mid-Oct; 👪; [S] 2/3 to Central Park North) [FREE] Get your bass on! You can borrow a rod and bait (corn kernels) for free catch-and-release fishing at the Harlem Meer from April through October. Photo ID is required. There are also free 'Birding Basics for Families' tours departing from here from March to May and September to November at 10am to 11am on Sunday.

MANHATTAN COMMUNITY BOATHOUSE — BOATING

Map p436 (www.manhattancommunityboathouse.org; W 72nd St; ⌚10am-5pm Sat & Sun Jun-early Sep; [S] 1/2/3 to 72nd St) [FREE] This volunteer-run boathouse offers free kayaking on summer weekends. If you want more than a 20-minute paddle, check out the boathouse downtown off N Moore St (www.downtownboathouse.org/pier26), which offers weekend trips out on the Hudson.

BELVEDERE CASTLE — BIRDWATCHING

Map p436 (☎212-772-0288; Central Park, at 79th St; ⌚10am-5pm; 👪; [S] 1/2/3, B, C to 72nd St) [FREE] For a DIY birding expedition with kids, borrow a 'Discovery Kit' at Belvedere Castle in Central Park. It comes with binoculars, a bird book, colored pencils and paper – a perfect way to get the kids excited about birds. Picture ID required.

TOGA BIKE SHOP — CYCLING

Map p436 (☎212-799-9625; www.togabikes.com; 110 West End Ave, btwn 64th & 65th Sts; rentals per 24hr $35-75; ⌚11am-7pm Mon-Fri, 10am-6pm Sat, 11am-6pm Sun; [S] 1 to 66th St-Lincoln Center) This friendly, long-standing bike shop is conveniently located between Central Park and the Hudson River bike path. Rental prices include a helmet.

FIVE BOROUGH BICYCLE CLUB — CYCLING

Map p436 (☎347-688-2925; www.5bbc.org) For a $25 annual fee, you can participate in this local club's myriad day rides as well as long-haul rides. Check the website for details of upcoming rides and meeting locations.

WOLLMAN SKATING RINK — SKATING

Map p436 (☎212-439-6900; www.wollmanskatingrink.com; Central Park, btwn 62nd & 63rd Sts; adult Mon-Thu $11, Fri-Sun $18, child $6, skate rentals $8, lock rental $5, spectator fee $5; ⌚10am-2:30pm Mon & Tue, to 10pm Wed-Sat, to 9pm Sun Nov-Mar; 👪; [S] F to 57 St, N/Q/R to 5th Ave-59th St) Larger than the Rockefeller Center skating rink, and allowing all-day skating, this rink is at the southeastern edge of Central Park and offers nice views. Cash only.

CENTRAL PARK TENNIS CENTER — TENNIS

Map p436 (☎212-316-0800; www.centralparktenniscenter.com; Central Park, btwn 94th & 96th Sts, enter at 96th St & Central Park West; ⌚6:30am-dusk Apr-Oct or Nov; [S] B, C to 96th St) This daylight-hours-only facility has 26 clay courts for public use and four hard courts for lessons. You can buy single-play tickets ($15) here, and can reserve a court if you pick up a $15 permit at the **Arsenal** (☎212-360-8131; www.nycgovparks.org; Central Park, at 5th Ave & E 64th St; ⌚9am-5pm Mon-Fri; [S] N/R/Q to 5th Ave-59th St). The least busy times are roughly from noon to 4pm on weekdays.

Harlem & Upper Manhattan

MORNINGSIDE HEIGHTS | HARLEM | EAST HARLEM | HAMILTON HEIGHTS & SUGAR HILL | WASHINGTON HEIGHTS & INWOOD | WEST HARLEM | INWOOD | HAMILTON HEIGHTS

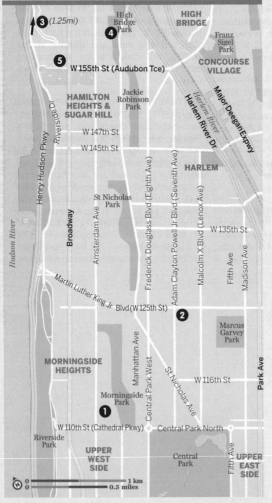

Top Five

1 Conceding that size *does* matter at the gloriously epic yet still-unfinished **Cathedral Church of St John the Divine** (p248), the largest place of worship in the US.

2 Seeing the world through African American eyes at the small but savvy **Studio Museum in Harlem** (p250).

3 Escaping the rat race and modernity at the **Cloisters Museum & Gardens** (p253), an architectural mishmash of monasteries housing medieval art.

4 Joining free Sunday jazz jams at the home of New York City's 'host with the most', **Marjorie Eliot** (p262).

5 Spending quiet time with Goya, El Greco, Velázquez and friends at the underrated **Hispanic Society of America Museum & Library** (p256).

For more detail of this area see Map p438

Explore

The top half of Manhattan is a lot of territory to cover, with numerous points of interest a distance away from each other. So pick a neighborhood (or better yet, a couple of contiguous neighborhoods) and stick to them. If you like your cities to feel a little bit country, then start with Inwood – which has invigorating parks and an extravagant museum – and then work your way down the western side to the gargantuan Cathedral Church of St John the Divine. Prefer an urban vibe? Then it's all about Harlem and Hamilton Heights, a bastion of African American culture jammed with swinging bars, soul-stirring churches and a few architectural treats.

It's worth noting that many of Harlem's major avenues have been renamed in honor of prominent African Americans; however, many locals still call the streets by their original names. Hence, Malcolm X Blvd is still frequently referred to as Lenox Ave.

Local Life

➡**Get your chic on** When Harlem peeps go out on the town, they usually dress to impress. Hit Atmos (p262) for killer kicks, Flamekeepers Hat Club (p262) for classic men's caps and hats, and in-the-know Trunk Show Designer Consignment (p262) for high-end threads at pre-loved prices.

➡**Tune in** For off-the-beaten-path musical events, nothing beats Morningside Heights. Riverside Church (p251), the Cathedral Church of St John the Divine (p248) and Columbia University (p251) all host regular concerts.

➡**Take a hike** New Yorkers jogging, hiking and biking is what you'll find at Inwood Hill Park (p256) on any given sunny day. Tie those laces and get moving.

Getting There & Away

➡**Subway** Harlem's main drag – 125th St – is just one subway stop from the 59th St–Columbus Circle Station in Midtown on the A and D trains. Other areas of Harlem and northern Manhattan can be reached on the A/C, B/D, 1/2/3 and 4/5/6 trains.

➡**Bus** Dozens of buses ply the north–south route between upper and lower Manhattan along all the major avenues. The M10 bus provides a scenic trip along the western side of Central Park into Harlem. The M100 and the M101 run east to west along 125th St.

Lonely Planet's Top Tip

Manhattan's uptown communities tend to be locally minded, with bars, restaurants and shops catering to a neighborhood scene. These tend to be sleepiest on weekday mornings and liveliest in the evenings and on weekends.

To make the most of your visit, hit one of the museums or other historic sights in the afternoon, then stick around for dinner when these areas come to life.

HARLEM & UPPER MANHATTAN

Best Places to Eat

➡ Red Rooster (p259)
➡ Dinosaur Bar-B-Que (p259)
➡ BLVD Bistro (p259)
➡ Charles' Pan-Fried Chicken (p260)

For reviews, see p258 ➡

Best Places to Drink

➡ Ginny's Supper Club (p260)
➡ Bier International (p261)
➡ Harlem Public (p260)
➡ Maison Harlem (p259)

For reviews, see p260 ➡

Best Places for Live Jazz

➡ Marjorie Eliot's Parlor Jazz (p262)
➡ Apollo Theater (p253)
➡ Minton's (p262)

For reviews, see p262 ➡

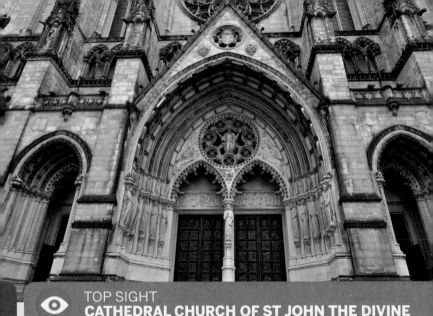

CATHEDRAL CHURCH OF ST JOHN THE DIVINE

The largest place of worship in America has yet to be completed – and probably won't be any time soon. But this glorious Episcopal cathedral nonetheless commands attention with its ornate Gothic-style facade, booming vintage organ and extravagantly scaled nave – twice as wide as London's Westminster Abbey.

An Unfinished History

The first cornerstone for the Cathedral was laid on St John's Day in 1892, though construction was hardly smooth. Engineers had to dig 70ft in order to find bedrock to which they could anchor the building. Architects died or were fired, and, in 1911, the initial Romanesque design was exchanged for a bigger, Gothic-inspired plan.

Depleted funds has seen construction regularly halted. The north tower remains unbuilt, and a 'temporary' domed roof, constructed out of terra-cotta tile in 1909, still shelters the Crossing. A raging fire in 2001 caused significant damage, including to the north transept, which is yet to be rebuilt.

If it is ever completed, the 601ft-long Cathedral will rank as the world's third-largest church, behind Rome's St Peter's Basilica and Côte d'Ivoire's Basilica of Our Lady of Peace at Yamoussoukro.

The Portal Sculptures

Framing the western entrance are two rows of sculptures carved in the 1980s and '90s by British artist Simon Verity. On the central pillar stands St John the Divine himself, author of the *Book of Revelation*.

DON'T MISS

→ Portal sculptures
→ Great Rose Window
→ Great Organ
→ Keith Haring Triptych

PRACTICALITIES

→ Map p438
→ ☏ tours 212-316-7540
→ www.stjohndivine.org
→ 1047 Amsterdam Ave, at W 112th St, Morning-side Heights
→ suggested donation $10, highlights tour $12, vertical tour $20
→ ⊙7:30am-6pm, highlights tour 11am & 2pm Mon, 11am & 1pm Tue-Sat, 1pm on selected Sun, vertical tour noon Wed & Fri, noon & 2pm Sat
→ Ⓢ B, C, 1 to 110th St-Cathedral Pkwy

(Note the Four Horsemen of the Apocalypse under his feet.) Themes of devastation are rife, but most unnerving is the statue of Jeremiah (third on the right), which stands on a base that shows the New York City skyline – Twin Towers included – being destroyed.

The Nave

Illuminated by the Great Rose Window (America's largest stained-glass window), the nave is lined with two magisterial sets of 17th-century tapestries. The Barberini Tapestries depict scenes from Christ's life, while the Mortlake Tapestries, based on cartoons by Raphael, show the Acts of the Apostles.

Great Organ

One of the most powerful organs in the world, the Great Organ was originally installed in 1911, then enlarged and rebuilt in 1952. It contains 8500 pipes arranged in 141 ranks. The 2001 fire damaged the instrument, but a careful five-year restoration brought it back.

Keith Haring Triptych

Behind the choir is the white-gold and bronze triptych 'Life of Christ,' carved by '80s pop artist Keith Haring (1958–90). It's one of the last works of art he produced prior to succumbing to an AIDS-related illness aged 31.

VISITING THE CATHEDRAL

One-hour highlight tours are offered at 11am and 2pm Monday, 11am and 1pm Tuesday to Saturday, and at 1pm on select Sundays. One-hour vertical tours, which take you on a steep climb to the top of the Cathedral (bring your own flashlight), are at noon Wednesday and Friday, as well as at noon and 2pm Saturday. Two services worth seeing are the Blessing of the Animals, a pilgrimage for pet owners held on the first Sunday of October, and the Blessing of the Bikes, held on a Saturday in mid- to late April, when local riders tool in on everything from sleek 10-speeds to clunky cruisers.

CIVIL RIGHTS

The Cathedral was involved in civil-rights issues back in the early 1950s and has regularly worked with members of the community on issues of inequity. It is also a long-running cultural outpost, hosting holiday concerts, lectures and exhibits, and it has been the site of memorial services for many famous New Yorkers, including trumpeter Louis Armstrong and artist Keith Haring.

TOP SIGHT
STUDIO MUSEUM IN HARLEM

This small, cultural treasure has been showcasing African American artists for more than four decades. Yet the museum is not just another art display center. It's an important point of connection for Harlem cultural figures of all stripes, who arrive to check out a rotating selection of exhibitions, attend film screenings or sign up for gallery talks.

From Loft to Museum

Founded in 1968, the museum originally came to life in a small loft space off 125th St that was sandwiched between a couple of garment factories and a supermarket. But it quickly became known for its thoughtful, contemporary-minded exhibits and vibrant event programming, which included concerts, poetry readings and lectures. Roughly a dozen years after its establishment, it moved to its present location, a renovated bank building that offered more room for exhibits, archives and its growing permanent collection.

Adjacent to the lobby is the museum's well-stocked gift shop, where you can pick up everything from art tomes and exhibition catalogs, to African jewelry and 'Black is Beautiful' T-shirts.

Collecting African American Artists

The permanent collection is small (less than 2000 objects), but it is rich. The Studio Museum has been an important patron to African American artists and the collection features work by more than 400 of them. This includes important pieces by painter Jacob Lawrence, photographer Gordon Parks and collagist Romare Bearden – all of whom are represented in major museum collections in the US.

In addition, its photography holdings include an extensive archive of work by James VanDerZee (1886–1983), an unparalleled chronicler of early-20th-century Harlem life. He shot portraits of prominent entertainers and black nationalists, and continued to take pictures well into his nineties. One well-known snap shows Jean-Michel Basquiat, the '80s graffiti artist and painter, sitting pensively with a Siamese cat on his lap.

'African American Flag'

Look up on your way in. One of the museum's most iconic works hangs right outside the front door: David Hammons' 1990 piece *African-American Flag*. Replacing the red, white and blue of the stars and stripes with the red, green and black of the pan-African flag, it's a sly comment on the country's African American presence.

Artists in Residence

The museum's long-running artist-in-residence program has provided crucial support to a long list of well-known creatives, including conceptualist David Hammons, figurative painter Mickalene Thomas and portraitist Kehinde Wiley. The residents' works can often be found on display in the basement gallery or in one of the small display areas upstairs. The museum also runs regular special events, from themed discussions to music performances – check the website.

DON'T MISS

- The African American Flag
- Rotating art exhibitions
- Photography by James VanDerZee
- The well-stocked gift shop

PRACTICALITIES

- Map p438
- ☎212-864-4500
- www.studiomuseum.org
- 144 W 125th St, at Adam Clayton Powell Jr Blvd, Harlem
- suggested donation $7, Sun free
- 🕐noon-9pm Thu & Fri, 10am-6pm Sat, noon-6pm Sun
- [S]2/3 to 125th St

⊙ SIGHTS

⊙ Morningside Heights

This neighborhood (between 110th and 125th Sts on the far west side) serves as a community for Columbia University, which occupies the neighborhood's southern half.

★CATHEDRAL CHURCH OF ST JOHN THE DIVINE   CHURCH
See p248.

COLUMBIA UNIVERSITY   UNIVERSITY
Map p438 (www.columbia.edu; Broadway, at 116th St, Morningside Heights; ⓢ1 to 116th St-Columbia University) Founded in 1754 as King's College downtown, the oldest university in New York is now one of the world's premiere research institutions. It moved to its current location (the site of a former asylum) in 1897, where its gated campus now channels a New England vibe and offers plenty of cultural happenings.

The principal point of interest is the main courtyard (located on College Walk at the level of 116th St), which is surrounded by various Italian Renaissance–style structures. Here, you'll find the statue of the open-armed *Alma Mater* seated before the Low Memorial Library. On the southern end of College Walk, on the corner of Amsterdam Ave, is Hamilton Hall, a key site during the infamous student uprising of 1968.

Your best bet for navigating the grounds is to download the self-guided audio tour by architectural historian Andrew Dolkart from the Columbia University website at www.columbia.edu/content/self-guided-walking-tour.html.

GENERAL ULYSSES S GRANT NATIONAL MEMORIAL   MEMORIAL
Map p438 (☏212-666-1640; www.nps.gov/gegr; Riverside Dr, at 122nd St, Morningside Heights; ⊙10am-5pm Wed-Sun; ⓢ1 to 125th St) FREE Popularly known as Grant's Tomb ('Who's buried in Grant's Tomb?' 'Who?' 'Grant, stupid!' goes a classic joke), this landmark holds the remains of Civil War hero and 18th president Ulysses S Grant and his wife, Julia. Completed in 1897 – 12 years after his death – the imposing granite structure is the largest mausoleum in America.

Seventeen Gaudi-inspired mosaic benches, designed by Chilean artist Pedro Silva in the 1970s, surround the mausoleum. It's a downright hallucinatory installation – and a good spot to contemplate the musings of the late, great comedian George Carlin, who was known to light up here back in the day.

RIVERSIDE CHURCH   CHURCH
Map p438 (☏212-870-6700; www.theriverside-churchny.org; 490 Riverside Dr, at 120th St, Morningside Heights; ⊙8am-5pm; ⓢ1 to 116th St) This imposing, neo-Gothic beauty was built by the Rockefeller family in 1930. While the sparseness of the interior evokes an Italian Gothic style, the stained-glass windows in the narthex are actually Flemish, dating back to the 16th century. The church rings its 74 carillon bells with an extraordinary 20-ton bass bell (the world's largest) at 10:30am, 12:30pm and 3pm on Sunday. Interdenominational services are held at 10:45am on Sunday, with free tours offered immediately after (at 12:30pm).

The church also hosts high-quality events, including concerts (see the website).

⊙ Harlem

Harlem is a place that is soaked in history – and then some. And while it remains one of the country's most fabled centers of African American life, it – like everywhere else in New York – is changing. National chains now blanket 125th St, Harlem's historic main drag. Of-the-moment eateries, luxury condos and young professionals (of all creeds and races) have also moved in. But the neighborhood nonetheless retains its trademark charm, from sidewalk vendors dispensing Malcolm X T-shirts to end-of-the-world types preaching hellfire.

★STUDIO MUSEUM IN HARLEM   MUSEUM
See opposite.

MALCOLM SHABAZZ HARLEM MARKET   MARKET
Map p438 (52 W 116th St, btwn Malcolm X Blvd & Fifth Ave, Harlem; ⊙10am-9pm; ⊕; ⓢ2/3 to 116th St) FREE This semi-enclosed market does a brisk trade in just about everything: leather goods, crafts, textiles, oils, drums, clothing, sculptures and a stupendous array of assorted African everything. It's also an excellent spot to get your hair braided. The market is run by the Malcolm Shabazz Mosque, the former pulpit of slain Muslim orator Malcolm X.

SCHOMBURG CENTER FOR RESEARCH IN BLACK CULTURE CULTURAL CENTER

Map p438 (☎917-275-6975; www.nypl.org/locations/schomburg; 515 Malcolm X Blvd, at 135th St, Harlem; ⏰10am-6pm Mon & Thu-Sat, to 8pm Tue & Wed; [S]2/3 to 135th St) [FREE] The nation's largest collection of documents, rare books and photographs relating to the African American experience resides at this scholarly center run by the New York Public Library. It's named after Arthur Schomburg, a black Puerto Rican activist who amassed a singular collection of manuscripts, slave narratives and other important artifacts. Regular exhibitions, lectures and film screenings are held on-site.

CRACK IS WACK PLAYGROUND PARK

Map p438 (www.nycgovparks.org/parks/M208E; Harlem River Park, E 127th St & 2 Ave; ⏰dawn-dusk; [S]4/5/6 to 125th St) [FREE] This far-flung playground is named for the bright orange 'Crack is Wack' mural painted by pop graffiti artist Keith Haring on a handball court back in October 1986. Restored and now visible through wire fencing, the work harkens back to a time when Haring's creations covered walls all over New York.

⊙ East Harlem

The working-class district of East Harlem above 96th St and east of Fifth Ave, known colloquially as Spanish Harlem or El Barrio, has been home to one of the city's biggest Puerto Rican communities since the 1950s. Today, it remains a vibrant Latino neighborhood, infused with a mix of Puerto Rican, Dominican, Mexican and South American immigrants.

EL MUSEO DEL BARRIO MUSEUM

Map p438 (☎212-831-7272; www.elmuseo.org; 1230 Fifth Ave, btwn 104th & 105th Sts, East Harlem; suggested donation adult/child $9/free; ⏰11am-6pm Tue-Sat; 📶; [S]6 to 103rd St) *Bienvenido* to one of New York's premiere Latino institutions, whose thoughtful, rotating exhibitions span all media, from painting and photography to video and site-specific installations. The shows often showcase El Museo's strong permanent collection, which includes pre-Columbian artifacts, traditional folk works and a stellar array of postwar art made by a wide gamut of Latino and Latin American artists.

The museum includes pieces by well-known historical figures like Chilean surrealist Roberto Matta and established contemporary artists such as Félix González-Torres and Pepón Osorio.

⊙ Hamilton Heights & Sugar Hill

Basically the northwestern extension of Harlem, Hamilton Heights takes its name from the former estate of Alexander Hamilton, one of the drafters of the US Constitution.

During the Harlem Renaissance, the northern edge of the neighborhood was dubbed 'Sugar Hill' as it was here that the Harlem elite came to live the 'sweet life.' This area is also tangentially linked to hip-hop history: Sugarhill Gang (whose single 'Rapper's Delight' became the first hip-hop tune to become a mainstream hit) takes its name from here, their home turf.

HAMILTON GRANGE HISTORIC BUILDING

Map p438 (☎646-548-2310; www.nps.gov/hagr; St Nicholas Park, at 141st St; ⏰9am-5pm Wed-Sun, guided tours 10am, 11am, 2pm & 4pm; [S]A/C, B/D to 145th St) [FREE] This Federal-style retreat belonged to US founding father Alexander Hamilton, who owned a 32-acre country estate here in the early 1800s. Unfortunately, Hamilton was only able to enjoy his abode for two short years, his life cut short in a fatal duel with political rival Aaron Burr. Moved from Convent Ave to its present location, the building is especially interesting to history and architecture buffs.

STRIVERS' ROW NEIGHBORHOOD

Map p438 (W 138th & W 139th Sts, btwn Frederick Douglass & Adam Clayton Powell Jr Blvds, Harlem; [S]B, C to 135th St) Also known as the St Nicholas Historic District, these streets were the darling of Harlem's elite in the 1920s. Its graceful row houses and apartments, many of which date back to the 1890s, were designed by three of the era's most celebrated architects: James Brown Lord, Bruce Price and Stanford White.

White's row of elegant Italianate creations along the northern side of W 139th St are arguably the most beautiful. Keep your eyes peeled for alleyway signs advising visitors to 'walk your horses.'

TOP SIGHT APOLLO THEATER

More than simply historic, Harlem's Apollo Theater is a swinging testament to Harlem's astounding musical legacy. Originally a whites-only burlesque joint, the neoclassical venue reinvented itself in 1934 with 'Jazz à la Carte.' Soon after, virtually every major black artist was crooning here, from Duke Ellington and Louis Armstrong to Count Bassie and Billie Holiday.

The revamped Apollo also introduced the legendary 'Amateur Night,' its long list of then-unknown competitors including Ella Fitzgerald, Gladys Night, Jimi Hendrix, the Jackson 5 and Lauryn Hill. The event still kicks on every Wednesday night, its wild and ruthless crowd as fun to watch as tomorrow's next big things. Beyond Amateur Night is a thriving, year-round program of music, dance, master classes and special events, with shows spanning anything from Cuban salsa tributes to Afro-Latin jazz suites.

While guided tours of the interior are only available for groups of 20 or more with advance reservation, individuals are welcome to join group tours based on availability. Take the tour and expect to see a fragment of the 'Tree of Hope,' a long-gone elm performers would rub for good luck before taking to the stage.

DON'T MISS

- Amateur Night
- The iconic theater marquee
- Guided tours
- Tree of Hope

PRACTICALITIES

- Map p438
- ☎212-531-5300, tours 212-531-5337
- www.apollotheater.org
- 253 W 125th St, btwn Frederick Douglass & Adam Clayton Powell Jr Blvds, Harlem
- tickets from $15
- [S]A/C, B/D to 125th St

HAMILTON HEIGHTS HISTORIC DISTRICT NEIGHBORHOOD
Map p438 (Convent Ave & Hamilton Tce, btwn 141th & 145th Sts, Hamilton Heights; [S]A/C, B/D to 145th St) Two parallel streets in Hamilton Heights – Convent Ave and Hamilton Tce – contain a landmark stretch of historic limestone and brownstone townhouses from the period between 1866 and 1931. Film fans may recognize the turreted building on the southeastern corner of Convent and 144st Aves from *The Royal Tenenbaums*.

Washington Heights & Inwood

Located at Manhattan's narrow, northern tip (above 155th St), Washington Heights takes its name from the first president of the US, who set up a Continental Army fort here during the Revolutionary War. For much of the 20th century, it has been a bastion of Dominican life – though it has recently seen an influx of downtown hipsters in search of affordable rent.

Inwood, at Manhattan's northern tip (from about 175th St), is a chilled-out residential zone with an almost suburban vibe.

CLOISTERS MUSEUM & GARDENS MUSEUM
Map p438 (www.metmuseum.org/cloisters; Fort Tryon Park; suggested donation adult/child $25/free; ⏰10am-5pm; [S]A to 190th St) On a hilltop overlooking the Hudson River, the Cloisters is a curious architectural jigsaw, its many parts made up of various European monasteries and other historic buildings. Built in the 1930s to house the Metropolitan Museum's medieval treasures, its frescoes, tapestries and paintings are set in galleries that sit around a romantic courtyard, connected by grand archways and topped with Moorish terra-cotta roofs. Among its many rare treasures is the the beguiling 16th-century tapestry series *The Hunt of the Unicorn*.

Also worth seeking out is the remarkably well-preserved 15th-century Annunciation Triptych (Merode Altarpiece). Then there's the stunning 12th-century Saint-Guilhem cloister and the Bonnefant cloister, the latter featuring plants used in medieval medicine, magic, ceremony and the arts.

ROBERT MIX / SHUTTERSTOCK ©

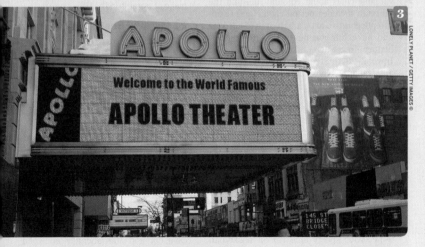

3

LONELY PLANET / GETTY IMAGES ©

...ownstones
...a walk along streets lined with classic
...nstone townhouses.

2. Harlem streets
Explore the soulful streets of Harlem,
the center of the city's African American
culture.

3. Apollo Theater (p253)
Don't miss 'Amateur Night' at the theater
where Ella Fitzgerald made her singing
debut.

HISPANIC SOCIETY OF AMERICA MUSEUM & LIBRARY MUSEUM

Map p438 (☎212-926-2234; www.hispanicsociety.org; Broadway, btwn 155th & 156th Sts, Washington Heights; ⌚10am-4:30pm Tue-Sun; [S]1 to 157th St) [FREE] Housed in the beaux-arts structure that naturalist John James Audubon once called home, this treasure contains the largest collection of 19th-century Spanish art and manuscripts outside of Spain – including paintings by El Greco, Goya and Velázquez. While Anna Hyatt Huntington's majestic sculpture of *El Cid* dominates the exterior courtyard, Goya's 1797 masterpiece *The Duchess of Alba* takes pride of place indoors. Another highlight is Joaquin Sorolla y Bastidas' show-stopping *Vision of Spain;* 14 giant paintings depicting Spain's geographic and cultural diversity.

The center's library features no less than 600,000 rare books, manuscripts and modern publications relating to the art, history and culture of Spain, Portugal, Latin America and the Philippines.

DYCKMAN FARMHOUSE MUSEUM MUSEUM

(☎212-304-9422; www.dyckmanfarmhouse.org; 4881 Broadway, at 204th St, Inwood; donation suggested; ⌚11am-4pm Thu-Sat, to 3pm Sun; [S]A to Inwood-207th St) Built in 1784 on a 28-acre farm, the Dyckman House is Manhattan's lone surviving Dutch farmhouse. Excavations of the property have turned up valuable clues about colonial life, and the museum includes period rooms and furniture, decorative arts, a half-acre of gardens and an exhibition on the neighborhood's history. To get here, take the subway to the Inwood–207th St station (not Dyckman St) and walk one block south.

INWOOD HILL PARK PARK

(www.nycgovparks.org/parks/inwoodhillpark; Dyckman St, at the Hudson River; [S]A to Inwood-207th St) This 196-acre oasis contains the last natural forest and salt marsh in Manhattan. It's a cool escape in summer and a great place to explore any time, as you'll find hilly paths for hiking and mellow, grassy patches and benches for quiet contemplation. It's so bucolic, in fact, that the treetops serve as frequent nesting sites for bald eagles.

Let your sporty side rip on basketball courts or soccer and football fields, or pack some produce and join locals who barbecue at designated grills on summer weekends.

Local Life
Harlem Soul

Harlem: the neighborhood where Cab Calloway crooned; where Ralph Ellison penned his epic novel, *Invisible Man,* on truth and intolerance; where acclaimed artist Romare Bearden pieced together his first collages. Simultaneously vibrant and effusive, brooding and melancholy, Harlem is the deepest recess of New York's soul.

1 Tom's Restaurant

Rev your engine with a cuppa joe and a side of nostalgia at Greek-American Tom's Restaurant (p259). Distinguished by its red-neon marquee, the diner's exterior stood in for the fictional Monk's Café in the TV comedy *Seinfeld.* The place is also immortalized in Suzanne Vega's iconic song 'Tom's Diner.'

2 Cathedral Church of St John the Divine

Vega's song includes the line: 'I'm listening to the bells of the cathedral.' The cathedral in question is the Cathedral Church of St John the Divine (p248), its epic scale more Old World than New. A yet to be completed blend of neo-Gothic and Romanesque styles, it's the largest place of worship in the US.

3 Malcolm Shabazz Harlem Market

Trawl the Malcolm Shabazz Harlem Market (p251), a low-key, semi-enclosed market run by the Malcolm Shabazz Mosque, former pulpit of slain Muslim orator Malcolm X. Pick up African jewelry, textiles, drums, leather goods and oils, or get your hair braided.

4 Studio Museum in Harlem

It might be small, but the Studio Museum in Harlem (p250) plays a vital role in the promotion and archiving of African American art. Its program of rotating exhibitions often features artists in its permanent collection, among them collagist Romare Bearden, satirical painter Robert Colescott and internationally renowned sculptor Richard Hunt.

Tom's Restaurant

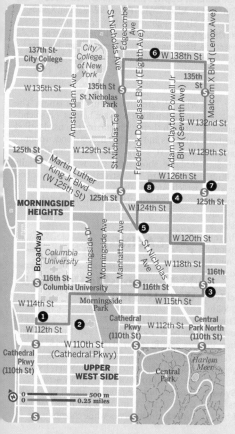

5 Flamekeepers Hat Club

Harlem's Gilded Age lives on at Flamekeepers Hat Club (p262), a friendly corner boutique lined with elegant hats and caps. If you simply can't decide, seek Marc Williamson's razor-sharp eye. The owner has quite a knack for picking the right piece for every face and shape. Just don't be surprised if you end up lingering; Williamson is also the consummate conversationalist.

6 Strivers' Row

On the blocks of 138th and 139th Sts, Strivers' Row (p252) is graced with 1890s townhouses. Earning its nickname in the 1920s when ambitious African Americans first moved here, these buildings have housed some of Harlem's greatest identities, among them songwriters Eubie Blake and Noble Sissle, blues veteran WC Handy and singer-dancer Bill 'Bojangles' Robinson.

7 Red Rooster

Taste the 'new Harlem' at Red Rooster (p259), where Ethiopean-born, Swedish-raised chef Marcus Samuelsson gives comfort food a competent, respectful makeover. The cornbread (paired with honey butter) is reason enough to roll in, while basement Ginny's Supper Club (p260) keeps the drinks and tunes flowing till the wee hours.

8 Apollo Theater

The best way to end any night in Harlem is 'where stars are born and legends are made,' the Apollo Theater (p253). Ella Fitzgerald made her singing debut here in November 1934, at one of the theater's earliest Amateur Nights. Eighty years on, Amateur Night kicks on every Wednesday, notorious crowds and all.

FULL PEWS: GOSPEL HARLEM CHURCH SERVICES

What started as an occasional pilgrimage has turned into a tourist-industry spectacle: entire busloads of travelers now make their way to Harlem every Sunday to attend a gospel service. The volume of visitors is so high that some churches turn away people due to space constraints. In some cases, tourists have been known to outnumber congregants.

Naturally, this has led to friction. Many locals are upset by visitors who chat during sermons, leave in the middle of services or show up in skimpy attire. Plus, for some, there's the uncomfortable sense that African American spirituality is something to be consumed like a Broadway show.

The churches, to their credit, remain welcoming spaces. But if you do decide to attend, be respectful: dress modestly (Sunday best!), don't take pictures and remain present for the duration of the service. Also, keep in mind that most churches will not allow large backpacks.

Sunday services generally start at 10am or 11am and can last for two or more hours. There are roughly five dozen participating churches. The superb Sunday gospel services at **Abyssinian Baptist Church** (Map p438; ☎212-862-7474; www.abyssinian.org; 132 W 138th St, btwn Adam Clayton Powell Jr & Malcolm X Blvds, Harlem; ⏲tourist gospel service 11am Sun early Sep-Jul; [S]2/3 to 135th St) are a raucous, soulful affair and the city's most famous. You'll need to arrive at least an hour before the service to queue up, and ensure you adhere to the strict entry rules: no tank tops, flip-flops, shorts, leggings or backpacks. Others include **Canaan Baptist Church** (Map p438; ☎212-866-0301; www.cbccnyc.org; 132 W 116th St, btwn Adam Clayton Powell Jr & Malcolm X Blvds, Harlem; ⏲service 10am Sun; 👪; [S]2/3 to 116th St), a neighborhood church founded in 1932, and **Convent Avenue Baptist Church** (Map p438; ☎212-234-6767; www.conventchurch.org; 420 W 145th St, at Convent Ave, Hamilton Heights; ⏲services 8am, 10:45am & 5pm Sun; [S]A/C, B/D or 1 to 145th St), which has been conducting traditional baptist services since the 1940s.

MORRIS-JUMEL MANSION MUSEUM HISTORIC BUILDING
Map p438 (☎212-923-8008; www.morrisjumel.org; 65 Jumel Tce, at 160th St, Washington Heights; adult/child $10/free, guided tours per person $12; ⏲10am-4pm Tue-Fri, to 5pm Sat & Sun; [S]C to 163rd St-Amsterdam Ave) Built in 1765 as a country retreat for Roger and Mary Morris, this columned mansion is the oldest house in Manhattan. It is also famous for having served as George Washington's headquarters after it was seized by the Continental Army in 1776. The mansion's beautifully appointed rooms contain many original furnishings, including a bed that reputedly belonged to Napoleon.

Across the street, along **10–18 Jumel Terrace** (10-18 Jumel Tce, Washington Heights; [S]C to 163rd St-Amsterdam Ave), stands a row of townhouses, designed in the 1890s by renowned architect Henri Fouchaux. At number 16 lived prolific entertainer and civil-rights activist Paul Robeson, who subsequently moved to 555 Edgecombe Ave (p260).

Around the corner lies storybook **Sylvan Terrace** (Sylvan Tce, Washington Heights; [S]C to 163rd St-Amsterdam Ave), still graced by its original, late-19th-century gas lamps. The street's striking wooden houses – resplendent with their high narrow stoops, dentiled canopies and boldly paneled wooden doors – were NYC's first attempt at building affordable abodes for city workers. Equally unique are the street's cobbled stones, which, unlike those of Lower Manhattan and Brooklyn, are Belgian, not Dutch.

🍴 EATING

🍴 Morningside Heights & West Harlem

TOM'S RESTAURANT DINER $
Map p438 (☎212-864-6137; www.tomsrestaurant.net; 2880 Broadway, at 112th St; mains $7-13; ⏲6am-1:30am Sun-Thu, 24hr Fri & Sat; [S]1 to 110th St) The exteriors of Tom's may look familiar if you're a fan of the TV series *Seinfeld,* but the interiors are all New York Greek diner. As in, *busy.* Reminisce about those Kramer scenes while chomping on

classic burgers, gyros, bagels or gut-warming homemade soups. Breakfast is served all day and it's open 24 hours Friday to Saturday. Cash only.

COMMUNITY FOOD & JUICE AMERICAN $$

Map p438 (☎212-665-2800; www.communityrestaurant.com; 2893 Broadway, btwn 112th & 113th Sts, Morningside Heights; sandwiches $11-15, mains $14-30; ⏰8am-9:30pm Mon-Thu, to 10pm Fri, 9am-10pm Sat, 9am-9:30pm Sun; 🥕👪; [S]1 to 110th St) Lofty and convivial, split-level Community is a brunch staple for frenzied families and hungover Columbia University students. Get here before 10:30am or be prepared to wait for your veggie scramble. Better yet, skip the weekend rush and bop in for a candlelit dinner. Both the warm lentil salad and grass-fed burger deserve an A, and there's no shortage of gluten-free options for sensitive tummies.

DINOSAUR BAR-B-QUE BARBECUE $$

Map p438 (☎212-694-1777; www.dinosaurbarbque.com; 700 W 125th St, at Twelfth Ave, Harlem; mains $12.50-25; ⏰11:30am-11pm Mon-Thu, to midnight Fri & Sat, noon-10pm Sun; [S]1 to 125th St) Jocks, hipsters, moms and pops: everyone dives into this honky-tonk rib bar for a rockin' feed. Get messy with dry-rubbed, slow-pit-smoked ribs, slabs of juicy steak and succulent burgers, or watch the waist with the lightly seasoned grilled-chicken options. The very few vegetarian options include a fantastic version of Creole-spiced deviled eggs.

🍴 Harlem

MAKE MY CAKE BAKERY $

Map p438 (☎212-932-0833; www.makemycake.com; 121 St Nicolas Ave, cnr 116th St, Harlem; cupcakes from $3; ⏰7:30am-8pm Mon-Thu, to 9pm Fri & Sat, to 7pm Sun; [S]2/3 to 116th St) Leave your diet at the door and treat yourself to some of the creamiest, dreamiest sweet treats this side of Central Park. Should you have the red velvet cupcake, the buttercream cupcake or a slice of gigantic strawberry cake? Heck, have them all!

★RED ROOSTER MODERN AMERICAN $$

Map p438 (☎212-792-9001; www.redroosterharlem.com; 310 Malcolm X Blvd, btwn 125th & 126th Sts, Harlem; mains $18-30; ⏰11:30am-10:30pm Mon-Thu, to 11:30pm Fri, 10am-11:30pm Sat, 10am-10pm Sun; [S]2/3 to 125th St) Transatlantic super- chef Marcus Samuelsson laces upscale comfort food with a world of flavors at his effortlessly cool, swinging brasserie. Here, mac 'n' cheese joins forces with lobster, blackened catfish pairs with pickled mango, and spectacular Swedish meatballs salute Samuelsson's home country. The prix-fixe lunch is a bargain at $25.

BLVD BISTRO AMERICAN $$

Map p438 (☎212-678-6200; www.boulevardbistrony.com; 239 Malcolm X Blvd, at 122nd St, Harlem; mains $16-36; ⏰11am-11pm Tue-Sat, 10am-6pm Sun; 🥕; [S]2/3 to 125th St) Tiny, bustling BLVD Bistro takes quality, seasonal produce and turns it into subtly tweaked southern soul food. Heading the kitchen is Mississippi-born Carlos Swepson, whose roots shine bright in dishes like blueberry-packed buttermilk pancakes, seven-cheese macaroni with pecan wood-smoked bacon, and one oh-so-fine potato salad. The menu includes vegetarian and gluten-free options, and the popular Sunday brunch runs all day. Praise the Lord!

MAISON HARLEM FRENCH, AMERICAN $$

Map p438 (☎212-222-9224; www.maisonharlem.com; 341 St Nicholas Ave, at 127th St, Harlem; lunch $10.50-26, dinner mains $12.50-29; ⏰11am-11pm Mon-Thu, to midnight Fri-Sun; 📶; [S]A/C, B/D to 125th St) Run by two French *amis,* this swinging little bar-bistro is like a second home for locals, who drop in at all hours to nibble on French toast, slurp on onion soup, or loosen their belt over decadent duck confit. For the full, effervescent effect, head here of an evening later in the week, when wine-fuelled merriment may just lead to dancing.

AMY RUTH'S RESTAURANT AMERICAN $$

Map p438 (☎212-280-8779; www.amyruthsharlem.com; 113 W 116th St, btwn Malcolm X & Adam Clayton Powell Jr Blvds, Harlem; waffles $10-18, mains $14-25; ⏰11am-11pm Mon, 8:30am-11pm Tue-Thu, 24hr Fri & Sat, to 11pm Sun; [S]B, C, 2/3 to 116th St) Perennially crowded Amy Ruth's serves up classic soul food, from fried catfish to mac 'n' cheese and fluffy biscuits. But it's the waffles that really merit a trip here – dished up 14 different ways, including with shrimp. Our all-time favorite is the 'Rev Al Sharpton,' waffles topped with succulent fried chicken.

🍴 East Harlem

EL AGUILA MEXICAN $

Map p438 (☎212-410-2450; www.elaguilanewyorkrestaurant.com; 137 E 116th St, at Lexington Ave, East Harlem; tacos from $2.50, burritos $7; ⏲24hr; [S]6 to 116th St) Get messy over cheap and cheerful chicken, tongue and *bistec* (grilled steak) tacos at this no-frills, tile-clad taqueria. Tasty alternatives include tamales, tostadas, *tortas* (sandwiches) and veggie burritos, all served with a side of blaring Mexican tunes and televised Mexican soaps. If you're heading in for breakfast, dig into the *pan dulce* (a sweet Mexican bun).

🍴 Inwood

NEW LEAF MODERN AMERICAN $$

(☎212-568-5323; www.newleafrestaurant.com; 1 Margaret Corbin Dr, Inwood; sandwiches & burgers $14, mains $23; ⏲11:30am-8pm Mon-Thu, 10am-9pm Fri-Sun; [S]A to 190th St) Nestled into Fort Tryon Park, a short jaunt from the Cloisters Museum & Gardens, this 1930s stone edifice feels like a country tavern. Settle in for seasonal produce made good in bistro-style dishes like mushroom risotto, Vermont maple salad with apple, goat's cheese, maple-candied bacon and balsamic, or a Maryland-style crab-cake sandwich. If possible, grab a table on the all-weather patio for that garden-party vibe.

LOCAL KNOWLEDGE

555 EDGECOMBE AVE

Completed in 1916, **555 Edgecombe Ave** (555 Edgecombe Ave, at 160th St, Washington Heights; [S]A/C to 163rd St-Amsterdam Ave, 1 to 157th St), a brick, beaux-arts giant, was Washington Heights' very first luxury apartment complex. It had a concierge, separate tradesmen entrance and no fewer than three elevators. Initially only available to white tenants, the area's transformation from a predominantly Irish and Jewish neighborhood to an African American one saw the building become predominately black by the 1940s. Its tenants would include some of New York's most prominent African Americans, among them boxer Joe Louis and music heavyweights Lena Horne, Count Basie, Duke Ellington and Billy Strayhorn. Today the building's cultural legacy lives on every Sunday afternoon, when veteran musician **Marjorie Eliot** (p262) throws open the doors of her apartment, inviting anyone and everyone into her living room for one of the city's most enchanting jazz jams.

🍴 Hamilton Heights

CHARLES' PAN-FRIED CHICKEN AMERICAN $

Map p438 (☎212-281-1800; 2839-2841 Frederick Douglass Blvd, btwn 151st & 152nd Sts; fried chicken from $10; ⏲11am-11pm Mon-Thu, to 1am Fri & Sat, to 8pm Sun; [S]B/D to 155th St) It's a hole-in-the-wall place, but the charismatic Charles Gabriel makes the best damn chicken we've ever tasted. Don't expect any designer details: just four unadorned tables, Styrofoam containers, and proof that a book (or chicken joint) must never be judged by its cover.

HARLEM PUBLIC AMERICAN $

Map p438 (☎212-939-9404; www.facebook.com/harlempublic; 3612 Broadway, at 149th St, Hamilton Heights; meals $9-15; ⏲noon-midnight Mon-Thu, to 1am Fri & Sat, 11am-midnight Sun; [S]1, A/C, B/D to 145th St) Amicable hipsters at the bar, old-school funk on the speakers, and finger-licking bar grub: gentrification ain't *always* bad. Celebrate new beginnings with mouthwatering feel-good food, whether it's the wicked peanut butter burger (peanut butter, brown sugar bacon and New York State cheddar) or the more virtuous two-bean vegetarian burger. Liquids focus on the local, from American craft beers to small batch New York liquors.

🍷 DRINKING & NIGHTLIFE

GINNY'S SUPPER CLUB COCKTAIL BAR

Map p438 (☎212-421-3821, brunch reservations 212-792-9001; www.ginnyssupperclub.com; 310 Malcolm X Blvd, btwn 125th & 126th Sts, Harlem; ⏲6-11pm Thu, to 3am Fri & Sat, 10:30am-2pm Sun; [S]2/3 to 125th St) Looking straight out of *Boardwalk Empire*, this roaring basement supper club is rarely short of styled-up punters sipping cocktails, nibbling on soul and global bites (from the Red Rooster kitchen upstairs), and grooving to live jazz from

WORTH A DETOUR

THE BRONX

The only borough on the US mainland, the 42-sq-mile, 1.4-million-strong Bronx lies just north of Manhattan between the Hudson, Harlem and East Rivers and Long Island Sound. It was named after Scandinavian sea captain Jonas Bronck, who settled here in 1639, in an area previously inhabited by the Lenape Nation.

Known for its very expensive team, its very expensive stadium ($1.5 billion; opened in 2009) and its 27 World Series wins, **Yankee Stadium** (☑718-293-4300, tours 646-977-8687; www.yankees.com; E 161st St, at River Ave; tours $20; ⓢB/D, 4 to 161st St-Yankee Stadium) channels the intimacy of the '23 original, so if you're into baseball – or *béisbol* or *beysbol* or *baseboll* – don't miss it.

If you're a culture vulture, the **Bronx Museum** (☑718-681-6000; www.bronxmuseum. org; 1040 Grand Concourse, at 165th St; ⊙11am-6pm Wed, Thu, Sat & Sun, to 8pm Fri; ⓢB/D to 167th St) FREE awaits 0.4 miles to the northeast, with well-executed exhibitions of contemporary and 20th-century art. A further 2.9-miles northeast along the Grand Concourse is **Edgar Allan Poe Cottage** (☑718-881-8900; www.bronxhistoricalsociety. org/poe-cottage; 2640 Grand Concourse, at Kingsbridge Rd; adult/child $5/3; ⊙10am-3pm Thu & Fri, to 4pm Sat, 1-5pm Sun; ⓢB/D to Kingsbridge Rd), former abode of the brooding author (1809–49). Resting peacefully a further 2.1 miles northeast is graceful **Woodlawn Cemetery** (☑718-920-0500; www.thewoodlawncemetery.org; Webster Ave, at E 233rd St; ⊙8:30am-4:30pm; ⓢ4 to Woodlawn), which dates back to the Civil War (1863). Its famous residents include Cuban singer Celia Cruz, jazz legends Miles Davis and Duke Ellington, and *Moby Dick* scribe Herman Melville.

Things are significantly livelier 1.2 miles southeast of Edgar Allan Poe Cottage, where the neighborhood of Belmont is best-known for its own Little Italy. At its heart is Arthur Ave, home to **Arthur Avenue Retail Market** (2344 Arthur Ave, btwn 186th St & Crescent Ave; ⊙daily, individual stalls vary; ⓢB/D to Fordham Rd, ⓡMetro-North to Fordham), an earthy indoor market peddling everything from olives and *pizza al taglio* (pizza by the slice) to T-shirts proclaiming, 'A friend will help you move, but a real friend will help you move a body'. A few doors up, veteran **Madonia Brothers Bakery** (☑718-295-5573; 2348 Arthur Ave, at 186th St; cannoli small/large $1.25/2; ⊙6am-7pm Mon-Sat, 6:30am-6pm Sun; ⓢB/D to Fordham Rd, ⓡMetro-North to Fordham) is worth a stop for its delectable Sicilian cannoli, filled fresh to order.

7:30pm Thursday to Saturday and DJ-spun beats from 11pm Friday and Saturday. For a spirited start to your Sunday, don't miss the weekly Sunday gospel brunch (reservations recommended).

CHIPPED CUP   CAFE
Map p438 (☑212-368-8881; www.chippedcupcoffee.com; 3610 Broadway, btwn 148th & 149th Sts, Hamilton Heights; ⊙7am-8pm Mon-Fri, 8am-8pm Sat & Sun; ☎; ⓢ1, A/C, B/D to 145th St) Hipsterdom gets all cozy here, where coffee-slurping scribes and students tap away among dainty teacups, worn novels and quirky artwork. If the weather is behaving, order a latte and *pain au chocolat,* grab a copy of the *New York Times,* and rediscover life's simpler pleasures in the leafy back garden.

BIER INTERNATIONAL   BEER HALL
Map p438 (☑212-280-0944; www.bierinternational.com; 2099 Frederick Douglass Blvd, at 113th St, Harlem; ⊙4pm-1am Mon, to 2am Tue-Thu, to 4am Fri, noon-4am Sat, noon-1am Sun; ⓢB, C, 1 to 110th St-Cathedral Pkwy, 2/3 to 110th St-Central Park North) A fun, buzzing beer garden that peddles more than a dozen drafts and a full menu of eats to choose from. The truffle fries with Parmesan make a great accompaniment to the Bier Stiefel ($15) – beer in a boot glass. Cash only.

PARIS BLUES   BAR
Map p438 (☑212-222-9878; www.parisbluesharlem.com; 2021 Adam Clayton Powell Jr Blvd, at 121st St, Harlem; ⊙noon-3am; ⓢA/C, B to 116th St, 2/3 to 125th St) This down-home dive is named after the 1961 Sidney Poitier and Paul Newman flick about two expats living and loving in Paris. It's a little worn in places and the booze selection is limited, but it makes up for it with buckets of charm, generous pours, and nightly jazz gigs from around 9pm.

ENTERTAINMENT

★MINTON'S JAZZ, CLUB

Map p438 (☎212-243-2222; www.mintonsharlem.com; 206 W 118th St, btwn St Nicholas Ave & Adam Clayton Powell Jr Blvd; ⏲6-11pm Wed-Sat, noon-3pm & 6-11pm Sun; [S]B/C, 2/3 to 116th St) Birthplace of bebop, this Harlem jazz-and-dinner club is a musical holy grail. Everyone from Dizzy Gillespie to Louis Armstrong have jammed here, and dinner (mains $20 to $46) or Sunday brunch (prix fixe $32) in its tinted-mirror dining room is an experience to behold. Book ahead, dress to impress and savor southern flavors while toe-tapping to live, honey-sweet jazz.

★MARJORIE ELIOT'S PARLOR JAZZ JAZZ

Map p438 (☎212-781-6595; 555 Edgecombe Ave, Apartment 3F, at 160th St, Washington Heights; ⏲3:30pm Sun; [S]A/C to 163rd St-Amsterdam Ave, 1 to 157th St) Each Sunday, the charming Ms Eliot provides one of New York's most magical experiences: free, intimate jazz jams in her own apartment. Dedicated to her two deceased sons, the informal concerts feature a revolving lineup of talented musicians, enchanting guests from all over the globe. Simply turn up and tap dem toes.

MAYSLES DOCUMENTARY CENTER CINEMA

Map p438 (☎212-537-6843; www.maysles.org; 343 Malcolm X Blvd, btwn 127th & 128th Sts, Harlem; suggested donation $10; [S]2/3 to 125th St) This small, not-for-profit cinema founded by the late director Albert Maysles (of *Grey Gardens* fame) shows documentary and other independent films. Check the website for details of upcoming screenings and events, which also include Q&A sessions with filmmakers, lectures and live performances.

SHOPPING

TRUNK SHOW DESIGNER CONSIGNMENT VINTAGE

Map p438 (☎212-662-0009; www.trunkshowconsignment.com; 275-277 W 113th St, at Eighth Ave; ⏲1:30-7pm Mon-Thu, usually by appointment Fri-Sun; [S]B, C to 110th St-Cathedral Parkway, 2/3 to 110th St-Central Park North) Step into this hot little consignment store for a unisex edit of fabulous pre-loved finds. With merchandise delivered every second day, you're pretty much assured of a couture catch. Opening times can vary, so consider calling ahead.

FLAMEKEEPERS HAT CLUB ACCESSORIES

Map p438 (☎212-531-3542; www.flamekeepershatclub.com; 273 W 121st St, at St Nicholas Ave; ⏲noon-7pm Sun-Wed, to 8pm Thu & Fri, to 9pm Sat; [S]A/C, B/D to 125th St) Sharpen your kudos at this sassy little hat shop, owned by affable Harlem local Marc Williamson. His carefully curated stock reads like a hat-lover's dream: buttery Barbisio fedoras from Italy, Selentino top hats from Czech Republic, and woolen patchwork caps from Ireland's Hanna Hats of Donegal. Prices range from $85 to $350, with an optional customization service for true individualists.

ATMOS SHOES

Map p438 (☎212-666-2242; http://atmosnyc.blogspot.com; 203 W 125th St, at Adam Clayton Powell Jr Blvd; ⏲11am-8pm Mon-Sat, noon-7pm Sun; [S]A/C, B/D, 2/3 to 125th St) Sneaker fetishists both high and low sprint to Atmos to pimp their feet (Method Man from the Wu-Tang Clan has been spotted here). A top spot for high-end kicks, limited-edition releases and re-releases, the Harlem store is well-known for its collaborations, with partners including Nike, Puma and K-Swiss.

SPORTS & ACTIVITIES

RIVERBANK STATE PARK HEALTH & FITNESS

Map p438 (☎212-694-3600; www.nysparks.com/parks/93; 679 Riverside Dr, at 145th St, Hamilton Heights; pool adult/child $2/1, fitness room $10, ice skating adult/child $5/3, roller skating $1.50, skate rental $6; ⏲hours vary; 📶👪; [S]1 to 145th St) This 28-acre, five-building facility, perched atop a waste refinery (not as crazy as it sounds), has an indoor Olympic-size pool, an outdoor lap pool, a fitness room, basketball and tennis courts, a running track around a soccer field, a playground and a roller-skating rink (with ice skating from November to March, weather permitting).

TREAD BICYCLE RENTAL

(☎212-544-7055; www.treadbikeshop.com; 250 Dyckman St; per hr/day $8/30; ⏲10am-7pm Mon-Sat, to 6pm Sun; 👪; [S]A to Dyckman St) Located in Inwood Hill Park, right off the New York Greenway Bike Trail, is this family-friendly rental shop – perfect for if you want to navigate the long and winding paths of Upper Manhattan on wheels.

Brooklyn

WILLIAMSBURG | BUSHWICK | BROOKLYN HEIGHTS | DOWNTOWN BROOKLYN | DUMBO | FORT GREENE | CLINTON HILL | BOERUM HILL | COBBLE HILL | CARROLL GARDENS | RED HOOK | GOWANUS | PARK SLOPE | PROSPECT HEIGHTS | BEDFORD-STUYVESANT | CROWN HEIGHTS | CONEY ISLAND | BRIGHTON BEACH

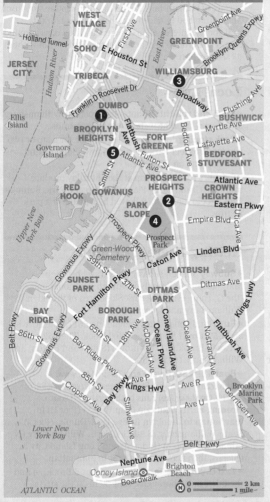

Neighborhood Top Five

1 Taking in the incredible views of Lower Manhattan from the waterfront **Brooklyn Bridge Park** (p265).

2 Catching the latest critically acclaimed art exhibitions at the **Brooklyn Museum** (p267) followed by a meal at Saul.

3 Downing cocktails at **Maison Premiere** (p288), one creative gastropub among the many that pack **Williamsburg**.

4 Strolling past meadows, the lakefront, scenic bridges and forest-covered hillocks in **Prospect Park** (p268).

5 Browsing a bygone era at **Dry Goods** (p300), one of many enticing boutiques along Atlantic Ave, followed by microbrews and snacks at a spot near Smith St such as **61 Local** (p294).

For more detail of this area see Map p440, p442, p444, p446 and p447 ➡

Lonely Planet's Top Tip

If you want to get a sense of what old New York was like, be sure to wander around Brighton Beach. Under the elevated tracks on Brighton Beach Ave, the bustling Russian district known as 'Little Odessa' is packed with greengrocers and emporiums dispensing smoked fish and pierogies. On the street, you'll find a cross section of humanity – from grandmas to sulky teens – chattering in dozens of different languages as the trains rumble overhead. It's unmistakably New York.

🍴 Best Places to Eat

- Roberta's (p279)
- Marlow & Sons (p279)
- Smorgasburg (p285)
- Cooklyn (p286)
- Zenkichi (p279)

For reviews, see p277

🍷 Best Places to Drink

- Maison Premiere (p288)
- Rookery (p289)
- Skinny Dennis (p288)
- Hotel Delmano (p288)
- 61 Local (p294)

For reviews, see p288

☆ Best Places to Channel Your Inner Hipster

- Bell House (p296)
- Brooklyn Bowl (p295)
- Royal Palms (p294)
- Jalopy (p296)
- Barbès (p296)

For reviews, see p295

Explore Brooklyn

If Brooklyn were its own city, it'd be the fourth largest in the US – bigger than Houston, Philadelphia and Phoenix. It is home to more than 2.6 million people and is a rambling 71 sq miles (easily three times larger than Manhattan). It is split in two, with one set of subway lines servicing the north end of the borough, and another set traveling to points south. So if you think you can see it all in a day, as old-school Brooklyners might say: 'Fuhgeddaboudit!'

For day-trip purposes, it is best to pick a neighborhood and stick to it. South Brooklyn, especially brownstone-studded Brooklyn Heights, offers lots of history and great Manhattan views. Fans of vintage amusement parks should head to Coney Island. For the night owls, the trendy enclave of Williamsburg lies just a single subway stop from Manhattan and is loaded with bars and restaurants.

If you are interested in other parts of town, ask around first. The borough may be all the rage, but it's not without its sketchy parts.

Local Life

- **Rock and roll** Hit the hot music spots in Williamsburg and Bushwick to hear the latest indie sounds.
- **Park sloping** Join the stroller brigade for a lap or two around Prospect Park. Or go window-shopping and cafe-hopping on Fifth Ave.
- **Farmers markets** Shop at the Saturday produce markets (Grand Army Plaza, Fort Greene Park, Borough Hall, McCarren Park), followed by a picnic at a park nearby.

Getting There & Around

- **Subway** Sixteen subway lines travel between Manhattan and Brooklyn, with an additional line (the G) connecting the Park Slope area of Brooklyn to Williamsburg and Queens.
- **Bus** Handy bus routes include the B61 (Atlantic Ave) and B57 (Court St) to reach Red Hook. The B62 runs between Brooklyn's downtown (Smith and Fulton) and Williamsburg (Driggs St).
- **Boat** The **East River Ferry** (Map p440; www.eastriverferry.com; S 8th St; 1-way weekday/weekend $4/6; [S] J/M/A to Marcy Ave) runs both north and south. Heading north, boats zip from Wall St (Pier 11) in Manhattan to Brooklyn Bridge Park/Dumbo (Pier 1), South Williamsburg (S 8th St), North Williamsburg (N 6th St), Greenpoint (India St) and Long Island City in Queens, then across to E34th St in Manhattan.
- **Taxi** Green Boro Taxis operate around Brooklyn and the other outer boroughs. Hail them on the street.

👁 TOP SIGHT
BROOKLYN BRIDGE PARK

This **85-acre park, nearing completion, is one of Brooklyn's most talked-about new sights. Wrapping around a bend on the East River, it runs for 1.3 miles from Jay St in Dumbo to the west end of Atlantic Ave in Cobble Hill. It has revitalized a once-barren stretch of shoreline, turning a series of abandoned piers into public park land.**

Empire Fulton Ferry State Park

Just east of the Brooklyn Bridge, in the northern section of Dumbo, you'll find this state park with a grassy lawn that faces the East River. Near the water is **Jane's Carousel** (Map p446; www.janescarousel.com; Brooklyn Bridge Park, Empire Fulton Ferry, Dumbo; tickets $2; ⏲11am-7pm Wed-Mon mid-May–mid-Sep, 11am-6pm Thu-Sun mid-Sep–mid-May; 👶; ⓈF to York St), a lovingly restored 1922 carousel set inside a glass pavilion designed by Pritzker Prize–winning architect Jean Nouvel. The park is bordered on one side by the **Empire Stores & Tobacco Warehouse** (Map p446; Water St, near Main St; ⓈF to York St; A/C to High St), a series of Civil War–era structures that house restaurants, shops and a theater.

Pier 1

A 9-acre pier just south of the Empire Fulton Ferry is home to a stretch of park featuring a playground, walkways and the Harbor and Bridge View lawns, both of which overlook the river. On the Bridge View Lawn, you'll find artist Mark di Suvero's 30ft kinetic sculpture *Yoga* (1991). From July through August, free outdoor films are screened on the Harbor View Lawn against a stunning backdrop of Manhattan. Other free open-air events (outdoor dance parties, group

DON'T MISS

➡ Views of downtown Manhattan from Pier 1

➡ Empire Fulton Ferry at sunset

➡ Refreshments at Fornino or Brooklyn Bridge Garden Bar

➡ A stroll across Brooklyn Bridge

PRACTICALITIES

➡ Map p446

➡ ☎718-802-0603

➡ www.brooklynbridge-park.org

➡ East River Waterfront, btwn Atlantic Ave & Adams St

➡ admission free

➡ ⏲6am-1am

➡ ⓈA/C to High St; 2/3 to Clark St; F to York St

WALKING THE BROOKLYN BRIDGE

To reach the bridge on foot, take the stairs at the north-eastern end of Cadman Plaza (on bicycle, enter at Tillary and Adams Sts). If you're coming from Dumbo, take Washington St straight uphill.

It's about a mile across the bridge (a 20- to 40-minute stroll depending on how often you stop to admire the view). Once on the Manhattan side, you'll arrive in City Hall Park, a 10-minute walk from Tribeca (west), Chinatown (north) or Wall St (south).

The pedestrian walkway affords a wonderful view of lower Manhattan; observation points under the support towers offer brass 'panorama' histories of the waterfront. Take care to stay on the side of the walkway marked for pedestrians – one half is designated for cyclists, who use it en masse for both commuting and pleasure rides, and frustrated pedalers have been known to get nasty with oblivious tourists who wander, camera pressed to an eye, into the bike lane. To beat the crowds, come early in the morning, when you'll have those views largely to yourself.

yoga classes, history tours) happen throughout the summer. The seasonal Brooklyn Bridge Garden Bar (p294; open April to October) can be found on the pier's north end. At the north end, you can catch the East River Ferry (p388).

Pier 6

At the southern end of the park, off Atlantic Ave, Pier 6 has a fantastic playground and a small water play area for tots (if you're bringing kids, pack swimsuits, towels). Neighboring Pier 5, just north, has walkways, sand volleyball courts, soccer fields and barbecue grills. There's also a few seasonal concessions (May to October), including wood-fired pizza, beer and Italian treats at **Fornino** (Map p446; 718-422-1107; www.fornino.com; Pier 6, Brooklyn Bridge Park; pizzas $12-25; 10am-10pm Apr-Oct; B45 to Brooklyn Bridge Park/Pier 6, S2/3, 4/5 to Borough Hall), which has a rooftop deck. A free seasonal ferry runs on weekends from Pier 6 to Governors Island (p75).

Brooklyn Bridge

The real star of the park is, of course, the architectural masterpiece linking New York's best-loved boroughs. The Brooklyn Bridge was the world's first steel suspension bridge. When it opened in 1883, the 1596ft span between its two support towers was the longest in history. Although its construction was fraught with disaster, the bridge became a magnificent example of urban design, inspiring poets, writers and painters. Today, the Brooklyn Bridge continues to dazzle – many regard it as the most beautiful bridge in the world.

The Prussian-born engineer John Roebling, who was knocked off a pier in Fulton Landing in June 1869, designed the bridge, which spans the East River from Manhattan to Brooklyn; he died of tetanus poisoning before construction of the bridge even began. His son, Washington Roebling, supervised construction of the bridge, which lasted 14 years and managed to survive budget overruns and the deaths of 20 workers. The younger Roebling himself suffered from the bends while helping to excavate the riverbed for the bridge's western tower and remained bedridden for much of the project; his wife Emily oversaw construction in his stead. There was one final tragedy to come in June 1883, when the bridge opened to pedestrian traffic. Someone in the crowd shouted, perhaps as a joke, that the bridge was collapsing into the river, setting off a mad rush in which 12 people were trampled to death.

TOP SIGHT
BROOKLYN MUSEUM

The five-story, 560,000-sq-ft beaux-arts building was designed by architectural firm McKim, Mead & White. Construction began in the early 1890s, with the intention of making it the largest single-site museum in the world. The plan lost steam in 1898, when Brooklyn was incorporated into NYC. Today, it houses more than 1.5 million objects, including ancient artifacts, 19th-century period rooms, and sculptures and paintings from across several centuries.

Egyptian Art

One of the highlights here is the excellent collection of Egyptian art, which spans a period of 5000 years. Housed in the 3rd-floor galleries, it includes bas-reliefs and Roman-era portraits, some of which are drawn from the museum's ongoing excavations in Egypt. A mummy chamber holds sarcophagi and ritual objects. But the most incredible piece is the so-called 'Bird Lady,' a delicate terra-cotta figurine with an abstracted face and claw-like hands, dating back to 3300–3650 BC. Look for her in a stand-alone vitrine.

American Art

An iconic portrait of George Washington by Gilbert Stuart; Childe Hassam's celebrated 1900 urban landscape, *Late Afternoon, New York, Winter*; and dozens of paintings by late-19th-century portraitist John Singer Sargent. The Brooklyn is in possession of one of the great collections of American art. Do not miss a trip to the 5th floor to see it.

A Room of Their Own

This is one of the few mainstream arts institutions to devote permanent space to showcasing women. The 8300-sq-ft Elizabeth A Sackler Center for Feminist Art on the 4th floor exhibits an engaging mix of one-person and historical shows that examine topics like women in video or pop art. At the gallery's core, you'll find Judy Chicago's seminal 1979 installation, *The Dinner Party*.

Other Highlights

There are other worthwhile galleries devoted to African sculpture, Latin American textiles and contemporary art. If you want a peek behind the scenes, head to the Visible Storage and Study Center on the 5th floor to see glass cases stuffed with everything from vintage bicycles to a bulbous Gaston Lachaise sculpture.

For dining, there's a casual snack counter, as well as gourmet fare in elegant Saul (p288), which serves creative farm-to-table fare.

On the first Saturday of every month (from 5pm to 11pm) the museum hosts a free evening of art, performances and live music (sometimes there's even a dance floor set up). It's a big draw for families.

DON'T MISS

➡ Egyptian collection
➡ Elizabeth A Sackler Center for Feminist Art
➡ Visible Storage
➡ American collection

PRACTICALITIES

➡ Map p444
➡ 718-638-5000
➡ www.brooklynmuseum.org
➡ 200 Eastern Pkwy
➡ suggested donation $16
➡ 11am-6pm Wed & Fri-Sun, to 10pm Thu
➡ S2/3 to Eastern Pkwy-Brooklyn Museum

TOP SIGHT
PROSPECT PARK

The creators of the 585-acre Prospect Park, Calvert Vaux and Frederick Olmsted, considered this an improvement on their other New York project, Central Park. Created in 1866, Prospect Park has many of the same features: a gorgeous meadow, a scenic lake, forested pathways and rambling hills that are straddled with leafy walkways. It receives roughly 10 million visitors a year.

DON'T MISS

- The peaceful view from the boathouse
- A stroll along Lullwater Creek
- A picnic and kite-flying on Long Meadow

PRACTICALITIES

- Map p444
- ☎718-965-8951
- www.prospectpark.org
- Grand Army Plaza
- 🕑5am-1am
- [S]2/3 to Grand Army Plaza; F to 15th St-Prospect Park

Grand Army Plaza

A large, landscaped traffic circle with a massive ceremonial arch sits at the intersection of Flatbush Ave and Prospect Park West. This marks the beginning of Eastern Pkwy and the entrance to Prospect Park. The arch, which was built in the 1890s, is a memorial to Union soldiers who fought in the Civil War. A greenmarket is held here from 8am to 4pm on Saturday year-round. On the first and third Sunday of warmer months (May through September), the plaza also sees a circle of food trucks dispensing gourmet goodies.

Long Meadow

The 90-acre Long Meadow, which is bigger than Central Park's Great Lawn, lies to the south of the park's formal entrance at Grand Army Plaza. It's a super strolling and lounging spot, filled with pick-up ball games and families flying kites. On the south end is Picnic House, with a snack stand and public bathrooms.

Children's Corner

Near Flatbush Ave, the Children's Corner contains a terrific 1912 carousel, originally from Coney Island, and the **Prospect Park Zoo** (Map p444; ☎718-399-7339; www.prospectparkzoo.com; Prospect Park, at Lincoln Rd & Ocean Ave; adult/child $8/5; 🕑10am-5:30pm Apr-Oct, to 4:30pm Nov-Mar; [S]2/3 to Grand Army Plaza). To the northeast of the carousel is the 18th century **Lefferts Historic House** (Map p444; ☎718-789-2822; www.prospectpark.org; Prospect Park, near Flabtush Ave & Empire Blvd; suggested donation $3; 🕑noon-5pm Thu-Sun May-Oct, noon-4pm Sat & Sun Nov-Apr; [S]B, Q to Prospect Park), which has plenty of old-fashioned toys to goof around with.

Audobon Center Boathouse

Sitting on a northern finger of Prospect Park Lake, the photogenic boathouse (aka Prospect Park Audubon Center) hosts a range of activities throughout the year (guided birdwatching sessions, free yoga classes, nature-themed art exhibitions, hands-on craft activities for kids). From here, there is a trailhead for 2.5 miles of woodsy nature trails (the route which takes you along Lullwater Creek is particularly scenic).

Lakeside Complex

After several years of construction (and a $74-million investment), Prospect Park's newest attraction continues to turn heads. The 26-acre Lakeside Complex features a pair of rinks for indoor and outdoor ice-skating in the winter, indoor roller skating in the summer (the outdoor rink becomes a watery splash area for small children) as well as a cafe, new walking trails and a small concert space. In the summer you can also hire paddleboats for a glide across the lake.

TOP SIGHT
CONEY ISLAND

Coney Island achieved worldwide fame as a working-class resort area at the turn of the 20th century. Though it is no longer the booming, peninsula-wide attraction it was then, it still draws crowds who come for the roller coaster rides, followed by hot dogs and beer on the boardwalk.

DON'T MISS

- Cyclone roller coaster
- Cold beer at Ruby's
- Nathan's Famous hot dogs

PRACTICALITIES

- Map p447
- www.coneyisland.com
- Surf Ave & Boardwalk, btwn W 15th & W 8th Sts
- [S]D/F, N/Q to Coney Island-Stillwell Ave

Historic Rides

Luna Park (Cyclone roller coaster; Map p447; www.lunaparknyc.com; Surf Ave, at 10th St; 🕐Apr-Oct; 👪; [S]D/F, N/Q to Coney Island-Stillwell Ave) is one of Coney Island's most popular amusement parks and contains one of its most legendary rides: the Cyclone ($9), a wood roller coaster that reaches speeds of 60mph and makes near-vertical drops. The pink-and-mint-green **Deno's Wonder Wheel** (Map p447; ☎718-372-2592; www.wonderwheel.com; W 12th St, btwn Surf Ave & the Boardwalk; ride $7; 🕐late Mar–mid-Oct; 👪; [S]D/F, N/Q to Coney Island-Stillwell Ave) dates all the way back to 1920. It is the best place to survey Coney Island from up high.

Hot Dogs & Beer

The hot dog was invented in Coney Island in 1867, and there's no better place to eat one than **Nathan's Famous** (Map p447; ☎718-333-2202; www.nathansfamous.com; 1310 Surf Ave, cnr Stillwell Ave, Coney Island; hot dog from $4; 🕐10am-midnight; [S]D/F to Coney Island-Stillwell Ave), established 1916. When thirst strikes, head to **Ruby's** (Map p447; ☎718-975-7829; www.rubysbar.com; 1213 Boardwalk, btwn Stillwell Ave & 12th St; 🕐11am-10pm Sun-Thu, to 1am Fri & Sat, closed Nov-Mar; [S]D, N/Q to Coney Island-Stillwell Ave), a legendary dive bar on the boardwalk.

SIGHTS

Williamsburg

There is a definite Williamsburg look: skinny jeans, multiple tattoos, a discreet body piercing, a beard for men, maybe some kind of retro head covering for a woman. Denizens of this raggedy and rowdy neighborhood across the East River on the L train seem to have time and money to slouch in cafes and party all night in bars; a fair share of older – early 30s – transplants from Manhattan and Europe qualify as elders.

The main artery is Bedford Ave between N 10th St and Metropolitan Ave, where there are boutiques, cafes, bars and cheap eateries. But cool spots have also sprouted along N 6th St and Berry St, and perhaps a sign of the times is that the uber-hip consider Williamsburg over and have moved on to colonizing next door Greenpoint, a traditionally Polish neighborhood, as well as the former warehouse buildings further out in Bushwick.

The Brooklyn Brewery hosts weekend tours, special events and pub nights.

WILLIAMSBURG BRIDGE BRIDGE

Map p440 (www.nyc.gov/html/dot/html/infrastructure/williamsburg-bridge.shtml; bike access at S 5th St & S 5th Pl, pedestrian access at Bedford Ave btwn S 5th & S 6th Sts; [S] J/M/Z to Marcy Ave) Built in 1903 to link Williamsburg and the Lower East Side, this steel-frame suspension bridge helped transform the area into a teeming industrial center. Its foot- and bike-paths offer excellent views of Manhattan and the East River. Bonus: unlike the more attractive Brooklyn Bridge, which is capped by less-than-interesting civic center zones, the Williamsburg connects two neighborhoods with plenty of bars and restaurants, offering the possibility of refreshments at both ends.

EAST RIVER STATE PARK PARK

Map p440 (www.nysparks.com/parks/155; Kent Ave, btwn 8th & 9th Sts, Williamsburg; ⏲9am-dusk; 👪; [S] L to Bedford Ave) The 7-acre waterfront East River State Park is a slice of greenery with sublime views of Manhattan. Its grassy lawn is home to a vast assortment of events and activities, including the odd summer concert. There is also summer-only ferry service to Governor's Island and year-round ferry service on the **East River Ferry** (Map p440; ☎800-533-3779; www.eastriverferry.com; N 6th St; 1-way weekday/weekend $4/6; [S] L to Bedford Ave). No pets allowed.

MCCARREN PARK PARK

Map p440 (www.mccarrenpark.com; 776 Lorimer St; pool admission free; skating adult/child $12/6, skate rental $6; 👪; [S] G to Nassau) The grassy 35-acre McCarren Park makes a good picnic spot on warm days, while on sweltering days you might want to head to the pool – a massive and historic pool that reopened in 2012 after being closed for almost three decades. Go early to avoid the worst of the crowds. From mid-November through January, there's also an ice rink.

BROOKLYN ART LIBRARY GALLERY, LIBRARY

Map p440 (☎718-388-7941; www.sketchbookproject.com; 103 N 3rd St, btwn Berry St & Wythe Ave, Williamsburg; ⏲10am-6pm Mon-Fri, 11am-7pm Sat & Sun; [S] L to Bedford Ave) [FREE] Lining the walls of this intriguing space are over 30,000 sketch books, which contain a wild mix of graphic design, collage, fine art, poetry, irreverent comics and personal essays. To browse the collection, sign up for a free library card, then do a search by subject matter, theme, artist name or country. In fact, contributors from over 130 countries have added their sketch books to the library. Ask the friendly librarian for personal favorites.

If you feel inspired after paging through a few books, join in the fun. You can buy a sketch book ($28 for the basic 32-page book), which once received will be added to the collection. There are no parameters, and you can always mail it in if you can't bring it in person.

BROOKLYN BREWERY BREWERY, PUB

Map p440 (☎718-486-7422; www.brooklynbrewery.com; 79 N 11th St, btwn Berry St & Wythe Ave, Williamsburg; tours free Sat & Sun, $12 Mon-Thu; ⏲tours 5pm Mon-Thu, 1-5pm Sat, 1-4pm Sun; tasting room 6-11pm Fri, noon-8pm Sat, noon-6pm Sun; [S] L to Bedford Ave) Harkening back to a time when this area of New York was a beer brewing center, the Brooklyn Brewery not only brews and serves tasty local suds, but offers tours of its facilities.

Tours Monday to Thursday include tastings of four beers, plus history and insight into the brewery; reserve a spot online. On weekends, tours are free (just show up) but don't include tastings. Instead, you can buy beer tokens ($5 each or five for $20) to sample the refreshing brews. Or you can skip the tour altogether and just while away a weekend afternoon in the bare-bones tasting room.

Interesting fact: the brewery's cursive logo was designed by none other than Milton Glazer, of 'I Heart New York' fame, who did the job in exchange for a share of the profits and free beer for life.

CITY RELIQUARY MUSEUM

Map p440 (☎718-782-4842; www.cityreliquary.org; 370 Metropolitan Ave, near Havemeyer St, Williamsburg; admission $5; 🕒noon-6pm Thu-Sun; [S]L to Lorimer Ave) A tiny community museum housed in a former bodega, the curiously fascinating City Reliquary is filled with New York–related ephemera. Cases and shelves are stuffed full of old shop signs, Statue of Liberty postcards, vintage pencil sharpeners, subway tokens, seltzer bottles and paint chips off the L train.

Bushwick

A couple of subway stops to the east of Williamsburg on the L train, the ramshackle blocks of Bushwick begin to appear. Today, Bushwick is home to artists and musicians, who've packed the hood in search of cheap rents. The neighborhood's western fringes are dotted with bars and industrial-chic restaurants. This area remains an industrial zone during the day but perks up on weekends when local bars and performance spaces come to life.

Before the hipsters invaded, Bushwick was known as a mixed community of African Americans, as well as Mexican, Ecuadoran, Puerto Rican and Dominican immigrants. It was also an important beer-brewing center in the late 19th and early 20th centuries. The stately homes of beer barons still line Bushwick Ave, some in decrepit condition.

Brooklyn Heights & Downtown Brooklyn

When Robert Fulton's steam ferries started regular services across the East River in the early 19th century, well-to-do Manhattanites began building stellar houses – Victorian Gothic, Romanesque, neo-Greco, Italianate and others – in Brooklyn Heights.

Strolling along the tree-lined streets to gaze at them now is a lovely afternoon activity; don't miss the 1881 Queen Anne–style landmark building that houses the Brooklyn Historical Society, which features a library (with some 33,000 grainy digitized photos from decades past), an auditorium and a museum devoted to the borough. The society also leads several walking tours.

Follow Montague St, the Heights' main commercial avenue, down to the waterfront until you hit the Brooklyn Heights Promenade, which juts out over the Brooklyn–Queens Expwy to offer stunning views of Lower Manhattan. Underneath the Expwy is the Brooklyn Bridge Park (p265), an 85-acre development of landscaped green space and pathways, built on piers stretching from the Brooklyn Bridge south to Atlantic Ave.

The 1848 beaux-arts **Brooklyn Borough Hall** straddles both Brooklyn Heights and downtown Brooklyn, characterized by its various courts. The small but fascinating New York Transit Museum has an amazing collection of original subway cars and transit memorabilia dating back more than a century. Near downtown Brooklyn is the Barclays Center (p297), home to the Brooklyn Nets pro basketball team and the NHL team the New York Islanders.

NEW YORK TRANSIT MUSEUM MUSEUM

Map p446 (☎718-694-1600; www.mta.info/mta/museum; Schermerhorn St, at Boerum Pl; adult/child $7/5; 🕒10am-4pm Tue-Fri, 11am-5pm Sat & Sun; 👪; [S]2/3, 4/5 to Borough Hall; R to Court St) Occupying an old subway station built in 1936 (and out of service since 1946), this kid-friendly museum takes on 100-plus years of getting around town. The best part is the downstairs area, on the platform, where you can climb aboard 13 original subway and elevated train cars dating to 1904. The museum's gift shop sells popular subway-map gifts.

BROOKLYN HEIGHTS PROMENADE LOOKOUT

Map p446 (btwn Orange & Remsen Sts; 🕒24hr; 👪; [S]2/3 to Clark St) All of the east–west lanes of Brooklyn Heights (such as Clark and Pineapple Sts) lead to the neighborhood's number-one attraction: a narrow park with breathtaking views of Lower Manhattan and New York Harbor. Though it hangs over the busy Brooklyn–Queens Expwy (BQE), this little slice of urban beauty is a great spot for a sunset walk.

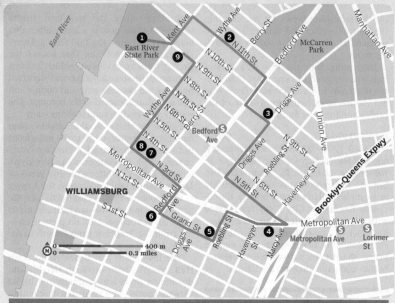

🏃 Local Life
Exploring Williamsburg

Williamsburg is essentially a college town without a college – it's New York's of-the-moment Bohemian magnet, drawing slouchy, baby-faced artists, musicians, writers and graphic designers. Once a bastion of Latino working-class life, it's become a prominent dining and nightlife center. There's lots to explore, from vintage cocktail dens to colorful stores selling one-of-a-kind creations from Brooklyn's craftmakers.

❶ Seeing Green

Offering fabulous Manhattan views, the East River State Park (p270) is an open green space that becomes a major draw in the summertime – with picnicking and the occasional concert.

❷ Homegrown Hops

Hearkening back to a time when the area was NYC's beer-brewing center, the Brooklyn Brewery (p270) not only brews and serves tasty local suds, it also offers tours.

❸ Fashion Finds

If you want to dress the part, stop in at Buffalo Exchange (p298), a much-loved vintage shop, where you'll find eye-catching fashions for men and women.

❹ Bodega Ephemera

For a glimpse of curious old objects from the days of yore, visit City Reliquary (p271),

which is packed with NYC relics, including exhibits on the 1939 World's Fair.

❺ American Detour

A fun little shop for browsing, Fuego 718 (p298) transports you south of the border with Day of the Dead boxes, colorful frames and mirrors, and kitsch and crafts from Mexico, Peru and beyond.

❻ Cocktails & Oysters

Crank that time machine back one more notch at Maison Premiere (p288), which features bespoke cocktails, oysters and other treats.

❼ Brooklyn Art Library

Sign up for a free account so that you can browse the myriad sketchbooks from artists around the world at this space (p270). Or buy a blank book and add your work to the collection.

AMANDA HALL / GETTY IMAGES ©

Manhattan and the Brooklyn Bridge from Empire Fulton Ferry State Park (p265)

❽ Brooklyn Oenology

Don't let the pretentious name deter you. Friendly **Brooklyn Oenology** (Map p440; ☎718-599-1259; www.brooklynoenology.com; 209 Wythe Ave, btwn 3rd & 4th Sts; 🕒4-10pm Mon, 2-10pm Tue-Thu, to midnight Fri & Sat, noon-10pm Sun; [S] L to Bedford Ave) offers sample wines, whiskeys, beers, ciders and other treats, all made in New York.

❾ Vinyl Valhalla

Williamsburg's massive new record shop (p298) is a dream for vinyl collectors. There are also frequent in-store concerts, many of which are free.

BROOKLYN HISTORICAL SOCIETY MUSEUM
Map p446 (☎718-222-4111; www.brooklynhistory.org; 128 Pierrepont St, near Clinton St; admission suggested $10; 🕒noon-5pm Wed-Sun; [S] A/C, F to Jay St; M, R to Court St; 2/3, 4/5 to Borough Hall) Housed in an 1881 Queen Anne–style landmark building (a gem in itself, with striking terra-cotta details on the facade), this library and museum is devoted to all things Brooklyn. Its priceless collection contains a rare 1770 map of New York City and a signed copy of the Emancipation Proclamation.

Be sure to check out the vintage library, with its original black-ash balcony from the 19th century. The society organizes regular exhibitions and neighborhood walks. Check the website for details.

◉ Dumbo

Dumbo's nickname is an acronym for its location: 'Down Under the Manhattan Bridge Overpass,' and while this north Brooklyn slice of waterfront used to be strictly for industry, it's now the domain of high-end condos, furniture shops and art galleries. Several highly regarded performing-arts spaces are located in the cobblestone streets and the **Empire Fulton Ferry State Park** hugs the waterfront and offers picture-postcard Manhattan views.

★**BROOKLYN BRIDGE PARK** PARK
See p265.

◉ Fort Greene & Clinton Hill

These appealing residential districts spread east and south from the Brooklyn side of the Manhattan Bridge (along the eastern side of Flatbush Ave). The neighborhoods are marked on the southwestern end by the **Williamsburgh Savings Bank Tower** (Map p442; 1 Hanson Pl, at Ashland Pl; [S] 2/3, 4/5 to Atlantic Ave; D, N/R to Atlantic Ave-Pacific St) [FREE], which was built in 1927 and for decades was the tallest building in Brooklyn. If you're lost, looking for the tower is a good way to regain your sense of direction.

If you're on the hunt for gorgeous 19th-century architecture, Washington and Clinton Aves in Clinton Hill are home to some beautiful clusters of post–Civil War row houses.

BROOKLYN ACADEMY OF MUSIC
CULTURAL CENTER

Map p442 (BAM; ☎718-636-4100; www.bam. org; 30 Lafayette Ave, at Ashland Pl, Fort Greene; ⒮D, N/R to Pacific St; 2/3, 4/5, B, Q to Atlantic Ave) Founded in 1861, BAM is the country's oldest performing-arts center and supplies New York City with its edgier works of modern dance, music and theater. The complex contains a 2109-seat opera house, an 874-seat theater, the four-screen Rose Cinemas and a 250-seat theater around the corner. Its stage has showcased Mercer Cunningham retrospectives, contemporary African dance and avant-garde interpretations of Shakespeare.

From September through December, BAM hosts the Next Wave Festival, which presents an array of avant-garde works and artist talks. The on-site bar and restaurant, BAMcafé, stages free jazz, R&B and pop performances on weekends.

MUSEUM OF CONTEMPORARY AFRICAN DIASPORAN ARTS
MUSEUM

Map p442 (MoCADA; ☎718-230-0492; mocada. org; 80 Hanson Pl, at S Portland Ave, Fortt Greene; adult/child $8/free; ⊙noon-7pm Wed-Sat, to 6pm Sun; ⒮C to Lafayette Ave; B/D, N/Q/R, 2/3 4/5 to Atlantic Ave) This small museum hosts a wide of range of thought-provoking installations that explore social and political issues facing people of the African diaspora. Photography, sculpture, sound, and multimedia works are all part of the rotation of temporary exhibitions. The museum also hosts performance pieces, music nights, artist talks and discussions. Don't miss the shop onsite with a range of one-of-a-kind art, jewelry, apparel and home decor by contemporary designers.

In 2018, the museum will move to roomier digs (tripling its exhibition space in fact) in a new building going up a few blocks away at Lafayette and Flatbush.

FORT GREENE PARK
PARK

Map p442 (www.fortgreenepark.org; btwn Myrtle & DeKalb Aves & Washington Park & Edward's St, Fort Greene; ⊙6am-1am; ⒧; ⒮B, Q/R to DeKalb Ave) This 30-acre park sits on land that housed military forts during the Revolutionary War. In 1847, the area was designated Brooklyn's first park (a measure supported by newspaper editor Walt Whitman), and by 1867, Calvert Vaux and Frederick Olmsted were redesigning the place into the attractive hilltop landscape

it is today. There are walkways, ball fields and a playground.

At the center of the park stands the Prison Ship Martyrs' Monument, supposedly the world's largest Doric column (it's 149ft high). Designed by Stanford White, it was built in 1905 to memorialize the 11,500 American prisoners of war who died in British prison ships during the Revolution.

BRIC HOUSE
CULTURAL CENTER

Map p442 (☎718-683-5600; www.bricartsmedia.org; 647 Fulton St, cnr Rockwell Pl; ⊙gallery 10am-6pm Tue-Sun; ☎; ⒮B, Q/R to DeKalb Ave; 2/3, 4/5 to Nevins St) This long-running Brooklyn arts organization (responsible for free summer concerts in Prospect Park among other things) moved into a permanent space in 2013 – and at 40,000 sq ft, it's quite impressive. The multidisciplinary arts complex stages art exhibitions, media events and a wide range of cultural fare – plays, concerts, dance performances – inside its 400-seat theater. There's also a branch of the Hungry Ghost cafe, and a glassworking facility (which also has exhibitions) next door.

⊙ Boerum Hill, Cobble Hill & Carroll Gardens

Just south of Brooklyn Heights and Downtown Brooklyn, this cluster of tree-lined brownstone neighborhoods – Boerum Hill (east of Court St), Cobble Hill (west of Court St) and Carroll Gardens (south of Degraw St) – is short on attractions but full of great places to stroll, eat and shop. In Boerum Hill, Smith St is a particularly enticing option. The roughly 13-block stretch south of Atlantic Ave is filled with restaurants, bookshops, bars and neat boutiques – a more chilled-out alternative to the consumer craziness of Manhattan. Atlantic Ave is broader and busier, with bars, restaurants, Middle Eastern groceries, clothing boutiques and antique shops, all concentrated into the blocks between Boerum Pl and Third Ave. To the south of Cobble Hill is Carroll Gardens, a long-time Italian neighborhood, which continues down to the Gowanus Expwy.

INVISIBLE DOG
GALLERY

Map p442 (☎347-560-3641; www.theinvisibledog.org; 51 Bergen St; ⊙1-7pm Thu-Sat, to 5pm Sun; ⒮F, G to Bergen St) In a converted factory off Smith St, the Invisible Dog is an interdisciplinary arts center that embodies the spirit of Brooklyn's creativity. Frequent exhibitions are held on the ground floor, while artist studios upstairs sometimes throw open their doors for group shows. Plays, film screenings, music performances and the odd market all add to the cultural appeal of this community-focused arts center.

Red Hook

Red Hook is a waterfront area with cobblestone streets and hulking industrial buildings. Though it's a bit of a hike from the subway line, the formerly gritty area is now home to a handful of bars and eateries, as well as a massive waterfront branch of Fairway, a beloved gourmet grocery with breathtaking views of NY Harbor. You can catch a ferry to Red Hook (near Ikea) from Lower Manhattan.

WATERFRONT MUSEUM MUSEUM

Map p442 (☎718-624-4719; www.waterfrontmuseum.org; 290 Conover St, at Pier 44; ⏲4-8pm Thu & 1-5pm Sat; 👪; 🚌B61 to Coffey St, [S]F to Smith St) [FREE] The former Lehigh Valley Railroad Barge #79 (built 1914) was purchased for a dollar by its current owner, a juggler, who rescued it from its partially submerged state under the George Washington Bridge. Now it serves as a floating museum with exhibits and events. The museum is free, but if you leave a donation you get a temporary tattoo. It's not a huge attraction, but sufficiently odd to be interesting.

Gowanus

To the east of the elevated subway station at Smith and 9th Sts, in an area surrounded by former industrial blocks, is the Gowanus Canal. Despite its toxic status, the area is home to a number of artist studios and frequently attracts intrepid urban explorers in search of moody (if not entirely stench-free) waterfront pictures. With the opening of new restaurants and gourmet grocer Whole Foods, the area is Brooklyn's 'next big thing.'

A former creek named after Gouwane, a Canarsie Native American chief, it was here that ships to New York Harbor came to unload their goods. It was also where local industrial operations unloaded all kinds of untreated waste. Today, it has been declared a clean-up site by the Environmental Protection Agency.

Park Slope

The Park Slope neighborhood is known for its classic brownstones, tons of great eateries and boutiques (especially along Fifth Ave, which is more cutting edge than the other major strip, Seventh Ave), lesbian residents and stroller-pushing couples who resemble those on the Upper West Side (but have a backyard attached to their apartment).

The 585-acre Prospect Park, created in 1866, is considered the greatest achievement of landscape designers Olmsted and Vaux, who also designed Central Park. Wander along its forested pathways, go for a run along its 3-plus-mile loop or jump on a boat that tours its 60-acre lake from May to October; a new skating rink is open in winter. Next door is the excellent 52-acre Brooklyn Botanic Garden (p276), which features impressive cherry-tree blossoms in spring. Beside the garden is the Brooklyn Museum (p267), with comprehensive collections of African, Islamic and Asian art, plus the Elizabeth A Sackler Center for Feminist Art.

★PROSPECT PARK PARK

See p268.

OLD STONE HOUSE BUILDING

Map p444 (☎718-768-3195; www.theoldstonehouse.org; Washington Park/JJ Byrne Playground, 3rd St, off Fifth Ave; suggested donation $3; ⏲11am-4pm Sat & Sun; 👪; [S]F, R to 4th Ave) This stone house, reconstructed by Robert Moses, is a replica of a 1699 Dutch farmhouse. There's a permanent exhibit devoted to the Battle of Long Island (as Brooklyn was known as c 1776), which includes period clothes and weapons. There's also a great playground for kids here.

Prospect Heights

Just across Flatbush Ave from Park Slope is the easygoing Prospect Heights. Once a home to Italian, Jewish and Irish residents, it began to attract African Americans and West Indians in the middle of the 20th

WORTH A DETOUR

HARBOR DEFENSE MUSEUM

Beneath the breathtaking Verrazano-Narrows Bridge and located inside Fort Hamilton, military buffs will discover a small treasure trove of artifacts at the **Harbor Defense Museum** (☎718-630-4349; www.harbordefensemuseum.com; 101st St & Fort Hamilton Pkwy; 🕐10am-4pm Mon-Fri; 👪; [S]R to Bay Ridge-95th St), the only army museum in New York City. Built between 1825 and 1831, this arched, brick fort is still an active army base (bring a photo ID to get in). The historic caponier, a freestanding bastion, houses the museum. The diverse collection includes helmets, weapons and uniforms from the Revolutionary War to WWII.

There is also an array of vintage artillery. Take a guided tour if you want to learn how to load a 19th-century cannon. (Interesting fact: future Confederate general Robert E Lee ran the fort in the 1840s.)

To get here, take the R train to Bay Ridge-95th St and then walk half-a-dozen blocks to the southwest along Fourth Ave. The museum is located in a small park adjacent to the Verrazano-Narrows Bridge.

century. Today, it draws a mix of young families and professionals who appreciate the proximity to Prospect Park. Most businesses are clustered along Vanderbilt and Washington Aves.

★BROOKLYN MUSEUM MUSEUM

See p267.

BROOKLYN BOTANIC GARDEN GARDENS

Map p444 (www.bbg.org; 1000 Washington Ave, at Crown St; adult/child $12/free, free Tue & 10am-noon Sat; 🕐8am-6pm Tue-Fri, 10am-6pm Sat & Sun; 👪; [S]2/3 to Eastern Pkwy-Brooklyn Museum) One of Brooklyn's most picturesque attractions, this 52-acre garden is home to thousands of plants and trees, as well as a Japanese garden where river turtles swim alongside a Shinto shrine. The best time to visit is late April or early May, when the blooming cherry trees (a gift from Japan) are celebrated in Sakura Matsuri, the Cherry Blossom Festival.

A network of trails connect the Japanese garden to other popular sections devoted to native flora, bonsai trees, a wood covered in bluebells and a rose garden.

There is a good cafe on-site with outdoor seating. There are multiple entrances. The best one is at Washington Ave, south of the Brooklyn Museum, which leads to a striking visitor center with a 'living' roof covered in 40,000 plants.

BROOKLYN PUBLIC LIBRARY LIBRARY

Map p444 (☎718-230-2100; www.bklynlibrary.org; 10 Grand Army Plaza, btwn Flatbush & Eastern Pkwy; 🕐9am-9pm Mon-Thu, to 6pm Fri & Sat, 1-5pm Sun; 👪; [S]B, Q to 7th Ave; 2/3 to Eastern Pkwy-Brooklyn Museum) [FREE] Brooklyn's Central Library is an art-deco masterpiece from 1941 that contains over one million books, magazines and multimedia items. The limestone-covered building is shaped like an open book and there are 15 bronze panels above its 50ft-high entrance featuring literary characters like Tom Sawyer and Moby Dick. Free events happen throughout the year, including film screenings, classical concerts and weekly story time for babies, toddlers and pre-schoolers.

Bedford-Stuyvesant & Crown Heights

Bedford-Stuyvesant is New York City's largest African American district – it's where Notorious BIG grew up and film director Spike Lee shot *Do the Right Thing*. The neighborhood sprawls across central Brooklyn between Flushing and Atlantic Aves and incorporates everything from picturesque row houses to bleak public-housing projects. South of Atlantic Ave, you'll find Crown Heights, a neighborhood of African Caribbean and African American residents, who throw a resplendent West Indian Day parade (held every year on Labor Day).

The Stuyvesant Heights Historic District (corner Lewis Ave and Decatur St; subway A/C to Utica Ave), located near Bed-Stuy's southern limits, vies with Brooklyn Heights and Park Slope for most gorgeous late-19th-century brownstones.

Parts of these neighborhoods bordering Bushwick and East New York can get sketchy. If you're keen on adventuring, ask around before setting out.

BROOKLYN CHILDREN'S MUSEUM MUSEUM
(☎718-735-4400; www.brooklynkids.org; 145 Brooklyn Ave, at St Marks Ave, Crown Heights; admission $11, free 2-6pm Thu; ☺10am-5pm Tue-Sun, till 6pm Thu; ☑; Ⓢ C to Kingston-Throop Aves; 3 to Kingston Ave) A bright yellow, L-shaped structure houses this hands-on kids' favorite, which was founded in 1899. The collection contains almost 30,000 cultural objects (musical instruments, masks and dolls) and natural history specimens (rocks, minerals and a complete Asian elephant skeleton). The museum is located next to Brower Park and is about a mile from the Grand Army Plaza.

WEEKSVILLE HERITAGE CENTER HISTORIC SITE
(☎718-765-5250; www.weeksvillesociety.org; 1698 Bergen St, btwn Rochester & Buffalo Aves, Crown Heights; admission $5; ☺tours 3pm Tue, Thu & Fri; Ⓢ A/C to Utica Ave) In 1838 a free African American by the name of James Weeks purchased a tract of land on the fringes of Brooklyn's settled areas to build a free African American community of entrepreneurs, doctors, laborers and craftsmen. Over time, the village was absorbed into Brooklyn, but three of the historic wooden houses (aka the Hunterfly Road Houses) can be visited.

The center continues to evolve: a 19,000-sq-ft gold-certified LEED (Leadership in Energy and Environmental Design) building opened in 2014, with oral media lab, resource center, gallery space and performance hall, as well as a new micro farm and botanic collection. It's a trek to get here, but worth it for history buffs.

WYCKOFF HOUSE HISTORIC BUILDING
(☎718-629-5400; wyckoffmuseum.org; 5816 Clarendon Rd, btwn 59th St & Ralph Ave, East Flatbush; adult/child $5/3; ☺grounds noon-4pm Fri & Sat, guided house tours 1pm & 3pm Fri & Sat; ☒B8 to Beverley Rd/Ralph Ave, Ⓢ B, Q to Newkirk Plaza) Built in 1652, the Pieter Claesen Wyckoff House is New York City's oldest structure. A working farm until 1901, this Dutch Colonial H-frame house has shingled walls and split Dutch doors. It's located in the East Flatbush section of Brooklyn. Reservations required. Call or check the websites for directions out here.

◉ Coney Island & Brighton Beach

★CONEY ISLAND NEIGHBORHOOD
See p269.

BRIGHTON BEACH NEIGHBORHOOD
About an hour by subway from Manhattan, this neighborhood is home to a large Ukrainian and Russian population. Like Coney Island next door, it has a boardwalk overlooking brown sands and Atlantic waters. The bigger draw, though, is the bustling thoroughfare (Brighton Beach Ave) under the elevated subway tracks, which is lined with shops, restaurants and cafes selling products from the Motherland. Welcome to 'Little Odessa.'

NEW YORK AQUARIUM AQUARIUM
Map p447 (www.nyaquarium.com; Surf Ave & W 8th St; admission $12; ☺10am-6pm Jun-Aug, to 4:30pm Sep-May; ☑; Ⓢ F, Q to W 8th St-NY Aquarium) This fun, kid-friendly aquarium offers an opportunity to peek at an ocean's worth of creatures. The sea lion show is the big draw, which takes place in an outdoor Aquatheater with stadium seating. The New York Aquarium is currently undergoing a massive $157-million expansion, adding an ambitious 500,000-gallon tank entitled 'Ocean's Wonders: Sharks!' slated for completion in late 2016. Expect higher prices – and state-of-the-art galleries – when it opens.

✗ EATING

✗ Williamsburg, Greenpoint & Bushwick

CHAMPS VEGAN $
Map p440 (☎718-599-2743; www.champsdiner.com; 197 Meserole St, at Humboldt St; sandwiches & salads $9-12; ☺8am-midnight; 🛜🅹; Ⓢ L to Montrose) 🍃 This airy little diner whips up delicious plates of comfort food – all made with vegan ingredients. The reasonable prices and all-day breakfasts keep things busy. Try the French toast slam (with tofu scramble and tempeh bacon), the chocolate chip and banana pancakes, mac 'n' cheese or

Neighborhood Walk
Brownstones & Bridges

START ST GEORGE HOTEL
END JANE'S CAROUSEL
LENGTH 2 MILES; TWO HOURS

Studded with historic structures, the area around Brooklyn Heights also has sublime views of Manhattan. Start at the corner of Clark and Henry Sts, at the base of the 30-story **1 St George Hotel**. Built between 1885 and 1930, it was once the city's largest hotel with 2632 rooms. Two blocks to the north, at Orange and Hicks Sts, is **2 Plymouth Church**. In the mid-19th century, Henry Ward Beecher led abolitionist sermons here, as well as 'mock auctions' to buy a slave's freedom. Continue west on Orange and then south on Willow St. At 70 Willow, the yellow 11-bedroom mansion served as **3 Truman Capote's house** while he was writing *Breakfast at Tiffany's*. Continue south, turning right on Pierrepont St, and follow as it bends to the left. The street turns into **4 Montague Tce**, a one-block lane lined with old brownstones. Thomas Wolfe penned *Of Time and the River* at No 5. From here, Remsen St travels west to reach the **5 Brooklyn Heights Promenade** (p271). This scenic park, with its staggering city views, was built by planner Robert Moses in 1942, as a way of placating locals irritated by the construction of the roaring expressway below. Head north along the Promenade, then north along Columbia Heights, and take the bouncy, pedestrian-only **6 Squib Park Bridge** down into Brooklyn Bridge Park. At the bottom, admire the view from the grassy Pier 1, part of **7 Brooklyn Bridge Park** (p265). Nearby is **8 Fulton Ferry Landing**. George Washington made an important hasty retreat here during the Battle of Long Island in 1776. From here, follow Water St under the **9 Brooklyn Bridge** (completed 1883), and past the **10 Empire Stores & Tobacco Warehouse** (p265), two Civil War–era brick structures. The walk ends at Empire Fulton Ferry, part of Brooklyn Bridge Park and home to the gleaming **11 Jane's Carousel** (p265).

a 'bacon cheeseburger' (a black bean burger with tempeh bacon and veggie cheese).

Energy-fueling juices, smoothies and lattes (with almond or soy milk) also available.

PETER PAN BAKERY BAKERY **$**

Map p440 (☎718-389-3676; peterpandonuts.com; 727 Manhattan Ave; snacks $1-3; 🕐5:30am-8pm Mon-Sat, to 7pm Sun; [S]G to Nassau Ave) On the main drag in Greenpoint, Peter Pan Bakery is a much-loved classic for its unfussy, well-made baked goods and excellent breakfast sandwiches on housebaked rolls or bagels (try the bacon-egg-and-cheese on a toasted poppy-seed roll), all at rock-bottom prices. Have a seat at the wraparound counter, or take it away and munch in McCarren Park.

ROBERTA'S PIZZA **$$**

Map p440 (☎718-417-1118; www.robertaspizza.com; 261 Moore St, near Bogart St, Bushwick; pizzas $14-18; 🕐11am-midnight Mon-Fri, from 10am Sat & Sun; ✎; [S]L to Morgan Ave) This hipster-saturated warehouse restaurant in Bushwick consistently produces some of the best pizza in New York. Service can be lackadaisical and the waits long (lunch is best), but the brick-oven pies are the right combination of chewy and fresh. The classic margherita is sublimely simple, though more adventurous palates can opt for the seasonal hits like Speckenwolf (mozzarella, speck, crimini and onion).

There is a garden bar where you can enjoy beer, wine or cocktails while you wait for your name to come up. On weekends, the brunch draws equally large crowds.

ZENKICHI JAPANESE **$$**

Map p440 (☎718-388-8985; zenkichi.com; 77 N 6th St, at Wythe Ave; small plates $9-18, tasting menu $65; 🕐6pm-midnight Mon-Sat, 5:30-11:30pm Sun; [S]L to Bedford Ave) A temple of refined Japanese cuisine, Zenkichi presents beautifully prepared dishes in an atmospheric setting that has wowed foodies from far and wide. The recommendation here is the *omakase* (a seasonal eight-course tasting menu, featuring highlights like konbu-cured sashimi, crunchy shrimp tempura with trumpet mushrooms, tender grilled black cod and a silky miso soup).

The experience starts just inside the unmarked door, where you'll be led past bamboo- and pebble-lined pathways lit by lanterns to a private booth enclosed by bamboo curtains. The buzzer on the table summons the server, who can expertly guide you through the menu. Given the atmosphere, it's a favorite on date night.

OKONOMI JAPANESE **$$**

Map p440 (www.okonomibk.com; 150 Ainsle St, btwn Lorimer & Leonard Sts, Williamsburg; set menu $17-23; 🕐9am-2pm & 6-11pm Mon-Fri, 10am-4pm Sat & Sun; [S]L to Lorimer St; G to Metropolitan Ave) 🌿 For a dazzling breakfast that doesn't involve eggs or French toast, make a pilgrimage to this exquisite little wood-lined eatery in East Williamsburg. Okonomi serves only set menus: a small vegetable dish, baked egg, brown rice (with the option of adding a poached egg) and tender fish (such as sake-braised tuna or smoked bluefish), accompanied by a tasty green tea with barley. Perfection!

By evening, the eatery transitions to a ramen spot, with equally fine attention to detail. Most seafood is sourced from the East Coast, and nothing goes to waste (fish bones and head are simmered for ramen stock).

MARLOW & SONS MODERN AMERICAN **$$**

Map p440 (☎718-384-1441; www.marlowandsons.com; 81 Broadway, btwn Berry St & Wythe Ave, Williamsburg; mains lunch $14-18, dinner $25-28; 🕐8am-midnight; [S]J/M/Z to Marcy Ave; L to Bedford Ave) The dimly lit, wood-lined space feels like an old farmhouse cafe, and hosts a buzzing nighttime scene as diners and drinkers crowd in for oysters, tip-top cocktails and a changing daily menu of locavore specialties (smoked pork loin, crunchy crust pizzas, caramelized turnips, fluffy Spanish-style tortillas). Brunch is also a big draw, though prepare for lines.

FIVE LEAVES MODERN AMERICAN **$$**

Map p440 (☎718-383-5345; fiveleavesny.com; 18 Bedford Ave, at Lorimer St, Greenpoint; mains lunch $11-16, dinner $15-28; 🕐8am-1am; ✎; [S]G to Nassau Ave) An anchor of the Greenpoint dining and drinking scene, Five Leaves draws a wide mix of neighborhood regulars who create a lively buzz both at the outdoor tables in front and in the vintage-filled interior. Stop by in the morning for ricotta pancakes, fresh pastries and great coffee (from Parlor Coffee), or at lunch for eggplant and quinoa falafel, truffle fries and chopped black kale salads. In the evening the market-fresh seasonal menu features the likes of ora king salmon with buckwheat pilaf and pork

Local Life
South Brooklyn

This 4-mile walk takes in some of Brooklyn's most fascinating neighborhoods, where new restaurants, shops, bars and cafes are rapidly changing the urban landscape. Along the way, you'll stroll through leafy neighborhoods, past brownstone-lined streets and across two pretty parks. To hit the flea markets and greenmarkets mentioned here, do this walk on a Saturday.

❶ Fort Greene Park

A stroll across pleasant 30-acre Fort Greene Park is a leisurely way to kick off the day. Climb the hill to the Prison Ship Martyr's Monument for views of Manhattan. On Saturday, there's a greenmarket just off the park on Cumberland St (we're fond of the apple-cider doughnuts).

❷ Smooch

The leafy neighborhood surrounding the park is also called Fort Greene. Take a stroll along restaurant-lined DeKalb Ave, Fort Greene's main thoroughfare. Stop for coffee at **Smooch** (Map p442; ☎718-624-4075; 264 Carlton Ave, btwn DeKalb & Willoughby, Fort Greene; ☺8am-9pm Mon-Wed, to 10pm Thu-Sun; ⓢC to Lafayette Ave; G to Fulton St). Peek down the side streets for a glimpse of some of Brooklyn's loveliest streets.

❸ Unique Finds

The **Brooklyn Flea Market** (Map p442; www.brooklynflea.com; 176 Lafayette Ave, btwn Clermont & Vanderbilt Aves, Fort Greene; ☺10am-5pm Sat Apr-Oct; ♿; ⓢG to Clinton-Washington Aves) hosts over 200 vendors who congregate to sell their wares, ranging from antiques and vintage clothes to enticing to-go snacks.

❹ Vanderbilt

Crossing Atlantic Ave you arrive in Prospect Heights, another charming Brooklyn hood. Vanderbilt Ave is the main drag. Stop in at Cooklyn (p286) for seasonal recipes with a deep connection to local purveyors.

❺ Grand Army Plaza

Continue down to **Grand Army Plaza** (Map p444; Prospect Park, Prospect Park West & Flatbush Ave; ☺6am-midnight; ♿; ⓢ2/3 to Grand Army Plaza; B, Q to 7th Ave), a giant traffic circle crowned by a massive arch. Just

Fort Greene Park

south, at the Prospect Park entrance, is a popular Saturday greenmarket.

❻ The Other Central Park

Prospect Park (p268), Brooklyn's version of Central Park, features many of the same landscape features but with far fewer crowds. A grassy meadow, forested trails and a scenic lake are the big draws.

❼ Hero's Supply

Strolling west out of the park, you enter Park Slope, with tree-lined streets and historic brownstones in every direction. Fifth Ave is one of the commercial drags (as is Seventh Ave). Visit the curious **Brooklyn Superhero Supply Co** (Map p444; ☎718-499-9884; www.superheosupplies.com; 372 Fifth Ave, btwn 5th & 6th Sts, Park Slope; ⊙11am-5pm; 👶; 🚇R to 9th St; F, G to 4th Ave) for capes, disguises and particle guns.

❽ Lavender Lake

Just west of Park Slope is Gowanus, a once-industrial neighborhood on the make. Take the picturesque wood-plank bridge on Carroll St and have a waterside look before stopping at Lavender Lake (p294), an enticing bar with a relaxing backyard open in the summer.

shank vindaloo. Add in wines and creative cocktails for the start to a great night.

RABBIT HOLE
MODERN AMERICAN **$$**

Map p440 (☎718-782-0910; www.rabbitholerestaurant.com; 352 Bedford Ave, btwn S 3rd & 4th Sts, Williamsburg; mains breakfast $9-14, dinner $15-22; ⊙9am-11pm; 🖉; 🚇L to Bedford Ave; J/M/Z to Marcy Ave) A warm and inviting spot in South Williamsburg, the very charming Rabbit Hole is a fine spot to disappear into, particularly if you're craving breakfast (served till 5pm). There's casual cafe seating up front for good coffee and even better house-made pastries. Head to the back, or the relaxing rear garden for creamy eggs Benedict or fresh fruit and granola.

In the evening, the quaint plank-floored, tin-ceilinged eatery transforms into a gastropub with lamb burgers, pan-seared striped bass, microbrews and old-fashioned cocktails.

MOMO SUSHI SHACK
JAPANESE **$$**

Map p440 (☎718-418-6666; www.momosushishack.com; 43 Bogart St, btwn Moore & Seigel Sts, Bushwick; sushi rolls $6-14; ⊙noon-4:30pm daily & 5:30-11pm Mon-Thu, to midnight Fri & Sat; 🖉; 🚇L to Morgan Ave) Three shared tables occupy this industrial-chic spot, where inventive Japanese tapas all come with instructions on how to eat them. Foodie preciousness aside, Momo's is staggeringly good, offering super-fresh classics and flamboyant contemporary creations, including rice croquettes with squash, sage, walnut and mozzarella. There are veggie options and a good list of sakes. Cash only.

MONTANA'S
TRAIL HOUSE
MODERN AMERICAN **$$**

(☎917-966-1666; montanastrailhouse.com; 445 Troutman, btwn Cypress & St Nicholas Aves, Bushwick; mains $15-24; 🚇L to Jefferson Ave) A wild repurposing of a former gas station, Montana's is all reclaimed plank walls, industrial light fixtures, taxidermy and bookshelves that hide a secret passageway to an outdoor patio. Order a cocktail (something with rye or black-pepper-infused bourbon) and dine on seasonal, creative comfort food like root-beer-braised brisket, fall harvest vegetables or smokey duck breast with burnt lemon.

It draws the trademark Bushwick crowd: young, hip and tattooed.

BROOKLYN EATING

PAULIE GEE'S PIZZA $$

(☎347-987-3747; www.pauliegee.com; 60 Greenpoint Ave, btwn West & Franklin Sts, Greenpoint; pizzas $14-18; ⏰6-11pm Mon-Fri, from 5pm Sat, 5-10pm Sun; [V] [👶]; [S]G to Greenpoint Ave) Greenpoint's best pizza place has a cozy cabin-in-the-woods vibe, with flickering candles and old-school beats playing overhead. Diners huddle over chunky wooden tables forking away at delicious, thin-crust creatively topped pizzas. For the full experience, add on craft brews, affordable wine selections, zesty salads and dessert decadence (flourless chocolate cake, Van Leeuwan ice cream).

Great vegan options (we're talking jackfruit meatballs and almond milk and onion cream).

MISS FAVELA BRAZILIAN $$

Map p440 (☎718-230-4040; www.missfavela.com; 57 S 5th St, cnr Wythe St, Williamsburg; mains $20-25, sandwiches $14; ⏰noon-midnight; [S]J/M to Marcy Ave; L to Bedford Ave) This ramshackle little spot near the Williamsburg Bridge serves hearty plates of Brazilian cooking like *moqueca* (a coconut-milk-flavored fish stew) and *picanha* (a juicy cut of prime steak), best preceded by *bolinhos de bacalhau* (codfish balls) and accompanied by a caipirinha or three.

Come on Saturdays for live samba and *feijoada* (black beans and pork stew) and on Sundays for live *forró* (music of northeastern Brazil). Sidewalk seating on warm days.

CUBANA SOCIAL CUBAN $$

Map p440 (☎718-782-3334; www.cubanasocial.com; 70 N 6th St, btwn Kent & Wythe; mains $19-23, sandwiches around $14; ⏰5pm-midnight Mon-Thu, to 4am Fri, 10am-4am Sat, 10am-midnight Sun; [S]L to Bedford Ave) True to name, Cubana Social boasts an old-school (circa 1950s) Havana vibe. In an open room fronted by a small stage, waitstaff bearing plates of slow-roasted pork, *ropa vieja* (a kind of beef stew) and empanadas glide among the small candelit tables. There's live music (jazz, Afro-Cuban, Latin) Thursday to Saturday nights.

WATER TABLE MODERN AMERICAN $$$

(☎917-499-5727; www.thewatertablenyc.com; 10 India St, Greenpoint; prix-fixe Sun $50, Fri & Sat $65-80; ⏰7:30-10pm Fri & Sat, 6-8pm Sun; [S]G to Greenpoint) Scoring high on novelty, the Water Table is set inside a rustically converted WWII navy patrol boat. The three-course

THE BEST OF NEW YORK PIZZA

New York is known for a lot of things: screeching subways, towering skyscrapers, bright lights. It is also known for its pizza, which comes in a variety of gooey, chewy, sauce-soaked varieties. Following is a list of some of the top places in the city to grab a pie or a slice:

➡ **DiFara Pizza** (☎718-258-1367; www.difara.com; 1424 Ave J, cnr E 15th St; pizza slice $5; ⏰noon-8pm Wed-Sat, from 1pm Sun; [👶]; [S]B, Q to Ave J) In operation since 1964 in the Midwood section of Brooklyn, this old-school slice joint is still lovingly tended to by proprietor Dom DeMarco, who makes the pies himself. Expect lines.

➡ **Totonno's** (p288) The classic Coney Island pizzeria makes pies till the dough runs out.

➡ **Grimaldi's** (Map p446; ☎718-858-4300; www.grimaldis-pizza.com; 1 Front St, cnr of Old Fulton St, Dumbo; pizzas $12-18; ⏰11:30am-11pm; [S]A, C to High St) Legendary lines and legendary pizza in Dumbo.

➡ **Juliana's** (p283) Celebrated return of pizza legend Patsy Grimaldi to Brooklyn in 2013.

➡ **Lucali** (p286) Neapolitan-style pies started as a hobby for this noted Carroll Gardens *pizzaiolo* (pizza maker).

➡ **Franny's** (p286) A contemporary eatery with an organic vibe serves simple pies in Park Slope.

➡ **Roberta's** (p279) Divine pies with cheeky names like 'Gorgon Ramsay' in Bushwick's artsy district.

If you want to try several pizzas in one go, sign up for an outing with **Scott's Pizza Tours** (☎212-913-9903; www.scottspizzatours.com; tours incl pizza $40-65), which will take you to the most vaunted brick ovens around the city by foot or by bus.

dinner (smoked scallop lobster bisque, kale salad, New England dry-rub chicken, and seafood stew were recent selections) would seem a bit pricey if not for the memorable experience of sailing past soaring skyscrapers and the Statue of Liberty by night. Reserve a spot online.

✕ Brooklyn Heights, Downtown Brooklyn & Dumbo

ARCHWAY CAFE   AMERICAN $
Map p446 (www.archwaycafe.com; 57 Pearl St, btwn Water & Front Sts, Dumbo; mains $9-12; ⊙11:30am-7:30pm Mon-Sat, to 6:30pm Sun; 🛜✎; ⓢA/C to High St; F to York St) One of the best places for a casual bite in Dumbo, Archway Cafe is a good anytime spot. Join the morning crowd over avocado toast, baked eggs with chorizo, or granola with fresh berries and yogurt, or stop in later for lunchtime sandwiches (BBQ pulled pork) or salads. It also has excellent espresso and fresh bakery items.

BROOKLYN ICE CREAM FACTORY   ICE CREAM $
Map p446 (☎718-246-3963; www.brooklynice creamfactory.com; Fulton Landing, Water & Old Fulton Sts, Brooklyn Heights; ice cream $4-7; ⊙noon-10pm; 🚻; ⓢA/C to High St) You can grab a cone or a milkshake within view of the Manhattan and Brooklyn Bridges at this shop located inside an old fireboat house. Expect long lines on warm days.

JULIANA'S   PIZZA $$
Map p446 (☎718-596-6700; www.julianaspizza. com; 19 Old Fulton St, btwn Water & Front Sts, Dumbo; pizza $17-32; ⊙11:30am-11pm; ⓢA/C to High St) Legendary pizza maestro Patsy Grimaldi has returned to Brooklyn, with delicious thin-crust perfection in both classic and creative combos (like the No 5, with smoked salmon, goat cheese and capers). It's in Dumbo and the Brooklyn waterfront.

Patsy and his wife Carol were the original owners of Grimaldi's (they sold the business to Frank Ciolli, who now runs the still famous Grimaldi's a few doors down). Now that there are two great pizza joints next to each other, the lines have thinned a bit, though it's still best to arrive early if you don't want a long wait. Who serves the better pie? Our money is on Juliana's.

VINEGAR HILL HOUSE   AMERICAN $$
Map p446 (☎718-522-1018; www.vinegarhill-house.com; 72 Hudson Ave, btwn Water & Front Sts, Vinegar Hill; mains brunch $13-17, dinner $23-32; ⊙6-11pm Mon-Sat, from 5:30pm Sun & 10:30am-3:30pm Sat & Sun; ✎; ⓢF to York St) Tucked into out-of-the-way Vinegar Hill, this homey spot is decked out in a charming array of thrift-store bric-a-brac. But don't let the low-key decor fool you: chef Brian Leth cooks up an evolving menu that is bracingly fresh and unfussy, such as sea trout with wild mushrooms, pork chop with grits and romesco sauce or corn risotto with eggplant.

There is a wine list stocked with French vintages (from $38 per bottle), as well as retro cocktails. This place is popular, especially in summer when the back patio is open. Show up near opening time if you don't want to wait.

ALMAR   ITALIAN $$
Map p446 (☎718-855-5288; www.almardumbo. com; 111 Front St, btwn Adams & Washington Sts, Dumbo; mains lunch $10-16, dinner $16-45; ⊙8am-10:30pm Mon-Fri, 9am-11pm Sat, 10am-5pm Sun; 🚻; ⓢF to York St; A/C/E to High St) This welcoming Italian eatery serves breakfast, lunch and dinner in a homey, wood-lined space in Dumbo. Alfredo's meatballs are top-notch, as is the rich and meaty lasagna Bolognese. But if you're into seafood, don't miss the simple and delicious *cavatelli* (small pasta shells) with mussels, clams, shrimp and cherry tomatoes – it doesn't skimp on the shellfish. Cash only.

The small, inviting bar is an ideal spot to sip wine and nibble on olives.

RIVER CAFÉ   AMERICAN $$$
Map p446 (☎718-522-5200; www.rivercafe. com; 1 Water St, Brooklyn Heights; brunch $55, fixed price dinner 3-/6-course $120/150; ⊙5:30-11:30pm daily, 11:30am-2:30pm Sat & Sun; ✎; ⓢA/C to High St) Situated at the foot of the Brooklyn Bridge, this floating wonder offers beautiful views of downtown Manhattan – not to mention solidly rendered Modern American cooking. It took a beating during Hurricane Sandy and finally reopened in early 2014. Specialties include Wagyu steak tartare, Hudson Valley foie gras, crispy lavender-glazed duck breast and poached Nova Scotia lobster.

The atmosphere is sedate (jackets are required after 5pm) but incurably romantic.

🍴 Fort Greene & Clinton Hill

ROMAN'S ITALIAN $$

Map p442 (☎718-622-5300; www.romansnyc.com; 243 Dekalb Ave, btwn Clermont & Vanderbilt; mains $18-28; ⏲5-11pm Mon-Fri, from noon Sat & Sun; [S]G to Clinton-Washington Aves) In a small buzzing space on restaurant-dotted Dekalb Ave, Roman's is a celebration of seasonal locavorism, with a focused menu that changes nightly. Dishes feature imaginative combinations (sourced from small, sustainable farms) and are beautifully executed: beets with oranges and anchovies, *maccheroni* (macaroni-like pasta) with pork sausage and ricotta, and striped bass filet with green olives.

Adroitly made cocktails and an esoteric wine list seal the deal.

WALTER'S MODERN AMERICAN $$

Map p442 (☎718-488-7800; www.walterfoods.com; 166 Dekalb Ave, cnr Cumberland St, Fort Greene; mains $18-28; ⏲11am-midnight Mon-Fri, from 9am Sat & Sun; [S]B, Q/R to Dekalb Ave) On an idyllic corner just off Fort Greene Park, quaint old-timey Walter's serves up rich Southern and bistro fare with a few flourishes. Favorites: beer-battered blackened catfish with red cabbage coleslaw, spicy fisherman's stew and a reliably good burger (add bacon for a touch of decadence).

Don't neglect the raw bar (oysters, lobster, littleneck clams), the craft cocktails or brunch (fried chicken and waffles is a hit).

🍴 Crown Heights & Bedford-Stuyvesant

★DOUGH BAKERY $

(☎347-533-7544; www.doughdoughnuts.com; 448 Lafayette Ave, cnr Franklin Ave, Clinton Hill; doughnuts around $3; ⏲6am-9pm; 📶; [S]G to Classon Ave) Situated on the border of Clinton Hill and Bed-Stuy, this tiny, out-of-the-way spot is a bit of a trek, but worth it if you're a pastry fan. Puffy raised doughnuts are dipped in a changing array of glazes, including pistachio, blood orange and hibiscus. Doughnut divinity for the tongue.

BERG'N MARKET $

Map p444 (www.bergn.com; 899 Bergen St, btwn Classon & Franklin, Crown Heights; mains $8-12; ⏲9am-late Tue-Fri, from 10am Sat & Sun; 📶🖉; [S]C to Franklin Ave) From the same team behind Brooklyn Flea, Berg'n is a large brick food hall in Crown Heights where you can feast on smoky brisket (Mighty Quinn's), roasted eggplant and beet hummus sandwiches (Samesa), slow-roasted pork burritos (Bklyn Burro), sea salt and caramel ice cream (Blue Marble) and other temptations.

It also has a bar serving microbrews and a coffee stand (Parlour). It's a casual bustling hall, with nights of trivia, board games, pro sports screenings and more.

PEACHES SOUTHERN $$

(☎718-942-4162; www.peachesbrooklyn.com; 393 Lewis Ave, Bedford-Stuyvesant; mains $16-21; ⏲11am-4pm & 5-10pm Mon-Sat, from 10am Sun; [S]A/C to Utica) The homey atmosphere and tasty Southern food make Peaches a Bed-Stuy favorite. The stone-ground grits with blackened catfish is popular at all hours, while the French toast with fresh berries is in demand at brunch. Black kale salad, roasted beet salad and sides like garlic-sautéed broccoli or gooey mac 'n' cheese are the best of the rather limited vegetarian options.

🍴 Boerum Hill, Carroll Gardens, Red Hook & Gowanus

WHOLE FOODS MARKET $

Map p442 (☎718-907-3622; www.wholefoodsmarket.com; 214 3rd St, btwn Third Ave & Bond St; ⏲8am-11pm; 📶; [S]R to Union) 🍃 Brooklyn's first Whole Foods is pretty impressive, with all the gourmet goodies you'd expect to find, plus a few surprises – including a 20,000-sq-ft greenhouse (where some of the produce is grown), an in-house coffee roaster and a sprawling prepared-foods counter (you'll also find records for sale). After browsing the staggering selection, head upstairs to the small bar and food counter.

You can order burgers, truffle-oil-flavored fries, mac 'n' cheese, kale salad and over a dozen unique microbrews on tap. There's outdoor seating with fine views over, uh, NYC's most polluted waterway.

FAIRWAY SUPERMARKET $

Map p442 (☎718-254-0923; www.fairwaymarket.com; 480-500 Van Brunt St, Red Hook; ⏲7am-11pm; 🖉; 🚌B61 to cnr Coffey & Van Brunt Sts, [S]F, G to Carroll St) This sprawling supermarket offers an array of breads, cheeses, olives and smoked meats, as well as delicious prepared foods. An on-site cafe serves simple breakfasts and lunch, and offers excellent views of the Red Hook waterfront.

FOUR AND TWENTY BLACKBIRDS BAKERY $

Map p442 (☎718-499-2917; www.birdsblack.com; 439 Third Ave, cnr 8th St, Gowanus; pie slice around $5; 🕙8am-8pm Mon-Fri, from 9am Sat, 10am-7pm Sun; 📶; [S]R to 9th St) Sister owners Emily and Melissa Elsen create flaky, buttery crusts and often use seasonal, regionally sourced fruits to create NYC's best pies, hands down. At this warm, old-fashioned spot, any time is just right to drop in for a slice and a steaming cup of Irving Farm coffee. You can also come for quiches, savory galettes, sandwiches and other light bites.

GOVINDA'S INDIAN, VEGETARIAN $

Map p442 (☎718-875-6127; www.radhagovindanyc.com; 305 Schermerhorn, btwn Nevins & Bond Sts, downtown; lunch $7-9; 🕙noon-3pm Mon-Fri; 🌿; [S]2/3, 4/5 to Nevins St; A/C, G to Schermerhorn St) On the bottom floor of a Hare Krishna temple, Govinda's prepares five or six different vegan options each day (eggplant parmesan, vegetable curry, lentil soup, samosas and the like), plus rich desserts, all served cafeteria style. There's not much ambience, but if you're vegetarian, you'll find this place a godsend (sorry).

SAHADI'S SELF-CATERING $

Map p442 (☎718-624-4550; www.sahadis.com; 187 Atlantic Ave, btwn Court & Clinton Sts, Boerum Hill; 🕙9am-7pm Mon-Sat; 🌿; [S]2/3, 4/5 to Borough Hall) The smell of fresh-roasted coffee and spices greets you as you enter this beloved Middle Eastern delicacies shop. The olive bar boasts two-dozen options and there are loads of breads, cheeses, nuts and hummus. It's a great place to assemble a picnic before heading to Brooklyn Bridge Park.

MILE END DELI $

Map p442 (☎718-852-7510; www.mileenddeli.com; 97A Hoyt St, Boerum Hill; sandwiches $12-16; 🕙8am-4pm & 5-10pm Mon-Fri, from 10am Sat & Sun; [S]A/C, G to Hoyt Schermerhorn Sts) You can almost taste the smoked meats as you enter this small Boerum Hill eatery, which has exposed brick walls and a couple of communal tables. Try a smoked beef brisket on rye with mustard ($14) – the bread is sticky soft and the meat will melt in your mouth.

LOCAL KNOWLEDGE

SMORGASBURG!

The biggest foodie event in Brooklyn, **Smorgasburg** (www.smorgasburg.com; 🕙11am-6pm Sat & Sun), brings more than 100 vendors selling an incredible array of goodness, along the lines of Italian street snacks, duck confit, Indian flatbread tacos, roasted mushroom burgers, gooey grilled-cheese sandwiches, Ethiopian vegan comfort food, sea salt caramel ice cream, passion-fruit doughnuts and much more. Smorgasburg locations tend to change from season to season, so check the website for the latest.

The market currently happens in Williamsburg (on the waterfront) on Saturdays and Prospect Park (near Lakeside) on Sundays from April to October and in Sunset Park on weekends the rest of the year.

You'll also find classic Montreal-style bagels and that delightful Quebecois mess, poutine (french fries topped with gravy and cheese curds).

★POK POK THAI $$

Map p442 (☎718-923-9322; www.pokpokpdx.com; 117 Columbia St, cnr Kane St, Columbia Street Waterfront District; sharing plates $12-20; 🕙5:30-10pm Mon-Fri, from 10am Sat & Sun; [S]F to Bergen St) Andy Ricker's NYC outpost is a smashing success, wowing diners with a rich and complex menu inspired by northern Thailand street food. Fiery fish-sauce-slathered chicken wings, spicy green papaya salad with salted black crab, smoky grilled eggplant salad and sweet pork belly with ginger, turmeric and tamarind are among the many unique dishes. The setting is fun and ramshackle. Reserve ahead.

BATTERSBY MODERN AMERICAN $$

Map p442 (☎718-852-8321; www.battersbybrooklyn.com; 255 Smith St, btwn Douglass & Degraw Sts; mains $17-32, tasting menu $75-95; 🕙5:30-11pm Mon-Sat, to 10pm Sun; [S]F, G to Bergen St) A top choice in Brooklyn, Battersby serves magnificent seasonal dishes. The small menu changes regularly, but be on the lookout for veal sweetbreads, pappardelle with duck ragu, Chatham cod with braised fennel and delightfully tender lamb. The space is Brooklyn-style quaint (plank floors, brick walls, tin ceiling), but tiny and cramped.

To get in without a long wait, plan ahead: arrive at opening time or make a reservation – accepted only for folks partaking of the tasting menu.

FRANKIES SPUNTINO
ITALIAN $$

Map p442 (☎718-403-0033; www.frankiesspuntino.com; 457 Court St, btwn 4th Pl & Luquer St, Carroll Gardens; mains $16-22; ⏰11am-11pm; ⒮F, G to Carroll St) Frankies is a neighborhood magnet, attracting local couples, families and plenty of Manhattanites with hearty pasta dishes like *cavatelli* with hot sausage and pappardelle with braised lamb. But as a *spuntino* (snack joint), this place is more about the small plates, with a seasonal menu that boasts excellent fresh salads, cheeses, cured meats and heavenly crostinis. No reservations.

LUCALI
PIZZA $$

Map p442 (☎718-858-4086; www.lucali.com; 575 Henry St, at Carroll St, Carroll Gardens; pizza around $25, toppings $3; ⏰6-10pm, closed Tue; 🚼; ⒮F, G to Carroll St) One of New York's tastiest pizzas comes from this unlikely spot (it looks like a living room) run by Mark Iacono. Pizzas are all one size, with chewy crusts, fresh tomato sauce and super-fresh mozzarella. Toppings are limited, but the Brooklyn accent is for real. Cash only; BYO beer or wine.

Plan ahead at this enormously popular spot: arrive at 6pm, give them your cell number, and plan on dining a few hours later.

BROOKLYN CRAB
SEAFOOD $$

Map p442 (☎718-643-2722; www.brooklyncrab.com; 24 Reed St, btwn Conover & Van Brunt Sts, Red Hook; mains $18-42, sandwiches $15-24; ⏰11:30am-10pm Wed, Thu & Sun, to 11pm Fri & Sat; 🚌B61 to Van Brunt & Van Dyke Sts, ⒮F, G to Smith-9th Sts) Across from Fairway, Brooklyn Crab is a casual three-story eatery, where diners hunker over picnic tables to feast on steamed crabs, oysters, fried cod, peel-and-eat shrimp and other delights from the sea. With waterfront views, tender crustaceans and refreshing drafts of Narragansett Lager, it's a great spot on a sunny day.

✕ Park Slope & Prospect Heights

CHUKO
JAPANESE $

Map p444 (☎718-576-6701; www.barchuko.com; 552 Vanderbilt Ave, cnr Dean St, Prospect Heights;

ramen $13; ⏰noon-3pm & 5:30-11pm; 🖉; ⒮B/Q to 7th Ave; 2/3 to Bergen St) This cozy wood-lined ramen shop brings a top-notch noodle game to Prospect Heights. Steaming bowls of al dente ramen are paired with one of several spectacularly silky broths, including an excellent roasted pork and a full-bodied vegetarian. The appetizers are *very* worthwhile, particularly the fragrant salt-and-pepper chicken wings.

TOM'S RESTAURANT
DINER $

Map p444 (☎718-636-9738; 782 Washington Ave, at Sterling Pl, Prospect Heights; mains $7-12; ⏰7am-4pm Mon-Sat, from 8am Sun; ⒮2/3 to Eastern Pkwy-Brooklyn Museum) Open since 1936, this diner looks like grandma's cluttered living room and delivers good, greasy-spoon cooking just three blocks from the Brooklyn Museum. Breakfast is served all day and it's a deal, with very few items costing more than $10. Copious wall signs advertise specials – the blueberry-ricotta pancakes with lemon zest are unrivaled.

If you want to go old school, order an egg cream (milk, soda with chocolate syrup). Lines are loooong for weekend brunch.

COOKLYN
MODERN AMERICAN $$

Map p444 (☎347-915-0721; cooklyn-nyc.com; 659 Vanderbilt Ave, btwn Prospect & Park Pl, Prospect Heights; mains $18-29; ⏰5:30-11pm Mon-Thu, to midnight Fri & Sat, to 10pm Sun; ⒮B, Q to 7th Ave; 2/3 to Grand Army Plaza) 🍃 On restaurant-lined Vanderbilt Ave, Cooklyn is a standout for its beautifully executed seafood pasta dishes (lobster mac 'n' cheese, squid-ink cavatelli) and grilled fish and meat dishes (including a thick double-cut pork chop). The service is friendly, solo diners can eat at the marble-topped bar, and there are also outdoor tables in back.

For a taste of the borough, Cooklyn lives up to its name, with many locally sourced products – bread from Brooklyn Bread Co, cheese from Stinky Cheese, beer from Brooklyn Brewery and coffee from Toby's Estate.

FRANNY'S
PIZZA $$

Map p444 (☎718-230-0221; www.frannysbrooklyn.com; 348 Flatbush Ave, btwn Sterling & St Johns Pl, Park Slope; pizzas $18-21; ⏰5:30-11pm Mon-Fri, noon-11:30pm Sat, noon-10pm Sun; 🖉; ⒮B, Q to 7th Ave) This Park Slope icon serves bubbling thin-crust pizza baked in a brick oven, all decorated with a simple lineup of choice organic toppings such as buffalo mozzarella and oregano. There is an array of appetizers (such as codfish croquettes and roasted squash with pepper, almonds and crème fraîche), as well as some well-rendered pastas.

CHERYL'S GLOBAL SOUL CAFE $$

Map p444 (☎347-529-2855; www.cherylsglobalsoul.com; 236 Underhill Ave, btwn Eastern Pkwy & St Johns Pl, Prospect Heights; sandwiches $8-14, mains $15-25; ⏲8am-4pm Mon, to 10pm Tue-Sun; [V] [kids]; [S]2/3 to Eastern Pkwy-Brooklyn Museum) Around the corner from the Brooklyn Museum and the Brooklyn Botanic Garden, this homey brick-and-wood favorite serves up fresh, unpretentious cooking that draws on a world of influences. Expect everything from sake-glazed salmon with jasmine rice to exceptional homemade quiche to a long list of tasty sandwiches. There are veggie options, as well as kid-friendly mac 'n' cheese or fish and chips.

LOT 2 MODERN AMERICAN $$

Map p444 (☎718-499-5623; www.lot2restaurant.com; 687 Sixth Ave, btwn 19th & 20th Sts, Park Slope; mains $17-28; ⏲6-10pm Tue-Sat, from 5pm Sun; [S]F to 7th Ave; R to Prospect Ave) This intimate rustic spot serves locally sourced, high-end comfort food in the southern end of Park Slope. The menu is small but big on flavors. Try the grilled-cheese sandwich with parsnip soup, pan-seared fluke with arborio rice or a juicy grass-fed burger with thick cut, duck-fat fries. Come on Sundays for the three-course special, a deal at $32.

GANSO JAPANESE $$

Map p446 (☎718-403-0900; www.gansonyc.com; 25 Bond St, btwn Fulton & Livingston Sts, downtown; ramen $14-16; ⏲11:30am-10pm Sun-Thu, to 11pm Fri & Sat; [S]2/3 to Hoyt St; A/C, G to Hoyt-Schermerhorn) Tucked away in an unlikely corner of Brooklyn (just off the Fulton St mall) Ganso is a cozy, wood-lined spot that serves up some of the best ramen in Brooklyn. Spicy miso with pork belly is a winner (there's also a vegetarian option).

The appetizers are delicious: crispy pork *gyoza* (dumpling), *hijiki* (brown sea vegetable) salad, and plump buns stuffed with short-rib meat or pork belly.

SAUL FRENCH $$$

Map p444 (☎718-935-9842; www.saulrestaurant.com; Brooklyn Museum, 200 Eastern Pkwy, Prospect Heights; mains lunch $22-26, dinner $27-36; ⏲noon-3pm Wed-Sun & 5:30-10pm Thu, 5:30-11pm Fri-Sun; [S]2/3 to Eastern Parkway-Brooklyn Museum) A veteran of French food temples like Le Bernardin and Bouley, chef Saul Bolton continues to wow diners at his high-end but minimalist dining room in

BROOKLYN COOKBOOKS

Locally sourced products, sustainability and no small dose of creativity are all hallmarks of Brooklyn's celebrated new dining scene. To learn more about the magic behind the cuisine – and more importantly how to make the dishes at home – check out the following titles:

➡ *The New Brooklyn Cookbook* (2010) Recipes, stories and culinary insight from 31 of Brooklyn's top restaurants.

➡ *Pok Pok* (2013) Andy Ricker delves deeply into Northern Thai cooking, with precise instructions on creating those complex and heady dishes.

➡ *Roberta's Cookbook* (2013) Diver scallops in plum juice, orecchiette with oxtail ragu and glorious pizza perfection.

➡ *Four and Twenty Blackbirds Pie Book* (2013) Take your pastry skills up a notch with these tantalizing recipes by the Elsen sisters.

➡ *Franny's: Simple, Seasonal, Italian* (2013) An essential reference for making memorable pizzas, pastas and gelato at home.

➡ *The Frankie's Spuntino* (2010) Beautifully designed cookbook packed with recipes of reimagined Italian-American comfort fare.

➡ *One Girl Cookie* (2012) Moist, tender whoopie pies and other sweet indulgences.

➡ *The Mile End Cookbook* (2012) Reinventing Jewish comfort food.

➡ *Brooklyn Brew Shop's Beer Making Book* (2011) Easy to follow guide for making refreshing brews at home.

For the latest on the borough's dining scene, seek out *Edible Brooklyn* magazine (www.ediblebrooklyn.com).

the Brooklyn Museum. The seasonal menu is compact and simple, with a focus on fresh produce (think pan-roasted bass with autumn ragout or pork with kale and sweet potato). Reservations recommended.

✖ Coney Island & Brighton Beach

VARENICHNAYA
RUSSIAN $

Map p447 (📞718-332-9797; 3086 Brighton 2nd St, Brighton Beach; mains around $10; ⊙noon-10pm; ⓢB, Q to Brighton Beach) This small, family-run hideaway serves up consistently fresh dumplings from a variety of former Soviet Bloc countries. There are *pelmeni* (Siberian meat dumplings), *vareniki* (Ukrainian ravioli) and *mantis* (Uzbek lamb dumplings). The borscht is divine, as are the sturgeon and lamb kebabs. On weekends, plan on waiting for a table.

TOTONNO'S
PIZZA $$

Map p447 (📞718-372-8606; www.totonnosconeyisland.com; 1524 Neptune Ave, cnr 16th St, Coney Island; pizza $18-22; ⊙noon-8pm Thu-Sun; 🅿; ⓢD/F, N/Q to Coney Island-Stillwell Ave) This old-school pizza parlor stays open until the dough runs out. The toppings menu is slim (check the board above the open kitchen), but this is the kind of pie that doesn't need lots of overwrought decoration: coal-fired dough is topped with mozzarella first, followed by tomato sauce, so your crust never gets soggy. Cash only.

A place of pilgrimage, complete with real-deal New York attitude.

🍷 DRINKING & 🍸 NIGHTLIFE

🍸 Williamsburg, Greenpoint & Bushwick

★MAISON PREMIERE
COCKTAIL BAR

Map p440 (📞347-335-0446; www.maisonpremiere.com; 298 Bedford Ave, btwn S 1st & Grand Sts, Williamsburg; ⊙4pm-2am Mon-Fri, from 11am Sat & Sun; ⓢL to Bedford Ave) We kept expecting to see Dorothy Parker stagger into this old-timey place, which features an elegant bar full of syrups and essences, suspended bartenders and a jazzy soundtrack to

further channel the French Quarter New Orleans vibe. The cocktails are serious business: the epic list includes more than a dozen absinthe drinks, various juleps and an array of specialty cocktails.

A raw bar doles out delicious oysters, while there's more serious dining (and an outdoor patio) behind the bar.

HOTEL DELMANO
COCKTAIL BAR

Map p440 (📞718-387-1945; www.hoteldelmano.com; 82 Berry St, at N 9th St, Williamsburg; ⊙5pm-2am Mon-Fri, from 2pm Sat & Sun; ⓢL to Bedford Ave) This low-lit cocktail bar aims for a speakeasy vibe, with old smoky mirrors, unpolished floorboards and vintage chandeliers. Nestle into one of the nooks in back or have a seat at the curving marble-topped bar and watch moustached barkeeps whip up a changing array of inventive cocktails (rye, gin and mescal are favored spirits).

It also offers charcuterie, cheese boards and a raw bar (oysters, littleneck clams, shrimp cocktail). Enter on N 9th St.

SKINNY DENNIS
BAR

Map p440 (www.skinnydennisbar.com; 152 Metropolitan Ave, btwn Wythe Ave & Berry St, Williamsburg; ⊙noon-4am; ⓢL to Bedford Ave) No need to fly to Austin. You can get your honky-tonk right here in Billyburg at this roadhouse saloon on bustling Metropolitan Ave. Aside from Kinky Friedman posters, a reverential painting of Willie Nelson, peanut shells on the floor and a Patsy Cline–heavy jukebox in the corner, you'll find country crooners playing nightly to a garrulous beer-swilling crowd.

SPUYTEN DUYVIL
BAR

Map p440 (📞718-963-4140; www.spuytenduyvil-nyc.com; 359 Metropolitan Ave, btwn Havemeyer & Roebling, Williamsburg; ⊙5pm-late Mon-Fri, from noon Sat & Sun; ⓢL to Lorimer St; G to Metropolitan Ave) This low-key Williamsburg bar looks like it was pieced together from a rummage sale. The ceilings are painted red, there are vintage maps on the walls and the furniture consists of tattered armchairs. But the beer selection is staggering, the locals from various eras are chatty and there's a decent-sized patio with leafy trees that is open in good weather. There's also a fine jukebox.

RADEGAST HALL & BIERGARTEN
BEER HALL

Map p440 (📞718-963-3973; www.radegasthall.com; 113 N 3rd St, at Berry St, Williamsburg;

⏲noon-2am Mon-Fri, from 11am Sat & Sun; [S]L to Bedford Ave) An Austro-Hungarian beer hall in Williamsburg offers up a huge selection of Bavarian brews as well as a kitchen full of munchable meats. You can hover in the dark, woody bar area or sit in the adjacent hall, which has a retractable roof and communal tables to feast at – perfect for pretzels, sausages and burgers.

SPRITZENHAUS BEER HALL

Map p440 (☎347-987-4632; www.spritzenhaus33.com; 33 Nassau Ave, Greenpoint; ⏲4pm-4am Mon-Wed, noon-4am Thu-Sun; [S]G to Nassau Ave) Beer lovers shouldn't miss this place. On the edge of McCarren Park, this open, somewhat industrial 6000-sq-ft beer hall has 20 or so beers on tap, and dozens of other choices by the bottle. German, Belgian and North American microbrews dominate, and there's lots of meaty pub grub (sausages mostly, but the Belgian fries with truffle oil are also a hit).

Seating is at the long serpentine bar or on rustic picnic tables, though in winter you may want to linger by the fire.

ROOKERY BAR

(www.therookerybar.com; 425 Troutman St, btwn St Nicholas & Wyckoff Aves, Bushwick; ⏲noon-4am; [S]L to Jefferson St) There's loads happening in Bushwick, with every week bringing a new crop of farm-to-table restaurants and creative drinking dens. A mainstay of the Bushwick scene is the industrialesque Rookery, with outdoor seating on mural-lined Troutman Ave. Come for cocktails, craft brews, reconfigured pub fare (curried goat shepherds pie, oxtail sloppy joe), obscure electro-pop and a relaxed vibe.

PINE BOX ROCK SHOP BAR

Map p440 (☎718-366-6311; www.pineboxrockshop.com; 12 Grattan St, btwn Morgan Ave & Bogart St, Bushwick; ⏲4pm-4am Mon-Fri, from 2pm Sat & Sun; [S]L to Morgan Ave) The cavernous Pine Box is a former Bushwick casket factory that has 16 drafts to choose from, as well as spicy, pint-sized Bloody Marys. Run by a friendly musician couple, the walls are filled with local artwork, and a performance space in the back hosts regular gigs.

LARRY LAWRENCE BAR

Map p440 (☎718-218-7866; www.larrylawrencebar.com; 295 Grand St, btwn Roebling & Havemeyer Sts, Williamsburg; ⏲6pm-4am; [S]L to Lorimer St) This speakeasy-style bar makes a great detour while exploring Williamsburg by night. Once you find the place, you're in; no door Gestapo here – just a spacious, low-lit drinking den, with a welcoming vibe, an easygoing crowd and no overly obtrusive music. The entrance is hard to find: look for the tiny word 'bar' over a nondescript door, then head down the long concrete hallway.

There's an outdoor balcony for smokers.

DESNUDA BAR

Map p440 (☎718-387-0563; www.desnudany.com; 221 S 1st St, btwn Roebling St & Driggs Ave, Williamsburg; ⏲6pm-midnight Mon-Wed, to 2am Fri & Sat, 5-11pm Sun; [S]J/M to Marcy Ave; L to Lorimer St; G to Metropolitan Ave) A great way to start the night is by feasting on delectable oysters, tangy ceviches and complex libations at this charming eat-and-drinkery. (There's also a Desnuda in the East Village.) Come on Sunday or Monday for $1 oysters all night, served with chutneys and spicy dipping sauces, or early (5pm to 8pm) the rest of the week for the same deal.

Adventurous diners: don't miss the 'bong-smoked' oysters, where fresh oysters take on just a note of smokiness (as in Lapsang tea leaves, not marijuana, lest you were wondering). Dine at the raw bar in front, or the more discreet cocktail bar in back, amid vintage map wallpaper and vaguely colonial-era decor.

OTB BAR

Map p440 (www.otbbk.com; 141 Broadway, btwn Bedford & Driggs Aves, Williamsburg; ⏲5pm-2am Mon-Fri, from 2pm Sat & Sun; [S]J/M to Marcy Ave) OTB, which stands for 'off-track betting,' pays homage to those gamble-worthy thoroughbreds with horse-themed decor (betting-form menus, black-and-white photos of shapely ponies and horse wallpaper in the bathrooms) – though low-lit chandeliers, flickering candles and dark-wood furniture somehow creates a classy rather than kitschy vibe.

You'll also find friendly waitstaff, a fun crowd, great beer selections, bespoke cocktails and oysters ($1 after 11pm or midnight). OTB also has lots of other nibbles (chicken wings, beet salad, coconut curry mussels, mac 'n' cheese).

BOSSA NOVA CIVIC CLUB CLUB

(www.bossanovacivicclub.com; 1271 Myrtle Ave, btwn Evergreen & Central Aves, Bushwick; ⏲7pm-4am; [S]M to Central Ave) Yet another reason why you never need to leave Brooklyn, this

GREEN-WOOD CEMETERY

If you really want to enjoy a slice of scenic Brooklyn in total peace and quiet, make for **Green-Wood Cemetery** (Map p444; www.green-wood.com; 500 25th St, at Fifth Ave; ⏰7:45am-7pm May-Sep to 6pm Apr & Oct, to 5pm Nov-Mar; ⓈR to 25th St) FREE. A historic burial ground set on the borough's highest point, it covers almost 500 hilly acres. Its myriad tombs, mausoleums and patches of forest are connected by a looping network of roads and trails, making this a perfect spot for some aimless rambling.

Founded in 1838, the cemetery is the final resting place of all kinds of notable personalities. In fact, some 600,000 people are buried here – that's at least 530 miles worth, if you laid them head-to-toe. This includes inventor Samuel Morse, mobster Joey Gallo, abolitionist Henry Ward Beecher, and '80s graffitist and Brooklyn son Jean-Michel Basquiat.

The best spot in the cemetery is **Battle Hill**, the highest point, where the Continental Army fought off British troops during the 1776 Battle of Long Island. The event is commemorated by the 7ft statue of Minerva, the Roman goddess of wisdom, who waves to the Statue of Liberty in the distance. The hill is located in the northeast sector of the cemetery, off Battle Ave. Maestro Leonard Bernstein and Brooklyn Dodgers owner Charles Ebbets are both buried in the vicinity.

You can pick up a free map at the entrance. On Wednesdays at 1pm, there is a two-hour trolley tour (per person $15). Note the squawking green parakeets nesting atop the Gothic entryway – these guys apparently broke out of an airport crate in 1980 and have lived here ever since.

Tip: pack mosquito repellent in the summer.

smallish hole-in-the-wall club is a great place to get your groove on, with DJs spinning a wide mix of sounds in a somewhat tropical-themed interior. Great sound system, fairly priced drinks (at least as far as clubs are concerned) and snacks on hand when hunger strikes (empanadas, slow-cooked pork, arepas).

Draws a celebratory crowd that's ready to dance. It's free Monday to Thursday, $10 on Friday and Saturday.

KINFOLK STUDIOS
CAFE, LOUNGE

Map p440 (☑347-799-2945; www.kinfolklife.com; 90 Wythe Ave, btwn 11th & 10th Sts, Williamsburg; ⏰9am-late Mon-Fri, from 11:30am Sat & Sun; ⓈL to Bedford Ave) Kinfolk is a great little space for socializing, though sometimes it feels a little too cool for school. High-ceilinged cafe and art space by day morphs into high-style drinking den by night, with DJs spinning rare beats while hipsters crowd around drinking Japanese beers.

IDES
BAR

Map p440 (☑717-460-8006; www.wythehotel.com/the-ides; 80 Wythe Ave, Williamsburg; ⏰4pm-midnight Mon-Fri, from 2pm Sat & Sun; ⓈL to Bedford Ave) The rooftop bar of the

Wythe Hotel offers magnificent views of Manhattan; come early to beat the crowds.

VERBOTEN
CLUB

Map p440 (www.verbotennewyork.com; 54 N 11th St, btwn Wythe & Kent Aves, Williamsburg; cover $20-40; ⏰11pm-5am Fri & Sat) In a former metal shop in a once-gritty part of Williamsburg, Verboten is a 10,000-sq-ft club with an industrial aesthetic that plays underground dance music to a fairly straight crowd. It has a top-notch sound system and a trippy light show that erupts over the dance floor. There's also a restaurant-lounge area, Cabaret, in a spacious separate room.

Verboten hosts a range of other events, including deep-house yoga, Saturday DJ brunches, and other events.

OUTPUT
CLUB

Map p440 (www.outputclub.com; 74 Wythe Ave, btwn N 12th & 11th Sts, Williamsburg; cover $20-30; ⏰10pm-4am Wed-Sun; ⓈL to Bedford; G to Nassau) Output boasts a great (Function-One) sound system and draws a laid-back but dance-loving crowd. The drinks are pricey but the views from the rooftop are stunning. When big-name DJs spin, arrive early to beat the long lines – and buy tickets in advance to save cash. Go online for the latest.

CLEM'S
PUB

Map p440 (☏718-387-9617; 264 Grand St, at Roebling St, Williamsburg; ⊗2pm-4am, from noon Sat & Sun; ⓈL to Bedford Ave; J/M/Z to Marcy Ave) This tidy Williamsburg pub keeps things chill. It has a long bar, friendly bartenders and a few outdoor tables that are perfect for summer people-watching. Stop by at happy hour (till 8pm) for a beer and a shot for only $5.

METROPOLITAN
GAY & LESBIAN

Map p440 (☏718-599-4444; www.metropolitan-barny.com; 559 Lorimer St, at Metropolitan Ave, Williamsburg; ⊗3pm-4am; ⓈL to Lorimer St; G to Metropolitan Ave) This low-key Williamsburg hangout draws a good blend of arty gays and lesbians with its cool staff, cheap drinks, outdoor patio and groovy DJs. During the summer, it's known for its Sunday backyard barbecues, and on Wednesday nights, it's all about the girls.

BERRY PARK
BAR

Map p440 (☏718-782-2829; www.berryparkbk.com; 4 Berry St, cnr 14th St, Williamsburg; ⊗2pm-late Mon-Fri, from 11am Sat & Sun; ⓈG to Nassau Ave; L to Bedford Ave) This sports-loving bar is the go-to spot during soccer premier league matches as well as NFL games, with several huge screens for watching the action unfold. Fourteen beers on tap, and plenty of bar snacks (plus brunch till 4pm) keep folks from going hungry. The best part, though, is the huge rooftop deck with fabulous views of the city.

On summer days, there's no better drinking spot in the 'Burg.

BLUE BOTTLE COFFEE
CAFE

Map p440 (☏718-387-4160; www.bluebottlecoffee.net; 160 Berry St, btwn 4th & 5th Sts, Williamsburg; coffee from $4; ⊗7am-6pm Mon-Thu, to 7pm Fri-Sun; ⓈL to Bedford Ave) For the coffee connoisseurs, this top-of-the-line Williamsburg outpost (located in a former rope shop) uses a vintage Probat roaster on its beans. All drinks are brewed to order, so be prepared to wait a spell for your Kyoto iced. A small selection of baked goods includes coffee cake made with a chocolate stout from Brooklyn Brewery. Talk about locally sourced.

TOBY'S ESTATE
CAFE

Map p440 (☏347-457-6155; www.tobysestate.com; 125 N 6th St, btwn Bedford Ave & Berry St, Williamsburg; coffee from $4; ⊗7am-7pm Mon-Fri, 8am-8pm Sat & Sun; ☏; ⓈL to Bedford Ave) This small-batch roaster brings serious flavor to the streets of Billyburg with bold aromatic pour-overs, creamy flat-whites and smooth *cortados* (espresso with a dash of milk). There are a few couches and several communal tables often crowded with MacBook users.

MATCHA BAR
CAFE

Map p440 (matchabarnyc.com; 93 Wythe Ave, btwn N 10th & 11th Sts, Williamsburg; drinks from $5.25; ⊗8am-7pm Mon-Fri, from 10am Sat & Sun; ⓈL to Bedford Ave) When you need a pick-me-up and want a break from espresso, head to this purveyor of powdered green tea, which froths up delicious Matcha lattes, as well as iced variants (with flavors like Fuji apple ginger or vanilla almond). Other Matcha treats include macaroons and doughnuts.

🍸 Brooklyn Heights & Dumbo

FLOYD
BAR

Map p446 (☏718-858-5810; www.floydny.com; 131 Atlantic Ave, btwn Henry & Clinton Sts, Brooklyn Heights; ⊗5pm-4am Mon-Thu, from 4pm Fri, from noon Sat & Sun; Ⓢ2/3, 4/5 to Borough Hall) This glass-front bar is home to young flirters who cuddle on tattered antique sofas while beer-swillers congregate around an indoor boccie court. A good local hang.

BROOKLYN ROASTING COMPANY
CAFE

Map p446 (☏718-855-1000; www.brooklynroasting.com; 25 Jay St, cnr John St; coffees $2-5; ⊗7am-7pm; ☏; ⓈF to York St; A/C to High St) This sprawling coffee house is also the headquarters of one of Brooklyn's most celebrated roasters. BRC takes its beans very seriously (all beans are Fair Trade and organic), and after sampling the goods (and perhaps a doughnut by Dough), you may be tempted to buy a few different roasts to take home.

BROOKLYN BRIDGE GARDEN BAR
BAR

Map p446 (brooklynbridgegardenbar.com; Pier 1, Brooklyn Bridge Park; ⊗noon-10pm Jun-Aug, to 6pm Apr, May, Sep & Oct; ⓈA/C to High St) For outdoor drinks with a view of the Brooklyn Bridge, you can't beat this hidden spot in Pier 1. Craft beers, sangria, and cocktails are the draw (less so the limited food menu).

MICHAEL MARQUAND / GETTY IMAGES ©

Dumbo (p273)
his Brooklyn neighborhood earns its name from
s location: Down Under the Manhattan Bridge
verpass.

Williamsburg (p270)
ngle with local hipsters at one of area's trendy
rs or pubs.

Doughnuts
dulge in tasty treats and baked goods at a
lliamsburg bakery.

Prospect Park (p268)
joy the beautiful features of this 585-acre park,
ich include waterfalls, forested pathways and
mbling hills.

JOSEFINE STENUDD / GETTY IMAGES ©

🍺 Fort Greene

DER SCHWARZE KÖELNER
PUB

Map p442 (📞347-841-4495; dsk-brooklyn.com; 710 Fulton St, cnr Hanson Pl, Fort Greene; ⏰3pm-1am Mon-Fri, from 2pm Sat & Sun; 🚇C to Lafayette Ave; G to Fulton St) This casual beer garden with checkered floors, lots of windows and a lively, mixed crowd is located just a few blocks away from the Brooklyn Academy of Music. There are 18 beers on tap, all of which go swimmingly with a hot *brezel* (soft German pretzel). A variety of other snacks are served all night.

If you're packing a toddler, don't miss the twice weekly Babies and Beer gatherings, where kids can play while the parents raise a glass or two. It happens at 2:30pm on Tuesdays and Thursdays.

🍺 Cobble Hill, Carroll Gardens, Gowanus & Red Hook

61 LOCAL
BAR

Map p442 (📞718-875-1150; www.61local.com; 61 Bergen St, btwn Smith St & Boerum Pl, Cobble Hill; ⏰7am-midnight Mon-Fri, from 9am Sat & Sun; 🛜; 🚇F, G to Bergen) A roomy brick-and-wood hall in Cobble Hill manages to be both chic and warm, with large communal tables, a mellow vibe and a good selection of craft beers (including KelSo, Ommegang and Allagash). There's a simple menu of charcuterie, cheese boards and other snacks, including pulled pork tacos, quiche and Mediterranean platters (hummus, labne, olives).

CLOVER CLUB
BAR

Map p442 (📞718-855-7939; www.cloverclubny. com; 210 Smith St, btwn Baltic & Butler Sts, Carroll Gardens; ⏰4pm-2am Mon-Fri, 10:30am-4am Sat, 10:30am-1am Sun; 🚇F, G to Bergen) This delightful cocktail parlor channels 19th-century elegance with a rich mahogany bar, vintage fixtures and vest-wearing barkeeps. Beautifully prepared cocktails draw in a mostly local crowd, who come for lively conversation fueled by refined recipes such as the improved whiskey cocktail (rye whiskey, maraschino, absinthe and bitters). Clover also serves big weekend brunches (matched by excellent Bloody Marys and other libations).

ROYAL PALMS
BAR

Map p442 (www.royalpalmsshuffle.com; 514 Union St, btwn 3rd Ave & Nevins St, Gowanus; ⏰6pm-midnight Mon-Thu, to 2am Fri, noon-2am Sat, noon-10pm Sun; 🚇R to Union St) If you're hankering for a bit of sport, but don't want to drift too far from the bar stool, the Royal Palms should figure high on your itinerary. Inside this 17,000-sq-ft space, you'll find 10 full shuffleboard courts, plus board games (massive Jenga, oversize Connect Four), draft brews, cocktails and filling snacks provided by a food truck (with a different rotation each week).

The ambience veers toward sub-tropical Floridian, though it's hipsters rather than old-timers finessing those discs across the shiny courts. It's strictly age 21 and up.

SUNNY'S
BAR

Map p442 (📞718-625-8211; www.sunnysredhook. com; 253 Conover St, btwn Beard & Reed Sts, Red Hook; ⏰6pm-2am Tue, 4pm-4am Wed-Fri, from 2pm Sat, 4-11pm Sun; 🚌B61 to Coffey & Conover Sts, 🚇F, G to Carroll St) Way out in Red Hook, this super-inviting longshoreman bar – the sign says 'bar' – is straight out of *On the Waterfront*. Every Saturday at 10pm it hosts a foot-stomping bluegrass jam. Other banjo-pickin' and curious events (like comedy nights and afternoon nude-figure drawing) happen throughout the week. Check the website to see what's on.

LAVENDER LAKE
BAR

Map p442 (📞347-799-2154; www.lavenderlake. com; 383 Carroll St, btwn Nevins & Bond Sts, Gowanus; ⏰4pm-midnight Mon-Thu, to 2am Fri, noon-2am Sat, noon-midnight Sun; 🚇F, G to Carroll St; R to Union St) This gem of a bar in a former horse stable serves carefully selected craft beers and a few seasonal cocktails such as the autumnal Loddy Doddy, a hot toddy with orange-clove-infused scotch. The light-strewn garden is a brilliant summery spot. Lots of good food on hand too (mains $13 to $18). Try the charred eggplant and chickpea hummus or a whiskey-brined pork chop.

🍺 Park Slope & Greenwood

FREDDY'S
BAR

Map p444 (📞718-768-0131; 627 Fifth Ave, btwn 17th & 18th Sts, Park Slope; ⏰noon-4am; 🚇R to Prospect Ave) In this old-time bar in the South Slope, you can tip one back at a vintage mahogany bar while admiring the crazy videos made by Donald, the co-owner. Check out the one behind the bar of a cat drinking. It also offers free live music (uke jams, honky tonk), comedy nights and the odd film screening.

GREENWOOD PARK BEER HALL

Map p444 (☎718-499-7999; www.greenwoodparkbk.com; 555 Seventh Ave, btwn 19th & 20th Sts, Greenwood; ⏰4pm-2am Mon-Thu, noon-2am Fri-Sun; 📶; [S]F, G to Prospect Park) Around the corner from the leafy Green-Wood Cemetery, this roomy beer hall is a clever reconfiguration of a former gas station and mechanic's shop. In an open, industrial setting, you'll find over two-dozen beers on draft, plus panini, burgers, salads and other pub fare.

The outdoor space, with its three boccie courts and weekend barbecues, draws laid-back crowds in the summer. It's a family-friendly space in the daytime, but strictly 21-and-up after about 7pm.

☆ ENTERTAINMENT

★BROOKLYN ACADEMY OF MUSIC PERFORMING ARTS

Map p442 (BAM; ☎718-636-4100; www.bam.org; 30 Lafayette Ave, at Ashland Pl, Fort Greene; 📶; [S]D, N/R to Pacific St; B, Q, 2/3, 4/5 to Atlantic Ave) At this performing-arts complex, the Howard Gilman Opera House and Harvey Lichtenstein Theater host their share of ballet, modern and world dance performances. Among other groups, it has presented the Alvin Ailey American Dance Theater, the Mark Morris Dance Group and the Pina Bausch Dance Theater.

Buy tickets early for the Next Wave Festival (September to December), featuring cutting-edge theater and dance from around the globe. Also onsite: the **BAM Rose Cinemas** (tickets $12-18), which screen first-run, indie and foreign films. Around the corner is the **BAM Fisher Building** (www.bam.org/fisher; 321 Ashland Pl, Fort Greene; [S]D, N/R to Pacific St; B, Q, 2/3, 4/5 to Atlantic Ave) with its more intimate 250-seat theater.

NITEHAWK CINEMA CINEMA

Map p440 (www.nitehawkcinema.com; 136 Metropolitan Ave, btwn Berry & Wythe, Williamsburg; [S]L to Bedford Ave) This triplex has a fine lineup of first-run and indie films, a good sound system and comfy seats, but Nitehawk's big draw is that you are able to dine and drink while watching a movie. Munch on hummus plates, sweet potato risotto balls or short rib empanadas, matched by a Blue Point toasted lager or perhaps a Negroni.

Even a bad Bruce Willis flick can't ruin the experience. Many shows sell out (especially on weekends). Purchase tickets in advance online to avoid disappointment. There's also a cozy bar downstairs, worthy of a pre- or post-show cocktail.

> **ℹ WHAT'S ON**
>
> Visit the websites of **Free Williamsburg** (www.freewilliamsburg.com) and **Brooklyn Based** (www.brooklynbased.com) to keep tabs on the latest music gigs, art openings and more.

BROOKLYN BOWL LIVE MUSIC

Map p440 (☎718-963-3369; www.brooklynbowl.com; 61 Wythe Ave, btwn 11th & 12th Sts, Williamsburg; ⏰6pm-2am Mon-Fri, from 11am Sat & Sun; [S]L to Bedford Ave; G to Nassau Ave) This 23,000-sq-ft venue inside the former Hecla Iron Works Company combines bowling (p301), microbrews, food and groovy live music. In addition to the live bands that regularly tear up the stage, there are NFL game days, karaoke and DJ nights. Aside from weekends (11am to 6pm), it's age 21 and up.

There's also excellent food on hand, courtesy of Blue Ribbon Fried Chicken.

BELL HOUSE LIVE MUSIC

Map p442 (☎718-643-6510; www.thebellhouseny.com; 149 7th St, Gowanus; ⏰5pm-4am; 📶; [S]F, G, R to 4th Ave-9th St) A big, old venue in the mostly barren neighborhood of Gowanus, the Bell House features live performances, indie rockers, DJ nights, comedy shows and burlesque parties. The handsomely converted warehouse has a spacious concert area, plus a friendly little bar in the front room with flickering candles, leather armchairs and 10 or so beers on tap.

NATIONAL SAWDUST LIVE PERFORMANCE

Map p440 (☎646-779-8455; nationalsawdust.org; 80 N 6th St, at Wythe Ave, Williamsburg; [S]L to Bedford Ave) Covered in wildly hued murals, this brand new arts space opened to much fanfare in 2015, with the promise of cutting-edge multidisciplinary programming. You can see daring works, like operatic singers with multimedia projections, electro-acoustic big-band jazz and concerts by experimental composers, along with more globally infused performances – Inuit throat singing, African tribal funk, and the singing of Icelandic sagas among other things.

JALOPY
LIVE MUSIC

Map p442 (📞718-395-3214; www.jalopy.biz; 315 Columbia St, at Woodhull St, Red Hook; 🚇F, G to Carroll St) This fringe Carroll Gardens/Red Hook banjo shop has a fun DIY space with cold beer for its bluegrass, country and uku-lele shows, including a feel-good Roots 'n' Ruckus show on Wednesday nights.

ST ANN'S WAREHOUSE
THEATER

Map p446 (📞718-254-8779; www.stannsware-house.org; 45 Water St, Dumbo; 🚇A/C to High St) This avant-garde performance com-pany hosts innovative theater and dance happenings that attract the Brooklyn lit-erati. The calendar has featured rock opera, genre-defying music by new composers, and strange and wondrous puppet theater. In 2015, St Ann's moved to a new location in the historic Tobacco Warehouse facing Brooklyn Bridge Park.

In an industrial, red-brick building that dates back to the Civil War, St Ann's first permanent home – a high-tech 320-seat theater – stages some of New York's most thought-provoking productions (such as an all-female rendition of Shakespeare's *Henry IV* set in a women's penitentiary).

BARBÈS
LIVE MUSIC

Map p444 (📞347-422-0248; www.barbesbrook-lyn.com; 376 9th St, at Sixth Ave, Park Slope; sug-gested donation for live music $10; ⏰5pm-2am Mon-Thu, 2pm-4am Fri & Sat, to 2am Sun; 🚇F to 7th Ave) This festive bar and performance space is owned by a French musician and longtime Brooklyn resident, Olivier Conan who some-times takes the stage with his Latin-themed band Las Rubias del Norte. The line-up is impressive and eclectic (the bar is named after the North African neighborhood in Paris), with Afro-Peruvian grooves, West African funk, French chanson and Tuvan throat singing among other sounds.

Don't miss the brassy Slavic Soul Party, which plays here most Tuesday nights (from 10pm). There are also DJ nights, readings and film screenings, too.

LOFTOPERA
OPERA

(www.loftopera.com; tickets from $30) True to its name, this Brooklyn-based outfit per-forms condensed operas at lofts in Gow-anus and elsewhere in Brooklyn. Even if you're not an opera fan, it's an extraordi-nary experience witnessing a first-rate per-formance in an intimate setting. Visit the website for tickets and venues.

THEATER FOR A NEW AUDIENCE
PERFORMING ARTS

Map p442 (📞tickets 866-811-4111; www.tfana. org; 262 Ashland Pl, cnr Fulton St, Fort Greene; 🚇2/3 4/5 to Nevins St; B Q/R to DeKalb Ave) Part

---

READING BROOKLYN

Brooklyn's literary roots run deep. The former Borough President Marty Markowitz described Brooklyn as 'New York's left bank', and given the range of local talents that have shaped American literature – not to mention the countless authors living here today – he may not be far off the mark.

The following are a few quintessential Brooklyn reads from celebrated Brooklynites present and past:

➡ *Leaves of Grass* (1855) Walt Whitman's poetic celebration of life; particularly poignant: 'Crossing Brooklyn Ferry.'

➡ *A Tree Grows in Brooklyn* (1943) Betty Smith's moving coming-of-age story set in the squalid tenements of Williamsburg.

➡ *Sophie's Choice* (1979) William Styron's blockbuster set in a boarding house in post-war Flatbush.

➡ *Motherless Brooklyn* (1999) Jonathan Lethem's brilliant and darkly comic tale of small-time hoods set in Carroll Gardens and other parts of Brooklyn.

➡ *Literary Brooklyn* (2011) Evan Hughes provides an overview of great Brooklyn writers and their neighborhoods over the years, from Henry Miller's Williamsburg to Truman Capote's Brooklyn Heights.

of the emerging cultural district surrounding BAM, the Theatre for a New Audience opened in late 2013, in a grand new building inspired by London's Cottesloe Theatre. The calendar features avant-garde productions of works by Shakespeare, Ibsen and Strindberg, as well as more recent works by playwrights like Richard Maxwell and his theater company the New York City Players.

Julie Taymor's wildly reconfigured *Midsummer Night's Dream* opened the theater's first season to much acclaim.

MUSIC HALL OF WILLIAMSBURG
LIVE MUSIC

Map p440 (www.musichallofwilliamsburg.com; 66 N 6th St, btwn Wythe & Kent Aves, Williamsburg; show $15-40; S L to Bedford Ave) This popular Williamsburg music venue is *the* place to see indie bands in Brooklyn. (For many groups traveling through New York, this is their one and only spot.) It is intimate and the programming is solid. Recent sold-out shows include Brooklyn-based legends They Might Be Giants and Aussie roots rockers the John Butler Trio.

BAMCAFÉ
LIVE MUSIC

Map p442 (☑718-636-4100, dinner reservations 718-623-7811; www.bam.org; 30 Lafayette Ave, at Ashland Pl, Fort Greene; S D, N/R to Pacific St; B, Q, 2/3, 4/5 to Atlantic Ave) This high-ceilinged restaurant and lounge in the upstairs part of the Brooklyn Academy of Music is the spot to hit for free Friday and Saturday evening shows. The room is beautiful and the lineup is generally mellow, covering jazz, R&B, world music and experimental rock.

The cafe opens two hours before most shows, and it's worth sticking around for a drink or a meal – recent selections from Chef Tsering Nyima's seasonal menu included red-wine-braised short ribs, pan-seared Cape Cod skate, and vegetarian spaetzle of roasted butternut squash.

WARSAW
LIVE MUSIC

Map p440 (☑718-387-5252; www.warsawconcerts.com; Polish National Home, 261 Driggs Ave, at Eckford St, Greenpoint; S L to Bedford Ave; G to Nassau Ave) A burgeoning New York classic, this stage is in the Polish National Home (with good views in the old ballroom) for bands ranging from indie darlings the Dead Milkmen to funk legends like George Clinton. Polish ladies serve pierogies and beers under the disco balls.

KNITTING FACTORY
LIVE MUSIC

Map p440 (☑347-529-6696; bk.knittingfactory.com; 361 Metropolitan Ave, at Havemayer St, Williamsburg; shows $8-20; S G, L to Lorimer St) A long-time outpost for folk, indie and experimental music in New York, Williamsburg's Knitting Factory is where you go to see everything from cosmic space jazz to rock. The stage is small and intimate. A separate bar room has a soundproof window with stage views.

BARCLAYS CENTER
BASKETBALL

Map p444 (☑917-618-6700; www.barclayscenter.com; cnr Flatbush & Atlantic Aves, Prospect Heights; S B/D, N/Q/R, 2/3, 4/5 to Atlantic Ave) The Dodgers still play baseball in Los Angeles, but the Brooklyn Nets in the NBA (formerly the New Jersey Nets) now hold court at this high-tech stadium that opened in 2012. Basketball aside, Barclays also stages major concerts and big shows – Vampire Weekend, Coldplay, Cirque de Soleil, Disney on Ice... Speaking of ice, Brooklyn hockey fans now have a home team: the New York Islanders began playing their home games here in 2015.

BARGEMUSIC
CLASSICAL MUSIC

Map p446 (☑718-624-4924; www.bargemusic.org; Fulton Ferry Landing, Brooklyn Heights; tickets $35-45; ; S A/C to High St) The chamber-music concerts held on this 125-seat converted coffee barge (built c 1899) are a unique, intimate affair. For nearly 40 years, it has been a beloved venue, with beautiful views of the East River and Manhattan. There are free children's concerts ('Music in Motion') on some Saturdays at 4pm.

PUPPETWORKS
PUPPET SHOW

Map p444 (☑718-965-3391; www.puppetworks.org; 338 Sixth Ave, cnr 4th St, Park Slope; adult/child $10/9; ; S D, N/R to 9th St; F, G to 4th Ave) In a tiny theater in Park Slope, this outfit stages delightful marionette shows, which earn rave reviews from pint-sized critics. Catch puppet adaptations of classics like *Beauty and the Beast*, *Goldilocks and the Three Bears* and *The Wizard of Oz*. Most shows happen on Saturdays and Sundays at 12:30pm and 2:30pm. Check the website for a schedule.

BROOKLYN CYCLONES
BASEBALL

Map p447 (☑718-372-5596; www.brooklyncyclones.com; MCU Park, 1904 Surf Ave, at 17th St, Coney Island; tickets $10-20, all tickets on Wed $10; S D/F, N/Q to Coney Island-Stillwell Ave) The

BROOKLYN ENTERTAINMENT

minor league baseball team Brooklyn Cyclones, part of the New York–Penn League, plays at a beachside park a few steps from the Coney Island boardwalk.

SHOPPING

Williamsburg, Greenpoint & Bushwick

ROUGH TRADE   MUSIC

Map p440 (☑718-388-4111; www.roughtradenyc.com; 64 N 9th St, btwn Kent & Wythe Aves, Williamsburg; ◷11am-11pm Mon-Sat, to 9pm Sun; ⓢL to Bedford Ave) This sprawling, 10,000-sq-ft record store – a London import – stocks thousands of titles on vinyl and CD. It also has in-store DJs, listening stations, art exhibitions, and coffee and tea from Greenpoint purveyor Five Leaves. A small concert hall onsite hosts live bands throughout the week (admission varies).

BEACON'S CLOSET
(GREENPOINT)   THRIFT STORE

Map p440 (☑718-486-0816; www.beaconscloset.com; 74 Guernsey St, btwn Nassau & Norman Aves, Greenpoint; ◷11am-8pm; ⓢL to Bedford Ave) Twenty-something groovers find this massive 5500-sq-ft warehouse of vintage clothing part goldmine, part grit. Lots of coats, polyester tops and '90s-era T-shirts are handily displayed by color, but the sheer mass can take time to conquer. You'll also find shoes of all sorts, flannels, hats, handbags, chunky jewelry and brightly hued sunglasses.

BEACON'S CLOSET
(BUSHWICK)   THRIFT STORE

Map p440 (☑718-417-5683; 23 Bogart St, Bushwick; ◷11am-8pm; ⓢL to Morgan Ave) Beacon's recently opened this 2000-sq-ft vintage store in the epicenter of Brooklyn's hipster hood of Bushwick. It's well worth stopping by when you need to add a bit of sparkle to your wardrobe: dresses, tops, button downs and accessories. There is a nicely curated selection of covetable wears on hand.

A&G MERCH   HOMEWARES

Map p440 (☑718-388-1779; aandgmerch.com; 111 N 6th St, btwn Berry & Wythe Sts, Williamsburg; ◷11am-7pm; ⓢL to Bedford Ave) A&G Merch is a fun little shop to explore, with its mix of whimsy and elegance. Check out antique plates adorned with animal heads (Uncle Herb the lion), rustic wicker baskets, cast-iron whale bookends, silver tree-branch-like candleholders, brassy industrial table lamps and more goods to give your nest that artfully rustic look so prominent in Brooklyn these days.

PINK OLIVE   GIFTS

Map p440 (pinkolive.com; 370 Bedford Ave, btwn S 4th & 5th Sts, Williamsburg; ◷noon-8pm Mon-Fri, to 7pm Sat, to 6pm Sun; ⓢJ/M to Marcy Ave; L to Bedford Ave) This small sunny shop has plenty of great gift ideas, including one-of-a-kind stationery, pretty things for baby (French bulldog pajamas, comfy socks), artwork for the home, delicate jewelry, soy candles, chocolate bars and lavender oatmeal soaps.

BUFFALO EXCHANGE   CLOTHING

Map p440 (☑718-384-6901; www.buffaloexchange.com; 504 Driggs Ave, at 9th St, Williamsburg; ◷11am-8pm Mon-Sat, noon-7pm Sun; ⓢL to Bedford Ave) This new and used clothing shop is a go-to spot for Brooklynites on a budget – featuring clothes (designer and not), shoes, jewelry and accessories. It's a generally well-curated collection, though you'll still want to bank on spending some quality time here.

SPOONBILL & SUGARTOWN   BOOKS

Map p440 (☑718-387-7322; www.spoonbillbooks.com; 218 Bedford Ave, at 5th St, Williamsburg; ◷10am-10pm; ⓢL to Bedford Ave) Williamsburg's favorite bookstore has an intriguing selection of art and coffee-table books, cultural journals, used and rare titles, and locally made works not found elsewhere.

Check the website for upcoming readings and book-launch parties.

FUEGO 718   HANDICRAFTS

Map p440 (☑718-302-2913; fuego718.com; 249 Grand St, btwn Roebling St & Driggs Ave, Williamsburg; ◷noon-8pm; ⓢL to Bedford Ave) A kaleidoscope of kitsch and crafts, Fuego 718 packs a riotous display of Day of the Dead boxes and figurines, Haitian metal art made from recycled products, Italian *milagros* (metal charms), Lotería boards (that iconic Mexican bingo) and ornate mirrors with vividly painted frames.

You can also browse the small whimsical paintings by Andras Bartos (reasonably priced at $48) and other artists, plus jewelry handcrafted by both Brooklyn and international designers.

BROOKLYN MARKETS

When the weekend arrives, Brooklynites are out and about, strolling the stoop sales and hitting the markets. Here are a few good places to unearth something unusual (and enjoy a good bite while you're at it):

➡ **Brooklyn Flea Market (Fort Greene)** (p280) On Saturdays from April to November, some 200 vendors sell their wares on the grounds of a school in Fort Greene. You'll find antiques, records, vintage clothes, craft items and enticing food stalls stuffed with a smorgasbord of tasty treats. In winter, the market moves indoors, either in Williamsburg or Fort Greene (check website for details).

➡ **Brooklyn Flea (Williamsburg)** (Map p440; www.brooklynflea.com; 50 Kent Ave btwn 11th & 12th Sts, ⏰10am-5pm Sun Apr-Oct; [S] L to Bedford Ave; G to Nassau Ave) On Sundays in the summer and fall, you can get more market action at this large outdoor space at the East River Waterfront in Williamsburg. You'll also find plenty of vintage furnishings, retro clothing and bric-a-bric, not to mention an array of lobster rolls, *pupusas* (corn tortillas filled with cheese, beans, meat or vegetables), tamales and chocolate. This area is also home to the popular Smorgasburg market on Saturdays in the summer, when food vendors from all over New York City descend on the area with tasty victuals.

➡ **Artists & Fleas** (Map p440; www.artistsandfleas.com; 70 N 7th Ave, btwn Wythe & Kent Aves, Williamsburg; ⏰10am-7pm Sat & Sun; [S] L to Bedford Ave) In operation since 2003, this is a popular artists, designers and vintage market in Williamsburg, where you can find an excellent selection of crafty goodness.

➡ **Grand Army Plaza Greenmarket** (Map p444; Grand Army Plaza, Prospect Park West & Flatbush Ave; ⏰8am-4pm Sat; [S] 2/3 to Grand Army Plaza) Open on Saturdays year-round, this greenmarket is a good spot to put together an impromptu picnic before heading into Prospect Park.

➡ **Neighborhood Greenmarkets** You'll find other year-round greenmarkets at **Brooklyn Borough Hall** (downtown Brooklyn; [S] 2/3, 4/5 to Borough Hall) on Tuesday, Thursday and Saturday; **Carroll Park** (Carroll Gardens; [S] F, G to Carroll St) on Sunday; and **Fort Greene Park** (Fort Greene; [S] B, Q/R to DeKalb Ave) on Saturday. Check www.grownyc.org for other NYC greenmarkets.

ACADEMY ANNEX MUSIC

(☎718-218-8200; academyrecordsnyc.wordpress.com; 85 Oak St, at Franklin St, Greenpoint; ⏰noon-8pm; [S] G to Greenpoint Ave) Serious vinyl vultures head to this Greenpoint mecca to browse bins stuffed full of rock, hip hop, jazz, blues, electronica and world music.

DESERT ISLAND COMICS BOOKS

Map p440 (www.desertislandbrooklyn.com; 540 Metropolitan Ave, btwn Union Ave & Lorimer St, Williamsburg; ⏰noon-9pm Mon-Sat, to 7pm Sun; [S] L to Lorimer St; G to Metropolitan Ave) Desert Island is an indie comic-book shop located inside a former bakery in Williamsburg. Inside, you'll find hundreds of comics, graphic novels, local zines, prints and cards. It also sells original prints and lithographs by artists like Adrian Tomine and Peter Bagge. Good tunes are provided by the turntable in back.

BROOKLYN INDUSTRIES CLOTHING

Map p440 (☎718-486-6464; www.brooklynindustries.com; 162 Bedford Ave, at 8th St, Williamsburg; ⏰10am-9pm Mon-Sat, to 8pm Sun; [S] L to Bedford Ave) This is where the cool kids shop for hooded sweatshirts, silk-screen T-shirts and slinky knit dresses. It may be a chain but this Brooklyn Industries has the cachet of actually being in Brooklyn.

🔒 Dumbo

POWERHOUSE BOOKS BOOKS

Map p446 (☎718-666-3049; www.powerhousebooks.com; 37 Main St, Dumbo; ⏰10am-7pm Mon-Fri, from 11am Sat & Sun; 📶; [S] A/C to High St, F to York St) An important part of Dumbo's cultural scene, Powerhouse Books hosts changing art exhibitions, book-launch parties and weird and creative events in its 5000-sq-ft space. You'll also find intriguing books on urban art, photography and pop culture – all imprints of its namesake publishing house.

MODERN ANTHOLOGY
CLOTHING

Map p446 (modernanthology.com; 68 Jay St, btwn Water & Front Sts, Dumbo; ⊙11am-7pm Mon-Sat, noon-6pm Sun; 🚇F to York St; A/C to High St) For the rugged, city-dwelling (and not poor) man, Modern Anthology has plenty of appeal. Among the finds: elegant but manly leather satchels, brassy beer bottle openers shaped like animal heads, woolly Pendleton blankets, leather boots, soft cotton button-downs and well-fitting dark-denim jeans.

There's also a branch on Smith St (near Dean St).

PS BOOKSHOP
BOOKS

Map p446 (☎718-222-3340; www.psbookshop-nyc.com; 76 Front St, at Washington St, Dumbo; ⊙10am-8pm; 🚇A/C to High St; F to York St) This is a good used-book shop with a delightful selection of art monographs, street books, children's books and vintage travelogues.

NATCHIE ART
ARTS

Map p446 (www.natchieart.com; 141 Front St, at Pearl St, Dumbo; ⊙noon-7pm; 🚇F to York St; A/C to High St) An Aussie expat living in NYC, Natchie creates whimsical, art-naïf prints of city icons, like the Brooklyn Bridge, the High Line, the Empire State Building and the Literary Walk in Central Park. As a bonus, each print also features a free download of a song – inspired by the image – written and performed by Natchie.

🏠 Boerum Hill, Cobble Hill, Carroll Gardens & Gowanus

DRY GOODS
ACCESSORIES

Map p442 (☎718-403-0090; 362 Atlantic Ave, btwn Hoyt & Bond Sts; ⊙noon-7pm Tue-Sun; 🚇A/C, G to Hoyt-Schermerhorn Sts) Strolling into this delightful little store, run by a mother and daughter team, is like stepping back in time. The old wooden shelves and cabinetry are packed with curiosities.

Vintage stationary and pencils, finely crafted Kent hairbrushes, papermaking kits for kids, eggwhite soap from Belgium, 18th-century mouthwash (a reputed favorite of Louis XV), Saint James meridian shirts (as worn by Brigitte Bardot and James Dean) and Legacy swing dresses are just a few items you'll find here. The emphasis is on heritage brands – denoting well-made products meant to last.

DRY GOODS
CLOTHING

Map p442 (☎718-855-4295; www.wpstorebrooklyn.com; 225 Smith St, cnr Butler St, Carroll Gardens; ⊙noon-7pm Mon-Sat, to 6pm Sun; 🚇F, G to Bergen St) The first American outpost of the Italian boutique retailer WP Lavori sells durable clothing that channels a rugged but classic style in its soft button-down shirts and cable-knit sweaters by Woolrich, fur-trimmed coats by Spiewalk, sleek Baracuta jackets and made-to-last Blundstone boots. It's set in an elegant brick-walled shop in Carroll Gardens.

BLACK GOLD
MUSIC

Map p442 (☎347-227-8227; www.blackgold-brooklyn.com; 461 Court St, btwn 4th Pl & Luquer St, Carroll Gardens; ⊙7am-3pm Mon, to 8pm Tue-Fri, 10am-9pm Sat, to 7pm Sun; 🚇F, G to Carroll St) Records, coffee, antiques and taxidermy await you in this tiny addition to the ever-expanding Carroll Gardens Court St scene. Sample vintage vinyl on the turntable from John Coltrane to Ozzy Osborne and enjoy a damn good cup of coffee, ground and brewed individually. Need a stuffed hyena from the Ozarks? Find one here.

NO RELATION VINTAGE
THRIFT STORE

Map p442 (☎718-858-4906; norelationvintage.com; 654 Sackett St, btwn Third & Fourth Aves; ⊙noon-8pm; 🚇D, N/R to Union St) This gigantic vintage shop in the Gowanus area has a staggering inventory with great deals for bargain hunters.

🏠 Park Slope & Prospect Heights

BEACON'S CLOSET (PARK SLOPE)
THRIFT STORE

Map p444 (☎718-230-1630; 92 Fifth Ave, cnr Warren St, Park Slope; ⊙noon-9pm Mon-Fri, 11am-8pm Sat & Sun; 🚇2/3 to Bergen St) An excellent thrift shop stocked full of shoes, jewelry and bright vintage finds. It is the sister store of the bigger Beacon's Closet in Greenpoint (p298).

FLIRT
CLOTHING

Map p444 (www.flirt-brooklyn.com; 93 Fifth Ave, btwn Park & Prospect Pls, Park Slope; ⊙11:30am-7:30pm; 🚇B/D, N/Q/R, 2/3, 4/5 to Atlantic Ave/Pacific St, G to Bergen St) The name says it all at this girlishly sexy Park Slope boutique, selling custom-made skirts (pick your cut and fabric) and tiny tops in soft knits.

SPORTS & ACTIVITIES

LAKESIDE
SKATING, BOATING

Map p444 (☎718-462-0010; www.lakesideprospectpark.com; Prospect Park, near Ocean & Parkside Aves; ice-skating $6-9, skate rental $6; ⌚10am-6:30pm Mon-Thu, to 9pm Fri, 11am-9pm Sat, 11am-6:30pm Sun Nov-Mar; 👪; [S]B, Q to Prospect Park) Two brand-new rinks (one open and one covered) in Prospect Park opened in late 2013 as part of Lakeside Center, a $74 million project which reconfigured 26 acres of parkland in a beautiful, ecofriendly showcase. In the summer, kids can splash about in wading pools and sprinklers; the other rink features old-school roller skating.

In the summer, pedal boats and kayaks are available for leisurely rides on the lake.

BROOKLYN BOULDERS
ROCK CLIMBING

Map p442 (www.brooklynboulders.com; 575 Degraw St, at Third Ave, Boerum Hill; day pass $28, shoe rental $6; ⌚8am-midnight; [S]R to Union St) It's Brooklyn's biggest indoor climbing arena for scaling aficionados and folks looking to reach new heights. Ceilings top out at 30ft inside this 18,000-sq-ft facility, and its caves and freestanding 17ft boulder and climbing walls offer numerous routes for beginners to experts. There are overhangs of 15°, 30° and 45°. Climbing classes are available.

BROOKLYN BOWL
BOWLING

Map p440 (☎718-963-3369; www.brooklynbowl.com; 61 Wythe Ave, btwn 11th & 12th Sts, Williamsburg; lane rental per hr $50, shoe rental $5; ⌚6pm-2am Mon-Fri, from 11am Sat & Sun ; [S]L to Bedford; G to Nassau Ave) This incredible alley is housed in the 23,000-sq-ft former Hecla Iron Works Company, which provided ornamentation for several NYC landmarks at the turn of the 20th century. There are 16 lanes surrounded by cushy sofas and exposed brick walls. In addition to bowling, Brooklyn Bowl hosts concerts throughout the week, and there's always good food on hand.

PROSPECT PARK TENNIS CENTER
TENNIS

Map p444 (☎718-436-2500; www.prospectpark.org/tennis; Prospect Park, cnr Parkside & Coney Island Aves; ⌚7am-11pm; [S]F to Fort Hamilton Pkwy; Q to Parkside Ave) Open all year, this 11-court facility takes permits or sells single-use tickets on location from mid-May to mid-November. Hourly rates range from $40 to $84.

RED HOOK BOATERS
KAYAKING

Map p442 (www.redhookboaters.org; Louis Valentino Jr Pier Park, Coffey St; ⌚1-5pm Sun Jun-Sep & 6-8pm Thu mid-Jun–mid-Aug; 🚌B61 to Van Dyke St, [S]F, G to Smith-9th Sts) [FREE] This boathouse, located in Red Hook, offers free kayaking in the small embayment off Louis Valentino Jr Pier Park. Check the website for the latest times before making the trip out.

AREA YOGA CENTER
YOGA

Map p442 (☎718-797-3699; www.areayogabrooklyn.com; 389 Court St, btwn 1st & 2nd Pl, Cobble Hill; class $15; ⌚classes 7am-9pm Mon-Sat, to 5pm Sun; [S]F, G to Carroll St) Area offers a wide range of classes and has locations in Cobble Hill, Brooklyn Heights and Park Slope.

ON THE MOVE
CYCLING

Map p444 (☎718-768-4998; www.onthemovenyc.com; 400 Seventh Ave, btwn 12th & 13th Sts, Park Slope; bike rentals per day (incl helmet) $40; ⌚2-7pm Mon-Fri, noon-5pm Sat & Sun; [S]F to 7th Ave) A couple of blocks south from Brooklyn's Prospect Park, On the Move rents and sells all manner of bikes and gear. They are closed in inclement weather and cut back hours from October to March.

BIKE AND ROLL
CYCLING

Map p446 (www.bikenewyorkcity.com; Old Fulton St, Brooklyn Bridge Park; bike hire per 2hr/half-/full day $12/39/44; ⌚11am-7pm Mar-Nov; [S]A/C to High St) Hire bikes here for a spin through Brooklyn Bridge Park (perhaps heading down to Red Hook), around Dumbo or the uphill hoof to the very crowded Brooklyn Bridge.

Queens

LONG ISLAND CITY | ASTORIA | JACKSON HEIGHTS | FLUSHING & CORONA | ELMHURST | WOODSIDE | MASPETH

Neighborhood Top Five

1 Feeling inspired at the Museum of Modern Art's cross-river sibling, **MoMA PS1** (p304). From painting and sculpture to site-specific installations, this cultural hub displays edgy, world-class artwork, not to mention lectures, performances and an electric summer party series.

2 Reliving your favorite film and TV moments at the **Museum of the Moving Image** (p306), Astoria's contemporary tribute to the small and silver screens.

3 Getting soaked, pummeled and pampered at **New York Spa Castle** (p316), Queens' sprawling aquatic wonderland.

4 Taking a snack crawl through Latin America, via food trucks along meltingpot Roosevelt Ave (p312).

5 Immersing yourself in bustling Asian street life and feasting on chewy Chinese noodles, plump dumplings and plenty more in **Flushing** (p306).

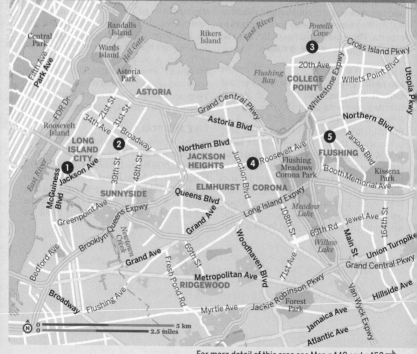

For more detail of this area see Map p448 and p450

Explore Queens

Of the city's five boroughs, Queens is top dog in size and runner-up in head count. Anywhere else, it would be a major city in its own right. So where to begin?

Assuming it's not Tuesday or Wednesday (when many galleries are closed), start with a day in Long Island City, home to contemporary art hubs MoMA PS1, Sculpture-Center and the Fisher Landau Center for Art. Watch the sun set from Gantry Plaza State Park, and sip-and-sup on neighborly Vernon Blvd.

Spend a day or two exploring neighboring Astoria, taste-testing a variety of eateries, sipping local brews, and checking out the Museum of the Moving Image. If it's summer, catch an alfresco film at Socrates Sculpture Park.

With its Hong Kong jumble of street foods, Asian groceries and kitschy malls, Flushing (home to NYC's biggest Chinatown) also merits a full-day adventure. Time poor? Spend the morning on Main St and Roosevelt Ave, then hit neighboring Corona for the Queens Museum or Louis Armstrong House.

If it's hot, tackle the surf at Rockaway Beach, home to NYC's coolest beach scene.

Local Life

➡**Hangouts** Brew fans head to Astoria Bier & Cheese (p315) for local suds, while hipsters *sans* attitude down single-origin joe at Queens Kickshaw (p315).

➡**Culture** Take an aerial tour of NYC without ever leaving the ground at the retro-cool Queens Museum (p307).

➡**Flushing** Snack on lamb dumplings in the Golden Shopping Mall (p314) basement, then ignite the palate at Hunan Kitchen of Grand Sichuan (p315) or Fu Run (p314).

Getting There & Away

➡**Subway** Twelve lines serve Queens. From Manhattan, catch the N/Q/R and M to Astoria, the 7 to Long Island City, Woodside, Corona and Flushing, and the A to Rockaway Beach. The E, J and Z lines reach Jamaica, while the G directly connects Long Island City to Brooklyn.

➡**Train** Long Island Rail Road (LIRR) has a handy connection from Manhattan's Penn Station to Flushing. It also runs to Jamaica, for the AirTrain to JFK.

➡**Bus** Routes include the M60, which runs from LaGuardia Airport to Harlem and Columbia University in Manhattan, via Astoria.

Lonely Planet's Top Tip

Don't miss the **Fisher Landau Center for Art** (p305) for free modern art without the crowds. Occupying an old parachute-harness factory in Long Island City, the core of its stellar collection of painting, photography, sculpture and installations spans from the 1960s to today. The rotating exhibitions feature works from A-listers such as Robert Rauschenberg, Cy Twombly and Jasper Johns.

QUEENS

Best Places to Eat

➡ Fu Run (p314)

➡ M Wells Dinette (p309)

➡ Pye Boat Noodle (p309)

➡ Bahari (p312)

➡ Roosevelt Ave (p312)

For reviews, see p309 ➡

Best Places to Escape the Grind

➡ Rockaway Beach (p307)

➡ New York Spa Castle (p316)

➡ Bohemian Hall & Beer Garden (p315)

➡ Gantry Plaza State Park (p305)

For reviews, see p305 ➡

Best for Culture Vultures

➡ MoMA PS1 (p304)

➡ Museum of the Moving Image (p306)

➡ Queens Museum (p307)

➡ Fisher Landau Center for Art (p305)

For reviews, see p305 ➡

TOP SIGHT
MOMA PS1

The smaller, hipper sibling of Manhattan's Museum of Modern Art, MoMA PS1 hunts down razor-sharp art and serves it up in an ex-school locale. Forget about lily ponds in gilded frames. Here you'll be peering at videos through floorboards and debating the meaning of nonstatic structures while staring through a hole in the wall. Nothing is predictable. Best of all, admission is free with your MoMA ticket.

DON'T MISS

- Temporary and long-term exhibitions
- Summer 'Warm Up' parties
- Sunday Sessions

PRACTICALITIES

- Map p448
- ☎718-784-2084
- www.momaps1.org
- 22-25 Jackson Ave, Long Island City
- suggested donation adult/child $10/free, free with MoMA ticket, Warm Up party admission online/at venue $18/20
- 🕒noon-6pm Thu-Mon, Warm Up parties 3-9pm Sat Jul & Aug
- [S]E, M to 23rd St-Court Sq, G, 7 Court Sq

Roots, Radicals & PS1 Classics

PS1 first hit the scene in the 1970s. This was the age of Dia, Artists' Space and the New Museum – new-gen projects showcasing the city's thriving experimental, multimedia art scene. In 1976, Alanna Heiss – a supporter of art in alternative spaces – took possession of an abandoned school building in Queens and invited artists such as Richard Serra, James Turrell and Keith Sonnier to create site-specific works. The result was PS1's inaugural exhibition, *Rooms*. Surviving remnants include Richard Artschwager's oval-shaped wall 'blimps' and Alan Saret's light-channeling *The Hole at P.S.1, Fifth Solar Chthonic Wall Temple*, on the north wing's 3rd floor. These works are part of the gallery's long-term installations, which also include Pipilotti Rist's video *Selbstlos im Lavabad* (Selfless in the Bath of Lava) – viewable through the lobby floorboards – and James Turrell's awe-inspiring *Meeting*, where the sky is the masterpiece. (Though note this last work was closed for restoration at last visit.)

Summer 'Warm Up' Parties

On Saturday afternoon from July to early September, rock on at one of New York's coolest weekly music/culture events, Warm Up. It's a hit with everyone from verified hipsters to plugged-in music geeks, who spill into the MoMA PS1 courtyard to eat, drink and catch a stellar lineup of top bands, experimental music and DJs. Featured artists have included acid-house deity DJ Pierre and techno pioneer Juan Atkins. It's like one big block party, albeit with better music and art than your usual neighborhood slap-up. Linked to it is the annual YAP (Young Architects Program) competition, in which one design team is selected to transform the museum courtyard with a large-scale structure that provides shade and a creative party space.

Sunday Sessions

Another cultural treat is the Sunday Sessions, on Sunday from September to May. Spanning lectures, film screenings, music performances, even architectural projects, the lineup has included experimental comedy, postindustrial noise jams and Latin art-house dance. One week you might catch a symphony debut, the next an architectural performance from Madrid. Upcoming events are listed on the MoMA PS1 website.

SIGHTS

The Queens Tourism Council (www.itsinqueens.com) website offers information on attractions and events, while the Queens Council on the Arts (Map p448; ☎347-505-3010; www.queenscouncilarts.org; 37-11 35th Ave, Astoria; [S]M, R to Steinway) promotes art in the borough. For a more personalized introduction, Hunter College urban-geography professor Jack Eichenbaum leads many unusual walking tours (p317) of Queens' ethnic neighborhoods, including a full-day walk/subway ride along the 7 train line.

Long Island City

It's a testament to Queens' long lack of cool that Long Island City remained undeveloped for decades. Now it has masses of new high-rise condominiums lining the riverfront with fantastic views of Manhattan. The area has also become a hub of art museums. PS 1 Contemporary Art Center is dedicated solely to new, cutting-edge works. On Saturdays from early July through September, the center's outdoor courtyard is transformed into an installation art space and crammed with the highest concentration of hipsters this side of the Mississippi. If the weather is pleasant, don't miss the waterside Socrates Sculpture Park, with its outdoor exhibits of massive, climbable sculptures by greats including Mark di Suvero, who founded the space.

★MOMA PS1 — GALLERY

See p304.

★FISHER LANDAU CENTER FOR ART — MUSEUM

Map p448 (www.flcart.org; 38-27 30th St, Long Island City; ⏲noon-5pm Thu-Mon; [S]N/Q to 39th Ave) [FREE] Surprisingly little visited, considering the caliber of the work shown, this private collection is a must for fans of modern and contemporary art. Whether it's Cy Twombly, Jenny Holzer, Agnes Martin or any other big name in art in the last 50 years, you'll see their work on display in this converted factory building.

Co-designed by late British architect Max Gordon (designer of London's Saatchi Gallery), the space also hosts the Columbia University School of Visual Arts MFA Thesis Exhibition each May – a highly respected showcase for talented up-and-coming artists.

NOGUCHI MUSEUM — MUSEUM

Map p448 (www.noguchi.org; 9-01 33rd Rd, Long Island City; adult/child $10/free, by donation 1st Fri of the month; ⏲10am-5pm Wed-Fri, 11am-6pm Sat & Sun; [S]N/Q to Broadway) The art and the building here are the work of Japanese-American sculptor, furniture designer and landscape architect Isamu Noguchi, famous for iconic lamps and coffee tables, as well as elegant abstract stone sculptures. They are on display here, in serene concrete galleries and a minimalist rock garden – a complete aesthetic vision and an oasis of calm.

The building itself was once a photo-engraving plant, located across the street from Noguchi's studio. Art aside, the space also hosts a small cafe and a gift shop, the latter stocking Noguchi-designed lamps and furniture, as well as a small range of other mid-20th-century design pieces.

SCULPTURECENTER — GALLERY

Map p448 (☎718-361-1750; www.sculpture-center.org; 44-19 Purves St, Long Island City; suggested donation $5; ⏲11am-6pm Thu-Mon; [S]7 to 45th Rd-Court House Sq, E, M to 23rd St-Ely Ave, G to Long Island City-Court Sq) Down a dead-end street, in a former trolley repair shop, SculptureCenter pages Berlin with its edgy art and industrial backdrop. Its hangarlike main gallery and cavernous underground space show both emerging and established artists. It's always a worthwhile add-on to a visit to nearby MoMA PS1.

SOCRATES SCULPTURE PARK — ART

Map p448 (www.socratessculpturepark.org; 32-01 Vernon Blvd, Long Island City; ⏲10am-dusk; [S]N/Q to Broadway) [FREE] First carved out of an abandoned dump by sculptor Mark di Suvero, Socrates is now a city park on the river's edge with beautiful views and a rotating series of installations. Try to time a visit with free events – such as yoga on weekends from mid-May to late September, and Wednesday-night movies in July and August.

GANTRY PLAZA STATE PARK — PARK

Map p448 (www.nysparks.com/parks/149; 4-09 47th Rd, Long Island City; [S]7 to Vernon Blvd-Jackson Ave) This 12-acre riverside park directly across the water from the United Nations has gorgeous uninterrupted views of the Manhattan skyline. It's nicely designed, with public lounges for panoramic chilling, and attracts a good mix of Queens families. The restored gantries – in service until 1967 – are testament to the area's past as a loading dock for rail-car floats and barges.

Dating back to 1936, the giant Pepsi-Cola sign at the park's northern end is an icon of Long Island City. It once topped a nearby Pepsi bottling plant, which has been since demolished.

Astoria

Home to the largest Greek community outside Greece, this is obviously the place to find amazing Greek bakeries, restaurants and gourmet shops, mainly along Broadway. An influx of Eastern European, Middle Eastern (Steinway Ave, known as 'Little Egypt,' is the place for falafel, kebabs and hookah pipes) and Latino immigrants have created a rich and diverse mix. A reminder that movie-making started in Astoria in the 1920s, the American Museum of the Moving Image exposes some of the mysteries of the craft with amazing exhibits and screenings in its ornate and recently renovated theater. In summer, cool off at the Astoria Pool (p316), the city's largest and oldest. Much of the neighborhood, as well as curious Manhattanites, can be found at the Bohemian Hall & Beer Garden (p315) during warm afternoons and evenings.

★MUSEUM OF THE MOVING IMAGE — MUSEUM

Map p448 (☎718-777-6888; www.movingimage.us; 36-01 35th Ave, Astoria; adult/child $12/6, 4-8pm Fri free; ⏲10:30am-5pm Wed & Thu, to 8pm Fri, 11:30am-7pm Sat & Sun; 📶; [S]M, R to Steinway St) This super-cool complex is one of the world's top film, television and video museums. Galleries show a collection of 130,000-plus artifacts, including Elizabeth Taylor's wig from *Cleopatra,* nearly everything related to *Seinfeld* and a whole room of vintage arcade games. Interactive displays – such as a DIY flipbook station – show the science behind the art.

You can also try your hand at film editing (including re-dubbing the 'We're not in Kansas anymore' scene from *The Wizard of Oz*), and get nostalgic over an impressive booty of vintage TVs and cameras. The museum's temporary exhibitions are usually fantastic, as are the regular film screenings – check the website for details.

GREATER ASTORIA HISTORICAL SOCIETY — MUSEUM

Map p448 (☎718-278-0700; www.astorialic.org; 35-20 Broadway, Astoria; ⏲noon-4pm Sat & by appt; [S]N/Q to Broadway; M, R to Steinway) Get a glimpse of old-time Astoria at this labor-of-love community space. There's always some exhibit of neighborhood ephemera, and the group hosts lectures and films as well.

Jackson Heights

JACKSON HEIGHTS HISTORIC DISTRICT — NEIGHBORHOOD

(btwn Roosevelt & 34th Aves, from 70th to 90th Sts; [S]7 to 74th St-Broadway, E, F/M, R to Roosevelt Ave-Jackson Heights) Spread out in a 50-block area to the north of the subway is one of the nicest NYC neighborhoods that few New Yorkers know about. Following the 1909 opening of the 59th St-Queensboro Bridge, the Jackson Heights Historic District was set up in 1917 as a 'garden city' (popular in England at the time), with six-story, chateau-style brick apartment buildings sharing long, well-landscaped, private gardens. There are a few good vantage points – try 80th or 81st Sts from 37th to 34th Aves.

Flushing & Corona

The intersection of Main St and Roosevelt Ave, downtown Flushing, can feel like the Times Square of a city a world away from NYC. Immigrants from all over Asia, primarily Chinese and Korean, make up this neighborhood bursting at the seams with markets and restaurants filled with delicious and cheap delicacies. The Long Island Rail Road station and terminal for the 7 train see around 100,000 people pass through daily. Flushing Meadows Corona Park (p308), meanwhile, is the home of Citi Field (p316), the USTA Billie Jean King National Tennis Center (p316) (the US Open is held here every August) and many lakes, ball fields, bike paths and grassy expanses, and was used for the 1939 and 1964 World's Fairs, of which there are quite a few faded leftovers – including Queens' most famous landmark, the stainless-steel *Unisphere,* standing 120ft high and weighing 380 tons. Kids can learn about science and technology through fun hands-on exhibits at the New York Hall of Science (p309); a quirky

WORTH A DETOUR

HITTING THE SHORE

Immortalized by the Ramones' 1977 song 'Rockaway Beach,' America's largest urban beach – and one of the city's best – is just a $2.75 trip on the A train from Manhattan. Less crowded than Coney Island and with a wilder feel, Rockaway Beach is a long stretch with two social hubs.

On the west end, **Jacob Riis Park**, part of the 26,000-acre Gateway National Recreation Area, draws families and young professionals with cash to spend on the 90-minute **ferry ride** (Map p410; ☎718-474-0593; www.newyorkbeachferry.com; Pier 11; return adult/child $30/15; 🕐Sat, Sun & public holidays summer; [S]2/3 to Wall St, J/Z to Broad St, 1 to South Ferry, R to Whitehall St) from Lower Manhattan to Riis Landing. This area is also home to the cool green ruins of Fort Tilden, a decommissioned coastal artillery installation from WWI.

On the east end, starting around Beach 108th St, is a burgeoning scene of hipsters, artists and locavore food options, fronting the city's only designated surfing beaches (at Beach 92nd St and going east). On the boardwalk here, concrete concession booths peddle treats such as lobster rolls, ceviche and hipster pizza.

Extending from near JFK international airport, the salty, marshy **Jamaica Bay Wildlife Refuge** covers the water north of the Rockaways' barrier island. As one of the most important migratory bird and wetland habitats along the eastern seaboard, it attracts more than 325 bird species in spring and fall, as they snap up all sorts of briny sea creatures like clams, turtles, shrimp and oysters. Each season brings different visitors. Spring features warblers and songbirds, and American woodcocks in late March. In mid-August shorebirds start to move south, landing here from Canada and fueling up for the trip to Mexico. Fall is when migrating hawks and raptors get mobile, along with ducks, geese, monarch butterflies and thousands and thousands of dragonflies. Birders and naturalists get the most action around the east and west ponds. Although the west pond was breached during Hurricane Sandy, it is still possible to walk the roughly 1.5-mile perimeter of the east pond. Just make sure to wear mud-resistant shoes, insect repellent and sunscreen, carry some water and watch out for poison ivy.

To get to the **visitor center** (☎718-318-4340; www.nyharborparks.org; Cross Bay Blvd, Broad Channel; 🕐9am-5pm; 🚌Q53 to Cross Bay Blvd/Wildlife Refuge, [S]A/S to Broad Channel) [FREE], exit at Broad Channel station, walk west along Noel Rd to Cross Bay Blvd, turn right (north) and walk for 0.7 miles, and the center will be visible on the left side of the road.

minigolf course is on the site. Also within this massive park is the Queens Museum.

QUEENS MUSEUM — MUSEUM

Map p450 (QMA; www.queensmuseum.org; Flushing Meadows Corona Park, Queens; suggested donation adult/child $8/free; 🕐noon-6pm Wed-Sun; 📶; [S]7 to 111th St or Mets-Willets Point) The Queens Museum is one of the city's most unexpected pleasures. Its most famous installation is the *Panorama of New York City*, a gob-smacking 9335-sq-ft miniature New York City, with all buildings accounted for and a 15-minute dusk-to-dawn light simulation. The museum also hosts top exhibitions of global contemporary art, reflecting the diversity of Queens.

The QM is housed in a historic building made for the 1939 World's Fair (and once home to the UN), and you'll find a retro-fabulous collection of memorabilia from both the '39 and '64 fairs on display (with reproductions in the gift shop).

LOUIS ARMSTRONG HOUSE — BUILDING

Map p450 (☎718-478-8274; www.louisarmstronghouse.org; 34-56 107th St, Corona; adult/child $10/7; 🕐10am-5pm Tue-Fri, noon-5pm Sat & Sun, last tour 4pm; [S]7 to 103rd St-Corona Plaza) At the peak of his career and with worldwide fame at hand, legendary trumpeter Armstrong settled in this modest Queens home, and lived there until his death in 1971. The place has been immaculately preserved in groovy style, down to the dazzling turquoise kitchen fixtures. Guided tours (45 minutes) tell Armstrong's story with audio clips and more.

LOCAL KNOWLEDGE

QUEENS: THE NEW BROOKLYN

Artist Julian Lesser gives the lowdown on his favorite New York borough (and why it should be your favorite, too).

The Best Thing About Queens

The cultural diversity. In Astoria alone you've got the original Greek population, plus everyone from Colombians and Brazilians to Egyptians. There's even a 'Little Egypt' on Steinway Ave, between Astoria Blvd and 30th Ave, with great kebab shops and strong coffee. Much of Queens is pretty mixed these days, but Flushing is incredibly Asian. The result is a really authentic shopping experience, with massive Asian grocery stores selling exotic-looking fruits and every conceivable type of still-wriggling seafood. Planes fly low over Flushing, so it's also cool if you're a plane-spotter.

Don't-Miss Eats

I love **Brooklyn Bagel & Coffee Company** (p312). It has amazing, huge bagels and a wide variety of cream cheeses. It creates a new flavor every week for its customers to try. **Queens Kickshaw** (p315) is also great, the team sourcing a lot of their ingredients locally. In Long Island City, I love **LIC Market**. It's like an intimate cafe but it does full service, and puts a lot of love into the food. It's also handy if you're visiting MoMA PS1.

Cultural Picks

For cutting-edge contemporary art, spend an afternoon at **MoMA PS1** (p304) and the nearby **SculptureCenter** (p305) in Long Island City. You could easily spend a few happy hours at the impressive **Museum of the Moving Image** (p306) in Astoria – it's a cool place to see props from classic films and TV shows. For a lesser-known treat, join one of the fascinating walking tours run by the **Greater Astoria Historical Society** (p306).

Satchmo shared the house with his fourth wife, Lucille Wilson, a dancer at the Cotton Club. Armstrong's den, of which he was most proud, features a portrait of the great painted by none other than Benedetto (aka Tony Bennett).

**FLUSHING MEADOWS
CORONA PARK** PARK
Map p450 (www.nycgovparks.org/parks/fmcp; Grand Central Pkwy, Corona; S 7 to Mets-Willets Point) FREE Central Queens' biggest attraction is this 1225-acre park, built for the 1939 World's Fair and dominated by Queens' most famous landmark, the stainless-steel *Unisphere* – it's the world's biggest globe, at 120ft high and weighing 380 tons. Facing it is the former New York City Building, now home to the fantastic Queens Museum (p307).

Just south are three weather-worn, Cold War–era New York State Pavilion Towers, part of the New York State Pavilion for the 1964 World's Fair. (You may recognize them as alien spaceships from the film *Men in Black*.) If entering the park from the north, via the 7 train, look for the 1964 World's Fair mosaics by Salvador Dalí and Andy Warhol. Also nearby is Citi Field (p316), and the USTA Billie Jean King National Tennis Center (p316). Head west over the Grand Central Pkwy to find a few more attractions, including the New York Hall of Science. The park has grounds, too, on its eastern and southern edges. The top-notch Astroturf soccer fields are popular for organized and pick-up soccer, and there's a pitch-and-putt golf course that's lit up for drunken golfers at night.

UNISPHERE MONUMENT
Map p450 (Flushing Meadows Park; S 7 to 111th St or Mets-Willets Point) Designed for the 1964 World's Fair, this 12-story-high stainless-steel globe is the focal point of Flushing Meadows Park, and the de facto icon of Queens. In summer, it's ringed with fountains; at other times, it's crisscrossed by skateboarders.

NEW YORK HALL OF SCIENCE   MUSEUM

Map p450 (☎718-699-0005; www.nysci.org; 47-01 111th St; adult/child $15/12, 2-5pm Fri & 10-11am Sun free; ⏰9:30am-5pm Mon-Fri, 10am-6pm Sat & Sun; ⓢ7 to 111th St) Occupying a weird 1965 building, rippling with stained glass, this science museum is unapologetically nerdy. An outdoor minigolf course and playground don't require as much brain power.

✖ EATING

Spanakopita? *Khao man gai? Sopa de mariscos?* If it exists, you can devour it in Queens. Head to Long Island City for locavore eateries, and to Astoria for anything from Greek to bagels – hot spots here include 30th Ave, Broadway (between 31st and 35th Sts) and 31st Ave. Steinway Ave between Astoria Blvd and 30th Ave is Astoria's 'Little Egypt.' Further east, Elmhurst is home to a cluster of straight-outta-Bangkok Thai options, while Roosevelt Ave is perfect for a Latin food-truck crawl. At the end of the 7 subway line lies Flushing, New York's 'Chinatown without the tourists.' For a clued-in exploration of the borough, join a World's Fare Tours (p316) adventure, run by food writer Joe DiStefano. Celebrity chefs Eric Ripert and Anthony Bourdain have both sought his wisdom.

✖ Long Island City

CANNELLE PATISSERIE   BAKERY $

Map p448 (☎718-937-8500; 5-11 47th Ave, Long Island City; pastries $3; ⏰6:30am-8pm Mon-Fri, from 7am Sat, 7am-5pm Sun; ⓢ7 to Vernon Blvd-Jackson Ave) A surprising source of flawless French pastry, this cafe sits on a slick block in new-build LIC – but one bite of a flaky croissant or a gemlike fruit tart will take you straight to Paris. This is a branch of the original business, set in an even more unlikely location: a dreary strip mall in Jackson Heights.

LIC MARKET   CAFE $$

Map p448 (☎718-361-0013; www.licmarket.com; 21-52 44th Dr, Long Island City; lunch $9-12, dinner mains $15-36; ⏰7am-3:30pm Mon, to 10pm Tue-Sat, 10am-3:30pm Sun; 🖥; ⓢE, M to 23rd St-

Ely Ave, 7 to 45th Rd-Court House Sq) 🍴 Local creatives and office workers mix at this cool little cafe, trimmed in local artwork and cooking pots. Breakfast winners include the 'sausage and onions' sandwich (fried eggs, breakfast sausage, cheddar and caramelized onion), while ever-changing lunch and dinner options can include scallops, soulful risottos and seasonal game.

M WELLS DINETTE   CANADIAN $$

Map p448 (☎718-786-1800; www.magasinwells.com; 22-25 Jackson Ave, Long Island City; mains $9-29; ⏰noon-6pm Thu-Mon; ⓢE, M to 23rd St-Court Sq, G, 7 Court Sq) Like being back at school (but with better grub), this cultish nosh spot sits inside school-turned-museum MoMA PS1 (no need to pay museum admission). Desk-like tables face the open kitchen, where Quebecois head chef Hugue Dufour gives regional ingredients a gutsy French-Canadian makeover: frisée salad with duck hearts, smoked egg and fried bread, for instance.

M WELLS STEAKHOUSE   STEAK $$$

Map p448 (☎718-786-9060; www.magasinwells.com; 43-15 Crescent St, Long Island City; mains $27-70; ⏰5:30-11pm Wed-Mon, also 11am-3pm Sun; ⓢE, M to 23rd St-Court Sq, G, 7 to Court Sq) Carnivores with a taste for the avant-garde will appreciate Quebecois chef Hugue Dufour's surreal yet satisfying take on steak. Pork chops, grilled over a wood fire, arrive in stacks like pancakes; the tomahawk chop is an almost terrifyingly huge beef rib (terrifying too for its $160 price tag). Loud, exuberant ambience. Reserve on weekends.

✖ Astoria

★PYE BOAT NOODLE   THAI $

Map p448 (☎718-685-2329; 35-13 Broadway, Astoria; noodles $10-13; ⏰11:30am-10:30pm, to 11pm Fri & Sat; 🍴; ⓢN/Q to Broadway, M, R to Steinway) An army of young Thai waitresses in matching fedoras greet you at this cute place decked out like an old-fashioned country house. The specialty is rich, star-anise-scented boat noodles, topped with crispy pork cracklings. It also does delicate seafood *yen ta fo* (mild seafood soup, tinted pink), a rarity in NYC. Good with a side of papaya salad (off-menu request: add funky fermented crab).

JAMIE GRILL / GETTY IMAGES ©

BRUCE YUANYUE BI / GETTY IMAGES ©

JUMPER / GETTY IMAGES ©

1. Queens (p302)
Be entertained by street musicians in Queens.

2. Rockaway Beach (p307)
Surf at NYC's best urban beach, famed for its natural scenery.

3. Flushing Meadows Corona Park (p308)
Visit Queens' most famous landmark and the world's largest globe, *Unisphere* (by Gilmore David Clarke and further refined by Peter Muller-Munk Associates).

4. Gantry Plaza State Park (p305)
Recline on public sunloungers and enjoy uninterrupted views of the Manhattan skyline.

ROOSEVELT AVE FOOD TRUCKS

When it comes to sidewalk grazing, it's hard to beat Roosevelt Ave and its army of late-night Latino food trucks, carts and stalls. Just one stroll from 90th St to 103rd St will have you sipping on *champurrados* (a warm, thick corn-based chocolate drink), nibbling on a *cemita* (Mexican sandwich) and making a little more room for some Ecuadoran fish stew. It's cheap, authentic and quintessentially Queens. Hungry? Then set off on a taste-testing mission of Roosevelt Ave's best.

On the south side or Roosevelt head for the intersection with Benham St. Here you'll find the legendary food truck Tia Julia, justifiably famous for its *cemitas* ($9).

A few steps further east along Roosevelt Ave lies food stall El Coyote Dormilon. The coyote might be snoozing, but the vendor is up and at it, busily turning masa from her bucket into warm, super-fresh tortillas. (Note: fresh masa and a tortilla press are a good sign at any stall.) Quesadillas ($3) are the specialty here – try the distinctive *cuitlacoche* (a mushroom that grows on corn) and *quesillo* (stringy, cow's milk cheese) combo. It's seriously fine.

Keep rolling along Roosevelt Ave to Warren St. A major Warren St star is El Guayaquileño, famous for its Ecuadoran fish stew made of yuca, tuna, cilantro, onion, lemon, cumin and toasted corn kernels. It's flavorsome, wonderfully textured and a meal in itself. That said, leave room for the *bollos de pescado* (mashed green plantain with tuna, steamed in a banana leaf and served with tomato and chopped onion; $10).

ROSARIO'S — PIZZA $

Map p448 (☎718-728-2920; 22-55 31st St, Astoria; slice $2; ⏰8:30am-7:30pm Mon-Sat; 🖉; [S]N/Q to Ditmars Blvd) Rosario's is a fully stocked Italian deli, its meats and cheeses dazzling in their own right. But its brilliant secret is its flawless, crisp-crust pizza, sold by the slice, cheese only (don't even bother asking for toppings). It's hidden at the back – ask the counterman if you don't see any in the display case.

The shop is a favorite of MTA staff on break (the N and Q trains end here). They favor big sandwiches and Rosario's rice balls.

BROOKLYN BAGEL & COFFEE COMPANY — BAKERY $

Map p448 (☎718-204-0141; www.brooklynbagelandcoffeecompany.com; 35-05 Broadway, Astoria; bagels $1.25; ⏰6am-4:30pm; [S]N/Q to Broadway; M, R to Steinway St) It may be in Queens, not Brooklyn, but there's little confusion about the caliber of the bagels here. With a good crust and chewy inside, they come in a number of drool-inducing variations, including sesame, onion, garlic, and wholewheat with oats and raisins. Mix and match with a dazzling repertoire of flavored cream cheese, including wasabi lox and baked apple.

★BAHARI — GREEK $$

Map p448 (☎718-204-8968; 31-14 Broadway, Astoria; oven dishes $9-15, grilled meats $12-29; ⏰noon-midnight; 🖉👪; [S]N/Q to Broadway) Many of Astoria's Greek restaurants are standard grill joints. Bahari branches out with the full range of casseroles and stews: moussaka with crusty-creamy bechamel, velvety slow-cooked beans, spinach-flecked rice. A meal of these rich dishes is a bargain, especially in the elegant surroundings. (Note: fish is pricier.) Excellent staff and plenty of room, compared with most NYC restaurants.

MOMBAR — EGYPTIAN $$

Map p448 (☎718-726-2356; 25-22 Steinway St, Astoria; dishes $10-24; ⏰5-10pm Tue-Sun; 🖉; [S]N/Q to Astoria Blvd) A legendary restaurant in the Steinway strip of Arab businesses, Mombar is worth a visit for the decor alone – its collage style of found objects was assembled over years as chef Mustafa saved money to open the place. It's a jewel-box setting for his refined Egyptian food; definitely get his signature *mombar*, a light, rice-stuffed sausage.

KABAB CAFE — EGYPTIAN $$

Map p448 (☎718-728-9858; 25-12 Steinway St, Astoria; dishes $12-26; ⏰1-5pm & 6-10pm Tue-Sun; 🖉; [S]N/Q to Astoria Blvd) Chef Ali is a larger-than-life personality and an anchor on the Steinway strip known as Little Egypt – though his creative, earthy food, often served straight from the frying pan to your plate, ranges much farther than his Alexandrian roots. Start with mixed apps, for fluffy green Egyptian-style falafel, then pick any lamb dish.

VESTA TRATTORIA & WINE BAR ITALIAN **$$**

Map p448 (☎718-545-5550; www.vestavino.com; 21-02 30th Ave, Astoria; pizzas $13-15, dinner mains $13-26; 🕒5-10pm Mon-Thu, to 11pm Fri, 11am-3pm & 4-11pm Sat, 11am-3pm & 4-10pm Sun; [S]N/Q to 30th Ave) Vesta is one of those neighborhood secrets, with chatty regulars at the bar, local art on the walls and organic produce from a Brooklyn rooftop farm. The menu is simple and seasonal, with nourishing *zuppe* (soups), bubbling thin-crust pizzas and tasty mains of mostly pasta and risotto dishes.

Star of the popular weekend brunch is the Hangover Pizza, with spicy tomato sauce, potatoes, pancetta and baked egg.

TAVERNA KYCLADES GREEK **$$**

Map p448 (☎718-545-8666; www.tavernakyclades.com; 33-07 Ditmars Blvd, Astoria; mains $15-30; 🕒noon-11pm Mon-Sat, to 10pm Sun; [S]N/Q to Ditmars Blvd) Kyclades is tops when it comes to Greek seafood – and repeat diner Bill Murray agrees. Simple classics include succulent grilled octopus and whole fish, backed up with *saganaki* (pan-fried cheese) and a hearty salad. Skip the overpriced Kyclades Special, and go early to beat the daunting line. (Ironically, the Manhattan location, in the East Village, is less crowded.)

🍴 Jackson Heights

AREPA LADY COLOMBIAN **$**

Map p448 (☎347-730-6124; 77-02 Roosevelt Ave, Jackson Heights; dishes $4-8; 🕒noon-11pm, to 1am Fri & Sat; 🥕; [S]7 to 74 St-Broadway, E, F, M, R to Roosevelt Ave-Jackson Heights) Many a street-food fanatic has made a pilgrimage to the sainted Arepa Lady, a legend of the Roosevelt Ave late-night food carts. Her sons have opened this shoebox of a storefront, open during daylight hours, with the same chewy, cheesy corn cakes that made Mom famous. Bonus: black walls, a cool jazz soundtrack and enthusiastic local family diners.

The address is on Roosevelt Ave, but the storefront is around the corner on 77th St.

LITTLE TIBET TIBETAN **$**

Map p448 (☎718-505-8423; 72-19 Roosevelt Ave, Jackson Heights; dishes $6-11; 🕒noon-11pm; [S]7 to 74 St-Broadway, E, F/M, R to Roosevelt Ave-Jackson Heights) Little Tibet could be the nickname for all of Jackson Heights, where traditionally Indian shops and restaurants are slowly giving way to entrepreneurs from the Himalayas, both Tibet and Nepal. This little place has exceptional neighborhood loyalty and a cozy, wood-paneled atmosphere. Wash down the *momos* (dumplings) with a huge list of Queens microbrews.

TIA JULIA MEXICAN **$**

(Benham St, at Roosevelt Ave, Jackson Heights; tacos $2.50, sandwiches $5-9; 🕒10am-5am; [S]7 to 90th St-Elmhurst Ave) Legendary food truck Tia Julia is justifiably famous for its *cemitas*, Mexican sandwiches stacked high with string cheese, chicken cutlet, chipotles and the refreshing herb *pápalo*. Its piled-high tacos are pretty impressive too.

EL GUAYAQUILEÑO ECUADORAN **$**

(Warren St, btwn Roosevelt Ave & 40th Rd, Jackson Heights; dishes from $5; 🕒8am-10.30pm Sun-Thu, to around 4am Fri & Sat; [S]7 to Junction Blvd) The best known of a cluster of Ecuadoran and Peruvian food carts on Warren St, El Guayaquileño is famous for its fish stew made of yuca, tuna, cilantro, onion, cumin and toasted corn. And save room for *bollos de pescado* (smashed green plantain with tuna, steamed in a banana leaf and served with tomato and onion).

EL COYOTE DORMILON MEXICAN **$**

(Roosevelt Ave, btwn Benham & Aske Sts, Jackson Heights; tacos $2.50, sandwiches $5; 🕒1-11pm Mon & Tue, to 4am Wed-Sun; [S]7 to 90th St-Elmhurst Ave) This tiny food cart has the whole range of Mexican snacks, from tacos to gorditas. It offers one rarely seen item: the *pambazo,* a pressed sandwich stuffed with cheese, chorizo and potatoes.

🍴 Elmhurst

PLANT LOVE HOUSE THAI **$**

Map p448 (☎718-565-2010; 86-08 Whitney Ave, Elmhurst; dishes from $5; 🕒noon-10pm; [S]M, R to Elmhurst Ave) Snug and adorable, this ultra-Thai cafe serves authentically modest portions of incendiary soups (*num tok*, enriched with pork blood, is a specialty) and improbably huge wedges of sweet toast

FARM LIFE

Frolic with cows, sheep and goats at the **Queens County Farm Museum** (☎718-347-3276; www.queensfarm.org; 73-50 Little Neck Parkway, Floral Park; ☺10am-5pm; 🚻; 🚌Q46 to Little Neck Parkway), the last patch of farmland within the city limits. It's a long way from Manhattan, but for anyone with an interest in urban agriculture – or kids who need a break from city energy – this is a tranquil destination. It hosts an annual pow-wow for tribes from all over America.

soaked in butter. Maybe not a balanced meal, but a satisfying and transporting one.

KHAO KANG　　　　　　　　THAI $
Map p448 (☎718-806-1807; 76-20 Woodside Ave, Elmhurst; plate $8; ☺11am-9pm Tue-Sun; 🚇E, F/M, R to Roosevelt Ave-Jackson Heights, 7 to 74 St-Broadway) New-era Thai food at its best, where you can eat like a business-luncher in Bangkok, pointing at two or three hot dishes – creamy-hot pumpkin with eggs and basil, caramelized pork, and more – to eat over rice. It's fast and inexpensive, but doesn't skimp on style. Desserts are a treat too.

🍴 Woodside

SRIPRAPHAI　　　　　　　　THAI $$
Map p448 (☎718-899-9599; www.sripraphai restaurant.com; 64-13 39th Ave, Woodside; mains $9-23; ☺11:30am-9:30pm Thu-Tue; 🚇7 to 69th St) The first restaurant in NYC to serve Thai food for Thai people, no punches pulled. In some ways it has been outpaced by newer, more single-minded restaurants (the menu here is epic, from all over the country), but it is still a legend and a satisfying place for a big dinner of everything from curries to heavenly fried soft-shell crab. Cash only.

🍴 Flushing & Corona

★**GOLDEN SHOPPING MALL**　　CHINESE $
Map p450 (41-28 Main St, Flushing; meals from $3; ☺10am-9:30pm; 🚇7 to Flushing-Main St) A chaotic jumble of hung ducks, airborne noodles and greasy Laminex tables, Golden Mall's basement food court dishes up fantastic hawker-style grub. Don't be intimidated by the lack of English menus. Most stalls have at least one English speaker, and the regulars are usually happy to point out their personal favorites, whether it's Lanzhou hand-pulled noodles or spicy pig ears.

Two must-tries are the lamb dumplings from Xie Family Dishes (stall 38) – best dipped in a little black vinegar, soy sauce and chili oil – and the spicy cumin lamb burger at Xi'an Famous Foods next door.

★**TORTILLERIA NIXTAMAL**　　MEXICAN $
Map p450 (☎718-699-2434; www.tortilleria nixtamal.com; 104-05 47th Ave, Corona; dishes $2.50-13; ☺11am-7pm Mon-Wed, to 9pm Thu & Sun, to 11pm Fri & Sat; 🚇7 to 103rd St-Corona Plaza) The red-and-yellow picnic benches at this lo-fi gem are never short of a roaming gastronome, here for super-authentic Mexican snacks. The secret weapon is the Rube Goldbergian machine, which transforms additive-free masa into super-tasty tacos and tamales.

The guys here are purists, their tacos adorned with a simple garnish of cilantro, onion and lime. Other must-tries include the pork-broth pozole soup, spiked with chopped onion, radish, oregano and crushed red peppers. Cool down with a *horchata fresca* (a spiced rice and almond milk drink) while cheering on El Tricolor.

FU RUN　　　　　　　　　CHINESE $
Map p450 (☎718-321-1363; www.furunflushing. com; 40-09 Prince St, Flushing; mains $9-24; ☺11:30am-midnight; 🚇7 to Flushing-Main St) Fu Run has a cult following for very good reason: its northeast Chinese cooking is extraordinary – rustic, sometimes subtle, always impeccably fried. Reconfigure your understanding of the country's flavors over sour cabbage–laced pork dumplings or the unforgettable Muslim lamb chop (deep-fried ribs dressed in dried chilies, cumin and sesame seeds).

HUNAN KITCHEN OF GRAND SICHUAN　　　　　CHINESE $$
Map p450 (☎718-888-0553; 42-47 Main St, Flushing; mains $10-24; ☺11am-12:30am; 🚇7 to Flushing-Main St) Work up a sweat at this respectable Flushing restaurant, best known

for its specialties from Hunan province. Standout dishes include a deliciously salty white-pepper smoked beef, tender chicken with hot red pepper, and lovely warming fish soup. If you're in a large group, order the house specialty: BBQ duck, Hunan-style.

✕ Maspeth

BUN-KER
VIETNAMESE $$

(☑718-386-4282; http://bunkervietnamese.com; 46-63 Metropolitan Ave, Maspeth; mains $14-26; ⊙5-10pm Tue & Wed, to 11pm Thu & Fri, noon-11pm Sat, to 10pm Sun; ◻Q54 to Metropolitan Ave/Woodward Ave, Ⓢ L to Jefferson St) NYC is short on good Vietnamese restaurants – so it's worth the adventure to head to this passion project in fringiest Queens. (Nascent hipster 'hood Ridgewood is the nearest residential spot.) The owners have great seafood connections and use best-quality meats, adding extra savor to dishes like ginger catfish and short ribs with lemongrass.

🍷 DRINKING & NIGHTLIFE

★BOHEMIAN HALL & BEER GARDEN
BEER GARDEN

Map p448 (☑718-274-4925; www.bohemianhall.com; 29-19 24th Ave, Astoria; ⊙5pm-1am Mon-Thu, to 3am Fri, noon-3am Sat, noon-midnight Sun; Ⓢ N/Q to Astoria Blvd) This Czech community center kicked off NYC's beer-garden craze, and nothing quite matches it for space and heaving drinking crowds, which pack every picnic table under the towering trees in summer. There's obligatory food (dumplings, sausages); the focus is on the cold and foamy Czech beers. Some nights, folk bands set up (with occasional cover charge of $5 or so).

ASTORIA BIER & CHEESE
BEER HALL

Map p448 (☑718-545-5588; www.astoriabierandcheese.com; 34-14 Broadway, Astoria; ⊙noon-11pm Mon-Thu, to midnight Fri & Sat, to 10pm Sun; Ⓢ N/Q to Broadway, M, R to Steinway) At this funky bar-shop hybrid in Astoria, you can foam that upper lip with 10 seasonal, mostly local drafts, or pick from hundreds of canned and bottled options, to take home or swill on-site. *Fromage* fiend Mike Fisher (formerly of Williamsburg's Bedford Cheese Shop) keeps the cheese se-lection inspired and surprising, with pairing plates available.

QUEENS KICKSHAW
BAR

Map p448 (☑718-777-0913; www.thequeenskickshaw.com; 40-17 Broadway, Astoria; ⊙7:30am-midnight Mon-Thu, to 1am Fri, 9am-1am Sat, to midnight Sun; 🛜; Ⓢ M, R to Steinway St) This Astoria hangout brings a little Brooklyn to Queens, with reclaimed wood, indie folk tunes, and communal tables lined with wi-fi-ing Macheads. Brainstorm over a single-origin brew, or loosen up with a craft ale or cider. The menu just happens to be vegetarian, with fantastic grilled sandwich-es (try the Gouda, with black beans, guava jam and pickled jalapeños).

STUDIO SQUARE
BEER GARDEN

Map p448 (☑718-383-1001; www.studiosquarebeergarden.com; 35-33 36th St, Astoria; Ⓢ M, R to 36th St, N/Q to 36th Ave) A next-generation beer garden, this place might not have big trees or Old World ambience, but it makes up for it with a massive beer menu, plenty of room to move and a Queens-inspired diverse clientele. Special events range from movie screenings to drag shows.

☆ ENTERTAINMENT

★TERRAZA 7
LIVE MUSIC

Map p448 (☑718-803-9602; http://terraza7.com; 40-19 Gleane St, Elmhurst; ⊙4pm-4am; Ⓢ 7 to 82nd St-Jackson Hts) Come to Queens for multicultural eats, then stay for equally diverse sounds at this cool bi-level performance space. It makes creative use of the tiny room, setting the live band in a loft above the bar. Latin jazz is the mainstay, but performers can hail from as far as Morocco.

CREEK AND THE CAVE
COMEDY

Map p448 (☑917-865-4575; www.creeklic.com; 10-93 Jackson Ave, Long Island City; ⊙11am-2am Sun-Thu, to 4am Fri & Sat; Ⓢ 7 to Vernon Blvd-Jackson Ave) The biggest and best known of a handful of fringy comedy clubs in the neighborhood, the Creek and the Cave has two stages, a Mexican restaurant, a chilled-out backyard and a bar with well-maintained pinball machines. With so much fun in one place, it's no surprise the place is a kind of clubhouse for young comedy scenesters.

SHOPPING

ARTBOOK
BOOKS

Map p448 (☎718-433-1088; www.artbook.com/artbookps1.html; 22-25 Jackson Ave, Long Island City; ⏰noon-6pm Thu-Mon; [S]E, M to 23rd St-Court Sq, G, 7 Court Sq) The bookshop at MoMA PS1 is, appropriately, well stocked with beautiful tomes and eye-popping periodicals.

SPORTS & ACTIVITIES

NEW YORK SPA CASTLE
SPA

(☎718-939-6300; http://ny.spacastleusa.com; 131-10 11th Ave, College Point; weekday/weekend $40/50; ⏰6am-midnight; 📶; [S]7 to Flushing-Main St) A slice of cutting-edge Korean bathhouse culture in an industrial corner of Queens, this 100,000-sq-ft spa complex is a bubbling dream of mineral and massage pools, saunas of dazzling variety, steam rooms and waterfalls. It also has a food court, beauty treatments and massages (from $75), and a gym ($5). Avoid the place on weekends as it gets packed.

A free shuttle bus runs to/from the corner of Northern Blvd and Union St, a few blocks north of the Flushing–Main St subway station. Shuttles depart every 10 and 40 minutes past the hour.

CLIFFS
INDOOR CLIMBING

Map p448 (☎718-729-7625; www.thecliffsclimbing.com; 11-11 44th Dr, Long Island City; admission $28, shoes/harness rental $6/5; ⏰7am-midnight Mon-Fri, 9am-10pm Sat & Sun; [S]E, M to 23rd St-Ely Ave, 7 to 45th Rd-Court House Sq) New York's largest indoor-climbing facility has more than 30,000 sq ft of climbing surface, with some 125 top rope stations, 16ft top-out bouldering and a rappel tower. If that's not enough of a workout for you, there's also a gym with cardiovascular machines and exercise equipment.

USTA BILLIE JEAN KING NATIONAL TENNIS CENTER
TENNIS

Map p450 (☎718-760-6200; www.usta.com; Flushing Meadows Corona Park, Corona; ⏰6am-midnight; [S]7 to Mets-Willets Pt) The US Open takes place in late August; tickets usually go on sale at Ticketmaster in April or May, but are hard to get for marquee games. General admission to early rounds is easier. For about $80, top bleachers on Court 7 can take in five matches at once. Scan the USTA website in January/February for updates.

The USTA has 12 indoor DecoTurf courts, 19 field courts, four climate-controlled clay bubbled courts, and three stadium courts that can be hired (per hour outdoor court $22 to $34, indoor court $24 to $68). Reservations can be made up to two days in advance. Hourly lessons are $90 to $120.

NEW YORK METS
BASEBALL

Map p450 (☎718-507-8499; www.mets.com; 123-01 Roosevelt Ave, Flushing; tickets $19-130; [S]7 to Mets-Willets Pt) In the National League since 1962, the Mets remain New York's 'new' baseball team, and still the working-class underdog compared with the glitzier, richer Yankees. Fans hold on to the magic of '86, when the Mets last won the World Series in a miraculous comeback. Cheer the boys to victory at Citi Field stadium, a 35-minute subway trip from Midtown.

WORLD'S FARE TOURS
WALKING TOUR

(www.chopsticksandmarrow.com; tours from $60) Dedicated Queens eater Joe DiStefano leads tours around Flushing's vibrant Chinatown and through the Himalayan dumpling eateries clustered in Jackson Heights. Grocery fiends can join a tour around Southeast Asian stores in Elmhurst, many of which also sell great snacks.

ASTORIA POOL
SWIMMING

Map p448 (☎718-626-8620; www.nycgovparks.org/parks/astoriapark; 19th St, at 23rd Dr, Astoria; ⏰11am-7pm late Jun-early Sep; [S]N/Q to Astoria Blvd) [FREE] This Works Progress Administration Olympic-size outdoor pool, built in 1936, is the biggest in the city, an elegant wonder with views of Manhattan and the Triborough Bridge. It's best for lounging, rather than serious laps, as it is only 3ft deep, and crowds can break 1000 on sunny summer days.

Note the city policy at pools: T-shirts or coverups must be white (no colors), and you must bring a combination lock.

CITI FIELD
STADIUM

Map p450 (www.mets.com; 120-01 Roosevelt Ave, Flushing; [S]7 to Mets-Willets Point) The home of the New York Mets, the city's underdog baseball team, Citi Field opened in 2009. It replaces the earlier Mets HQ, Shea Stadium. It also houses a small Mets Hall of Fame and museum.

QUEENS HISTORICAL SOCIETY TOURS

Map p450 (☎718-939-0647; www.queenshistoricalsociety.org; 143-35 37th Ave, Flushing; admission $5, tours from $20; ⏰2:30-4:30pm Tue, Sat & Sun; [S]7 to Flushing-Main St) Set in the 18th-century Kingsland Homestead, this group has a small museum and offers walking tours through various neighborhoods in Queens. These include nearby sites associated with early religious-freedom movements and later Underground Railroad efforts.

GEOGRAPHY OF NEW YORK CITY WITH JACK EICHENBAUM WALKING TOUR

(☎718-961-8406; www.geognyc.com; tour $39) Urban geographer Jack Eichenbaum leads insightful walking (and sometimes subway) tours around Queens, focusing on the strange collisions between planning and reality, history and diverse modern use.

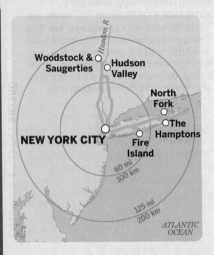

Day Trips from New York City

The Hamptons p319
New York's version of Malibu is a sweeping coastline studded with opulent mansions that host see-and-be-seen summer parties. Surprises include Native American sites, charming village main streets and wild state parks.

Fire Island p321
This car-free getaway ramps up in summer with tiny rental bungalows, chill beach bars and, at one end, a famous gay scene, roaring with drag queens and a carefree clubs. The wild setting, with sand streets and miles of beaches, restores calm.

North Fork p323
Wine-tasting at Long Island's vineyards is a fun day's ramble, capped by main-street strolling and alfresco dining at waterside Greenport.

Hudson Valley p325
You could spend weeks exploring this region, with great hiking, open-air sculpture, charming towns and historic homes of American greats (Irving, Roosevelt and Vanderbilt included).

Woodstock & Saugerties p328
Supplement your pilgrimage to hippiedom with a round of antiquing and quiet walks in protected parks.

The Hamptons

Explore

This string of villages on Long Island's South Fork is a summer escape for Manhattan's wealthiest, who commute to mansions by helicopter. The beaches are lovely, but the towns are a frenetic scene of jetsetters, celebrities and curious wannabes, and absolutely everything costs a pretty penny out here, with most inns charging well over $300 a night in summer. Prices do drop a bit and traffic jams disappear about a month after Labor Day. This lessening of crowds, combined with the balmy weather of the fall harvest season, make autumn an appealing time to visit. Montauk, out at the end of the island, is a generally calmer scene year-round.

The Best...

→**Sight** Parrish Art Museum (p320)
→**Place to Eat** Westlake Fish House (p321)
→**Place to Drink** Montauket (p321)

Top Tip

Those in search of summer solitude should plan a visit on a weekday, as the weekends are stuffed to the gills with refugees from the urban jungle.

Getting There & Away

→**Car** Take the Midtown Tunnel out of Manhattan onto I-495/Long Island Expwy. Follow this for about 1½ hours until you reach exit 70 to Sunrise Hwy East/Rte 24. After about 10 miles merge onto Montauk Hwy/Rte 27, which goes directly to Southampton. Continue along Rte 27 to get to all towns east of there.

→**Bus** The **Hampton Jitney** (212-362-8400; www.hamptonjitney.com; one way $32) is a 'luxury' express bus. Its Montauk line departs from Manhattan's East Side: Lexington Ave between 85th and 86th Sts, then 69th St, 59th St and 40th St. It makes stops at villages along Rte 27 in the Hamptons.

→**Train** The **Long Island Rail Road** (LIRR; 511; www.mta.info/lirr; furthest zone one way off-peak/peak $20.50/28.25) leaves from Penn Station in Manhattan, and Hunterspoint Ave and Jamaica Stations in Queens, making stops in West Hampton, Southampton, Bridgehampton, East Hampton and Montauk. (But these communities are difficult to appreciate without a car.) You can buy tickets in advance online and reserve round-trip fares in summer.

Need to Know

→**Area Code** 631
→**Location** 100 miles east (East Hampton) of Manhattan
→**Information** (631-283-0402; www.southamptonchamber.com; 76 Main St; 10am-4pm Mon-Fri, to 2pm Sat)

◉ SIGHTS

The Hamptons is actually a series of villages, most with 'Hampton' in the name. Those at the western end – or 'west of the canal,' as locals call the spots on the other side of the Shinnecock Canal – include Hampton Bays, Quogue and Westhampton. They are less frenzied than those to the east, which start with the village of Southampton.

◉ Southampton

Compared with some of its neighbors, Southampton is an old-money, rather conservative spot. It's home to sprawling old mansions, a main street with no 'beachwear' allowed, and some lovely beaches. Pick up maps and brochures about the town at the Southampton Chamber of Commerce, squeezed among a group of high-priced, artsy-crafty shops and decent restaurants.

SOUTHAMPTON HISTORICAL MUSEUM   MUSEUM
(631-283-2494; www.southamptonhistorical museum.org; 17 Meeting House Ln; adult/child $4/free; 11am-4pm Wed-Sun Mar-Dec) Before the Hamptons was the Hamptons, there was this clutch of nicely maintained old buildings, including a whaling captain's mansion.

WORTH A DETOUR

LONG BEACH

Beautiful Long Beach, one of the best stretches of sand in the area, is only a few miles outside New York City's limits. It's easily accessible by train and has clean beaches, a hoppin' main strip with ice-cream shops and eateries within walking distance of the ocean, a thriving surf scene and many city hipsters. The downside is a $12 day-use fee. Long Island Rail Road runs 'beach getaways,' which include discounted admission and round-trip train fare during the summer, with departures from both Penn Station and Atlantic Terminal in Brooklyn.

SHINNECOCK NATION CULTURAL
CENTER & MUSEUM   MUSEUM
(☑631-287-4923; www.shinnecockmuseum.
com; 100 Montauk Hwy; adult/child $15/8.50;
⊙11am-5pm Thu-Sun; ⛟) The 1300-member
Shinnecock tribe runs this museum and
living-history village, one of the few re-
minders of Native American life on Long
Island.

PARRISH ART MUSEUM   MUSEUM
(☑631-283-2118; www.parrishart.org; 279 Montauk Hwy, Water Mill; adult/child $10/free, free
Wed; ⊙10am-5pm Wed-Mon, to 8pm Fri) In a
sleek long barn designed by Herzog & de
Meuron, this institution spotlights local
artists such as Jackson Pollock, Willem de
Kooning and Chuck Close.

For more Pollock, make reservations to
see his nearby paint-drizzled studio and
home.

◉ Bridgehampton & Sag Harbor

To the east of Southampton, Bridgehamp-
ton is tiny but packed with trendy boutiques and restaurants. Turn north here
and go 7 miles north to reach the old whaling town of Sag Harbor, on Peconic Bay,
edged with historic homes. You can pick
up a walking-tour map at the Sag Harbor
Chamber of Commerce on Long Wharf at
the end of Main St.

The Sag Harbor **Whaling & Historical
Museum** (☑631-725-0770; www.sagharbor
whalingmuseum.org; 200 Main St, Sag Harbor;
adult/child $6/2; ⊙10am-5pm Mon-Sat mid-Apr–
mid-Oct) is fascinating, and the village's tiny
Cape Cod–style streets are a joy to stroll;
there are many excellent restaurants to
discover.

A quick ride on the South Ferry will take
you to sleepy Shelter Island, which sits like
a pearl in the claw formed by Long Island's

North and South Forks. Think of it as a
low-key Southampton, a moneyed hideaway with a touch of maritime New England
style. Check out www.shelter-island.org, a
listings website run by the nonprofit Shelter Island Club, for the latest information.

A highlight of Shelter Island is the
Mashomack Nature Preserve (☑631-749-
1001; www.nature.org/mashomack; Rte 114, Shelter Island; donation adult/child $3/2; ⊙9am-5pm
Mar-Sep, to 4pm Oct-Feb), which is dotted with
hiking trails.

◉ East Hampton

This is Long Island's trendiest town.

OSBORN-JACKSON HOUSE   MUSEUM
(☑631-324-6850; www.easthamptonhistory.org;
101 Main St; donation $4; ⊙10am-4pm Tue-Sat)
Check out East Hampton's colonial past
with a visit to the East Hampton Historical
Society. The Society tends to five historical
attractions around East Hampton, including several old colonial farms, mansions
and a marine museum.

POLLOCK-KRASNER HOUSE   ARTS CENTER
(☑631-324-4929; 830 Springs-Fireplace Rd;
adult/child $10/5; ⊙tours hourly 11am-4pm
Thu-Sat May-Oct) Tour the former home of husband-
and-wife art stars Jackson Pollock and Lee
Krasner – worth it just to see the paint-
spattered floor of Pollock's studio. Reservations required.

◉ Montauk

Once a sleepy and humble stepsister to the
Hamptons, these days Montauk, at the far
eastern end of Long Island, has developed a
cool reputation for the surfing beach Ditch
Plains. Now there are affluent hipsters and
boho-chic hotels, but the area is still far

SLEEPING IN THE HAMPTONS

Bridge Inn (☑631-537-2900; www.hamptonsbridgeinn.com; 2668 Montauk Hwy, Bridge-hampton; r from $209; ✳🐾🛜) Get your foot in the Hamptons door at this clean and sleek motel, tucked behind hedges like all the neighboring mansions.

Sunrise Guesthouse (☑631-668-7286; www.sunrisebnb.com; 681 Old Montauk Hwy, Montauk; r $130, ste $195; ✳🛜) A good old-school option a few miles west of town, just across the road from the beach.

Ocean Resort Inn (☑631-668-2300; www.oceanresortinn.com; 95 S Emerson Ave, Montauk; r from $135, ste from $185; ✳🛜) All rooms at this small, L-shaped hotel open onto a large porch or balcony. It's walking distance to the beach and the main town.

more of a democratic scene than the Hamptons, with proudly blue-collar residents and casual seafood restaurants.

'The End,' as Montauk is affectionately called, is buffered from the Hamptons by the forested dunes of Hither Hills State Park, where camping, fishing and hiking are options. The road divides just before the park – go straight through, or meander along the beachfront on Old Montauk Hwy. The roads converge in town, then wind up at the far eastern tip of the island, in **Montauk Point State Park** (☑631-668-3781; 2000 Montauk Hwy; admission per vehicle $8; ☉sunrise-sunset), with **Montauk Point Lighthouse** (☑631-668-2544; www.montauk lighthouse.com; 2000 Montauk Hwy; adult/child $10/4; ☉10:30am-5:30pm summer, reduced hours rest of year) as a marker.

✖ EATING & DRINKING

CANDY KITCHEN   DINER $
(☑631-537-9885; 2391 Montauk Hwy, Bridge-hampton; mains $5-12; ☉7am-7:30pm; 🍴) An antidote to glitz, this corner diner has been serving good soups, ice cream and other staples since 1925.

★WESTLAKE FISH HOUSE   SEAFOOD $$
(☑631-668-3474; 352 W Lake Dr, Montauk; mains $21-36; ☉noon-9pm Thu-Sun, to 10pm Fri & Sat; 🍴) In the marina of the same name, this is a great place for seafood, all caught the same day.

LOBSTER ROLL   SEAFOOD $$
(1980 Montauk Hwy, Amagansett, Montauk; mains $14-28; ☉11:30am-10pm summer) 'Lunch' is the sign to look for on the roadside west of Montauk, marking the clam-and-lobster shack that's been in operation since 1965.

NICK & TONI'S   MEDITERRANEAN $$$
(☑631-324-3550; 136 North Main St, East Hampton; pizzas $17, mains $24-42; ☉6-10pm Wed-Mon, to 11pm Fri & Sat, plus 11:30am-2:30pm Sun) A good bet for celebrity sightings, this institution serves Italian food with ingredients from nearby farms.

MONTAUKET   BAR
(☑631-668-5992; 88 Firestone Rd, Montauk; ☉from noon Thu-Sun) Experts agree: this is the best place to watch the sun go down on Long Island.

Fire Island

Explore

Fire Island is a skinny, 50-mile-long barrier island most notable for the absence of cars. Sand streets, concrete paths and boardwalks connect the dozen or so tiny residential communities, and the only traffic is fat-tire bikes and the little wagons regulars haul their belongings in. Several enclaves are famed getaways for the gay community, but there's something for everyone here, including families, couples and single travelers – gay and straight alike. The island is federally protected as the Fire Island National Seashore, and much of it is wild dunes and windswept forest. In summer, expect hamlets jam-packed with nightclubs next to neighboring stretches of sand where you'll find nothing but pitched tents and deer. Don't forget bug repellent: the mosquitoes are both fierce and abundant on Fire Island. While day trips are easy here, staying for a night or two is a real treat (even if hotel offerings aren't great), especially in the quieter spring and fall.

The Best...

→**Activity** Sunken Forest

→**Place to Eat** Sand Castle

→**Place to Drink** CJ's

Top Tip

On summer weekends, skip out before 3pm on Sunday or (better) spend the night and leave Monday – the line for the ferry on Sunday evenings is impossible.

Getting There & Away

→**Car** Take the Midtown Tunnel out of Manhattan onto I-495/Long Island Expwy. For Sayville ferries (to The Pines, Cherry Grove and Sunken Forest), get off at exit 57 on to the Veterans Memorial Hwy. Make a right on Lakeland Ave and take it to the end, following signs for the ferry. For Davis Park Ferry from Patchogue (to Watch Hill), take the Long Island Expwy to exit 63 southbound (North Ocean Ave). For Bay Shore ferries (all other Fire Island destinations), take the Long Island Expwy to exit 30E, then get onto the Sagtikos Pkwy to exit 42 south, to Fifth Ave terminal in Bay Shore. To get to Robert Moses State Park by car, take exit 53 off the Long Island Expwy and travel south across the Moses Causeway.

→**Train** The Long Island Rail Road makes stops in Bay Shore, Sayville and Patchogue, where you can catch a summer-only shuttle service (or walk or taxi) to the ferry terminal.

→**Ferry** Fire Island Ferries (☑631-665-3600; www.fireislandferries.com; 99 Maple Ave, Bay Shore) run from near the Bay Shore LIRR station (one way adult/

child $10/5) to Kismet, Ocean Beach and other western communities. Sayville Ferry Service goes from Sayville to Cherry Grove and Fire Island Pines. Davis Park Ferry goes to Davis Park and Watch Hill – the easternmost ferry-access point of the island. Fire Island Water Taxi offers on-demand service across the bay.

Need to Know

→**Area Code** ☑631

→**Location** 60 miles east of Manhattan

→**Information** (www.fireisland.com)

SIGHTS

The gemlike parts of Fire Island are the car-free zones in the center (rather than the ends, reached by causeways). Davis Park, Fair Harbor, Kismet, Ocean Bay Park and Ocean Beach combine small summer homes with tiny clusters of basic grocery stores and restaurants. Of these communities, Ocean Beach ('OB' to locals) is the liveliest, with a miniature downtown by the ferry port and a little strip of bars. Perhaps the most infamous villages are those that have evolved into gay destinations: Cherry Grove and The Pines, in the center of Fire Island. Biking between towns isn't feasible, as streets turn into deep sand. For exploring further than you can walk, Fire Island Water Taxi runs a lateral ferry service along the bay side – but this shuts down in October, along with most other tourist-oriented businesses.

SUNKEN FOREST FOREST
(☑631-597-6183; www.nps.gov/fiis; ☺visitors center mid-May–mid-Oct) **FREE** This 300-year-old forest, a surprisingly dense stretch of

---

SLEEPING ON FIRE ISLAND

Watch Hill Campground (☑631-567-6664; www.watchhillfi.com; Fire Island; tent sites $25; ☺early May–late Oct) A tidy camping area in a wooded patch on the east end of Fire Island; a marina, snack bar and store are all on-site. Take the ferry from Patchogue.

Seashore Condo Motel (☑631-583-5860; www.seashorecondomotel.com; Bayview Ave, Ocean Bay Park; r from $219; ☜) Small, wood-paneled rooms without many frills, despite the price.

Madison Fire Island (☑631-597-6061; www.themadisonfi.com; 22 Atlantic Walk, Fire Island Pines; r from $250;❉☜☎) Fire Island's first 'boutique' hotel, which rivals anything Manhattan has to offer in terms of amenities, but also has killer views from a rooftop deck and a gorgeous pool (and pool boys).

JONES BEACH

The appeal of **Jones Beach State Park** (☑516-785-1600; www.nysparks.com; 1 Ocean Pkwy; parking $10, lounge chairs $10, pools adult/child $3/1, mini-golf $5; ☺10am-7pm, though hours vary by area) is simple: 6.5 miles of clean sand covered with sun-worshippers. Its character differs depending on which 'field' you choose – for example, 2 is for the surfers and 6 is for families, and there's a gay beach way east – but it's a scene no matter where you spread your blanket. The ocean gets quite warm by midsummer (up to about 70°F, 21°C) and there are plenty of lifeguards. In between sunning and riding waves you might also hop into one of the two massive on-site pools for a swim; play shuffleboard or basketball on beachside courts; stroll the 2-mile boardwalk; visit the still waters of the bay beach; or, at Castles in the Sand, learn how master builder Robert Moses transformed Long Island with the creation of Jones Beach in the 1940s.

Biking and running are allowed along a 4-mile path that stretches through the park, and there are places to rent bikes along the beach. When the sun goes down, you can grill at one of the many barbecues in the sand, grab burgers at the few local restaurants near the beach, or head to the **Jones Beach Theater** (☑516-221-1000; www. jonesbeach.com; 1000 Ocean Pkwy, Wantagh), where alfresco concerts under the stars feature big names in pop.

Jones Beach is about 33 miles east of NYC, and it takes roughly 45 minutes to get here using public transportation. The Long Island Rail Road offers round trips from Manhattan's Penn Station and Brooklyn's Flatbush Ave Station (transfer required at Jamaica) to Freeport Station on Long Island; in summer, a round-trip combo ticket is available for $20.50.

If you have your own vehicle, take the Midtown Tunnel from Manhattan onto I-495/Long Island Expwy (LIE); turn off exit 38 to the eastbound Northern State Pkwy, then look for exit 33 for the Wantagh Pkwy. That goes straight to Jones Beach State Park. (You can also take the LIE to exit 31S for the Cross-Island Pkwy and then exit 25A onto the Southern State Pkwy to get to the Wantagh Pkwy.)

trees behind the dunes, is easily accessible via a boardwalk trail looping through. It's pleasantly shady in summer, and vividly colored when the leaves change in fall. It's accessible by its own ferry stop (Sailors Haven, where there's also a visitor center), or a long walk in the winter season, after the ferry shuts down.

The beach straight south of here is also an impressively wild, yet reasonably accessible, stretch of the island.

✗ EATING & DRINKING

CJ'S   AMERICAN **$$**
(☑631-583-9890; www.cjsfireisland.com; 168 Cottage Walk, Ocean Beach; mains $12-18) Open year-round, CJ's is raucous and fun and a great place to wait for your ferry. It's packed on summer weekend nights, so get here early.

SAND CASTLE   SEAFOOD **$$**
(☑631-597-4174; www.fireislandsandcastle.com; 106 Lewis Walk, Cherry Grove; mains $15-30;

☺11am-11pm in season, kitchen closed Wed) One of Fire Island's only oceanfront (rather than bayfront) options, Sand Castle serves up satisfying appetizers (fried calamari, portobello fries) and lots of seafood temptations (mussels, crabcakes, seared sea scallops). Nice cocktails and people watching.

North Fork

Explore

Once synonymous with beachy hideaways, Long Island is now also known for its grapes. What was a lone winery in 1973 has become a thriving industry that takes up more than 3000 acres of land, most in the North Fork. East of Riverhead, Rte 25 is marked with green 'wine trail' signs. (The South Fork also has a handful of vineyards; you can continue on to them, if you choose, via Shelter Island and two ferries.) On summer and fall weekends, the tasting-room scene can be rather lively, as limos full of celebrating groups hop from place to place.

The Best...
→**Sight** Greenport
→**Place to Eat** Claudio's
→**Place to Drink** At the wineries (take your pick!)

Top Tip
The North Folk wineries are an easy DIY adventure. Consider taking the train out to Long Island and renting a car there (Riverhead is a good place to look). Prices are cheaper than in Manhattan and you'll save time, gas and frustration.

Getting There & Away
→**Bus** The Hampton Jitney picks up passengers on Lexington Ave at 86th St in Manhattan, and also 69th, 59th and 44th Sts. It makes stops in 10 North Fork villages.

→**Car** Take the Midtown Tunnel out of Manhattan, which will take you onto the I-495/Long Island Expwy. Take this until it ends, at Riverhead, and follow signs onto Rte 25. Stay on Rte 25 for all points east.

→**Train** The Long Island Rail Road's line is the Ronkonkoma Branch, with trips leaving from Penn Station and Brooklyn and running all the way out to Greenport.

→**Ferry** To get from the North Fork to the South Fork (or vice versa), take the North Ferry and South Ferry services to and from Shelter Island.

Need to Know
→**Area Code** ☑631
→**Location** 100 miles east of Manhattan
→**Information** Long Island Wine Council (☑631-369-5887; www.liwines.com)

SIGHTS

Harvest time is in fall, which, combined with foliage and pumpkin-picking opportunities, makes it an ideal time to visit North Fork (although most places are open year-round). A drive along the back roads east of Riverhead affords some beautiful, unspoiled vistas of farms and rural

LOCAL KNOWLEDGE

NORTH FORK WINERIES

Early on, North Fork wineries gained a reputation for Merlot and Cabernet Franc, but in recent years, more have excelled with whites such as Chenin Blanc. The following are some of the most notable operations, whether for wine or simply good atmosphere in the tasting rooms.

Bedell Cellars (☑631-734-7537; www.bedellcellars.com; 36225 Main Rd, Cutchogue; wine tasting from $15; ☺11am-5pm Sun-Thu, to 7pm Fri & Sat) ✔ This estate prides itself on sustainable production practices. A gorgeous tasting room, though the wines skew oaky.

Pindar Vineyards (☑631-734-6200; www.pindar.net; 37645 Main Rd, Peconic; wine tasting $10; ☺11am-6pm) One of the earliest vineyards, now with 500 acres. Offers tours of facilities and live music.

Lenz Winery (☑631-734-6010; www.lenzwine.com; 38355 Rte 25, Peconic; ☺10am-5pm, to 6pm in summer) One of the oldest North Fork wineries, with excellent sparkling wines and Gewürztraminer.

Pugliese Vineyards (☑631-734-4057; www.pugliesevineyards.com; 34515 Main Rd, Cutchogue; tastings from $5; ☺11am-5pm, to 6pm Sat) More nice sparkling wines, in a small-scale, family-run tasting room.

North Fork Tasting Room (☑631-727-9513; www.northforktastingroom.com; 3225 Sound Ave, Riverhead; bottles from $24; ☺5-9pm Fri, from noon Sat & Sun) If you want to taste the wine without the travel, head straight to this winery, 4.5 miles northwest of Riverhead. Here you can sample a range of wines, local brews and snacks.

If driving yourself doesn't appeal, **Vintage Tours** (☑631-765-4689; www.vintagetour1.com; tour per person incl lunch $88-99) and **North Fork Trolley Co** (☑631-369-3031; www.northforktrolley.com; tour per person $79) can shepherd you around.

SLEEPING IN NORTH FORK

Greenporter Hotel (☑631-477-0066; www.greenporterhotel.com; 326 Front St, Greenport; r from $199; ❊❈❋❊) An older motel redone with white walls and Ikea furniture, this place is good value for the area. Its on-site restaurant, Cuvée, is very good.

North Fork Table & Inn (☑631-765-0177; www.nofoti.com; 57225 Main Rd, Southold; r from $250) A favorite foodies' escape, this four-room inn has an excellent farm-to-table restaurant (three-course prix-fixe $75), run by alums of the esteemed Manhattan restaurant Gramercy Tavern.

Pridwin Beach Hotel & Cottages (☑631-749-0476; www.pridwin.com; 81 Shore Rd, Shelter Island; r from $245; ❊❈❋❊) Nestled on a prime piece of property surrounded by woods and fronting a small beach and the bay, Pridwin Beach Hotel & Cottages on Shelter Island has standard hotel rooms as well as private water-view cottages, some renovated in high-designer style.

residential areas. The level terrain is also very bike-friendly; rent from or tour with Long Island Bicycle Tours.

The most charming town in the area is **Greenport**, which has a picturesque waterfront, where kids flock to a century-old carousel. Peaceful, pedestrian-friendly streets nearby are dotted with shops, cafes and eateries. Completists can head all the way out at the eastern tip of the North Fork to Orient Beach State Park.

 **EATING & DRINKING**

FOUR & TWENTY BLACKBIRDS   DESSERTS **$**
(☑347-940-6717; 1010 Village Ln, Orient; pie slice $5; ☺8am-6pm Wed-Mon mid-May–Sep, weekends only Oct-Apr) An outpost of the Brooklyn pie experts, with delectable fruit and chocolate varieties.

LOVE LANE KITCHEN   MODERN AMERICAN **$$**
(☑631-298-8989; 240 Love Ln, Mattituck; mains lunch $12-15, dinner $16-30; ☺8am-9:30pm Thu-Mon, 7am-4pm Tue & Wed) At this popular place on a cute street, local meat and vegetables drive the global-diner menu: burgers, of course, plus spicy chickpeas and duck tagine.

CLAUDIO'S   SEAFOOD **$$$**
(☑631-477-0627; 111 Main St, Greenport; mains $25-36; ☺11:30am-9pm, to 10pm Fri & Sat May-Oct) A Greenport legend, owned by the Portuguese Claudio family since 1870. For a casual meal, hit Claudio's Clam Bar, on the nearby pier.

Hudson Valley

Explore

Winding roads along the Hudson River take you by picturesque farms, Victorian cottages, apple orchards and old-money mansions built by New York's elite. Painters of the Hudson River School romanticized these landscapes – you can see their work at art museums in the area as well as in NYC. Autumn is a particularly beautiful time for a trip up this way. The eastern side of the river feels more populated – less so the further north you go – while the western side has a rural feel, with hills leading into the Catskills mountain region.

The Best...

➡**Sights** Dia Beacon (p326)

➡**Place to Eat** Blue Hill at Stone Barns (p327)

➡**Place to Drink** The Hop (p327)

Top Tip

Foodies should gravitate towards Rhinebeck or Beacon, which have some of the best restaurants in the area.

Getting There & Away

➡**Car** From Manhattan, take the Henry Hudson Pkwy across the George Washington Bridge (I-95) to Palisades Pkwy. Head for the New York State Thruway to Rte 9W or Rte 9, the principal scenic river routes. You can also take the

Taconic State Pkwy north from Ossining, a pretty road in autumn.

⇒**Bus** Short Line (www.coachusa.com; 710 W State St) Buses runs regular trips to Rhinebeck ($51).

⇒**Train** The Metro-North (📞511; www. mta.info/mnr) commuter train line makes several stops on the Lower and Middle Hudson Valleys (take the Hudson Line). Amtrak runs to Hudson.

Need to Know

⇒**Area Code** 📞845

⇒**Location** 95 miles north (Hyde Park) of Manhattan

⇒**Information** Dutchess County Tourism (📞800-445-3131; www.dutchesstourism. com; 3 Neptune Rd, Poughkeepsie), Hudson Valley Network (www.hudson valleyvoyager.com)

◉ SIGHTS & ACTIVITIES

◉ Lower Hudson Valley

Several magnificent homes can be found near Tarrytown and Sleepy Hollow, east of the Hudson. Further north, the village of Cold Spring offers good hiking on trails not far from the train station. For arts, the formerly industrial Beacon, also easily reached by train, has been revived as an outpost of the avant-garde. If you have a car, cross to the Hudson's west bank to explore Harriman State Park and adjacent Bear Mountain State Park, with views down to Manhattan from its 1303ft peak.

★**DIA BEACON**   GALLERY
(Beacon; 📞845-440-0100; www.diaart.org; 3 Beekman St, Beacon; adult/child $12/free; ⊙11am-6pm Thu-Mon Apr-Oct, 11am-4pm Fri-Mon Nov-Mar) This former factory houses monumental contemporary sculpture by the likes of Richard Serra and Dan Flavin, plus ever-changing, always surprising installations.

HARRIMAN STATE PARK   OUTDOORS
(📞845-947-2444; www.nysparks.com; Seven Lakes Dr, Ramapo; parking per car $8) This park on the west side of the Hudson covers

72 sq miles and provides swimming, hiking, camping and a visitor center.

BEAR MOUNTAIN STATE PARK   OUTDOORS
(📞845-786-2701; www.nysparks.com; Palisades Pkwy, Bear Mountain; parking per car $8 summer; ⊙8am-dusk) The main draw is views of the Manhattan skyline from the 1303ft peak (accessible by car), but there's also ice skating in winter and boating and swimming in summer. There are several scenic roads snaking their way past secluded lakes with gorgeous vistas.

KYKUIT   HISTORIC SITE
(📞914-366-6900; www.hudsonvalley.org; 381 N Broadway, Sleepy Hollow; tour adult/child $25/23; ⊙tour hours vary May–early Nov, closed Tue) This onetime Rockefeller summer home has a remarkable collection of modern art.

SUNNYSIDE   HISTORIC BUILDING
(📞914-591-8763, Mon-Fri 914-631-8200; www. hudsonvalley.org; 3 W Sunnyside Ln, Sleepy Hollow; adult/child $12/6; ⊙tours 10:30am-3:30pm Wed-Sun May-Oct; 🅿) Washington Irving, famous for tales such as *The Legend of Sleepy Hollow,* built this imaginative home. Tour guides in 19th-century costume tell good stories.

STORM KING ART CENTER   GALLERY
(📞845-534-3115; www.stormking.org; 1 Museum Rd, New Windsor; adult/child $15/8; ⊙10am-5:30pm Wed-Sun Apr-Oct, to 4:30pm Nov) 🅿 This 500-acre sculpture park, established in 1960, has works by Mark di Suvero, Andy Goldsworthy and others, all carefully placed in nooks formed by the land's natural breaks and curves.

◉ Poughkeepsie & Hyde Park

FRANKLIN D ROOSEVELT HOME   HISTORIC BUILDING
(📞845-486-7770; www.nps.gov/hofr; 4097 Albany Post Rd, Hyde Park; adult/child $18/free, museum only adult/child $9/free; ⊙9am-5pm) FDR served three terms as president and instituted lasting progressive programs; he also made the decision to drop the A-bomb on Japan to end WWII. A tour of his home, relatively modest considering his family wealth, is interesting, but it can be unpleasantly crowded in summer.

In this case, better to focus on the excellent museum, built around FDR's own library, where he recorded his groundbreaking radio program of 'fireside chats.' You can also visit **Val-Kill** (☏845-229-9422; www.nps.gov/elro; 54 Valkill Park Rd, Hyde Park; adult/child $10/free; ⊙9am-5pm daily May-Oct, Thu-Mon Nov-Apr), Eleanor Roosevelt's cottage hideaway.

VANDERBILT MANSION   HISTORIC SITE
(☏877-444-6777; www.nps.gov/vama; 119 Vanderbilt Park Rd, Hyde Park; grounds free, tours adult/child $10/free; ⊙9am-5pm) The railroad-wealthy Vanderbilt family's summer 'cottage' is a Beaux-Arts spectacle, with most of the original furnishings.

WALKWAY OVER THE HUDSON   PARK
(☏845-454-9649; www.walkway.org; 61 Parker Ave, Poughkeepsie; ⊙7am-sunset) Once a railroad bridge crossing the Hudson, this is now the world's longest pedestrian bridge – 1.28 miles – and a state park.

◉ Rhinebeck & Hudson

★OLANA   HISTORIC SITE
(☏518-828-0135; www.olana.org; 5720 Rte 9G, Hudson; tours adult/child $12/free, grounds per vehicle $5; ⊙grounds 8am-sunset daily, tours 10am-4pm Tue-Sun May-Oct, self-guided tour only 2-5pm Sat) In pure aesthetic terms, this is the finest of the Hudson Valley mansions, as landscape painter Frederic Church designed every detail, inspired by his travels in the Middle East and his appreciation of the river view.

✗ EATING

THE HOP   MODERN AMERICAN $$
(☏845-440-8676; 554 Main St, Beacon; sandwiches $15, mains $24-36; ⊙noon-10pm Wed-Mon, to midnight Fri & Sat) Craft beer and cider is this casual spot's raison d'etre, and it goes perfectly with local cheeses and hearty creations like the Huff-n-Puff, a pork burger with ham and bacon.

HELSINKI   MODERN AMERICAN $$
(☏518-828-4800; www.helsinkihudson.com; 405 Columbia St, Hudson; mains $13-25; ⊙5-10pm Thu-Tue) This restored carriage house is a sort of clubhouse for the valley's working artists. A music venue showcases rock, jazz and even global touring acts, while the restaurant does locally sourced cuisine like garlicky kale salads.

BLUE HILL AT STONE BARNS   MODERN AMERICAN $$$
(☏914-366-9600; www.bluehillfarm.com; 630 Bedford Rd, Pocantico Hills; prix fixe $218; ⊙cafe & farm 10am-4:30pm Wed-Sun, restaurant 5-10pm Wed-Sat, from 1pm Sun) ✔ Go maximum locavore at chef Dan Barber's farm (it also supplies his Manhattan restaurant). By day, visitors are welcome to tour the fields and pastures, and there's a very basic cafe.

BOCUSE   MODERN FRENCH $$$
(☏845-451-1012; www.ciarestaurantgroup.com; 1946 Campus Dr, Hyde Park; mains $26-31; ⊙11:30am-1pm & 6-8:30pm Tue-Sat) One of several excellent student-run restaurants at the Culinary Institute of America, this

---

SLEEPING ON THE HUDSON

Roosevelt Inn (☏845-229-2443; www.rooseveltinnofhydepark.com; 4360 Albany Post Rd, Hyde Park; r $85-115; ⊙closed Jan & Feb; ❋☎) A fantastically clean roadside motel; its pine-paneled 'rustic' rooms are a bargain.

Wm Farmer and Sons (☏518-828-1635; www.wmfarmerandsons.com; 20 S Front St, Hudson; r from $149; ❋☎) This rustic-chic former boarding house, steps from the train station and a short walk to Warren St, has rough-hewn furniture and claw-foot tubs. Its restaurant gets high marks.

Mohonk Mountain House (☏845-255-1000; www.mohonk.com; 1000 Mountain Rest Rd, New Paltz; d all-inclusive from $558; ❋☎❀⊞) This rustic castle perches over a dark lake, offering guests all the luxuries, from lavish meals to golf to spa services, plus a full roster of outdoor excursions, such as hiking and trail rides. Rates include all meals and most activities. Day visitors are welcome too, for a meal (reserve ahead) or a fee (adult/child $26/21) – the hiking trails are good for all ages, a somewhat easier way to see the area than in the neighboring Mohonk Preserve.

place does traditional truffles and modern tableside tricks like liquid-nitrogen ice cream. Lunch is good value. For a snack, head for **Apple Pie Cafe** (☑845-905-4500; 1946 Campus Dr, Hyde Park; sandwiches $10-15; ☺7:30am-5pm Mon-Fri).

Woodstock & Saugerties

Explore

In the southern Catskills, the town of Woodstock symbolizes the tumultuous 1960s, when young people questioned authority, experimented with freedom and redefined popular culture. Today, it's a combination of quaint and hip – an artists' colony full of young urbanites. The Woodstock Guild is a good source for finding out the latest goings-on in the arts and culture scene, such as the annual Woodstock Film Festival in October, which attracts film fans from all over.

Saugerties, which sees far fewer tourists, has a quaint main street and picturesque lighthouse.

The Best...

➡**Sight** Opus 40

➡**Activity** Overlook Mountain, Catskill Forest Preserve

➡**Place to Eat** Cucina

Top Tip

Bring an empty bag – you never know what you'll unearth in the many antique shops and markets (plus weekend yard sales!) found in the area.

Getting There & Away

➡**Car** Take the New York State Thruway (via the Henry Hudson Pkwy north from Manhattan) or I-87 to Rte 375 for Woodstock, Rte 32 for Saugerties or Rte 28 for other points.

➡**Bus** Frequent buses to Saugerties and Woodstock are operated by Trailways (☑800-858-8555; www.trailwaysny.com).

Need to Know

➡**Area Code** ☑845

➡**Location** 110 miles north (Saugerties) of Manhattan

◉ SIGHTS & ACTIVITIES

A minor technicality: the 1969 music *festival* was actually held in Bethel, an hour away. Nonetheless, the *town* of **Woodstock** still cultivates the free spirit of that era, with rainbow tie-dye style and local grass-roots everything, from radio to movies to a farmers market (Wednesdays in summer; fittingly billed as a 'farm festival'). Just 7 miles east, **Saugerties** is not nearly as quaint and feels by comparison like the big city, but the lighthouse on the point in the Hudson is well worth a visit.

For a very rural drive, head to **West Saugerties** (FYI, rock aficionados: site of Big Pink, the house made famous by Bob Dylan and The Band) and take Platte Clove Rd (Cty Rd 16) northwest. The seven winding miles are some of the most scenic in the Catskills. The road eventually emerges around Tannersville.

OPUS 40   SCULPTURE PARK
(☑845-246-3400; www.opus40.org; 50 Fite Rd, Saugerties; adult/child $10/3; ☺11am-5:30pm Thu-Sun May-Sep) Beginning in 1938, artist Harvey Fite worked for nearly four decades to coax an abandoned quarry into an immense work of land art, all sinuous walls, canyons and pools.

SAUGERTIES LIGHTHOUSE   LIGHTHOUSE
(☑845-247-0656; www.saugertieslighthouse. com; 168 Lighthouse Dr, Saugerties; tour suggested donation adult/child $5/3; ☺sunrise-sunset, tours noon-3pm Sun summer) **FREE** A half-mile nature trail leads to this 1869 landmark on the point where Esopus Creek joins the Hudson. You can also stay the night in the lighthouse's two-room B&B ($225), but you must book at least six months ahead.

BETHEL WOODS CENTER
FOR THE ARTS   ARTS CENTER
(☑866-781-2922; www.bethelwoodscenter. org; 200 Hurd Rd; museum adult/child $15/6; ☺museum 10am-7pm daily May-Sep, 10am-5pm

SLEEPING IN WOODSTOCK & SAUGERTIES

Roxbury Motel (☑607-326-7200; www.theroxburymotel.com; 2258 County Rd 41, Roxbury; r $158-550; ❇🐾) Every room is a work of art: sleep in a glam version of a Flintstones cave, Oz's Emerald City or even a dreamy cream pie. (A couple of more subdued rooms are available for $100.) Breakfast is continental but generous, and there's a full spa.

White Dove Rockotel (☑845-306-5419; www.thewhitedoverockotel.com; 148 Tinker St, Woodstock; r from $165, ste from $225; 🐾) A couple of Phish fans run this purple-painted Victorian. The four party-ready rooms are decorated with psychedelic concert posters, record players and vintage vinyl.

Thu-Sun Oct-Apr) The site of the Woodstock Music & Art Fair, on Max Yasgur's farm outside Bethel, is 70 miles from the town of Woodstock. It's now home to an amphitheater with great summer concerts and an evocative museum dedicated to the hippie movement and the 1960s.

CATSKILL FOREST PRESERVE PARK
(www.dec.ny.gov/lands/5265.html) For memorable hiking, head to this park, a huge swath of land that contains the vital watershed feeding NYC's ravenous thirst, and hundreds of miles of trails. One of the most accessible parts of the park near Woodstock is **Overlook Mountain**. Reach it by taking Rock City Rd (next to the village green), which turns into Meads Mountain Rd. The trailhead parking lot is up about 2 miles. The 4.8-mile trail takes in great views, plus the ruins of a 1920s lodge, and a metal firetower, which you can climb if you're not scared of heights.

TOWN TINKER TUBE RENTAL WATER SPORTS
(☑845-688-5553; www.towntinker.com; 10 Bridge St, Phoenicia; tubes per day $15, package incl transportation $25; 🚽) Visit this outfitter for everything you need to ride an inner tube down wet and wild (and cold!) Esopus Creek.

 EATING

LAST CHANCE CHEESE AMERICAN $$
(☑518-589-6424; 6009 Main St, Tannersville; mains $9-20; ⊙11am-midnight Fri & Sat, to 9pm Sun, to 4pm Mon) This four-decade-old institution is part roadhouse with live bands, part candy store and part restaurant, serving hearty meals.

CUCINA ITALIAN $$
(☑845-679-9800; 109 Mill Hill Rd, Woodstock; mains $16-26; ⊙5am-late, from 11am Sat & Sun) Sophisticated seasonal Italian fare, including thin-crust pizzas, in a farmhouse with a large communal table.

🛏 Sleeping

In general, accommodations prices in New York City do not abide by any high-season or low-season rules; wavering rates usually reflect availability. With over 50 million visitors descending upon the city every year, you can expect that hotel rooms fill up quickly – especially in summer. Accommodations options range from boxy cookie-cutter rooms in Midtown high-rises to stylish boutique options downtown. You'll also find a few B&Bs set in residential neighborhoods.

Booking Accommodations

In New York City, the average room rate is well over $300. But don't let that scare you as there are great deals to be had – almost all of which can be found through savvy on-line snooping. To get the best deals, launch a two-pronged approach: if you don't have your heart set on a particular property, then check out the generic booking websites. If you do know where you want to stay – it might sound simple – but it's best to start at your desired hotel's website. These days it's not uncommon to find deals and package rates directly on the site of your accommodation of choice.

Room Rates

New York City doesn't have a 'high season' in the common way that beach destinations do. Sure, there are busier times of the year when it comes to tourist traffic, but at over 50 million visitor per annum, the Big Apple never needs to worry when it comes to filling up beds. As such, room rates fluctuate based on availability; in fact, most hotels have a booking algorithm in place that spits out a price quote relative to the number of rooms already booked on the same night, so the busier the evening the higher the price goes.

If you're looking to find the best room rates, then flexibility is key – weekdays are often cheaper, and you'll generally find that accommodations in winter months have smaller price tags. If you are visiting over a weekend, try for a business hotel in the Financial District, which tends to empty out when the workweek ends.

Beyond Hotels & Hostels

We can all thank little Plaza-dweller Eloise for conjuring up fanciful dreams of hanging one's hat in a luxury New York City hotel room, but these days, finding a place to sleep in the city that never does is hardly restricted to the traditional spectrum of lodging.

Websites such as **Airbnb** (www.airbnb.com) are providing a truly unique – and not to mention economical – alternative to the wallet-busting glitz and glam. Selling 'unique spaces' to tourists looking for their home away from home, such sites offer locals the opportunity to rent out their apartments while they're out of town, or lease a space (be it a bedroom or pull-out couch) in their home. Airbnb is an undeniable hit in NYC, where space comes at a premium and obscenely high real estate prices act as quite the incentive for locals to supplement their housing income.

Lonely Planet's Top Choices

NoMad Hotel (p342)
A beaux-arts beauty, where
Franco-American chic meets
meticulous wining and dining.

Wythe Hotel (p347) Boutique
style in trendy Williamsburg,
with industrial chic rooms, a
roof terrace and a great Brooklyn location.

Gramercy Park Hotel
(p339) This grande dame with
gorgeous bars and a guest-only
rooftop terrace offers keys to
the coveted park below.

3B (p348) Charming four-room
Brooklyn haunt run by a creative, arts-loving collective.

Truck-a-Float (p349)
Artfully designed cabins floating
in a marina near Rockaway
Beach.

Best by Budget

$
Local NYC (p349)
New York Loft Hostel
(p347)
Harlem Flophouse (p346)

$$
Citizen M (p340)
Wall Street Inn (p333)
Boro Hotel (p349)

$$$
Knickerbocker (p342)
Hôtel Americano (p337)
Plaza (p342)

Best for Views

Standard (p337)
Z Hotel (p350)
Four Seasons (p342)

Best for Families

Hotel Beacon (p345)
Bubba & Bean Lodges
(p344)
Nu Hotel (p348)

Best Boutique Digs

Crosby Street Hotel (p334)
Andaz Fifth Avenue (p342)
Ace Hotel (p343)

Best for Honeymooners

1871 House (p344)
London NYC (p343)
Andaz Fifth Avenue (p342)

Best for Jetsetters

Hotel Gansevoort (p337)
Bowery Hotel (p336)
McCarren Hotel & Pool
(p348)

NEED TO KNOW

Prices
The following price ranges
refer to the standard range
in rates for a standard double room regardless of the
time of year. Unless otherwise stated, breakfast is
included in the price.

$	less than $150
$$	$150 to $350
$$$	more than $350

Reservations
Reservations are essential
– walk-ins are practically
impossible and rack rates
are almost always unfa-
vorable relative to online
deals. Reserve your room
as early as possible and
make sure you understand
your hotel's cancellation
policy. Expect check-in to
always be in the middle of
the afternoon and check-
out times to be in the late
morning.

Websites
➝ **newyorkhotels.com**
(www.newyorkhotels.com)
The self-proclaimed
official website for hotels
in NYC.

➝ **NYC** (www.nycgo.com/
hotels) Loads of listings
from the NYC Official
Guide.

➝ **Lonely Planet**
(lonelyplanet.com/usa/new-
york-city/hotels) Accom-
modations reviews and
online booking service.

Tipping
You must always tip the
maid – leave $3 to $5 per
night in an obvious location
with a note. Porters should
receive a dollar or two, and
service staff bringing items
to your room should be
tipped as well.

Where to Stay

Neighborhood	For	Against
Lower Manhattan & the Financial District	Convenient to Tribeca's nightlife and ferries. Cheap weekend rates at business hotels.	The area can feel impersonal, corporate and even a bit desolate after business hours.
SoHo & Chinatown	Shop to your heart's content right on your doorstep.	Crowds (mostly tourists) swarm the commercial streets of SoHo almost any time of day.
East Village & Lower East Side	Funky and fun, the area feels the most quintessentially 'New York' to visitors and Manhattanites alike.	Not tons to choose from when it comes to hotel sleeps.
West Village, Chelsea & the Meatpacking District	Brilliantly close-to-everything feel in a thriving, picturesque part of town that has an almost European feel.	Prices soar for traditional hotels, but remain reasonable for B&Bs. Rooms can sometimes be on the small side, even for NYC.
Union Square, Flatiron District & Gramercy	Convenient subway access to anywhere in the city. You're also steps away from the Village and Midtown in either direction.	Prices are high and there's not much in the way of neighborhood flavor.
Midtown	In the heart of the postcard's version of NYC: skyscrapers, museums, shopping and Broadway shows.	One of the most expensive areas in the city; expect small rooms. Midtown can often feel touristy and impersonal.
Upper East Side	You're a stone's throw from top-notch museums and the rolling hills of Central Park.	Options are scarce and wallet-busting prices are not uncommon; you're not particularly central.
Upper West Side & Central Park	Convenient access to Central Park and the Museum of Natural History.	Tends to swing a bit too far in the familial direction if you're looking for a livelier scene.
Harlem & Upper Manhattan	Great neighborhood vibe, better prices, close to Central Park.	Long subway rides (or pricey cab rides) to the action downtown and in Brooklyn.
Brooklyn	Better prices; great for exploring some of NYC's most creative neighborhoods.	It can be a long commute to Midtown Manhattan and points north.
Queens	Much cheaper than Manhattan. Digs in Long Island City are a short subway ride from Midtown.	Industrial setting can make for a less charming stay.

🛏 Lower Manhattan & the Financial District

Most hotels in the Financial District are geared towards business travelers, which often means discounted rates on weekends. To the north, hipper Tribeca harbors a handful of forever-fashionables, among them Robert De Niro's Greenwich Hotel.

WALL STREET INN HOTEL $$

Map p410 (☎212-747-1500; www.thewallstreetinn.com; 9 S William St; r from $209; ❄📶; [S]2/3 to Wall St) The sedate stone exterior of this inn belies its warm, Colonial-style interior. Beds are big and plush, and rooms have glossy wood furnishings and long drapes. The bathrooms are full of appreciated touches, like Jacuzzis in the deluxe rooms and tubs in the others. Wi-fi is complimentary.

The building is a piece of history, too – the 'LB' tile in the entry dates from the previous tenants, the Lehman Brothers banking company.

GILD HALL BOUTIQUE HOTEL $$

Map p410 (☎212-232-7700; www.thompsonhotels.com/hotels/gild-hall; 15 Gold St, at Platt St; r from $289; ❄📶; [S]2/3 to Fulton St) Boutique and brilliant, Gild Hall's entryway leads to a bi-level library and wine bar that exudes hunting-lodge chic. Rooms fuse Euro elegance and American comfort, with high tin ceilings, glass-walled balconies, Sferra linens, and mini-bars stocked with Dean & DeLuca treats. Hermès designed the leather headboards on the king-size beds, which work perfectly in their warmly hued, minimalist surroundings. Rates often drop on weekends.

CLUB QUARTERS WORLD TRADE CENTER HOTEL $$

Map p410 (☎212-577-1133; clubquartershotels.com/new-york/world-trade-center; 140 Washington St, at Albany St; r from $259; ❄@📶; [S]R to Cortland St; A/C, 2/3, 4/5, J/Z to Fulton St; 1 to Rector St) Right opposite the World Trade Center site, this 252-room chain hotel keeps things affordable with clean, modern, cookie-cutter rooms at reasonable prices. Perks include free wi-fi, unlimited bottled water, coffee and tea, complimentary wi-fi printing and iPad use, on-site fitness room and laundry facilities. Eleven subways lines are within walking distance.

COSMOPOLITAN HOTEL HOTEL $$

Map p410 (☎212-566-1900; www.cosmohotel.com; 95 W Broadway, at Chambers St; d from $289; ❄@📶; [S]1/2/3, A/C to Chambers St) Cosmo is a hero if you'd rather save your bills for the area's chic eateries and boutiques. The 129-room hotel isn't much to brag about – clean, carpeted rooms with private bathrooms, a double bed or two, and Ikea-knock-off furnishings. But it's clean and comfortable, with Frette linen and towels, CO Bigelow bath amenities, and major subway lines at your feet.

Advance purchases (at least a month ahead) can see room rates drop below $200.

★GREENWICH HOTEL BOUTIQUE HOTEL $$$

Map p410 (☎212-941-8900; www.thegreenwichhotel.com; 377 Greenwich St, btwn N Moore & Franklin Sts; r from $595; ❄📶🏊; [S]1 to Franklin St; A/C/E to Canal St) From the plush drawing room (complete with crackling fire) to the lantern-lit pool inside a reconstructed Japanese farmhouse, nothing about Robert De Niro's Greenwich Hotel is generic. Each of the 88 individually designed rooms feature dark, aged wood across the floors; and opulently tiled Carrara marble or Moroccan tiled bathrooms. Floor-to-ceiling French doors open onto a Tuscan-inspired courtyard in some of the Courtyard and Greenwich rooms.

ANDAZ WALL ST BOUTIQUE HOTEL $$$

Map p410 (☎212-590-1234; newyork.wallstreet.andaz.hyatt.com; 75 Wall St, at Water St; r from $445; ❄@📶; [S]2/3 to Wall St) A favorite of hipper downtown business types, the 253-room Andaz takes sleek and handsome, and gives it a relaxed, new-school vibe. Guests are checked-in on iPads, and treated to complimentary wi-fi, local calls and mini-bar soda and snacks. Rooms are spacious, contemporary and elegantly restrained, with 7ft-high windows, oak floors and sublimely comfortable beds with 300-thread-count cotton sheets.

Slurp craft brews at Andaz's seasonal Beer Garden or crafty cocktails at year-round Dina Rata, then work it all off at the spa or 24-hour fitness center. Weekend rates can drop well below $300.

SMYTH TRIBECA BOUTIQUE HOTEL $$$

Map p410 (☎212-587-7000; www.thompsonhotels.com/hotels/smyth-tribeca; 85 W Broadway, btwn Warren & Chambers Sts; r from $415; ❄📶; [S]A/C, 1/2/3 to Chambers St) Revamped by

Gachot Studios, the Smyth delivers the same combo of luxury and laid-back hipness that you'll find at sister Thompson hotels Gild Hall and the Beekman. Modernist furniture, rugs and book-lined shelves give the lobby a snug, chic, Scandinavian vibe, while the sound-proofed rooms are a soothing combo of charcoal carpets, walnut paneling, and slinky bathrooms with irresistible rain showers.

Extra in-house perks include a fine-dining, season-driven restaurant from A-list restaurateur Andrew Carmellini; a complimentary town car service; and twice-daily housekeeping service.

🛏 SoHo & Chinatown

Style fiends hyperventilate over SoHo's fashion-conscious streets and hoteliers have taken note. There's no shortage of coveted accommodations options to choose from along these star-studded lanes, but they come at quite a cost. Is it worth it? Totally. You'll have some of the world's best shopping, drinking and dining at your doorstep, and you're a short subway hop or taxi ride from some of Manhattan's other great neighborhoods. Slightly cheaper digs await in the borderlands of Chinatown and Nolita. For true budget options, however, you'll need to leave the neighborhood and go further afield.

BOWERY HOUSE HOSTEL $

Map p412 (☎212-837-2373; www.thebowery-house.com; 220 Bowery, btwn Prince & Spring Sts; s/d with shared bath from $100/140; ❄📶; [S]J/Z to Bowery) Across the street from the New Museum, this former 1920s-era flophouse has been resurrected as an upmarket hostel, its rooms decked out with Bowery-themed film posters and custom-made mattresses (ie shorter and narrower), while communal bathrooms feature rain showers and heated floors. There's also a stylish lounge area with Chesterfield sofas and chandeliers, a buzzing bar and a roof terrace.

Light sleepers should avoid this place, which attracts a nightlife-loving crowd; earplugs come standard with every room.

LEON HOTEL HOTEL $$

Map p415 (☎212-390-8833; www.leonhotelnyc.com; 125 Canal St, btwn Bowery & Chrystie St; r from $250; ❄📶; [S]B/D to Grand St) At the entrance to the Manhattan Bridge and surrounded by hectic streets, this boxy space offers clean, no-frills accommodations that is decent value in wallet-draining NYC. Rooms are comfortable, if minimally furnished, and some have fetching views of Lower Manhattan and taller-than-thou One World Trade Center. The staff are friendly and the location is super-handy for exploring Chinatown, Nolita and the Lower East Side.

Regular online deals can see room rates drop well below $300, with doubles often beginning at $250 a night

NOMO SOHO BOUTIQUE HOTEL $$

Map p412 (☎646-218-6400; www.nomosoho.com; 9 Crosby St, btwn Howard & Grand Sts; r from $279; ❄📶; [S]N/Q/R, J/Z, 6 to Canal St) Neo-baroque playfulness underscores the plush, smallish rooms at this beautiful downtown property, where creamy whites and dreamy blues meet flouncy sconces and marble bathrooms. Indeed, upper-level rooms will leave you feeling like you're gazing out at Manhattan from a cloud. The garden-inspired restaurant serves fine modern American flavors under a maelstrom of crystal chandeliers, while the bar sees guests sipping behind a secret bookshelf door.

BEST WESTERN BOWERY HANBEE HOTEL HOTEL $$

Map p415 (☎212-925-1177; www.bw-boweryhanbeehotel.com; 231 Grand St, at Bowery; r from $279; ❄📶; [S]B/D to Grand St; J/Z to Bowery) Clean, comfortable, simple rooms is what you get at this reliable chain hotel. While the place lacks any real character or charm, it's one of the few midrange options in this part of town, slap bang in Chinatown and within walking distance of uber-hip SoHo, Nolita and the Lower East Side. There's an on-site gym.

CROSBY STREET HOTEL BOUTIQUE HOTEL $$$

Map p412 (☎212-226-6400; www.firmdalehotels.com; 79 Crosby St, btwn Spring & Prince Sts; r from $675; ❄@📶; [S]6 to Spring St; N/R to Prince St) Step into Crosby Street for afternoon tea and you'll never want to leave. It's not just the scones and clotted cream that will grab you, but the eccentric, loft-like lobby, buzzing bar, film-screening room, and one-of-a-kind rooms. While some of the latter are starkly black and white, and others as pretty and floral as an English garden, all are plush, refined and subtly playful.

MERCER
BOUTIQUE HOTEL $$$

Map p412 (☎212-966-6060; www.mercerhotel. com; 147 Mercer St, at Prince St; r from $625; ✴️🖥; ⓢN/R to Prince St) Right in the heart of SoHo's brick lanes, the grand Mercer is where stars sleep. Above the leisurely lobby full of fat, plush sofas, the 75 rooms offer a slice of chic loft life in a century-old warehouse. Flat-screen TVs, dark-wood floors and white-tiled bathrooms (some with soaking tubs under a skylight) add a modern touch to rooms that nod to the building's industrial roots.

JAMES NEW YORK
BOUTIQUE HOTEL $$$

Map p412 (☎212-465-2000; www.jameshotels. com/new-york; 27 Grand St, btwn Ave of the Americas & Thompson St; r from $403; ✴️@🖥🏊; ⓢA/C/E, 1 to Canal St) The James plays with a variety of architectural elements in each of the hotel's different spaces, and somehow they all work beautifully. The public areas – especially the designated lobbies – blend abundant natural light with playful touches (we love the computer-key mural). Upstairs, rooms are light-filled and relatively simple, with chocolate-hued accents, reclaimed timber floors, and a motorized screen separating each from its copper-hued bathroom.

Added sex appeal is provided by the rooftop plunge pool, complete with slinky bar for see-and-be-seen cocktails.

LAFAYETTE HOUSE
GUESTHOUSE $$$

Map p412 (☎212-505-8100; www.lafayettenyc. com; 38 E 4th St , btwn Fourth Ave & Lafayette St; r $250-450; ✴️🖥; ⓢ6 to Bleecker St; B/D/F/M to Broadway-Lafayette St) A former townhouse, this Victorian beauty offers eight homely rooms with big beds, thick drapes, marble fireplaces and old-fashioned armoires. Two rooms feature their own private garden, while another two come with private terrace or balcony. Light sleepers beware: rooms facing the street can feel a bit noisy.

BROOME
BOUTIQUE HOTEL $$$

Map p412 (☎212-431-2929; www.thebroomenyc. com; 431 Broome St, at Crosby St; r from $400; ✴️🖥; ⓢN/R to Prince St; 6 to Spring St) Occupying a handsomely restored, 19th-century federal-style building, the Broome opened to much fanfare in 2014. Spread across five stories its 14 rooms are the epitome of simple, muted elegance, each with locally sourced fittings including furnishings by Mitchell Gold + Bob Williams and

oversized mirrors from BDDW. Topping it off are beautiful, personable service and a soothing, tranquil vibe that offers respite from SoHo's relentless energy.

NOLITAN HOTEL
BOUTIQUE HOTEL $$$

Map p412 (☎212-925-2555; www.nolitanhotel. com; 30 Kenmare St, btwn Elizabeth & Mott Sts; r from $479; ✴️🖥🏊; ⓢJ/Z to Bowery; 6 to Spring St; B/D to Grand St) Set behind a memorable facade of floating positive-negative Tetris bricks, the Nolitan is a great find situated between two of the most popular New York neighborhoods: SoHo and the Village. Tuck into a good book in the inviting lobby lounge, or head upstairs to your stylish pad – a scene that looks straight out of a CB2 catalog.

Wi-fi and bike use is complimentary, as are the vino and cheese during happy hour (Monday to Saturday). Online room rates can slide well below $300, so always keep an eye out.

🛏️ East Village & Lower East Side

Statement-making structures have been cropping up in these once grittier neighborhoods, giving the area a fun, world-in-one feel that still remains distinctly New York in style. Visitors seeking that true city feel will be perfectly happy taking up residence along these low-numbered streets, especially if you've got the dime for a room at the Bowery or Cooper Sq hotels. Stay west if subway convenience is a primary concern – underground transportation thins as you head east, especially beyond First Ave.

BLUE MOON BOUTIQUE HOTEL
HOTEL $$

Map p418 (☎347-294-4552; www.bluemoonboutiquehotel.com; 100 Orchard St, btwn Broome & Delancey Sts; dm/d from $85/170; ✴️🖥; ⓢF to Delancey St; J/M to Essex St) You'd never guess that this welcoming brick guesthouse – full of festive yellows, blues and greens – was once a foul tenement back in the day (the day being 1879). With touches including original wood shutters and wrought-iron bed frames, Blue Moon's small, spare rooms are vintage-inspired and comfortable. The best rooms are bright, with balconies that have fine views.

The Blue Moon also has two dorm rooms with four single beds each (no bunk beds) – one mixed room, one for females only.

EAST VILLAGE HOTEL HOTEL $$
Map p416 (☎646-429-9184; www.eastvillagehotel.com; 147 First Ave, at 9th St; d from $270; ❄📶; Ⓢ6 to Astor Pl) In a vibrant location in the East Village, this place has clean, simple rooms with exposed brick walls, comfy mattresses, wall-mounted flat-screen TVs and small kitchenettes. Street noise is an issue (beware, light sleepers), and it's in an old building, so you'll have to walk your luggage up a few flights.

There's no lobby or other common areas. Guests receive an access code to the door to come and go as they please, so there's little interaction with other guests.

LUDLOW HOTEL $$
Map p418 (☎212-432-1818; ludlowhotel.com; 180 Ludlow St, btwn Houston & Stanton Sts; d from $325; ❄📶; ⓈF to 2nd Ave) Nearly a decade in the making, this 184-room boutique hotel finally opened its doors in 2014 to much fanfare. Rooms are beautifully designed with unique features (some have tree-trunk nightstands made of petrified wood), mosaic-tiled bathrooms and small balconies. On the downside, the least expensive rooms are tiny and extremely cramped.

There's a gorgeous lobby bar and outdoor patio, plus a stylish French bistro.

BOWERY HOTEL BOUTIQUE HOTEL $$$
Map p416(☎212-505-9100; www.theboweryhotel.com; 335 Bowery, btwn 2nd & 3rd Sts; r from $475; ❄@📶; ⓈF/V to Lower East Side-Second Ave; 6 to Bleecker St) Pick up your old-fashioned gold room key with its red tassel in the dark, hushed lobby – filled with antique velvet chairs and faded Persian rugs – then follow the mosaic floors to your room. There you can dock your iPod, use the wi-fi, check out the 42in plasma, watch some DVDs, or raid your bathroom goodies (courtesy of CO Bigelow).

Rooms have huge factory windows with unobstructed views, simple white spreads with red piping, and elegant four-poster beds. The Bowery's zinc-topped bar, outside garden patio, and rustic Italian eatery, Gemma, are always packed.

STANDARD EAST VILLAGE HOTEL $$$
Map p416(☎212-475-5700; www.standardhotels.com; 25 Cooper Sq (Third Ave), btwn 5th & 6th Sts; r from $475; ❄📶; ⓈN/R to 8th St-NYU; 4/6 to Bleecker St; 4/6 to Astor Pl) Rising above the East Village like an unfurled sail, Cooper Sq's gleaming white structure looms strikingly out of place in low-rise East Village – even with the ersatz graffiti wall its designers placed at the entrance. For a more authentic glimpse at the old East Village, head to the outdoor patio bars. From there you can look right into the apartments in neighboring tenements – a mere 29in away.

The rooms are well equipped with comfy beds, big windows (most are floor-to-ceiling), Bluetooth audio speakers and high-end bath amenities.

West Village, Chelsea & the Meatpacking District

Real estate in the desirable West Village in the Meatpacking District is the highest in the city, and this plays out in hotel tariffs as well. Staying here, however, is well worth opening your wallet a bit wider as you'll be treated to a wonderful neighborhood vibe at some of the more memorable properties in town. Just a few blocks up in Chelsea, you'll find a spike in new development with a horde of swankified properties promising cutting-edge design befitting the pages of a Scandinavian design magazine. Nights in Chelsea will ensure convenient (read: walkable) access to boutique shopping, eating and drinking downtown.

CHELSEA HOSTEL HOSTEL $
Map p424 (☎212-647-0010; www.chelseahostel.com; 251 W 20th St, btwn Seventh & Eighth Aves; dm $40-80, s $75-100, d from $130; ❄@📶; ⓈA/C/E, 1/2 to 23rd St, 1/2 to 18th St) Occupying some serious real estate in the desirable Chelsea neighborhood, this old bastion of backpackerdom is a good pick if location ranks at the top of your list. Walkable to the Village and Midtown, Chelsea Hostel capitalizes on its convenience with somewhat steep prices, but it's kept clean (even a tad sterile at times) and there's access to common rooms and kitchens where other budget travelers often meet and hang.

JANE HOTEL HOTEL $
Map p420 (☎212-924-6700; www.thejanenyc.com; 113 Jane St, btwn Washington St & West Side Hwy; r with shared/private bath from $115/275; [P]❄📶; ⓈL to Eighth Ave; A/C/E to 14th St; 1/2 to

Christopher St-Sheridan Sq) The claustrophobic will want to avoid the Jane's tiny 50-sq-ft rooms, but if you can stomach living like a luxury sailor, check into this renovated red-brick gem, which was built for mariners in the early 20th century (survivors from the *Titanic* also stayed here in 1912).

The small cabin rooms have shared bathrooms; the more expensive captain's quarters come with private commodes. The gorgeous ballroom/bar looks like it belongs in a five-star hotel. The excellent but affordable Cafe Gitane is here as well.

LARCHMONT HOTEL HOTEL $

Map p420 (☎212-989-9333; www.larchmonthotel.com; 27 W 11th St, btwn Fifth & Sixth Aves; s/d with shared bath from $130/150; ❄📶; [S]4/5/6, N/Q/R to 14th St-Union Sq) Housed in a prewar building that blends in with the other fine brownstones on the block, a stay at the Larchmont is all about location. The carpeted rooms are basic and in need of updating, as are the communal bathrooms, but it's still a good deal for the price.

COLONIAL HOUSE INN B&B $$

Map p424 (☎212-243-9669, 800-689-3779; www.colonialhouseinn.com; 318 W 22nd St, btwn Eighth & Ninth Aves; r $150-350; ❄📶; [S]C/E to 23rd St) Friendly and simple, this 20-room gay-friendly inn is tidy but a bit worn and small. Most rooms have small walk-in closets (with a small TV and refrigerator) and sinks. When the weather is nice, the rooftop deck sees some nude sunbathing. The smaller rooms have shared baths, while the deluxe suite has a private bath and private access to the back garden.

CHELSEA PINES INN B&B $$

Map p420 (☎212-929-1023, 888-546-2700; www.chelseapinesinn.com; 317 W 14th St, btwn Eighth & Ninth Aves; s/d from $229/269; ❄📶; [S]A/C/E to 14th St; L to Eighth Ave) With its five walk-up floors coded to the rainbow flag, the 26-room Chelsea Pines is serious gay-and-lesbian central, but guests of all stripes are welcome. It helps to be up on your Hitchcock beauties, as vintage movie posters not only plaster the walls but rooms are named for starlets such as Kim Novak, Doris Day and Ann-Margret.

There's a sink in the walk-in closet of standard rooms, with clean bathrooms down the hall. The small lounge downstairs opens to a tiny courtyard out back.

INCENTRA VILLAGE HOUSE B&B $$

Map p420 (☎212-206-0007; www.incentravillage.com; 32 Eighth Ave, btwn 12th & Jane Sts; r from $259; ❄📶; [S]A/C/E to 14th St; L to Eighth Ave) Boasting a great location in the West Village, these two red-brick, landmark townhouses were built in 1841 and later became the city's first gay-friendly inn. Today, the 11 rooms get booked way in advance; call early to get in on its gorgeous Victorian parlor and antique-filled, serious-Americana rooms. The Garden Suite has access to a small garden in back and there's wi-fi access in the parlor.

TOWNHOUSE INN OF CHELSEA B&B $$

Map p424 (☎212-414-2323; www.townhouseinnchelsea.com; 131 W 23rd St, btwn Sixth & Seventh Aves; r from $350; ❄📶; [S]F/V, 1 to 23rd St) Housed in a lone 19th-century, five-story townhouse on busy 23rd St, this 14-room B&B is a Chelsea gem. Bought in 1998 and extensively renovated by the Fisherman family (who wisely installed an elevator), the rooms are big and welcoming, with fanciful fabrics on big brass or poster beds and TVs held in huge armoires.

There's an honor-system bar and an ol' piano for you to play boogie-woogie on in the lounge, and a 2nd-floor, all-Victorian library that doubles as a breakfast room.

HÔTEL AMERICANO HOTEL $$$

Map p424 (☎212-216-0000; www.hotel-americano.com; 518 W 27th St, btwn Tenth & Eleventh Aves; r from $385; ❄📶🏊;[S]A/C/E to 23rd St) Design geeks will go giddy when they walk into one of Hôtel Americano's perfectly polished rooms. It's like sleeping in a bento box, but the food's been replaced by a carefully curated selection of minimalist and muted furniture. Oh, and that thing hanging from the ceiling that looks like a robot's head? It's a suspended fireplace, of course. Other accoutrements await, from Turkish towels to Japanese washing cloths, and all controls are activated by your personal iPad. When you're ready to venture from your museumeqsue cocoon, explore surrounding Chelsea on a guest bike. There's also a rooftop deck with a small pool.

STANDARD BOUTIQUE HOTEL $$$

Map p420 (☎212-645-4646; www.standardhotels.com; 848 Washington St, at 13th St; r from $521; ❄📶; [S]A/C/E to 14th St; L to Eighth Ave) Hipster hotelier André Balazs has built a wide, boxy, glass tower that straddles the High Line. Every room has sweeping Meatpacking District views and is filled with cascading sunlight, which makes the Standard's glossy, wood-framed beds and marbled bathrooms glow in a particularly homey way. There's also a hyper-modern Standard (p336) in the East Village.

The amenities are first-rate, with a buzzing German beer garden and a brasserie at street level (and ice rink in winter), and a plush nightclub on the top floor. The location is unbeatable, with the best of NYC right outside your door.

HOTEL GANSEVOORT LUXURY HOTEL **$$$**
Map p420 (☎212-206-6700; www.hotelgansevoort.com; 18 Ninth Ave, at 13th St; r from $450; ❄📶🏊🐾; [S]A/C/E, 1/2/3 to 14th St; L to Eighth Ave) Coated in zinc-colored panels the 14-floor Gansevoort has been a swank swashbuckler of the Meatpacking District since it opened in 2004. Rooms are luscious and airy, with fudge-colored suede headboards, plasma-screen TVs and illuminated bathroom doors. Rooftop bar Plunge attracts long lines up top and guests swim in the skinny pool overlooking the Hudson River.

There's also a street-level restaurant and a very swanky cocktail lounge/nightclub called Provacateur.

MARITIME HOTEL BOUTIQUE HOTEL **$$$**
Map p424 (☎212-242-4300; www.themaritimehotel.com; 363 W 16th St, btwn Eighth & Ninth Aves; r from $425; ❄📶; [S]A/C/E to 14th St; L to Eighth Ave) This white tower dotted with portholes has been transformed into a marine-themed luxury inn by a hip team of architects. It feels like a luxury *Love Boat* inside, as its 135 rooms, each with their own round window, are compact and teak-paneled, with gravy in the form of 20in flat-screen TVs and DVD players.

The most expensive quarters feature outdoor showers, a private garden and sweeping Hudson views. The building was originally the site of the National Maritime Union headquarters (and then a shelter for homeless teens).

DREAM DOWNTOWN HOTEL **$$$**
Map p424 (☎212-229-2559; www.dreamdowntown.com; 355 W 16th St, btwn Eighth & Ninth Aves; r from $535; ❄📶🏊; [S]A/C/E to 14th St; L to Eighth Ave; 1 to 18th St) The Dream Downtown is a looming behemoth that sinks its circle-themed footprint deep in the heart of Chelsea. The metallic facade is punctuated by portholes that look like the windows of Captain Nemo's would-be space vessel; a generous smattering of ellipses echo throughout, including bedroom walls and the subtle tiling of the narrow pool – a refreshing oasis on unbearable summer days.

Ample public space is a priority here, which takes the shape of several cocktail lounges and restaurants that attract weekenders in the know.

🛏 Union Square, Flatiron District & Gramercy

Countless visitors lay their weary heads under the blinding lights of Times Square for convenience, but consider for a second that Union Square and its neighbors are just as handy. A quick glance at the subway map will show a handful of lines that crisscross in this busy downtown hub – you're a straight shot to Lower Manhattan and the museums on the Upper East Side, with the adorable nooks of the Village at your doorstep. The area's slumber options are varied and eclectic, ranging from the high-priced chic-boutique to a few shared-bathroom, penny-saving options.

CARLTON ARMS HOTEL **$**
Map p426 (☎212-679-0680; www.carltonarms.com; 160 E 25th St, at Third Ave; d with shared/private bath $120/150; ❄📶; [S]6 to 23rd St or 28th St) If only these walls could talk… The Carlton Arms has gone through many incarnations during its 100 years as a hotel, from nights of subterfuge (the lobby was a speakeasy during Prohibition) to days of dereliction (as a refuge for addicts and prostitutes in the 1960s). These days the Carlton Arms feels equal parts art gallery and budget hotel.

Artwork adorns the interiors, with murals following the walls up five flights of stairs, and into each of the tiny guest rooms and shared bathrooms (there is a small sink in each guest room). Not surprisingly, it draws an eclectic mix of Bohemian travelers, who don't mind the rustic accommodations in exchange for big savings. Prepare to work those legs: there's no lift.

WYNDHAM GARDEN HOTEL **$$**

Map p426 (☎212-243-0800; www.wyndham.com; 37 W 24th St, btwn Fifth & Sixth Aves; r from $280; ❄📶; [S]F/M, N/R to 23rd St) Nearly equidistant from Chelsea and Union Square, the Wyndham's colorful checked entrance fits in with the uniqueness of its surrounding neighborhoods. The whimsy disappears once you're inside, it's beige walls, taupe carpet and plain work stations typical of a chain hotel. Despite this and the somewhat poor soundproofing, it's a fantastic location and has free wi-fi, clean rooms and helpful staff.

MARCEL AT GRAMERCY BOUTIQUE HOTEL **$$**

Map p426 (☎212-696-3800; www.themarcelatgramercy.com; 201 E 24th St, at Third Ave; r from $300; ❄@📶; [S]6 to 23rd St) The minimalist, 97-room Marcel is a poor-man's chic boutique, and that's not a bad thing. Rooms are simple yet modern, their grey-and-beige color scheme shaken up by bold, canary-yellow Chesterfield bedheads. Bathrooms are uninspired but clean, while rooms on the avenue have decent views. Downstairs, the sleek lounge makes for a nifty place to unwind from a day of touring. Room wi-fi is an extra $10 per day.

HOTEL 17 HOTEL **$$**

Map p426 (☎212-475-2845; www.hotel17ny.com; 225 E 17th St, btwn Second & Third Aves; d with shared bath from $150; ❄📶; [S]N/Q/R, 4/5/6 to 14th St-Union Sq, L to Third Ave) Right off Stuyvesant Sq, this popular, eight-floor townhouse is where Woody Allen shot a frightening dead-body scene for his film *Manhattan Murder Mystery* (1993). The 120 rooms are small and basic, with old-school chintzy furnishings and a lack of natural light, and only four have private bathrooms (but all are free of dead bodies).

If this place is booked, ask about its sister property in Midtown, **Hotel 31** (Map p428; ☎212-685-3060; www.hotel31.com; 120 E 31st St, btwn Lexington & Park Aves, Midtown East; d with private/shared bathroom from $199/159; ❄📶; [S]N/R, 6 to 28th St).

★**GRAMERCY PARK HOTEL** BOUTIQUE HOTEL **$$$**

Map p426 (☎212-920-3300; www.gramercyparkhotel.com; 2 Lexington Ave, at 21st St; r from $500; ❄📶; [S]6, N/R to 23rd St) Formerly a grand old dame, the Gramercy's major face-lift has it looking young and sexy. Dark wood paneling and red suede rugs and chairs greet you in the lobby, while the rooms – overlooking nearby Gramercy Park – deliver customized oak furnishings, 400-count Italian linens, and big, feather-stuffed mattresses on sprawling beds. Colors are rich and alluring, fit for a Spanish grandee.

The largest rooms – sprawling suites with French doors dividing living and sleeping areas – start at $800. Add zest to your life with drinks at the celebrity-studded Rose and Jade bars, and dinner at Maialino (p167), Danny Meyer's rustic Italian eatery.

Midtown

If you want to be in the heart of the action, consider Midtown East, which encompasses the area around Grand Central Terminal and the UN. It's not as crazy and eclectic as Midtown West, but options are endless, from a design-conscious 'budget' option with shared bathrooms to thousand-dollar suites with private terraces overlooking Gotham's blinking lights. Light sleepers beware – Midtown West is a 24-hour kind of place, though it's especially convenient for Broadway fans.

PARK SAVOY HOTEL **$**

Map p432 (☎212-245-5755; www.parksavoyny.com; 158 W 58th St, btwn Sixth & Seventh Aves; d from $145; ❄📶; [S]N/Q/R to 57th St-7th Ave) The best thing about the Park Savoy is the low price and nifty location near the lovely gateway of Central Park. More money saved on lodgings means more to spend at nearby Fifth Ave boutiques and top Broadway shows. Naturally, there is a trade-off and that's the rooms: worn carpets, cheap bedspreads, and showers with trickling water pressure, to say nothing of the unhelpful staff.

★**CITIZEN M** HOTEL **$$**

Map p432 (☎212-461-3638; www.citizenm.com; 218 W 50th St, btwn Broadway & Eighth Ave, Midtown West; r from $246; ❄📶; [S]1, C/E to 50th St) A few steps from Times Square, Citizen M is a true millennial. Speedy self-service counters provide lightning-fast check-in and check-out, communal areas are upbeat, contemporary and buzzing, and rooms are smart and compact. A tablet in each controls lighting, blinds and room temperature, and the plush mattresses, free movies and soothing rain showers keep guests purring. On-site perks include gym, rooftop bar and 24-hour canteen.

★YOTEL HOTEL **$$**

Map p432 (☎646-449-7700; www.yotel.com; 570 Tenth Ave, at 41st St, Midtown West; r from $130; ❄📶; [S]A/C/E to 42nd St-Port Authority Bus Terminal; 1/2/3, N/Q/R, S, 7 to Times Sq-42nd St) Part futuristic spaceport, part Austin Powers set, this uber-cool 669-room option bases its rooms on airplane classes: Premium Cabin (Economy), First Cabins (Business) and VIP Suites (First); some First Cabins and VIP Suites include a private terrace with hot tub. Small but cleverly configured, Premium Cabins include automated adjustable beds, while all cabins feature floor-to-ceiling windows with killer views, slick bathrooms and iPod connectivity.

Perks include free morning muffins, a gym and the city's largest outdoor hotel terrace, complete with a stunning skyscraper backdrop (naturally).

IVY TERRACE B&B **$$**

Map p428 (☎516-662-6862; www.ivyterrace.com; 230 E 58th St, btwn Second & Third Aves, Midtown East; r from $225; ❄📶; [S]4/5/6 to 59th St; N/Q/R to Lexington Ave-59th St) Especially popular with couples, Ivy Terrace is a criminally charming B&B. The spacious, Victorian-inspired rooms cozily combine elegant drapes, antique furniture (the Rose Room features a canopy bed), hardwood floors and kitchens with breakfast supplies. One of the suites even has a flagstone balcony. There's a three-night minimum stay (sometimes five to seven nights), and no elevator.

Its location is just east of the Midtown fray but close to Bloomingdales and the mega shopping strips of Madison and Fifth Aves.

PARK CENTRAL HOTEL **$$**

Map p432 (☎212-247-8000; www.parkcentralny.com; 870 Seventh Ave, btwn 55th & 56th Sts, Midtown West; d from $270; ❄📶; [S]N/Q/R to 57th St-7th Ave) Close to Carnegie Hall, Broadway and Central Park, the Park Central is positively massive (761 rooms!), a fact that becomes apparent in the sometimes lengthy waits for an elevator. Following a multimillion-dollar overhaul in 2013, the hotel is in good nick, though some rooms still seem a bit dated with cramped bathrooms, and service is hit or miss.

Wi-fi is included in a somewhat cheeky $25 facilities fee, which also includes access to the fitness center and unlimited local and domestic long-distance calls.

HOTEL ELYSÉE BOUTIQUE HOTEL **$$**

Map p428 (☎212-753-1066; www.elyseehotel.com; 60 E 54th St, btwn Madison & Park Aves, Midtown East; r from $207; ❄@📶; [S]E/M to Lexington Ave-53rd St; 6 to 51st St) Adorned with antiques and classic detailing, this intimate hotel has been bedding the famous and fabulous since 1926. Come evening, star-spot over complimentary wine and cheese in the lounge, or in the deco-glam Monkey Bar restaurant, co-owned by Vanity Fair editor Graydon Carter and featured in both *Mad Men* and *Sex and the City*.

There's no gym on-site, but passes to NY Sports Club are complimentary.

HOTEL PENNSYLVANIA HOTEL **$$**

Map p432 (☎212-736-5000; www.hotelpenn.com; 401 Seventh Ave, at 33rd St, Midtown West; d from $229; ❄📶; [S]1/2/3 to Penn Station-34th St) When it opened in 1919, the Hotel Pennsylvania was the largest hotel in the world. Although it's lost its title (and much of its luster), this place still feels vast, with a seemingly endless maze of guestrooms spread across 18 floors. Despite not having the most comfortable beds in town, rooms are adequate and fair value, with some offering views of the Empire State Building.

ROW NYC HOTEL **$$**

Map p432 (☎212-869-3600; rownyc.com; 700 Eighth Ave, btwn 44th & 45th Sts, Midtown West; d from $223; ❄📶; [S]A/C/E to 42nd St-Port Authority Bus Terminal) In the heart of the theater district, Row NYC serves up slick, contemporary rooms with minimal space and tiny bathrooms. It's a big hotel, with a noisy lobby, so not ideal for those seeking solitude. On the other hand, if you can score a deal, it's a decent mid-range option – particularly if you're hankering for quick access to Times Square and Broadway.

As elsewhere in this part of town, street noise is a problem on the lower levels.

POD 39 HOTEL **$$**

Map p428 (☎212-865-5700; www.thepodhotel.com; 145 E 39th St, btwn Lexington & Third Aves, Midtown East; r from $240; ❄📶; [S]S, 4/5/6, 7 to Grand Central-42nd St) It's a case of good things coming in very small packages at funky Pod 39. The sibling of budget-luxe

Pod 51, its 366 rooms offer hip-n-functional design, private bathroom and city views in Pod's trademark tiny dimensions. Cranking up the millennial cred is a Technicolor taqueria, eclectic lobby lounge, light-strung rooftop bar, and games room (complete with oh-so-retro ping-pong table).

POD 51 HOTEL $$
Map p428 (☎212-355-0300; www.thepodhotel.com; 230 E 51st St, btwn Second & Third Aves, Midtown East; r with shared/private bathroom from $175/255; ❄📶; [S]6 to 51st St; E/M to Lexington Ave-53rd St) A dream come true for folks who would like to live inside their iPod – or at least curl up and sleep with it – this affordable hot spot has a range of room types, most barely big enough for the bed. 'Pods' have bright bedding, tight workspaces, flat-screen TVs, iPod docking stations and 'raindrop' showerheads. In the warmer months, sip a drink on the perky rooftop deck.

MURRAY HILL EAST SUITES HOTEL $$
Map p428 (☎212-661-2100; murrayhillsuites.com; 149 E 39th St, btwn Lexington & Third Aves, Midtown East; r from $130; ❄📶; [S]4/5/6, 7 to Grand Central) The dated brick facade is a suitable introduction to the rooms, where uninspiring furniture and carpet page the eras of flares and shoulder pads. If you can overlook the design shortcomings, you'll enjoy remarkably spacious quarters, with separate sitting areas and kitchenettes. A plethora of great eating and drinking options are nearby. The catch: a minimum 30-day stay.

SETON HOTEL HOTEL $$
Map p428 (☎212-889-5301; www.setonhotelny.com; 144 E 40th St, btwn Lexington & Third Aves, Midtown East; d from $232; ❄@📶; [S]4/5/6, 7 to Grand Central-42nd St) Near Grand Central Terminal, the Seton Hotel offers a range of clean, modern rooms that are generally good value. On the downside, some quarters are rather dark, and street noise (and poorly soundproofed doors) can be a problem for light sleepers. As to be expected at these prices, the rooms are quite small. The location in the heart of Midtown Manhattan, however, is excellent.

RESIDENCE INN NEW YORK MANHATTAN/MIDTOWN EAST HOTEL $$
Map p428 (☎212-980-1003; www.marriott.com; 148 E 48th St, btwn Lexington & Third Aves, Midtown East; d from $254; ❄📶; [S]6 to 51st St) Popular for its occasional deals, this Residence Inn offers no surprises to those familiar with the Marriott brand. Rooms are clean, comfortable and in good condition, with serviceable kitchenettes (a big draw for families). Some quarters, however, are cramped and rather gloomy, so try to take a look before committing.

The extensive breakfast buffet gets crowded – go early to score a seat (and plan on sometimes lengthy waits for the elevator in the morning). Take advantage of the complimentary ear plugs if sleeping on the lower floors.

ECONO LODGE BUDGET HOTEL $$
Map p432 (☎212-246-1991; www.econolodgetimessquare.com; 302 W 47th St, at Eighth Ave, Midtown West; r from $195; ❄📶; [S]C/E to 50th St; N/Q/R to 49th St) A budget option only steps away from the Times Square action, Econo Lodge has a small, no-frills lobby that leads to small, no-frills rooms. Some have double beds and can hold four, and others are kings, with just enough room to squeeze in an armoire and A decent-sized bathroom.

When the rates come down in off-season, the prices are more in line with the hotel's offerings.

★**NOMAD HOTEL** BOUTIQUE HOTEL $$$
Map p428 (☎212-796-1500; www.thenomadhotel.com; 1170 Broadway, at 28th St, Midtown West; r from $479; ❄📶; [S]N/R to 28th St) Crowned by a copper turret and featuring interiors designed by Frenchman Jacques Garcia, this beaux-arts dream is one of the city's hottest addresses. Rooms channel a nostalgic NYC-meets-Paris aesthetic, in which recycled hardwood floors, leather-steam-trunk minibars and clawfoot tubs mix it with flat-screen TVs and high-tech LED lighting. Wi-fi is free, while in-house restaurant/bar NoMad is one of the neighborhood's most coveted hangouts.

★**KNICKERBOCKER** BOUTIQUE HOTEL $$$
Map p432 (☎212-204-4980; theknickerbocker.com; 6 Times Sq, at 42nd St; d from $515; ❄📶; [S]N/Q/R, S, 1/2/3, 7 to Times Sq-42nd St) Originally opened in 1906 by John Jacob Astor, the 330-room Knickerbocker is back in business after a luxurious, $240-million refurbishment. Unlike its Times Square location, the place exudes a restrained, monochromatic elegance. Rooms are dashingly chic,

hushed and modern, decked out with adjustable 55-inch flat-screen TV, bedside tablet and USB charging ports. Carrara-marble bathrooms come with a spacious shower, with some offering standalone tub.

Hotel facilities include a sophisticated lounge, cocktail bar and Modern American noshery, as well as a fabulous rooftop bar, complete with bookable private nooks, cigars and nightly DJs.

★PLAZA LUXURY HOTEL **$$$**

Map p428 (☎212-759-3000, 888-850-0909; www.theplaza.com; 768 Fifth Ave, at Central Park S; r from $875; ❄📶; [S]N/R to Fifth Ave-59th St) Suitably set in a landmark French Renaissance–style building, the iconic Plaza's 282 guestrooms are a regal affair, with sumptuous Louis XV–style furniture and 24-carat gold-plated bathroom faucets. Onsite drawcards include the wine-therapy Caudelié Spa and fabled Palm Court, the latter famed for its stained-glass ceiling and afternoon tea. Less enticing is the hotel's $14.95 wi-fi surcharge.

★ANDAZ FIFTH AVENUE BOUTIQUE HOTEL **$$$**

Map p428 (☎212-601-1234; newyork.5thavenue.andaz.hyatt.com; 485 Fifth Ave, at 41st St, Midtown East; r from $465; ❄📶; [S]S, 4/5/6 to Grand Central-42nd St; 7 to Fifth Ave; B/D/F/M to 42nd St-Bryant Park) Youthful, chic Andaz ditches stuffy reception desks for hip, mobile staff who check you in on iPads in the art-laced lobby. The hotel's 184 rooms are svelte and contemporary, with NYC-inspired details like 'Fashion District' rolling racks and subway-inspired lamps. We especially love the sexy, spacious bathrooms, complete with rain showers, black porcelain foot baths and Beekman 1802 amenities.

It also has a 'secret' basement bar serving limited-edition spirits and locavore-focused dishes, and regular talks by guest artists and curators. Check the website for special deals.

★ACE HOTEL BOUTIQUE HOTEL **$$$**

Map p428 (☎212-679-2222; www.acehotel.com/newyork; 20 W 29th St, btwn Broadway & Fifth Ave, Midtown West; r from $329; ❄📶; [S]N/R to 28th St) A hit with cashed-up creatives, the Ace's standard and deluxe rooms recall upscale bachelor pads – plaid bedspreads, quirky wall stencils, leather furnishings and fridges. Some even have Gibson guitars and turntables. All have free wi-fi. For cool kids with more 'cred' than 'coins,' there are 'mini' and 'bunk' rooms (with bunk beds), both of which can slip under $200 in winter.

The Ace vibe is upbeat and fun, with a hipster-packed lobby serving up live bands and DJs, superlative espresso bar Stumptown Coffee Roasters (p201) and two of the area's top nosh spots – turf-centric **Breslin Bar & Dining Room** (Map p428; ☎212-679-1939; www.thebreslin.com; 16 West 29th St, btwn Broadway & Fifth Ave; lunch mains $16-24, dinner mains $23-37; ⏰7am-midnight; [S]N/R to 28th St) and surf-centric John Dory Oyster Bar (p195).

★QUIN LUXURY HOTEL **$$$**

Map p432 (☎212-245-7846; www.thequinhotel.com; 101 W 57th St, at Sixth Ave, Midtown West; d from $492; ❄📶; [S]F to 57th St) Opened to much acclaim in late 2013, the Quin delivers opulence with a dash of new-school verve. Its beautiful, slinky common areas are anything but 'common' – the hotel lounge comes complete with 15ft video wall for showcasing art installations. Rooms are quiet, exceedingly comfortable and elegantly restrained, with custom-made, king-sized Duxiana beds, svelte marble bathrooms with glass-enclosed shower, and Nespresso machines.

★FOUR SEASONS LUXURY HOTEL **$$$**

Map p428 (☎ 212-758-5700; www.fourseasons.com/newyork; 57 E 57th St, btwn Madison & Park Aves, Midtown East; r from $825; ❄📶; [S]N/Q/R to Fifth Ave-59th St) Housed in a 52-floor tower designed by IM Pei, the five-star Four Seasons delivers seamless luxury. Even the smallest of the neutrally hued rooms are generously sized, with spacious closets and HD TVs in the Tuscan-marble bathrooms. The views over Central Park from the 'Park View' rooms are practically unfair, with oohs and aahs also induced by the hotel's esteemed spa.

ROYALTON BOUTIQUE HOTEL **$$$**

Map p428 (☎212-869-4400; www.royalton.com; 44 W 44th St, btwn Fifth & Sixth Aves, Midtown East; d from $374; ❄📶; [S]B/D/F/M to 42nd St-Bryant Park) This modern-classic creation by Ian Schrager and Philippe Starck makes a grand introduction with its mahogany-rich lobby, laced with African art. Up the dark hallways are mid-size rooms with short, wide beds and soft, muted, pastel-hued furnishings. Some rooms have circular 'soaking tubs,' deluxe rooms feature a fireplace, and there's an iPad in every room. There's a fitness center to boot.

LONDON NYC LUXURY HOTEL $$$

Map p432 (☎212-307-5000; www.thelondonnyc.com; 151 W 54th St, btwn Sixth & Seventh Aves, Midtown West; ste from $349; ❄📶; [S]B/D, E to Seventh Ave) This sophisticated hotel salutes the British capital in savvy ways, including a silk-stitched tapestry of Hyde Park (or is it Central Park?) in the lobby, a restaurant by Gordon Ramsay, and complimentary calls to London. But the real draw is the huge, plush rooms – all called suites, and all with separate bedroom and living area, 2000-thread-count linens and spacious bathrooms with showers for two. Amenities include an equally sleek gym.

LIBRARY HOTEL BOUTIQUE HOTEL $$$

Map p428 (☎212-983-4500; www.libraryhotel.com; 299 Madison Ave, at 41st St, Midtown East; d from $240; ❄📶; [S]S, 4/5/6, 7 to Grand Central-42nd St) With hushed reading rooms and a gentlemen's club atmosphere, this elegant, bookish oasis dedicates each floor to one of the major categories of the Dewey Decimal System: Social Sciences, Literature, Philosophy and so on, with over 6000 volumes split up between quarters. Rooms are petite yet cunningly designed with all the amenities of the larger suites, and the rooftop bar pours literary-inspired cocktails.

Adding further appeal is the complimentary wi-fi, breakfast and evening wine-and-cheese sessions.

MUSE NEW YORK BOUTIQUE HOTEL $$$

Map p432 (☎212-485-2400; www.themusehotel.com; 130 W 46th St, btwn Sixth & Seventh Aves, Midtown West; d from $419; ❄📶; [S]B/D/F/M to 47th-50th Sts-Rockefeller Ctr) Near the epicenter of the theater district, the Muse is a shimmering 200-room high-rise brought to you by the Kimpton group, famed for its boutique hotels. The rooms set up a svelte, sultry vibe with their silvery, blue-gray color scheme, luxurious beds and high-end furnishings. Staff are generally helpful and added perks include evening wine reception, complimentary bike usage and in-room spa services.

70 PARK HOTEL $$$

Map p428 (☎212-973-2400; www.70parkave.com; 70 Park Ave, at 38th St, Midtown East; r from $259; ❄📶🐾; [S]S, 4/5/6, 7 to Grand Central-42nd St) Beyond the plush and cozy lobby lounge, adorned with a limestone fireplace, this slumber number offers 205 slinky rooms packed with state-of-the-art technology (including great sound systems); comfy plush beds featuring Frette linens; and a palate of black, white, purple and chrome. Adjoining rooms can be turned into large suites for families. Pets are welcome, staff are friendly and spa treatments are offered in-room. Bliss.

REFINERY HOTEL BOUTIQUE HOTEL $$$

Map p428 (☎646-664-0310; www.refineryhotelnewyork.com; 63 W 38th St, btwn Sixth & Fifth Aves; d from $299; ❄📶; [S]B/D/F/M to 42nd St-Bryant Park) What was once a hat factory is now a hip slumber spot, its 12 floors of design-literate, faintly deco rooms fusing dark oak hardwood floors with custom furnishings, high-tech gadgetry and walk-in rain showers. Topping it off (literally) is the fabulous rooftop bar, a great spot to sip a martini with one eye on the Empire State Building.

Last but not least is the location: a short stroll from atmospheric Bryant Park and the dazzle of Broadway theaters.

PIERRE LUXURY HOTEL $$$

Map p428 (☎212-838-8000; www.lhw.com; 2 E 61st St, at Fifth Ave, Midtown East; r from $845; ❄📶; [S]N/Q/R to Fifth Ave-59th St) Opulent, historic and obscenely romantic, the Pierre is a destination in itself. The lobby looks like a Gilded Age period piece, the on-site restaurant (Sirio Ristorante) is owned by celebrated restaurateur Sirio Maccioni, and the spacious rooms (in muted tones with delicate accent colors) beckon with wide beds, sweeping views of Central Park (at the hotel's front door) and decadent, full-size bathrooms.

The Pierre's 49 suites have gracious sitting areas – some with fireplaces and antique desks for business – that are both lavish and tranquil, and the on-site spa beckons with treatments based on traditional Indian teachings, herbs and oils. Wi-fi will set you back $12.95 per day.

RITZ-CARLTON LUXURY HOTEL $$$

Map p432 (☎212-308-9100; www.ritzcarlton.com; 50 Central Park S, at Sixth Ave; r from $995; ❄📶; [S]N/Q/R to 57th St-Seventh Ave; F to 57th St) Pure, unadulterated luxury: this landmark building comes with views of Central Park so epic you almost can't see New York.

All 259 rooms feature French colonial undertones, with tasseled armchairs, beautiful inlaid-tile bathrooms and loads of space for your countless Louis Vuitton cases, dahhhling. Park-view rooms come with a *Birds of New York* field guide set by a telescope.

The hotel's Auden Bistro offers modern takes on classic bistro fare, while the high-end spa will pamper and polish you with La Prairie products. Unfortunately, room wi-fi will set you back $14.95 per day.

Upper East Side

The Upper East Side contains some of the wealthiest zip codes in the country, so accommodations aren't cheap. But that's the price you pay for being walking distance from some of New York's grandest cultural attractions.

BUBBA & BEAN LODGES

B&B $$

Map p434 (☑917-345-7914; www.bblodges.com; 1598 Lexington Ave, btwn 101st & 102nd Sts; r $190-280; ❈⟨; Ⓢ6 to 103rd St) Owners Jonathan and Clement have turned a charming Manhattan townhouse into an excellent home-away-from-home. The five guest rooms are simply furnished, with crisp, white walls, hardwood floors and navy linens, providing the place with a modern, youthful feel. All units are equipped with private baths as well as kitchenettes.

THE FRANKLIN

HOTEL $$

Map p434 (☑800-607-4009, 212-369-1000; www.franklinhotel.com; 164 E 87th St, btwn Lexington & Third Aves; r from $260; ❈⟨; Ⓢ4/5/6 to 86th St) Fronted by a classic red-and-gold awning, this long-time spot channels a 1930s feel – starting with the vintage elevator. As with many old-timey New York spots, the rooms and bathrooms are tiny. But the decor is modern, the staff congenial and the location couldn't be more ideal – walking distance from Central Park and many museums.

In addition, wine and cheese are served in the evenings. Rooms facing the back are quieter.

BENTLEY HOTEL

BOUTIQUE HOTEL $$

Map p434 (☑212-644-6000; www.bentleyhotel-nyc.com; 500 E 62nd St, at York Ave; r from $340; ❈⟨; ⓈN/Q/R to Lexington Ave/59th St) Featuring great East River views, the Bentley overlooks FDR Dr, as far east as you can go. Formerly an office building, the hotel has shed its utilitarian past in the form of chic boutique-hotel stylings, a swanky lobby and sleek rooms. The downside of staying here is the long walk to subway, restaurants and other essentials.

1871 HOUSE

HISTORIC HOTEL $$

Map p434 (☑212-756-8823; www.1871house.com; 130 E 62nd St, btwn Park & Lexington Aves; r from $285; ❈⟨; ⓈN/Q/R to Lexington Ave-59th St) Named for the year it was built, this historic home now serves as a quaint five-room inn. Each unit (including two multi-room suites) is like a mini-apartment, with a kitchenette, private bath, queen beds, working fireplace and period-style furnishings. All the rooms are light-filled, with airy 12ft ceilings, while the suites, on the upper floors, can sleep up to five.

This is a good-value place for the neighborhood. But note that this is a character-ful, vintage structure: there is no elevator, the floors are a bit creaky, and in winter, heat is provided by steam radiators. Breakfast costs extra.

THE MARK

HOTEL $$$

Map p434 (☑212-744-4300; www.themarkhotel.com; 25 E 77th St, at Madison Ave; d from $725; ❈⟨; Ⓢ6 to 77th St) French designer Jacques Grange left his artful mark on The Mark with bold geometric shapes and rich, playful forms that greet visitors in the lobby (the zebra-striped marble floor is pure eye candy). Upstairs, the beautifully renovated rooms and suites boast a more subdued aesthetic, though equally embracing of high style.

Light and airy rooms are set with coffered ceilings, fine Italian linens and elegant custom-made furnishings. Touch-screen panels control temperature, the lighting scheme and sound, which comes courtesy of Bang & Olufsen. Black-and-white-tiled bathrooms have more than a whiff of art deco (and there's a separate shower and soaking tub), though technology makes its appearance here as well – with a flat-screen TV embedded in the mirror. On the downside, the least expensive rooms can feel small, and service can sometimes be a little hipper-than-thou.

🛏 Upper West Side & Central Park

If you're after culture, the Upper West Side has obvious appeal, with celebrated theaters, cinemas and concert halls (particularly Lincoln Center) right at your doorstep. Proximity to the lush oasis of Central Park and peaceful Riverside Park adds to the allure. Sleeping options here run the gamut from budget-minded hostels to pricey luxury hotels.

JAZZ ON THE PARK HOSTEL   HOSTEL $

Map p436 (☎212-932-1600; www.jazzhostels.com; 36 W 106th St, btwn Central Park West & Manhattan Ave; dm $46-70, d $155-200; ✻@≋; 🄢B, C to 103rd St) This flophouse-turned-hostel right off of Central Park is generally a good bet, with clean dorms sporting four to 12 bunks in co-ed and single-sex configurations. This is a great place to meet other travelers, with free nightly activities (comedy and movie nights, pub crawls, summer barbecues). The downstairs lounge, aka 'the dungeon', has a pool table, couches and big-screen TV.

There's also an area for eating, an accessible rooftop and several small terraces.

HOSTELLING INTERNATIONAL NEW YORK   HOSTEL $

Map p436 (HI; ☎212-932-2300; www.hinewyork.org; 891 Amsterdam Ave, at 103rd St; dm $58-75; ✻≋; 🄢1 to 103rd St) This red-brick mansion from the 1880s houses HI's 672 well-scrubbed bunks. It's rather 19th-century industrial, but benefits include good public areas, a backyard (that sees barbecue action in the summer), a communal kitchen and a cafe. There are loads of activities on offer, from walking tours to club nights. There are attractive private rooms with private bathrooms, too. The hostel is alcohol-free. Wi-fi throughout the building.

HOTEL BEACON   HOTEL $$

Map p436 (☎212-787-1100, reservations 800-572-4969; www.beaconhotel.com; 2130 Broadway, btwn 74th & 75th Sts; d from $315; ≋▥; 🄢1/2/3 to 72nd St) Adjacent to the Beacon Theatre (p243), this family favorite offers a winning mix of attentive service, comfortable rooms and convenient location. The

Beacon has 260 units (including one- and two-bedroom suites) decorated in muted shades of Pottery Barn green. The units are well-maintained and quite roomy – and all come with coffee makers and kitchenettes.

Upper stories have views of Central Park in the distance. A good deal.

HOTEL NEWTON   HOTEL $$

Map p436 (☎212-678-6500; www.thehotelnewton.com; 2528 Broadway, btwn 94th & 95th Sts; d from $210; ✻≋; 🄢1/2/3 to 96th St) The nine-story Newton isn't going to win any interior-design awards, but it's clean and managed well, making it a solid budget option. The 110 guest rooms are small but tidy, and come stocked with TVs, mini-refrigerators, coffee makers and microwaves. The bathrooms are all well-maintained. Larger 'suites' are roomier and feature a sitting area. Wi-fi costs extra.

LUCERNE   HOTEL $$

Map p436 (☎212-875-1000; www.thelucernehotel.com; 201 W 79th St, cnr Amsterdam Ave; d from $281; ✻≋▥; 🄢B, C to 81st St) This unusual 1903 structure breaks away from beaux arts in favor of the baroque with an ornately carved, terra-cotta-colored facade. Inside is a stately 200-room hotel, ideal for couples and families with children (Central Park and the American Museum of Natural History are a stone's throw away). Nine types of guest rooms evoke a contemporary Victorian look.

Think: flowered bedspreads, scrolled headboards and plush pillows with fringe. Service is courteous and there is a nice French-Mediterranean restaurant on-site.

YMCA   HOSTEL $$

Map p436 (☎212-912-2625; www.ymcanyc.org; 5 W 63rd St, at Central Park West; d $210, tr/q with shared bath from $170/180; ✻@≋▥; 🄢A/C, B/D to 59th St-Columbus Circle) Just steps from Central Park, this grand art-deco building has several floors – 8th to the 13th – of basic, but clean, rooms. Guests have access to extensive, but old-school, gym, racquetball courts, pool and sauna. There's wi-fi on the ground floor. Four other YMCAs in town offer accommodation, including branches in Midtown, the Upper East Side and Harlem.

NYLO HOTEL
BOUTIQUE HOTEL $$$

Map p436 (📞212-362-1100; www.nylo-nyc.com; 2178 Broadway, at 77th St; r from $285; ❄️🛜; 🚇1 to 77th St) This modern boutique hotel has 285 casually stylish rooms with warm earth tones. Niceties include plush bedding, wood floors, elegant lighting, roomy (for New York) bathrooms, coffee makers and flat-screen TVs. 'NYLO Panoramic' rooms have furnished private terraces and extravagant Manhattan views. The handsomely designed lounge and bar areas on the ground floor are great places to decamp after a day spent exploring. Friendly service and a great location.

EMPIRE HOTEL
HOTEL $$$

Map p436 (📞212-265-7400; www.empirehotelnyc.com; 44 W 63rd St, at Broadway; r from $370; ❄️🛜🏊; 🚇1 to 66th St-Lincoln Center) If you're in town for culture, you can't beat this location, just across the street from the Lincoln Center. This old hotel was remade a few years back, complete with canopied pool deck, sexy rooftop bar and a dimly lit lobby lounge studded with zebra-print settees. The 400-plus rooms come in various configurations, and feature brightly-hued walls with plush dark leather furnishings.

🛏 Harlem & Upper Manhattan

Harlem is home to a handful of satisfying slumber options, including graceful guesthouses in historic townhouses.

HARLEM FLOPHOUSE
GUESTHOUSE $

Map p438 (📞212-662-0678; www.harlemflophouse.com; 242 W 123rd St, btwn Adam Clayton Powell Jr & Frederick Douglass Blvds, Harlem; r with shared bath from $125; 🛜; 🚇A/B/C/D, 2/3 to 124th St) Rekindle Harlem's Jazz Age in this 1890s townhouse, its nostalgic rooms decked out in brass beds, polished wood floors and vintage radios (set to a local jazz station). It feels like a delicious step back in time, which also means shared bathrooms, no air-con and no TVs. The owner is a great source of local information, and his indie rock band rehearses at the property during off-hours. Last but not least is friendly house cat Phoebe, who completes the homely, welcoming vibe.

ALOFT HARLEM
HOTEL $$

Map p438 (📞212-749-4000; www.aloftharlem.com; 2296 Frederick Douglass Blvd, btwn 123rd & 124th Sts, Harlem; d from $235; ❄️🛜; 🚇A/C, B/D, 2/3 to 125th St) Designed for younger travelers, Aloft channels a W Hotel vibe but at a far cheaper price. Guest rooms are snug (285 sq ft) but chic, with crisp white linens, fluffy comforters and colorful, striped bolsters. The modern bathrooms are small (no tubs), but are highly functional and feature amenities courtesy of Bliss.

A basement lounge with pool tables can get boisterous, but it'll be stumbling distance to your room. All around, it's convenient (the Apollo Theater and the bustling 125th St commercial district are nearby) and a good deal.

ALLIE'S INN
B&B $$

Map p438 (📞646-283-3068, 212-690-3813; www.alliesinn.com; 313 W 136th St, btwn Frederick Douglass Blvd & Edgecombe Ave, Harlem; r from $175; ❄️🛜; 🚇A/C, B to 135th St) This Harlem charmer has just three guest rooms, all clean and comfortable, with oak floors, simple modern furnishings and small kitchen units. It's a refreshing alternative to the Midtown towers and ideal for those wanting to explore Harlem's rich culture. There's a growing number of notable eateries and bars in the neighborhood, and the subway station is just around the corner. Minimum two-night stay.

102 BROWNSTONE
HOTEL $$

Map p438 (📞212-222-1212; www.102brownstone.com; 102 W 118th St, btwn Malcolm X & Adam Clayton Powell Jr Blvds, Harlem; r from $157; ❄️🛜; 🚇A/C, B, 2/3 to 116th St) This intimate five-room guesthouse is a charming and convenient spot for travelers who want to explore the city but come to a little peace and quiet at the end of the day. All of the units have antique-style furnishings, private bathrooms and mini-fridges. The Zen suite – decorated in lemony tones – has a full kitchen and a Jacuzzi bath.

MOUNT MORRIS HOUSE B&B
GUESTHOUSE $$

Map p438 (📞917-478-6213; www.mountmorrishousebandb.com; 12 Mt Morris Park W, btwn 121st & 122nd Sts, Harlem; ste/apt from $175/225; ❄️🛜; 🚇2/3 to 116th St) Set inside a stunning Gilded Age townhouse from 1888, this cozy inn offers four extravagantly spacious slumber options: a one-bedroom suite, a two-bedroom suite and a studio apartment with a fully equipped kitchen. Each one impresses with period-style furnishings, including four-poster beds, Persian-style rugs and brocaded settees, not to mention fireplaces and vintage bathtubs. Breakfast isn't offered, though complimentary coffee, tea and cakes are available all day.

The property is an easy walk to 125th St. Cash preferred.

LA MAISON D'ART GUESTHOUSE **$$**

Map p438 (☎718-593-4108; www.lamaisondartny.com; 259 W 132nd St, btwn Adam Clayton & Frederick Douglas Blvds, Harlem; r from $183; ❄📶; [S]2/3 to 135th St) Situated above an art gallery, this welcoming Harlem abode harbors five comfy rooms bursting with character. Each has unique features, ranging from antiques and a four-poster bed to an oversize Jacuzzi bath (the lilac-painted walls and gold curtains in the Victorian room may not be everyone's cup of tea). Adding delight is a garden out back, perfect for some low-key R&R.

It's in a classic Harlem brownstone, with decent eating and drinking options in the area. It's also an easy subway ride to Midtown and other Manhattan neighborhoods.

SUGAR HILL HARLEM B&B **$$**

Map p438 (☎212-234-5432; www.sugarhillharleminn.com; 460 W 141st St, btwn Amsterdam & Convent Aves, Sugar Hill; r from $156; ❄📶; [S]A/C, B/D to 145th St) The suites at this airy, turn-of-the-century townhouse are named after African American jazz greats. All are well-appointed, with antique-style furnishings and private bathroom (not necessarily en suite). Most have ample bay windows, while a couple also come equipped with kitchens. A few additional guest rooms are located in a second renovated townhouse around the corner on Convent Ave.

While the three-level building lacks an elevator, it makes amends with its soothing garden.

Brooklyn

A short train ride across the East River and you'll find bigger and (sometimes) brighter rooms – and a lot more bang for your buck.

Note: Brooklyn is more than 70 sq miles and transport within the borough can be a challenge, so pick an area (north or south) that offers the best proximity to the sights you want to see.

★NEW YORK LOFT HOSTEL HOSTEL **$**

Map p440 (☎718-366-1351; www.nylofthostel.com; 249 Varet St, btwn Bogart & White Sts, Bushwick; dm $40-85, d $140; ❄[@]📶; [S]L to Morgan Ave) This renovated 1913 warehouse building in Bushwick is a good choice for urban pioneers. It has spacious, brick-lined dorms, with two or three beds in each. Amenities include a communal kitchen, a large patio area with picnic tables and a small terrace. With loads of activities on offer – outdoor barbecues, film screenings, bar crawls – this is a great place to meet other travelers.

It's not the prettiest part of Brooklyn, but there are plenty of good restaurants and bars nearby. A good place to get your hipster on.

★WYTHE HOTEL BOUTIQUE HOTEL **$$**

Map p440 (☎718-460-8000; wythehotel.com; 80 Wythe Ave, at N 11th St, Williamsburg; r from $325; ❄📶; [S]L to Bedford Ave; G to Nassau Ave) Set in a converted 1901 factory, the red-brick Wythe Hotel brings a serious dash of style to Williamsburg. The industrial-chic rooms have beds made from reclaimed lumber, custom-made wallpaper (from Brooklyn's own Flavor Paper), exposed brick, polished concrete floors and original 13ft timber ceilings.

On the ground floor, Reynard dishes up brasserie classics in a lovely setting of tile floors, brick walls, soaring wood ceilings and vintage fixtures. The top-floor Ides Bar is a great spot for sunset cocktails, craft brews and memorable skyline views of Manhattan.

MCCARREN HOTEL & POOL BOUTIQUE HOTEL **$$**

Map p440 (☎718-218-7500; www.chelseahotels.com; 160 N 12th St, btwn Bedford Ave & Berry St, Williamsburg; d from $255; ❄📶🏊; [S]L to Bedford; G to Nassau) This hipster hotel on the fringes of Williamsburg is insufferably chic, offering minimalist rooms with bamboo flooring and marble-filled bathrooms. Pricier rooms have balconies and rain showers. The large saltwater pool is surrounded by design-conscious loungers, while the upper-level bar and lounge with retractable rooftop offers jaw-dropping views of Manhattan.

It also has an appealing fern- and animal-portrait-filled restaurant (Oleanders) and free bicycles for guests.

BLUE PORCH B&B $$

Map p444 (☎718-434-0557; www.blueporchnyc.com; 15 DeKoven Court, at Foster Ave & Rugby Rd, Ditmas Park; r from $176; 📶; [S]B/Q to Newkirk Ave) A lovely 1904 Victorian with two bright, airy guest rooms is located in the sleepy district of Ditmas Park (south of Prospect Park). The bathrooms are beautifully kept, the rooms have polished wood floors and the continental breakfasts are generous. It's a good deal if you don't mind the 40-minute trip into Manhattan. A two-night minimum is required.

BOX HOUSE HOTEL HOTEL $$

Map p440 (☎718-383-3800; www.theboxhousehotel.com; 77 Box St, at McGuinness Blvd, Greenpoint; d from $300; ❄📶; [S]7 to Vernon Blvd-Jackson Ave; G to Greenpoint Ave) In an industrial stretch of North Brooklyn, this hotel has inviting lofts with oak floors, 16ft ceilings, oversized windows, and vintage furnishings and decorations. Each loft has a lounge (and full-sized pull-out sofa) and kitchen on the main level, and a sleeping area (queen-sized bed) upstairs. The price is steep for the area, but you get a lot of space for your money – making it good for small groups.

The immediate surroundings are a bit of a wasteland, but it's a 15-minute walk to the buzzing eateries and drinkeries of Greenpoint. Free shuttle service in a 1970s taxi cab is a bonus. Discounted deals for extended weekend (three-night) stays.

SERENITY AT HOME B&B $$

Map p444 (☎646-479-5138; www.serenityah.com; 57 Rutland Rd, btwn Bedford & Flatbush Aves; r with shared/private bathroom for 3 nights from $250/430; ❄📶; [S]B, Q, S to Prospect Park) A short stroll from Prospect Park in Brooklyn, this charming guesthouse is set in a lovely pre-war row house. Each of four guestrooms has wooden floors, attractive furnishings and high-quality mattresses and bedding. Note that three rooms share bathrooms, while there's one spacious room with its own private bathroom (boasting a clawfoot tub no less).

Zenobia, the owner, makes guests feel right at home, and has loads of useful advice for exploring the neighborhood and the city beyond. Minimum three-night stay.

AKWAABA MANSION INN B&B $$

Map p442 (☎718-455-5958, 866-466-3855; www.akwaaba.com; 347 MacDonough St, btwn Lewis & Stuyvesant Aves, Bedford-Stuyvesant; r $195-225; ❄📶; [S]A/C to Utica Ave) Sitting on a tree-lined block of tidy, century-old townhouses in Bedford-Stuyvesant, this graceful B&B is tucked into a sprawling mansion built by a local beer baron back in 1860. Period design flourishes include brass beds, marble fireplaces, the original parquet floors and a screened-in wraparound porch – the perfect spot to settle in with a good book.

African textiles and vintage photographs add a personal touch. The mansion has four roomy suites, each with private bathroom, while a couple of the units have Jacuzzi tubs for two.

★3B B&B $$

Map p446 (☎347-762-2632; www.3bbrooklyn.com; 136 Lawrence St, Brooklyn; d with shared bathroom $184; ❄📶; [S]A/C, F, R to Jay St-Metro Tech) 🍃 The 3rd-floor unit of this downtown Brooklyn brownstone has been turned into a bright and contemporary four-room B&B. It has high ceilings, wood floors and comfy furnishings. On the downside: all rooms share bathroom facilities (one full bathroom and one half bathroom), and street noise may be a problem for light sleepers.

It's in a central downtown Brooklyn location, within easy walking distance of Fort Greene, Carroll Gardens or Brooklyn Heights. Hosts are friendly and eco-minded, with 100% of electricity supplied by wind energy. Good breakfasts.

NU HOTEL HOTEL $$

Map p446 (☎718-852-8585; www.nuhotelbrooklyn.com; 85 Smith St; d from $280; ❄@📶; [S]F, G to Bergen St) The 93 rooms in this downtown Brooklyn hotel are of the stripped-down variety, featuring lots of crisp whiteness (sheets, walls, duvets). Furnishings are made from recycled teak and the floors are cork. For something more daring, book a Nu Perspectives room, adorned with colorful murals by Brooklyn artists.

There is a small lounge and bikes are available. Ask for a room away from busy Atlantic Ave if you are a light sleeper.

ALOFT NEW YORK BROOKLYN

BOUTIQUE HOTEL $$

Map p446 (☑718-256-3833; www.aloftnewyork-brooklyn.com; 216 Duffield St, btwn Willoughby & Fulton Sts; d from $320; ※☎❄; Ⓢ2 to Hoyt St) A cheery, modern boutique-y spot in downtown, Aloft is walking distance from the sights in Cobble Hill and Carroll Gardens. Its 176 rooms are simple and cozy, with 9ft ceilings, minimalist furnishings, bright pillows and plenty of wood trim. Bathroom amenities are by Bliss. But the best feature is the dizzying rooftop beer garden that is open till 2am on weekends.

HENRY NORMAN

BOUTIQUE HOTEL $$$

Map p440 (☑718-951-6000; www.henrynorman-hotel.com; 251 N Henry St, btwn Norman & Meserole Aves; d from $354; ※☎; ⓈG to Nassau Ave) Set in a former 19th-century warehouse, this striking brick building (once home to artists' lofts) offers bohemian chic in its high-ceilinged rooms. Each has hardwood floors, muted color schemes (decorated in white and gray), artwork on the walls and iPod docking stations. Pricier rooms have terraces and better-equipped kitchenettes.

It's on an industrial stretch of roadway, but the hipster bars, shops and cafes of Greenpoint are about a 15-minute walk away. Or take the complimentary shuttle service to avoid the bleak cityscape.

🛏 Queens

This sprawling borough still lags behind Manhattan and Brooklyn in terms of boutique and B&B charmers, but a rash of new hotels in Long Island City offer killer views of Manhattan and easy access to Midtown. They are mostly chains, with a few independents, and all can offer some excellent deals.

★ TRUCK-A-FLOAT

CABIN $

(www.truckafloat.com; 59-14 Beach Channel Dr, Rockaway Beach; r weekday/weekend $75/110; ⓈA to Beach 60th St) 🅿 Four shipshape little cabins, creatively designed and topped with fiberglass truck covers, are moored in a marina – think glamping, but bobbing on the water. (Bathrooms are down the pier at the marina office.) The cabins look onto the bay, for a cool urban-wild view of bird life and airplanes; the beach is a 20-minute walk across the barrier island.

LOCAL NYC

HOSTEL $

Map p448 (☑347-738-5251; www.thelocalny.com; 13-02 44th Ave, Long Island City; dm/d from $58/159; ※☎; ⒺE, M to Court Sq-23rd St) This hostel has clean and small, simply designed rooms, with comfy mattresses and plenty of natural light. The airy cafe-bar is a fine place to meet other travelers, with good coffees by day, and wine and beer by night. Throughout the week, there's a regular line-up of events (movie nights, live music, pub quizzes).

Friendly staff are helpful in highlighting some of NYC's lesser-known gems. Don't miss the view from the rooftop.

PLAYLAND MOTEL

DESIGN HOTEL $

(☑347-954-9063; www.playlandmotel.com; 97-20 Rockaway Beach Blvd, Rockaway Beach; d with shared/private bathroom from $80/152; ※☎; ⓈA, S to Beach 98th St) This creative confection in the Rockaways features 12 wild rooms, each designed by a Brooklyn artist. The beds are comfy, but the bathrooms are communal (unless you book the suite). There's a lively bar on site, with DJs and creative cocktails. Bring earplugs if you plan to actually *sleep* here during the rowdy summer season.

The location is best for a dedicated beach party within city limits; it's a *looong* commute to Manhattan (at least an hour on the subway).

BORO HOTEL

DESIGN HOTEL $$

Map p448 (☑718-433-1375; www.borohotel.com; 38-28 27th St, Long Island City; r from $299; 🅿※☎❄; ⒺN/Q to 39th Ave) The Boro offers minimalist city luxe (Frette linens, plush robes, soaking tubs) for far less than you'd pay in Manhattan – with the benefit of glittering skyline views from the floor-to-ceiling windows. The hyper-minimalist, wood-floor rooms have high ceilings; many have expansive balconies. Continental breakfast is better than average, with flaky croissants and Greek yogurt.

PAPER FACTORY HOTEL

HOTEL $$

Map p448 (☑718-392-7200; www.thepaperfactoryhotel.com; 37-06 36th St, Long Island City; d from $199; ※☎; ⒺM, R to 36th St) In the buzzing, semi-industrial neighborhood of Long Island City, you'll find this whimsical gem. It's set in a former paper factory and warehouse, and its 123 rooms and appealing common areas evoke industrial chic. Reclaimed lumber and polished concrete (with vintage maps embedded in the floors) feature prominently in the lobby, and there's a smattering of artwork and artfully displayed old machine parts throughout the hotel.

The rooms themselves continue the vintage aesthetic, albeit with comfy modern beds, good showers and big-city views. The 12ft ceilings and large windows add to the spacious feel, and locally created artwork and old-fashioned furniture make each room feel unique. The graffiti-stained rooftop has entrancing views of Manhattan, and the in-house restaurant, Mundo, serves eclectic global fare.

Z HOTEL BOUTIQUE HOTEL $$

Map p448 (☎212-319-7000, 877-256-5556; www.zhotelny.com; 11-01 43rd Ave, Long Island City; r from $225; ❄📶; [S]F to 21st-Queensbridge; E, M to Court Sq-23rd St) Its location screams 'industrial wasteland,' but this design-savvy tower delivers jaw-dropping views of Manhattan. The 100 rooms are snug but stylish, in dark, contemporary shades. More astounding views (and a pizza oven) await at the rooftop bar, while the downstairs restaurant is a salt-of-the-earth combo of American comfort food and Sunday football games. One drawback is the chilly exterior hallway.

Freebies include wi-fi, local and international calls, and bike rental. Bargain room rates may be available online.

Understand New York City

New York City Today

With almost 60 million smitten visitors pouring into the city each year, New York remains a mighty force to be reckoned with. Statement architecture is reinvigorating the skyline, while ambitious greenhouse targets attest to a city determined to build a cleaner, greener future. Yet, like any metropolis, the world's 'can-do' capital is not without its challenges, from rising crime rates to social harmony in the Age of Terror.

Best on Film

Annie Hall (1977) Oscar-winning romantic comedy by the king of New York neuroses, Woody Allen.

Manhattan (1979) Allen's at it again with tales of twisted love set among NYC's concrete landscape.

Taxi Driver (1976) Martin Scorsese's tale of a troubled Vietnam vet turned taxi driver.

Requiem for a Dream (2000) An unusual tale of a Brooklyn junkie and his doting Jewish mother.

The Wolf of Wall St (2013) Leonardo DiCaprio depicts the breathtaking rise and fall of a notorious NYC stockbroker.

Best in Print

The Amazing Adventures of Kavalier & Clay (Michael Chabon; 2000) Beloved Pulitzer Prize–winning novel that touches upon Brooklyn, escapism and the nuclear family.

10:04 (Ben Lerner; 2014) Rising star Lerner tells the story of a New York City novelist juggling work, life, art and a heart condition that could prove deadly.

A Tree Grows in Brooklyn (Betty Smith; 1943) An Irish American family living in the Williamsburg tenements at the beginning of the 20th century.

Down These Mean Streets (Piri Thomas; 1967) Memoirs of tough times growing up in Spanish Harlem.

Seasoned Tolerance

Following the 2015 terrorist attacks in Paris and California, city authorities took swift action to engage NYC's 800,000-strong Muslim community, many of whom feared becoming victims of Islamophobic hate crimes. A meeting between the New York Police Department (NYPD) and 40 (mostly Muslim) community leaders was organized six days after the November 13 Paris atrocity to foster greater trust between Muslim New Yorkers and law enforcement officers. Two days after the December 2 attack in San Bernardino, California, mayor Bill de Blasio addressed a crowd at the Jamaica Muslim Center (Masjid Al-Mamoor) in Queens, re-enforcing his promise to robustly investigate any hate-related crimes committed against Muslims in NYC. Despite concerns about an anti-Muslim backlash, the number of incidents reported to the Hate Crime Task Force actually fell by 43% between 2014 and 2015 according to the NYPD, indicating the city's seasoned tolerance is far from dead.

De Blasio Blues

According to a *Wall Street Journal*–NBC4 New York–Marist poll taken in late 2015, mayor Bill de Blasio's approval rating slid from 44% in the spring to just 38% in the fall, suggesting the love affair between de Blasio and NYC could be on the rocks. The swing was especially significant among black voters, among whom his approval rating tumbled from 59% to 50% in the same period. White voters are even less impressed according to a poll by the *New York Times* and Siena College, which declared their support for the mayor to be just 28% in late 2015. Some detractors argue that the city's two-year rise in gun crime (the first increase in almost two decades) reflects de Blasio's 'soft' stance on law enforcement. The Democrat is a prolific critic of the 'stop and frisk' policy supported by former mayor Michael Bloomberg, which allows police officers to randomly stop, question, and search citizens. In early December 2014, de Blasio openly criticized a grand jury decision not to indict NYPD officer Daniel Pantaleo for the July 17 death of Eric Garner, a ruling that sparked anti-police protests across the country. When, in late December 2014, two NYPD officers were shot, execution-style, by a man who had posted anti-police comments on social media, police union president Patrick Lynch blamed City Hall for condoning anti-police sentiments. Despite widespread criticism of Lynch's comment, hundreds of NYPD officers turned their backs on de Blasio at one of the slain officer's funeral.

Clean & Green

Never one to take things lying down, NYC is fighting climate change with impressive fervor. The city's current goal is to slash citywide greenhouse gas emissions 80% below 2005 levels by 2050. The goal compliments de Blasio's 'One City, Built to Last', a scheme in which 3000 city-owned buildings will be upgraded with more efficient power, cooling and heating systems by 2025. Private buildings will be given ambitious target reductions, which, if not met voluntarily, will be followed by mandated reductions. Given around three-quarters of NYC's total greenhouse gases are produced by buildings, the program will go a long way to meeting the 2050 targets. De Blasio's recent commitments build on the original New York City Carbon Challenge launched by his predecessor, Michael Bloomberg. Kick-started in 2007, the program encouraged universities, businesses and other private bodies to slash their greenhouse gas emissions by 30% in 10 years.

Thin Is In

New York's Midtown skyline is undergoing an upgrade thanks to a new wave of pencil-thin, super-tall towers. Mostly residential, these architecture supermodels include recently completed 432 Park Ave, a 1396ft-tall, elongated cube tower designed by Uruguayan architect Rafael Viñoly. Currently NYC's tallest building to roof level, it will be superceded by 1522ft Central Park Tower (aka Nordstrom Tower) in 2019. The latter's total height will reach 1550ft, making it the world's tallest residential building both by both roof and total architectural height. The building – located at 225 W 57th St – is the work of Chicago-based firm Adrian Smith + Gordon Gill Architecture (AS+GG), the team behind the record-breaking, kilometer-high Jeddah Tower currently under construction in Saudi Arabia. Just up the street from Central Park Tower, the 1438ft-tall 111 W 57th St condominium will take slender to a whole new level with a width-to-height ratio of 1:24, which will make it the city's skinniest show pony. The most spectacular newcomer, however, will arguably be 53W53 at 53 West 53rd, a mixed-use tower designed by French architect Jean Nouvel with a head-turning, skeletal form.

population per sq mile

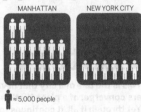

MANHATTAN   NEW YORK CITY

👤 ≈ 5,000 people

housing

(% of population)

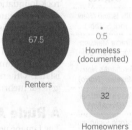

67.5
Renters

0.5
Homeless (documented)

32
Homeowners

if New York City were 100 people

34 would be Caucasian
28 would be Hispanic/Latino
23 would be African American
13 would be Asian
2 would be other

History

This is the tale of a city that never sleeps, of a kingdom where tycoons and world leaders converge, of a place that's seen the highest highs and the most devastating lows. Yet through it all, it continues to reach for the sky (both figuratively and literally). And to think it all started with $24 and a pile of beads...

Living Off The Land

Long before the days of European conquest, the swath that would eventually become NYC belonged to Native Americans known as the Lenape – 'original people' – who resided in a series of seasonal campsites. They lived up and down the eastern seaboard, along the signature shoreline, and on hills and in valleys sculpted by glaciers after the Ice Age left New York with glacial debris now called Hamilton Heights and Bay Ridge. Glaciers scoured off soft rock, leaving behind Manhattan's stark rock foundations of gneiss and schist. Around 11,000 years before the first Europeans sailed through the Narrows, the Lenape people foraged, hunted and fished the regional bounty here. Spear points, arrowheads, bone heaps and shell mounds testify to their presence. Some of their pathways still lie beneath streets such as Broadway. In the Lenape language of Munsee, the term Manhattan may have translated as 'hilly island.' Others trace the meaning to a more colorful phrase: 'place of general inebriation.'

> **NYC's Top Historical Sights**
> ....
> Ellis Island (New York Harbor)
> ....
> Gracie Mansion (Upper East Side)
> ....
> Merchant's House Museum (NoHo)
> ....
> Jane's Carousel (Brooklyn)
> ....
> Historic Richmond Town (Staten Island)

A Rude Awakening

The Lenape people lived undisturbed until European explorers muscled in, firstly by way of the French vessel *La Dauphine*, piloted by Florentine explorer Giovanni da Verrazano. He explored the Upper Bay in 1524, deemed it a 'very beautiful lake,' and, while anchored at Staten Island, attempted to kidnap some of the Native Americans he encountered. This began several decades of European explorers raiding Lenape villages, and cultivated the Lenape's deep mistrust of outsiders. By the time the Dutch West India Company employee Henry Hudson arrived

TIMELINE	c AD 1500	1625–26	1646
	About 15,000 Native Americans live in 80 sites around the island. The groups include the feuding Iroquois and Algonquins.	As the population of New Amsterdam reaches 200, the Dutch West India Company imports slaves from Africa to work in the fur trade and construction.	The Dutch found the village of Breuckelen on the East River shore of Long Island, naming it after Breukelen in the Netherlands; it will remain an independent city until 1898.

in 1609, encounters with Native Americans were often dichotomized into two crude stories that alternated between 'delightful primitives' and 'brutal savages.'

Buying Manhattan

The Dutch West India Company sent 110 settlers to begin a trading post here in 1624. They settled in Lower Manhattan and called their colony New Amsterdam, touching off bloody battles with the unshakable Lenape. It all came to a head in 1626, when the colony's first governor, Peter Minuit, became the city's first – but certainly not the last – unscrupulous real estate agent, purchasing Manhattan's 14,000 acres from the Lenape for 60 guilders ($24) and some glass beads.

Peg Leg, Iron Fist

Following the purchase of Manhattan in 1626, the colony quickly fell into disrepair under the governance of Willem Kieft. Then Peter Stuyvesant stepped in and busily set about fixing the demoralized settlement, making peace with the Lenape, establishing markets and a night watch, repairing the fort, digging a canal (under the current Canal St) and authorizing a municipal wharf. His vision of an orderly and prosperous trading port was partially derived from his previous experience as governor of Curaçao. The burgeoning sugar economy in the Caribbean inspired an investment in slave trading that soon boosted New Amsterdam's slave workforce to 20% of the population. After long service, some were partially freed and given 'Negroe Lots' near today's Greenwich Village, the Lower East Side and City Hall. The Dutch West India Company encouraged the fruitful connection to plantation economies on the islands, and issued advertisements and offered privileges to attract merchants to the growing port. Although these 'liberties' did not at first extend to the Jews who fled the Spanish Inquisition, the Dutch West India Company turned Stuyvesant's intolerance around. By the 1650s, warehouses, workshops and gabled houses were spreading back from the dense establishments at the river's edge on Pearl St.

By 1664, the English showed up in battleships, ready for a fight. Stuyvesant was tired, though, and avoided bloodshed by surrendering without a shot. King Charles II promptly renamed the colony after his brother, the Duke of York. New York became a prosperous British port with a population of 11,000 by the mid-1700s. The city grew in prominence as the change point for the exchange of slaves and goods between worlds. The honeymoon, however, was short-lived.

NYC Names & their Dutch Origins

Gramercy: Kromme Zee ('crooked lake')

Coney Island: Konijneneiland ('rabbits island')

Yonkers: jonker ('squire')

Bowery: bouwerij (old-fashioned word for 'farm')

Bronx: named for Jonas Bronck

1754	1776	1789	1791
The first institution of higher learning, King's College, is founded by royal charter from George II. After the American Revolution, it's reborn as Columbia University.	American colonies sign the *Declaration of Independence* on July 4. Figures who helped create this document include John Hancock, Samuel Adams and Benjamin Franklin.	Following a seven-day procession from his home in Mount Vernon, George Washington is inaugurated at Federal Hall as the country's first president.	*Bill of Rights* adopted as constitutional amendments articulating citizen's rights including free speech, religion and the press; and the right to bear arms.

Freedom of the Press & the Great Negro Plot

New York City was the first capital of the United States – George Washington took his first presidential oath at Federal Hall in 1789.

Rising tensions were evident in the colonial press, as John Peter Zenger's *New York Weekly Journal* flayed the king and royal governor so regularly that the authorities tried to convict Zenger for seditious libel in 1733. He was acquitted and that was the beginning of what we know today as 'freedom of the press.'

In 1741, a spate of fires occurred across the city, including one at Fort George, then home of Lieutenant Governor George Clarke. The blazes were widely blamed on African American slaves, and rumors quickly spread of a planned rebellion by blacks and poorer white settlers to burn down New York City. Despite contradictory accounts and a lack of solid evidence, the so-called Great Negro Plot led to the arrest and execution of numerous slaves and their alleged conspirators.

Revolution & War

Patriots clashed in public spaces with Tories, who were loyal to the king, while Lieutenant Colonel Alexander Hamilton, an intellectual, became a fierce anti-British organizer. Citizens fled the city, sensing the oncoming war, and revolutionary battle began in August of 1776, when General George Washington's army lost about a quarter of its men in just a couple of days. He retreated, and fire encompassed much of the colony. But soon the British left and Washington's army reclaimed their city. After a series of celebrations, banquets and fireworks at Bowling Green, General Washington bade farewell to his officers at what is now the Fraunces Tavern Museum and retired as commander-in-chief.

On December 16, 1835, a gas line broke in a dry-goods store near Hanover Square, causing a massive fire to quickly spread south down Stone St and northeast toward Wall St. Raging for over a day, it destroyed much of what remained of the original Dutch and British colonial city.

However, in 1789, to his surprise, the retired general found himself addressing crowds at Federal Hall, gathered to witness his presidential inauguration. Alexander Hamilton, meanwhile, began rebuilding New York and became Washington's secretary of the treasury, working to establish the New York Stock Exchange. But people distrusted a capitol located adjacent to the financial power of Wall St merchants, and New York lost the seat of the presidency to Philadelphia shortly thereafter.

Population Bust, Infrastructure Boom

The 19th century brought with it plenty of setbacks: the bloody Draft Riots of 1863, massive cholera epidemics, rising tensions among 'old' and new immigrants, and the serious poverty and crime of Five Points, the city's first slum, located where Chinatown now lies. Eventually, though, the city was prosperous and found resources to build mighty public works. A great aqueduct system brought Croton Water to city

1811	1825	1853	1863
Manhattan's grid plan is developed by Mayor DeWitt Clinton, which leads to reshaping the city by leveling hills, filling in swamps and laying out plans for future streets.	The Erie Canal, considered one of the greatest engineering feats of the era, is ceremoniously completed, greatly influencing trade and commerce in New York.	The State Legislature authorizes the allotment of public lands, which removes 17,000 potential building sites from the real-estate market for what will later become Central Park.	The Civil War Draft Riots erupt in New York, lasting for three days and ending only when President Lincoln dispatches combat troops from the Federal Army to restore order.

dwellers, relieving thirst and stamping out the cholera that was sweeping the town. Irish immigrants helped dig a 363-mile 'ditch' – the Erie Canal – linking the Hudson River with Lake Erie. The canal's chief backer, Mayor DeWitt Clinton, celebrated the waterway by ceremonially pouring a barrel of Erie water into the sea. Clinton was also the mastermind behind the modern-day grid system of Manhattan's street layout – a plan created by his commission to organize the city in the face of an oncoming population explosion.

And there was yet another grand project afoot – one to boost the health of the people crammed into tiny tenement apartments – in the form of an 843-acre public park. Begun in 1855 in an area so far uptown that some immigrants kept pigs, sheep and goats there, Central Park was both a vision of green reform and a boon to real-estate speculation.

Another vision was realized by German-born engineer John Roebling, who sought a solution to a series of winter freezes that had shut down the ferry system connecting downtown Manhattan to Brooklyn, then an independent city. He designed a soaring symphony of spun wire and Gothic arches to span the East River, and his Brooklyn Bridge accelerated the fusion of the neighboring cities.

By the turn of the 20th century, elevated trains carried one million people a day in and out of the city. Rapid transit opened up areas of the Bronx and Upper Manhattan, spurring mini building booms in areas near the lines. At this point, the city was simply overflowing with the masses of immigrants arriving from southern Italy and Eastern Europe, who had boosted the metropolis's population to around three million. The journey from immigrant landing stations at Castle Garden and Ellis Island led straight to the Lower East Side. There, streets reflected these myriad origins with shop signs in Yiddish, Italian, German and Chinese.

Class Lessons

All sorts of folks were living in squalor by the late 19th century, when the immigration processing center at Ellis Island opened, welcoming one million newcomers in just its first year. They crammed into packed tenements, shivered in soup lines and shoveled snow for nickels.

Meanwhile, newly wealthy folks – boosted by an economy jump-started by financier JP Morgan, who bailed out sinking railroads and led to the city becoming the headquarters of Standard Oil and US Steel – began to build increasingly splendid mansions on Fifth Ave. Modeled on European chateaux, palaces such as the Vanderbilt home, on the corner of 52nd St and Fifth Ave, reached for new summits of opulence. Tapestries adorned marble halls, mirrored ballrooms reflected bejeweled

HISTORY CLASS LESSONS

New York's Brooklyn Bridge opened with suitable fanfare on May 24, 1883. After New York mayor Franklin Edison and Brooklyn mayor Seth Low led President Chester Arthur and Governor Grover Cleveland across the structure, more than 150,000 members of the public followed suit, each paying a penny for the honor.

1870	1882	1883	1886
After four years of lobbying for a national institution of art by a civic group led by lawyer John Jay, New York City's Metropolitan Museum of Art is founded.	Thomas Edison switches on the city's first electric lights at the JP Morgan bank at 23 Wall St. On the same November day, electricity is delivered to 85 Manhattan addresses.	The Brooklyn Bridge, which was built at a cost of $15.5 million (and 27 lives), opens; 150,000 people walk across its span at the inaugural celebration.	The Statue of Liberty's pedestal is completed, allowing the large lady to be presented to New York at a dedication ceremony that takes place before thousands of citizens.

revelers, and liveried footmen guided grand ladies from their gilded carriages in a society where Astors, Fricks and Carnegies ruled. Reporter and photographer Jacob Riis illuminated the widening gap between the classes by writing about it in the *New York Tribune* and in his now-classic 1890 book, *How the Other Half Lives,* eventually forcing the city to pass much-needed housing reforms.

Factory Tragedy, Women's Rights

Wretched factory conditions – low pay, long hours, abusive employers – in the early 20th century were highlighted by a tragic event in 1911. The infamous Triangle Shirtwaist Company fire saw rapidly spreading flames catch onto the factory's piles of fabrics, killing 146 of 500 female workers who were trapped behind locked doors. The event led to sweeping labor reforms after 20,000 female garment workers marched to City Hall. At the same time, suffragists held street-corner rallies to obtain the vote for women. Nurse and midwife Margaret Sanger opened the first birth-control clinic in Brooklyn, where 'purity police' promptly arrested her. After her release from jail in 1921, she formed the American Birth Control League (now Planned Parenthood), which provided services for young women and researched methods of safe birth control.

Forgotten-NY.com is Queens native Kevin Walsh's compendium of historical NYC, with not-found-elsewhere tales about everything from old subway stations to cemeteries.

The Jazz Age

The 1920s saw the dawning of the Jazz Age, when Prohibition outlawed the sale of alcohol, encouraging bootlegging and speakeasies, as well as organized crime. Congenial mayor James Walker was elected in 1925, Babe Ruth reigned at Yankee Stadium and the Great Migration from the South led to the Harlem Renaissance, when the neighborhood became a center of African American culture and society. It produced poetry, music, painting and an innovative attitude that continues to influence and inspire. Harlem's daring nightlife in the 1920s and '30s attracted the flappers and gin-soaked revelers who marked the complete failure of Prohibition, and provided a foretaste of the liberated nightlife New Yorkers enjoy today. But the fun could not last forever – economic collapse was looming.

Hard Times

The stock market crashed in 1929, beginning the Great Depression of the 1930s, which the city dealt with through a combination of grit, endurance, rent parties, militancy and a slew of public-works projects. The once-grand Central Park blossomed with shacks, derisively called Hoovervilles, after the president who refused to help the needy.

1898	1904	1913	1931
The *Charter of New York* is ratified and the five boroughs of Brooklyn, Staten Island, Queens, the Bronx and Manhattan unite to become the largest city in America.	Luna Park in Coney Island opens, followed by Dreamland amusement park. Meanwhile, the IRT subway carries 150,000 passengers on its very first day of operation.	Though not yet complete, Grand Central Terminal opens for business on February 2. Over 150,000 people visit the new station on its opening day.	The Empire State Building (1454ft tall) supersedes the Chrysler Building as the world's tallest skyscraper; the World Trade Center's north tower steals the crown in 1970.

But mayor Fiorello La Guardia found a friend in President Franklin Roosevelt, and worked his Washington connections to great effect to bring relief money – and subsequent prosperity – home.

WWII brought troops galore to the city, ready to party down to their last dollar in Times Square, before being shipped off to Europe. Converted to war industries, the local factories hummed, staffed by women and African American workers who had rarely before had access to good, unionized jobs. The explosion of wartime activity led to a huge housing crunch, which brought New York its much-imitated, tenant-protecting Rent Control Law.

There were few evident controls on business, as Midtown bulked up with skyscrapers after the war. The financial center marched north, while banker David Rockefeller and his brother, Governor Nelson Rockefeller, dreamed up the Twin Towers to revitalize downtown.

Enter Robert Moses

Working with mayor La Guardia to usher the city into the modern age was Robert Moses, an urban planner who would influence the physical shape of the city more than anyone else in the 20th century – either wonderfully or tragically, depending on whom you ask. He was the mastermind behind the Triborough Bridge (now the Robert F Kennedy Bridge), Jones Beach State Park, the Verrazano–Narrows Bridge, the West Side Hwy and the Long Island parkway system – not to mention endless highways, tunnels and bridges. His vision was one of doing away with intimate neighborhoods of brownstones and townhouses, and of creating sweeping parks and soaring towers. The approach got preservationists fired up and their efforts to stop him from bulldozing neighborhoods led to the formation of Landmarks Preservation Commission in 1965.

Three Women Who Changed New York

➡ **Margaret Sanger** (1879–1966) A nurse, midwife and activist, Margaret Sanger opened the first birth-control clinic in the country in NYC in 1916. She eventually founded the American Birth Control League, which would later become Planned Parenthood.

➡ **Jane Jacobs** (1917–2006) Sprung into action against Robert Moses' plan to clear a huge tract of her neighborhood for public housing, Jane Jacobs defended preservation and inspired the creation of the Landmarks Preservation Commission (the first such US group).

➡ **Christine Quinn** (b 1966) In 2006, Christine Quinn became the first woman and open lesbian to become City Council Speaker, breaking gender and sexuality boundaries as the second-most powerful official (after the mayor) in NYC.

NYC's Tallest Buildings

Woolworth Building (792ft; 1913–1930)

Chrysler Building (1046ft; 1930–31)

Empire State Building (1454ft; 1931–1972 & 2001–12)

World Trade Center (1368ft; 1972–2001)

One World Trade Center (1776ft; 2012–present)

1941	1945	1963	1969
Duke Ellington's band leader Billy Strayhorn, inspired by the subway line that leads to Harlem, composes 'Take the A Train,' which becomes the band's signature song.	The United Nations, headquartered on Manhattan's east side, is established after representatives of 50 countries meet in San Francisco to agree on a charter.	The original Penn Station is demolished to build Madison Square Garden; outcry leads to the foundation of the Landmarks Preservation Commission.	On June 28, eight police officers raid the gay-friendly Stonewall Inn. Patrons revolt, sparking days of rioting and the birth of the modern gay-rights movement.

Move to the Beats

The 1960s ushered in an era of legendary creativity and anti-establishment expression, with many artists centered right downtown in Greenwich Village. One movement was Abstract Expressionism, a large-scale outbreak of American painters – Mark Rothko, Jackson Pollock, Lee Krasner, Helen Frankenthaler and Willem de Kooning among them – who offended and intrigued with incomprehensible squiggles and blotches and exuberant energy. Then there were the writers, such as Beat poets Allen Ginsberg and Jack Kerouac and novelist/playwright Jane Bowles. They gathered in Village coffeehouses to exchange ideas and find inspiration, which was often found in the form of folk music from burgeoning big names, such as Bob Dylan.

'Drop Dead'

David Berkowitz (nicknamed Son of Sam) terrified New York from 1976 to 1977 with a spate of shootings that killed six and wounded seven. The attacks were ruthless and unexpected, with several victims shot while sitting in their cars. When caught in August 1977, Berkowitz quipped 'What took you so long?'.

By the early 1970s, deficits had created a serious fiscal crisis, effectively demoting the elected mayor Abraham Beame to a figurehead, turning over the city's real financial power to Governor Carey and his appointees. President Ford's refusal to lend federal aid – summed up nicely by the *Daily News* headline 'Ford to City, Drop Dead!' – marked the nadir of relationships between the US and the city it loved to hate. As massive layoffs decimated the city's working class, untended bridges, roads and parks reeked of hard times.

The traumatic '70s – which reached a low point in 1977 with a citywide blackout and terrorizing serial killer David Berkowitz – saw rents fall, which helped nourish an exciting alternative culture that staged performances in abandoned schools, opened galleries in unused storefronts and breathed new life into the hair-dye industry with the advent of the punk-rock aesthetic. The fees from shooting the movie *Fame* at PS 122 at 9th St and First Ave, for example, helped pay for the renovation of the still-popular performance space. Ramones-loving punks turned former warehouses into pulsing meccas of nightlife, transforming the former industrial precincts of SoHo and Tribeca. Immortalized in Nan Goldin's famous photographic performance piece *The Ballad of Sexual Dependency*, this renaissance challenged gender roles and turned the East Village into America's center of tattooing and independent filmmaking.

Out Of the Ashes

During the 1970s, a wave of arson attacks reduced blocks of apartment houses in the South Bronx to cinders. Amid the smoke, an influential hip-hop culture was born, fueled by the percussive rhythms of Puerto Rican salsa. Rock Steady Crew, led by 'Crazy Legs' Richie Colón, pio-

1976–77	1977	1980	1988
David Berkowitz, the 'Son of Sam' killer, says a demon in a dog told him to commit a string of murders around the city. He kills six and wounds seven others using a .44 revolver.	Following a lightning strike at a power substation, a summer blackout leaves New Yorkers in the dark for 24 sweltering hours, which leads to rioting around the city.	Mark David Chapman kills John Lennon in front of Lennon's home at the Dakota, on Manhattan's Upper West Side.	Squatters, who had turned the East Village's Tompkins Square Park into a massive homeless encampment, riot when cops attempt to remove them from their de-facto home.

neered athletic, competitive break dancing. Kool DJ Herc spun vinyl for break beat all-night dance parties. Afrika Bambaataa, another founding hip-hop DJ, formed Zulu Nation, bringing DJs, break dancers and graffiti writers together to end violence.

Daring examples of graffiti dazzled the public with train-long graphics. The best-known 'masterpiece' belied the graf writers' reputation as vandals: Lee 163, with the Fab 5 crew, painted a whole car of trains with the message 'Merry Christmas, New York.' Some of these maestros of the spray can infiltrated the art world, most notably Jean-Michel Basquiat, once known by his tag, 'Samo.'

Some of the money snagged in the booming stock markets of the 1980s was spent on art, but even more was blown up the noses of young traders. While Manhattan neighborhoods struggled with the spread of crack cocaine, the city reeled from the impact of addiction, citywide crime and an AIDS epidemic that cut through communities.

Dot-Com Days

A *Time* magazine cover in 1990 sported a feature story on 'New York: The Rotting Apple.' Still convalescing from the real-estate crash at the end of the 1980s, the city faced crumbling bridges and roads, jobs leaking south and Fortune 500 companies hopping the rivers to suburbia. And then the dot-com market roared in, turning geeks into millionaires and the New York Stock Exchange into a speculator's fun park. Buoyed by tax receipts from IPO (initial public offering) profits, the city launched a frenzy of building, boutique-ing and partying unparalleled since the 1920s.

With pro-business, law-and-order-loving Rudy Giuliani as mayor, the dingy and destitute were swept from Manhattan's yuppified streets to the outer boroughs, leaving room for Generation X to score digs and live the high life. Mayor Giuliani grabbed headlines with his campaign to stamp out crime, even kicking the sex shops off notoriously seedy 42nd St. The energetic mayor succeeded in making New York America's safest big city, by targeting high-crime areas and using statistics to focus police presence. Crime dropped, restaurants boomed, real-estate prices sizzled, and *Sex & the City* beamed a vision of sophisticated singles in Manolos around the world.

Still, things were faltering in New York at the dawn of the new millennium, and, when that fateful day came in 2001, it forever changed the perspective of both the city and the world.

History on the Pages

The Historical Atlas of New York City: A Visual Celebration of 400 Years of New York City's History (Eric Homberger, 1998)

Gotham: A History of New York City to 1898 (Edwin G Burrows and Mike Wallace, 2003)

The Restless City: A Short History of New York from Colonial Times to the Present (Joanne Reitano, 2006)

Taxi! A Social History of the New York City Cabdriver (Graham Russell Gao Hodges, 2007)

New York: The Novel (Edward Rutherfurd, 2010)

1993	2001	2008–09	2010
On February 26, terrorists detonate a bomb below the North Tower of the World Trade Center. The explosion kills six people and injures more than 1000.	On September 11, terrorist hijackers fly two planes into the Twin Towers, destroying the World Trade Center and killing nearly 3000 people.	The stock market crashes due to mismanagement by major American financial institutions. The Global Financial Crisis spreads worldwide.	Mayor Michael Bloomberg is sworn into a third term after winning an election that he personally made possible by abolishing the local term-limits law.

September 11

On September 11, 2001, terrorists flew two hijacked planes into the World Trade Center's Twin Towers, turning the whole complex to dust and rubble and killing nearly 3000 people. Downtown Manhattan took months to recover from the ghastly fumes wafting from the ruins as forlorn missing-person posters grew ragged on brick walls. While the city mourned its dead and recovery crews coughed their way through the debris, residents braved constant terrorist alerts and an anthrax scare. Shock and grief drew people together, uniting the oft-fractious citizenry in a determined effort not to succumb to despair.

Protests, Storms & Political Change

The decade after September 11 was a period of rebuilding – both physically and emotionally. In 2002, then-mayor Michael Bloomberg began the unenviable task of picking up the pieces of a shattered city that had thrust all of its support behind his predecessor, mayor Giuliani, whose popularity rose in the wake of September 11.

Much to Bloomberg's pleasure, New York saw much renovation and reconstruction, especially after the city hit its stride with spiking tourist numbers in 2005. In 2008, however, the economy buckled under its own weight, in what has largely become known as the Global Financial Crisis. Anger towards the perceived recklessness of America's financial institutions saw thousands take to the Financial District's Zuccotti Park on September 17, 2011, in a stand against the nation's unfair division of personal wealth. Known as Occupy Wall Street, the protest subsequently spread to hundreds of other cities across the world.

Fury of the meteorological kind hit New York in 2012, in the form of superstorm Hurricane Sandy. While a pre-storm surge on October 28 turned parts of Brooklyn and New Jersey into a New World Venice, Sandy saved its ultimate blow for the following day. Cyclonic winds and drenching rain pounded the city, causing severe flooding and property damage, including to the NYC subway system, Hugh L Carey Tunnel and World Trade Center site. A major power blackout plunged much of Lower Manhattan into surreal darkness, while trading at the New York Stock Exchange was suspended for two days in its first weather-related closure since 1888.

The winds of political change swept through the city in November 2013, when Bill de Blasio became the city's first Democratic mayor since 1989. The 52-year-old self-proclaimed 'progressive' also became the first white mayor of NYC with an African American spouse.

The September 11 terrorist attacks caused an estimated $60 billion in damages to the World Trade Center site, including damage to infrastructure, the subway system and surrounding buildings. It took 3.1 million hours of labor to clean up 1.8 million tons of debris, at a cost of $750 million.

2011	2012	2013	2016
On June 24, New York becomes the sixth US state to legalize same-sex marriage. The act is signed into law by Governor Andrew Cuomo.	Superstorm Sandy hits NYC in October, causing major flooding and property damage, cutting power and shutting down the New York Stock Exchange for two days.	Bill de Blasio wins the NYC mayoral election, defeating opponent Joseph J Lhota and becoming the city's first Democratic mayor in almost 20 years.	Architect Santiago Calatrava's World Trade Center Transportation Hub opens in Lower Manhattan. The project's final price tag is $3.9 billion, almost double the original estimate.

The NYC Table

Unlike California or the South, New York is never really referred to as having one defining cuisine. Ask for some 'New York food' and you'll wind up with anything from a hot dog to a Gallic-inspired tasting menu at Le Bernardin. Cuisine in the multicultural town is global by definition, a testament to the immigrants who have unpacked their bags and recipes on its streets. And just like the city itself, it's a scene that's constantly evolving, driven by insatiable ambition.

Urban Farm to Table

Whether it's upstate triple-cream Kunik at Bedford Cheese Shop or Montauk Pearls oysters at fine-dining Craft, New York City's passion for all things local and artisanal continues unabated. The city itself has become an unlikely food bowl, with an ever-growing number of rooftops, backyards and community gardens finding new purpose as urban farms.

While you can expect to find anything from organic tomatoes atop Upper East Side delis to beehives on East Village tenement rooftops, the current queen of the crop is Brooklyn Grange (www.brooklyngrange farm.com), an organic farm covering two rooftops in Long Island City and the Brooklyn Navy Yards. At 2.5 acres, it's purportedly the world's biggest rooftop farm, producing more than 50,000lb of organically cultivated goodness annually, from eggs to carrots, chard and heirloom tomatoes. The project is the brainchild of young farmer Ben Flanner. Obsessed with farm-to-table eating, this former E*Trade marketing manager kick-started NYC's rooftop revolution in 2009 with the opening of its first rooftop soil farm – Eagle Street Rooftop Farm – in nearby Greenpoint. Flanner's collaborators include some of the city's top eateries, among them Marlow & Sons and Roberta's in Brooklyn, and Dutch in Manhattan.

Food Specialties

While the concept of 'New York cuisine' is inherently ambiguous, this town is not without its edible icons. It's the bites with the longest histories that folks usually have in mind when they refer to NYC specialties. Among these are bagels and pizza, introduced by Eastern European Jews and Italians, among the earliest wave of immigrants here. Have one! Have three! But leave room for the cheesecake, egg creams and dogs.

Bagels

Bagels may have been invented in Europe, but they were perfected around the turn of the 19th century in NYC – and once you've had one here, you'll have a hard time enjoying one anywhere else. It's a straightforward masterpiece: a ring of plain-yeast dough that's first boiled and then baked, either left plain or topped with various finishing touches, from sesame seeds to chocolate chips. 'Bagels' made in other parts of the country are often just baked and not boiled, which makes them nothing more than a roll with a hole. And even if they do get boiled elsewhere, bagel-makers

Bargain-savvy gastronomes love the biannual NYC Restaurant Week. Taking place in January to February and July to August, it sees many of the city's restaurants, including some of its very best, serve up three-course lunches for $25, or three-course dinners for $38. Check www.nycgo.com/restaurantweek for details and reservations.

here claim that it's the New York water that adds an elusive sweetness never to be found anywhere else. Which baker creates the 'best' bagel in New York is a matter of (hotly contested) opinion, but most agree that Manhattan's Ess-a-Bagel and Queens' Brooklyn Bagel & Coffee Company rank pretty high. The most traditionally New York way to order one is by asking for a 'bagel and a schmear,' which will yield you said bagel with a small but thick swipe of cream cheese. Or splurge and add some lox – thinly sliced smoked salmon – as was originally sold from pushcarts on the Lower East Side by Jewish immigrants back in the early 1900s.

Pizza

Pizza is certainly not indigenous to Gotham. But New York–style pizza is a very particular item, and the first pizzeria in America was Lombardi's in Manhattan's Little Italy, which opened in 1905.

While Chicago-style pizza is 'deep dish' and Californian tends to be light and doughy, New York prides itself on pizza with a thin crust, an even thinner layer of sauce and triangular slices (unless they're Sicilian-style, in which case they're rectangular). Pizza made its way over to New York in the 1900s through Italian immigrants and its regional style soon developed, the thin crust allowing for faster cooking time in a city where everyone is always in a hurry.

Today there are pizza parlors about every 10 blocks, especially in Manhattan and most of Brooklyn, where you'll find standard slices for $3. The style at each place varies slightly – some places touting cracker-thin crust, others offering slightly thicker and chewier versions, and plenty of nouveau styles throwing everything from shrimp to cherries on top. The city's booming locavore movement has also made its mark, with hipster pizzerias like Roberta's in Brooklyn peddling wood-fired pies topped with sustainable, local produce.

Hot Dogs

The hot dog made its way to New York via various European butchers in the 1800s. One, Charles Feltman of Germany, was apparently the first to sell them from pushcarts along the Coney Island seashore. But Nathan Handwerker, originally an employee of Feltman's, opened his own shop across the street, offering hot dogs at half the price of those at Feltman's and put his former employer out of business. Today, the original and legendary Nathan's still stands in Coney Island, while its empire has expanded on an international scale. There is barely a New York neighborhood that does not have at least a few hot-dog vendors on its street corners, although some locals would never touch one of those 'dirty-water dogs,' preferring the new wave of chi-chi hot-dog shops that can be found all over town. Enjoy yours, wherever it's from, with 'the works': smothered with spicy brown mustard, relish, sauerkraut and onions.

Egg Creams

Now don't go expecting eggs or cream in this frothy, old-school beverage – just milk, seltzer water and plenty of chocolate syrup (preferably the classic Fox's U-Bet brand, made in Brooklyn). When Louis Auster of Brooklyn, who owned soda fountains on the Lower East Side, invented the treat back in 1890, the syrup he used was indeed made with eggs and he added cream to thicken the concoction. The name stuck, even though the ingredients were modified, and soon they were a staple of every soda fountain in New York. While Mr Auster sold them for 3¢ apiece, today they'll cost you anywhere from $1.50 to $4.50, depending on where you find one – which could be from old-school institutions such as Katz's Delicatessen in the Lower East Side or Tom's Restaurant in Brooklyn.

Food truck fans with a smartphone can download the free Tweat.it app, which offers a real-time food-truck map and vendors' tweets denoting locations, daily specials and discounts. The app also works on iPad and iPod Touch.

City Harvest (www.cityharvest.org) is a nonprofit organization that distributes unused food to around 1.4 million struggling New Yorkers each year. A whopping 150,000lb of food is rescued daily from city restaurants, bakeries and catering companies. Individuals wanting to make a monetary donation can do so via the City Harvest website.

New York–Style Cheesecake

In one form or another, cheesecake has been around for quite a while. Look back 2400 years and you'll notice that Greek historian Thucydides and his posse were already kneading honey into fresh feta and baking it over hot coals for a sweet treat. Centuries later, the Romans adopted it, tweaking the concept by incorporating spelt flour for a more 'cake-like' form. This would be followed by countless more tweaks across the continent and centuries.

It would, however, take the error of a 19th-century New York farmer to create the key ingredient in New York–style cheesecake: cream cheese. A botched attempt at making French Neufchâtel cheese resulted in a curious product with the texture of polyethylene plastic. Enter James Kraft, founder of Kraft Foods, who picked it up in 1912, reformulated it, wrapped it in foil and introduced the country to the wonder of cream cheese.

Classic, New York cheesecake would be immortalized by Lindy's restaurant in Midtown. Opened by Leo Lindemann in 1921, the particular type of confection served there – made of cream cheese, heavy cream, a dash of vanilla and a cookie crust – became wildly popular in the '40s. Today, this calorific local masterpiece is a staple on countless dessert menus, whether you're at a Greek diner or haute cuisine hot spot. The most famous (and arguably best) cheesecake in town is that from Brooklyn stalwart Junior's (www.juniorscheesecake.com), whose well-known fans include Barack Obama.

> **NYC Master Chef Cookbooks**
>
> *Daniel: My French Cuisine*
> (Daniel Boulud & Sylvie Bigar)
>
> *The Babbo Cookbook*
> (Mario Batali)
>
> *A Girl and Her Greens*
> (April Bloomfield)
>
> *Momofuku*
> (David Chang & Peter Meehan)

Drink Specialties

Cocktails

New York City is a master of mixed libations. After all, this is the home of Manhattans, legendary speakeasies and Cosmo-clutching columnists with a passion for fashion. Legend has it that the city's namesake drink, Manhattan – a blend of whiskey, sweet vermouth and bitters – began life on the southeastern corner of 26th St and Madison Ave,

---

THE COFFEE LOWDOWN

Adam Craig, founder of specialty coffee shop **Culture Espresso** (p201).

What are your coffee shop recommendations? In Manhattan, definitely try Ninth Street Espresso in the East Village, Third Rail in the West Village and Stumptown Coffee Roasters in Midtown. In Brooklyn, top specialty spots include my former cafe Variety in Greenpoint and Cafe Pedlar in Carroll Gardens. Williamsburg is home to Bay Area roaster Blue Bottle Coffee. In Astoria, Queens, head to Queens Kickshaw.

What do the coffee cognoscenti drink? Most commonly, espresso-machine drinks made using single-origin coffee; coffee sourced from a specific geographic region. African-sourced coffee is a little more citrus-like, South American varieties are nuttier and more full-bodied, while Asian coffee often has 'blueberry' and 'chocolate' coming through. Non-espresso drinks include the light-bodied 'pour over', in which coffee is extracted through a cone over two-and-a-half to three minutes, and the 'Chemex coffee,' another filtered variety whose tea-like consistency highlights the subtler nuances of the beans.

And on a hot day? Wised-up New Yorkers opt for a 'cold brew,' prepared using two different methods. The first, known as 'full immersion', is made by steeping coarsely ground coffee in water for 16 hours to create a concentrate. The concentrate is then brought back with water to create a drink that's full-bodied, chocolatey and low in acidity. The second method, called 'Kyoto cold drip,' sees coffee passed through a ceramic filter at about one drop every two seconds for 16 to 18 hours. The result, served on ice, is super concentrated and akin to drinking cognac.

at the long-gone Manhattan Club. The occasion was a party in 1874, allegedly thrown by Jennie Churchill (mother of British Prime Minister Winston) to celebrate Samuel J Tilden's victory in the New York gubernatorial election. One of the barmen decided to create a drink to mark the occasion, naming it in honor of the bar.

Another New York classic was born that very year – the summer-centric Tom Collins. A mix of dry gin, sugar, lemon juice and club soda, the long drink's name stems from an elaborate hoax in which hundreds of locals were informed that a certain Tom Collins had been sullying their good names. While many set out to track him down, clued-in bartenders relished the joke by making the drink and naming it for the fictitious troublemaker. When the aggrieved stormed into the bars looking for a Tom Collins, they were served the drink to cool their tempers.

These days, NYC's kicking cocktail scene is big on rediscovered recipes, historical anecdotes and vintage speakeasy style. Once-obscure bartenders such as Harry Johnson and Jerry Thomas are now born-again legends, their vintage concoctions revived by a new generation of braces-clad mixologists. Historic ingredients such as Crème de Violette, Old Tom gin and Batavia Arrack are back in vogue. In the Financial District, cocktail bar Dead Rabbit has gone one further, reintroducing the 17th-century practice of pop-inns, drinks that fuse ale, liqueurs, spices and botanicals.

Then there are the city's revered single-spirit establishments, among them tequila- and mescal-focused Mayahuel in the East Village, whiskey-versed Ward III in Tribeca, and the self-explanatory Brandy Library and Rum House, in Tribeca and Midtown respectively.

Borough Brews

Beer brewing was once a thriving industry in the city – by the 1870s, Brooklyn boasted a belly-swelling 48 breweries. Most of these were based in Williamsburg, Bushwick and Greenpoint, neighborhoods packed with German immigrants with extensive brewing know-how. By the eve of Prohibition in 1919, the borough was one of the country's leading beer peddlers, as famous for kids carrying growlers (beer jugs) as for its bridges. By the end of Prohibition in 1933, most breweries had shut shop. And while the industry rose from the ashes in WWII, local flavor gave in to big-gun Midwestern brands.

Fast-forward to today and Brooklyn is once more a catchword for a decent brewski as a handful of craft breweries put integrity back on tap. Head of the pack is Brooklyn Brewery, whose seasonal offerings include a nutmeg-spiked Post Road Pumpkin Ale (available August to November) and a luscious Black Chocolate Stout (a take on Imperial Stout, available October to March). The brewery's comrades-in-craft include SixPoint Craft Ales (www.sixpoint.com), Threes Brewing (www.threesbrewing.com) and Other Half Brewing Co (www.otherhalfbrewing.com). Justifiably famed for its piney, hoppy Imperial IPA Green Diamonds, Other Half Brewing Co gathers its hops and malts from local farms.

Up-and-coming Queens is home to nanobrewery Transmitter Brewing (www.transmitterbrewing.com) and beach-born Rockaway Brewing Company (www.rockawaybrewco.com). The borough's dominant player remains SingleCut Beersmiths (www.singlecutbeer.com), whose launch in 2012 saw Queens welcome its first brewery since Prohibition. Its offerings include unusual takes on lager, among them the Jan White Lagrrr, brewed with coriander, chamomile flowers, oranges, matzo and Sichuan peppercorns. Further north, the Bronx lays claim to Bronx Brewery and Gun Hill Brewing Co, the latter making waves with its Void of Light, a jet-black, roastalicious stout.

The first public brewery in America was established by colonial governor Peter Minuit (1580–1638) at the Market (Marckvelt) field in what is now known as the Financial District in Lower Manhattan. Minuit is credited with 'purchasing' Manhattan from the native Lenape people in May 1626.

The Arts

The spectacles of Broadway, the gleaming white-box galleries of Chelsea, joints playing jazz, music halls blaring moody indie rock and opera houses that bellow melodramatic tales – for more than a century, New York City has been America's capital of cultural production. And while gentrification has pushed many artists out to the city's fringes and beyond, New York nonetheless remains a nerve center for the visual arts, music, theater, dance and literature.

NYC: An Art Heavyweight

That New York claims some of the world's mightiest art museums attests to its enviable artistic pedigree. From Pollock and Rothko, to Warhol and Rauschenberg, the city has nourished many of America's greatest artists and artistic movements.

The Birth of an Arts Hub

In almost all facets of the arts, New York really got its sea legs in the early 20th century, when the city attracted and retained a critical mass of thinkers, artists, writers and poets. It was at this time that the homegrown art scene began to take shape. In 1905, photographer (and husband of Georgia O'Keeffe) Alfred Stieglitz opened Gallery 291, a Fifth Ave space that provided a vital platform for American artists and helped establish photography as a credible art form.

In the 1940s, an influx of cultural figures fleeing the carnage of WWII saturated the city with fresh ideas – and New York became an important cultural hub. Peggy Guggenheim established the Art of this Century gallery on 57th St, a space that helped launch the careers of painters such as Jackson Pollock, Willem de Kooning and Robert Motherwell. These Manhattan-based artists came to form the core of the Abstract Expressionist movement – also known as the New York School – creating an explosive and rugged form of painting that changed the course of modern art as we know it.

On any given week, New York is home to countless art exhibits, installations and performances. Get a comprehensive listing of happenings at www.nyartbeat.com.

An American Avant-Garde

The Abstract Expressionists helped establish New York as a global arts center. Another generation of artists then carried the ball. In the 1950s and '60s, Robert Rauschenberg, Jasper Johns and Lee Bontecou turned paintings into off-the-wall sculptural constructions that included everything from welded steel to taxidermy goats. By the mid-1960s, pop art – a movement that utilized the imagery and production techniques of popular culture – had taken hold, with Andy Warhol at the helm.

By the '60s and '70s, when New York's economy was in the dumps and much of SoHo lay in a state of decay, the city became a hotbed of conceptual and performance art. Gordon Matta-Clark sliced up abandoned buildings with chainsaws and the artists of Fluxus staged happenings on downtown streets. Carolee Schneemann organized performances that utilized the human body. At one famous 1964 event, she had a crew of nude dancers roll around in an unappetizing mix of paint, sausages and dead fish in the theater of a Greenwich Village church.

Art Now

Today, the arts scene is mixed and wide-ranging. The major institutions – the Metropolitan Museum of Art, the Museum of Modern Art, the Whitney Museum, the Guggenheim Museum and the Brooklyn Museum – deliver major retrospectives covering everything from Renaissance portraiture to contemporary installation. The New Museum, on the Lower East Side, is more daring, while countless smaller institutions, among them the excellent Bronx Museum, El Museo del Barrio and the Studio Museum in Harlem, focus on narrower slices of art history.

New York remains the world's gallery capital, with more than 800 spaces showcasing all kinds of art all over the city. The blue-chip dealers can be found clustered in Chelsea and the Upper East Side. Galleries that showcase emerging and mid-career artists dot the Lower East Side, while prohibitive rents have pushed the city's emerging and experimental scenes further out, with current hot spots including Harlem and the Brooklyn neighborhoods of Bushwick, Greenpoint, Clinton Hill and Bedford-Stuyvesant (Bed-Stuy).

Graffiti & Street Art

Contemporary graffiti as we know it was cultivated in NYC. In the 1970s, the graffiti-covered subway train became a potent symbol of the city and work by figures such as Dondi, Blade and Lady Pink became known around the world. In addition, fine artists such as Jean-Michel Basquiat, Kenny Scharf and Keith Haring began incorporating elements of graffiti into their work.

The movement received new life in the late 1990s when a new generation of artists – many with art-school pedigrees – began using materials such as cut paper and sculptural elements (all illicitly). Well-known New York City artists working in this vein include John Fekner, Stephen 'Espo' Powers, Swoon and the twin-brother duo Skewville.

A Musical Metropolis

This is the city where jazz players such as Ornette Coleman, Miles Davis and John Coltrane pushed the limits of improvisation in the '50s. It's where various Latin sounds – from cha-cha-cha to rumba to mambo – came together to form the hybrid we now call salsa, where folks singers such as Bob Dylan and Joan Baez crooned protest songs in coffeehouses, and where bands such as the New York Dolls and the Ramones tore up the stage in Manhattan's gritty downtown. It was the ground zero of disco. And it was the cultural crucible where hip-hop was nurtured and grew – then exploded.

For comprehensive coverage of the American jazz scene, log on to www.jazztimes. com, which features plenty of stories about all the established and rising New York acts.

The city remains a magnet for musicians to this day. The local indie rock scene is especially vibrant: groups including the Yeah Yeah Yeahs, LCD Soundsystem and Animal Collective all emerged out of NYC. Williamsburg is at the heart of the action, packed with clubs and bars, as well as indie record labels and internet radio stations. The best venues for rock include the Music Hall of Williamsburg and the Brooklyn Bowl, as well as Manhattan's Bowery Ballroom.

All That Jazz

Jazz remains a juggernaut – from the traditional to the experimental. The best bets for jazz are the Village Vanguard in the West Village and the Jazz Standard near Madison Square Park. For more highbrow programming, there's Midtown's Jazz at Lincoln Center, which features a wide array of solo outings by important musicians, as well as tribute concerts to figures such as Dizzy Gillespie and Thelonious Monk.

Classical & Opera

The classics are alive and well at Lincoln Center. Here, the Metropolitan Opera delivers a wide array of celebrated operas, from Verdi's *Aida* to Mozart's *Don Giovanni*. The New York Philharmonic (the symphony that was once directed by one of the 20th-century's great maestros, Leonard Bernstein) is also normally based here, although a refurbishment of its home, David Geffen Hall, saw it looking for a temporary home in late 2015. Carnegie Hall, the Merkin Concert Hall and the Frick Collection also offer wonderful – and more intimate – spaces to enjoy great classical music.

For more avant-garde fare, try the Center for Contemporary Opera and the Brooklyn Academy of Music (BAM) – the latter is one of the city's vital opera and classical music hubs. Another excellent venue, featuring highly experimental work, is St Ann's Warehouse in Brooklyn. If you like your performance *outré*, keep an eye on their calendar.

On Broadway & Beyond

In the early 20th century, clusters of theaters settled into the area around Times Square and began producing popular plays and suggestive comedies – a movement that had its roots in early vaudeville. By the 1920s, these messy works had evolved into on-stage spectacles like *Show Boat,* an all-out Oscar Hammerstein production about the lives of performers on a Mississippi steamboat. In 1943, Broadway had its first runaway hit – *Oklahoma!* – that remained on stage for a record 2212 performances.

Today, Broadway musicals are shown in one of 40 official Broadway theaters, lavish early-20th-century jewels that surround Times Square, and are a major component of cultural life in New York. If you're on a budget, look for off-Broadway productions. These tend to be more intimate, inexpensive, and often just as good.

NYC bursts with theatrical offerings beyond Broadway, from Shakespeare to David Mamet to rising experimental playwrights including Young Jean Lee. In addition to Midtown staples such as Playwrights Horizons and Second Stage Theatre, the Lincoln Center theaters and smaller companies like Soho Rep are important hubs for works by modern and contemporary playwrights.

Across the East River, BAM, PS 122 and St Ann's Warehouse all offer edgy programming. Numerous festivals, such as FringeNYC, BAM's epic Next Wave Festival and the biennial Performa offer brilliant opportunities to catch new work.

Bust a Move: Dance & the City

For nearly 100 years, New York City has been at the center of American dance. It is here that the American Ballet Theatre (ABT) – led by the fabled George Balanchine – was founded in 1949. The company promoted the idea of cultivating American talent, hiring native-born dancers and putting on works by choreographers such as Jerome Robbins, Twyla Tharp and Alvin Ailey.

But NYC is perhaps best known for nurturing a generation of modern-dance choreographers – figures such as Martha Graham, who challenged traditional notions of dance with boxy, industrial movements on bare, almost abstract sets. The boundaries were pushed ever further by Merce Cunningham, who disassociated dance from music. Today, companies such as STREB are pushing dance to its limits.

Lincoln Center and Brooklyn Academy of Music host regular performances, while up-and-coming acts feature at spaces including Chelsea's Kitchen, Joyce Theater and New York Live Arts, as well as Midtown's Baryshnikov Arts Center (http://bacnyc.org).

THE ARTS ON BROADWAY & BEYOND

For comprehensive theater listings, news and reviews (both glowing and scathing), click onto www. nytimes.com/ pages/theater. You'll also find listings, synopses and industry news at www. playbill.com.

Brooklyn has a hopping indie music scene, with local bands performing regularly in Williamsburg and Bushwick. To hear the latest sounds, log on to www.newtown radio.com.

A NEW YORK HIP-HOP PLAYLIST

New York is the cradle of hip-hop. Rap to the following classics from the city's finest:

'Rapper's Delight', Sugarhill Gang (1979) – The single that launched the commercial birth of hip-hop, from a New York–New Jersey trio

'White Lines,' Grandmaster Flash and the Furious Five (1983) – The ultimate '80s party song from the Bronx

'It's Like That,' Run DMC (1983) – That's just the way it is from the legendary Queens trio

'Fat Boys,' Fat Boys (1984) – Brooklyn's ultimate beat-boxers

'No Sleep Till Brooklyn,' Beastie Boys (1986) – The NYC trio who fought for their right to party

'Ain't No Half Steppin',' Big Daddy Kane (1988) – Mellifluous rhymes from a Brooklyn master

'Fight the Power,' Public Enemy (1989) – A politically charged tour de force from Long Island's hip-hop royals

'C.R.E.A.M.,' Wu-Tang Clan (1993) – The rules of street capitalism rapped out by Staten Island's finest crew

'N.Y. State of Mind,' NAS (1994) – From from the debut album of a Brooklyn-born, Queens-raised rap deity

'99 Problems,' Jay-Z (2004) – This Bed-Stuy, Brooklyn boy is now a music mogul (and Beyoncé's other half)

New York in Letters

The city that is home to the country's biggest publishing houses has also been home to some of its best-known writers. In the 19th century, Herman Melville (*Moby Dick*), Edith Wharton (*The House of Mirth*) and Walt Whitman (*Leaves of Grass*) all congregated here. But things really got cooking in the early part of the 20th century. There were the liquor-fueled literary salons of poet-communist John Reed in the 1910s, the acerbic wisecracks of the Algonquin Round Table in the 1920s and the thinly veiled novels of Dawn Powell in the '40s, a figure whose work often critiqued New York's media establishment.

The 1950s and '60s saw the rise of writers who began to question the status quo. Poet Langston Hughes examined the condition of African Americans in Harlem and Beat poets such as Allen Ginsberg rejected traditional rhyme in favor of free-flowing musings. The last few decades of the 20th century offered a wide gamut to choose from, including Jay McInerney, chronicler of the greed and coke-fueled '80s, to new voices from under-represented corners of the city such as Piri Thomas and Audre Lorde.

NYC scribes continue to cover a vast array of realities in their work – from zombies (Colson Whitehead) and postmodern narrative techniques (Jennifer Egan), to the crazy impossibility that is New York in Michael Chabon's Pulitzer-winning *The Amazing Adventures of Kavalier & Clay*. Among the latest crop of Gotham-based talent is award-winning Ben Lerner, whose metafiction novel *10:04* is as much about the city's visceral intensity as it is about its neurotic, heart-troubled protagonist.

Architecture

New York's architectural history is a layer cake of ideas and styles – one that is literally written on the city's streets. Humble colonial farmhouses and graceful Federal-style buildings can be found alongside ornate beaux-arts palaces from the early 20th century. There are the revivals (Greek, Gothic, Romanesque and Renaissance) and the unadorned forms of the International Style. And, in recent years, there has been the addition of the torqued forms of deconstructivist architects. For the architecture buff, it's a bricks-and-mortar bonanza.

Colonial Foundations

New York's architectural roots are modest. Early Dutch colonial farmhouses were all about function: clapboard-wood homes with shingled, gambrel roofs were positioned to take advantage of daylight and retain heat in winter. A number of these have somehow survived to the present.

Above One World Trade Center (left; p70) and Woolworth Building (right; p76)

The most remarkable is the Pieter Claesen Wyckoff House in East Flatbush, Brooklyn. Originally built in 1652 (with additions made over the years), it is the oldest house in the entire city.

After the Dutch colony of New Netherlands became the British colony of New York in 1664, architectural styles moved to Georgian. Boxy, brick and stone structures with hipped roofs began to materialize. In the northern Manhattan district of Inwood, the Morris-Jumel Mansion from 1765 is an altered example of this: the home was built in the Georgian style by Roger Morris, then purchased by Stephen Jumel, who added a neo-Classical facade in the 19th century. Another British colonial building of interest is the Fraunces Tavern, where George Washington bid an emotional farewell to the officers who had accompanied him throughout the American Revolution. Today the structure contains a museum and restaurant.

On the ceremonial end is St Paul's Chapel, south of City Hall Park. Built in the 1760s, it is the oldest surviving church in the city. Its design was inspired by the much bigger St Martin-in-the-Fields church in London.

AIA Guide to New York (5th edition) is a comprehensive guide to the most significant buildings in the city.

Architecture in the New Republic

In the early 1800s, architecture grew lighter and more refined. The so-called Federal style employed classical touches – slim, columned entrances, triangular pediments at the roof line and rounded fanlights over doors and windows. Some of the best surviving examples are tied to municipal government. City Hall, built in 1812, owes its French form to émigré architect Joseph François Mangin and its Federal detailing to American-born John McComb Jr. The interior contains an airy rotunda and curved cantilevered stairway.

Uptown, on the Upper East Side, 1799 Gracie Mansion, the official residence of New York City's mayor since 1942, is a fine example of a Federal residence, with its broad, river-view porch and leaded glass sidelights. This stretch of riverfront was once lined with buildings of the sort – a sight that impressed Alexis de Tocqueville during his tour of the United States in the early 19th century.

Other Federal-style specimens include the 1793 James Watson House at 7 State St right across from Battery Park, and the 1832 Merchant's House Museum, in NoHo. The latter still contains its intact interiors.

Must-See Buildings

Chrysler Building

Grand Central Terminal

Morris-Jumel Mansion

Empire State Building

Temple Emanu-El

New Museum of Contemporary Art

Greek, Gothic & Romanesque: The Revivals

Following the publication of an important treatise on Greek architecture in the late 1700s, architects began to show a renewed interest in pure, classical forms. In the US, a big instigator of this trend was Minard Lafever, a New Jersey–born carpenter turned architect turned author of pattern books. By the 1830s, becolumned Greek revival structures were going up all over New York.

Manhattan contains a bevy of these buildings, including the gray granite St Peter's Church (1838) and the white-marble Federal Hall (1842) – both of which are located in the Financial District. In Greenwich Village, a row of colonnaded homes built on the north side of Washington Square (Numbers 1–13) in the 1820s are fine residential interpretations of this style.

Starting in the late 1830s, the simple Georgian and Federalist styles started to give way to more ornate structures that employed Gothic and Romanesque elements. This was particularly prominent in church construction. An early example was the Church of the Ascension (1841) in Greenwich Village – an imposing brownstone structure studded with pointed arches and a crenelated tower. The same architect – Richard Upjohn – also designed downtown Manhattan's Trinity Church (1846) in the same style.

Brooklyn Bridge (p266)

By the 1860s, these places of worship were growing in size and scale. Among the most resplendent are St Patrick's Cathedral (1858–79) and the perpetually under construction Cathedral Church of St John the Divine (1911–), in Morningside Heights. Indeed, the style was so popular that one of the city's most important icons, the Brooklyn Bridge (1870–83), was built à la Gothic Revival.

Romanesque elements (such as curved arches) can be spotted on structures all over the city. Some of the most famous include the Joseph Papp Public Theater (formerly the Astor Library) in Greenwich Village, built between 1853 and 1881, and the breathtaking Temple Emanu-El (1929) on Fifth Ave on the Upper East Side.

Esteemed New York architecture critic Ada Louise Huxtable gathers some of her most important essays in the book *On Architecture: Collected Reflections on a Century of Change.*

Beaux-Arts Blockbusters

At the turn of the 20th century, New York entered a gilded age. Robber barons such as JP Morgan, Henry Clay Frick and John D Rockefeller – awash in steel and oil money – built themselves lavish manses. Public buildings grew ever more extravagant in scale and ornamentation. Architects, many of whom trained in France, came back with European design ideals. Gleaming white limestone began to replace all the brownstone, first stories were elevated to allow for dramatic staircase entrances, and buildings were adorned with sculptured keystones and Corinthian columns.

McKim Mead & White's Villard Houses, from 1884 (now the Palace Hotel), show the movement's early roots. Loosely based on Rome's Palazzo della Cancelleria, they channeled the symmetry and elegance of the Italian Renaissance. Other classics include the central branch of the New York Public Library (1911) designed by Carrère and Hastings, the 1902 extension of the Metropolitan Museum of Art by Richard Morris Hunt, and Warren and Wetmore's stunning Grand Central Terminal (1913), which is capped by a statue of Mercury, the god of commerce.

Chrysler Building (p188) detail

Reaching Skyward

By the time New York settled into the 20th century, elevators and steel-frame engineering had allowed the city to grow up – literally. This period saw a building boom of skyscrapers, starting with Cass Gilbert's neo-Gothic 57-story Woolworth Building (1913). To this day, it remains one of the 50 tallest buildings in the United States.

Others soon followed. In 1930, the Chrysler Building, the 77-story art-deco masterpiece designed by William Van Alen, became the world's tallest structure. The following year, the record was broken by the Empire State Building, a clean-lined moderne monolith crafted from Indiana limestone. Its spire was meant to be used as mooring mast for dirigibles (airships) – an idea that made for good publicity, but which proved to be impractical and unfeasible.

The influx of displaced European architects and other thinkers who had resettled in New York by the end of WWII fostered a lively dialogue between American and European architects. This was a period when urban planner Robert Moses furiously rebuilt vast swaths of New York – to the detriment of many neighborhoods – and designers and artists became obsessed with the clean, unadorned lines of the International Style.

One of the earliest projects in this vein was the UN buildings (1948–52), the combined effort of a committee of architects, including the Swiss-born Le Corbusier, Brazil's Oscar Niemeyer and America's Wallace K Harrison. The Secretariat employed New York's first glass curtain wall – which looms over the ski-slope curve of the General Assembly. Other significant modernist structures from this period include Gordon Bunshaft's Lever House (1950–52), a floating, glassy structure on Park Ave and 54th St, and Ludwig Mies van der Rohe's austere, 38-story Seagram Building (1956–58), located just two blocks to the south.

The New Guard

By the late 20th century, numerous architects began to rebel against the hard-edged, unornamented nature of modernist design. Among them was Philip Johnson. His pink granite AT&T Building (now Sony Tower; 1984) – topped by a scrolled, neo-Georgian pediment – has become a postmodern icon of the Midtown skyline.

What never become an icon was Daniel Libeskind's twisting, angular design for the One World Trade Center (2013) tower, replaced by a boxier architecture-by-committee glass obelisk. On the same site, budget blowouts led to tweaks of Santiago Calatrava's luminous design for the World Trade Center Transportation Hub (2016). According to critics, what should have looked like a dove in flight now resembles a winged dinosaur. The latest WTC site controversy involves Two World Trade Center, its original Sir Norman Foster design recently scrapped for one by Danish firm Bjarke Ingels Group (BIG). According to the Chief Operating Officer of 21st Century Fox, James Murdoch, Foster's design was too conventional for what will become the media company's new base. BIG responded with its trademark unconventionalism: a tower of giant, differently sized boxes, soaring playfully into the sky.

Not that Sir Foster is a hack at cutting-edge style. The British architect's Hearst Tower (2006) – a glass skyscraper zigzagging its way out of a 1920s sandstone structure – remains a Midtown trailblazer. The building is one of numerous daring 21st-century additions to the city's architectural portfolio, among them Brooklyn's sci-fi arena Barclays Center (2012), Thom Mayne's folded-and-slashed 41 Cooper Square (2009) in the East Village, and Frank Gehry's rippling, 76-storey apartment tower New York by Gehry (2011) in the Financial District.

Starchitects on the Line

Frank Gehry's IAC Building (2007) – a billowing, white-glass structure often compared to a wedding cake – is one of a growing number of starchitect creations appearing around railway-turned-urban-park, the High Line. The most prolific of these is Renzo Piano's new Whitney Museum (2015). Dramatically asymmetrical and clad in blue-grey steel, the building has received significant praise for melding seamlessly with the elevated park. Turning heads eight blocks to the north is 100 Eleventh Ave (2010), a 23-storey luxury condominium by French architect Jean Nouvel. Its exuberant arrangement of angled windows is nothing short of mesmerizing, both cutting-edge in its construction and sensitive to the area's heritage. That the facade's patterning evokes West Chelsea's industrial masonry is not coincidental.

The area's next darling is set to be Zaha Hadid's apartment complex at 520 West 28th St. Rising 11 stories, the luxury structure will be the late Iraqi-British architect's first residential project in the city, its voluptuous, sci-fi curves to be complimented by a 2500-sq-ft sculpture deck showcasing art presented by Friends of the High Line.

Public Art: New York by Jean Parker Phifer, with photos by Francis Dzikowski, is an informative guide to the city's public monuments.

Queer City: From Stonewall to Marriage Equality

New York City is out and damn proud. It was here that the Stonewall Riots took place, that the modern gay rights movement bloomed and that America's first Pride march hit the streets. Yet even before the days of 'Gay Lib,' the city had a knack for all things queer and fabulous, from Bowery sex saloons and Village Sapphic poetry to drag balls in Harlem. It hasn't always been smooth sailing, but it's always been one hell of a ride.

Before Stonewall

Subversion in the Villages

By the 1890s, New York City's rough-and-ready Lower East Side had established quite a reputation for scandalous 'resorts' – dancing halls, saloons and brothels – frequented by the city's 'inverts' and 'fairies.' From Paresis Hall at 5th St and Bowery to Slide at 157 Bleecker St, these venues offered everything from cross-dressing spectaculars and dancing to back rooms for same-sex shenanigans. For closeted middle-class men, these dens were a secret thrill – places reached undercover on trains for a fix of camaraderie, understanding and uninhibited fun. For curious middle-class straights, they were just as enticing – salacious destinations on voyeuristic 'slumming tours.'

As New York strode into the 20th century, writers and bohemians began stepping into Greenwich Village, lured by the area's cheap rents and romantically crooked streets. The unconventionality and free thinking the area became known for turned the Village into an Emerald City for gays and lesbians, a place with no shortage of bachelor pads, more tolerant attitudes and – with the arrival of Prohibition – an anything-goes speakeasy scene. A number of gay-owned businesses lined MacDougal St, among them the legendary Eve's Hangout at number 129. A tearoom run by Polish Jewish immigrant Eva Kotchever (Eve Addams), it was famous for two things: poetry readings and a sign on the door that read 'Men allowed but not welcome.' There would have been little chance of welcome drinks when police raided the place in June 1926, charging Eve with 'obscenity' for penning her *Lesbian Love* anthology, and deporting her back to Europe. Three years later, Eve was honored by a Greenwich Village theater group, who staged a theatrical version of her book at Play Mart, a basement performance space on Christopher St.

Divas, Drag & Harlem

While Times Square had developed a reputation for attracting gay men – many of them working in the district's theaters, restaurants and speakeasy bars – the hottest gay scene in the 1920s was found further north, in Harlem. The neighborhood's flourishing music scene included numerous

America's first gay-rights rally was held in New York City in 1964. Organized by the Homosexual League of New York and the League for Sexual Freedom, the picket took place outside the Army Induction Center on Whitehall St, where protestors demanded an end to the military's anti-gay policies.

gay and lesbian performers, among them Gladys Bentley and Ethel Waters. Bentley – who was as famous for her tuxedos and girlfriends as she was for her singing – had moved her way up from one-off performances at cellar clubs and tenement parties to headlining a revue at the famous Ubangi Club on 133rd St, where her supporting acts included a chorus line of female impersonators.

Even more famous were Harlem's drag balls, which became a hit with both gay and straight New Yorkers in the Roaring Twenties. The biggest of the lot was the Hamilton Lodge Ball, organized by Lodge #710 of the Grand United Order of Odd Fellows and held annually at the swank Rockland Palace on 155th St. Commonly dubbed the Faggot's Ball, it was a chance for both gay men and women to (legally) cross-dress and steal a same-sex dance, and for fashionable 'normals' to indulge in a little voyeuristic titillation. The evening's star attraction was the beauty pageant, which saw the drag-clad competitors compete for the title of 'Queen of the Ball.' Langston Hughes proclaimed it the 'spectacles of color' and the gay writer was one of many members of New York's literati to attend the ball. It was also attended by everyone from prostitutes to high-society families, including the Astors and the Vanderbilts. Even the papers covered the extravaganza, its outrageous frocks the talk of the town.

The Stonewall Revolution

The relative transgression of the early 20th century was replaced with a new conservatism in the following decades, as the Great Depression, WWII and the Cold War took their toll. Conservatism was helped along by Senator Joseph 'Joe' McCarthy, who declared that homosexuals in the State Department threatened America's security and children. Tougher policing aimed to eradicate queer visibility in the public sphere, forcing the scene further underground in the 1940s and '50s. Although crackdowns on gay venues had always occurred, they became increasingly common.

Yet on June 28, 1969, when eight police officers raided the Stonewall Inn – a gay-friendly watering hole in Greenwich Village – patrons did the unthinkable: they revolted. Fed up with both the harassment and corrupt officers receiving payoffs from the bars' owners (who were mostly organized crime figures), they began bombarding the officers with coins, bottles, bricks and chants of 'gay power' and 'we shall overcome.' The police were also met by a line of high-kicking drag queens and their now legendary chant, 'We are the Stonewall girls, we wear our hair in curls, we wear no underwear, we show our pubic hair, we wear our dungarees, above our nelly knees...'

Their collective anger and solidarity was a turning point, igniting intense and passionate debate about discrimination and forming the catalyst for the modern gay-rights movement, not just in New York, but across the US and in countries from the Netherlands to Australia.

LGBTI HISTORY

1927
New York State amends a public-obscenity code to include a ban on the appearance or discussion of gay people onstage in reaction to the increasing visibility of gays on Broadway.

1966
On April 21, gay rights organization Mattachine Society stages a 'Sip-In' at NYC's oldest gay drinking hole, Julius Bar, challenging a ban on serving alcohol to LGBTI people.

1969
Police officers raid the Stonewall Inn in Greenwich Village on June 28, sparking a riot that lasts several days and gives birth to the modern gay-rights movement.

1987
ACT UP is founded to challenge the US government's slow response in dealing with AIDS. The activist group stages its first major demonstration on March 24 on Wall St.

2011
New York's Marriage Equality Act comes into effect at 12:01am on July 24. A lesbian couple from Buffalo take their vows just seconds after midnight in Niagara Falls.

2015
Out@NBCUniversal becomes the first LGBT group to march in the city's annual St Patrick's Day parade after organizers lift their ban on openly LGBTI groups.

QUEER CITY: FROM STONEWALL TO MARRIAGE EQUALITY THE STONEWALL REVOLUTION

In the Shadow of AIDS

LGBTI activism intensified as HIV and AIDS hit world headlines in the early 1980s. Faced with ignorance, fear and the moral indignation of those who saw AIDS as a 'gay cancer,' activists such as writer Larry Kramer set about tackling what was quickly becoming an epidemic. Out of his efforts was born ACT UP (AIDS Coalition to Unleash Power) in 1987, an advocacy group set up to fight the perceived homophobia and indifference of then president Ronald Reagan, as well as to end the price gouging of AIDS drugs by pharmaceutical companies. One of its boldest protests took place on September 14, 1989, when seven ACT UP protesters chained themselves to the VIP balcony of the New York Stock Exchange, demanding pharmaceutical company Burroughs Wellcome lower the price of AIDS drug AZT from a prohibitive $10,000 per patient per annum. Within days, the price was slashed to $6400 per patient.

The epidemic itself had a significant impact on New York's artistic community. Among its most high-profile victims were artist Keith Haring, photographer Robert Mapplethorpe and fashion designer Halston. Yet out of this loss grew a tide of powerful AIDS-related plays and musicals that would not only win broad international acclaim, but would become part of America's mainstream cultural canon. Among these are Tony Kushner's political epic *Angels in America* and Jonathan Larson's rock musical *Rent*. Both works would win Tony Awards and the Pulitzer Prize.

Queer Screen Classics

Torch Song Trilogy (1988)

The Boys in the Band (1970)

Paris Is Burning (1990)

Angels in America (2003)

Jeffrey (1995)

Marriage & the New Millennium

The LGBTI fight for complete equality took two massive steps forward in 2011. On September 20, a federal law banning LGBTI military personnel from serving openly – the so-called 'Don't Ask, Don't Tell' policy – was repealed after years of intense lobbying. Three months earlier, persistence had led to an even greater victory – the right to marry. On June 15, by a margin of 80 to 63, the New York State Assembly passed the Marriage Equality Act. On June 24, the very eve of New York City Gay Pride, it was announced that the Act would be considered as the final bill of the legislative session. Considered and amended, the bill was approved by a margin of 33 to 29 and signed into law at 11.55pm by New York Governor Andrew Cuomo. State victory became a national one on June 26, 2015, when the US Supreme Court ruled that same-sex marriage is a legal right across the country, striking down the remaining marriage bans in 13 US states.

In the same year, organizers of New York City's St Patrick's Parade lifted their long-standing ban on LGBTI groups, allowing Out@ NBCUniversal – a group consisting of gay, lesbian, bisexual and transgender people working for NBCUniversal – to join the parade. The lifting of the ban no doubt met with the approval of New York City mayor Bill de Blasio, who had famously boycotted the event in protest against the ban.

Despite these significant triumphs, New York City is not immune to intolerance and prejudice. In 2013, New Yorkers reeled when a Brooklyn man, Mark Carson, was fatally shot in Greenwich Village, one of Manhattan's most historically tolerant neighborhoods. Carson and a friend had been walking along 8th St in the early hours of May 18 when, after a short altercation with a group of men hurling homophobic abuse, the 32-year-old was shot at point-blank range. The attack prompted a midnight vigil in Carson's memory, as well as a sobering reminder that even in liberal New York City, not everyone is happy to live and let live.

LGBTI Reads

Dancer from the Dance (Andrew Holleran)

Last Exit to Brooklyn (Hubert Selby)

Another Country (James Baldwin)

City Boy (Edmund White)

NYC on Screen

New York City has a long and storied life on screen. It was on these streets that a bumbling Woody Allen fell for Diane Keaton in *Annie Hall*, that Meg Ryan faked her orgasm in *When Harry Met Sally*, and that Sarah Jessica Parker philosophized about the finer points of dating and Jimmy Choos in *Sex & the City*. To fans of American film and television, traversing the city can feel like one big déjà vu of memorable scenes, characters and one-liners.

Hollywood Roots & Rivals

Believe it or not, America's film industry is an East Coast native. Fox, Universal, Metro, Selznick and Goldwyn all originated here in the early 20th century, and long before Westerns were shot in California and Colorado, they were filmed in the (now former) wilds of New Jersey. Even after Hollywood's year-round sunshine lured the bulk of the business west by the 1920s, 'Lights, Camera, Action' remained a common call in Gotham.

The Kaufman Astoria Legacy

The heart of the local scene was Queens' still-kicking Kaufman Astoria Studios. Founded by Jesse Lasky and Adolph Zukor in 1920 as a one-stop-shop for their Famous Players–Lasky Corporation, the complex would produce a string of silent-era hits, among them *The Sheik* (1921) and *Monsieur Beaucaire* (1924), both starring Italian-born heartthrob Rudolph Valentino, and *Manhandled* (1924), starring early silver-screen diva Gloria Swanson. Renamed Paramount Pictures in 1927, the studios became known for turning Broadway stars into big-screen icons, among them the Marx Brothers, Fred Astaire and Ginger Rogers, the latter making her feature-film debut as a flapper in *Young Man of Manhattan* (1930).

Despite Paramount moving all of its feature film shoots to Hollywood in 1932, the complex – renamed Eastern Services Studio – remained the home of Paramount's newsreel division. Throughout the 1930s, it was also known for its 'shorts,' which launched the careers of homegrown talents including George Burns, Bob Hope and Danny Kaye. After a stint making propaganda and training films for the US Army between WWII and 1970, what had become known as the US Signal Corps Photographic Center was renamed the Kaufman Astoria Studios by George S Kaufman (the real estate agent, not the playwright) in 1983. Modernized and expanded, the studio has gone on to make a string of flicks, including *All that Jazz* (1979), *Brighton Beach Memoirs* (1986), *The Stepford Wives* (2004) and *Men in Black III* (2012). It was here that the Huxtables lived out their middle-class Brooklyn lives in the 1980s' TV sitcom *The Cosby Show,* and it's still here that small-screen favorites *Sesame Street* and *Orange is the New Black* are taped.

Film Locations

Central Park
Countless cameos, including in Woody Allen's Annie Hall, Manhattan *and* Hannah & Her Sisters

64 Perry St
Carrie Bradshaw's apartment exterior in Sex & the City

Katz's Delicatessen Where Meg Ryan faux climaxes in When Harry Met Sally

Tom's Restaurant Stand-in for Monk's Café in Seinfeld

Tiffany & Co Where Audrey Hepburn daydreams in Breakfast at Tiffany's

Beyond Astoria

Slap bang in the historic Brooklyn Navy Yard, the 26-acre Steiner Studios is the largest studio complex east of LA. Its film credits to date include *The Producers* (2005), *Revolutionary Road* (2008), *Sex & the City* 1 and 2 (2008, 2010), and *The Wolf of Wall Street* (2013). The studios have also been used for numerous TV shows, among them Martin Scorsese's critically acclaimed gangster drama *Boardwalk Empire* and fellow HBO series *Vinyl*, a new rock drama by Scorsese, Mick Jagger and Terence Winter.

Back in Queens you'll find the city's other big gun, Silvercup Studios. Its list of features include NYC classics such as Francis Ford Coppola's *The Godfather: Part III* (1990) and Woody Allen's *Broadway Danny Rose* (1984) and *The Purple Rose of Cairo* (1985), plus TV gems such as mafia drama *The Sopranos* and the equally lauded comedy *30 Rock*, the latter starring Tina Fey as a TV sketch writer and Alec Baldwin as a network executive at the Rockefeller Center.

In reality, the Rockefeller Center is home to the NBC TV network, its long-running variety show *Saturday Night Live* the real inspiration behind Fey's *30 Rock* project. Other media networks dotted across Manhattan include the Food and Oxygen Networks, both housed in the Chelsea Market, as well as Robert De Niro's Tribeca Productions, based in the Tribeca Film Center.

Beyond the studios and headquarters are some of the top film schools – New York University's (NYU) Tisch Film School, the New York Film Academy, the School of Visual Arts, Columbia University and The New School. But you don't have to be a student to learn, with both the Museum of the Moving Image in Astoria, Queens, and the Paley Center for Media in Midtown Manhattan acting as major showcases for screenings and seminars about productions both past and present.

> Metro Goldwyn Mayer's famous 'Leo the Lion' logo was designed by Howard Dietz. His inspiration was the mascot of New York's Columbia University, where the publicist had studied journalism. Leo's famous roar was first added to films in 1928.

Lights, Landmarks, Action
Downtown Drama to Midtown Romance

It's not surprising that NYC feels strangely familiar to many first-time visitors – the city itself has racked up more screen time than most Hollywood divas put together and many of its landmarks are as much a part of American screen culture as its red-carpet celebrities. Take the Staten Island Ferry, which takes bullied secretary Melanie Griffith from suburbia to Wall St in *Working Girl* (1988); Battery Park, where Madonna bewitches Aidan Quinn and Rosanna Arquette in *Desperately Seeking Susan* (1985); or the New York County Courthouse, where villains get their just deserts in *Wall Street* (1987) and *Goodfellas* (1990), as well as in small-screen classics such as *Cagney & Lacey*, *NYPD Blue* and *Law & Order*. The latter show, famous for showcasing New York and its characters, is honored with its own road – Law & Order Way – that leads to Pier 62 at Chelsea Piers.

Few landmarks can claim as much screen time as the Empire State Building, famed for its spire-clinging ape in *King Kong* (1933, 2005), as well as for the countless romantic encounters on its observation decks. One of its most famous scenes is Meg Ryan and Tom Hanks' after-hours encounter in *Sleepless in Seattle* (1993). The sequence – which uses the real lobby but a studio-replica deck – is a tribute of sorts to *An Affair to Remember* (1957), which sees Cary Grant and Deborah Kerr make a pact to meet and (hopefully) seal their love atop the skyscraper.

Film Festivals

Dance on Camera (January/February)

New York International Children's Film Festival (February/March)

Tribeca Film Festival (April)

Human Rights Watch International Film Festival (June)

NewFest: LGBT Film Festival (October)

New York Film Festival (September/October)

NYC CELLULOID SHORTLIST

It would take volumes to cover all the films tied to Gotham, so fire up your imagination with the following celluloid hits:

Taxi Driver (Martin Scorsese, 1976) Starring Robert De Niro, Cybill Shepherd and Jodie Foster. De Niro is a mentally unstable Vietnam War vet whose violent urges are heightened by the city's tensions. It's a funny, depressing, brilliant classic that's a potent reminder of how much grittier this place used to be.

Manhattan (Woody Allen, 1979) Starring Woody Allen, Diane Keaton and Mariel Hemingway. A divorced New Yorker dating a high-school student (the baby-voiced Hemingway) falls for his best friend's mistress in what is essentially a love letter to NYC. Catch romantic views of the Queensboro Bridge and the Upper East Side.

Desperately Seeking Susan (Susan Seidelman, 1985) Starring Madonna, Rosanna Arquette and Aidan Quinn. A case of mistaken identity leads a bored New Jersey housewife on a wild adventure through Manhattan's subcultural wonderland. Relive mid-1980s East Village and long-gone nightclub Danceteria.

Summer of Sam (Spike Lee, 1999) Starring John Leguizamo, Mira Sorvino and Jennifer Esposito. Spike Lee puts NYC's summer of 1977 in historical context by weaving together the Son of Sam murders, the blackout, racial tensions and the misadventures of one disco-dancing Brooklyn couple, including scenes at **CBGB** (315 Bowery, btwn 1st & 2nd Sts; S F to 2nd Ave; 6 to Bleecker St) and Studio 54.

Angels in America (Mike Nichols, 2003) Starring Al Pacino, Meryl Streep and Jeffrey Wright. This movie version of Tony Kushner's Broadway play recalls 1985 Manhattan: crumbling relationships, AIDS out of control and a closeted Roy Cohn – advisor to President Ronald Reagan – doing nothing about it except falling ill himself. Follow characters from Brooklyn to Lower Manhattan to Central Park.

Party Monster (Fenton Bailey, 2003) Starring Seth Green and Macaulay Culkin, who plays the famed, murderous club kid Michael Alig, this is a disturbing look into the drug-fueled downtown clubbing culture of the late '80s. The former Limelight club is featured prominently.

Precious (Lee Daniels, 2009) Starring Gabourey Sidibe and based on the novel *Push* by Sapphire. This unflinching tale of an obese, illiterate teenager who is abused by her parents takes place in Harlem, offering plenty of streetscapes and New York–ghetto 'tude.

Birdman (Alejandro G. Iñárritu, 2014) Oscar-winning black-comedy/drama starring Michael Keaton and featuring Zach Galifianakis, Edward Norton, Andrea Riseborough, Amy Ryan, Emma Stone and Naomi Watts. Birdman documents the struggles of a has-been Hollywood actor trying to mount a Broadway show.

Sarah Jessica Parker is less lucky in *Sex & the City* (2008), when a nervous Chris Noth jilts her and her Vivienne Westwood wedding dress at the New York Public Library. Perhaps he'd seen *Ghostbusters* (1984) a few too many times, its opening scenes featuring the haunted library's iconic marble lions and Rose Main Reading Room. The library's foyer sneakily stands in for the Metropolitan Museum of Art in *The Thomas Crown Affair* (1999), in which thieving playboy Pierce Brosnan meets his match in sultry detective Rene Russo. It's at the fountain in adjacent Bryant Park that DIY sleuth Diane Keaton debriefs husband Woody Allen about their supposedly bloodthirsty elderly neighbor in *Manhattan Murder Mystery* (1993). True to form, Allen uses the film to showcase a slew of New York locales, among them the National Arts Club in Gramercy Park and one of his own former hangouts, Elaine's at 1703 Second Ave. It's here, at this since-closed Upper East Side restaurant, that Keaton explains her crime theory to Allen and dinner companions Alan Alda and Ron Rifkin.

The restaurant was a regular in Allen's films, also appearing in *Manhattan* (1979) and *Celebrity* (1998).

Across Central Park – whose own countless scenes include Barbra Streisand and Robert Redford rowing on its lake in clutch-a-Kleenex *The Way We Were* (1973) – stands the **Dakota Building** (Map p436; 1 W 72nd St, at Central Park West; [S]B, C to 72nd St), used in the classic thriller *Rosemary's Baby* (1968). The Upper West Side is also home to Tom's Restaurant, whose facade was used regularly in *Seinfeld.* Another neighborhood star is the elegant Lincoln Center, where Natalie Portman slowly loses her mind in the psychological thriller *Black Swan* (2010), and where love-struck Brooklynites Cher and Nicolas Cage meet for a date in *Moonstruck* (1987). The Center sits on what had previously been a rundown district of tenements, captured in Oscar-winning gangland musical *West Side Story* (1961).

The more recent Oscar-winner *Birdman* (2014) shines the spotlight on Midtown's glittering Theater District, in which a long-suffering Michael Keaton tries to stage a Broadway adaptation at the St James Theatre on W44th St. Locked out of the building, a mortified Keaton fronts Times Square in nothing but his underwear. A few blocks further east, he spars over his play with Lindsay Duncan at historic drinking den Rum House.

NYC TV Shows

Over 70 TV shows are filmed in NYC, from hit series such as Law & Order: Special Victims Unit and The Good Wife, to long-standing classics including The Tonight Show Starring Jimmy Fallon and Saturday Night Live. Combined, the city's TV and film industries spend $8.7 billion on production annually and support 104,000 jobs. Over a third of professional actors in the US are based here.

Dancing in the Streets

Knives make way for leotards in the cult musical *Fame* (1980), in which New York High School of Performing Arts students do little for the city's traffic woes by dancing on Midtown's streets. The film's graphic content was too much for the city's Board of Education, who banned shooting at the real High School of Performing Arts, then located at 120 W 46th St. Consequently, filmmakers used the doorway of a disused church on the opposite side of the street for the school's entrance, and Haaren Hall (Tenth Ave and 59th St) for interior scenes.

Fame is not alone in turning Gotham into a pop-up dance floor. In *On the Town* (1949), starstruck sailors Frank Sinatra, Gene Kelly and Jules Munshin look straight off a Pride float as they skip, hop and sing their way across this 'wonderful town,' from the base of Lady Liberty to Rockefeller Plaza and the Brooklyn Bridge. Another wave of campness hits the bridge when Diana Ross and Michael Jackson cross it in *The Wiz* (1978), a bizarre take on *The Wizard of Oz*, complete with munchkins in Flushing Meadows Corona Park and an Emerald City at the base of the WTC Twin Towers. The previous year, the bridge provided a rite of passage for a bell-bottomed John Travolta in *Saturday Night Fever* (1977), who leaves the comforts of his adolescent Brooklyn for the bigger, brighter mirror balls of Manhattan. Topping them all, however, is the closing scene in Terry Gilliam's *The Fisher King* (1991), which sees Grand Central Terminal's Main Concourse turned into a ballroom of waltzing commuters.

The infamous subway grill scene in *The Seven Year Itch* (1955) – in which Marilyn Monroe enjoys a dress-lifting breeze – was shot at 586 Lexington Ave, outside the since-demolished Trans-Lux 52nd Street Theatre.

Location Tours

Movie- and TV-location guided tours such as On Location Tours are a good way to visit some of the spots where your screen favorites were shot, including *The Devil Wears Prada, Spider-Man, How I Met Your Mother* and more. Alternatively, you can do it yourself after visiting the wonderfully comprehensive On the Set of New York website (www.onthesetofnewyork.com), which offers free downloadable location maps covering much of Manhattan.

Survival Guide

Transportation

ARRIVING IN NEW YORK CITY

With its three bustling airports, two main train stations and a monolithic bus terminal, New York City rolls out the welcome mat for millions of visitors who come to take a bite out of the Big Apple each year.

Direct flights are possible from most major American and international cities. Figure six hours from Los Angeles, seven hours from London and Amsterdam, and 14 hours from Tokyo. Consider getting here by train instead of car or plane to enjoy a mix of bucolic and urban scenery en route, without unnecessary traffic hassles, security checks and excess carbon emissions.

Flights, tours and rail tickets can be booked online at lonelyplanet.com/bookings.

John F Kennedy International Airport

John F Kennedy International Airport (JFK; ☎718-244-4444; www.kennedyairport.com; [S]) is 15 miles from Midtown in southeastern Queens, has eight terminals, serves nearly 50 million passengers annually and hosts flights coming and going from all corners of the globe.

Taxi

From JFK, taxis charge a flat rate of $52 to any destination in Manhattan (not including tolls or tip); it can take 45 to 60 minutes to most destinations. A yellow taxi from Manhattan to the airport will use the meter; prices (often about $60) depend on traffic – it can take 45 to 60 minutes. To/from a destination in Brooklyn, the metered fare should be about $45 (Coney Island) to $65 (downtown Brooklyn). Note that the Williamsburg, Manhattan, Brooklyn and Queensboro–59th St Bridges have no toll either way, while the Queens–Midtown Tunnel and the Hugh L Carey Tunnel (aka the Brooklyn–Battery Tunnel) cost $8 going into Manhattan.

Vans & car service

Shared vans, like those offered by **Super Shuttle Manhattan** (www.supershuttle.com), cost around $20 to $26 per person, depending on the destination. If traveling to the airport from NYC, car services have set fares from $45.

Express bus

The **NYC Airporter** (www.nycairporter.com) runs to Grand Central Station, Penn Station or the Port Authority Bus Terminal from JFK. The one-way fare is $17.

Subway

The subway is the cheapest but slowest way of reaching Manhattan. From the airport, hop on the AirTrain ($5, payable as you exit) to Sutphin Blvd-Archer Ave (Jamaica Station) to reach the E, J or Z line (or the Long Island Rail Road). To take the A line instead, ride the AirTrain to Howard Beach station. The E train to Midtown has the fewest stops. Expect the journey to take at least 1½ hours to Midtown.

Long Island Rail Road (LIRR)

This is by far the most relaxing way to arrive in the city. From the airport, take the AirTrain ($5, as you exit) to Jamaica Station. From there, LIRR trains go frequently to Penn Station in Manhattan or to Atlantic Terminal in Brooklyn (near Fort Greene, Boerum Hill and the Barclay Center). It's about a 20-minute journey from station to station. One-way fares to either Penn Station or Atlantic Terminal cost $7.50 ($10 at peak times).

LaGuardia Airport

Used mainly for domestic flights, **LaGuardia** (LGA; ☎718-533-3400; www.panynj.gov) is smaller than JFK but only 8 miles from midtown Manhattan; it sees about 26 million passengers per year.

Taxi

A taxi to/from Manhattan costs about $42 for the approximately half-hour ride.

Car service

A car service to LaGuardia costs around $35.

Express bus

The **NYC Airporter** (www.nycairporter.com) costs $14 and goes to/from Grand Central, Penn Station and the Port Authority Bus Terminal.

Subway & bus

It's less convenient to get to LaGuardia by public transportation than the other airports. The best subway link is the 74 St–Broadway station (7 line, or the E, F, M and R lines at the connecting Jackson Heights-Roosevelt Ave station) in Queens, where you can pick up the new Q70 Express Bus to the airport (about 10 minutes to the airport).

Newark Liberty International Airport

Don't write off New Jersey when looking for airfares to New York. About the same distance from Midtown as JFK (16 miles), **Newark** (EWR; ☎973-961-6000; www.panynj.gov) brings many

New Yorkers out for flights (there's some 36 million passengers annually).

Car service

A car service runs about $45 to $60 for the 45-minute ride from Midtown – a taxi is roughly the same. You'll have to pay a whopping $15 to get into NYC through the Lincoln (at 42nd St) and Holland (at Canal St) Tunnels and, further north, the George Washington Bridge, though there's no charge going back through to NJ. There are a couple of cheap tolls on New Jersey highways, too, unless you ask your driver to take Hwy 1 or 9.

Subway/train

NJ Transit (☎973-275-5555; www.njtransit.com) runs a rail service (with an AirTrain connection) between Newark airport (EWR) and New York's Penn Station for $13 each way. The trip takes 25 minutes and runs every 20 or 30 minutes from 4:20am to about 1:40am. Hold onto your ticket, which you must show upon exiting at the airport.

Express bus

The **Newark Liberty Airport Express** (www.newarkairportexpress.com) has a bus service between the airport and Port Authority Bus Terminal, Bryant Park and Grand Central Terminal in Midtown ($16 one way). The 45-minute ride goes

every 15 minutes from 6:45am to 11:15pm and every half hour from 4:45am to 6:45am and 11:15pm to 1:15am.

Port Authority Bus Terminal

For long-distance bus trips, you'll arrive and depart from the world's busiest bus station, the **Port Authority Bus Terminal** (Map p432; ☎212-564-8484; www.panynj.gov; ⊠A/C/E, N/Q/R, 1/2/3, 7), which sees over 65 million passengers each year. Bus companies leaving from here include the following:

Greyhound (Map p432; ☎800-231-2222; www.greyhound.com) Connects New York with major cities across the country.

Peter Pan Trailways (☎800-343-9999; www.peterpanbus.com) Daily express services to Boston, Washington, DC, and Philadelphia.

Short Line Bus (☎212-736-4700; www.shortlinebus.com) Serves northern New Jersey and upstate New York, focusing on college towns such as Ithaca and New Paltz; part of Coach USA.

Penn Station

Penn Station (33rd St, btwn Seventh & Eighth Aves; ⊠1/2/3, A/C/E to 34th St-Penn Station) The departure point for all **Amtrak** (☎800-872-7245; www.amtrak.com)

CLIMATE CHANGE & TRAVEL

Every form of transport that relies on carbon-based fuel generates CO_2, the main cause of human-induced climate change. Modern travel is dependent on aeroplanes, which might use less fuel per kilometrer per person than most cars but travel much greater distances. The altitude at which aircraft emit gases (including CO_2) and particles also contributes to their climate change impact. Many websites offer 'carbon calculators' that allow people to estimate the carbon emissions generated by their journey and, for those who wish to do so, to offset the impact of the greenhouse gases emitted with contributions to portfolios of climate-friendly initiatives throughout the world. Lonely Planet offsets the carbon footprint of all staff and author travel.

trains, including the Acela Express services to Princeton, NJ, and Washington, DC (note that this express service will cost twice as much as a normal fare). All fares vary, based on the day of the week and the time you want to travel. There's no baggage-storage facility at Penn Station.

Long Island Rail Road (LIRR; 📞511; www.mta.info/lirr; furthest zone one-way off-peak/peak $20.50/28.25) The Long Island Rail Road serves over 300,000 commuters each day, with services from Penn Station to points in Brooklyn and Queens, and on Long Island. Prices are broken down by zones. A peak-hour ride from Penn Station to Jamaica Station (en route to JFK via AirTrain) costs $9.50 if you buy it at the station (or a whopping $16 onboard!).

NJ Transit (📞973-275-5555; www.njtransit.com) Also operates trains from Penn Station, with services to the suburbs and the Jersey Shore.

New Jersey PATH (📞800-234-7284; www.panynj.gov/path) An option for getting into NJ's northern points, such as Hoboken and Newark. Trains ($2.50) run from Penn Station along the length of Sixth Ave, with stops at 33rd, 23rd, 14th, 9th and Christopher Sts, as well as at the reopened World Trade Center site.

Metro-North Railroad (📞511; www.mta.info/mnr) The last line departing from Grand Central Terminal, the Metro-North Railroad serves Connecticut, Westchester County and the Hudson Valley.

Bus Stations

A growing number of budget bus lines operate from locations just outside **Penn Station** (33rd St, btwn Seventh & Eighth Aves; 🚇1/2/3, A/C/E to 34th St-Penn Station).

BoltBus (📞877-265-8287; www.boltbus.com; 📶) Services from New York to Philadelphia, Boston, Baltimore and Washington, DC. The earlier you purchase tickets, the better the deal. Notable for its free wi-fi, which occasionally actually works.

megabus (http://us.megabus.com; 📶) Travels from New York to Boston, Washington, DC, and Toronto, among other destinations. Free (sometimes functioning) wi-fi.

Vamoose (Map p432; 📞212-695-6766; www.vamoosebus.com; 🚇1 to 28th St; A/C/E, 1/2/3 to 34th St-Penn Station) Buses head to Arlington, Virginia, near Washington, DC.

GETTING AROUND NEW YORK CITY

Once you've arrived in NYC, getting around is fairly easy. The 660-mile subway system is cheap and (reasonably) efficient and can whisk you to nearly every corner of the city. There are also buses, ferries, trains, pedicabs and those ubiquitous yellow taxis (though don't expect to see many available when it's raining) for zipping around and out of town when the subway simply doesn't cut it.

The sidewalks of New York, however, are the real stars in the transportation scheme – this city is made for walking. Increasingly, it's also made for bicycles, with the addition of hundreds of miles of new bike lanes and greenways over the last few years.

Subway

The New York subway system, run by the **Metropolitan Transportation Authority** (MTA; 📞511; www.mta.info), is iconic, cheap ($2.75 per ride, regardless of the distance traveled), round-the-clock and often the fastest and most reliable way to get around the city. It's also safer and (a bit) cleaner than it used to be.

It's a good idea to grab a free map from a station attendant. If you have a smartphone, download a useful app (like the free Citymapper), with subway map and alerts of service outages. When in doubt, ask someone who looks like they know what they're doing. They may not, but subway confusion (and consternation) is the great unifier in this diverse city. And if you're new to the underground, never wear headphones when you're riding, as you might miss an important announcement about track changes or skipped stops.

CHINATOWN BUSES

Maniacally driven Chinatown buses, operating around Canal St, were once the cheapest and probably most dangerous way to travel to Boston, Philadelphia, Washington, DC, and other areas on the East Coast. After a series of deadly accidents over the past decade (including one in 2011 that killed 15 people), the Federal Motor Carrier Safety Administration clamped down on these bus lines, some of which continued to operate illegally even after their licenses were revoked; others simply changed their names and logos. Keep in mind the risks involved in traveling with one of these cut-rate operators.

SUBWAY CHEAT SHEET

The following are a few tips for understanding the madness of the New York subway:

Numbers, letters, colors

Color-coded subway lines are named by a letter or number, and most carry a collection of two to four trains on their tracks.

Express & local lines

A common mistake is accidentally boarding an 'express train' and passing by a local stop you want. Know that each color-coded line is shared by local trains and express trains; the latter make only select stops in Manhattan (indicated by a white circle on subway maps). For example, on the red line, the 2 and 3 are express, while the slower 1 makes local stops. If you're covering a greater distance – say from the Upper West Side to Wall St – you're better off transferring to the express train (usually just across the platform from the local) to save time.

Getting in the right station

Some stations – such as SoHo's Spring St station on the 6 line – have separate entrances for downtown or uptown lines (read the sign carefully). If you swipe in at the wrong one – as even locals do on occasion – you'll either need to ride the subway to a station where you can transfer for free, or just lose the $2.75 and re-enter the station (usually across the street). Also look for the green and red lamps above the stairs at each station entrance; green means that it's always open, while red means that that particular entrance will be closed at certain hours, usually late at night.

Weekends

All the rules switch on weekends, when some lines combine with others, some get suspended, some stations get passed, others get reached. Locals and tourists alike stand on platforms confused, sometimes irate. Check www.mta.info for weekend schedules. Sometimes posted signs aren't visible until after you reach the platform.

Taxi

Hailing and riding in a cab are rites of passage in New York – especially when you get a driver who's a neurotic speed demon, which is often (don't forget to buckle up). Still, most taxis in NYC are clean and, compared to those in many international cities, pretty cheap.

Taxi & Limousine Commission (TLC; www.nyc.gov/html/tlc/html/home/home.shtml) The taxis' governing body has set fares for rides (which can be paid with credit or debit card). It's $2.50 for the initial charge (first one-fifth of a mile), 50¢ for each additional one-fifth mile as well as per 60 seconds of being stopped in traffic, $1 peak surcharge (weekdays 4pm to 8pm), and a 50¢ night surcharge (8pm to 6am), plus a NY State sur-

charge of 50¢ per ride. Tips are expected to be 10% to 15%, but give less if you feel in any way mistreated; be sure to ask for a receipt and use it to note the driver's license number.

Passenger rights The TLC keeps a Passenger's Bill of Rights, which gives you the right to tell the driver which route you'd like to take, or ask your driver to stop smoking or turn off an annoying radio station. Also, the driver does not have the right to refuse you a ride based on where you are going. Tip: get in first, then say where you're going.

Private car These services are a common taxi alternative in the outer boroughs. Fares differ depending on the neighborhood and length of ride, and must be determined beforehand, as they have no meters. These 'black cars' are

quite common in Brooklyn and Queens, however, it's illegal if a driver simply stops to offer you a ride – no matter what borough you're in. A couple of car services in Brooklyn include **Northside** (☑718-387-2222; 207 Bedford Ave; ☉24hr) in Williamsburg and **Arecibo** (☑718-783-6465; 170 Fifth Ave, at Degraw St; ☉24hr) in Park Slope.

Boro Taxis Green Boro Taxis operate in the outer boroughs and Upper Manhattan. These allow folks to hail a taxi on the street in neighborhoods where yellow taxis rarely roam. They have the same fares and features as yellow cabs, and are a good way to get around the outer boroughs (from, say, Astoria to Williamsburg, or Park Slope to Red Hook). Drivers are reluctant (but legally obligated) to take passengers

CITI BIKES

Hundreds of miles of designated bike lanes have been added over the past decade. Add to this the excellent bike-sharing network **Citi Bike** (www.citibikenyc.com; bike hire per 24hr/7 days $11/27) and you have the makings for a surprisingly bike-friendly city. Hundreds of Citi Bike kiosks in Manhattan and parts of Brooklyn house the iconic bright blue and very sturdy bicycles, which have reasonable rates for short-term users.

You'll find routes and bike lanes for every borough on **NYC Bike Maps** (www.nycbikemaps.com). For downloadable maps and point-to-point route generator, visit **NYC DOT** (www.nyc.gov/html/dot/html/bicyclists/bikemaps.shtml). Free bike maps are also available at most bike shops.

into Manhattan as they aren't legally allowed to take fares going out of Manhattan south of 96th St.

Ferry

East River Ferry (www.eastriverferry.com; one-way $4-6) Runs year-round commuter service connecting a variety of locations in Queens and Brooklyn with Manhattan.

New York Water Taxi (☎212-742-1969; www.nywatertaxi.com; hop-on, hop-off 1-day pass $31) Has a fleet of zippy yellow boats that provide hop-on, hop-off service around Manhattan and Brooklyn.

Staten Island Ferry (Map p410; www.siferry.com; Whitehall Terminal, 4 South St, at Whitehall; ⏲24hr; [S]1 to South Ferry) [FREE] Another bigger, brighter ferry (this one's orange) is the commuter-oriented ferry to Staten Island, which makes constant free journeys across New York Harbor.

Train

Long Island Rail Road (LIRR; ☎511; www.mta.info/lirr; furthest zone one-way off-peak/peak $20.50/28.25), **NJ Transit** (☎973-275-5555; www.njtransit.com), **New Jersey PATH** (☎800-234-7284; www.panynj.gov/path) and **Metro-North Railroad** (☎511; www.mta.info/mnr) all offer useful services for getting around NYC and surrounds.

TOURS

There are loads of options in NYC when it comes to guided tours. You can take a historical walking tour, taste your way around ethnically rich neighborhoods, or do something more active on a bicycling, kayaking or bird-watching tour.

Big Apple Greeter
(☎212-669-8159; www.bigapplegreeter.org) For an inside take on the NYC experience, book a walking tour in the neighborhood of your choice led by a local volunteer who just can't wait to show off their city to you. You'll be matched with a guide who suits your needs, whether that means speaking Spanish or American Sign Language, or knowing just where to find the best wheelchair-accessible spots in the city. Reserve four weeks in advance.

Big Onion Walking Tours
(☎888-606-9255; www bigonion.com; tours $20) Choose from nearly 30 tours, including Brooklyn Bridge and Brooklyn Heights, the 'Official' Gangs of New York Tour, a Gay and Lesbian History Tour – Before Stonewall, and Chelsea and the High Line. 'Each tour has a very extensive script,' says Big Onion founder Seth Kamil. It's that attention to fine detail in this grand city that makes the award-winning Big Onion whose tours 'explore the many layers of history' – stand apart, and gives it a stellar reputation.

Bike the Big Apple
(☎877-865-0078; www.bikethebigapple.com; tours incl bike & helmet around $95) Biking tours let you cover more ground than walking tours and give you a healthy dose of exercise to boot. Bike the Big Apple, recommended by NYC & Company (the official tourism authority of New York City and operators of www.nycgo.com), offers 10 set tours. The most popular is the 15-mile, six-hour 'Back to the Old Country – the Ethnic Apple Tour', covering a bit of Queens, northern Brooklyn and the Lower East Side of Manhattan. Other tours visit the Bronx, Little Italy, city parks, Brooklyn chocolate shops and several night rides.

Circle Line Boat Tours
(Map p432; ☎212-563-3200; www.circleline42.com; Pier 83, 42nd St, at Twelfth Ave, Midtown West; cruises from adult/child $29/20; 🚌westbound M42 or M50, [S]A/C/E to 42nd-Port Authority) The classic Circle Line guides you through all the big sights from the safe distance of a boat. Options include a 2.5-hour full-island cruise, a shorter (90-minute) 'semi-circle' journey and a two-hour evening cruise. From May to October, the outfit also operates adrenaline-fueled cruises aboard the high-speed *Beast*. See the website for schedules.

Foods of New York (☎212-913-9964; www.foodsofny.com; tours from $52) The official foodie tour of NYC & Company offers various three-hour tours that help you eat your way through gourmet shops and eateries in either the West Village, Chelsea, Chinatown or Nolita. Prepare yourself for a moving feast of French bread, fresh Italian pasta, sushi, global cheeses, real New York pizza, local fish and freshly baked pastries.

Gray Line (☎212-445-0848; www.newyorksightseeing.com; tours $44-69) The most ubiquitous guided tour in the city, Gray Line is responsible for bombarding New York streets with the red double-decker buses that aren't much loved by locals. For an overview of the city, though, it's not a bad option. The company offers various routes, the best being both of the popular hop-on, hop-off loops of Manhattan. Tours are available in various languages, including Spanish, French, German, Italian and Japanese.

Liberty Helicopter Tours (Map p410; ☎1-800-542-9933; www.libertyhelicopters.com; Pier 6, East River, Lower Manhattan; per person for 12-15min $185; [S]1 to South Ferry; R to Whitehall St) Enjoy a bird's-eye view of the city in a very Donald Trump sort of way as a helicopter whisks you high above New York's concrete jungle. Just get ready to shell out for the privilege.

New York City Audubon (Map p426; ☎212-691-7483; www.nycaudubon.org; 71 W 23rd St, Suite 1523, at Sixth Ave; tours & classes free-$170; [S]F/M to 23rd St) Throughout the year, the New York City Audubon Society runs bird-watching field trips (including seal and waterbird spotting on New York Harbor and eagle-watching in the Hudson Valley), lectures and beginning birding classes.

New York Gallery Tours (Map p424; ☎212-946-1548; nygallerytours.com; 526 W 26th St, at Tenth Ave; tours $25; [S]C/E to 23rd St) You know you're supposed to check out the array of amazing modern-art galleries in Chelsea. But where to begin? This excellent guided tour takes you to a slew of galleries and provides helpful commentary along the way. It also runs gay and lesbian tours that focus on a 'queer aesthetic'. Scheduled tours happen every Saturday at different times and locations; see the website for information.

On Location Tours (☎212-683-2027; www.onlocationtours.com; tours $25-49) Face it: you want to sit on Carrie Bradshaw's apartment stoop and check out the bar Michael Keaton frequents in *Birdman*. This company offers various tours – covering *Gossip Girl*, *Sex and the City*, *The Sopranos*, general TV and movie locations, and movie locations in Central Park – that let you live out your entertainment-obsessed fantasies. A couple of the tours are also available in French or German.

Strayboots (☎877-787-2929; www.strayboots.com; tours from $12) The self-guided tours fuse interesting urban info with a scavenger-hunt element to help New York neophytes find their way around the neighborhood of their choice. Go at your own pace as you text in your answers to central command to receive your next clue. Download the app to give it a go.

Wildman Steve Brill (☎914-835-2153; www.wildmanstevebrill.com; tours up to $20) New York's best-known naturalist – betcha didn't know there were any! – has been leading folks on foraging expeditions through city parks for more than 30 years. He'll trek with you through Central Park, Prospect Park, Inwood Park and many more, teaching you to identify natural riches including sassafras, chickweed, ginkgo nuts, garlic and wild mushrooms along the way. It's wild.

Directory A–Z

Customs Regulations

US Customs allows each person over the age of 21 to bring 1L of liquor and 200 cigarettes into the US duty free. Agricultural items including meat, fruits, vegetables, plants and soil are prohibited. US citizens are allowed to import, duty free, up to $800 worth of gifts from abroad, while non-US citizens are allowed to import $100 worth. If you're carrying more than $10,000 in US and foreign cash, traveler's checks or money orders, you need to declare the excess amount. There is no legal restriction on the amount that may be imported, but undeclared sums in excess of $10,000 will probably be subject to investigation. If you're bringing prescription drugs, make sure they're in clearly marked containers. Obviously, leave the illegal narcotics at home. For updates, check www.cbp.gov.

Discount Cards

If you plan on blitzing the major sights, consider buying one of the numerous multi-attraction passes (see www.nycgo.com/attraction-passes). Getting one of these discount cards will save you a wad of cash. Go online for more details, and to purchase these passes.

New York CityPASS (www.citypass.com) Buys you admission to six major attractions (including the Empire State Building) for $114, saving around 40% if purchased separately.

The New York Pass (www.newyorkpass.com) This pass gives you one-day access to some 80 different sites for $90. Multiday passes also available (from two to 10 days).

Downtown Culture Pass (www.downtownculturepass.org) Purchase this $25 pass for free admission (and shop discounts) at a handful of sites in Lower Manhattan, including the Museum of American Finance and the Museum of Jewish Heritage – both locations where you can purchase the pass in person.

Explorer Pass (www.smartdestinations.com) A pass that lets you choose between three and 10 attractions that you wish discounted admission to. You pick the sites from among 60 options, including the Museum of Modern Art (MoMA), the Intrepid Museum, Sightseeing cruises and the Top of the Rock.

Electricity

The US electric current is 110V to 115V, 60Hz AC. Outlets are made for flat two-prong plugs (which often have a third, rounded prong for grounding). If your appliance is made for another electrical system (eg 220V), you'll need a step-down converter, which can be bought at hardware stores and drugstores. Most electronic devices (laptops, camera-battery chargers etc) are built for dual-voltage use, however, and will only need a plug adapter.

120V/60Hz

120V/60Hz

Emergency

Local directory ☎411

Municipal offices & information ☎311

National directory information ☎1-212-555-1212

Operator ☎0

Fire, police & ambulance ☎911

Internet Access

It's rare to find accommodations in New York City that doesn't offer wi-fi, though it isn't always free. Public parks with free wi-fi include the High Line, Bryant Park, Battery Park, Tompkins Square Park and Union Square Park. Other public areas with free wi-fi include **Columbia University** (Map p438; www.columbia.edu; Broadway, at 116th St, Morningside Heights; [S]1 to 116th St-Columbia University) and **South Street Seaport** (Map p410; www.southstreetseaport.com; [S]A/C, J/Z, 2/3, 4/5 to Fulton St). Internet kiosks can be found at the scatter of Staples and FedEx Office locations around the city, and you can also try Apple stores.

Legal Matters

If you're arrested, you have the right to remain silent. There is no legal reason to speak to a police officer if you don't wish to – especially since anything you say 'can and will be used against you' – but never walk away from an officer until given permission. All persons who are arrested have the legal right to make one phone call. If you don't have a lawyer or family member to help you, call your consulate. The police will give you the number upon request.

Medical Services

Before traveling, contact your health-insurance provider to find out what types of medical care will be covered outside your hometown (or home country). Overseas visitors should acquire travel insurance that covers medical situations in the US, as nonemergency care for uninsured patients can be very expensive. For non-emergency appointments at hospitals, you'll need proof of insurance or cash. Even with insurance, you'll most likely have to pay up front for non-emergency care and then wrangle with your insurance company afterwards in order to get your money reimbursed.

Clinics

Callen-Lorde Community Health Center (☎212-271-7200; www.callen-lorde.org; 356 W 18th St, btwn Eighth & Ninth Aves; 🕒8:15am-8:15pm Mon-Thu, to 4:45pm Fri, 8:30-3:15pm Sat; [S]A/C/E, L to 8th Ave-14th St) This medical center, dedicated to the LGBTI community and people living with HIV/AIDS, serves people regardless of their ability to pay.

New York County Medical Society (☎212-684-4670; www.nycms.org) Provides doctor referrals over the phone, based on type of problem and language spoken.

Planned Parenthood (☎212-965-7000; www.plannedparenthood.org; 26 Bleecker St, btwn Mott & Elizabeth Sts; [S]B/D/F/V to Broadway-Lafayette St; 6 to Bleecker St) Provides birth control, STD screenings and gynecological care.

Travel MD (☎212-737-1212; www.travelmd.com; 952 Fifth Ave, btwn 76th & 77th Sts; 🕒24hr; [S]6 to 77th St) Care specifically for visitors to NYC; hotel appointments can be made.

Emergency Rooms

Emergency services can be stress-inducing and slow (unless your medical condition is absolutely dire); a visit should be avoided if other medical services can be provided to mitigate the situation.

Bellevue Hospital Center (☎212-562-4141; www.nychhc.org/bellevue/html/home/home.shtml; 462 First Ave, at 27th St, Midtown East; [S]6 to 28th St) Major public hospital with emergency room and trauma center.

Lenox Hill Hospital (☎212-434-2000; 100 E 77th St, at Lexington Ave; 🕒24hr; [S]6 to 103rd St) A good hospital with a 24-hour emergency room and multilingual translators, in the Upper East Side.

Mount Sinai Hospital (☎212-241-6500; www.mountsinai.org; 1468 Madison Ave, at 101st St; 🕒24hr; [S]6 to 103rd St) An excellent hospital in the Upper East Side.

New York-Presbyterian Hospital (☎212-305-2500; 630 W 168th St, at Ft Washington Ave; [S]A/C, 1 to 168th St) Reputable hospital.

Pharmacies

New York is bursting with 24-hour 'pharmacies,' which are handy all-purpose stores where you can buy over-the-counter medications anytime; the pharmaceutical prescription counters have more limited hours. Major pharmacy chains include CVS, Duane Reade, Rite Aid and Walgreens. The latter also has walk-in medical care (www.drwalkin.com) at a number of Manhattan locations. Hospital-affiliated doctors are available to offer diagnosis and treatment. For locations, visit the website.

Money

ATMs

ATMs are on practically every corner. You can either use your card at banks – usually in a 24-hour-access lobby, filled with up to a dozen monitors at major branches – or you can opt for the lone wolves, which sit in delis, restaurants, bars and grocery stores, charging fierce service fees that average $3 but can go as high as $5.

Most New York banks are linked by the New York Cash Exchange (NYCE) system, and you can use local bank cards interchangeably at ATMs – for an extra fee if you're banking outside your system.

Changing Money

Banks and moneychangers, found all over New York City (including all three major airports), will give you US currency based on the current exchange rate.

Travelex (☎212-265-6063; www.travelex.com; 1578 Broadway, btwn 47th & 48th Sts, Midtown West; ⏰9am-7pm Mon-Sat, to 8pm Sun, extended hr in summer; [S]N/Q/R to 49th St) A city-wide currency exchange, which includes this branch at Times Square.

Credit Cards

Major credit cards are accepted at most hotels, restaurants and shops throughout New York City. In fact, you'll find it difficult to perform certain transactions, such as purchasing tickets to performances and renting a car, without one.

Stack your deck with a Visa, MasterCard or American Express, as these are the cards of choice here. Places that accept Visa and MasterCard also accept debit cards. Be sure to check with your bank to confirm that your debit card will be accepted in other states or countries – debit cards from large commercial banks can often be used worldwide.

If your cards are lost or stolen, contact the company immediately.

Opening Hours

Standard business hours are as follows:

Banks 9am–6pm Monday–Friday, some also 9am–noon Saturday

Bars 5pm–4am

Businesses 9am–5pm Monday–Friday

Clubs 10pm–4am

Restaurants Breakfast 6am–11am, lunch 11am–around 3pm, and dinner 5pm–11pm. Weekend brunch 11am–4pm.

Shops 10am–around 7pm weekdays, 11am–around 8pm Saturday, and Sunday can be variable – some stores stay closed while others keep weekday hours. Stores tend to stay open later in the neighborhoods downtown.

Post

Visit the **US Postal Service** (www.usps.com) website for up-to-date information about postage prices and branch locations throughout the city. Alternatives to post-office mailing include various mail stores, such as the chain Mailboxes Etc, which has many options around Manhattan. The upside is there's always a much shorter wait, and there are more branches to choose from; the downside is that it's much more expensive.

Post Office (Map p432; ☎800-275-8777; usps.com; James A Foley Bldg, 380 W 33rd St, at Eighth Ave, Midtown West; ⏰7am-10pm Mon-Fri, 9am-9pm Sat, 11am-7pm Sun; [S]A/C/E to 34th St-Penn Station) The beautiful New York General Post Office can help with all your postal requirements, as can the various branch offices, which are listed on the US Post website.

Public Holidays

Major NYC holidays and special events may force the closure of many businesses or attract crowds, making dining and accommodations reservations difficult.

New Year's Day January 1

Martin Luther King Day Third Monday in January

Presidents' Day Third Monday in February

Easter March/April

Memorial Day Late May

Gay Pride Last Sunday in June

Independence Day July 4

Labor Day Early September

Rosh Hashanah and Yom Kippur Mid-September to mid-October

Halloween October 31

Thanksgiving Fourth Thursday in November

Christmas Day December 25

New Year's Eve December 31

Telephone

Phone numbers within the US consist of a three-digit area code followed by a seven-digit local number. If you're

393

DIRECTORY A–Z TIME

PRACTICALITIES

Newspapers & Magazines

There are loads of periodicals to choose from. What else would you expect from one of the media capitals of the world? Newspapers include the following:

New York Post (www.nypost.com) The *Post* is known for screaming headlines, conservative political views and its popular Page Six gossip column.

New York Times (www.nytimes.com) 'The gray lady' has become hip in recent years, adding sections on technology, arts and dining out.

Village Voice (www.villagevoice.com) Owned by national alternative-newspaper chain New Times, the legendary *Voice* has less bite but still plenty of bark.

Wall Street Journal (www.wallstreetjournal.com) This intellectual daily focuses on finance, though its new owner, media mogul Rupert Murdoch, has ratcheted up the general coverage to rival that of the *Times*.

Magazines that give a good sense of the local flavor include the following:

New York Magazine (www.nymag.com) A biweekly magazine with feature stories and great listings about anything and everything in NYC, plus an indispensable website.

New Yorker (www.newyorker.com) This highbrow weekly covers politics and culture through its famously lengthy works of reportage; it also publishes fiction and poetry.

Time Out New York (www.timeout.com/newyork) A weekly magazine, its focus is on mass coverage, plus articles and interviews on arts and entertainment.

Radio

NYC has some excellent radio options beyond commercial pop-music stations. An excellent programming guide can be found in the *New York Times* Entertainment section on Sunday. Our top pick is **WNYC** (820AM and 93.9FM; www.wnyc.org), NYC's public radio station that is the local NPR affiliate and offers a blend of national and local talk and interview shows, with a switch to classical music in the day on the FM station.

Smoking

Smoking is strictly forbidden in any location that's considered a public place; this includes subway stations, restaurants, bars, taxis and parks.

calling long distance, dial ☑1 + the three-digit area code + the seven-digit number. To make an international call from NYC, call ☑011 + country code + area code + number. When calling Canada, there is no need to use the 011.

Area Codes in NYC

No matter where you're calling within New York City, even if it's just across the street in the same area code, you must always dial 1 + the area code first.

Manhattan ☑212, 646
Outer boroughs ☑347, 718, 929
All boroughs (usually cell phones) ☑917

Cell Phones

Most US cell (mobile) phones besides the iPhone operate on CDMA, not the European standard GSM – make sure you check compatibility with your phone service provider. North Americans should have no problem, though it is best to check with your service provider about roaming charges.

If you require a cell phone, you'll find many store fronts – most run by Verizon, T-Mobile or AT&T – where you can buy a cheap phone and load it up with prepaid minutes, thus avoiding a long-term contract.

Time

New York City is in the Eastern Standard Time (EST)

zone – five hours behind Greenwich Mean Time (London), two hours ahead of Mountain Standard Time (including Denver, Colorado) and three hours ahead of Pacific Standard Time (San Francisco and Los Angeles, California). Almost all of the USA observes daylight-saving time: clocks go forward one hour from the second Sunday in March to the first Sunday in November, when the clocks are turned back one hour. (It's easy to remember by the phrase 'spring ahead, fall back.')

Toilets

Considering the number of pedestrians, there's a noticeable lack of public restrooms around the city. You'll find spots to relieve yourself in Grand Central Terminal, Penn Station and Port Authority Bus Terminal, and in parks, including Madison Square Park, Battery Park, Tompkins Square Park, Washington Square Park and Columbus Park in Chinatown, plus several places scattered around Central Park. The good bet, though, is to pop into a Starbucks (there's one about every three blocks), a department store (Macy's, Century 21, Bloomingdale's) or a neighborhood park like Tompkins Square in the East Village or Bleecker Playground (at W 11th & Hudson) in the West Village.

Tourist Information

In this web-based world you'll find infinite online resources to get up-to-the-minute information about New York City. In person, try one of the official bureaux of **NYC & Company** (www.nycgo.com).

Times Square (Map p432; ☎212-484-1222; www.nycgo.com; Seventh Ave, at 44th St, Midtown West; 🕘9am-6pm; [S]N/Q/R, S, 1/2/3, 7 to Times Sq-42nd St)

Macy's Herald Square (Map p432; ☎212-484-1222; www.nycgo.com; Macy's, 151 W 34th St, at Broadway; 🕘9am-7pm Mon-Fri, from 10am Sat, from 11am Sun ; [S]B/D/F/M, N/Q/R to 34th St-Herald Sq)

City Hall (Map p410; ☎212-484-1222; www.nycgo.com; City Hall Park, at Broadway; 🕘9am-6pm Mon-Fri, 10am-5pm Sat & Sun; [S]4/5/6 to Brooklyn Bridge-City Hall; R to City Hall; J/Z to Chambers St)

The **Brooklyn Tourism & Visitors Center** (Map p446; ☎718-802-3846; www.nycgo.com; 209 Joralemon St, btwn Court St & Brooklyn Bridge Blvd, Downtown; 🕘10am-6pm Mon-Fri; [S]2/3, 4/5 to Borough Hall) has all sorts of info on this much-loved borough.

Outer Borough Tourism Portals

The outer boroughs each have a special tourism website:

Brooklyn (www.explorebk.com) In-depth coverage of Brooklyn.

Bronx (www.ilovethebronx.com) The lowdown on all things Bronx-related.

Queens (www.itsinqueens.com) Gateway to Queen's rich, multicultural neighborhoods.

Staten Island (www.statenislandusa.com) Highlights and goings-on in one of NYC's least-visited boroughs.

Neighborhood Tourism Portals

Many of the city's most popular neighborhoods have their own websites (either official or 'unofficial') dedicated to exploring the area. Some of our favorites include the following:

Lower East Side (www.lowereastsideny.com)

Chinatown (www.explorechinatown.com)

Upper East Side (www.uppereast.com)

Soho (www.sohonyc.com)

Williamsburg (www.freewilliamsburg.com)

Travelers with Disabilities

Office for People with Disabilities (☎212-639-9675; www.nyc.gov/html/mopd; 🕘9am-5pm Mon-Fri) Federal laws guarantee that all government offices and facilities are accessible to people with disabilities. For information on specific places, you can contact the mayor's Office for People with Disabilities, which can send you a free copy of its *Access New York* guide.

Big Apple Greeter (www.bigapplegreeter.org/what-is-the-access-program) [FREE] Another excellent resource is the Big Apple Greeter program, which has over 50 volunteers on staff with physical disabilities who are happy to show off their corner of the city.

Accessibility Line (☎511; http://web.mta.info/accessibility/stations.htm) Call or visit the website for detailed information on subway and bus wheelchair accessibility.

Also visit www.nycgo.com/accessibility.

Visas

Visa Waiver Program

The US Visa Waiver Program (VWP) allows nationals from 38 countries to enter the US without a visa, provided they are carrying a machine-readable passport. For the up-to-date list of countries included in the program and current requirements, see the **US Department of State** (http://travel.state.gov/visa) website.

Citizens of VWP countries need to register with the **US Department of Homeland Security** (www.cbp.gov/travel/international-visitors/esta) three days before their visit. There is a $14 fee for registration application; when approved, the registration is valid for two years or until your passport expires, whichever comes first.

Visas Required

You must obtain a visa from a US embassy or consulate in your home country if you:

- Do not currently hold a passport from a VWP country.
- Are from a VWP country, but don't have a machine-readable passport.
- Are planning to stay longer than 90 days.
- Are planning to work or study in the US.

Behind the Scenes

SEND US YOUR FEEDBACK

We love to hear from travelers – your comments keep us on our toes and help make our books better. Our well-traveled team reads every word on what you loved or loathed about this book. Although we cannot reply individually to your submissions, we always guarantee that your feedback goes straight to the appropriate authors, in time for the next edition. Each person who sends us information is thanked in the next edition – the most useful submissions are rewarded with a selection of digital PDF chapters.

Visit **lonelyplanet.com/contact** to submit your updates and suggestions or to ask for help. Our award-winning website also features inspirational travel stories, news and discussions.

Note: We may edit, reproduce and incorporate your comments in Lonely Planet products such as guidebooks, websites and digital products, so let us know if you don't want your comments reproduced or your name acknowledged. For a copy of our privacy policy visit lonelyplanet.com/privacy.

OUR READERS

Many thanks to the travelers who used the last edition and wrote to us with helpful hints, useful advice and interesting anecdotes: Allison Phillips, Barbara Gougoulis, Elena Barrela, Else Lunøe, Heather Monell, Isabelle Bourgey, John Guy, Linda Rath, Nathalie Jacob, Rhonda Gharib, Richard Johnson, Sam Pulfer, Sommyr Pochan, Sören Dobberschütz.

AUTHOR THANKS

Regis St Louis

I'm grateful to many folks – friends and strangers alike – who shared tips on their favorite places in the city. Special thanks to my talented co-authors Cristian Bonetto and Zora O'Neill for their excellent contributions that showcase this ever-changing city, and to Wesley Clark for providing a home away from home. As always, biggest thanks go to my wife, Cassandra, and our daughters, Genevieve and Magdalena, who make this whole enterprise worthwhile.

Cristian Bonetto

Sincere thanks to Kathy Stromsland, Charles Isherwood, Eben Freeman, Chris Crowley, Kim Anderson, Christa Larwood, Mark Webster and Steven Ritzel for their tips, insight and friendship. Also, a big shout out to my ever-diligent co-writers, Regis St Louis and Zora O'Neill, and to Rebecca Warren for her support and professionalism.

Zora O'Neill

Thanks to Michael LoBianco, Robbi Kearns and Olga Kuchukov for Catskills tips, to Brooke Donnelly and Marla Garfield for guidance on Long Island, and to Ali El Sayed and Jeff Orlick for Queens wisdom. As always, thanks to Peter Moskos for accompanying me.

ACKNOWLEDGEMENTS

Cover photograph: Exterior of The Solomon R. Guggenheim Museum, ©SRGF, NY. Used with permission. Luigi Vaccarella/4Corners ©

Illustration pp232-3 by Javier Zarracina

New York City Subway Map © 2015 Metropolitan Transportation Authority. Used with permission.

THIS BOOK

This 10th edition of Lonely Planet's *New York City* guidebook was researched and written by Regis St Louis, Cristian Bonetto and Zora O'Neill. Regis and Cristian also worked on the previous edition. Cristian worked on the 8th edition with Brandon Presser and Carolina A Miranda. This guidebook was produced by the following:

Destination Editor
Rebecca Warren
Product Editors
Anne Mason, Tracy Whitmey
Senior Cartographer
Alison Lyall
Book Designers
Michael Buick, Jessica Rose
Assisting Editors
Carolyn Boicos, Bruce Evans, Paul Harding, Helen Koehne, Fionnuala Twomey, Amanda Williamson

Cover Researcher
Naomi Parker

Thanks to David Carroll, Daniel Corbett, Ryan Evans, Andi Jones, Wayne Murphy, Jenna Myers, Claire Naylor, Karyn Noble, Darren O'Connell, Kirsten Rawlings, Dianne Schallmeiner, Ellie Simpson, Lyahna Spencer, Angela Tinson, Tony Wheeler, Dora Whitaker

Index

EATING

New York City Maps

Sights

- Beach
- Bird Sanctuary
- Buddhist
- Castle/Palace
- Christian
- Confucian
- Hindu
- Islamic
- Jain
- Jewish
- Monument
- Museum/Gallery/Historic Building
- Ruin
- Shinto
- Sikh
- Taoist
- Winery/Vineyard
- Zoo/Wildlife Sanctuary
- Other Sight

Activities, Courses & Tours

- Bodysurfing
- Diving
- Canoeing/Kayaking
- Course/Tour
- Sento Hot Baths/Onsen
- Skiing
- Snorkeling
- Surfing
- Swimming/Pool
- Walking
- Windsurfing
- Other Activity

Sleeping

- Sleeping
- Camping

Eating

- Eating

Drinking & Nightlife

- Drinking & Nightlife
- Cafe

Entertainment

- Entertainment

Shopping

- Shopping

Information

- Bank
- Embassy/Consulate
- Hospital/Medical
- Internet
- Police
- Post Office
- Telephone
- Toilet
- Tourist Information
- Other Information

Geographic

- Beach
- Gate
- Hut/Shelter
- Lighthouse
- Lookout
- Mountain/Volcano
- Oasis
- Park
- Pass
- Picnic Area
- Waterfall

Population

- Capital (National)
- Capital (State/Province)
- City/Large Town
- Town/Village

Transport

- Airport
- BART station
- Border crossing
- Boston T station
- Bus
- Cable car/Funicular
- Cycling
- Ferry
- Metro/Muni station
- Monorail
- Parking
- Petrol station
- Subway/SkyTrain station
- Taxi
- Train station/Railway
- Tram
- Underground station
- Other Transport

Note: Not all symbols displayed above appear on the maps in this book

Routes

- Tollway
- Freeway
- Primary
- Secondary
- Tertiary
- Lane
- Unsealed road
- Road under construction
- Plaza/Mall
- Steps
- Tunnel
- Pedestrian overpass
- Walking Tour
- Walking Tour detour
- Path/Walking Trail

Boundaries

- International
- State/Province
- Disputed
- Regional/Suburb
- Marine Park
- Cliff
- Wall

Hydrography

- River, Creek
- Intermittent River
- Canal
- Water
- Dry/Salt/Intermittent Lake
- Reef

Areas

- Airport/Runway
- Beach/Desert
- Cemetery (Christian)
- Cemetery (Other)
- Glacier
- Mudflat
- Park/Forest
- Sight (Building)
- Sportsground
- Swamp/Mangrove

WEEHAWKEN

Hudson River

CROTONA PARK

BRONX

MORRISANIA

HARLEM

LONGWOOD

HUNTS POINT

UNION CITY

Central Park

Randalls Island

East River

Rikers Island

ASTORIA

JACKSON HEIGHTS

FLUSHING

MANHATTAN

LONG ISLAND CITY

SUNNYSIDE

QUEENS

HOBOKEN

East River

GREENPOINT

MASPETH

JERSEY CITY

WILLIAMSBURG

RIDGEWOOD

GLENDALE

BUSHWICK

Ellis Island

Liberty Island

Governors Island

DUMBO

BROOKLYN HEIGHTS

DOWNTOWN BROOKLYN

BROOKLYN

PROSPECT HEIGHTS

NEW LOTS

RED HOOK

Upper New York Bay

PROSPECT PARK

18 Coney Island & Brighton Beach (4.5mi)

LOWER MANHATTAN & THE FINANCIAL DISTRICT *Map on p410*

LOWER MANHATTAN & THE FINANCIAL DISTRICT

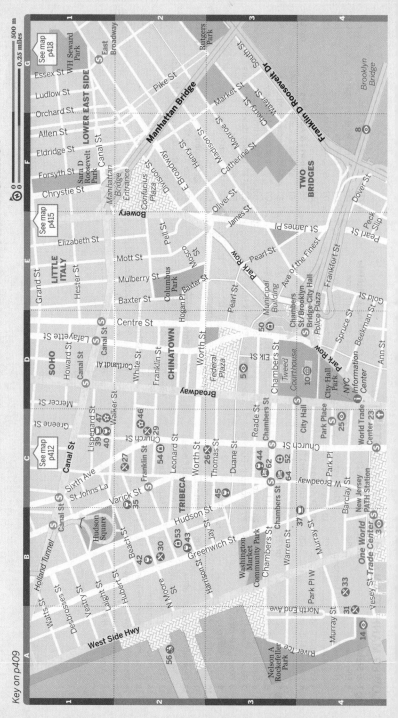

500 m
0.25 miles

See map p418

See map p415

See map p412

WH Seward Park
Sara D Roosevelt Park
Essex St
Ludlow St
Orchard St
Allen St
Eldridge St
Forsyth St
Chrystie St
East Broadway
Pike St
Canal St
LOWER EAST SIDE

Rutgers Park
Manhattan Bridge
Market St
South St
Water St
Cherry St
Monroe St
Madison St
Henry St
Catherine St
Oliver St
James St
St James Pl
Pearl St
Confucius Plaza
Division St
E Broadway
Bowery
Manhattan Bridge Entrance

Franklin D Roosevelt Dr
Brooklyn Bridge
TWO BRIDGES
Dover St

Elizabeth St
Mott St
Mulberry St
Baxter St
Hester St
Grand St
LITTLE ITALY
Columbus Park
Hogan Pl
Pell St
Mosco St
Baxter St
Park Row
Pearl St
Municipal Building
Ave of the Finest
Spruce St
Frankfort St
Gold St
Beekman St
Ann St
Peck Slip
Frankfort St
Pearl St

Centre St
Lafayette St
Canal St
Howard St
Canal St
SOHO
Mercer St
Greene St
Sixth Ave
St Johns La
Varick St
Canal St
Walker St
Lispenard St
Cortlandt Al
White St
Franklin St
Worth St
Federal Plaza
CHINATOWN
Broadway
Worth St
Chambers St
Elk St
Tweed Courthouse
City Hall Park
Park Row
Chambers St/Brooklyn Bridge-City Hall
Police Plaza
NYC Information Center

Mercer St
Greene St
Canal St
Franklin St
Leonard St
Worth St
Thomas St
Duane St
Reade St
Chambers St
Church St
City Hall
Park Place
World Trade Center 23
TRIBECA
Hudson St
Beach St
N Moore St
Jay St
Harrison St
Washington Market Community Park
Chambers St
Warren St
Murray St
Park Pl
W Broadway
Barclay St
New Jersey PATH Station
One World Trade Center

Watts St
Desbrosses St
Vestry St
Laight St
Hubert St
Holland Tunnel
Hudson Square
West Side Hwy
Nelson A Rockefeller Park
River Tce
North End Ave
Vesey St
Murray St
Park Pl W

39 40 47
46
27
54
29
26
44
62
52
64
45
53
43
42
30
35
56
50
5
10
25
37
33
31
14
8

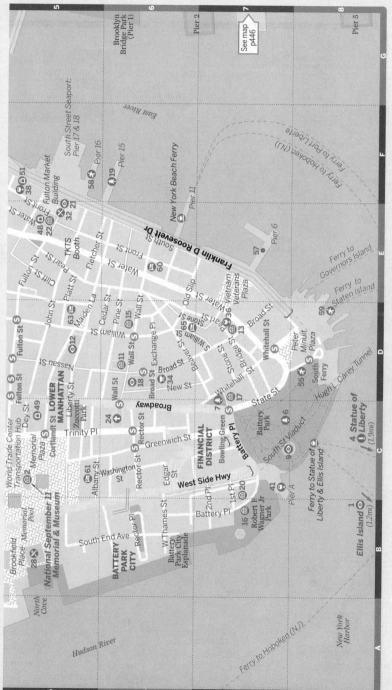

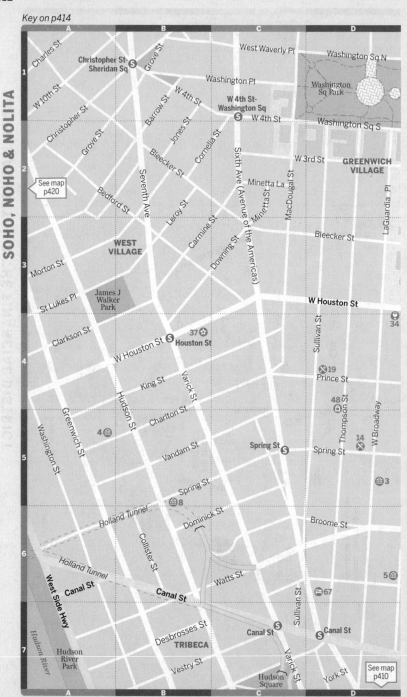

SOHO, NOHO & NOLITA

Charles St
W 10th St
Christopher St
Grove St
Christopher St-Sheridan Sq Ⓢ
Grove St
West Waverly Pl
Washington Sq N
Washington Pl
W 4th St
W 4th St-Washington Sq Ⓢ
W 4th St
Washington Sq Park
Washington Sq S
Barrow St
Jones St
Cornelia St
W 3rd St
GREENWICH VILLAGE
Bleecker St
Minetta La
Minetta St
MacDougal St
LaGuardia Pl
See map p420
Bedford St
Seventh Ave
Leroy St
Carmine St
Downing St
Sixth Ave (Avenue of the Americas)
Bleecker St
WEST VILLAGE
Morton St
St Lukes Pl
James J Walker Park
W Houston St
Sullivan St
Ⓧ 34
Clarkson St
W Houston St Ⓢ
37 ✪ **Houston St**
Ⓧ **19**
Prince St
King St
Varick St
Hudson St
Charlton St
48 ⒜
Thompson St
W Broadway
Greenwich St
4 ⒜
Vandam St
Spring St Ⓢ
Spring St
14 Ⓧ
Washington St
Spring St
⒜ 3
8 ⒜
Dominick St
Broome St
Holland Tunnel
Collister St
5 ⒜
Holland Tunnel
Watts St
Sullivan St
West Side Hwy
Canal St
Canal St
⒠ 67
Hudson River
Desbrosses St
TRIBECA
Canal St Ⓢ
Ⓢ **Canal St**
Hudson River Park
Vestry St
Hudson Square
Varick St
York St
See map p410

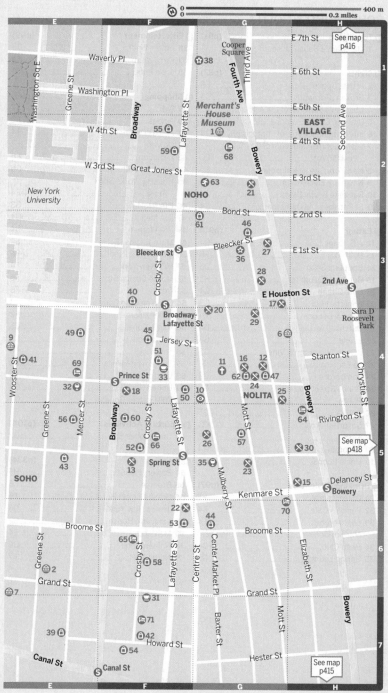

SOHO, NOHO & NOLITA *Map on p412*

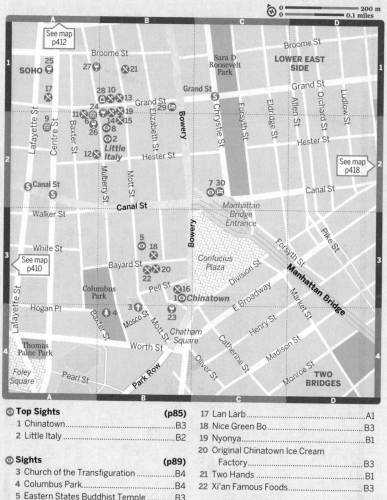

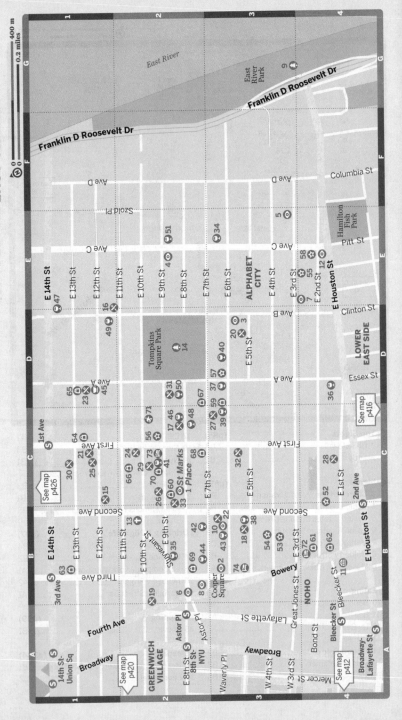

EAST VILLAGE

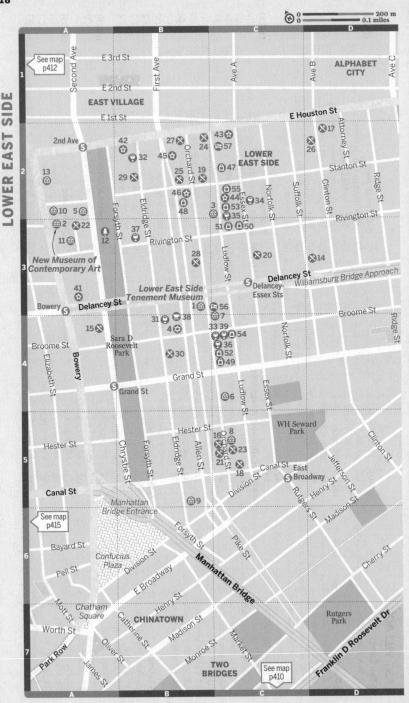

LOWER EAST SIDE

LOWER EAST SIDE

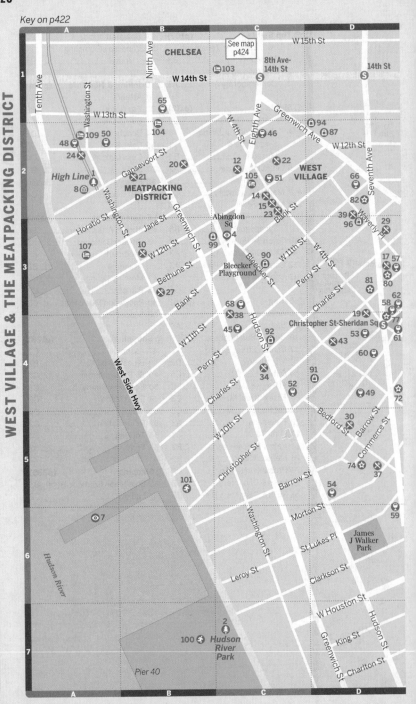

Key on p422

WEST VILLAGE & THE MEATPACKING DISTRICT

See map p424

CHELSEA

W 14th St

8th Ave-14th St

14th St

Tenth Ave

Washington St

Ninth Ave

W 13th St

Greenwich Ave

W 12th St

Seventh Ave

High Line

MEATPACKING DISTRICT

Gansevoort St

Horatio St

Washington St

Greenwich St

Jane St

W 4th St

Eighth Ave

WEST VILLAGE

Abingdon Sq

Bleecker Playground

Bank St

Bleecker St

W 11th St

Perry St

W 4th St

Charles St

Christopher St-Sheridan Sq

Bethune St

Bank St

W 11th St

Perry St

Charles St

Hudson St

West Side Hwy

W 10th St

Christopher St

Barrow St

Bedford St

Barrow St

Commerce St

Morton St

St Lukes Pl

James J Walker Park

Hudson St

Leroy St

Clarkson St

W Houston St

Greenwich St

King St

Hudson River

Hudson River Park

Pier 40

Charlton St

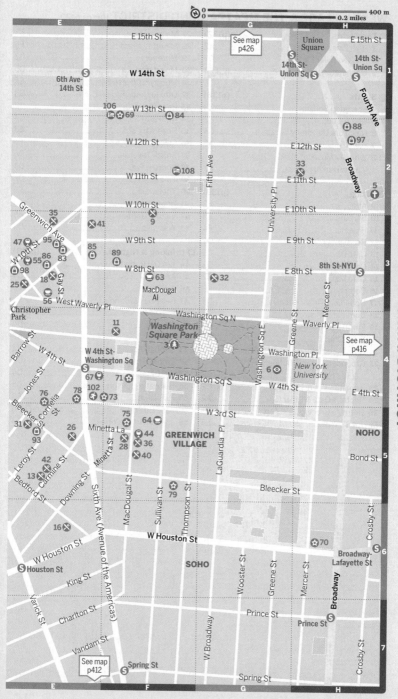

WEST VILLAGE & THE MEATPACKING DISTRICT *Map on p420*

WEST VILLAGE & THE MEATPACKING DISTRICT

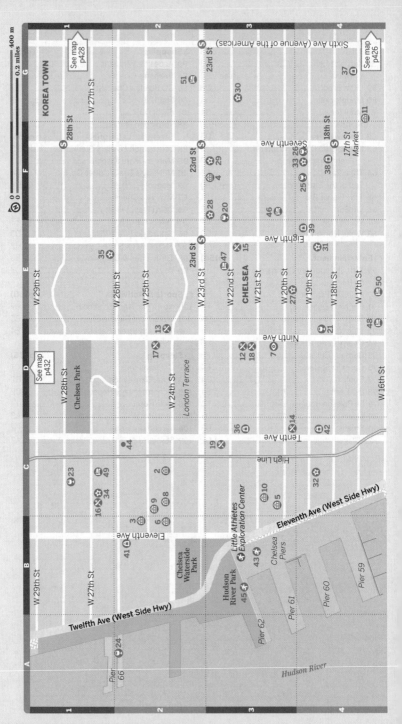

CHELSEA

0 400 m
0 0.2 miles

KOREA TOWN

See map p428

See map p432

Chelsea Park

London Terrace

CHELSEA

High Line

Little Athletes Exploration Center

Chelsea Waterside Park

Hudson River Park

Chelsea Piers

Twelfth Ave (West Side Hwy)

Eleventh Ave (West Side Hwy)

Eleventh Ave

Tenth Ave

Ninth Ave

Eighth Ave

Seventh Ave

Sixth Ave (Avenue of the Americas)

See map p426

17th St Market

Hudson River

W 29th St
W 27th St
W 28th St
W 26th St
W 25th St
W 24th St
W 23rd St
W 22nd St
W 21st St
W 20th St
W 19th St
W 18th St
W 17th St
W 16th St

28th St
23rd St
23rd St
23rd St
18th St
17th St

Pier 66
Pier 59
Pier 60
Pier 61
Pier 62

35
13
17
44
23
16 34
49
41
3
6 9
8
2
19
36
14
42
12 18
7
21
27
31
15
47
28
20
46
39
25
33 26
38
4 29
51
30
37
11
50
48
32
10 5
43
45
24

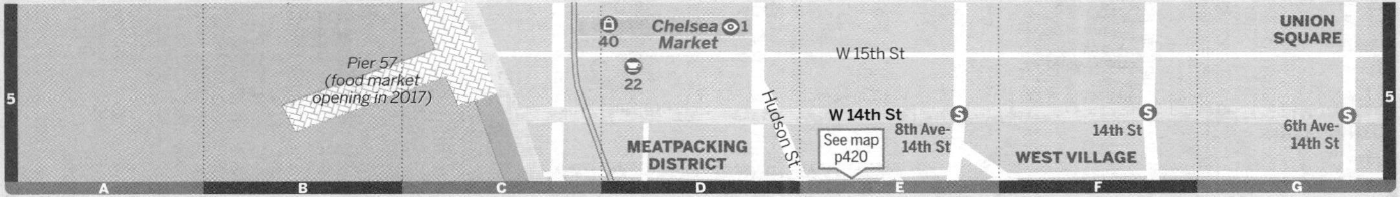

Pier 57 (food market opening in 2017)
40
Chelsea Market 1
22
MEATPACKING DISTRICT
Hudson St
W 15th St
W 14th St
See map p420
8th Ave-14th St
14th St
WEST VILLAGE
UNION SQUARE
6th Ave-14th St
A
B
C
D
E
F
G
5
5

Top Sights (p134)
1 Chelsea Market ... D5

Sights (p137)
2 Barbara Gladstone Gallery ... C2
3 Cheim & Read ... B2
4 Chelsea Hotel ... F3
5 David Zwirner ... C3
6 Gagosian ... B2
7 General Theological Seminary ... D3
8 Mary Boone Gallery ... C2
9 Pace Gallery ... C2
10 Paula Cooper Gallery ... C3
11 Rubin Museum of Art ... G4

Eating (p148)
12 Blossom ... D3
Chelsea Market ... (see 1)
13 Co ... D2
14 Cookshop ... C3
15 Foragers City Table ... E3
16 Heath ... C1
17 Jun-Men ... D2
18 Le Grainne ... D3
19 Tía Pol ... C3

Drinking & Nightlife (p153)
20 Barracuda ... F3
21 Bathtub Gin ... D4
22 Blue Bottle ... D5
23 Eagle NYC ... C1
24 Frying Pan ... A2
25 G Lounge ... F4
Gallow Green ... (see 34)
26 Peter McManus Tavern ... F4

Entertainment (p154)
27 Atlantic Theater Company ... E3
28 Chelsea Bow Tie Cinema ... F3
29 Gotham Comedy Club ... F3
30 Irish Repertory Theater ... G3
31 Joyce Theater ... E4
32 Kitchen ... C4
33 New York Live Arts ... F4
34 Sleep No More ... C1
35 Upright Citizens Brigade Theatre ... E1

Shopping (p159)
36 192 Books ... C3
37 Housing Works Thrift Shop ... G4
38 INA (Chelsea) ... F4
39 Nasty Pig ... E4
40 Posman Books ... D5
41 Printed Matter ... B2
42 Story ... C4

Sports & Activities (p160)
43 Chelsea Piers Complex ... B3
44 New York Gallery Tours ... C2
45 Schooner Adirondack ... B3

Sleeping (p336)
46 Chelsea Hostel ... F3
47 Colonial House Inn ... E3
48 Dream Downtown ... D4
49 Hôtel Americano ... C1
50 Maritime Hotel ... E4
51 Townhouse Inn of Chelsea ... G2

UNION SQUARE, FLATIRON DISTRICT & GRAMERCY

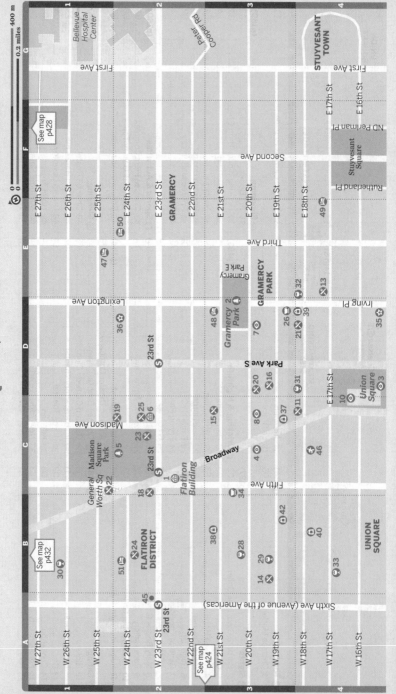

UNION SQUARE, FLATIRON DISTRICT & GRAMERCY

WEST VILLAGE · **GREENWICH VILLAGE** · **EAST VILLAGE**

◎ Top Sights	(p163)
1 Flatiron Building	C2
2 Gramercy Park	D3
3 Union Square	D4

◎ Sights	(p165)
4 Lord & Taylor Building	C3
5 Madison Square Park	C3
6 Metropolitan Life Tower	C2
7 National Arts Club	D3
8 Theodore Roosevelt Birthplace	C3
9 Tibet House	B5
10 Union Square Greenmarket	C4

⊗ Eating	(p166)
11 ABC Kitchen	C4
12 Artichoke Basille's Pizza	D3
13 Bar Jamón	E4
14 Boqueria Flatiron	B3
15 Cosme	C3
16 Craft	D3
17 Dos Toros Taqueria	D5
18 Eataly	C2
19 Eleven Madison Park	D3
20 Gramercy Tavern	D4
21 Javelina	C1
22 Mad Sq Eats	(see 48)
23 Shake Shack	C2
24 Tacombi Café El Presidente	B2
25 The Clocktower	C2
26 71 Irving Place	F5
27 Beauty Bar	E4
28 Boxers NYC	C5
29 Flatiron Lounge	B3
30 Flatiron Room	B1
31 Old Town Bar & Restaurant	D4
32 Pete's Tavern	E4
33 Raines Law Room	B4
34 Toby's Estate	C3

◆ Drinking & Nightlife	(p168)

☆ Entertainment	(p173)
35 Irving Plaza	D4
36 Peoples Improv Theater	D2

⊕ Shopping	(p173)
37 ABC Carpet & Home	C3
38 Abracadabra	B3
39 Bedford Cheese Shop	D4
40 Books of Wonder	B4
41 DSW	C5
42 Idlewild Books	B3
Union Square Greenmarket	(see 10)
43 Whole Foods	D5

⊕ Sports & Activities	(p174)
44 Jivamukti	D5
45 New York City Audubon	A2
46 Soul Cycle	C4

⊟ Sleeping	(p338)
47 Carlton Arms	E1
48 Gramercy Park Hotel	D3
49 Hotel17	E4
50 Marcel at Gramercy	E2
51 Wyndham Garden	B2

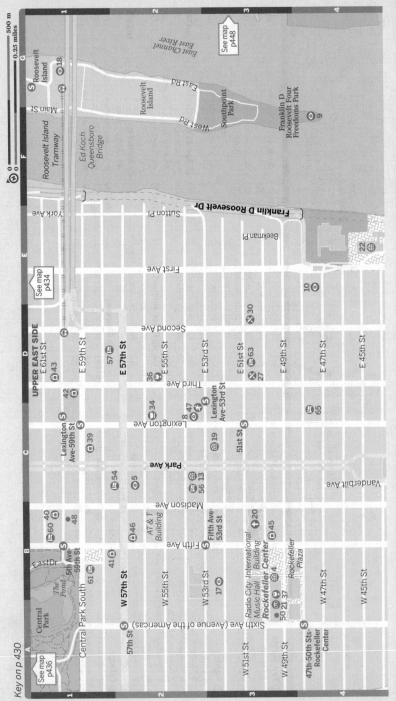

Key on p 430

500 m
0.25 miles

See map p436

Central Park

The Pond

East Dr

5th Ave-59th St

Central Park South

Sixth Ave (Avenue of the Americas)

Fifth Ave

Madison Ave

Park Ave

Lexington Ave

Third Ave

Second Ave

First Ave

York Ave

See map p434

UPPER EAST SIDE

Roosevelt Island Tramway

Ed Koch Queensboro Bridge

Roosevelt Island

Main St

Roosevelt Island

West Rd

East Rd

East Channel East River

Southpoint Park

Franklin D Roosevelt Four Freedoms Park

See map p448

Franklin D Roosevelt Dr

Sutton Pl

Beekman Pl

Vanderbilt Ave

Fifth Ave-53rd St

AT&T Building

Radio City International Music Hall Building

Rockefeller Center

Rockefeller Plaza

47th-50th Sts-Rockefeller Center

W 57th St

W 55th St

W 53rd St

W 51st St

W 49th St

W 47th St

W 45th St

E 61st St

E 59th St

E 57th St

E 55th St

E 53rd St

E 51st St

E 49th St

E 47th St

E 45th St

Lexington Ave-59th St

Lexington Ave-53rd St

51st St

57th St

5th Ave 59th St

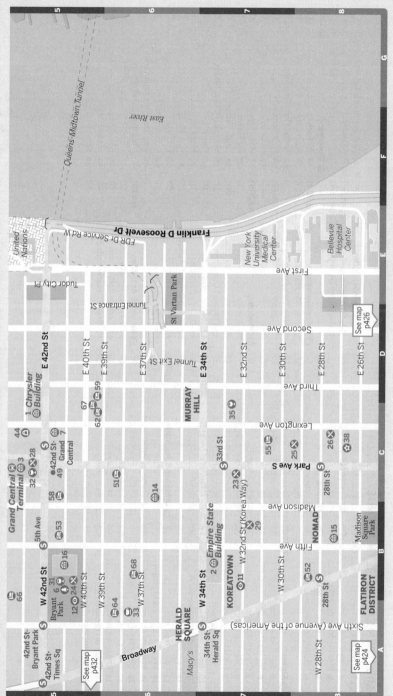

East River

Queens-Midtown Tunnel

Franklin D Roosevelt Dr

FDR Dr Service Rd W

United Nations

New York University Medical Center

Bellevue Hospital Center

See map p426

Tudor City Pl

St Vartan Park

Tunnel Entrance St

Tunnel Exit St

First Ave

Second Ave

Third Ave

Lexington Ave

Park Ave S

Madison Ave

Fifth Ave

Sixth Ave (Avenue of the Americas)

Broadway

E 42nd St

E 40th St

E 39th St

E 37th St

E 34th St

E 32nd St

E 30th St

E 28th St

E 26th St

33rd St

28th St

W 32nd St (Korea Way)

W 39th St

W 37th St

W 34th St

W 30th St

28th St

W 28th St

Chrysler Building

Grand Central Terminal

5th Ave

42nd St-Grand Central

Empire State Building

MURRAY HILL

NOMAD

KOREATOWN

HERALD SQUARE

FLATIRON DISTRICT

Madison Square Park

Bryant Park

42nd St-Bryant Park

42nd St-Times Sq

34th St-Herald Sq

Macy's

W 42nd St

W 40th St

See map p432

See map p424

1

2

3

44

32 28

49

7

67

62 59

51

14

35

55

25

26

38

23

29

15

52

11

53

58

66

31

6

12 24

16

64

33

68

MIDTOWN EAST & FIFTH AVENUE

MIDTOWN WEST & TIMES SQUARE

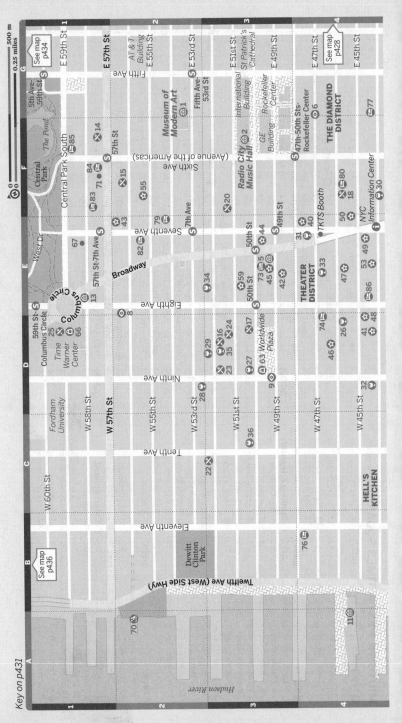

Key on p431

See map p436

See map p434

See map p428

500 m
0.25 miles

Hudson River

Twelfth Ave (West Side Hwy)

Eleventh Ave

Tenth Ave

Ninth Ave

Eighth Ave

Broadway

Seventh Ave

Sixth Ave (Avenue of the Americas)

Fifth Ave

Central Park

The Pond

Central Park South

West Dr

Columbus Circle

Time Warner Center

Fordham University

Dewitt Clinton Park

HELL'S KITCHEN

THEATER DISTRICT

THE DIAMOND DISTRICT

Rockefeller Center

Radio City Music Hall

Museum of Modern Art

St Patrick's Cathedral

International Building

GE Building

AT & T Building

47th-50th Sts-Rockefeller Center

TKTS Booth

NYC Information Center

Worldwide Plaza

W 60th St
W 58th St
W 57th St
W 55th St
W 53rd St
W 51st St
W 49th St
W 47th St
W 45th St

E 59th St
E 57th St
E 55th St
E 53rd St
E 51st St
E 49th St
E 47th St
E 45th St

5th Ave-59th St
59th St-Columbus Circle
57th St
57th St-7th Ave
50th St
49th St
Fifth Ave-53rd St

Columbus Circle

Fifth Ave-53rd St

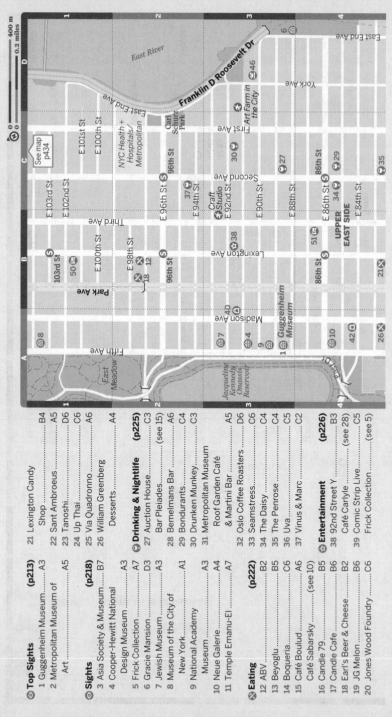

UPPER EAST SIDE

Map labels: Metropolitan Museum of Art, Central Park, Conservatory Water, The Pond, Hunter College, Rockefeller University, John Jay Park, Franklin D Roosevelt Dr, East End Ave, York Ave, First Ave, Second Ave, Third Ave, Lexington Ave, Park Ave, Madison Ave, Fifth Ave, East River, Ed Koch Queensboro Bridge, Roosevelt Island Tramway.

UPPER WEST SIDE & CENTRAL PARK

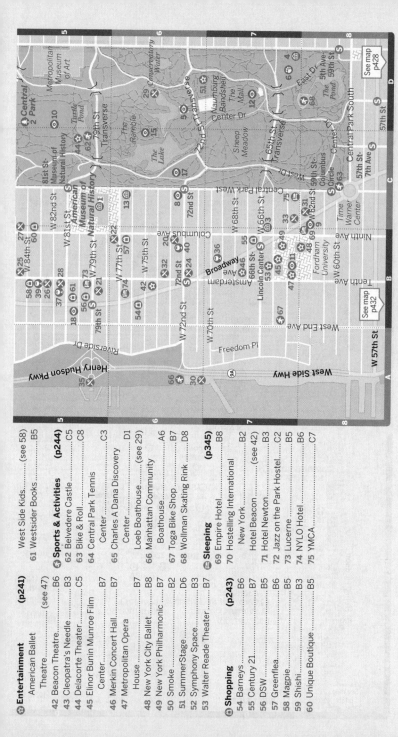

UPPER WEST SIDE & CENTRAL PARK

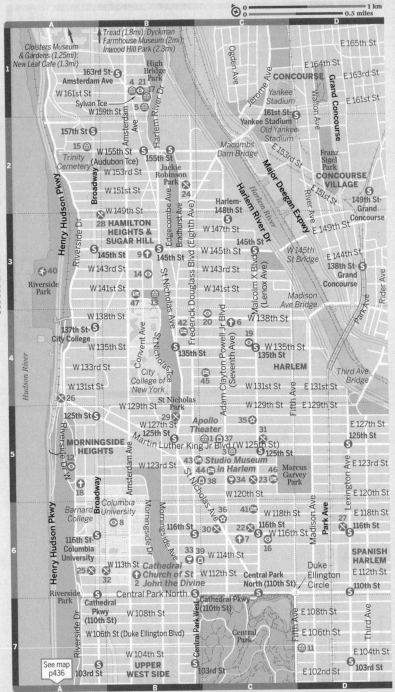

See map
p434

WILLIAMSBURG

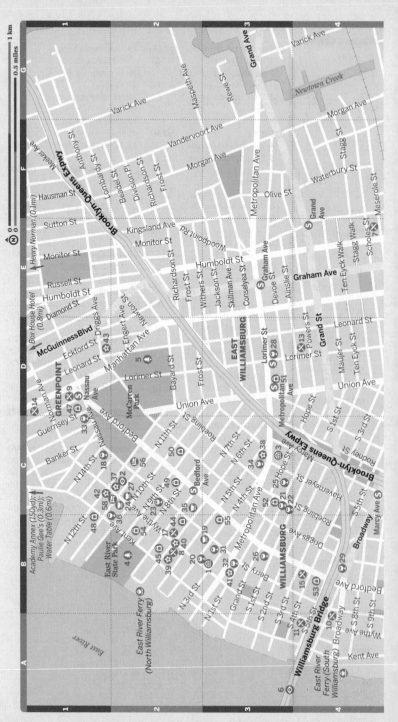

0.5 miles
1 km

Academy Annex (150yd);↑
Paulie Gee's (0.3mi);
Water Table (0.6mi)

East River
(North Williamsburg)

East River Ferry
(North Williamsburg)

East River Ferry (South
Williamsburg)

East River
(South Williamsburg)

GREENPOINT

**EAST
WILLIAMSBURG**

WILLIAMSBURG

McCarren
Park

East River
State Park

Newtown Creek

McGuinness Blvd

Brooklyn-Queens Expwy

Brooklyn-Queens Expwy

Williamsburg Bridge

Grand Ave

Graham Ave

Grand St

Broadway

Box House Hotel
(0.8mi)

Henry Norman (0.1mi)

◎ Sights (p251)

1 Brooklyn Art Library	B3
2 Brooklyn Brewery	C2
3 City Reliquary	C3
4 East River State Park	C3
5 McCarren Park	D2
6 Williamsburg Bridge	A3

⊗ Eating (p259)

7 Champs	E4
8 Cubana Social	B2
9 Five Leaves	D1
10 Marlow & Sons	A4
11 Miss Favela	A4
12 Momo Sushi Shack	G5
13 Okonomi	D4
14 Peter Pan Bakery	D1
15 Rabbit Hole	B4
16 Roberta's	G5
17 Zenkichi	B2

⊙ Drinking & Nightlife (p260)

18 Berry Park	C1
19 Blue Bottle Coffee	B3
20 Brooklyn Oenology	B2
21 Clem's	C3
22 Desnuda	C3
23 Hotel Delmano	C2
Ides	(see 58)
24 Kinfolk Studios	C2
25 Larry Lawrence	C3
26 Maison Premiere	B3
27 Matcha Bar	C2
28 Metropolitan	D3
29 OTB	B4
30 Pine Box Rock Shop	G5
31 Radegast Hall & Biergarten	B3
32 Skinny Dennis	G5
33 Spritzenhaus	C1
34 Spuyten Duyvil	C3
35 Toby's Estate	C2
36 Verboten	B2

⊙ Entertainment (p262)

37 Brooklyn Bowl	C2
38 Knitting Factory	C3
39 Music Hall of Williamsburg	B2
40 National Sawdust	B2
41 Nitehawk Cinema	B3
42 Output	C1
43 Warsaw	D1

⊙ Shopping (p262)

44 A&G Merch	B4
45 Artists & Fleas	G5
46 Beacon's Closet (Bushwick)	B3
47 Beacon's Closet (Greenpoint)	D1
48 Brooklyn Flea (Williamsburg)	B1
49 Brooklyn Industries	C2
50 Buffalo Exchange	C2
51 Desert Island Comics	D3
52 Fuego 718	C3
53 Pink Olive	B4
54 Rough Trade	B2
55 Spoonbill & Sugartown	B3

⊙ Sports & Activities (p262)

Brooklyn Bowl	(see 37)

⊙ Sleeping (p347)

56 McCarren Hotel & Pool	C2
57 New York Loft Hostel	G5
58 Wythe Hotel	C2

BOERUM HILL, CARROLL GARDENS, COBBLE HILL, FORT GREENE & RED HOOK

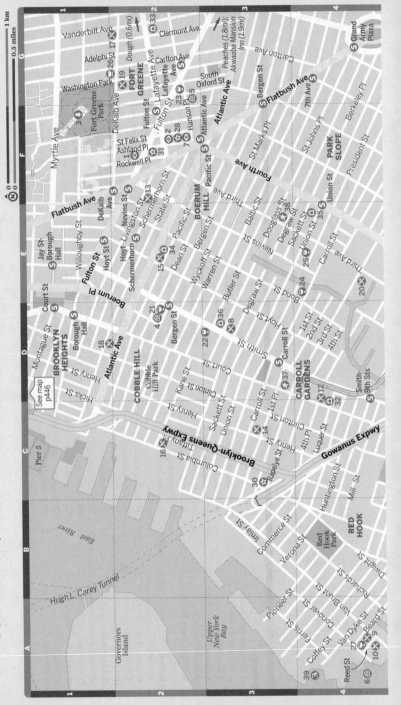

0.5 miles
1 km

See map p446

BOERUM HILL, CARROLL GARDENS, COBBLE HILL, FORT GREENE & RED HOOK

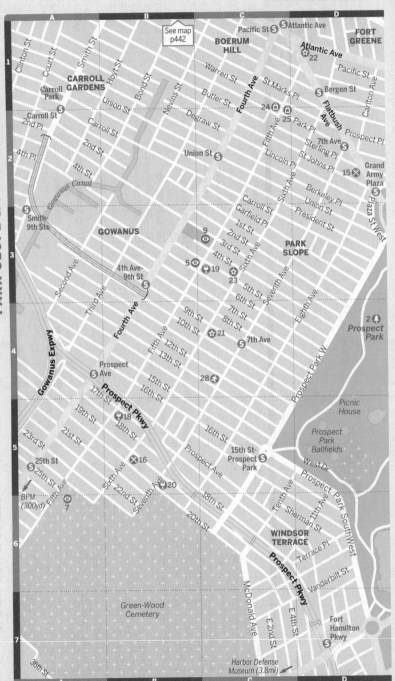

See map
p442

Pacific St
Atlantic Ave
FORT
GREENE

BOERUM
HILL

Atlantic Ave
22

Pacific St

CARROLL
GARDENS

Warren St

St Marks Pl

Bergen St

Carroll
Park

Union St

Butler St

Fourth Ave

24

Flatbush
Ave

Carroll St

Degraw St

Park Pl

7th Ave

Carroll St
2nd Pl

Fifth Ave

25

Sterling Pl

St Johns Pl

Prospect Pl

4th Pl

2nd St

Union St

Lincoln Pl

15

Grand
Army
Plaza

4th St

Gowanus Canal

Sixth Ave

Carroll St
Garfield Pl

Berkeley Pl
Union St
President St

Plaza St West

Smith-
9th Sts

GOWANUS

9

1st St
2nd St

PARK
SLOPE

4th Ave-
9th St

5

19

3rd St
4th St

23

5th St

Sixth Ave

Seventh Ave

Eighth Ave

2
Prospect
Park

Second Ave

Third Ave

Fourth Ave

Fifth Ave

9th St
10th St

21

6th St
7th St
8th St

7th Ave

Prospect Park W

12th St
13th St

Prospect
Ave

28

Picnic
House

Gowanus Expwy

17th St

15th St
16th St

16th St

Prospect
Park
Ballfields

18

19th St

21st St

18th St

Prospect Pkwy

Prospect Ave

15th St-
Prospect
Park

West Dr

23rd St

16

Sixth Ave

Seventh Ave

Prospect Park Southwest

25th St

20

Tenth Ave

Eleventh Ave

25th St

7

22nd St

18th St

Sherman St

BPM
(300yd)

Fifth Ave

20th St

WINDSOR
TERRACE

Terrace Pl

Vanderbilt St

Green-Wood
Cemetery

McDonald Ave

Prospect Pkwy

E 2nd St

E 4th St

Fort
Hamilton
Pkwy

36th St

Harbor Defense
Museum (3.8mi)

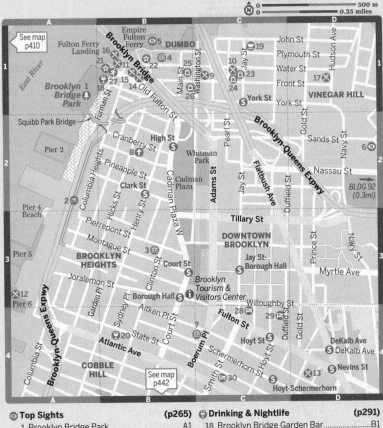

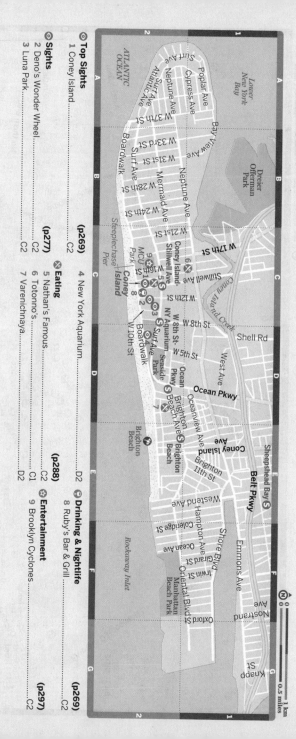

Map scale: 0.5 miles / 1 km

ASTORIA

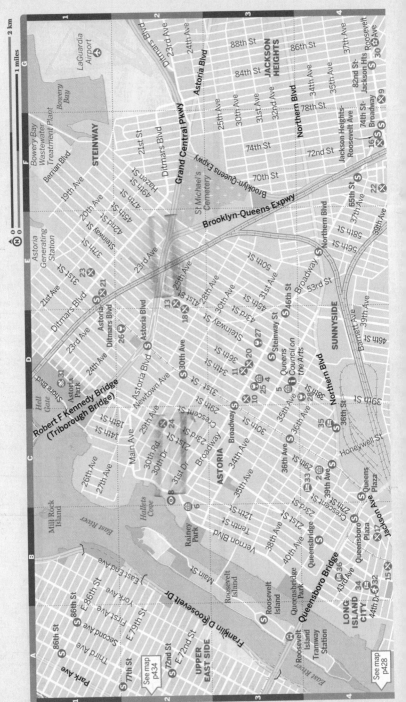

FLUSHING

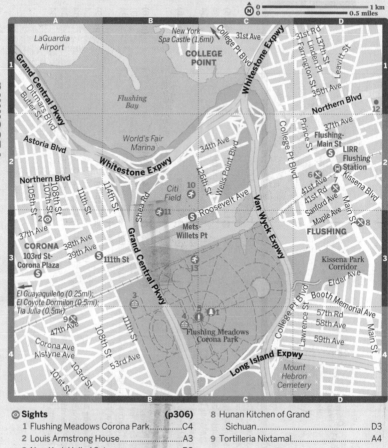